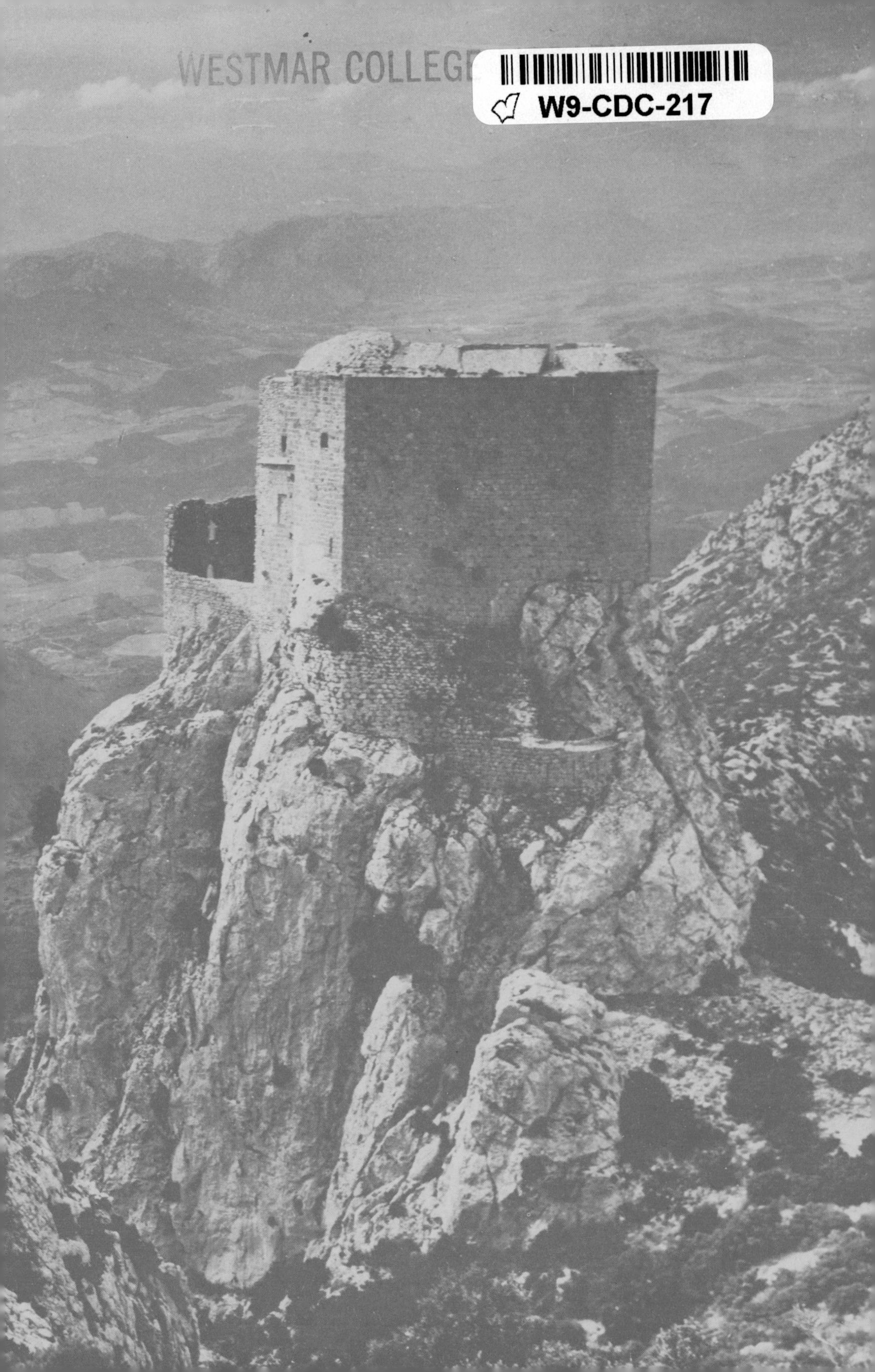

Medieval Heresy

To my wife

Medieval Heresy

Popular Movements from Bogomil to Hus

M. D. Lambert

Edward Arnold

Copyright © M. D. Lambert 1977

First published 1977 by
Edward Arnold (Publishers) Ltd
25 Hill Street, London W1X 8LL

ISBN: 0 7131 58948

Printed in Great Britain by
Willmer Brothers Limited, Birkenhead

Contents

Maps

Illustrations

Acknowledgements

I owe the idea of writing about medieval heresy to Professor N. Cantor. For the opportunity of studying at the Monumenta Germaniae Historica I am indebted to the Alexander von Humboldt Stiftung, whose generosity to its beneficiaries extends beyond academic interests. For hospitality and guidance I am grateful to the late Professor H. Grundmann; for bibliographical advice I am indebted to Dr H. Lietzmann, and for help to Dr M. Polock, Professors J. M. Bak, S. Čirković, J. Šidak and Mr D. Bethell. I am grateful also to the seminars of Professor E. Werner at Leipzig and Professor B. Töpfer in East Berlin for stimulus, even where I disagreed, and to Professor D. C. Douglas and Mr W. K. Ford for encouragement. I received from the Colston Research Fund a welcome grant, and the staff of Bristol University library, especially Mr J. Edwards and those handling inter-library loans, have given valuable help.

Miss S. Rainey has worked on proofs and index; Dr J. V. Fearns and Dr J. Fines gave me access to their theses; Mrs Y. Burns has contributed a fresh translation of the Testament of Gost Radin, with important new readings.

I am indebted to a series of scholars for commenting on chapters and correcting errors. Professor J. B. Russell read drafts on eleventh century heresy, Dr R. I. Moore on the Cathars, Miss B. Bolton on Innocent III and the Free Spirit, Dr J. A. F. Thomson and Mr J. W Sherborne on the Lollards, Professor F. Seibt and Dr A. V. Antonovics on the Hussites, Dr A. V. Antonovics also on introductory material on the late Middle Ages. Professor R. E. Lerner read an early draft of the whole; Dr A. V. Murray and Professor C. N. L. Brooke read a more recent version and gave many hints. Professor W. L. Wakefield commented fully on the first seven chapters, and showed me the Cathar sites near Toulouse.

My father first interested me in historical research and commented shrewdly to the end of his life on all I wrote. It is my keenest regret that he has not lived to see publication.

The dedication is but a poor return for all that I owe my wife in comment, encouragement and practical assistance at every stage. In a real sense, she has been a co-author, and I do not think I would have finished the book without her.

University of Bristol   M.D.L.

A*

Preface

This book is a working synthesis of the state of research on popular heretical movements in Western Europe from the eighth to the fifteenth centuries, intended both for the undergraduate reader who needs a one-volume introduction and for the scholar working in one portion of this vast field who wants a handbook for quick reference on the subject as a whole. 'Popular' has been taken to mean movements with a substantial following amongst laymen. Individual heretical episodes involving small numbers may only be included in so far as they reveal a stage in the growth of a movement on a larger scale. Intellectual heresy would make another book; it has not been studied here, except in those cases where it gave a direct impetus to a popular heresy. Thus the case of Abelard, despite the general interest it aroused, is excluded; Wyclif, on the other hand, because of his effect on the Lollards, is given a chapter, and space is devoted to learned disputes about Wyclif and his teaching in the University of Prague because they are essential to the understanding of the Hussite revolt, which was a popular movement.

No hard and fast dates can be given for a subject of this type. I glance initially at the glimmerings of heresy in the West in the eighth century and the contemporaneous popular movement of Paulicianism, but my first substantial point of departure is the origins of Bogomilism in Bulgaria with the village priest Bogomil in the tenth century. An excursus into the history of this Eastern heresy, which spread from Bulgaria into Byzantium, has been necessary in order to explain the origins of the Western heresy of Catharism, the direct descendant of Bogomilism; the attention given to Byzantine and Balkan heresy also provides a helpful unit of contrast with the history of Western heresy. My survey stops short of the Reformation. Certain medieval heresies, those of the Hussites, the Waldensians, the Lollards and the Bohemian *Unitas Fratrum*, survived into the Reformation period but the exact nature of their influence and possible connections with the beliefs of the Reformers is still under investigation and the position is far from clear. Only detailed local studies of the sixteenth century will solve the problem; I do no more than glance at this theme in my epilogue. The story of the Hussites, in which major forces in a kingdom challenged the medieval Church on issues of doctrine, forms a natural conclusion. Although different strands within the Hussite revolt continued their existence after the fifteenth century, the agreement at Jihlava, whereby the moderate Hussites victorious over their more radical enemies in Bohemia made their submission to the Church and to their ruler in 1436, marks the end of a major phase in the history of this heresy and a conclusion to the book.

The history of medieval heresy is a history of failure, for none of the movements surveyed succeeded either in imposing their views on the Western Church or in gaining toleration for their opinions and practices. Condemnation of their beliefs as heretical by the papacy, whatever the time-lag or the vicissitudes on the way, led either to effective repression and so to extinction, as in the case of the Cathars, or to an underground, often precarious, survival, as in the case of the Lollards or the Waldensians. Substantial doctrinal unity in the Church was maintained partly by force, and partly by a continuing public commitment to the cause of orthodoxy; when this broke down, and beliefs condemned as heretical maintained themselves successfully against all efforts at repression, the Middle Ages was at an end.

I have written as a historian, not a theologian. I have taken heresy to mean whatever the papacy explicitly or implicitly condemned during the period. It has to be recognized, of course, that the growth of heresies and the failure of local authorities to deal effectively with them was one factor in the extension of papal power in the Church, and that it was some time before a clear legal concept of heresy emerged from the uncertainties of the eleventh and twelfth centuries: nevertheless, this definition will be a convenient working tool. It may incidentally lead to criticism in relation to the Hussites: some historians, not without reason, regard the moderate wing of the Hussites as reformers rather than heretics, and note that the condemnation of Hus was the work of a Council that itself had unorthodox views of the papacy. Yet Hus denied the medieval doctrine of the papacy, and even the moderate Utraquists received papal condemnation. I have therefore, with consistency, treated the Hussite movement as heretical. Where Byzantine heresy is concerned, I have followed the decisions of the patriarchate of Constantinople; for early heresy, I have followed the decisions of the great councils of the undivided Church.

When dealing with certain Western heresies, I have felt justified in making a distinction between 'real' heresies, that involved a major distortion of orthodox belief or practice, and 'artificial' heresies, which as an ensemble in a living context did not exist, as in the case of the Free Spirit of the late Middle Ages. The case of the poverty of Christ and the heresy of the *fraticelli* occupies a curious position. A real heresy was present, it seems to me, and predated the counter-actions of authority. The distortions of the ideal of poverty involved threatened to overturn the balance of Christian ethics; yet the actual decisions, whereby the pope of the time condemned them and tried to uproot the basis of their ideas in the Franciscan order, were in fact based on technical issues, and may fairly be called 'artificial'. The concept of 'artificial' heresy also enables me to give attention to the cases in which unpopular groups or individuals were smeared with slanderous charges by authority at various levels or by local opinion and to allude, but no more, to the closely allied subject of witchcraft.

Allocation of space has been dictated by consideration of the intrinsic importance of a particular movement and by the availability of secondary literature. Catharism and its antecedents has been given substantial space, justified by the importance of the counteraction which it inspired in the Church and by the lack of summaries in English; on the other hand,

Waldensianism, the one condemned movement to survive in continuity from the twelfth century to the present, has less than its due because, despite the present flow of research on it, it is not ripe for synthesis on any scale. Both Joachimism and the problems of the Franciscans have already been given extensive up-to-date treatment in English: the accounts of these, therefore, are cut short. Lollardy post-1414, well recorded in English from the point of view of prosecutions, is studied at a length greater than the importance of its adherents alone would deserve because it affords us a valuable body of information from a limited area about the conduct of heretics under persecution. Hussitism is given the largest space of all because of its significance as the movement which had the greatest potential to destroy the doctrinal supremacy of the Roman Church. Politics in this case is inextricably intertwined with the growth of heresy, so that any meaningful account must be a long one. A separate chapter on the apparently dualist church of Bosnia, as part of the account of Catharism, has had to be excised for lack of space and is replaced by a short summary and bibliography.[1]

Lack of space and of time for research has caused me to leave on one side the Spanish kingdoms and Poland. But all the major popular movements will be found here, and some mention of the regions of western Europe most seriously affected by heresy.

Certain cruxes, where research is inadequate or mistaken, or the source-material is defective, I have resolved in my own way, sometimes in disagreement with a general trend, or with an established authority, or in accord with little-known and minority views. They may be listed as follows.

(i)   The revival of heresy in the West in the eleventh century was touched by Byzantine Bogomilism, as were a number of episodes in early twelfth-century heresy. A hypothesis of Bogomil infiltration in successive shallow movements, intensifying into the 1140s, seems to me more tenable than the viewpoint which erects a barrier in the 1140s, accepting a Bogomil doctrinal presence then, but denying its earlier existence.[2]

(ii) Dr K. V. Selge's revisionist view of the origins of the Waldensian movement, which makes the desire for poverty in it secondary to the desire to preach, is not justified by the original sources.[3]

(iii) Waldensianism in the later Middle Ages was not a significant force, and its importance as a background to Hussitism can easily be exaggerated.[4]

(iv) The fall of Catharism was the prime battle-honour of the Inquisition, and while peaceful counter-preaching and changes in the spiritual climate helped to destroy it, force mattered most.[5]

(v)   Heresy was stirring among the Franciscans, their tertiaries and sympathizers in the Franciscan province of Provence well before 1318, and was not primarily 'created' by John XXII and his persecution.[6]

---

[1]Below, pp. 142–50. For a Waldensian synthesis, see also p. 151, n. 1.

[2]Below, ch. 3, 5; see esp. pp. 32, 53–4.

[3]See exposition of Waldensian origins below, pp. 67–70, and criticism of Selge's hypothesis, appendix C.

[4]Below, ch. 9; see also pp. 294, 336–8.

[5]Below, ch. 8, s. 2 (esp. pp. 134–41).

[6]Below, pp. 197–9, 203.

(vi) Lollardy, not mere anticlericalism, went on existing in England after *c.* 1430; this is demonstrable from the records of prosecutions for possession of suspect books. On the other hand, it was not a very important factor in changing public opinion on the eve of the Reformation.[7]

(vii) The importance of towns for the origins of heresy has been exaggerated. The interesting hypothesis of Norman Cohn, who sees a prime stimulus to millenarian heresy in the psychology of disorientated artisans in certain towns, rests, in part at least, on a faulty appreciation of evidence for medieval heresy.[8] On a wider front, historians have too readily assumed that casual references to preaching in towns, conventional terminology for adherents of sects and the use of towns as natural centres for the tracking down of heresy by persecutors demonstrate that heretical movements were more often born in towns. There is no case for this, and there was much rural heresy.[9]

Every historian of heresy must encounter the conflict of emphasis between the supporters of religious and of socio-economic factors as prime movers in the genesis of heresy. It dates back at least as far as the still-living work of G. Volpe, and it has received fresh impetus by political divisions amongst scholars since the war. To my mind, the late Professor H. Grundmann is the best single guide to popular medieval heresy; like him, I believe that the first necessity for the historian of heresy is to examine the religious and intellectual climate of orthodoxy in order to understand deviations from it. On the other hand, supporters of the 'religious' view, among whom I am to be numbered, have not always been ready enough to visualize the concrete situation in which heresy arises, and have been too easily satisfied with merely negative refutations of the most simplified socio-economic views. I am convinced that there is more to be said on this side, and that detailed analysis of cases of heresy, preferably in the late Middle Ages, where the sources are much fuller, will advance understanding in the future.[10] In reading the controversial secondary literature, I have been struck by the absence of concrete information on the origins, social class and wealth of heretics, which must be essential preliminaries for any general discussion. There is still too little collaboration between the religious and the economic historian, and we know too little of the basic facts.

The format of a one-volume introduction necessarily tends to put greatest emphasis on the religious aspect; as I write, I have been conscious that I have been able to say less about the often subtle social and economic background to these movements than I could have wished. The maps showing the distribution of heresy which I have included, none the less, may do something to rectify that deficiency. They are sketches, and in most cases they are necessarily incomplete; for they tell us, not about the total distribution of

---

[7]Below, pp. 263–4, 338–9.

[8]For his work, see below, pp. 47–8.

[9]For refs to the subject in this book, see note appended to this preface.

[10]The suggestions for an anthropological approach in J. L. Nelson, 'Society, Theodicy and the Origins of Heresy: towards a Reassessment of the Medieval Evidence', in *SCH*, ix, pp. 65–77, should be noted. A general survey of hypotheses is in J. B. Russell, 'Interpretations of the Origins of Medieval Heresy', *MS*, xxv (1963), pp. 26–53.

heresy in a locality, but about the distribution of detected heresy, which may be a very different matter; they are subject to all the idiosyncrasies of evidence which attach to underground movements, yet I hope that they will act as a stimulus to further and fuller investigation of the reasons why heresy settled in certain localities. The gazetteer to the first map, based on fresh analysis of the sources for Western heresy in the eleventh century, demonstrates the negative conclusion, that no generalization about the social class of these heretics can be made at all, since the sources are deficient on the point. The map of the Waldensians in Austria, taken from Dr M. Nickson's work, shows how a heresy may be embedded in the countryside; so, too, does the map of Cathars in the Lauragais, derived from Dr Y. Dossat's work, which, combined with his evidence of the incidence of certain punishments in the inquisition held there in 1245–6, gives a clue to the numbers then involved in heresy. The map of the spread of the Waldensians from the original nucleus at Lyons in the first century of their existence, taken from the work of Dr J. V. Fearns, shows the variety of environments in which heresy could take hold; the sketch of the fall of the Bosnian Church, based on the work of Professor S. Ćirković, demonstrates that in this instance, contrary to common assumptions, the growth of trade and contact with the outside world, so far from aiding the development of heresy, helped to bring it to an end. The map of Lollardy underground, based on the work on prosecutions by Dr J. A. F. Thomson and Dr. J. Fines, shows how heresy may fan out in villages and hamlets from the effects of a preacher's activity, and illustrates the relationship which existed in late Lollardy between heresy and textile areas. A further map, based on an analysis of Foxe's *Martyrs*, plots for contrast with Lollardy the places of origin and of burning of the Marian martyrs. It is hoped that it may be of some assistance to others elucidating the relation between medieval heresy and the Reformation. One other map, that of the dualist Churches and the spread of conflict among the heretics, is not concerned with geographical distribution or social origin of heresy, but rather is designed to recall to the reader the degree to which late twelfth-century Catharism was dependent on the dualists of the Balkans and Byzantium.

The pioneer of the study of medieval heresy in modern times for the English reader was H. C. Lea, the historian of the Inquisition; his work, in three volumes,[11] seriously outdated on many aspects, remains the most comprehensive treatment of the subject, and may still be used with profit. Lea wrote with a powerful indignation. He hated the Middle Ages and its Church, and he lacked any sympathetic understanding of the persecuting churchmen and their ideals. Yet the reader who disagrees with Lea and his lack of perspective while admiring his detailed scholarship, must still be reminded that the history of medieval heresy is a terrible story—one of persecution of men and women for their religious opinions.

[11]H. C. Lea, *A History of the Inquisiton of the Middle Ages*, New York, 1888; review: J. Dahlberg–Acton, *EHR* III (1888), 773–88.

NOTE

Heresy, Town and Country On eleventh-century heresy, see appendix D s. 1 (esp. the section on social composition and the notes); for J. B. Russell's analysis of geographical location of early heresy, see p. 35, n. 38.

Note especially the rural origin in an Alpine backwater of Peter of Bruis's heresy (pp. 51–5), and Tanchelm's preaching, not only in Antwerp, but also in undeveloped Zeeland (p. 56); Eon de L'Étoile may not be a heretic at all (p. 60) but if he is, he is certainly a rural figure (p. 59). Note the place of rural nobility in the rise of Languedocian Catharism (pp. 86, 114; for the Lauragais, p. 136 and map four). In Languedoc there was no gulf between town and country. For Waldensians in the countryside, see pp. 158–61, and in the mountains, p. 153; for Dolcino's peasant following, p. 195; for late English Lollardy in the countryside, pp. 238, 239, 252, 256–7, 258, 262–5, 269 and map 9.

Valdes's conversion was stimulated by the commercial environment of a town (pp. 67–8), and preaching fanned out from Lyons (p. 70); towns were of great importance for heresy also in Northern Italy (pp. 82–4, 117); the Beguins of the Franciscan province of Provence were found principally in towns, no doubt because the Franciscans were there (p. 199); Wyclif's heresy originated in the university town of Oxford (chap 14), and the city and university of Prague were vital for the rise of Hussitism (chapters 16, 17). But much Lollard preaching took place in the country; location of centres is due to the placing of patrons (pp. 241, 252, 257, 258), and Tabor was the centre of a peasant movement (pp. 310–11, 316–8).

For terminology, see pp. 30, 40, and for Inquisition evidence, pp. 169–71

Part One

The Beginnings

I

The Problem of Heresy

Heresy, and the horror it inspires, intertwines with the history of the Church itself. Jesus warned his disciples against the false prophets who would take His name and the Epistle to Titus states that a heretic, after a first and second abomination, must be rejected. But Paul, writing to the Corinthians, said, 'Oportet esse haereses', as the Latin Vulgate translated his phrase—'there must be heresies, that they which are proved may be manifest among you'[1]— and it was understood by medieval churchmen that they must expect to be afflicted by heresies.

Heresy was of great importance in the early centuries in forcing the Church progressively to define its doctrines and to anathematize deviant theological opinions. At times, in the great movements such as Arianism and Gnosticism, heresy seemed to overshadow the Church altogether. Knowledge of the individual heresies and of the definitions which condemned them became a part of the equipment of the learned Christian; the writings of the Fathers wrestled with these deviations, and lists of heresies and handbooks assimilated this experience of the early centuries and handed it on to the Middle Ages.

Events after Christianity became the official religion of the Empire also shaped the assumptions with which the Church of the Middle Ages met heresy. After Constantine's conversion, Christians in effect held the power of the State and, despite some hesitations, they used it to impose a uniformity of belief. Both in the eastern and in the western portions of the Empire it became the law that pertinacious heretics were subject to the punishments of exile, branding, confiscation of goods, or death. These regulations survived the fall of the Empire, and so did the assumption that it was the right of the Church to call on the State to put down heresy.

Heresy was not thought to be the product of the individual speculative intelligence, or of devout men and women seeking a higher ethical life—still less of oppressed lower classes demanding better conditions and masking their economic objectives in the outwardly religious forms of their age. All these interpretations have been put forward by modern historians of medieval heresy, but they are quite alien to the assumptions of churchmen, whether of

---

[1] Titus 3.10; 1 Cor. 11.19. H. Grundmann, 'Oportet et haereses esse. Das Problem der Ketzerei im Spiegel der mittelalterlichen Bibelexegese', *AKG*, XLV (1963), pp. 129–64. For the meaning of the Greek term from which 'heresy' is derived in Titus and other early sources, see L. Goppelt, *Apostolic and Post-Apostolic Times*, trans. R. A. Guelich (London, 1970), pp. 165–77. I owe this reference to Mr W. K. Ford.

the Middle Ages or of the early centuries of the Church. They believed that heresy was the work of the devil. Descriptions of heretics were couched in sets of favourite adjectives and texts, passed on from author to author, and only too often imposed with scant discrimination on the heretics, their beliefs and practices.[2] Some were an inheritance passed onto the Middle Ages from the age of the Fathers; others were developed in the Middle Ages themselves. The descriptions served primarily to develop a set of conventional characteristics of the type-figure of the heretic: his pride, which must be a feature, for he has set himself up against the teaching of the Church; his superficial appearance of piety, which must be intended to deceive, and cannot be real, since he is in fact the enemy of the faith; and his secrecy, which is contrasted to the openness of Catholic preaching. He may well be described as unlettered (even if this is not entirely true), since *a priori* he lacks the equipment of the orthodox churchman; he may be accused of counterfeiting piety while actually indulging in libertinism—an accusation which strangely repeats those made by pagan writers against early Christians, and sometimes appears to feed on the same material. His beliefs may be crudely assimilated to the heresies of the patristic age, even when they are quite unrelated, though this tendency fades as more accurate knowledge of actual medieval heresy penetrates the conventions. The bulk of sources emanate from the repressing forces or the chroniclers on the Catholic side, and their descriptions are thus shaped by these conventions. Surviving work of the heretics, in which we can see for ourselves the nature of their teaching, is very much less, either because the heresy was conveyed more often by word of mouth than by writing, or because repression has destroyed documents.

The historian thus faces acute problems of evidence when he wishes to study the behaviour, motives and beliefs of the medieval heretic. He is dealing much of the time with underground movements existing behind a barrier of secrecy—and because Church and State are most often combined against them, they are willy nilly secret opposition movements hostile to authority. As a modern historian, he must elucidate motives from sources which are very rarely concerned with them, and scrape off layers of convention and prejudice from his originals in order to reach a true delineament of the heretics.

The subject is also two-sided. It takes two to create a heresy: the heretic, with his dissident beliefs and practices; and the Church, to condemn his views and to define what is orthodox doctrine. It was in the persistent resistance to the teaching of the Church that heresy consisted: error became heresy when, shown his deviation, the obstinate refused to obey and retract. In the thirteenth century Robert Grosseteste's definition stated that 'a heresy is an opinion chosen by human perception contrary to holy Scripture, publicly avowed and obstinately defended.' The Church, confronted from the twelfth century onwards with a challenge from hostile sects, was forced, step by step, to recognize how these sects differed from those of late antiquity, and to take new measures to deal with them. A machinery was created both for defining doctrine and for uncovering and putting down those who refused to accept the

---

[2]H. Grundmann, 'Der Typus des Ketzers in mittelalterlicher Anschauung', *Kultur-und Universalgeschichte Festschrift für Walter Goetz*. Leipzig and Berlin, 1927), pp. 91–107 (fundamental for approach to sources).

decisions of authority.[3] Not all these developments have been fully studied by medievalists, for, although we have known much since Lea of the origins and workings of one of the instruments of repression, the inquisition, much more needs to be known about the doctrinal decision-making of ecclesiastical authority and the way in which the medieval concept of heresy was built up. Moreover, the search for understanding of the motives of the heretic will take the historian into the study of medieval societies and economic changes and into the issues of the morale of the faithful, the conditions in regional Churches and the effect of abuse in stimulating heresies. All are subjects open to investigation, where often enough no final word, even within the limitations of our sources, has yet been said.

In view of these difficulties, both of the multifarious nature of the subject and of the problematic, sometimes prejudiced, sources, it is hardly surprising that the study of medieval heresies has tended to lag behind research on other facets of medieval history. Yet heresies are an integral part of the medieval scene in a number of countries, and their growth is a phenomenon which runs side by side with, often directly influencing, such well known developments as the rise of papal power, the growth of the canon law, the emergence of religious orders and the development of the crusading ideal. The need for detection and repression of heresy shaped the western Church for the future for good and ill, and in political history was occasionally of decisive importance, as for example the Albigensian crusades in French history and the Hussite crisis for the lands of the Bohemian crown. The heretical movements of the Middle Ages failed in their purpose, but they nevertheless left their imprint on the course of events.

Comparative neglect has in recent years given way to an upsurge of interest among scholars; a number of discoveries have enlarged the store of works written by heretics themselves, or have enabled us at least to get closer to their ideas and to shake off some of the distortions of the Catholic source material. The time is ripe for a summary in English, to survey the whole field, and to give a guide to recent progress—bearing in mind always that fresh research in a subject in rapid flux is bound to change current generalizations, and that the 'refracting mirror' of medieval assumptions about heresy and the scarcity of the requisite type of sources will always tend to inhibit our vision of the truth.

Not only the existence of the assumption that State and Church have a duty to persecute, and the emergence of a machinery to detect and examine religious dissidents, shaped the conditions of existence of the medieval heretic. He was also subject to one basic principle of medieval Christianity generally: that the heretic who wilfully persisted in his error was condemned to the pains of hell for eternity. The persistent dissident was thus not only defying a visible authority—and, as we shall see, that authority was not always very clearly in evidence, or actively pursuing heretics; he was also challenging the fear of damnation, and backing his own judgement or that of his group against

---

[3] On the medieval notion of heresy, see *MBPH*, pp. 1–7 (note esp. the analogy between heresy and disease), and *The Concept of Heresy: the Middle Ages* (*Medievalia Lovanensia*, IV (forthcoming)). See also prologue to G. Leff, *Heresy in the Later Middle Ages. The Relation of Heterodoxy to Dissent c. 1250–c. 1450*, Manchester, New York, 1967, 2v (Survey stressing intellectual factors); reviews, H. S. Offler, in *EHR* LXXXIV (1969), 572–6; M. D. Lambert, in *History* LV (1970), 75–9.

a spiritual authority with the power to decide his eternal future. That groups of men and women in medieval society were prepared to make this defiance is one of the striking facts to record, and one major theme of this book will be the examination, where possible, of the motives which led them to do it. Second only in interest to this question is that of the failure of all medieval heretical movements who made this defiance to survive in the long term. Why, we may ask, having once challenged authority, were these heretics severally unable to maintain the independence of their beliefs?

2

Early Western Heresy and Eastern Dualism

Introduction

Dualism must be accounted one of the perennial beliefs of mankind.[1] Its presence has been found in areas as geographically distinct as China and the hunting-ground for the Iroquois Indians, and at epochs as widely divided as 2000 B.C. and the twentieth century. It is fundamentally inimical to orthodox Christianity: the dualist exaggerates and distorts the ascetic, world-renouncing texts of Scripture and postulates an evil material creation. What can be seen is evil: flesh itself is the creation of an evil God or of a fallen creature, given over to evil. What is unseen is spiritual. The ultimate purpose of existence is to escape from the evil material world. The effects of this set of beliefs on orthodox doctrine are profound: the incarnation of Christ is made void; Christ cannot truly have taken on man's nature, since human flesh is a part of the evil creation. With the denial of the Incarnation, the orthodox doctrine of Redemption is void; the sacraments of the Church, in so far as they use evil matter—water in baptism, bread and wine in the Eucharist—must also be repudiated. Attitudes to sin and freewill are changed. Meat-eating is rejected. Logically, marriage must be eschewed, for it perpetuates the human body, which is part of the evil creation.

Dualist beliefs have the strong superficial attraction of simplicity; they present a clear-cut world picture to an ignorant convert, or one passing from paganism, and they appear to provide a solution to the perennial theological problem of the presence of evil in a world created by a good God.

In the early centuries of the Church's existence various forms of dualist belief presented a major challenge. The schools of thought known collectively as the Gnostics lived beside, and intertwined with, the Christian Churches in the early centuries.[2] Only after some vicissitudes were their beliefs declared heresy and their teachers banished from the congregations; a considerable struggle was needed to maintain orthodoxy against them. Manichaeism, the third-century heresy which blended ancient Zoroastrianism with the original revelations of its leader, the Iranian priest Mani, could in its time boast of

---

[1]U. Bianchi, 'Le Dualisme en Histoire des Religions', *RHR*, CLIX (1961), pp. 1–46.

[2]H. Jonas, *The Gnostic Religion*, 2nd edn (Boston, 1963). I have relied on this for my view of Gnosticism. For survey of dualism from Gnosticism to the Cathars, see S. Runciman, *The Medieval Manichee* (Cambridge, 1947), review by R. Manselli in *RR*, xx (1949), pp. 65–94; from Mani and Priscillian to Byzantine and Western dualism, see R. Manselli, *L'Eresia del Male* (Napoli, 1963). I am indebted to the Reverend F. R. Walters for advice.

adherents from Turkestan to the West. Within the sphere of interest of the Byzantine Church, it gained many adherents, and outlasted Gnostic dualism; indeed, it survived till the persecutions of the Emperors Justin and Justinian, and was only broken in the Byzantine world and reduced to a fragment there by the seventh century.

In both the eastern and western portions of the undivided Church there existed the same repugnance towards heresy. In both that repugnance was manifested ultimately in an apparatus of law, intended to restrain its appearance and punish its persistent adherents. Circumstances, however, ensured that the laws against heresy were employed much more heavily in the east than in the Latin West. The eastern Church's area of jurisdiction abutted on the homelands of religious syncretism in the Near East, whence religious speculations flowed into Byzantine lands, and where heretics of all kinds, in flight from persecution, might find both a refuge and a springboard for further incursions. The Greek mind was more subtle and more fertile in producing novelties than the Latin; no massive influx of barbarians succeeded in bringing about a catastrophic fall in the level of culture, as it did in the West, with a by-product in the extinction of the speculative intellectual tradition that had so often spawned heresy in late antiquity.

The Byzantine emperors worked hard to eradicate heresy and had much success (as we have seen) in the case of the persecutions of Justinian. But, though they demolished some heresies, others came to take their place. In Byzantium heresies of various kinds continued to exist on the same lines as they had done in the early centuries of the Church—that is, as movements with organization, leaders and a body of doctrine which was handed on from one generation to the next. There is never a time in the history of the Byzantine Church in which heresy is completely eliminated.

Early Western Heresy

In the West the effects of the barbarian invasions provided a kind of *tabula rasa* for orthodoxy. Catholicism under the pope at Rome came to win almost total victory in the territories under his jurisdiction.[3] Arianism, the fourth-century heresy which denied the true divinity of Christ, brought to central German tribes by the preaching of Wulfilas, had for a time hindered the achievement of uniformity but was finally overcome. Events had altered the environment in which the heresies of the early centuries had once spread. Churchmen were preoccupied with the needs of defence and the spread of the gospel among the heathen barbarians. There was no longer a cultivated laity. The centuries following the fall of Rome were filled with warfare. Heresy of the old pattern virtually ceased to exist, its place being taken by the resistance to Christianity of paganism and supersition—in short, of apostasy rather than heresy proper.[4]

Such outbreaks of doctrinal dissidence that did occur were treated mildly by the authorities, presumably because they presented no significant

[3] H. I. Marrou, 'L'Héritage de la Chrétienté', *HS*, pp.51–4, at p. 53 (see *HS* for wide-ranging articles on heresies and society, and pages of accompanying discussion from original colloquy at Royaumont).

[4] A. Gieysztor, 'Mouvements para-hérétiques en Europe centrale et orientale du 9e au 11e Siècle: Apostasies', in *HS,* pp. 159–67.

challenge to the Church:[5] they tend either to be the work of individual theologians who develop a real heresy but gather no movement, or that of rustic preachers who hold crowds in their hands but are themselves hardly more than isolated rebels and eccentrics. Four such episodes, dating from the eighth and early ninth centuries, a time of greater order and tranquillity, may be taken to illustrate the point. One is the case of the ascetics whom Boniface met in Germany, some being abstainers from foods 'ordained by God for our use', others men who lived on milk and honey, perhaps recalling God's promises for the land of Canaan or adapting John the Baptist's diet of locusts and wild honey.[6] Two others are rural preachers. Aldebert, from Boniface's time, who first emerged in the region of Soissons declared himself a saint, distributed his hair clippings and nail parings to followers, and, claiming to lead the apostolic life, travelled round preaching to large crowds. Theuda in the ninth century followed a similar career in the villages round Mainz, claiming a special revelation and a knowledge of the date of the imminent end of the world.[7] A fourth and very different case is that of Claudius, bishop of Turin, one-time master of a school in Aquitaine, who was appointed to his see by the favour of Louis the Pious between 814 and 820.[8] He denounced the use of images in Christian worship, and ordered them to be removed from his diocese. The cult of the Cross excited his disapproval: in a *reductio ad absurdum* he asked why, if the Cross was venerated, all virgin girls should not on similar grounds be paid reverence, since Christ was nine months in the womb of a virgin and only six hours on the Cross. He rejected the cult of the saints, and questioned the value of pilgrimages. The pope's authority was put in doubt on the grounds that Peter's primacy was personal to him and ceased at his death; apostolic authority rested on good life rather than any institutional position. Thus uncannily a ninth century theologian anticipated a part of the English Lollard heresy of the fifteenth century.[9]

Of the four, Theuda was an eccentric prophetess of a kind recurrent at all periods of the Church's history. Aldebert had a little more positive doctrinal content in his preaching—a rejection of wealth seems implicit in his simple costume and his claim to the apostolic life. The German ascetics are hard to place. It is natural to assume a Scriptural basis for their behaviour but, unless they were arguing that their diet was necessary for all Christians, they were not strictly heretics. All differ from Claudius, who was giving vent to a dogmatic heresy, if not a very profound one; he, however, left no following and no tradition.

At this stage popular impulses to dissidence are not combining with doctrinal heresy to form movements against the Church. The Adoptionism taught by Felix of Urgel in the eighth century in his diocese of Toledo, though it reached the people, hardly qualifies as an exception. There, as

---

[5] For all early Western heresy, J. B. Russell, *Dissent and Reform in the Early Middle Ages* (Berkeley & Los Angeles, 1965), esp. pp. 251–2. I am indebted to Professor Russell for helpful comment and free use of his maps—the more generous in view of our difference of academic judgement.

[6] The latter is Russell's suggestion (op. cit., p. 11); for the episode, see ibid, pp. 10–11, and further the same writer's 'St Boniface and the Eccentrics', *CH*, xxxiii (1964), pp. 3–15.

[7] Russell, pp. 102–8.

[8] Ibid., pp. 13–17.

[9] See below, chap. 15.

elsewhere in this period, we do not meet the dedicated sectary with doctrinal apparatus and organization, of the kind that existed in the early centuries and was still to be found in Byzantium. Heresy in the West at this time remains rare, sporadic and formless.

In the renewed period of disorder which followed the death of Louis the Pious and the breakdown of the Carolingian Empire, we meet no recorded cases of heresy at all in the West for a period of a hundred years.[10] Western churchmen used the traditional texts of the Fathers and the councils of the early centuries in which heresy is denounced and categorized, and continued to believe that it was a deadly sin and a principal weapon of the devil against the Church; but by the late tenth century there was no one among them with any personal experience of a living heresy.

The Paulicians

In the Byzantine world, by contrast, the eighth century and much of the ninth witnessed the growth of a sect on the soil of Asia Minor, equipped with a doctrinal tradition reaching back to the early centuries, which actually came to offer a military challenge to the Byzantine Empire. The Paulicians, so called because of their reputed adherence to 'the wretched little Paul'—the third-century Adoptionist heretic Paul of Samosata—had originated in the kingdom of Armenia, a neighbour of Byzantium.[11] They retained a number of beliefs characteristic of early Syriac Christianity, which had been a missionary influence in Armenia: a great veneration of baptism, a mistrust of the use of images in worship, and the belief that Christ was not God by nature but by grace, being 'adopted' by the Father at His baptism when He was thirty years old.[12] Hellenizing reforms in the Armenian Church had turned members of this early Syriac party formally into heretics, and initiated persecution. From Armenia they passed obscurely into Byzantium, then for a time received the favour of eighth-century emperors who favoured Iconoclasm and were sympathetic to them because of their dislike of images.[13] By the beginning of the ninth century they thus already had a long history behind them, linking them in an unbroken line of descent to the beliefs of the earliest centuries.

Early in the ninth century the appearance of a great leader in the sect, Sergius, a founder of churches and ally of the Moslems in military raids on the Empire, coupled with the waning of support for Iconoclasm in the imperial court, caused a fresh outbreak of persecution. The Paulicians, numerous in the Asiatic Themes, fought back.[14] Under Karbeas, a former imperial staff officer who had fled during the persecution in 843, they built up an independent State on the upper Euphrates near the western border of Armenia. Under his successor Chrysocheir, also a one-time soldier from the

[10]Russell, pp. 17–18.

[11]All previous work on the Paulicians is superseded by N. G. Garsoïan, *The Paulician Heresy* (The Hague & Paris, 1967); for their name, see pp. 145, 213–4; review by J. V. A. Fine, jr, in *Speculum* XLIV (1969), pp. 285–8. Further lit. is in M. Loos, *Dualist Heresy in the Middle Ages* (Prague, 1974); the author believes in Marcionite influence on the Paulicians. Garsoïan is preferable.

[12]Garsoïan, *Paulician Heresy*, pp. 220–30.

[13]Ibid., pp. 122–4.

[14]Ibid., pp. 125–30; see also pp. 72, 119–20.

Byzantine army, the Paulicians raided the Empire as far west as Nicaea and Ephesus, and dared to respond to an embassy from Constantinople with a claim on all the provinces east of the Bosphorus. But the armies of Basil I took revenge, destroyed their capital Tephrikē in 871–2, and removed them for good from the imperial provinces of Asia Minor. Remnants fled beyond the eastern frontiers, to the Arabs and to their ancient homelands in Armenia, where they long survived, if less dramatically than in the Empire. On the western frontier in the Balkans a group already existed, having been settled there as a garrison in Thrace against the Bulgars by the Iconoclast emperor Constantine V in 747, at a time when the heretics were in favour.[15] It was in this area that the sect scored its next success against Byzantium.

Well before the fall of the Paulician State, in an obscure mutation beginning probably with Sergius and completed in Karbeas's day, in the ninth century, a substantial portion of the Paulicians in the Empire exchanged their Adoptionist heresy for dualist beliefs.[16] In place of the orthodox doctrine of the creation of heaven and earth by one god, they came to postulate the existence of two beings, one the Heavenly Father to whom the Future belonged but who had no power in the visible world, the other an evil being, Satan, who had created the visible world and held domain over it.[17] Other heresies followed from this: Christ could no longer be regarded, as in orthodox doctrine, as true man and true God—to have had a body like other men would have made Him a part of Satan's evil creation. His body was held to have been brought from heaven. He was not born of Mary; the term *theotokos* which Byzantine churchmen used of her was applied instead to the heavenly Jerusalem. Since Christ did not have an ordinary man's body, He could not truly have suffered at the Crucifixion. Sacraments which made use of the matter which Satan had created were rejected; the bread and wine of the eucharist was interpreted allegorically as meaning the teaching of Christ. Baptism in the Byzantine Church by water was repudiated by citing Christ's words, 'I am the living water.' The evil being who is the creator of the visible world was equated with Jehovah, the God of the Jews, and His revelation in the Old Testament treated as the work of Satan.

The influence of the earlier Syro-Armenian tradition was not completely supplanted, for it modified the new dualism. In place of the extreme asceticism usual in dualist sects, rejecting marriage as perpetuating Satan's creation and demanding from adepts strict renunciation of food and drink, the Byzantine Paulicians retained the attitudes of their Armenian predecessors, refusing the customary fasts in the Byzantine Church, eating cheese and milk during Quadragesima and accepting marriage. One unusual doctrine, the rejection of Mary's virginity, was carried over from the previous tradition. The rejection of the veneration of the Cross, though compatible

---

[15]Ibid., pp. 122–3. The chronicler Georgius Cedrenus says that Paulicians were settled in Constantinople.

[16]Reconstruction by Garsoïan, based on reassessment of the relative weight to be given to Armenian and Greek sources. I accept her hypothesis on the late date and compilatory character of Peter of Sicily, the crux of the book. On the historical context of the mutation, see ibid., pp. 182–5.

[17]Ibid., pp. 169–73.

with dualism, was also a legacy from the past. By this internal doctrinal development in the ninth century a sect which had already shown resilience in its resistance to persecution took into its armoury the potent weapon of dualism.

It is a characteristic of dualist heresy that it needs scant basis for a resurrection; defeated, it may easily rise again. It is a form of belief that may appear simply through spontaneous combustion, or at least be fanned into flames again from a few smouldering ashes—a small surviving nucleus of teachers, a limited amount of written material. Such seems to have been the case in the Byzantine Empire: Gnostic dualism had faded out; Manichaeism was almost destroyed;[18] and mutated Byzantine Paulicianism came to take their place. Its function in the history of Byzantine heresy was to act as a receptacle, an organized body for the transmission of dualism to later generations.

Bulgarian Bogomilism

After the fall of Tephrikē in 872 and the destruction of the Paulicians in Asia Minor, the next major landfall for dualism was in Bulgaria some sixty years later. Emphasis thus shifts from the heartland of Byzantium to a fringe area, a mission outpost for the Byzantine Church and a buffer State, which only began to be incorporated in the Empire in 972. Bulgaria was a land of barbarians where an aristocracy drawn from the Bulgars, a Turco-Tatar tribe from south Russia, ruled a Slav peasantry.[19] It had long been a threat to the western frontier of the Empire. In 864 its ruler Boris I, under pressure from a Byzantine army, accepted baptism from the Greek Orthodox Church. Missionaries could now set about the work of conversion, but they found themselves in a situation of confusion. Paganism, aided by the fears of the aristocracy about the aims of Boris in introducing the new religion, was in the early years strong enough to bring about two reactions to the old gods, and influences from different faiths and countries—Greek, Armenian, Catholic, Jewish and Islamic—competed for the allegiance of a backward people.[20]

In this difficult terrain Byzantine churchmen never succeeded in building up a strong Church, largely for political reasons. Hostility between Bulgaria and Byzantium was of longer standing than the introduction of Christianity, and the Church, despite the use of a Slavonic liturgy and the development of a flourishing school of translators for religious texts, was unable to overcome the baleful effects of the association between Greek Orthodoxy and the hated political power on the country's frontier. Byzantinization increased the gulf between the Bulgar aristocracy, who in cultural matters looked towards

[18]H .C. Puech and A. Vaillant, *Le Traité contre les Bogomiles de Cosmas le Prêtre* (Paris, 1945) (the standard, subtle account of Bogomil doctrines, relevant also for Catharism), p. 304.

[19]Background by D. Obolensky, 'The Empire and its Northern Neighbours, 565–1018', in *CMH*, IV, i, ed. J. M. Hussey, 2nd edn (Cambridge, 1966), pp. 473–518; and *The Bogomils* (Cambridge, 1948) (narrative of Bogomil history with hypothesis of continuity from Mani), pp. 59–110; for inferences from Cosmas by A. Vaillant, see Puech-Vaillant, *Traité*, pp. 19–37. Useful lit. in Loos, *Dualist Heresy*, but with hypothesis of Marcionite influence.

[20]Evidence of the *Responsa ad consulta Bulgarorum*. The Catholic contact was brief and slight. I. Dujčev, 'Die Responsa Nicolai I. Papae ad Consulta Bulgarorum als Quelle für die bulgarische Geschichte', in *Medioevo Bizantino–Slavo*, 1 (Rome, 1965), pp. 125–48.

Constantinople and whose economic arrangements were like some of the worst developments in the contemporary Empire, and their oppressed peasantry. In the Church parallel developments opened a division between a wealthy Greek or Greek-orientated upper clergy, the *presviteri*, often contemptuous of their charges, and a poor, ill-educated Bulgarian-speaking village priesthood. Heresy which could canalize patriotic opposition to a pro-Byzantine Church and a dislike of peasants for their lords thus had a natural platform in Bulgaria.

Paulicianism had a foothold in the neighbouring terrain of Thrace through the establishment of the garrison there by Constantine V. In the eighth century these heretics would still have been adherents of the Adoptionist wing of the sect; in the ninth they were open to the mutation into dualism which affected the tradition of the Byzantine Paulicians, or to the influence of dualists dispersed after the fall of Tephrikē, and were thus a potential fount of dualist missionary activity; in the mid-tenth century a history of the Paulicians written in Byzantium, falsely attributed to Peter of Sicily, said that the heretics were sending missionaries into Bulgaria.[21] A decade or less earlier Theophylact Lecapenus, Patriarch of Constantinople, asked for his advice about a new heresy in Bulgaria by its Tsar Peter, categorized it as 'Manichaeism mixed with Paulicianism.' 'Manichaeism' is commonly used in Byzantine polemical sources as a general term for dualist heresy; the second term makes the references more precise.[22] John the Exarch, the eminent Bulgarian churchman, in a source datable possibly to 915, certainly before 927, referred to 'filthy Manichaeans and all pagan Slavs' in Bulgaria, who said that the devil was the eldest son of God.[23] The suggestion of alliance between pagan reaction and dualism may well be significant. The earliest school of translators in Bulgaria selected for translation a number of Byzantine polemical works directed wholly or partly against dualist heresy—a fact which suggests that the young Church was facing dualism as a practical problem not long after the age of conversion.[24]

Bogomil, a Bulgarian priest who had probably taken the name, meaning 'worthy of the pity of God', as a pseudonym,[25] organized the heretical ideas already to be found in the country and blended them with others to form a

[21]Garsoïan, *Paulician Heresy*, pp.55, 57. Dating of 954–9 suggested ibid., p. 77, n. 182.

[22]Obolensky's translation (*Bogomils*, p. 115). As evidence, the letter is contaminated by literary material of no certain relevance (Puech, in Puech–Vaillant, pp. 132–4). 'Paulicianism' is a correction for 'Paulianism' in the original. See Garsoïan, p. 216, for the absence of contact between Paulicianism and Manichaeism and the reasons for the loose use of the term in Byzantium (pp. 186–97).

[23]Obolensky's translation (*Bogomils*, p. 95); for description and dating, see Puech–Vaillant, pp 20–3 (Vaillant), 132 (Puech).

[24]I. Dujčev, 'I Bogomili nei paesi slavi e loro storia', in *Medioevo Bizantino-Slavo*, I, pp. 251–82.

[25]Vaillant's derivation is in Puech–Vaillant, *Traité*, p. 27, and Puech's ibid., pp. 282–3, to be preferred to Obolensky, *Bogomils*, p. 117, n. 4. Historicity of Bogomil questioned by V. S. Kiselkov in 'Szöstesztvuvalli e pop Bogomil?', *IP*, xiv (1958), pp. 57–67 (in Bulgarian); for a summary of the controversy, see E. Werner, 'Theophilos-Bogumil', *BS*, vii (1966), pp. 49–60 (in German), and 'Bogomil—eine literarische Fiktion?', *FF*, xxxiii (1959), pp. 24–8; Werner's view of historicity preferred, but not his derivation of the name; see also Puech, in Puech–Vaillant, pp. 283–9. Further argument for authenticity by I. Dujčev, in *Medioevo Bizantino-Slavo*, I; for Bogomil's work. Puech, in Puech–Vaillant, pp. 289–90.

new heresy during the reign of the Tsar Peter (927–969). Cosmas, a member of the Bulgarian clergy who answered his heresy in a treatise written probably in 972, said that Bogomil preached heresy 'for the first time' in the land of Bulgaria;[26] but the evidence for Paulician influence there enables us to go beyond this view.

The heresy, whose adherents came to be known as Bogomils[27] in the following century, amounts to a fresh mutation of dualism.[28] Bogomils believed that the devil was the creator of the visible world of matter. Though Cosmas only refers ambiguously to the point, we may assume from his incidental comments and some later evidence about the sect that this had the same consequences as it did for the Paulicians, in a heretical belief that Christ had no ordinary body, was not born of Mary, and did not truly suffer.[29] The sacraments which make use of matter, the devil's creation, were rejected;[30] Christ did not institute the eucharist. References to eucharistic bread and wine were glossed to mean the four gospels and the Acts of the Apostles. Orthodox baptism with water was rejected in favour of initiation rites in which the laying on of hands and not water was used.[31] The devil was identified with Jehovah, whose revelation in the Old Testament was repudiated.[32] Thus far the negations taught by the sect corresponded to those of Paulicianism.

But the Bogomils were only partially influenced by these elements in the dualist Byzantine Paulician amalgam of doctrine which derived from their Syro-Armenian past. Like the Paulicians, they repudiated the veneration of the Cross: if crosses came into their hands, they chopped them up and used them for tools.[33] It seems as if they followed the Byzantine Paulicians in denying the virginity of Mary, though Cosmas's language is again vague.[34] Where the Bogomils differed from their Paulician predecessors was in the realm of ethics. Unlike other dualist sects, the Paulicians did not demand an extreme asceticism from their adepts. The Bogomils did.[35] They condemned marriage *per se*; it consecrated sexual relations, which continued Satan's rule over man. Similarly, the procreation of children, which perpetuated the flesh, part of Satan's evil creation, was prohibited. Bogomil hostility to procreation was vented on the children themselves. Whenever they saw children of baptismal age, Cosmas tells us, the Bogomils would turn away as from a bad smell, spit and hold their noses.[36] Meat, the product of procreation, was also forbidden; to touch it, they argued, was to obey the command of Satan. Wine too was condemned.

[26]Puech-Vaillant, p. 54.

[27]Ibid., pp. 280–3.

[28]Sensitive reconstruction, setting Cosmas against later sources, by Puech, in Puech-Vaillant, pp. 129–343; chronological development in Obolensky, pp. 59–110.

[29]Ibid., pp. 205–9. All further reference unless otherwise stated are to Puech's analysis, which includes textual references.

[30] Ibid., pp. 223–30.

[31]Ibid., pp. 250–60.

[32]Ibid., pp. 168–74.

[33]Ibid., p. 58 (text); 234–7 (Puech).

[34]Ibid., pp. 208–9.

[35]For their asceticism, see ibid, pp. 260–72.

[36]Ibid., p. 81 (text).

In their rejection of the Greek Orthodox Church the heretics were as radical as it is possible to be.[37] They rejected church buildings, and would not venerate icons, images or crosses. The liturgy they regarded merely as a human invention of Chrysostom. All the sacraments of the Church were repudiated, including, of course, confession to the Orthodox priesthood. They rejected the saints whom the Church accepted, with the exception of the Apostles and the martyrs who refused to worship idols.[38] Sundays were not observed as feast days, but used both for fasting and for work. The normal apparatus for the interpretation of Scripture was discarded,[39] and the Fathers were not taken as a standard. A later source tells us that they had special hostility for the masters of the Orthodox Church, Basil, Gregory of Nazianzus, John Chrysostom.[40] Texts were allegorized according to a personalized, subjective exegesis which, for example, made all the miracle stories of the gospels into merely symbolic narratives.[41]

In place of the priesthood of Orthodoxy, with its liturgy, instruction and machinery of worship, the Bogomils set an extremely simple community.[42] They avoided even applying the term 'Church' to themselves, though they declared that they were the only true Christians. The prayer of the sect consisted solely in the Lord's Prayer repeated four times every day and four times every night. Confession was made within the group, not apparently to any designated body of men but to members of the sect indiscriminately, women as well as men. There were inner mysteries, only hinted at by Cosmas.[43] Some in the sect had special understanding of Scripture and could foretell the future. There is a suggestion of *gnosis* in the phrase of Cosmas about the Bogomils believing themselves to be already the inhabitants of heaven;[44] he describes them as teaching that manual labour is to be despised, and as citing the words of Jesus about taking no thought for the morrow.[45] The analogy of other dualist sects suggests that there must have been some division between adepts, who were expected to practise all the renunciations, and simple adherents, who were not.[46] But Cosmas says nothing directly of this.

Two innovations in Bogomilism distinguish them from other heresies. One was the restriction of all prayer to the *Pater Noster*. The other consisted in no single doctrine or practice, but in an element of innovation within their cosmological myths. Cosmas is not interested in retailing these 'fables' to his hearers, but attention to later sources enables us to discover what they were.[47] The myths explained in an attractive narrative form the origins of evil in the fall from heaven of a once good being, and the nature of his work of creation of

[37]For this and the following items, see Puech's analysis, ibid., pp. 213–37.

[38]Ibid., p. 216; compare Obolensky, *Bogomils*, p. 214, n. 8.

[39]Puech-Vaillant, pp. 174–7.

[40]Ibid., p. 217.

[41]Ibid., pp. 209–10. 214–15; Obolensky, *Bogomils*, pp. 217–18 on a Byzantine Bogomil commentary on Matthew's gospel.

[42]Puech's analysis, Puech-Vaillant, pp. 237–60.

[43]Ibid., pp. 161–3.

[44]Ibid., p. 77 (text).

[45]Ibid., pp. 276–7. Puech would apply this only to initiates.

[46]Ibid., pp. 277–9. This is a fair hypothesis, but one must note the frailty of direct evidence for the existence of two baptisms in tenth-century Bulgaria (ibid., pp. 250–5).

[47]Ibid., pp. 188–96.

the visible world and of man. The Bogomils appear to have added to these tales an interpretation of the parable of the prodigal son in which the devil was once the eldest son of God and Christ the second, the devil being demoted through disobedience to the Father. The other novelty was the insertion of further detail into a story about the devil's creation of man, which was intended to demonstrate in a picturesque fashion the utter disparity between man's soul, the creation of the good god, and his body, the creation of the devil.[48]

In Bulgaria the heresy has a long history: its last traces disappear there only in the seventeenth century.[49] Cosmas gives, or implies, some reasons for its popularity in his time.[50] A prime reason in his view lay in the state of the Bulgarian clergy, the division between its upper and lower sections, the ignorance of the village priests, and the unwillingness of the upper clergy to instruct them; opposition to the use of Slavonic, which we know about from other sources, is evidence of this unwillingness. The state of the clergy explains the vehemence of the heretics' attacks on the priests—'blind pharisees',[51] drunken and lazy—and the bishops who do not restrain them, and also the extremely radical nature of their rejection of everything to do with the Greek Orthodox Church.

Analogous to this is the hostility of the heretics to civil authority. The heretics, Cosmas says, 'teach their own people not to obey their masters, they revile the wealthy, hate the Tsar, ridicule the elders, condemn the boyars, regard as vile in the sight of God those who serve the Tsar, and forbid every serf to work for his lord'.[52] In the social conditions of the tenth century, with the spread of the *prostasia* type of holding and the oppression of the peasants, this was bound to win adherents. The use of the term 'mammon' for the devil and the curious phrase in which children are described by the Bogomils as 'the children of riches' point to the heretics' concern at the position of the wealthy in Bulgaria.[53]

A heresy which simplified doctrine and appeared to offer an answer to the perennial problem of the existence of evil in a world created by a good God held its place among a freshly converted people. Cosmas cites a question which we can imagine being put by a Bulgarian Christian: 'Why does God allow the devil to attack man?'[54] The polemist did not think much of the

---

[48]Ibid., pp. 190–2, 198–201, 336. Creation myths are known from Byzantine sources; for narratives, see Obolensky, *Bogomils,* pp. 180–1, 208.

[49]Puech-Vaillant, p. 167.

[50]Vaillant's analysis (Puech-Vaillant, pp. 27–35) (with strong social stress); also Puech (ibid., pp. 163–4).

[51]Ibid., p. 64 (text).

[52]Trans, and comment in Obolensky, *Bogomils,* pp. 137–8; Puech-Vaillant, p. 86 (text), 275 (Puech). Marxist exposition, interpreting such statements as fundamental, in D. Angelov's review of Obolensky (*Byzantinoslavica,* x (1949), pp. 303–12 (in French)) and his *Bogomilstvoto v Bulgarija* (Sofia, 1957) (in Bulgarian); review by E. Werner (fellow-Marxist), in *Byzantinoslavica,* xviii (1957), pp. 97–103 (in German); comment (incl. 2nd edn), in 'Die Bogomilen in Bulgarien: Forschungen und Fortschritte', *SM,* 3rd ser., iii (1962), pp. 249–79. A French version of Angelov (D. Anguélov, *Le Bogomilisme en Bulgarie* (Toulouse, 1972), with introduction by J. Duvernoy, pp. 7–15) was published after these notes were written.

[53]Vaillant, in Puech-Vaillant, pp. 28–9.

[54]Ibid., p. 75 (text).

question; but it was still a cogent one, and the dualists appeared to have an answer to it.

There are signs in the doctrines of Bogomilism and the arguments put forward to support them of ill-instructed logical thinking at work.[55] When the heretics refused the veneration of the Cross, they alleged in support the argument, 'If someone had killed the son of the king with a piece of wood, could this wood be dear to the king? So it is with the cross for God.'[56] The analogy implies a total misunderstanding of the doctrine of redemption, comparable to the response of the barbarian ruler Clovis on hearing for the first time the narrative of the Passion of Christ, 'Had I and my armies been present, I would have avenged his injuries.'

Cosmas stresses the importance of ignorance in preparing the ground for the heretics' teaching, but he does not bring out so clearly the genuine misunderstanding and the search for truth in the teachers of the sect themselves. Restriction of prayer to the *Pater Noster* alone is plainly a result of a direct reading, and over-rigid interpretation of the words of Christ in Scripture. Possibly the Paulicians' rejection of the Old Testament took root in Bulgaria because of a practical deficiency; Cosmas speaks of a shortage of books, and lower clergy who joined the sect were perhaps the more inclined to the exclusion of the Old Testament because they had not access to portions of it.[57]

In one other way the Bulgarian background facilitated the progress of the heresy. The Orthodox Church had awoken among some Bulgarians a veneration for the monastic life. Numerous monasteries had been founded, and in the disturbed conditions of the tenth century there was a flight to monasticism,[58] Cosmas reproves parish clergy who leave their wives and children to become monks.[59] At the same time there was disorder; unworthy postulants were accepted in the religious houses, and there were wandering, unsatisfactory monks. The Bogomil adept, pale from fasting, poor and humbly dressed, seemed like a good monk, distinguished from the unworthy by his obvious virtures, and his teaching seemed at first hearing that of orthodoxy, Dualism was, so to speak, the temptation of Greek Orthodox monasticism. Its extreme asceticism had drawing power for the zealous monk; conversely heretical teachers could profit by the veneration for monasticism among Orthodox Christians.

The case of Bogomilism is a rarity in the history of heresy. Nowhere else, with the possible exception of Hungary in the eleventh century, is a heresy formed in a country so near to heathenism. Reactions to paganism are common in countries converted in the Dark Ages through the agency of the ruler; they are an expression at once of conservatism in religion and of dislike of the expanding power of rulers. Heresy proper only comes at a further stage, when Christianity has conquered the countryside and beliefs have been

[55]D. Angelov, 'Aperçu sur la Nature et l'Histoire du Bogomilisme en Bulgarie', in *HS*, pp. 75–81 (Marxist view), esp. p. 81; R. Morghen, 'L'Origine de l'Hérésie au Moyen Âge', ibid., pp. 121–38, at pp. 125–6 (stressing literal appeal to Scripture by Bogomils).
[56]Puech-Vaillant, p. 59 (text).
[57]Ibid., p. 33.
[58]Obolensky, *Bogomils*, pp. 101–8.
[59]Puech-Vaillant, pp. 93–4.

assimilated by the population.[60] Bulgaria will not fit this pattern: it had two pagan reactions of the usual type in 866 and 889. But in the tenth century, probably as early as the 940s, a Christian heresy was formed at a stage when orthodoxy had not yet been fully assimilated.

The reasons lie in the existence from an early stage in Bulgaria of an organized, coherent alternative to the Greek Orthodox Church in the form of Paulicianism, and in the ability of the village priest Bogomil to adapt its dualism for his people.[61] Pagan gods were not capable of transplantation in the Dark Ages; even the updated heathenism which the Oborodites defended on the eastern borders of the Western Empire against the Christian German settlers of the eleventh and twelfth centuries was a religion for themselves alone, not easily transferable elsewhere. A heresy, however, has a universal quality, and can as readily be transplanted as orthodoxy.

Through its dualist beliefs Bogomilism deserves to rank as a mutation of one of the universal religions. In Bulgaria, its appeal obviously owed much to a localized protest against authority in Church and State, not dissimilar to the popular feeling which lay behind pagan reactions in freshly converted countries. Once formed, however, the new heresy had an objective religious appeal transcending the Bulgarian frontiers. In an unusual sequence, the heresy then passed from the mission field back into the Byzantine Empire, to win adherents in Asia Minor and in the capital itself, Constantinople.

The Spread of Bogomilism in Byzantium.
The pathway lay via the western regions of Asia Minor, where in the Thracesian Theme, Smyrna and the Opsikion Theme a 'pseudo-monk', John Tzurillas, spread the heresy until condemnation after trial in the diocese of Acmonia, probably early in the eleventh century.[62] In the Opsikion Theme the heretics were known as Phundagiagitai; in the Kibyrrhaeot Theme, farther to the southwest in Asia Minor, and 'in the West', i.e. the Balkan provinces of the Empire on the borders of Bulgaria, they were known as Bogomils.[63] In the eleventh century they were in the capital, where Euthymius, monk of the Peribleptos monastery and anti-Bogomil polemist, uncovered four converts amongst his fellow-monks.[64] In the mid-eleventh century a heresy was reported in Thrace, which on the face of it appeared to

[60]A. Gieysztor, in *HS*, pp. 159–69; on the limitations of early missionizing, see L. G. D. Baker, 'The shadow of the Christian symbol', *SCH*, VI, pp. 17–28.

[61]On relation of Bogomilism to earlier heresies, see Puech in Puech-Vaillant, pp. 292–336; on Paulicianism, pp. 317–25; compare Vaillant, ibid., p. 27, Dujčev in *Medieovo Bizantino-Slavo*, I, pp. 265–9 (for judgement on Bogomil's originality, see p. 269; and for attitude to Psellos, p. 258).

[62]For Byzantine Bogomilism, see Obolensky, *Bogomils*, pp. 168–229; his summary, stressing supra-national character of sect implicit in Byzantine transplantation, is in 'Bogomilism in the Byzantine Empire', in *Actes du VIᵉ Congrès International des Études Byzantines*, I (Paris, 1950), pp. 289–97; for contrast of approach with Angelov, see his 'Le Christianisme oriental et les Doctrines dualistes', *L'Oriente cristiano nella storia della civiltà*, Accademia Nazionale dei Lincei, (Rome, 1964), pp. 643–53; and D. Angelov, 'Le Mouvement bogomile dans les Pays slaves balkaniques et dans Byzance', ibid., pp. 607–18. Dating of Tzurillas trial given in Obolensky, *Bogomils*, p. 174. Recorded distribution of Bogomils, below, map 1 and Appendix D, s. 1.

[63]G. Ficker, *Die Phundagiagiten* (Leipzig, 1908); Obolensky, *Bogomils*, p. 177; above, p. 14.

[64]Ibid., pp. 174–83; on Euthymius, see Puech, in Puech-Vaillant, pp. 140–2.

consist of Bogomilism and Messalianism,[65] another form of Byzantine dualism going back to the early centuries, in which evil took the form of a demon in the heart of man, implanted at every pregnancy. In the early twelfth century an investigation by the Emperor Alexius revealed that Bogomilism had found a following among the aristocratic families of Constantinople, taught by a doctor, Basil, who had been active in the sect for fifty-two years.[66]

It is obvious that our information shows us only a portion of the total extent of Bogomil heresy in the Byzantine Empire in the eleventh century. Sources are relatively meagre. The heretics showed a missionary zeal: Euthymius of Peribleptos describes them drawing lots in the manner of the Apostles in order to apportion among themselves their regions for preaching. As in Bulgaria, they remained an undercover movement, attending church, accepting baptism, kissing the icon, even accepting communion, while in secret practising their beliefs and holding prayer meetings.[67] Their ritual practices were very simple. Euthymius describes one of the meetings, the leader starting off with injunction to prayer, 'Let us adore the Father, the Son and the Holy Spirit', the group replying, 'It is meet and right', and then embarking on repetitions of the Lord's Prayer with prostrations, 'bobbing their heads up and down like men possessed.' In Constantinople under the leadership of Basil they appear to have adapted to the needs of a more sophisticated membership, stressing their cosmology more, and appealing to wealthier converts who liked to dabble in speculations.[68]

At the same time asceticism continued to carry great weight. The dedication of the initiate had its own impact. 'A Bogomil', wrote Anna Comnena, the emperor's daughter and chronicler, 'looks gloomy and is covered up to the nose and walks with a stoop . . .'[69] The leaders had personality. Tzurillas, in the village of Chilioi Kapnoi—perhaps his home— had so won the inhabitants that scarcely ten remained orthodox, and three years of his preaching carried the word widely through western Asia Minor. Basil when captured clung grimly to his faith, and faced burning with courage, clapping his hands, slapping his thigh, and turning away his eyes when he saw the pyre, but keeping up his spirits with the prospect of a divine rescue.

Repression was not efficient. Through much of the eleventh century Byzantine government faced overwhelming secular problems. The Church had long lived with a presence of heresy in some part or another of the territory under its jurisdiction. There was no regular machinery designed for the detection of heresy, and only chance or the pertinacity of an individual

---

[65]Michael Psellos; the source is unreliable. Contrast Obolensky, *Bogomils*, pp. 183–8 (cautious acceptance) with Dujčev, *Medioevo Bizantino-Slavo*, I, pp. 257–8 (Psellos evidence only for fact that a heresy existed); Angelov, *Bogomilstvoto* (see Werner in *SM*, 3rd ser., III (1962), pp. 249–79, but note his citation of P. Joannou, 'Les Croyances démonologiques au XIᵉ Siècle à Byzance', *Actes du VIᵉ Congrès des Études Byzantines*, I, pp. 245–60). On Messalianism, see below, p. 22, n.82.

[66]Obolensky, *Bogomils*, pp. 197–205.

[67]On the motives for this, Puech-Vaillant, pp. 149–61.

[68]Obolensky, *Bogomils*, p. 202.

[69]Obolensky's trans. (ibid., p. 199).

churchman uncovered it. The long, uninterrupted career of Basil is witness to the relative ineffectiveness of Byzantine police action against heresy.

Byzantine sources fill out our picture of rites and doctrines.[70] There were two initiation ceremonies: a *baptisma* for the neophyte, with the gospel of John being laid on his or her head and the *Pater Noster* repeated; a *teleiosis* for the initiate, granted only after proof of fasts, renunciations and prayer, and with the assent of the other members, the gospel of John being again laid on the head, followed by men and women members laying on hands and singing a hymn. The two ceremonies corresponded to a gradual initiation into the mysteries of the sect and the full rigours of its renunciation. Instruction began simply, with basic doctrine and injunctions, then went deeper, carrying the neophyte farther and farther from the teaching of the Byzantine Church. Orthodox baptism with water linked its recipient with Satan's evil creation and the Church which lay under his power. In the *teleiosis* the ceremony of initiation itself was preceded by a ritual purification in which a washing with sponges of dirty water effaced all traces of the effects of this Satanic baptism.

Behind the initiation lay a cosmology whose essential starting-point lay in the assumption that the very act of creation of the visible world and of man was the work of an evil power. In the teaching of the Bogomils the devil, by his original name Satanael, was the first-born Son of God who once sat on a throne at His right hand and had the same form and garment, acting as a steward and ordainer on behalf of the Father over all the powers of heaven.[71] But his position went to his head, and he raised a rebellion among the angels of God, drawing them into his plan by promises that he would lighten their burdens. Like the unjust steward of the parable,[72] he went from one to another, asking what their debts, i.e. duties, to his master were. 'A hundred measures of oil.' 'Then take your bill', replied he 'and write fifty.' The Father learnt of the rebellion, and precipitated Satan and his angels out of heaven.

Ejected, Satan yet retained the creative power of a Son of God, and set about a work of creation with the aid of the angels and powers who had fallen with him.[73] He created a firmament, a second heaven, for his own residence, then the visible world, stage by stage as it is described in Genesis. The body of Adam he created out of earth and water, but tried in vain to animate it; water flowed out of the big toe of the right foot, and the elements would not hold together.[74] Then he breathed into the body to give it life; but still the breath escaped by the toe, and went to animate the trickle of water that had already escaped, thus becoming the Serpent, Satan's agent. Finally, powerless to animate Adam, he called to the Father whose spirit, the *pneuma*, at last gave him life. In another version[75] the soul was stolen by the devil from God and

[70]Principally Euthymius Zigabenus, commissioned to write by Alexius. Puech in Puech-Vaillant, pp. 142–3; summary in Obolensky, *Bogomils*, pp. 206–19. His description of initiation relates primarily to Basil's group. See Puech, in Puech-Vaillant, pp. 250–5, blending Byzantine sources.

[71]Ibid., pp. 181–96. On myths of the devil, H. I. Marrou, 'Un Ange déchu, un Ange pourtant', *Satan (EC*, xxvii (1948)), pp. 28–43; H. C. Puech, 'Le Prince des Ténèbres en son Royaume', ibid., pp. 136–74; below, p. 22, n. 83.

[72]Luke 16, 1–8.

[73]Puech, Puech-Vaillant, pp. 196–201.

[74]Version of Euthymius Zigabenus; summary in Obolensky, *Bogomils*, p. 208.

[75]Euthymius of Peribleptos; summary in Obolensky, *Bogomils*, p. 180.

pushed into the body he had made, but always escaped. For three hundred years the devil left the inanimate body of Adam, then, returning, stopped up the apertures of the body to prevent the soul's escape, and vomited into Adam's mouth unclean creatures that would sully the soul and keep it prisoner in the body.

Eve's creation followed on Adam's. Sexual desire between Adam and Eve was the work of the devil, who first seduced Eve himself and gave her children, Cain, then a daughter, Calomena.[76] Then Eve tempted Adam to sexual intercourse, and they procreated children, beginning with Abel, thus by the imprisonment of souls in the bodies made by the devil perpetuating his reign.

By adultery with Eve the devil lost his robe, his divine form and his creative power: he became black and ugly. One story has it that a further stage of his degradation was reached with the descent of Christ to Hell, when He seized the devil and bound him. The final '-el', a sign of his once great powers, disappeared from his name, and Satanael, former son of God, became Satan. The Old Testament narratives, it was believed, recorded Satanael's tyranny in first creating the world and then, after intercourse between the daughters of men and fallen angels had produced giants who defied him, sending a flood against them. Finally, as he learnt of the Father's plan to send Christ into the world, he secured the allegiance of Moses, giving to him the Law in Sinai, which should bind men to his power. The Father, seeing the sufferings of the souls imprisoned under Satan, sent out his Son, Christ, for 33 years in the years 5500 to 5533 from the beginning of the world.[77] He was not born of Mary but entered her by her ear; he did not truly suffer on the Cross, but only appeared to do so, and left his body in the air at the Ascension before returning to the Father, to be resolved into Him. Satan, defeated, had none the less not lost all his power, and a struggle continued which would be finally ended, not in a resurrection of body and soul, but in a destruction of the body, with all Satan's evil creation, and an assumption of the souls into the heaven of the Father with his angels.

Through the rites of the Bogomils and the prayers and renunciations associated with them a man made his escape from the power of Satan. The knowledge, communicated to him by the sectaries, of the true meaning of the Old Testament and of the place of the Byzantine Church, of the nature of the visible world and, above all, of the nature of man—a forced composition of incompatible elements from the Father's and Satan's respective creations— showed him his true predicament and the means of his escape. Renunciations, which for the Byzantine Bogomils included an order to shed no blood,[78] and abstinence from other products of procreation, cheese and eggs, as well as meat,[79] removed the initiate as far as humanly possible from the world of

[76]For what follows, see Puech, in Puech-Vaillant, pp. 201–5. His use of the *Interrogatio Johannis*, the twelfth-century apocryphal writing in Latin, based on a Bulgarian source, should be noted. See below, p.122.

[77]Puech, in Puech-Vaillant, pp. 178–81, 205–9, 211–13.

[78]Euthymius of Peribleptos; Obolensky, *Bogomils*, p. 182. Obolensky (ibid., pp. 143–4) distinguishes pacifist Bogomils from warlike Paulicians; Angelov (Werner, in *SM*, 3rd ser., III (1962), pp. 249–79) argues that pacifism and refusal of work are practices of the initiates, not rank and file.

[79]Euthymius Zigabenus; Obolensky, *Bogomils*, p. 214.

matter. *Teleiosis* consummated his escape. After it he received gifts of spiritual illumination and was known as one of the *theotokoi* who through teaching gave birth to the Word and who alone were able to put the demons to flight.[80]

Students of the heresies of the early Church will recognize from this description the number of ways in which Bogomilism resembles a Gnostic heresy. Developed within the jurisdiction of the Byzantine Church in the late ninth and early tenth centuries, it inevitably made use of much Christian symbolism and terminology, but had the pre-eminent characteristic of early Gnosticism of being able to take over the outer husk of language, names, and ceremonies from another religion, while filling that husk with its own kernel of belief. Like the Christian Gnostics, Bogomils effectively evacuated the core of orthodox belief in the Incarnation, Redemption and the Trinity to replace it by their own understanding of the evil nature of the visible world and of salvation from it by the *gnosis* and the ascetic exercises of a select group of initiates. Drastic denials of Greek Orthodox religious belief and practice, together with a certain radical, 'logical' way of thinking about the Christian life which was the Bogomils' own, came together with this kernel of Gnostic-type belief to form a new heresy.

Part of the heresy is of spontaneous growth; part, as we have seen, derived directly from the Paulicians. The influence of other sects is less likely. The Manichees might be responsible for predisposing Bogomils to an ascetic dualism, but the differences between them and the Bogomils are too great for much contact to be likely.[81] Manichees believed in a principle of evil co-equal and co-eternal with the principle of good: they were not mitigated dualists, believing in an ultimate control of good over the forces of evil, like the Bogomils were. Messalians, who believed that a demon existed in the heart of men, and that once the demon was driven out he became sinless, probably influenced Bogomilism in Byzantium from the twelfth century onwards.[82] Like Bogomilism, Messalianism had a natural appeal to monks. But no doctrine of pre-twelfth century Bogomilism can be put down as of a distinctively Messalian nature.

We know little of the details of the mythology of the Paulicians. They may have some responsibility for transmission to the Bogomils. The obvious channel, however, is the Gnostic and Gnostic-influenced writings which survived from the early days of heresy.[83] Doctrinal standards in the early centuries were not as rigid as they later became, and writings which circulated then might contain work tending towards a Docetic Christology or some

---

[80]Puech, in Puech-Vaillant, pp. 257–60.

[81]Puech, in Puech-Vaillant, pp. 185–8, 304–16.

[82]Ibid., pp. 325–36; for Puech's method, see ibid., pp. 292–304. Obolensky, *Bogomils*, p. 251, disagrees. I prefer Puech's sceptical approach to the sources, and incline to place Messalian influence later than Obolensky and generally to stress it less.

[83]Background in Jonas, *Gnostic Religion*; Byzantine apocryphal writings in Runciman, *Medieval Manichee*, pp. 21–5. Obolensky and Runciman give glimpses of J. Ivanov, *Bogomilski knigi i legendi* (Sofia, 1925) (in Bulgarian). Dependence on ancient literature demonstrated (correcting Ivanov) by E. Turdeanu, 'Apocryphes bogomiles et pseudo-bogomiles', *RHR*, CXXXVIII (1950), pp. 22–52, 176–218, A. Vaillant, 'Un Apocryphe pseudo-bogomile: La Vision d'Isaïe', *RES*, XLII (1963), pp. 109–21. Possible channels for descent of heresy are discussed in M. Dando, *Les Origines du Catharisme*, Paris, 1967.

heresy on the Trinity. Narratives which had a Gnostic flavour still circulated freely in the Byzantine world. The living context of Gnosticism had long vanished, and the writings were used harmlessly as vehicles for a fairy-tale literature. In the hands of the Bogomils they were made to yield poison: through them ancient materials, going back to late Judaic apocalyptic as well as to Gnosticism, was used to body out heretical doctrine.

Thus a long sequence of events produced on the terrain of Byzantium the developed heresy of Bogomilism, with a body of doctrine radically distinct from that of orthodoxy and a class of initiates, dedicated, aware of the gulf which separated them from the Church, and eager to spread their message. In the eleventh century, as the first map of heresy shows,[84] they had their representatives in the western Themes of Asia Minor and in Constantinople. The older dualism of the Paulicians survived in the Balkans, less, it would seem, in the form of undercover communities than the Bogomils, but in ancient settlements. Sometimes they produced troops to fight for the Emperor; more often they allied themselves with enemies of Byzantium such as the Cumans and the Pechenegs.[85] Western soldiers met them on the way to the First Crusade; Bohemond and his Normans burnt a fortified town inhabited by them in the Macedonian district of Pelagonia; and their name, transmuted to the sinister term 'Publicani', passed into the vocabulary of western heresiologists as a general description of 'heretic'. In Philippopolis they long remained and kept their idiosyncratic beliefs, being converted to Catholicism as late as the seventeenth century.[86]

Over on the eastern fringes of the Empire and in Armenia the Adoptionist wing of the Paulicians survived.[87] Though not dualist, they shared certain beliefs with their dualist cosectaries and with the Bogomils, rejecting images and the veneration of the Cross. The eleventh century was a hard time for them, for they were persecuted in Armenia in the early years, when the imperial armies aided the repressions set in hand by the Armenian clergy, and again in mid-century when the imperial collaborator, Gregory Magistros, hunted them down in the districts of Armenia under his control. But they still survived, some fleeing farther east into their old homeland in Syria, where they were to be found in Moslem armies fighting against the crusaders, others living on undercover in Armenia even into the nineteenth century.

---

[84]Below, p. 34.
[85]Garsoïan, *Paulician Heresy*, pp. 13–17; Obolensky, *Bogomils*, pp. 188–95.
[86]Runciman, pp. 45–6.
[87]Garsoïan, pp. 139–45 (history), 151–67 (doctrine), 231–3 (summary).

3

The Revival of Heresy in the West, 1000–1051

While Bogomil and his fellows were preaching their heresy in Bulgaria, the records of heresy of any kind in the West are quite blank. As Bogomilism spread into Byzantium proper in the late tenth or early eleventh centuries, first intimations of a return of heretical episodes are heard in the West. Doctrinal dissent began to appear again as life grew slowly more settled. The Viking disturbances came to an end; internal order gradually increased; *pari passu* came fresh economic life, the stirrings of reform in the Church and a little heresy. The table below shows the sequence of outbreaks from *c*. 970 to 1100 together with conciliar and other denunciations of heresy.[1]

Heretical Episodes in the West, *c*. 970–1100

Sardinia		Csanád	1030–46
(also Italy, Spain)	*c*. 970	Ravenna	1030–46
Châlons-sur-Marne	*c*. 1000	Venice	1030–46
Liège	1010–24	Verona	1030–46
Aquitaine	1018	Châlons-sur-Marne	*c*. 1046–8
Toulouse	*c*. 1022	Liège	*c*. 1048–50
Orléans	1022	*Rheims*	
Liège	1025	(*council denouncing heresy*)	1049
Arras	1025	Upper Lorraine	1051
Monforte	*c*. 1028	*Sisteron*	
Charroux		(*letter denouncing 'Afros' in ancient*	
(*council denouncing heresy*)	1027–8	*formula*)	1060
		Nevers	1075

[1]List inferred from Russell (*Dissent and Reform*), omitting Mainz 1012 as case of conversion to Judaism (Giezstor, in *HS*, pp. 160, 166), Rome 1016 as unfounded suspicion of heresy (H. Theloe, *Die Ketzerverfolgungen im 11. und 12. Jahrhundert* (Berlin and Leipzig, 1913), p.8), Liège *c*. 1048–54 as more probably datable to the twelfth century (below, p. 62, n. 56). My map, 'Bogumilen, Paulikianer and westliche Häresien, *ca.* 970–1100', in *Atlas zur Kirchengeschichte: die christliche Welt in Geschichte und Gegenwart*, ed. H. Jedin, K. S. Latourette, J. Marten (Freiburg im Breisgau, 1970), p. 57, needs correction on these points. Analysis of episodes, but not general denunciations, in gazetteer below, appendix D, s.1. Brief account in A. Borst, *Die Katharer* (Stuttgart, 1953), pp. 71–80 (the book is the definitive account of Cathars, esp. on doctrine and ethics); with sources in Ilarino da Milano, 'Le eresie popolari del secolo XI nell' Europa occidentale', in *Studi Gregoriani*, ed. G. B. Borino, II (Rome, 1947), pp. 43–89. E. Werner, 'Häresie und Gesellschaft im 11 Jahrhundert', *SSAWL, Philologisch-historische Klasse CXVII*, v (1975), pp. 5–83, and G. Cracco, *Riforma ed Eresia in momenti della Cultura Europea tra X e XI secolo* (Florence, 1972) reached me too late to use in the chapter.

At first outbreaks were on a very limited scale, with only four cases recorded between 970 and 1018. In the decade 1018 to 1028 approximately the incidence rises sharply, with reports of heresy for France, Italy and the Low Countries. After that the incidence drops again till the phase ends with the discovery of a group of heretics in Upper Lorraine, who were taken by their duke to the imperial court at Goslar and there hanged in 1051.[2] Thereafter silence descends on the chroniclers and, while accusations of heresy were made in the polemics of the Gregorian reform movement and their opponents,[3] no further authenticated cases of true heresy occur till 1100, save for the ambiguous evidence of a letter from Nicholas II to Sisteron denouncing heresy[4] and one line by a single chronicler recording a case at Nevers in 1075.

Outbreaks are also isolated. With the exception of the diocese of Châlons-sur-Marne and the city of Liège, heresy is never revealed twice in the same place during this period. We must allow for the inadequacies of record in an ill-documented era; none the less it looks as if repression at this time is succeeding in extinguishing heretical circles once they are discovered, without leaving a remnant of proselytizers from the group ready to revive their heresy when the publicity of an investigation is over.

Geographically discontinuous, eleventh-century Western heresy is also doctrinally idiosyncratic. To judge by the five cases[5] where the chroniclers leave us enough information to attempt a detailed reconstruction of the heretics' teaching, it cannot be ticketed solely in terms of any earlier heresy or regarded as forming part of any homogenous movement. Each outbreak has its individuality, the ensemble of doctrines taught—even if partly derivative, as will be suggested, from Bogomilism—being developed as a whole within the heretical circle in a particular locality. Western Europe is not yet ripe to give birth to a continuous heretical movement of the kind represented in Byzantium by the Bogomil and Paulician heresies. In its sporadic and individual character, eleventh-century Western heresy resembles still the type of casual and unorganized heresy which appears occasionally in the eighth and ninth centuries.[6]

Yet if attention is concentrated on the cases where doctrinal reconstruction is possible, especially those which lie within the active decade 1018 and 1028, a difference between this revived heresy and that of earlier centuries becomes plain. Where in the past we meet a theologian such as Claudius of Turin with a full dogmatic heresy but no group following, or alternatively a rural agitator such as Theuda or Aldebert who has a group following but no substantial

---

[2]On this and all other episodes in Borst, *Katharer* and Russell, *Dissent*, see gazetteer below appendix D, s.1; other authors are cited as necessary.

[3]Russell, *Dissent*, ch. 5, *passim*.

[4]Ibid., pp. 182, 198–9; for dismissal of the Sisteron source's relevance, see R. I. Moore 'The origins of medieval heresy', *History*, LV (1970), pp. 21–36 (survey of early heresy, with some new orientation) at p. 24 n. 1. For denunciations of heresy at the councils of Charroux and Rheims (above p. 24), see Russell, pp. 35, 41–2.

[5]Arras 1025 (see also Liège 1025), Châlons-sur-Marne *c*. 1000, Liege *c*. 1048–50, Monforte *c*. 1028, Orléans 1022.

[6]In this I agree with Moore (loc. cit., pp. 32–3), but I still believe there is an extra element in the eleventh century which he declines to recognize. See below, pp. 31–3 and appendix A, s. 1.

dogmatic heresy, now we find episodes in which a teacher with a dogmatic challenge to the Church has assembled a living heretical circle around him.[7]

In the first of these, about the year 1000, the peasant Leutard in the village of Vertu near Châlons-sur-Marne,[8] after being tormented in a dream by bees who entered his body through his private parts, went home from the fields, dismissed his wife 'as though he effected the separation by command of the gospel', went to the church and broke the crucifix, and thereafter gathered a hearing for his views among the peasants—aided, no doubt, by his welcome belief that it was not necessary to pay tithes. Part of his appeal was based on Scripture, used selectively; he is said to have taught 'that the prophets had set forth some useful things, and some not to be believed.'[9] The bishop exposed the weaknesses of this rustic agitator, who then committed suicide by throwing himself into a well; but some fifteen years later adherents of his were still in evidence.[10] The oddities, the bees and the claim to special revelation that he made, put him in the same class as Aldebert and Theuda; nevertheless, across the ambiguities of a weak chronicler we seem to catch glimpses of some more serious dogmatic heresy. It is difficult to be sure, but the dismissal of his wife 'as though . . . . by command of the gospel' sounds like a rejection of marriage, and the demonstration in the church like a rejection of crosses and images.

A second case, at Orléans in 1022, is better recorded.[11] A distinguished group, possibly to the number of twenty, including canons of the church of Holy Cross, nuns and other women, clergy, members of the nobility, and a one-time confessor to the queen of France, were implicated in a thoroughgoing heresy, traces of which in Orléans went back to about 1015. The core of their beliefs lay in a *gnosis*, entry to which was conferred by a ceremony of laying-on of hands. Initiates, relieved of the stain of all sin, were filled by the gift of the Holy Spirit which gave them full understanding of Scripture. Orthodox doctrines connected with Christ's possession of a human body were denied in the group: 'Christ was not born of the Virgin Mary. He did not suffer for men. He was not really buried in the sepulchre, and was not raised from the dead.[12] There was wholesale denial of validity to the sacraments of the Church: 'In baptism there was no washing away of sins;[13] Ordination was rejected, as was the mass. 'There is no sacrament', it was reported to be their belief, 'in the consecration by a priest of the body and

---

[7]Above, pp. 8–10.

[8]Source trans. with these quotation in *WEH*, pp. 72–3 (largest collection of translated texts, with historical sketch, pp. 1–55). I am indebted for information to Professor Wakefield.

[9]Not a distinction between 'acceptable' and 'unacceptable' OT writers, as Borst (*Katharer*, p. 73) and C. Thouzellier ('Tradition et Résurgence dans l'Hérésie médiévale', in *HS*, pp. 105–120, at p. 107) imply.

[10]J. B. Russell, 'Á Propos du Synode d'Arras', *RHE*, LVII (1962), pp. 66–87, at p. 86.

[11]See gazetteer (p. 362) and appendix A, s. 1. Exposition of doctrine rests on a selection of reliable from unreliable sources. The story of the orgy is omitted as interpolation. Trans. of Paul of S. Père de Chartres in *WEH*, pp. 76–81; *MBPH*, pp 10–15 (which contains the latest introduction to popular heresy of eleventh and twelfth centuries and translations of original texts).

[12]Moore's trans. (loc. cit., p. 26).

[13]'in baptismo nullam esse sclerum ablutionem' (*Gesta Synodi Aurelianensis*, in Bouquet, X, p. 536).

blood of Christ.'[14] Penance was also rejected. The initiate who had gained inner illumination was superior to these things, having entered on another level of being where he fed on heavenly food and saw angelic visions. Priesthood and Church are thus demoted by comparison with the experience of illumination.

The rejection of marriage by the Orléans group and, in one source, their apparent rejection of flesh-eating point towards another motive in the denial of the sacraments—an abhorrence of matter. When the sectaries were brought to trial before the king of France and some of his bishops, the leaders explained their denial of orthodoxy in terms of a blend of scepticism and an other-wordly rejection of earthly things. To the bishop of Beauvais's exposition of the reality of Christ's suffering and resurrection, they replied, 'We were not there, and we cannot believe that to be true', and to his question on the Virgin Birth, 'What nature denies is always out of harmony with the Creator.' When he asked them whether they believed in the doctrine of creation by the Father through the Son, they defied him, contrasting their knowledge of the Law written on the heart by the Holy Spirit and derived directly from the Creator with the bishop's teaching, fit to be related to 'those who have earthly wisdom and believe the fictions of carnal men, scribbled upon animal skins,'[15]

In a third outbreak the sectaries, probably townsmen and without any formal learning, originated in Italy, where they had been taught by an Italian called Gundulf, and came to Liège and Arras with the intention of making converts.[16] Their rejection of the sacramental system was at least as drastic as that of the Orléans group. They dismissed baptism, described the mass as a *vile negotium*, 'a dirty transaction for gain', and rejected penance and confession. In a sweeping rejection of the whole material apparatus of worship of the Church, they attacked the use of church buildings, altars and incense, bells and singing in church, the practice of burial by priests in consecrated ground, images of Christ and the saints and the practice of venerating the Cross. In its place they set their group's experience of the way of righteousness (*justitia*), in which they abandoned the world, 'restrained our flesh', as they put it, 'from carnal longings', lived by manual labour and showed kindness to all who were zealous to follow their way of life.

The practice of this moral life did away with any necessity for baptism. If *justitia* was observed, they argued, baptism was superfluous; if not, it could not save. Anticlerical feeling and insistence on individual responsibility influenced them against the sacrament, in a way to become familiar in the twelfth century in the West. It was invalid because of the evil life of its

---

[14]Trans., *WEH*, p. 78 (adapted).

[15]Ibid., p. 81. For reconstructions of Orléans heresy which differ from mine, see Moore, loc. cit., pp. 25–8, 33, and Manselli, *Eresia*, pp. 125–9.

[16]On site and dating, I follow Russell in *RHE*, LVII (1962), pp. 66–87. Partial trans. of synodal proceedings, *WEH*, pp. 82–5 (generally used here) and *MBPH*, pp. 15–19. Russell (*Dissent*, pp. 23–7) argues for a discrepancy between the confession of the heretics in the proceedings and the bishop's exposition. The bishop, he says, arbitrarily imposed dualism on the heretics. I disagree. There is no evidence of literary contamination of the bishop's account; he does not call the heretics Manichaeans; and both the bishop and the confession stress *justitia* as the guiding principle of the heretics.

ministrants, the certainty that sins renounced in it would be repeated in later life, and the impossibility of an adult making renunciations on behalf of a child. Rigorism went far at Arras. It excluded confessors from veneration, leaving only the Apostles and martyrs. It apparently, as the bishop in his synod concluded, interpreted the restraint of 'carnal longings', which they claimed is an evangelical principle, as meaning that those who married could not be saved.[17] It restricted the Scriptures 'to the precepts of the gospels and the Apostles.'

In a fourth case of heresy detected some three years later at a castle above Monforte in Piedmont, but derived, in the chronicler's view, 'from some unknown part of the world outside Italy', the social class of the participants, which included a countess and nobility, resembled that of the group at Orléans, as did the experience of illumination central to their beliefs.[18] Absolution for sin lay not in the hands of pope, bishop or priest. 'We do not have that Roman pontiff,' Gerard, the representative of the sect, replied to the archbishop of Milan, 'but another, who daily visits our brothers, scattered throughout the world, and when he brings God to us, pardon of our sins is granted.[19]

The group practised austerities. Sexual intercourse was prohibited as wrong in itself. Virgins were expected to preserve virginity, married men to treat their wives as though they were their mothers or sisters. Asked about the group's understanding of procreation as the end of marriage, Gerard answered that, if the human race agreed 'not to experience corruption' (i.e. engage in sexual intercourse), it would then be begotten 'without coition, like bees.' The heretics ate no meat, fasted and kept no private property. In a mysterious phrase, Gerard said, 'None of us ends his life without torments, that we may thus avoid eternal torments'[20]; it transpired that this meant that when a member of the sect was near death, he was killed 'in some way' by one of his fellows. The Scriptures—Old and New Testaments—and the 'holy canons' were read daily.

But the scriptural reading coexisted with beliefs which apparently denied the existence of Christ as a historical person and voided the orthodox doctrine of the Trinity. The Son, Gerard said, was 'the soul of man beloved of God', and the Holy Spirit 'the comprehension of divine truths by which all things are separately governed.' Pressed on the exact nature of his Christological belief, Gerard repeated his point, and added an identification of Mary with Scripture. 'He whom you call Jesus Christ is the soul of man, in the flesh born of the Virgin Mary, that is, born of sacred Scripture'.[21] Implicit in the group's

---

[17]'dicentes conjugatos id sortem fidelium nequaquam computandos' (Mansi, XIX, col. 449).

[18]Possibly Monforte d'Alba in diocese of Alba, but Glaber gives Asti diocese; see Ilarino da Milano in *Studi Gregoriana*, II, p. 68, n. 35. For sources, see gazetteer (p. 361), Appendix D, s. 1 Trans. of Landulf Senior in *WEH*, pp. 86–9, *MBPH*, pp. 19–21. A differing interpretation from mine is in C. Violante, *La società Milanese nell'età precomunale* (Bari, 1953), pp. 176–86. Runciman (*Medieval Manichee*, pp. 117–18) believes they were dualists.

[19]Trans. in *WEH* p. 88.

[20]Ibid., p. 87. Parallel in abjuration formula for Cathars from Moissac, *c.* 1150, in R. Manselli, 'Per la storia dell'eresie nel secolo XII. Un abiura del XII secolo dell'eresia catara', *BISIAM*, LXVII (1955), pp. 212–34.

[21]*WEH*, pp. 87–8.

beliefs was a denial of the Church, as radical as that of the Arras group but without their anticlericalism. Asked about the power of the priesthood to consecrate the body and blood of Christ, Gerard answered by dismissing all priesthood in favour of direct experience of the actions of the Spirit. 'There is no other pontiff beside our Pontiff,' the chronicler reports him as saying, 'though he is without tonsure of the head or any sacred mystery.' An organization in the sect can be glimpsed through a mention of the leaders, who pray in rotation night and day so that no hour is left without prayer to God, and of the elders (*maiores*) whose permission is apparently needed before neophytes who have lost their virginity can be accepted. But, given the radical rejection of the material world characteristic of the group, we would not expect the elders to have sacramental functions. At the end, the townsmen forced them to choose between a cross and a pyre—conceivably because the heretics rejected the veneration of the cross.

In a fifth case, we learn from a letter of 1048–50 sent by Théoduin, bishop of Liège, to Henry I of France of heretics (whom the bishop erroneously believed to be followers of the theologian Berengar of Tours) who denied the reality of Christ's body, saying it was a shadow, rejected marriage, and undermined the doctrine of infant baptism.[22]

The Character of Eleventh-century Heresy.

The radical nature of the dogmatic challenge to the Church in every one of these five episodes must make one consider that some novel elements are stirring in the popular religious consciousness of the West. Common to all the heresies is a stress on flight from the world, a concern for purity, a positive repugnance, it would seem, for material objects, and for human flesh and its desires, shown in the fact that each of these groups, with the possible exception of Leutard, condemned marriage.[23] The same world-renouncing trait comes across as part of the descriptions of heresy in two other contemporaneous outbreaks in Aquitaine (1018) and Châlons-sur-Marne (1046–8) where a shortage of information or possible inaccuracy of the chronicler prohibits detailed analysis. It is plainly related to the existence of a reform movement, strongly influenced by monastic ideals, which at this time was beginning to stir the laity. Beginning with the foundations of Cluny and Gorze in the previous century, a revival of monasticism was purging moribund monasteries over western Europe, and by a natural overspill affecting the lay world as well. Increasingly, the desire for reform made itself felt in the secular

---

[22]See summary in J. B. Russell, 'Les Cathares de 1048–1054 à Liège', *BSAHDL*, xliv (1961), pp. 1–8, at pp. 6–7; on the whole article, see below, Appendix D. For Russell's change of attitude since 1961 on the nature of the heresy, cf. *Dissent*, p. 206. Beliefs as described by Théoduin can hardly be linked to the work of the controversial theologian Berengar of Tours. However, Dr M. Gibson, contrary to the accepted view (Russell, *Dissent*, pp. 163–4), tells me that Berengar had some popular following; see her 'The Case of Berengar of Tours' (*SCH*, vii, pp. 61–8) for Berengar's condemnation. I regret that I have been unable to follow up the references she has given me.

[23]Contrast Moore's opinion, that there was 'little in common' between the groups, (loc. cit., p. 33). His view rests partly on his interpretation of sources for Orléans and Arras, which makes them more idiosyncratic than I would accept. Contrast Borst, *Katharer*, pp. 71 (title), 80: 'a Bible movement hostile to the world.'

Church, with a call to greater purity and devotion among the clergy. Monks were often instigators of reform and their ideals those most widely diffused, with a concomitant tendency to consider the world of little worth. A radical pessimism about the natural order is a strong feature of this reform. So, too, is the contrast preached by reformers between the Church of the Apostles as evidenced in Scripture, and the state of the contemporary priesthood and hierarchy.

These two features help to account for the reaction in these heresies against the material world towards an ascetic withdrawal, and also for the appeal which they made, however confusedly, to Scripture as against the contemporary Church and its practices.[24] In a sense, a segment of the lay world in the more advanced countries of the West was experiencing a conversion in the eleventh century. The fortress Christianity of the Dark Ages was giving way, in the more propitious social circumstances of the age, to a religion which could touch the intellect of the layman. There are signs of this in some of these outbreaks; it is especially marked at Arras, with the insistence on adult responsibility in the refusal of infant baptism, and at Orléans, in the form of scepticism towards the Virgin Birth. Thus, as so often, heresy in the eleventh century runs parallel to orthodoxy, reflecting and distorting the more widespread movements of opinion within the Church.

All social classes are touched in these episodes—aristocrats and clergy at Orléans, aristocrats at Monforte, townsmen probably at Arras and Liège, peasants in perhaps four other cases.[25] The situation is confused by the convention of ecclesiastical writers referring scornfully to heretics as men of low standing, *plebs, rustici* and the like, because they are unlearned men interfering in ecclesiastical matters that are not properly their concern[26]. The terms are imprecise and abusive. Above all, the social factors behind the heresy remain elusive because we know so little about social composition in the outbreaks; at the most, the number of outbreaks where composition is known is eight out of a total of seventeen cases (or a little more than seventeen, if we include as evidence the general denunciations of heresy in certain sources). Moreover, of these eight some rest on frail evidence indeed.[27] Yet the social and economic side cannot be wholly left out of account, even though perforce it stays imprecise. At this time developing economic life was opening routes for trade, which in turn aided the diffusion of ideas. Rising population created new problems, horizons widened. In particular, the movement which

[24]*RB* (classic interpretation of medieval heresy), pp. 476–83; a more exclusively 'Western' explanation of these heresies is in R. Morghen, *Medioevo cristiano* (Bari, 1953), from *ADRSP*, LXVII (1944) pp. 97–151, arousing controversy in A. Dondaine, 'L'Origine de l'Hérésie médiévale', *RSCI*, VI (1952), pp. 43–78; further work by Morghen in *HS*, bibliography and pp. 121–38 (see esp. E. Delaruelle's question, p. 137); facts given by Thouzellier (ibid., pp. 105–16) and Russell (*Dissent*) (with central theme of Western generating of heresy, but adding new dimension of pre-1000 heresy); survey by C.N.L. Brooke, 'Heresy and Religious Sentiment: 1000–1250', *BIHR*, XLI (1968), pp. 115–31 (reprinted in his *Medieval Church and Society* (London, 1971), pp. 139–61).
[25]See gazetteer below, Appendix D, s. 1.
[26]Grundmann in *Kultur und Universalgeschichte. Festchrift W. Goetz* (Leipzig and Berlin, 1927), pp. 91–107. Cf. P. Riché, 'Recherches sur l'Instruction des Laïcs du Xᶜ au XIIᶜ siècle', *CCM*, V (1962), pp. 175–82; Moore, loc. cit., p.30, n. 42.
[27]The best analysis of social factors is in Russell, *Dissent*, pp. 230–41 (covering episodes before and after the eleventh century).

later creates the independent communes is stirring at this time. As towns developed, communities of a new kind came into existence. This fact may suggest one reason for the novel phenomenon in eleventh-century heresy—the adherence of groups under a leader, and the preference, clearly expressed at Orléans, Arras and Monforte, for the experience of the group as against the teaching of the Church. The religious, economic and social developments of the first half of the eleventh century provided the conditions in which heresy once again could appear in a new guise in the West. Alone, however, they do not account for some surprising features in the five cases under review.

The ensemble of doctrines in each case includes elements which it is not easy to derive either from a Western reform movement or any other of the stirrings in society of the period. They require that we postulate the intervention of a non-Western force.[28] The heretics at Orléans and those at Liège described in bishop Théoduin's letter of 1048 to 1050, who said that Christ did not have a human body, or those at Monforte, who appear to have believed that He did not exist at all, were cutting across some of the most fundamental teaching of the Church. The influence of monastic ideas, misunderstood and taken to mean that matter in itself was evil, hardly seems sufficient to account for these drastic denials of the Incarnation. The rejection of marriage is easier to account for in Western terms, when one recalls the language of some reformers, the monastic strain so powerful in this century, and some Pauline sayings about the division between flesh and spirit. Yet at Arras and Monforte the heretics go well beyond a demand for celibacy for some Christians, and on to the extreme position, that marriage and sexual intercourse are of themselves sinful. Even marriage for the purpose accepted by all orthodox writers, that of procreation, is explicitly excluded at Monforte. This accords uneasily with the Western tradition.[29] So at Arras does the rejection of the Old Testament implied in the heretics' exclusive reliance on the gospels and the Apostles. This is not usual later in the Middle Ages in heresy of purely Western origin. The Waldensians, who were second to none in their stress on the New Testament, never toppled over into a denial of authority to the Old Testament because of their enthusiasm for the New.[30] Again, at Arras the extreme radicalism of the heretics' attitude to the material objects and concomitants of worship, including even the practice of singing in church, is startling; and as a whole it is an unobvious derivation from Western thinking.

The Cross as a symbol had many centuries of hallowed usage behind it, and

---

[28]The assumption of pioneer I. von Döllinger, *Beiträge zur Sektengeschichte des Mittelalters*, I (München, 1890), pp. 51–74; Dondaine in *RSCI*, VI (1952), pp. 43–78 (but note criticism of H. C. Puech, 'Catharisme médiévale et Bogomilisme', in *Oriente ed Occidente nel Medio Evo* (Rome, 1957), pp. 84–104); Borst, *Katharer*, pp. 71–80; and, with more subtle technique of dogmatic analysis than Dondaine, applied to Arras, J. V. Fearns, 'Peter von Bruis und die religiöse Bewegung des 12 Jahrhunderts', *AKG*, XLVII (1966), pp. 311–35. I am indebted to Dr Fearns for comments and information.

[29]Professor Russell reminds me of some hard sayings in the Fathers about sexual activity; R. Bultot, *La Doctrine du Mépris du Monde*, (Louvain and Paris, 1963) is informative. But the tenets of the heretics yet seem extreme to me.

[30]See Fearns, loc. cit., p. 326.

its repudiation at Châlons-sur-Marne, Arras and Monforte represents a sharp breach with the Western practice. Possible as it is for such a repudiation to be evolved spontaneously in a heretic's mind, as the case of Claudius of Turin shows,[31] it is still an unlikely tenet. The extreme rarity of this view in purely Western-influenced heresy in the twelfth century proves the point.[32] Finally, at Orléans we appear to be dealing with a Gnostic sect, with an initiation ceremony and a gift of special illumination for the chosen few. Any readers of Scripture could see in Acts the importance for the early Church of the laying on of hands, but whether he would easily find precedents for the kind of development recorded at Orléans is very doubtful.

The chances of spontaneous incubation in the West alone, despite the more *outré* nature of the belïefs, are obviously higher when we are dealing with only one tenet of this kind in a given outbreak. If, as in the five cases under discussion, we come across clusters of such beliefs, we shall be impelled to look beyond the orthodox developments in the Western Church to the tradition of Bogomilism, which we know to have been spreading in Byzantium during this century. Each of the doctrines discussed forms a part of the teaching of the Byzantine Bogomils, as we have seen. They said that Christ had no body and was not truly born, crucified or resurrected. They rejected marriage and sexual intercourse as sinful *per se*. They repudiated the Old Testament. They rejected formal liturgy, singing in church, church buildings altogether. They would not accept the eucharist. They rejected veneration of the Cross. They admitted initiates, as Zigabenus tells us, by laying-on of hands. From the time of John Tzurillas, if not earlier, they rejected flesh-eating altogether, as some of the Western heretics did.

Though every one of these beliefs could, in theory, be incubated spontaneously and alone in the West out of a distorted understanding of the Christian tradition, to derive clusters of them from Byzantine Bogomilism is the likelier hypothesis. Seeds of Byzantine dualism, carried into the West by trade contacts or by deliberate missionizing, possibly via the Greek colonies still existing in Italy,[33] fell here and there on fertile ground, prepared by the impact of the Western reform tradition with its strong ascetic overtones and, more faintly, the stirrings of a questioning lay spirit.

The writers who recorded these episodes knew nothing of Bogomilism. Certain of them described the heretics as Manichees—a description which in the strict sense was false, for Manichaeism had died out in the West some five centuries earlier, and there is no trace of its distinctive doctrines and organization in these outbreaks. Adémar of Chabannes made most energetic use of the phrase, applying it to three of the episodes between 1018 and 1028 and the denunciation made at the council of Charroux convoked to deal with heresy. Landulf Senior applied it to the Monforte sectaries, one other chronicler applied it to the heretics in Upper Lorraine, and a bishop, reporting heresy in Châlons-sur-Marne, contaminated his account of it by

[31]Russell, pp. 16–17. Dating and situation make an influence of dualism on Iconoclasm from Byzantium or elsewhere improbable.

[32]Fearns, loc. cit., pp. 324–5.

[33]H. Sproemberg, review of Borst's *Katharer* (*DLZ*, LXXVIII (1957), cols 1095–1104). Sproemberg never completed the map of which he speaks here (information from Professor E. Werner); I owe the idea of compiling one to his review.

recording that its adherents believed that Mani was the Holy Ghost. It is unlikely in fact that these dissidents had ever heard of Mani at all. Writers used the term solely because they smelt dualism in the outbreaks, and Manichaeism was the most famous form of dualism for Western writers, owing to the experience of Augustine.[34] None the less it was by a rightful instinct that the label reappeared in the chroniclers from 1018, for from this time, if not earlier, a form of oriental dualism was exerting its influence on indigenous heresy.

Contacts with Bogomilism in the eleventh century were too slight for the importation of a full-blown dualism. A heretical cosmology is only once in evidence, and then faintly.[35] As has been pointed out, in some cases where Bogomil beliefs are taught, Bogomil reasons are not given for them.[36] At Monforte, for example, the heretics, holding the Bogomil belief that sexual intercourse was of itself sinful, yet implied through the mouth of Gerard a desire for the continuation of the race, which a member of the Byzantine sect would surely have rejected. Outbreaks differ in the extent to which they have accepted a Bogomil penetration. The nearest to Bogomilism is the upper-class circle at Orléans, with its denial that Christ had a body, its rejection of marriage and flesh-eating, its body of initiates, and its use of the imposition of hands to confer a special illumination—corresponding to the *teleiosis* of the Byzantine sources. At Arras, though we have the drastic rejection of the Church characteristic of the Bogomils, the distaste for church buildings, the rejection of the Cross and of church singing, the stress on *justitia* is personal to the group and the rejection of baptism is a Western-type tenet. *Gnosis* seems to be quite lacking. Of them all, Monforte is the most idiosyncratic, with beliefs such as that Christ was the soul of man beloved of God that will not readily fit either Western reform dissidence or the Bogomil tradition. In all cases indigenous Western factors remain more potent than Bogomil ones; without the former there would have been no heresy in the West at this date. A native movement, still half-formed and not yet capable on its own of sustaining a challenge to the doctrines of the Church, has been penetrated but not taken over by Bogomilism. The heresies are *sui generis*, impossible fully to categorize,[37] a half-way house between Western dissidence and Eastern dualism, best described as 'proto-dualism'.

Distribution and Origins of Heresy
The map below plots in parallel Western proto-dualism and other heresies in the eleventh century and the contemporaneous incidence of dualism in the Byzantine empire and her neighbours, to show the geographical setting in which this penetration took place. It depicts the Paulicians at a late stage of their development, dispersed from Asia Minor to the frontiers, the Adoptionist wing lying on the Armenian side, the dualists in the Balkans. The

[34]Russell, pp. 192–6; for use of 'Manichei,' etc, see p. 208. Eleventh-century usage dates from *c.* 1018 entry for Aquitaine in Adémar.

[35]In the bishop's query at Orléans on creation *ex nihilo* through the Son, see Paul of S. Père de Chartres (Bouquet, x, p. 539). The Bogomils believed creation was through the devil. But the framing of the question in a source written long after the event could easily be fortuitous.

[36]Moore, loc. cit., p. 30.

[37]Cp. A. Borst, in *Atti del X Congresso Internazionale di Scienze Storiche* (Rome, 1957), pp. 349–50.

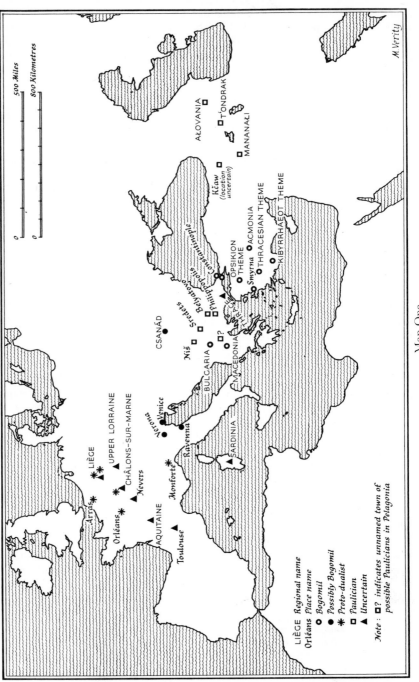

LIÈGE *Regional name*
Orléans *Place name*

○ Bogomil
● Possibly Bogomil
✳ Proto-dualist
▢ Paulician
▲ Uncertain

Note: ▢? indicates unnamed town of
possible Paulicians in Pelagonia

500 *Miles*

800 *Kilometres*

Arras
LIÈGE
UPPER LORRAINE
CHÂLONS-SUR-MARNE
Orléans
Nevers
AQUITAINE
Monforte
Toulouse
Verona
Venice
Ravenna
SARDINIA

CSANÁD
Niš
BULGARIA
Srediec
Beljatovo
Philippopolis
MACEDONIA
THR
Constantinople
OPSIKION THEME
Smyrna
ACMONIA
THRACESIAN THEME
KIBYRRHAEOT THEME
Kíaw *(location uncertain)*
ALOVANIA
T'ONDRAK
MANANAŁI
?

M. Verity

Map One
Western Heretics and Eastern Dualists

Bogomils are in Bulgaria and parts of Byzantium, including the capital. On the other side of the map proto-dualist episodes are scattered from Liège and Arras in the north to Monforte in the south. As far as our meagre sources go, large parts of Europe were untouched by heresy—the Holy Roman Empire apart from Upper Lorraine, Spain (apart from the elusive heresy linked by Glaber with Sardinia), all southern Italy, the British Isles, the Scandinavian lands.[38] The concentration of episodes, proto-dualist and unknown, lies in France, above all in the north, and in the Low Countries—that is, in some of the forward areas of western Europe at this time. There is some link with Italy or with the land route thereto. Châlons-sur-Marne, with two episodes, is a diocese that includes the fairs that formed the trade link between the north and the Mediterranean. Arras, where the heretics arrived from Liège and ultimately from Italy, had a link with the Mediterranean world through its cloth manufacture. Orléans, according to one weak source, gained its heresy from the activity of a woman missionary from Italy.[39] Italy itself is by Monforte, Venice, Verona and Ravenna. Sardinia, however, the farthest south of the heresy-bearing localities, is an oddity: In this case the chronicler's description is too muddled for us to know anything about persons or doctrines.

Csanád, Ravenna, Verona and Venice offer the possibility of an intermediate stage between the areas of Western heresy and Byzantine dualism, which otherwise lie so far apart on the map; but it lacks any solid confirmation owing to the vagaries of our informant, St. Gerard of Csanád.[40] Gerard, originally a monk from the Venetian monastery of San Giorgio, worked as a missionary bishop in the recently Christianized land of Hungary, where he composed a rambling commentary on the *Hymnum trium puerorum* at some stage between his appointment in 1030 and martyrdom in 1046. There he tells us of a heresy active in the region of his mission with features that sound suspiciously like Bogomilism. Immediately afterwards he speaks of heresy in France, Greece and Italy, giving specific mention of the three towns near the head of the Adriatic, where there were active trade links with the East. Csanád, at the junction of Latin and Byzantine spheres of influence, abutted on the cradle of Bogomilism in Bulgaria. But though the geographical setting fits well enough to a hypothesis of Bogomil infiltration, Gerard's understanding of the term '*haereses*' is too imprecise, the links in his mind between the heresy in Hungary and that in the Italian towns too uncertain, for it to remain more than an intriguing possibility.

Eleventh-century Western heresy has all the interest for the historian which is attached to the study of origins. After a hundred-year gap heresy revives. It is marked by novel elements. The heresies themselves are individual compositions—in a sense collector's pieces—with features not repeated later. A fresh stage is reached in the growth of Western dissidence, recognizable not

[38] Discussed in Russell, pp. 243–7.

[39] Raoul Glaber, *Les cinq Livres de ses Histoires (900–1044)*, ed. M. Prou, iii, viii (Paris, 1886), pp. 74–81.

[40] *Sancti Gerardi Chanadiensis scripta et acta*, ed. Ignatius, Count Batthyány (Alba-Carolinae, 1790), pp. 98–9; corrected by G. Silagi, *Untersuchungen zur 'Deliberatio supra Hymnum Trium Puerorum' des Gerhard von Csanád* (München, 1967), pp. 97–8 (fols 46ʳ–7ʳ of the original); misunderstood by Döllinger in *Beiträge*, i pp. 61–2. I am indebted to Dr Silagi for discussion. See also below appendix A, s. 2.

only by modern analysts of doctrine but also by contemporaries. A fresh climate of opinion affected not only the heretics themselves but also their opponents. In certain cases after 1018 the heretics meet with violence.[41] Generally it is the laity who are responsible. At Orléans it is the king who gives the order to burn the recalcitrant, the queen who pokes out the eye of her confessor with a stick, the mob who attempt to lynch the heretics. At Goslar it was the emperor who hanged the heretics from Upper Lorraine because they refused the test of killing a chicken. But the clergy evidently assented to these capital sentences, and the bishop of Cambrai-Arras applied force to try to lever confessions out of the Arras group. On the other hand, bishop Wazo of Liège pleaded for a measure of toleration. Let the wheat grow with the tares till the time of harvest, he argued.[42] This was advice not generally heeded in the Middle Ages. The new currents of religious thought affected both sides, carrying a few groups in this century into heresy, pushing the orthodox into fierce reactions against it.

Yet the historian's expectations are for ever doomed to disappointment by the thinness of the record. Here and there we seem to catch a fragment of the actual words of the heretics in their characteristic posture, attempting to conceal unorthodox belief behind bland-sounding phrases, and being drawn out by persistent questioning.[43] For the majority of the cases language is too ambiguous, entries in chronicles too curt, for us to form a satisfactory judgement. Even in the major episodes where reconstruction is possible, one is always conscious that a hypothesis is delicately balanced on a thin edge of evidence. Nor, given the documentation of the period, can we hope for a major new discovery to shed light on the problem. Heresy in this period will always remain obscure and tantalizing.

Perhaps the reason lies not only in the inadequacy of the literary equipment of the age, or the inexperience of the interrogators coping with a new problem who fail to draw out in full the heretics' thought; it may lie also in the lack of a developed, logical understanding of their own beliefs by the heretics themselves, innocent, ill-equipped seekers after purity. Unable to explain themselves adequately, they leave a blurred imprint on the sources.

We are after all dealing only with the prolegomena to the continuous history of Western heresy. After the resurgence of heresy in the second decade of the century—snuffed out, it may be, by vigorous counteraction by clergy and laity—heresy fades, reappears and then, after mid-century, vanishes as mysteriously as it had come. Bogomilism makes its first impact, but is unable to achieve that more permanent marriage which in the twelfth century gives birth to the Cathar churches. East and West met fleetingly, then parted again.

---

[41]On repression generally, see Russell, pp. 249–56.

[42]Ibid., p. 40; *MBPH*, pp. 21–4.

[43]At Arras, Monforte (in some measure: compare earlier and later answers of Gerard according to Landulf Senior) and Orléans; contrary view in Morghen, *Medioevo*, pp. 204–81.

Part Two

The Twelfth Century

4

Orthodox Reform and Heresy

The Nature of Twelfth-century Heresy.

Early in the twelfth century half a century's silence in the history of Western heresy was broken. A new rhythm becomes apparent:[1] heretical episodes occur more frequently. Heresy changes character. The heretical groups of the eleventh century sought a flight from the world to practise their austerities. They were generally content with a personal abnegation and a set of idiosyncratic views to be discussed within the closed circle of the chosen. The new breed of heretics are aggressive reformers who insist on changes in the Church that will bring Catholicism into line with their own ideas. The eleventh-century groups spread their views quietly, through personal contacts; in the best documented example, at Orléans, a heretical group among the clergy existed secretly, expanding through quiet missionizing for years before attracting notice from authority. Twelfth-century heretics have other assumptions. Heresy is spread more by open and aggressive preaching. Hearers are stimulated to positive action. It may be that crosses are torn down and burnt, that women give up their jewellery, or, as in the case of Henry the monk at Le Mans, a whole town rebels against its overlord. Heresiarchs are not afraid to use physical force: Eon de l'Étoile mobilizes a peasant force to rob churches in Brittany; Arnold of Brescia allies himself with the forces of republicanism to hold Rome against the pope; Tanchelm of Antwerp, whether suspect reformer or heretic leader, uses a bodyguard of soldiers.

The heretics and their supporters demand that the Church as a whole shall hear them and stir itself to follow. There is a new concern for the social implications of the Gospel, or a desire for radical changes among the clergy and in the relations between the Church and society.

We will not have far to seek the reasons for this change. An orthodox reform movement, first issuing from monks and from inferior strata in the hierarchy, then taken up vigorously by the papacy, had begun to stir the consciences of the laity at large.[2] Pamphlet and preaching warfare between the imperial and

---

[1]Borst, *Katharer*, p. 83; for latest work on twelfth-century heresy, see H. Grundmann, *Ketzergeschichte des Mittelalters, Die Kirche in ihrer Geschichte: Ein Handbuch* ed. K. D. Schmidt, E. Wolf, II, G. Pt. I (Göttingen, 1963), pp. 15–20, his 'Neue Beiträge zur Geschichte der religiösen Bewegungen im Mittelalter', *AKG*, XXXVII (1955), pp. 129–68 (research report) also in *Relazioni*, III, 357–402, *RB*, pp. 487–524 (2nd edn only). R. I. Moore, *The Origins of European Dissent*, will provide a fresh analysis, with discussion of social factors.

[2]G. Volpe, *Movimenti religiosi e sette ereticali nella società medievale Italiana (secoli XI–XIV)* (Firenze, 1926) (a stimulating survey, still of use); *RB*, pp. 13–16.

papal parties had taken discussion of the rightful place of the Church in the world into circles hitherto unaffected by such matters. Under Gregory VII the papacy had been led by a dominating personality prepared to open issues of principle to general discussion and to offer support for enthusiasts in rebellion against a simoniacal clergy.

The case of the lay movement of the Pataria in Milan, whose origins pre-dated the investiture controversies, is especially illuminating for the forces stirred by the reform movement.[3] The preaching of the deacon Ariald unleashed a formidable rebellion against the power of a simoniacal and unchaste upper clergy. Social tensions played a part as humbler citizens, sneered at by an opponent as 'inhabitants of the district of the rag-market',[4] attacked the power of a feudal nobility allied with the cathedral clergy, who lived an unregenerate life hardly distinguishable from that of their fellow nobles. Other cross-currents were the patriotism of a city and archbishopric with a distinguished past, and the rival interests of pope and emperor. Held together by an oath like a communal movement, the Pataria continued their inflammatory agitation from 1057 to 1075, and carried their influence into the cities of Brescia, Piacenza and Cremona. From Florence and the reform movement of St John Gualbert they drew uncorrupt priests to serve their needs in Milan.[5]

Lay participation was considerable, though lower clergy as well came to support the agitation, and two laymen, the knight Erlembald and his brother Landulf, notary of the Milan church, were leaders. In the fiercest language unworthy clergy were attacked, their houses were plundered, and the sacraments which they administered were boycotted. Landulf was quoted as saying that the people should think of their masses as if they were dogs' dung, and their churches as if they were cattle sheds; layman as he was, he preached, it would seem, without specific authorization, and was attacked by a chronicler for doing so. Accusations of heresy were flung about, the conservatives in Milan accusing the reformers of being heretics, while distinguished members of the reform party in Rome in the same period made free with the word 'heresy' as a term of abuse for moral faults in the clergy.[6] The reformers wrote as controversialists at a time when scant attention had been given to setting a strict and technical boundary between heresy and orthodoxy; nevertheless the use of the word was important. If simony in the

[3]C. Violante, *La pataria milanese e la riforma ecclesiastica.* I, *Le premesse (1045–57)* (Rome, 1955) (the standard work); H. E. J. Cowdrey, 'The Papacy, the Patarenes and the Church of Milan', *TRHS,* 5th ser., XVIII (1968), pp. 25–48; G. Miccoli, 'Per la storia della pataria Milanese', *BISIAM,* LXX (1958), pp. 43–123; E. Werner, *Pauperes Christi* (Leipzig, 1956), pp. 114–64 (Marxist survey with hypothesis of Bogomil influence which I do not accept); comment in E. Dupré Theseider, *Introduzione alle Eresie Medievali* (Bologna, 1953), pp. 77–94.

[4]The derivation of the name Patarene is controversial, but I prefer Muratori's hypothesis. See Borst, *Katharer,* p. 250, Werner, *Pauperes Christi,* pp. 142–3, Manselli, *Eresia,* p. 138, A. Frugoni, in *BISIAM,* LXV (1953), pp. 129–35, A. Dondaine in *AHDLMA* XXVII (1952), pp. 110–4, and *AFP,* XXIX (1959), pp. 275–6, Werner in *IP,* XIII (1957), pp. 16–31, and most recently C. Thouzellier, *Hérésie et Hérétiques,* (Rome, 1969), pp. 204–21.

[5]C. Violante, 'Hérésies urbaines et Hérésies rurales en Italie du 11e au 13e Siècle', *HS,* pp. 171–98 (individual hypothesis on the social reasons for Italy's fertility in heresy), at p. 177.

[6]J. Leclercq, 'Simoniaca haeresis', in *Studi Gregoriani,* I, pp. 523–30. I owe the ref. to Mr D. Bethell.

clergy was to be equated with heresy, extreme action to bring it to an end might seem justified. At the end of his career Erlembald went close to usurping a clerical function for himself, when he made a decision about the administration of baptism. To avoid use of chrism consecrated by the unworthy, he had a chrism made and administered by a Patarene priest.

Strictly, no action of the Patarenes went beyond the lines authorized by orthodox reformers in the Easter synod at Rome in 1059 which forbade laymen to hear the masses of married priests. They were not heretics: they lacked the will to proceed against the sacramental and doctrinal system of the Catholic Church.[7] But the reservations which even that most radical reformer St Peter Damiani expressed about the actions of the Pataria had some justification, for their reforming zeal tended to shake all Church authority, and set forces in motion whose direction could not be foreseen. This did not check the support which Gregory VII gave to the movement before and during his pontificate: influenced by him, Alexander II had given a banner to Erlembald, making him a kind of *gonfalonier* of the Roman Church. When Erlembald was killed in street fighting in 1075, Gregory honoured him as a martyr. The same public justification for action against unreformed clergy and the boycott of their sacraments was explicit in Gregory's rehabilitation of Ramihrdus, a priest in Cambrai burnt as a heretic after refusing to receive the sacrament from the hands of unworthy clergy. Ramihrdus roused a movement in Cambrai and its region that had affinities with the Pataria and he was very likely no more than a fiery reformer like Ariald.[8] Yet the line was perilously thin between the boycott of the masses of unreformed clergy and the heresy, to which we may refer for convenience as Donatist, that the masses of unworthy clergy were invalid, and in the atmosphere of reform, with preaching and pamphlets stressing the vices of the unreformed clergy, the step into that heresy was easy to take. By calling on him to take action against unworthy clergy, the Gregorian movement demanded from the layman a certain personal responsibility. This, a relatively new sentiment in the West, was to be fateful for the future development of heresy.

Church reform and heresy have important links. The revolutionary programme of the Gregorians set before the Church ideals which could never be wholly realized, and gave to some clergy and numbers of laymen a vision of a free Church that, in the social and political circumstances of the time, could never be expected to be wholly realized. At first, the Gregorians, as in the Pataria and elsewhere, could work with popular lay movements: thus the zeal of the common man who had been awakened to reform in the more advanced centres of western Europe found an orthodox channel. That fact will explain the relative absence of heresy in the half century that lay between the executions at Goslar and the reappearance of popular heresy.[9]

But in time the direction of papal reform tended to change, and its aims became more narrowly clerical and juridical. At worst, it might separate

[7]Dupré Theseider, p. 77.

[8]Russell, *Dissent*, pp. 43–4; *MBPH*, pp. 24–6.

[9]*RB*, p. 483; Brooke in *BIHR*, XLI (1968), p. 119. I have not examined the history of the followers of Berengar of Tours in the eleventh century, which might modify generalizations about the absence of heresy after 1051. See above, p. 29. n. 22.

clergy from laity without necessarily raising the devotion and efficiency of the former. The momentous question of the freedom of the Church and the worthiness of candidates for bishoprics tended to contract into the lesser issue of the right to deliver to the bishop the symbols of his sacred office; and, as compromise was reached on this at the Concordat of Worms in 1122, it might well be felt that some of the early call to purification had failed in its effect, and that the orthodox reform movement was turning into disputes over minutiae. Before Worms, reform in its most immediate impact on the lay world was beginning to run into the sands, and as this happened the number of heretical episodes began to rise. A first cause for the recrudescence of heresy in the West lay in the expectations roused by Gregorian reform and its failure to fulfil them.

Where the papacy scored its most lasting popular success was in the crusades. Here Urban II and his successors aroused a genuine popular enthusiasm, the driving force which outlasted so many military and political failures, and found expression in such obviously spontaneous and unrehearsed movements as the crusade of Peter the Hermit, which preceded the first crusade proper, or the children's crusade of the thirteenth century. How deep into the popular consciousness the crusades had penetrated is apparent from the belief of the inhabitants of the primitive region of western France on the borders of Brittany, Anjou and Maine, that the hermits of the woods who emerged as wandering preachers in shaggy attire were Saracens who had arrived by a concealed tunnel from their own land to betray the West from within.[10]

Crusade preaching stirred millennial enthusiasms. The Holy Land was represented as being literally a land flowing with milk and honey; the success of the crusade would, it was believed, issue in the new kingdom at Jerusalem that would reconcile men's quarrels, and usher in the era of plenty that would precede the End. The crusades aroused a deep popular feeling for the sufferings of Christ at the Crucifixion and a corresponding hatred for the Jews: pogroms accompanied the summons to the Crusade in a number of towns, and aided the spread of a mood of eschatological enthusiasm, in which the slaughter of the enemies of Christ was expected to lead to the events preceding the end of the world. A mood of religious enthusiasm was created that could lead to the rise of extravagant leaders and might easily run into unorthodox channels.[11]

The machinery of the crusades and the setting up of crusaders' kingdoms in Palestine that was their most obvious result, led to a renewed contact with Eastern heresy. Direct contact of crusaders with heresy is hardly recorded. In only one instance do we have such information, and that was when they came across a *castrum* inhabited by heretics, most probably Paulicians. The

[10]Bernard of Tiron, *Vita* (*PL*, CLXXII, col. 1409b).

[11]On aberrations linked to the crusades, see N. Cohn, *The Pursuit of the Millennium* (London, 1957), trans. into German, 1961, French, 1962, Italian, 1965; reviews, M. E. Reeves, in *MA* XXVIII (1959), pp. 225-9; B. Smalley, in *EHR*, LXXIV (1959), pp. 101-3; E. Winter, in *DLZ*, LXXXIII (1962), cols 998-1001, H. Grundmann, in *HZ*, CXCVI (1963), pp. 661-6; R. Manselli, in *RSLR*, III (1967), pp. 532-8. See summary of Cohn's theory and definition of terms in his 'Medieval Millenarism: its Bearing on the Comparative Study of Millenarian Movements', in *Millennial Dreams in Action*, ed. S. L. Thrupp (The Hague, 1962), pp. 31-43.

crusaders' reaction was to destroy the place and its inhabitants.[12] Yet the crusades were an important link in the chain binding closer the peoples of western Europe to Byzantium and the Balkans,[13] and the increased commercial activity stimulated, in part, by the existence of the crusader States would no doubt have facilitated formal and informal contacts with the underground Bogomil churches in Constantinople, Asia Minor and the Balkans.

Unmistakable evidence of the presence of Bogomilism emerges in the 1140s, but it is probable that it can be demonstrated earlier. Features in heretical episodes before that date, notably at Bucy-le-Long in 1114, look suspiciously like fragments of Bogomil doctrine, and, as we shall see, there is ground for believing that the early heretic, Peter of Bruis, had experienced some Bogomil influence. A hypothesis of gradually increasing Bogomil contact, culminating in the formation of fully-fledged dualist churches later in the century, seems best to fit the known facts. The crusades form one link among others in the chain of contacts that helped to make this influence more real in the West.

Nevertheless, dualism would never have made its re-entry into the West had not the soil been well prepared for the reception of heresy. A reaction against orthodoxy, an undogmatic dissatisfaction with the Church, was the necessary first stage if dissentient circles were ever to be able to accept, *en masse* and for a long period of time, elements of drastically ascetic religion well on the margins of Catholicism. This dissatisfaction was the product of a reform that for some had gone sour, or the effects of a rigidity and conservatism in the Church that was unable to accept new interpretations of the Christian life.

Most of a century was required before ecclesiastical authority was able to adapt its outlook and establish a coherent policy; in the doubts and hesitations, in the reaction to crude and sweeping condemnations, themselves the products of the uncertainty of authority, heretical groups found occasion to cut themselves off from the Church. The long, simmering crisis found for the first time the outline of a solution in the hands of Innocent III in the early thirteenth century. Till then, the anxieties of churchmen about the spread of heresy were not unjustified, for the Church of the twelfth century as a whole did not understand the forces at work behind the popular heretical movements, and had no effective answer to them.

Orthodox Wandering Preachers.
What made the heresy of the twelfth century insidious was its relatively unformed nature, its lack (at least until Catharism began to solidify towards the end of the century) of concise dogmatic positions, and its close relationship to the ideals and pre-occupations of orthodox piety. Most popular heresies are initiated, before the rise of the printing press, by a period of spontaneous wandering preaching. Those of the twelfth century were no exception. But the

[12] See gazetteer, Appendix D, s, 1 (Pelagonia).
[13] C. Thouzellier, 'Hérésie et Croisade au XIIe Siècle', *RHE*, XLIX, (1954), pp. 855–72 (hypothesis linking development of heretical doctrine to crusaders from second crusade; for its weakness, A. Borst, *DA*, XI (1954–5), pp. 617–8, R. Manselli, in *BISIAM* LXVII (1955), p. 221n.), S. Runciman, in *JEH*, XVIII (1967), pp. 89–90; see now revised version of Thouzellier's article in her *Hérésie et Hérétiques*, pp. 17–37 (note diagram on p. 37).

preaching, which stirred the populace and unconsciously helped to make them ready for the reception of the principal 'evangelical' and dualistic heresies of the century, often had an orthdox origin. We have seen it in operation in the Milan Pataria. In France it was carried on by wandering hermits well known in Catholic history as the founders of · religious congregations. It was not a work of planned missionizing by some organized sect. Its aim was the entirely orthodox one of the preaching of penance, the call of clergy and people to reform. Here we have a kind of spontaneous overspill of the fierce asceticism of the woods of western France, the work of reformers and monks who had not found full satisfaction in the normal outlets of cloister, canons or life among the secular clergy. Their work of preaching was not disapproved by the Church; some could show a papal permission for wandering preaching, analogous to the permission given to preach for the first and second crusades; but the preachers themselves were fiery and idiosyncratic and their preaching tours had consequences that were not always comfortable.

The earliest to be discussed by Johannes von Walter in his pioneer work on the wandering preachers of France was Robert of Arbrissel, and the case was typical for the reaction against the conventional ways of religion.[14] Robert was once in the household of the Bishop of Rennes, and had been a participant in the Gregorian reform movement, but he threw up a conventional career in the Church for the life of a hermit in the great wood of Craon, where he attracted followers and set out on preaching tours. Another case of reaction against a customary pattern of religious life is that of his follower Bernard of Tiron, who had become a monk, then prior of St Savin-sur-Gartempe where he came into conflict over the simony issue with Abbot Gervasius, then again Abbot of St Cyprian near Poitiers, where he clashed with his monks who did not want to accept reforms. After an unsuccessful dispute with Cluny, he was forced to leave. His solution was to turn his back on the unprofitable world of monastic communities and suits at Rome, and flee to the woods at Craon.

Another of the wandering preachers, Vitalis of Savigny, had been chaplain to Count Robert of Mortain and canon of the church of St Ebrulf at Mortain; but a love of poverty drove him into the waste and made him a hermit at Dompierre, east of Mortain, for seventeen years. The best known of von Walter's group was Norbert of Xanten, who had found the work of reform in circles of canons insufficient and took to the roads as a wandering preacher. As with the others, his zeal was not easy to incorporate into existing religious structures—an early attempt to make him leader of a group of Augustinian canons in Laon failed because of the canons' resistance to his reforms and he was led, in co-operation with the bishop of Laon, to found a new association which flowered into the Premonstratensians.

Though the backgrounds might differ, there are similarities within the group of wandering preachers which bear witness to some interesting new

[14]*Die ersten Wanderprediger Frankreichs*, (Leipzig, 1903–6), 2 vols. An ingenious but basically unsuccessful attack by H. Böhmer is in *TLZ*, xxix (1904), pp. 330–4, with reply from von Walter, *Wanderprediger*, ii, pp. 169–79. Full modern exposition by J. Becquet, 'L'Érémitisme clérical et laie dans l'Ouest de la France', in *L'Eremitismo nei Secoli* xi *e* xii (Milan, 1965), pp. 182–211; and his 'Érémitisme et hérésie au moyen age', in *HS*, pp. 139–45.

strands in popular piety. Their love of poverty is striking. Robert appeared on the preaching tours in rags almost to the point of indecency, with a beard and a grey cowl, going barefoot; Bernard of Tiron in shaggy attire, barefoot or riding on a donkey as a sign of humility. In the woods they lived on fruits and berries or on the product of rough manual labour, like turning or the products of simple gardens, worked by themselves without any lay brothers or hired labour. There were eccentricities: Robert of Arbrissel had a special calling for the religious care of women, and was accused by an opponent of undue intimacies—which in fact reflected no more than a characteristic lack of discretion. Bernard wept continually in his reflections on the sufferings of Christ all through the mass, and went about with his shoulders perpetually damp from his tears.

The audiences that these idiosyncratic figures drew on their preaching tours are a tribute, not only to their preaching power, but also to a diffused reverence for extreme asceticism and poverty. Poverty and preaching were closely linked: the lack of a stipend and the complete dependence of the preacher on the spontaneous offerings of his hearers were a guarantee of the preacher's independence and sincerity. Followers were speedily attracted, partly in the normal fashion, as the hermit who flees to the woods is seldom long there without attracting some visitors who come to seek a holy man's blessing and advice,[15] partly as mixed bodies of men and women attached themselves to the preachers as they travelled round the countryside. The denunciations of a married clergy and the general abuses of the pre-Gregorian world which were so much part of Robert's sermons probably drew to him the cast-off wives of reformed clergy, which a reformer might well describe as prostitutes.[16]

These mixed bodies created some not wholly unjustified alarm on the part of authority. There were questions about the permission to preach; Norbert, for example, was queried in 1119 about the legitimacy of his wandering tours. Influence was brought to bear on the preachers to cause their followers to settle down and choose a stable form of religious life in community. Thus, partly out of a normal zeal, partly at the instance of a reforming diocesan concerned for the spiritual benefit of his own locality—as in the case of Hermann of Laon,[17] and partly out of the pressure of anxious authorities, wandering preachers became founders of monasteries and orders.

The idiosyncrasy prevailed, however, here: the foundations were not of a conventional kind. Some, like Robert, revived the long disused idea of the double monastery. All were distinguished by a special care for poverty and a rejection of certain kinds of property. The foundations contributed to the variety of religious life in the first half of the twelfth century. Prémontré developed on the Slav frontier a missionary aim. But this was the exception. Robert of Arbrissel's foundation at Fontevrault, beginning as a pioneering work, with an unusual care for the status of women, ended as a religious house for the daughters and widows of the French court and nobility. Despite

[15]H. Grundmann, 'Zur Vita S. Gerlaci eremitae', *DA*, xviii (1962), pp. 539–54; economic interpretation of hermit movement in Werner, *Pauperes Christi*, pp. 25–52.

[16]Böhmer, in *TLZ*, xxix (1904), pp. 330–4.

[17]C. Dereine, 'Les Origines de Prémontré', *RHE*, xlii (1947), pp. 352–78.

certain original features, the apostolic life, as interpreted in terms of wandering preaching and poverty, could not be realized within these monasteries. That life was replaced for the followers of the preachers by withdrawal from the world in a stable pattern of life under vows.

It is striking how the sources, both for heretical movements and for the wandering preachers, speak of the apostolic life as a mark of these spontaneous phenomena. The clothing of the preachers amounted to a special uniform, with bare feet, minimal clothing and the donkey as the sign of the special humility of those practising the apostolic life. The noteworthy feature is that the apostolic life is no longer being interpreted exclusively along traditional lines, as the life of the monk or nun in community according to the pattern of the early Christians at Jerusalem, who held their goods in common and continued a life of prayer and charity to those in need. A new understanding of the apostolic life has come into being—based on the texts in Matthew and Luke about Christ sending out the Seventy to wander preaching through the villages, having neither scrip nor purse nor shoes and taking no money with them.[18]

The older view formed the scriptural justification for the life of the monks; it was very ancient and continued to hold considerable sway in the twelfth century, a period of vigorous development in new forms of monastic life.

But the spread of the reforms of the canonical life encouraged the development of the second, modern view of the apostolic life. The great stress on poverty in this interpretation is partly explained by the ascetic roots of these movements, with a strong semi-monastic tinge, partly by the post-Gregorian reaction against an over-endowed Church. That poverty had extraordinary popularity is apparent, for example, from the existence of an order like the Grandmontines, with its frail constitution and overwhelming emphasis on renunciation of worldly goods. A few entered to share the austerities; many more in the world remained outside to admire.

The poverty movements represented a reaction against the wealthy Church and a developing bourgeoisie in a time of rapid economic growth.[19] Wealth was notably concrete and visible, displayed in the finery of a merchant and his family. Behind the criticism of the Church as over-wealthy lay also an increasing popular rationalism, capable in a groping way of making comparisons with a new historical sense between the simple Church of the Apostles and the elaborate hierarchical Church of the twelfth century. What a leader and prophet of the Church in St Bernard of Clairvaux might set down for the Pope in the *De consideratione*, urging on him the example of the simplicity of the early Church, might also be understood in a cruder way at more popular levels, and, mishandled, turn towards heresy. A historian describing an encounter he had with a heretic at Bonn in the first half of the century described his scorn for the members of the Church hierarchy who

---

[18]C. Dereine, art. 'Chanoines', in *DHGE*; 'La Problème de la Vie commune chez les Canonistes, d'Anselm de Lucques à Gratien', *Studi Gregoriani*, III, pp. 287–98. M. D. Chenu, 'Moines, Clercs, Laïcs au Carrefour de la Vie évangélique (XIIe Siècle)', *RHE*, XLIX (1954), pp. 59–89.

[19]Outline by H. Grundmann, 'Soziale Wandlungen-Kaufleute, Bürger, Städte', in *Über die Welt des Mittelalters: Propyläen Weltgeschichte, Summa historica* (Berlin, etc., 1965), pp. 435–42. M. Mollat, 'La Notion de la Pauvreté au moyen âge. Position de Problèmes,' *Revue d' Histoire del' Église de France* LII (1966), 6–23.

lived so wrongfully (*irrationabiliter*)—the word is illuminating for the forces which operated below the surface against a traditional, conservative minded hierarchy.[20]

Against this diffused advance in understanding, the dissemination of a new logic at more popular levels, the Church had relatively slight defences. The great crowds which turned out for a popular preacher expressed the need for more coherent instruction, which the Church was in substance not meeting at the lower levels. As is well known, proposals to set up training centres for the clergy and to use cathedrals as foci for a popular theology broke down. Before the coming of the friars standards of training remained low. Systematic instruction of the laity was rare. Contemporary descriptions reveal sometimes in a flash the nature of the situation in the growing towns, against which reformers had to contend. A startling example is the new industrial town of Antwerp in the early twelfth century in the time of Tanchelm, where the only church for the entire town was allegedly served by a simoniac who lived in sin with his niece. Only relatively slowly did the Church begin to cope with the problems caused by the lack of a developed cure of souls within the towns.[21]

Here lay, in outline, the opportunities for the heretics—in the existence of much popular zeal, which reacted against a conservative Church still much in need of reform, a kind of primitive rationalism no longer satisfied with the fortress Church of the barbarian age, a new understanding of certain texts of Scripture, which had entered the popular consciousness[22] and could not be brought into accord with the ecclesiastical practices that the zealous few saw around them and, again among the few, a rejection of a still coarse and bloodstained age, with its crude materialism. Their yearning for a new way of apostolic life becomes explicable when set against this background. A preacher of skill, who came out of an ascetic background and denounced abuses, was sure of a hearing, and this remained true whether his views were essentially within the bounds of orthodox reform or not. These facts explain the success of the wandering preachers of France—but also the success of the heretical preachers nearly contemporary with them.

Cohn's *Millennium.*　Cohn examines forms of millennial expectation in popular movements from the eleventh century to the sixteenth, including Tanchelm, Eon de l'Étoile, the Pastoureaux, Flagellants and Taborites, in order to demonstrate that mass support for aberrations was produced by psychological disturbance of oppressed peasants and, especially, of artisans in overcrowded industrial towns (Cohn, pp. 24–32). Certain ideas recur, he claims: of an elite of amoral supermen, a sleeping saviour king or emperor. Cohn has stimulating value for tutorial teaching, great range, many sidelights, especially on religious lunacy and gallantly tackles the issue of motivation of

---

[20]Morghen, *Medioevo Cristiano*, p. 253; Ekbert of Schönau, *PL*, cxcv, col. 88. *Ratio* can mean 'right'; Morghen argues for meaning of illogicality implicit here as well as of moral fault. I owe comment to Professor C. N. L. Brooke.

[21]Russell, *Dissent*, pp. 60, 283; colourful anecdotes of moral failure generally in Lea, *Inquisition*, I, pp. 1–56; sketch of more subtle approach to relation between heresy and pastoral deficiencies in C. N. L. Brooke, 'The Church in the towns, 1000–1250', in *SCH*, vi, pp. 59–83, esp. p. 79; fuller discussion below, pp. 89–91.

[22]Morghen, *Medioevo cristiano*, pp. 204–81 *passim*.

heretics. But the book has weaknesses (i) in treatment of sources; (ii) in assumptions about medieval economic history and town life. Under (i) we must note how popular apocalyptic ideas need delicate handling. Of his examples, Tanchelm may well have been a slandered Gregorian reformer (below, pp. 55–7), Eon de l'Étoile a brigand feigning madness (below, pp. 59–60), and the Free Spirit an artificial heresy heavily 'developed' by persecutors. (below, ch. 11, s. 2). The exposition on Joachim fails to distinguish between Joachim and wild followers. Under (ii) we must note the distinction between 'family group' industries working for a local market and large-scale enterprises subject to the fluctuations of an international market. Under the latter uprooted ex-peasants found themselves unprotected; their disorientation made them hearers of millennial enthusiasts. But how many towns were the seat of such industries, where there was a psychological gulf between town and country, and was heresy so heavily the product of towns? Industrial towns of the Netherlands fit his description best; yet the author does not explain why early fourteenth-century disturbances there had so little religious, let alone millenarian flavour (op. cit. pp. 95, 98).

5

Heretical Preachers and the Rise of Catharism

Henry the Monk and Peter of Bruis

Henry the Monk provides a good example of a development in one wandering preacher from the ideas of drastic reform, largely still on the lines of the Gregorians, to a theological heresy, in which, nevertheless, issues of practical conduct still held first place.[1] In this he was typical of the theologically unformed protest of the twelfth century, in contradistinction to the more developed ideas of the thirteenth.

His origins are unknown. His success as a preacher in French-speaking areas suggests strongly that he himself was born somewhere in France or in a French-speaking part of the Empire. Henry was an apostate monk, probably also a priest, who had taken to the roads as a preacher of penance. The first detailed account of his activities comes from Le Mans, where he entered the city in 1116 preceded by two disciples carrying a cross on an iron-tipped staff, bearded, barefoot with poor clothing.[2] He was at first welcomed by the bishop, who unwisely left him in freedom there for some months while he set off for Rome. On his return he found the city had been turned upside down, the clergy denounced and stripped of all reverence among the people, who were brought to repentance by Henry's extraordinary eloquence.

Henry was still at this stage a radical Gregorian preacher, full of scathing denunciation for the sins of the clergy. But he showed some particular social concern, powerful enough to override the usual call to celibacy. His followers were exhorted to marry converted prostitutes as a charitable work, and dowries were forbidden. The stress on poverty was great. There were burnings of ornaments—but not the same emphasis as that of other preachers on asceticism, particularly in diet. As a preacher he had a long career, reappearing to move the populace against the clergy at various times in Lausanne, Poitiers and Bordeaux, as well as Le Mans, before moving into the lands of the Count of Toulouse, where his traces are lost after 1145. An

---

[1] My principal source is J. V. Fearns, 'The Contra Petrobrusianos of Peter the Venerable' (Ph.D. thesis, Univ. of Liverpool, 1963), pt I, ch. 3, 'Peter of Bruis and Henry of Lausanne'; some conclusions are in *AKG* XLVIII (1966), pp. 311–35. I am indebted to Dr Fearns for generously putting his thesis at my disposal. Early work in von Walter, *Wanderprediger*, II, pp. 130–40; new text with commentary in R. Manselli, 'Il monaco Enrico e la sua eresia', *BISIAM*, LXV (1953), pp. 1–63; see his *Studi sulle eresie del secolo XII*, (Rome, 1953), pp. 45–67 (survey linking evangelical heresies of Henry, Peter of Bruis, Valdes; critique in Ilarino da Milano, *RSCI*, IX (1955), pp. 424–31). For preachers, R. B. Brooke, *The Coming of the Friars* (London, 1975).

[2] Trans. of original text, the *Actus pontificum Cennomannis*, in *WEH*, pp. 108–14, *MBPH*, pp. 33–8.

C

attempt was made to divert him from heresy at the council of Pisa in 1135, where he promised to enter a monastery and give up wandering preaching, the council handling him relatively mildly and denouncing only three tenets.

This restrained treatment by the council, at a time when churchmen were not specially disposed to leniency towards heresy, suggests that at this time he was still rather a wild radical preacher than a heretic proper.[3] We know from a refutation of Henry's teaching by an unknown monk, William, that nevertheless in the end he did become a heretic of a dangerous kind.[4] The keynote of his heresy was its radical anticlericalism. Henry rejected the medieval role of the clergy as the dispensers of God's grace in favour of the responsibility of the individual.[5] This was carried to extreme lengths, involving Pelagianism.[6] Original sin was rejected: the individual fell by his own act, not by any taint from Adam. Baptism was a personal act of responsibility and could not thus be conferred on infants without understanding. In a similar way, prayers for the dead had no value, for this would cut across their own responsibility in life for their acts.

These two denials were of themselves not so significant, for they accompanied the normal reaction of an awakening laity to their responsibilities in the twelfth century. But what impresses in Henry is his denial of any useful part to the clergy. The sacramental life of the Church, as administered by an ordained priesthood, simply ceased to exist. The sacrifice of the mass was repudiated, the eucharist rejected, the power of binding and loosing denied to the priests, and sacerdotal confession replaced by a reciprocal confession of sins among the laity. In matrimony the consent of the individuals concerned was adequate: no place at all was left for any intervention by the clergy.

Behind these denials lay a burning desire for simplicity. Church buildings were unnecessary. All the accretions, as Henry saw them, which had grown up since the days of the New Testament were to be cast aside. The clergy were to hold neither money nor honours—an extreme, but not heretical view. Worship was to be simplified in accord with the text of the New Testament. Chrism and oil in baptism, having no warrant in Scripture, were to be eliminated, as were the ring, the mitre and the pastoral staff. A fervent acceptance of the New Testament, not for the first or last time, led to a wholesale rejection of practices which appeared to have no explicit scriptural warrant.

Henry's ideal was a poor wandering clergy, without sacramental functions, but with a vital preaching and exhorting role, wholly without institutional backing and apparatus, and he took such ideas to their most dramatic conclusion. While the orthodox reformers stressed the need to reform clerical morals, Henry cut the knot simply by removing the special functions of the clergy altogether. No doubt he began by taking up the very common heretical

---

[3] Fearns's argument is in 'Contra Petrobrusianos', p. lxxxvii. Trans. of text, *WEH*, pp. 114–5, *MBPH*, p. 39.

[4] See below, p. 51, n. 10; text ed. Manselli in *BISIAM* LXV (1953), pp. 36–62, trans. *WEH*, pp. 115–7, *MBPH*, pp. 46–60. Possibly William was William of St Thierry.

[5] For this exposition I am much indebted to Fearns, 'Contra Petrobrusianos'.

[6] See Manselli's comments (*Studi*, pp. 57–9).

position, that it was the unworthiness of the clergy which invalidated the sacraments, especially the mass administered by them. But he proceeded to the unusual position of eliminating the mass altogether. Could he have arrived at this position out of reflections on the Gregorian ideal and his own experience? Certainly this is a possibility. Nevertheless it is tempting to see an outside hand influencing his steps. J. V. Fearns suggests that the final step from radical preacher to heretic was facilitated by the influence of Peter of Bruis, the heretic leader from the mountains of the Embrun region, who, like Bogomil, began his career as a village priest.

Peter the Venerable, the abbot of Cluny and our prime source on the views and career of Peter of Bruis, believed when he wrote his tract against the sect, the *Contra Petrobrusianos*, that Henry was a faithful member of Peter's sect.[7] Later, when he wrote his introductory letter to the tract, he had learnt more of Henry and had come to give him a greater independence. He saw that Henry had had an independent career as wandering agitator before he encountered Peter of Bruis. A comparison of views of the two men confirms the dependence of Henry on Peter, but also his eclecticism. On a number of points they coincided, perhaps most strikingly in the total rejection of the eucharist, but also in the attacks on Church tradition, on offerings for the dead, and in the rejection of church buildings. The contemporary source, the *Actus pontificum Cennomannis*, says that, after Henry received permission to leave the synod of Pisa, he took up a new course with a fresh sect.[8] This can hardly be anything other than the Petrobrusians. Yet he did so with significant variations.

Despite Henry's zeal for the simplicities of the New Testament, he never followed Peter of Bruis in his rejection of the Old Testament or in his repudiation of the veneration of the Cross. Henry began his career in the evangelical, post-Gregorian tradition of reform and, though aided across the frontiers of orthodoxy by the more dogmatic heretic Peter, he and his followers always remained closer than the Petrobrusians to the tradition of evangelical heresy.[9] This is revealed by his attitude to poverty and the *apostolica vita*. For Henry, in the tradition of the wandering preachers, the poor life was a vital prerequisite for the clerical state; for Peter and his followers this played no special part. The right to preach freely mattered for Henry as it did for his orthodox predecessors. Like some of them, he claimed it from Christ's command to preach the gospel to all creatures. We hear little of this in the Petrobrusians.

The *Actus*, if we accept the identification of the new sect with the Petrobrusians, places the crucial meeting of Peter and Henry after the Synod of Pisa in 1135.[10] This would fit well with the career of Peter, who had long preached heresy in obscurity in the mountains; but, it would seem, shortly

---

[7] Ed. J. V. Fearns in *Corpus Christianorum, Continuatio mediaevalis,* x (Turnhout, 1968); for dating, see Fearns, 'The Contra Petrobrusianos', ch. 4.

[8] Ed. J. Mabillon in *Vetera Analecta* (Paris, 1723), col. 323A; Fearns, 'Contra Petrobrusianos', p. lxxxviii; *WEH*, p. 115. Introductory letter, subsequent to Peter's tract, ed. Fearns, *Corpus Christianorum*, loc. cit., pp. 3–6; it should be dated *c.* 1139–40 (see *MBPH*, p. 60; trans. ibid., pp. 60–2, *WEH*, pp. 118–21).

[9] Fearns, 'Contra Petrobrusianos', p. xcii.

[10] I have preferred Fearns's dating, (ibid., p. lxxxvii) to that of Manselli in *BISIAM*, LXV (1953), pp. 1–63: the date of appearance of the refutation by William the Monk is the crucial point.

before the *Contra Petrobrusianos* was written, extended his activities to the prosperous lands of Languedoc. Henry returning from Italy could readily have met him, then commenced his career as an agitator in southern France.

The setting for the preaching of the two heretics is significant. When Peter, the obscure mountain priest, came to extend his range, he roved through the prosperous towns of south-western France addressing great gatherings. At the time Peter the Venerable wrote, the heresy had spread into the province of Narbonne, westwards to Toulouse and the surrounding plain, and finally, by the time he had completed his prefatory letter, into the diocese of Arles and into Gascony.[11] At St Gilles, Peter ended his career with a violent death.

Henry was taken by the archbishop of Arles to the synod of Pisa, and thus may be presumed to have been active as a preacher in his province. After his return from Pisa, he began a second career in Languedoc, reaching the end of his tours in Toulouse, where St Bernard, if we believe his panegyrist, robbed Henry of his hold on the populace.[12] But the damage had been done. It can hardly be accidental that the area of Peter and Henry's success in the third decade of the century bears some similarity to that infiltrated by Catharism in the latter half of the century, where the Church had to face its greatest crisis. Peter and Henry deserve to be remembered, not only as founders of heretical groups in the age of rebirth of heresy, but also as forerunners of the Cathar success in Languedoc.[13]

The origins of Peter's heresy raise problems. Peter began as a parish priest, and then was ejected from his cure. Probably after this he began a career as a heretical agitator which lasted some twenty years, from about 1119 to his death in approximately 1139–40. Bruis was a small village in the canton of Rosans in the Hautes-Alpes; it was either Peter's birthplace or his parish. Peter's early years of preaching were spent in the mountainous regions of Embrun, Gap and Die. What surprises us is the geographical origins of this heresy: the Hautes-Alpes one would expect to be a backward area, a possible fount for heathen survivals, but not for a 'modern' heresy in the twelfth century. Of course, Peter could himself have incubated his own heresy. He is too shadowy a figure in our sources for us to be able to come to any useful conclusions on his personality and capacities. A clue, however, on a possible source is to be found in the geography of Bruis. It lies on one of the Alpine routes to Italy. Here would be a passage way to the mountain villages for novel heretical ideas, disseminated by travellers to and from that part of western Europe that was most open to external influences.[14]

Peter's theology was more interesting and idiosyncratic than Henry's, since only a part of his teaching resembled the common ideas of earlier and

[11] Fearns, 'Contra Petrobrusianos', p. xliv; trans. of Peter the Venerable's letter, in *WEH*, pp. 118–21; geographical references in text and introductory letter, ed. Fearns, *Corpus Christianorum*, pp. 3,10.

[12] See texts trans. *WEH*, pp. 122–6, *MBPH*, pp. 39–46. The *Vita prima* of St Bernard (*PL*, CLXXXV, col. 313) says Henry was captured and brought to the bishop in chains. This may have been in 1145; see *WEH*, p. 680.

[13] E. Griffe, *Les Débuts de l'Aventure cathare en Languedoc (1140–1190)* (Paris, 1969) (survey of early Midi Cathars with strong feeling for locality), pp. 21–48.

[14] Fearns, in *AKG*, XLVIII (1966), p. 329, n.92; on possible contact with Bogomil-infected regions, cf. p. 332 and n. 100.

contemporary twelfth-century sects. The teaching of the sect was radical and violent. Views were conveyed by vigorous practical demonstration, and it was in the course of one of these, while inciting the people at St Gilles to make a bonfire of their crucifixes, that Peter met his end, being pushed in himself and burnt by his opponents. At other times he and his followers would drag monks from their monasteries and force them to marry or, in a ceremony which foreshadows some actions of the radical group of Lollards at Norwich in the fifteenth century, would eat meat on Good Friday.[15]

Beneath their various tenets lay a belief in the Church as the spiritual unity of the congregation of the faithful.[16] The accretions of later ages are all stripped away to reveal the underlying true nature of the Church. The keynote, as among the Henricians they influenced, was a rejection of all external forms. The negative tenets of the sect, which naturally enough form the staple of Peter the Venerable's attack, are the repudiation of the authority of the Old Testament, of the Fathers and all the traditions of the Church, the rejection of infant baptism, of the doctrine of the eucharist and the sacrifice of the mass and of prayers for the dead. The use of church buildings was condemned, as was the veneration of the Cross and the practice of singing in church. But behind the denials lay some varied strands of thought, not all readily reconcilable with the common ferment of popular religious ideas of Peter's own time. The rejection of so many of the externals of worship springs from the desire for a de-materialization of worship. The formal objects of veneration—buildings, crosses, altars—are seen as positive incumbrances to true religion, and violently cast aside.

Behind the rejection of the eucharist, as celebrated in the contemporary Church, and the practice of infant baptism, lay the literal appeal to the Gospels. The eucharistic denial did not spring from the usual rejection of the unworthiness of the ministers of the sacrament, but from an extremely literal reading of Scripture. As they understood the Gospels, the transformation of the bread and wine into the Body and Blood took place once only at the Last Supper, and was a miracle never since performed by anyone else. Christ had no intention of instituting a rite to be repeated on the altars of the Church; not even a symbolic rendering of the act was open to consideration in their group. This is an exceptionally radical viewpoint, not easy to parallel: it will not fit with the dualism either of the Bogomils earlier, or of the Cathars later, for the Petrobrusians were not denying that Christ did offer his body and blood in the Upper Room. They were not forced by a rejection of matter, as among the Bogomils, to interpret Christ's actions on that occasion purely figuratively. The likelihood seems, as Fearns suggests, that on this issue Peter made a personal contribution to heresy.[17]

Four unusual Petrobrusian tenets may lead us to consider that the founder Peter had at some time been exposed to a Bogomil influence. They are the repudiation of the cult of the Cross, the rejection of the Old Testament, of church buildings, and of church music and singing. For these, parallels in the first half of the twelfth century are generally lacking, though they are not

[15]Below, p. 258
[16]Fearns, 'Contra Petrobrusianos', p. xlvii.
[17]Ibid., pp. lvii–lix.

absent at Arras in the eleventh century or from our sources for the Bogomils. Just as among the Petrobrusians supporters ripped down crucifixes and burnt them, so among the Bogomils the Cross was exposed to violent desecration, and its wood used for tools.[18] The rejection of the Old Testament is also a strong feature of Bogomilism. To find a rejection as clear and unequivocal as that of Peter of Bruis, one would have to turn to the dualists. Rejection of the Old Testament out of a consuming passion for the New does not seem to be quite enough. Again, on the question of church buildings, the twelfth century offers no parallels before the time of the Waldensians apart from Henry, whom we know to have been influenced by the Petrobrusians. The Waldensians later said that prayer could be offered to God from stables or private rooms; but for an earlier parallel one is led again to the Bogomils and Paulicians, whose denial that specially appointed places of worship were desirable was the outcome of their dualism.[19] Otherwise one would need to look back for precedents to the heretics of Arras, who believed that an altar and a church was no more than cement and stone, not better fitted for worship than rooms in a private house.[20] The fourth tenet, the rejection of church music and singing altogether, again binds together Arras heretics, Bogomils and Petrobrusians. A reaction against the multiplying of ritual observances and of elaboration in worship was common in monastic circles: the success of the Cistercians against Cluny is a witness to the force of this development, and such ideas infiltrated the laity. The Petrobrusian denial, as reported by Peter the Venerable, is however of an extreme and radical kind, rejecting not merely a superfluity of singing, but the whole practice of music in worship.

In sum, a dogmatic analysis reveals four points: the rejection of the Old Testament, the repudiation of the Cross, of church music and singing, and of church buildings, which are all to be found together in the tenets of the Petrobrusians, the Arras heretics and the Bogomils. The conjunction of four doctrines seems a little too much to be explained by incubation or dissemination from other Western sects, and gives weight to the hypothesis of external Bogomil influence, argued by Fearns.[21] One may postulate a theory of lingering remnants of the views of heretics of the Arras type, lasting unnoticed in the mountains; or alternatively the impact of travellers coming afresh from Bogomil areas and scattering the seed of their heresy over an Alpine route.[22] The Arras heresy, it will be remembered, was carried from Italy. Yet, if we argue for a Bogomil influence, we must accept that it was only an imperfect reflection of its original, quite lacking the dualist metaphysic and the Gnostic creation narratives. Peter, a hearer already predisposed to heresy, adopted what he needed for his own system. The negatives of Bogomilism fitted better to the Western situation. 'He chose and adapted what accorded with his aims, and the alien theology and ritual, which ran counter to those aims, he ignored'.[23] He was not a dualist, but he did act as a kind of John the

---

[18]Fearns, in *AKG*, XLVIII, pp. 324–5.

[19]Above, pp. 14–15

[20]Above, p. 27; Fearns, in *AKG*, XLVIII, p. 327.

[21]Fearns, 'Contra Petrobrusianos', pp. lx–lxix.

[22]Note the comment on possible effects of casual transmission (ibid., p. lxxvii).

[23]Ibid., p. lxxvi.

Baptist to the organized dualist churches of the second half of the century, preparing a way for them among the people.

In one other outbreak, two peasants, Clement and Ebrard, from the village of Bucy-le-Long near Soissons, about 1114 preached a heresy which also resembles Bogomilism.[24] Christ did not in reality take on flesh; the bread and wine were not really transformed into the Body and Blood; the mouth of the priest is the opening of hell. They spoke of themselves as followers of the apostolic life, and lived in a rigid asceticism. The mention of the *vita apostolica* and the denunciation of the unworthy priesthood place them in the Western stream of heresy; but the Docetism is not common in spontaneous Western heresy, and would assimilate them to the Bogomils. Especially significant is the nature of their renunciations. They refused everything that had been procreated as a result of sexual intercourse. The peasants revered them as men of God, but they ended their lives burnt by a mob.

In another rural setting at the village of Ivoy in the first quarter of the century, a group of heretics met secretly and taught their followers to reject the eucharist and the baptism of infants.[25] The case may be taken as typical of the episodes in which the sources are inadequate to reveal fully the nature of the heresy. We catch only a gleam of the popular concern for the individual's religious responsibility—the usual motive for the rejection of infant baptism.

Tanchelm and Arnold of Brescia

Tanchelm of Antwerp and Arnold of Brescia, well separated in time—one in the Netherlands, the other in Italy—show how the ferment of reform ideals in the post-Gregorian age could lead to heresy. The case of Tanchelm is controversial. Norman Cohn has used him to show how the psychological pressure of social conditions gave rise to a following for certain kinds of heresy in the Middle Ages.[26] A rabble-rouser of a fantastic and unbalanced imagination, he argues, Tanchelm was able to gain adherents in one of the overcrowded towns of the Netherlands, where sudden industrialization had carried men away from the bonds of family and custom in peasant life on the manor, and exposed them to the well-known troubles of an economy dependent through the wool trade and the international market on the vagaries of boom and slump.

But one is bound to ask whether the sources bear out the millenarian heresy, which, Cohn has said, prevailed above all in these new industrial areas.[27] Tanchelm has been taken as a type-figure for these developments,[28] but it is questionable whether he can bear the weight of theory which has been erected over his head. According to the traditional account, Tanchelm owed his rise to the glaring neglect of the Church authorities for the developing town of Antwerp. Disgusted by the state of the Church, Tanchelm began his preaching, soon held a dominance over the religious life of the town, carried

---

[24]Borst, *Katharer*, p. 84; another interpretation in Russell, *Dissent*, pp. 78–81 (note the comment on bishop Joscelin's creed); source in *WEH* pp. 102–4. I assume the story of the orgy is not authentic.

[25]Russell, *Dissent*, pp. 54–6; source in *WEH*, pp. 105–7.

[26]Cohn, *Millennium*, pp. 35–8.

[27]Background of hypothesis given, ibid., pp. 21–32; see above, p. 48.

[28]Grundmann, in *HZ*, cxcvi (1963), 661–6.

his preaching tours into Flanders, Zeeland and Brabant. His hearers came from the lower classes, but the success of his sermons in Zeeland must prove that they were far from exclusively drawn from townsmen, for this remained economically a relatively undeveloped land of fishermen and farmers. Tanchelm totally rejected the Church and its sacraments, and said the Church had become a brothel. The best-known source, a letter of the cathedral chapter at Utrecht, describes some fantastic scenes as Tanchelm declared himself God, entered into a symbolic marriage with a statue of Mary, and, accompanied by a former priest and a smith, made his way through Antwerp dressed in golden robes and with an armed guard.[29] The common people revered him as God, and drank his bathwater. But the interlude of fantasy came to an end after only three years, in 1115, when he was struck down by a priest.

Individualistic as his cult was, followers remained for a while after his death. Tanchelm benefitted, it has been argued, from both the internal pressures of town life, which made the oppressed artisans eager to accept a deliverer who should rescue them from earthly sufferings and usher in an age of plenty, and also from trends to millenarian thinking set in motion by the impact of the crusades.[30]

Not all the features of the cult in Antwerp need excite suspicion. The odd episode of the bathwater has been variously interpreted, as a sign of the overwhelming reverence of credulous followers, or as a misunderstanding by the writer, who had not understood Tanchelm's distribution to his followers of a watered wine;[31] connoisseurs of the twilight region of popular cults may recall in favour of the first hypothesis that Garibaldi's servant found a good sale, all unknown to his master, for his bathwater. Yet other features in the usual description are not quite convincing. Why, if Tanchelm's original platform was the wickedness of the orthodox Church and the immorality of its priesthood, was he also a libertine, who used his sway over women to satisfy his sexual needs?[32] Libertinism is almost on automatic accusation for a popular heretic who influences his women hearers. The principal source emanates from the enemies of Tanchelm in the chapter of Utrecht who sought to denounce him in 1112 to Frederick, archbishop of Cologne, and might be expected to press any possible hostile rumour on Tanchelm into service. Not everything in the case meets the eye. Behind the accusations of heresy could well lie an episode in the Gregorian—anti-Gregorian contest, much as accusations of heresy without much cause had been bandied about in the affairs of the Pataria in Milan and Ramihrdus in Cambrai, and were again to be in the case of Lambert le Bègue in Liège.[33] Such an interpretation is made more plausible by the evidence of direct borrowing of detail in the letter from Utrecht from the sixth-century chronicler Gregory of Tours.[34]

[29]Trans. in *WEH*, pp. 96–100; *MBPH*, pp. 28–31.

[30]Cohn's general hypothesis.

[31]Borst, *Katharer*, p. 85, n. 13.

[32]Ibid., Russell, *Dissent*, p. 65 (the best account of sources and dating, pp. 265–9, 282–3).

[33]Ibid., pp. 90–6; on Lambert, see *MBPH*, pp. 101–11.

[34]W. Mohr, 'Tanchelm von Antwerpen, eine nochmalige Überprüfung der Quellenlage,' *Annales Universitatis Saraviensis* III (1954), pp. 234–47; rejected by Werner (*Pauperes Christi*, pp. 205–7).

Pirenne brought some light when he inferred that Tanchelm was an agent of Count Robert II of Flanders, a supporter of the Gregorians, who wanted to use his party support in order to gain for the Flemish bishopric of Tournai a part of the bishopric of Utrecht, then in the hands of the imperialist party.[35] Tanchelm, on this view, played the part of the demagogue, stirring the populace against a lax imperialist clergy, and making manifest the need for a Gregorian reform in this area, which in turn might facilitate the diocesan rearrangements which the count desired. Pirenne made the connection too close: he was mistaken in thinking that Tanchelm was a layman, and a one-time notary of the Count.

It now appears that Tanchelm is to be numbered among the heretical leaders who sprang from the clergy. But was he already a Gregorian when he appealed to the Count for aid? Much rests on timing.[36] The letter of Utrecht can be read not as a hostile and discrediting account of a popular preacher with Gnostic undertones, but as a collection of slanders which wilfully distort Tanchelm's reforming activities. The letter might enable us to conclude that Tanchelm was first active in Zeeland,[37] not in the fevered area of Antwerp's artisan dwellings, and that he was active there in the first instance because this was the area which it was intended should be taken from the bishopric of Utrecht. The letter says that Tanchelm rejected the Church; for that one might understand the local Church, tainted by immorality and its imperialist connections. The rejection of Transubstantiation one might read as a rejection of the ministrations of unworthy priests, and the alleged union with God supposed to give Tanchelm divine powers one might read as an orthodox exhortation to mystical union with Christ. The betrothal with Mary, using rings, might be a version of a campaign to persuade women to give up luxuries and bestow their rings on a statue of Mary. An interpretation on these lines, as suggested by W. Mohr, would then give us in place of the unbalanced millenarian agitator a Gregorian reformer. Difficulties remain, even if this revision is accepted; there is still a hostile tradition, not necessarily dependent on the Utrecht letter, in other sources. The truth will never be quite clear, but we are on secure ground if we assume that there was much less heresy and excess than the sources suggest, and that we are probably right if we think of Tanchelm as a Gregorian who, especially at the end, slipped into Donatism.[38]

In the case of Arnold of Brescia the sources are not obscure, although they lack the confirmation of the direct words or writing of the heresiarch himself. Arnold first showed his hand when ruling a community of canons regular in his native city of Brescia, once influenced by the Pataria agitation, and in the 1130s the scene of a struggle for the bishopric between Villano and Manfred, supporters of the rival claims to the papal tiara of Anacletus II and Innocent

---

[35]H. Pirenne, 'Tanchelin et le Projèt de Démembrement du Diocèse d'Utrecht vers 1100,' *ARBB* 5th ser., XIII (1927), pp. 112–9.

[36]I follow Russell (*Dissent*, p. 282).

[37]Not first aroused by clerical deficiency (as Borst, *Katharer*, p. 84); correction by Russell (p. 283).

[38]Russell (p.64) goes farther in attributing heresy than I, partly on the analogy of the eccentric backwoods prophet Aldebert in the eighth century. I am more impressed by the possibilities of slander, and think excess more likely in a man of Aldebert's than Tanchelm's background.

II.[39] In the absence of Manfred, the successful candidate, from his city, Arnold allied himself with the supporters of a commune, and used the opportunity to set about a drastic reform of the clergy. Manfred incurred Arnold's hostility, not because he was some idle nobleman in episcopal orders, but simply because his moderate reforming plans, which had already come up against the hostility of the local clergy, did not go far enough. For Arnold the pattern of apostolic life was realized in the lives of strict canons regular, and the solution to the problems of wealthy, simoniacal and unchaste clergy was to impose on them *tout court* what was in effect the life of canons regular.

Arnold's movement, though it loosely resembled the Pataria and the agitation of Ramihrdus of Cambrai, went beyond their ideas in some respects. Nor did Innocent II give Arnold the support Gregory VII had once given to the Pataria. Condemned in 1139, Arnold was forced to leave Italy and make for Paris, where he had formerly studied under Peter Abelard. There his attacks on the clergy and, surprisingly, on St Bernard of Clairvaux earned him a condemnation at the Council of Sens in 1140, somewhat rhetorically associated as pupil with the ruin of his master Abelard. In flight, he was befriended by Guy, papal legate to Bohemia, who persuaded him to submit and accept penance. Misguidedly, Pope Eugenius III invited him to Rome to keep him under his eye, only to discover that the spectacle of abuses of the curia and the involvement of the papacy in temporal affairs caused a revival of his agitation in a fiercer form. 'The pope himself', he came to believe, 'was not what he professed to be—an apostolic man and shepherd of souls—but a man of blood who maintained his authority by fire and sword . . .'[40] The grievances of Rome's citizens offered him a better platform than the communal movement at Brescia, and with their aid he expelled the pope and declared the independence of the city, where he attempted to realize his ideal of the poor clergy—preaching, administering the sacraments, wholly unencumbered by possessions or political power. For a time his views, especially his rejection of the Donation of Constantine and his belief that the emperor should receive his crown from the citizens of Rome rather than the pope, recommended him to the imperial party. The pope, though he returned with the aid of military force, was again expelled in 1150. But Arnold's reform plans of that year revealed what a radical he was, and he could only retain his place through a conspiracy of faithful followers of the inferior class and without further aid from the nobles. The logic of his own radical religious positions led him into an extreme democratic position in politics. It was as a revolutionary holding on to power with limited numerical support that he was finally hunted down under Pope Hadrian IV and executed in 1155.

His eloquence and appeal to the crowds assimilate him to the inspired wandering preachers of France, and he is fully in accord with the ideas of the time in his stress on the overwhelming value of poverty. But he differed from

[39]A. Frugoni, *Arnaldo da Brescia nelle fonti del secolo XII* (Rome, 1954) (stresses influence of gospel on Arnold in Morghen tradition); review by Ilarino da Milano (*RSCI*, IX (1955), pp 417–33); comment by Dupré Theseider (*Introduzione*, pp. 134–7); Violante (*HS*, p. 177) discusses relative absence of heresy in Italy before Arnold.

[40]John of Salisbury, *Historia Pontificalis*, tr. M. Chibnall (London, 1956) (under 1149); and *WEH*, p. 148. See also texts trans. in *MBPH* pp. 66–71.

the wandering preachers in his readiness to use political force to gain his ends, and in the fact that he offered a programme, not merely for the salvation of the individual, but also for the Church at large—a programme he was prepared to enforce with the sword. Its fundamental tenet was that clergy and monks who had possessions could not be saved. There were other, sacramental errors in his beliefs, which linked with the central position on poverty. The sacraments were not denied in themselves, but there was a sweeping application of the common post-Gregorian position, that the sacraments had become invalid through the unworthiness of ministers. As one might expect from the pragmatic nature of Arnold, there was no deep dogmatic difference with orthodoxy, and in fact he was never formally arraigned for heresy.[41] The spiritual power of Rome was denied because of its involvement with the things of this world. Preaching was open to all, and depended, not on a particular training or authorization, but simply on the life of the preacher.

In practice nearly all shrank from the drastic renunciations which Arnold demanded of the hierarchy. He was too radical to be at ease with reformers within the Church. The sympathy of Guy, the cardinal legate in Bohemia, and his earlier readiness to repent showed that initially he was not far from the Church. But the emotional experience of contact with the darker side of Rome and his own temperament carried him beyond reconciliation.

The Arnoldists as an organized force never again played a significant part in Italy, for their power was broken by the events which followed the re-establishment of the commune in 1150. Arnold, however, was one of those dissident leaders whose power is derived, not from any great originality of thought, but from their ability to focus widespread discontents, and these long outlived his movement. The tenets of Arnoldists were thought worthy of refutation by Bonacursus of Milan in his polemical work, the *Manifestatio haeresis Catharorum*, written between 1176 and 1190, which included a section attacking the belief that evangelical poverty was obligatory, that laymen who practised it had full rights of preaching, and that their sins incapacitated priests and hierarchy from administering the sacraments and holding the power of binding and loosing.[42] Though at that date Arnoldism may well have represented a current of thought rather than a sect, the name passed into the catalogue of heresies to be periodically denounced by Popes, continuing to exist in bulls, though surely not in reality, down to 1511.[43]

Eon (or Eudo) de l'Étoile

The case of Eon carries us back to the wild rural agitators, Aldebert, Theuda and Leutard.[44] Though lettered and probably a younger son of the Breton nobility, Eon's following consisted exclusively of credulous peasants. The sources say that he gathered his followers to pray in secluded places, that he

---

[41]Grundmann, *Ketzergeschichte*, p. 20.

[42]Ilarino da Milano, 'La "Manifestatio heresis catarorum",' *Aevum*, XII (1938), pp. 281–333 (see third section of treatise); Arnoldists discussed in his *L'Eresia di Ugo Speroni nella confutazione del Maestro Vacario* (Vaticano, 1945), pp. 444–52. Note warning by W. L. Wakefield, (*WEH*, p. 146) that the links between Arnold and the Arnoldists are not wholly assured.

[43]D. Kurze, 'Die festländischen Lollarden', *AKG*, XLVII (1965), p. 68, n. 1. (article important for terminology and study of popular religion).

[44]Russell, pp. 118–24; note discussion of his name, pp. 120–1, 289.

was opposed to church buildings, and with his followers attacked them and stripped them of ornaments. He believed himself the Son of God, and persuaded his followers into believing that he was 'eum' of the Latin phrase probably known to him from the formula of an exorcism: Jesus Christ who would return in glory—'per eum qui venturus est cum gloria judicare vivos et mortuos et seculum per ignem'.[45] His disciples he called by the names of angels, prophets and apostles. His staff was, as it were, a sceptre shaped in the form of a Y—as long as the Y pointed upwards, two-thirds of the world belonged to God the Father, one to Eon; if he inverted the fork, the position would be reversed. The council of Rheims in 1148 heard these revelations with laughter, and banished Eon to prison, where he soon died.

Some commentators have, reasonably, thought that he was mad; others have noted apparently Gnostic elements.[46] Werner notes the deep superstitions of Brittany, which had established so strong a hold that in the seventeenth century part needed in effect to be freshly converted by the Jesuits.[47] Russell depicts him as sincere but deranged. Mad, or only 'mad north north west', with an eye to church plunder and escaping the death sentence at Rheims, one certain feature of the case is the pitiable condition of the followers of Eon. Their heresy was manifestly based on a profound ignorance.

The Early Cathars.

Heresy in the first three decades of the century tended to depend heavily on the personality of one preacher; his influence removed, the following he collected falls back into obscurity, or disappears completely. In Eon's time (the 1140s), the first signs appear that this phase in the history of Western dissent is coming to an end as writers and chroniclers describe the stirrings of a fully international movement, named differently in different countries, but having distinctive elements of belief and organization in common.[48] These betray a connection with the Bogomils of Byzantium and the Balkans.

The anonymity of the new heresy alarmed some orthodox observers. St Bernard, on hearing of it, exclaimed at the contrast between it and the heresies of the early Church, named after their founders, Mani and the Manichees, Sabellius and the Sabellians, Arius and the Arians.[49] Events bore out his fears, as over the following two decades this Bogomil-influenced heresy spread widely in the West.

The first outbreak to be recorded took place in the Rhineland, where in 1143–4 the Premonstratensian provost Everwin of Steinfeld described to St Bernard of Clairvaux the traits of a heresy detected at Cologne which had its own bishop and organization.[50] There were three ranks of adherents—

[45]Borst, *Katharer*, p. 87n. Or derivation from 'per eundem dominum nostrum Jesum Christum' (Russell, p. 120). Sources trans. in *WEH*, pp. 141–6, *MPBH* pp. 62–6.

[46]Refs, *WEH*, pp. 685–6, Russell, p. 120 and n. I agree with Russell in thinking there is little in this.

[47]*Pauperes Christi*, p. 180.

[48]Borst, *Katharer*, pp. 89–96.

[49]*Sermo* 66, (*PL*, CLXXXIII, col. 1094); *RB*, p. 50n.

[50]*PL*, CLXXXII, cols 676–80; trans. in *WEH*, pp. 127–32; on this correspondence, see Manselli, *Studi*, pp. 89–109; *MBPH*, pp. 74–8.

auditors, believers and elect, entry from the lowest category to that of believers, and from believers to elect being gained by a ceremony of laying-on of hands and a process of testing. The baptism thus obtained through the laying-on of hands 'in fire and the Spirit' was contrasted with the baptism by water of John the Baptist. The group refused to drink milk or consume anything produced as a result of coition, and rejected marriage. At daily meals, Everwin reported, they 'consecrated' their food and drink with the *Pater Noster*. They claimed their belief went back to the time of the martyrs, and that they had fellow adherents in 'Greece' (i.e. Byzantium) and 'certain other lands'. The bishop, his assistant and some others stood their ground in debate, and when they refused to recant were burnt by the people.

The distinctions among adherents, the existence of a category of adepts, the elect, the double initiation ceremony with the laying-on of hands, like the *baptisma* and the *teleiosis* known in Byzantium to Euthymius Zigabenus,[51] the contrast between this and the baptism in water of John, the rejection of milk, the products of coition and the repudiation of marriage, and finally the belief in the existence of co-religionists in Byzantium—all are good evidence of a Bogomil infiltration more substantial than any yet seen. What is missing in Everwin's account is any mention of Docetism or of a dualist cosmogony, perhaps because Everwin had not adequately penetrated the sect's beliefs, perhaps because dualism was not of great importance to these heretics.

Everwin's description illuminates the reasons why Bogomil influences should have established themselves in the West at this time. The Cologne heretics claimed, he said, that 'theirs alone is the Church, inasmuch as only they follow in the footsteps of Christ. They continue to be the true imitators of the apostolic life, seeking not those things which are of the world, possessing no house, or lands, even as Christ had no property . . . "You, however," they say to us, "add house to house, field to field, and seek the things that are of this world. You do this to the point that they who are considered the most perfect among you, such as monks and canons regular, although owning nothing of their own and holding everything in common, nevertheless possess all these things." Of themselves they say, "We, the poor of Christ, who have no fixed abode and flee from city to city like sheep amidst wolves, are persecuted as were the apostles and the martyrs . . ."'[52]

Apostolic life had been the turning point.[53] Where authority claimed apostolicity for the Church because of the succession of its bishops from the Apostles and the tradition of its doctrine from the early Church, the heretics bypassed that claim by their plea for realization of the apostolic life. It is conceived by the heretics, and plainly also by their hearers, as the wandering insecure life of the disciples on the pattern of the sending of the Seventy. Orthodox Gregorian preachers, of whom the hermits of western France are the best-known examples, helped to create a demand for this pattern of apostolic life. Through conservatism this demand was never met by orthodoxy in this period. The heretics were the beneficiaries.

Not all of the Cologne heretics accepted the Bogomil influence, however.

[51]Above, p. 20
[52]*WEH*, p. 129.
[53]*RB*, pp. 18–27.

Another group described by Everwin had beliefs of a 'western' type, rigorist in morality, pleading for a simple spiritual Church free of the tainted Catholic clergy and putting weight on the response of the individual conscience. They denied the validity of Catholic masses, Everwin said, 'because no priests of the Church are validly ordained. For, they say, the apostolic office has been corrupted through involvement in secular business . . . he who sits in the chair of Peter has lost the power to ordain which was bestowed upon Peter. And because the apostolic see does not have this power, the archbishops and bishops, who lead worldly lives within the Church, cannot receive from that see the power to ordain anyone.' They accepted the baptism of adults, 'baptized by Christ, no matter who may actually administer the sacrament', but rejected infant baptism as not in accord with Scripture. Texts again buttressed their idiosyncratic doctrine that only marriage between virgins was lawful, and also their rejection of purgatory. Penance they found unnecessary, 'because, on whatever day the sinner shall have lamented his sins, all are forgiven.'[54] Only observances established by Christ or the Apostles were acceptable.

Alike in their ethical concern and their attacks on the clergy, the groups thus diverged markedly in their more positive beliefs. Dissension between them led to their discovery.

In 1145 St Bernard of Clairvaux, engaged on his few days' preaching against the followers of Henry the Monk in Toulouse, may have brushed another heresy, described in an imprecise phrase apparently as that of 'weavers and Arians.'[55] At Liège a group was discovered with its own hierarchy and with a division among its adherents between initiates, called 'believers', and 'auditors', who were neophytes in the heresy. They rejected wholesale the sacraments, including marriage.[56]

A profession of faith and formula for abjuration amongst the manuscripts of the abbey of Moissac in the south of France dating from mid-century implies the existence of a heresy rejecting baptism, the eucharist, marriage and meat eating, which included among its beliefs the view that remission of sins could only be obtained through the imposition of hands, or the 'martyrdom' of their sect.[57]

In Périgord about 1160 a monk described heretics who followed the apostolic life, eating no meat, drinking no wine beyond a measure every third day, refusing to handle money, and making a hundred genuflections daily—but, significantly, refusing to adore the Cross. They had adherents among the clergy, as well as monks and nuns, who chanted the mass 'as a tactic of

[54]*WEH*, pp. 130–1.

[55]*PL*, clxxxv, col. 411; Manselli, 'Una designazione dell'eresia Catara "Arriana Haeresis"', *BISIAM*, lxviii (1956), pp. 233–46; Griffe, *Débuts*, pp. 33–7. R. I. Moore ('St Bernard's Mission to the Languedoc in 1145', *BIHR*, xlvii (1974), pp. 1–10) argues that Bernard did not meet the type of heresy of the first Cologne group there, as is sometimes alleged.

[56]*WEH*, pp. 139–41; *MBPH*, pp. 78–9. I have preferred H. Silvestre, in *RHE*, lviii (1963), pp. 979–80; P. Bonenfant, in *LMA*, lxix (1963), pp. 278–9 on dating to J. B. Russell ('Les Cathares de 1048–54 à Liège', *BSAHDL*, xlii (1961), pp. 1–8) who places the source, a letter from the faithful of Liège to the pope 'L', in the pontificate of Leo IX (1048–54). See gazetteer, Appendix D, s. 1, under Liège.

[57]Manselli, in *BISIAM*, lxvii (1955), pp. 212–34; summary, id., *Eresia*, pp. 165–8.

deception', and then threw the host down beside the altar or thrust it into the missal, for they believed that it remained nothing but a morsel of bread. Their use of a doxology customary in the Byzantine Church and not in the West reveals the origin of a portion at least of their beliefs.[58]

In the Rhineland a trial at Cologne in 1163 showed that the burnings two decades earlier had been ineffective; a Western-type heresy still existed there, but it had, according to the description of the prime source, Ekbert, later Benedictine abbot of Schönau, blended with the Bogomil-influenced group.[59] Amongst their errors, some held the belief that only marriage between virgins was legitimate—a sign that the 'Western' heresy still had its influence. But dissension between the groups seemed to have disappeared, and the 'Westerners' now existed as an outer circle, taught dissenting evangelical beliefs, while an inner circle of adepts had a secret doctrine which included belief in a Docetic Christology, transmigration of souls, and the creation of the world by an evil god. Initiation to the circle of adepts was obtained in a secret ceremony by the laying-on of hands. Ekbert believed that the heresy had an international character. In Flanders, whence the heretics had come, he said, they were called 'Piphles', in France 'Texerant' because of their weaving, and in Germany 'the Cathars', a Greek term meaning the 'pure ones,.[60] The latter has been taken most widely by modern writers as a term for the new heresy of the twelfth century, formed by the coalescence of Western evangelical heresy and Bogomil influences from the East.

Ekbert's sermons in one way represented a step forward in the progress of the Church's polemic against heresy, for they attempted to expound in full the dogmatic basis on which the Cologne heresy rested. Yet, progressive as this attitude was by contrast with that of the mass of writers hitherto, content with fleeting and superficial notices of denials of orthodoxy, Ekbert's work was largely vitiated by his fatal penchant for transferring bodily the doctrines of the Manichees of the fourth century, attacked by Augustine, to the account of the Cologne sectaries.[61] His description of the teachings of the adepts, with their thoroughgoing dualism, must be treated with scepticism: it is possible to infer merely that the first group at Cologne described in the 1140s by Everwin had survived, that it had dualist beliefs and, further, that rationalist propaganda was being used to attract followers. Although the true basis for the rejection of the mass lay in their rejection of bread and wine as part of an evil creation, the heretics used a primitive logic. Christ's body, they said, must have been as big as a mountain to feed the faithful for so long.[62]

Two years after the Cologne outbreak, a conference held at Lombers, a

---

[58]*PL*, CLXXXI, Cols 1721–2; trans. in *WEH*, pp. 138–9, *MBPH*, pp. 79–80 (Moore's dating is convincing). See Borst, *Katharer*, p. 92n. The doxology (Wakefield's trans.) runs, 'For Thine is the kingdom and Thou shalt rule over all creation, for ever and ever. Amen.'

[59]*Adversus Catharos PL*, CXCV, cols 11–102; extract trans. in *MBPH*, pp. 88–94; reconstruction of events in Russell, pp. 220–4.

[60]'Hos nostra Germania Catharos, Flandria Piphles, Gallia Texerant ab usu texendi appellat' (*PL*, CXCIII, col. 193); terminology for heretics generally in *RB*, pp. 29–38. But I think Grundmann underestimates the significance of references here and elsewhere to weaving; see below, p. 115. The term 'Cathar' should strictly only be applied to the leading class in the heresy; I have used the term as a generic one for the sect because it is so well established.

[61]Borst, *Katharer*, pp. 6–7; Manselli, *Eresia*, pp. 163–4.

[62]Noticed by Manselli (ibid., p. 164).

castle near Albi, in the south of France, revealed the relative freedom of Cathar heretics on a favourable terrain.[63] Local heretical leaders, known as 'the good men', debated with their opponents before a distinguished gathering which included, as well as William, the diocesan, the archbishop of Narbonne, other bishops, the viscount of Béziers, in whose lands Lombers lay, and Constance, countess of Toulouse and sister of the king of France.

The representatives of orthodoxy had to restrict their exposition so as to cite proof-texts only from the New Testament, since the heretics did not recognize the Old. The 'good men' stressed the evils of the way of living of churchmen, and their own superiority in this sphere. 'They said also' the record of the assembly runs, 'that Paul stated in his Epistle what kind of bishops and priests were to be ordained in the churches, and that, if the men ordained were not such as Paul had specified, they were not bishops and priests, but ravening wolves, hypocrites and seducers, lovers of salutations in the market place . . . desirous of being called rabbis and masters contrary to the command of Christ, wearers of albs and gleaming raiment, displaying bejewelled gold rings on their fingers, which their Master Jesus did not command . . .'[64] The ecclesiastics tried to draw their opponents on to the fields of dogma, in order to expose their deviations from othodoxy. But the heretics were not to be drawn. They are reported as saying that they did not want to be forced to reply about their faith. Eventually, as the bishops seemed to be getting the better of it, the 'good men' appealed to the people, and made a declaration which sounded quite Catholic. But they refused to swear to it since, following texts in James and the Gospels, they held that all oaths were unlawful. In any case they had said enough to be convicted of heresy, though the bishops never penetrated to the core of their beliefs.

The debate, it is plausibly argued, was intended to be a kind of legal pleading in the presence of eminent laity, in which the fact that the 'good men' were preaching heresy should be made manifest, and the secular authority consequently moved to action.[65] At Cologne there had been formal trial, which led instantly to punishment; at Lombers adjudication against the beliefs of the 'good men' had no effect at all.

A similar demonstration of the strength and independence of Catharism in the Midi took place some two years after Lombers in the international council of dualists held at the village of Saint Félix in the Lauragais, at which the territory most affected by Catharism was divided up into bishoprics, delimited territorially on the Catholic pattern.[66] In Lombardy a Cathar mission established itself in the fifth, or early in the sixth, decade of the century. A narrative, probably based on oral tradition, recounted a century later by the inquisitor Anselm of Alessandria, described how a party of heretics from northern France made their way into northern Italy, and converted a gravedigger called Mark from the Milan area who became the apostle of Cathar Italy, and with his friends John Judeus, a weaver, and

[63]Bouquet, XIV, pp. 431–4; trans. *WEH*, pp. 190–4; *MBPH*, pp. 94–8; the best analysis is by Griffe (*Debuts*, pp. 59–67).
[64]Trans. in *WEH*, p. 191.
[65]Griffe, *Débuts*, pp. 60–1.
[66]See below, p. 128.

Joseph, a smith, established a base for mission at Concorezzo near his birthplace.[67] Fragments of later information on the spread of Byzantine heresy through the French conquerors of Constantinople in 1204,[68] and on the flight of Cathars from the Midi before the inquisition to the area of Cuneo in the thirteenth century, jostle each other in this semi-legendary account.[69] But we may retain from it the fact, elsewhere attested, that Catharism reached Lombardy and established its hold before 1167 and, less certainly but with high probability, the surprising conclusion that stimulus to it was given by missionaries from northern France. Under Mark's leadership the heresy spread in Lombardy and thence into the March of Treviso and Tuscany.

In addition to these established examples, other outbreaks imperfectly recorded, such as the case of the clerk Jonas in Cambrai,[70] an episode in Vézelay in 1167,[71] or that of the party of strangers from either the Rhineland or Flanders who landed in England, only to be branded at the council of Oxford in 1166 and turned adrift to starve,[72] have the smell of Catharism, and may well have formed part of the same movement.[73] There is evidence, but no details, of a strong Cathar following being established early on in northern France.[74]

The greatest strength of the movement lay in its ethical appeal to populations who had been sufficiently affected by the religious sentiment of the age to value poverty and self-sacrifice, yet lacked orthodox instruction. The key figures were a number of highly dedicated missionaries whose fiercely ascetic way of life had an immediate impact, and whose courage before the fire impressed the Catholic chroniclers. Their distinctive rites, their total opposition to the Church, which was yet coupled with considerable skill in the arts of evasion, gave a new stiffening to pre-existing movements of dissent, some of whose tenets they shared. Writers on the Catholic side still lacked the skill fully to penetrate the inner beliefs of the movement; probably ethics remained for some time more important than dogma, even to the adepts.

[67]A. Dondaine, 'La Hiérarchie cathare en Italie', *AFP*, xix (1949), pp. 282–312; xx (1950), pp. 234–324 (ms. discoveries with analysis, lists of heretical bishops, important for internal history of Italian Cathars). Discussion of Anselm in *AFP*, xx (1950), pp. 259–62; this portion of Anselm's text is in *TDH*, pp. 308–9; trans. in *WEH*, pp. 168–70. See below, p. 127.

[68]This seems to me the plain meaning of 'postea francigene iverunt Constantinopolim ut subiugarent terram et invenerunt istam secta, et multiplicati fecerunt episcopum, qui dicitur episcopus latinorum' (*sic*) (*AFP*, xx (1950), p. 308). I reject Dondaine's supposition that this could mean the second crusade (art. cit., p. 240).

[69]E. Dupré Theseider, 'Le Catharisme languedocien et l'Italie', *CF*, iii, pp. 299–316; at p. 300.

[70]Russell, pp. 217–8.

[71]H. Maisonneuve, *Études sur les Origines de l'Inquisition* (Paris, 1960), pp. 115–16 (account of legislative aspect of inquisition, with survey of heresy).

[72]Russell, *Dissent*, pp. 224–6; for dating and sources, see ibid., pp. 309–10; trans. in *WEH*, pp. 245–7. See A. Morey and C. N. L. Brooke, *Gilbert Foliot and his Letters* (Cambridge, 1965), pp. 241–3.

[73]. I suspect that the sect described by Gerhoh of Reichersberg in his work on Antichrist of 1161–2 is solely of literary provenance. For text, see K. Heisig, 'Eine gnostische Sekte im abendländischen Mittelalter', *ZRG*, xvi (1964), pp. 271–4.

[74]Evidence of Anselm of Alessandria (*AFP*, xx (1950), p. 308), on foundation of a bishopric of Northern France; for hypothesis of siting in diocese of Châlons-sur-Marne at Montwimers, alias Mont-Aimé, see Borst, *Katharer*, pp. 91, 93 and cf. pp. 123n., 231. The issue is complicated by the uncertain dating of the Liège letter mentioning Montwimers. Borst opts for 1144–5, as I have done (above, p. 62).

In roughly two decades from the undoubted appearance of Bogomil influence at Cologne, the new heresy was disseminated from the Rhine to the Pyrenees, and into the Italian peninsula.[75] The beliefs and practices which had secured converts among the Bulgarians fresh from paganism, and equally among Christians of generations' standing in the villages of Asia Minor and in the monasteries and sophisticated aristocratic circles of Constantinople, now showed their powers among clergy and people in western Europe in an after-phase of the Gregorian reforms.

[75]Borst, *Katharer*, p. 92.

6

The Waldensians and the Deepening Crisis

In the last thirty years of the twelfth century Catharism was the heresy which preoccupied authority. It was not put down: in northern and central Italy and in Languedoc it actually succeeded in increasing its hold. At the same time, the other currents of heresy maintained themselves and, within the evangelical tradition, two new groups emerged: the Humiliati and the Waldensians, simple gospel-based movements whose members desired the right to exhort their fellow Christians. Both fell foul of authority on the issue of the right to preach; both, though at the outset apparently untainted by heresy, passed after their experience of rejection from disobedience into unorthodoxy. The papacy under Lucius III made a more strenuous and broader-based attempt to grapple with the problem of efficient repression of heresy, but could not find a solution;[1] at the end of the century there was more heresy than ever before. The zeal of the Humiliati and Waldensians had been lost to the Church, and in the two most dangerous regions in Italy and Languedoc heretical teachers were able to spread their ideas almost in freedom.

The Waldensians and the Humiliati

The Waldensians, the last and the most tenacious of the twelfth century wandering-preacher movements, are the classic example of the would-be reform movement drawn into heresy by the inadequacies of ecclesiastical authority. Valdes, the founder,[2] was a rich businessman of Lyons who was touched by a jongleur's version of the life of St. Alexius, the penitent son of a rich man who rejected a bride and went away to live in poverty, returning after many years to die unrecognized, destitute in his father's house. The sequel was that Valdes, after consulting a master of theology, decided to give

[1] See the discussion of *Ad abolendam* below, p. 72. Up-to-date survey on papal policy in B. Bolton, 'Tradition and Temerity: Papal Attitudes to Deviants, 1159–1216', in *SCH*, IX, pp. 79–91; see *RB*, pp. 50–69.

[2] K. V. Selge, *Die ersten Waldenser*. I, *Untersuchung und Darstellung;* II, *Der Liber antiheresis des Durandus von Osca* (Berlin, 1967) (summary on Valdes and early history, ch. 3; see my analysis below, Appendix C; review by H. Grundmann, *DA*, XXIV (1968), pp 572–3; French version in Selge's 'Caractéristiques du premier Mouvement vaudois et Crises au cours de son Expansion', in *CF*, II, pp. 110–42; sources given in *EFV* (standard collection of Waldensian sources), and analysis by G. Gonnet in his 'La Figure et l'Oeuvre de Vaudès dans la Tradition historique et selon les dernières Recherches', in *CF*, II, 87–109; H. Böhmer, 'Die Waldenser', in *RPTK*, XX, cols 799–840 (partly outdated by MS. discoveries, but still valuable).

up his wealth and the world. There was a Franciscan touch in his religious passion, throwing money on the street, rejecting the usurious business methods that had brought him wealth, insisting on receiving his food from others and having to be forced by the archbishop to eat with his wife. He made provision for his wife, endowed his daughters so that they might enter Fontevrault, but did not himself enter a monastery. His aim was the apostolic life of poverty and preaching on the lines of the gospel texts of the sending of the Seventy.[3] What distinguishes him from earlier wandering preachers, however, is his concern as a layman for self-instruction through vernacular translations of Scripture and the Fathers. Étienne de Bourbon, who supplements the edifying account of his conversion in the anonymous chronicle of Laon, tells us that he 'was not well-educated, but on hearing the gospels was anxious to learn more precisely what was in them',[4] set about commissioning translations, then drew followers. He desired to preach, and he and his followers set about doing so.

Soon he came into conflict with authority. The traditional interpretation of orders in the Church gave the right of preaching and of the cure of souls to the pope and the bishops, as successors of Peter and the Twelve, and to the priests, as successors of the Seventy.[5] Canon law restricted preaching to the clergy, and there were few exceptions.[6] Valdes's movement was a popular success, likely to arouse both the fears and the jealousies of the local clergy. From a controversial local situation the group appealed to the pope,[7] and sent representatives to the third Lateran Council in 1179 at Rome, showing their translations, and asking for his authorization of preaching. The response, according to Walter Map, the chronicler and servant of Henry II, was a theological examination designed to show their fitness to preach, in which that worldly cleric exposed their weaknesses by asking them in turn whether they believed in God the Father, the Son, the Holy Spirit, and then the mother of Christ. To each question they replied, 'We do', only to be laughed at when they gave the same response to the question about Mary, whether through their naïvety in seeming to put Mary on equality with the Trinity, or because of Nestorian implications in their answer. They withdrew, Map said, in confusion.

Map need not be taken seriously. He intended to make fun of the Waldensians, just as he deliberately garbled his account of the Cathars immediately preceding this anecdote.[8] But we may infer from him at least that there was some examination, and that no full, blanket permission to preach

---

[3]Matt. 10, 7–13. *Chronicon universale anonymi Laudunensis*, ed. G. Waitz, in *MGH Scriptores*, XXVI, p. 447; *WEH*, pp. 200–2 *MBPH*, pp. 111–13; conversion 1173 (Laon), 1176 (Böhmer, in *RPTK* XX, col. 806).

[4]A. Lecoy de la Marche, *Anecdotes historiques, Légendes et Apologues tirées du Recueil inédit d'Etienne de Bourbon, Dominicain du XIII*e *siècle* (*SHF Publications*, CLXXXV) (Paris, 1887), p. 291; *WEH*, p. 209. On the language of the translation commissioned (that of the region of Grenoble), see M. Carrières, 'Sur la Langue de la Bible de Valdo', *BSSV*, LXXXV (1946), pp. 28–34.

[5]*RB*, p. 63; A. Dondaine, 'Aux Origines de Valdéisme: une Profession de Foi de Valdès', *AFP*, XVI (1946), pp. 191–235 (document and survey of background); see below, p. 69.

[6]Selge, *Waldenser*, I, pp. 22n., 23n. and refs.

[7]Ibid., p. 23; see discussion, pp. 21–35, 243–59.

[8]W. Map, *De nugis curialium*, ed. M. R. James (Oxford, 1914, pp. 60–2); trans. in *WEH*, pp. 202–4. I owe the interpretation to Professor C. N. L. Brooke.

was then given to the group. The Laon chronicler says that Pope Alexander III embraced Valdes, 'approving his vow of voluntary poverty, but forbidding preaching by either himself or his followers unless welcomed by the local priests.'[9] Local clergy were not welcoming, and so the Pope's decision in practice was the near-equivalent of total refusal.

The approval of the vow of poverty coupled with the grave caution about preaching are characteristic of the traditional attitude. The practice of a dedicated way of life, in or on the margins of monasticism, was applauded; preaching remained the proper function of the clergy. Map's account recalls another facet of the situation—the clergy's fear of the consequences of any breach of their exclusive position. After describing the way of life of the Waldensians—going about two by two, barefoot, clad in woollen garments, owning nothing, holding all things common like the Apostles, naked, following a naked Christ—he added the sharp observation, 'They are making their first moves now in the humblest manner because they cannot launch an attack. If we admit them, we shall be driven out.'[10]

The following year Valdes and his followers were still in the Church. The papal legate Henri de Marcy, a leading Cistercian who had become the principal in high-level attempts to check the growth of Catharism in the Midi, presided over a diocesan council at Lyons in which Valdes assented to a profession of orthodox faith.[11] The great fear of authority, it would seem from this document, was that Waldensian enthusiasm would be infiltrated by the Cathar heresy. The profession was prophylactic, intended to alert Valdes to the dangers, and secure his specific rejection of a number of dualist tenets, taken either from twelfth-century experience in the field or derived from a profession of faith compiled in the fifth century and formerly used in the consecration of bishops under the Gallican rite. Other, non-dualist tenets, such as the Donatist rejection of sacraments administered by evil priests, common coin among quite varied twelfth century groups, may well also have stemmed from experience of Cathars in the Midi. There was in addition a careful enumeration of the sacraments to be accepted, one or two other errors, probably unrelated to Catharism, to be repudiated, and a conclusion relating specifically to the Waldensians, in which Valdes declared his intention to renounce the world, to be poor and take no thought for the morrow, to accept neither gold nor silver, and to accept the precepts of the Gospel as commands. It was a programme derived from the sending of the Seventy—but there was a total and significant silence on the right to preach. Valdes showed his will to obedience and orthodoxy by making the profession of faith; in return, as it were, he was able to state the intention of his group.

Trouble again came out of local conditions. At the end of the profession Valdes had repudiated unorthodox zealots who took the name of his association; perhaps he had not in the event been able to prevent their

---

[9]*Chronicon universale*, ed. Waitz, p. 449, trans. in *WEH*, p. 203. On problems of chronology, see Gonnet in *CF*, ii, pp. 94-7.

[10]*De nugis*, in *WEH*, p. 204.

[11]Text by Dondaine in *AFP*, xvi (1946), pp. 231-2, Selge, *Waldenser*, ii, pp. 3-6, Gonnet, in *EFV*, pp. 31-6; analysis in C. Thouzellier, *Catharisme et Valdéisme en Languedoc*, 2nd edn (Louvain & Paris, 1969), pp. 27-36 (see esp. for deep analysis of contemporary controversial literature), trans. *WEH*, pp. 204-8; dating, p. 709 n. 1. Either 1180 or 1181 is possible.

infiltration. Étienne de Bourbon sourly describes the indiscriminate preaching which aroused hostility, of those 'stupid and uneducated' persons who 'wandered though the villages, entered homes, preached in the squares and even in the churches . . .'[12] John of Canterbury, archbishop of Lyons, possibly after a vain attempt to bring them under control through the appointment of a provost, prohibited their preaching; they refused, and were excommunicated and driven from the lands where the archbishop held temporal power.[13]

For the disobedience a number of factors were responsible. One, to judge by later Waldensian writing, was the sense that Valdes had a direct mission from God; another was the state of the Church, and feeling against unworthy clergy; another may well have been the ambiguous language of the profession of faith, in which Valdes declared his resolve to follow the precepts of the Gospel as commands. Had not the Saviour enjoined his disciples to preach, in the same passage in which they were told to take neither gold nor silver, to carry neither scrip nor staff? The disciples, whom the Waldensians imitated, had been told to preach the Gospel to every creature, and Peter before the Sanhedrin had appealed to a higher obligation when he said that one should obey God rather than men. Fidelity to Scripture and the divine call seemed to require preaching. So the association was carried into schism.

Similar forces were at work among the Humiliati of Northern Italy.[14] Like other penitential associations, they aimed to lead a purer ethical life in the world in accord with the gospels without renouncing marriage. In reaction to the commercial life of Italy, free from the temptations of usury, they earned their bread in a number of Lombard towns by simple manual work, largely in the wool industry. As a sign of their humility they wore garments of undyed wool, and received their name either because of their way of life or their dress. A strict and literal interpretation of the gospels led them to reject oaths as well as lies, and the practice of litigation. Social origins were varied, and included clergy. They repudiated the accumulation of wealth, and gave away all superfluity in alms.[15]

The impulse to apostolic life here had another outlet, which did not include wandering begging, but did include a demand to preach and the wish to exercise a ministry with the direction of souls. First of all the orthodox groups in the Church, they seem to have hit on the idea of preaching to refute heresy, while themselves following an interpretation of the gospels and apostolic life

---

[12]Lecoy de la Marche, *Anecdotes*, p. 291; *WEH*, p. 209.

[13]Also known as Bellesmains: see P. Pouzet, *L'anglais dit John Bellesmains* (Lyon, 1927), pp. 7–9, C. T. Clay, in *Yorkshire Archaeological Journal*, xxxv (1940–3), pp. 11–19. I owe these refs to Professor C. N. L. Brooke. Events and Waldensian motives given by Selge, *Waldenser*, ɪ, pp. 76, 84, 184–5, 254–9 (dating 1181–2; Gonnet (*CF*, ɪɪ, p. 97) prefers 1182 or 1183); texts on Waldensians generally and trans. in J. B. Russell, *Religious Dissent in the Middle Ages* (New York, 1971), pp. 41–53.

[14]B. Bolton, 'Innocent III's Treatment of the Humiliati', in *SCH*, vɪɪɪ, pp. 73–82. Documents in G. Tiraboschi, *Vetera Humiliatorum Monumenta*, ɪ–ɪɪɪ (Milan, 1766–8); L. Zanoni, *Gli Umiliati* (Milan, 1911); older summary in E. S. Davison, *Forerunners of St Francis* (New York, 1927), ch. 5; F. Vernet, 'Humiliés', in *DTC*, vɪɪ, cols. 313–21; *RB*, pp. 157–61.

[15]B. Bolton, 'The poverty of the Humiliati'(unpublished). I am grateful to Miss Bolton for use of this and advice.

no less strict than that of the leading heretics.[16] Once again there was an attempt to cross the line which divided the practice of a better moral life, whether in or out of monasticism, from the right to a cure of souls; and it received the same rebuff as had the Waldensians. Alexander III heard and rejected their request to be allowed to preach. Like the Waldensians, they insisted on continuing and fell under the ban of the Church.

The Waldensians and the Humiliati came under consideration at Verona in 1184. In one sense, the legislation which issued as a byproduct of the reconciliation between pope and emperor after their long disputes represented a step forward in the Church's battle against heresy. The bull *Ad abolendam*, which involved the active co-operation of the emperor Frederick Barbarossa, is the first attempt in the whole century to try to deal with the challenge of heresy from a supra-national point of view. Hitherto the onus of action had lain heavily on the individual bishop, exercising his duty as successor of the Apostles to act as guardian of orthodoxy and to repress heresy, little aided from above. He had reacted to the presence of heresy in his diocese in very different ways, according to his own predilections.[17] Some bishops were quite inactive; others who did act were uncertain what procedure to follow. In the case of the peasant brothers suspect of heresy at Bucy-le-Long, discussed above, the bishop of Soissons had first applied the primitive procedure of the ordeal by water, found that one of his suspects failed the test and, uncertain what to do next, went off to seek advice; while he was away the mob burst into the prison and burnt the suspects.[18] A council at Rheims in 1157 had specifically mentioned a duty of the laity to aid the bishop in reporting cases of heresy, but still no detailed procedure was laid down.[19]

The papacy gave vacillating direction. In the case of Flemish townsmen accused of heresy who came to appeal to Alexander III, the pope first attempted to send them back with letters to the Archbishop of Rheims from whom they had appealed and, then, when they demurred, decided to confer further with the archbishop, Louis VII of France and others. His letter to the archbishop urged restraint rather than strictness, but offered no direction as to how that prelate was to set about establishing whether or not the townsmen really were heretics.[20]

The one locality which concerned the Popes over generations, and where they repeatedly exhorted against heresy, was Languedoc—and not only its heartland (where the problem ultimately became acute) but Gascony and Provence as well.[21] From the time of the council of Toulouse in 1119, a scattering of provincial councils under papal presidency warned against the presence of heresy, and urged local secular leaders not to give heretics

---

[16]*RB*, p. 65.

[17]Ibid., pp. 51–2; also Maisonneuve, *Études*, ch. 2; C. Thouzellier, 'La Répression de l'Hérésie et les Débuts de l'Inquisition', in *Histoire de l'Église*, ed. A. Fliche and V. Martin, x (Paris, 1950), pp. 291–340.

[18]Above, p. 55, n. 24.

[19]Maisonneuve, *Études*, pp. 108–11.

[20]*RB*, pp. 55–7.

[21]Ibid., pp. 52–5; on definition of Languedoc, see below, p. 85, n. 62. The county of Provence lay in imperial territory.

protection. Evidently it was the toleration of heresy by lords which created anxiety.

Ad abolendam attempted more than provincial legislation for the Midi, for it surveyed the field of heresy generally, not merely in the south of France, and it attempted to invigorate the bishops' pursuit of heresy.[22] It dealt seriously with heresy in Italy, the place of origin of a good proportion of the sects condemned. In the Church at large all exemption from the bishops' jurisdiction in matters of heresy was abolished; the bishop or his representatives were required to visit the parishes where heresy was believed to exist once or twice a year, and impose oaths on local inhabitants who would then declare any knowledge they might have of heresy in the locality. Secular authorities were to assist this inquisition under pain of penalties both secular and ecclesiastical. Maximum publicity was to be given by higher ecclesiastics to these regulations.

These decisions failed, however, to sway the situation to the Church's advantage. Discovery of heresy was still dependent on the accidents of popular denunciations—effective enough where there was general feeling against heresy, as in northern France, of little use in areas such as the regions of Languedoc or northern Italy, where there was more inertia or toleration. Procedure for proving or disproving the existence of heresy in formal trial remained primitive: it still included the oath and the ordeal, and did not impose the appropriate solution, i.e., the interrogation of suspects by experienced theologians. The bull of Lucius III reorganized the episcopal inquisition, but provided no means for ensuring that bishops in fact observed their duty to maintain it. Finally, and most deleteriously, *Ad abolendam* offered no solution to the problem of recognition and classification of heresy. A series of groups were named and anathematized—'the Cathars and the Patarenes, and those who falsely call themselves the Humiliati or Poor of Lyons, the Passagini, the Josephini, the Arnoldists . . .';[23] the only distinction made was that between those who preached without authority and those who preached actual error. The Waldensians and Humiliati were in the first category—linked in the Latin by *vel*, not necessarily because they had joined forces, but because, in an abusive word-play, they are linked together as liars, falsely taking to themselves the name of 'the humble' or 'the poor' without justification for the title.[24] For the author of the document, neither the humility nor the poverty could be genuine, because it was unaccompanied by a saving obedience to the Church's authority; in a common anathema they are lumped together with the profound heresy of the Cathars, to which they were bitterly opposed. The faithful are merely informed how heretics may be recognized by their unauthorized preaching, by their errors against the sacraments, or by declarations made by the bishops. This is a crude labelling technique; we have no word about the inner core of false doctrine that has led the sectaries into their denials of the sacraments or their preaching, and no

[22]Mansi, xxii, cols. 476–8; Maisonneuve, *Études*, pp. 151–6: On the changing attitude to repression of heresy 1179–84, see R. Manselli, 'De la "persuasio" à la "coercitio",' in *CF*, vi, pp. 175–97.

[23]Mansi, xxii, col. 477. On Passagians, see *WEH*, pp. 173–85, Manselli, 'I Passagini', *BISIAM*, lxxv (1963), pp. 189–210, on Josephini, *WEH*, p. 31.

[24]*RB*, p. 67, n. 120, comments pp. 68–9; Selge, *Waldenser*, i, p. 177, n. 151.

encouragement to the churchmen who might wish to distinguish more subtly between the recalcitrant and those who could be led more gently back to the Church.

So *Ad abolendam* completed the rejection of the Waldensians. There followed an equivocal phase, in which the edict was only partially effective.[25] In practice, Waldensianism as an enemy took second or third place to the Cathars, and the general inefficiency of repression helped to preserve them. The penalty of expulsion, often the most serious punishment applied, did no more than disseminate their influence more widely. The sequel to the decisions of 1184 was, moreover, muffled. In Languedoc the Archbishop of Narbonne, Bernard-Gaucelin, made an enquiry into Waldensian beliefs and issued a condemnation, probably between 1185 and 1187. But it was not effective. The populace approved their moral life; some lower clergy regarded them as auxiliaries and were sympathetic. Their preachers moved about freely, and were even invited to participate in debates which allowed expression to heretical and orthodox points of view. Only in Montpellier, where Count William VIII was hostile, does there seem to have been effective counteraction. In Aragon, Alfonso II in 1194 and Pedro II in 1198 issued edicts against Waldensians, the latter imposing the death penalty for obstinacy. Perhaps these edicts were aimed as much at conditions in the fiefs of the kings of Aragon on the French side of the Pyrenees as in the kingdom itself: in neither area do they appear seriously to have handicapped the preachers. To the north of Languedoc in Lorraine and in the border lands between France and the Empire, Waldensian missions gained success, although in Toul in 1192 the bishop ordered the rounding-up of 'Wadoys'. In Metz at the end of the century the authorities were so ill-informed that, when they came across laymen reading the Scriptures in unauthorized gatherings, they failed to realize that they were Waldensians. In Italy the inability of the hierarchy to get on top of heresy in the cities meant that the Waldensians shared in the general atmosphere of liberty. Only in the period 1196–1206, for example, was the archbishop of Milan able to enforce the destruction of a school that they had long held undisturbed in the city.

Much the same applied to the Humiliati,[26] who spread in the cities, sometimes also in the *contado* where some of their groups had originated. They appealed to industrial workers and artisans or to peasants lately come to the towns; their workshops and houses were usually found in the *faubourgs* where artisans lived.

The Waldensians, spreading through the zeal to preach the gospel, their mission expedited rather than hampered by the expulsion from Lyons following the excommunication by Archbishop John, found a home in the anticlerical atmosphere of Lombardy and became more radical in consequence.[27]

---

[25]For this phase and examples given below, see Thouzellier, *Catharisme et Valdéisme*, pp. 50–1, 133–8; Selge, *Waldenser*, I, pp. 131n., 279–81, 287, 290–1; M. H. Vicaire, *Saint Dominic and his Times*, (orig. *Histoire de Saint Dominique* (Paris 1957), trans. K. Pond (London, 1964) the standard biography), p. 75; Innocent III, *Epistolae*, xii, 17, (*PL*, CCXVI, col 29f.) on school in Milan.

[26]Above, p. 70, n. 14; suggestions on class by Bolton, in *SCH*, VIII, pp. 79–80; note on workshops by Violante, in *HS*, p. 179.

[27]Selge, *Waldensen*, I, pp. 259–63, 284–8.

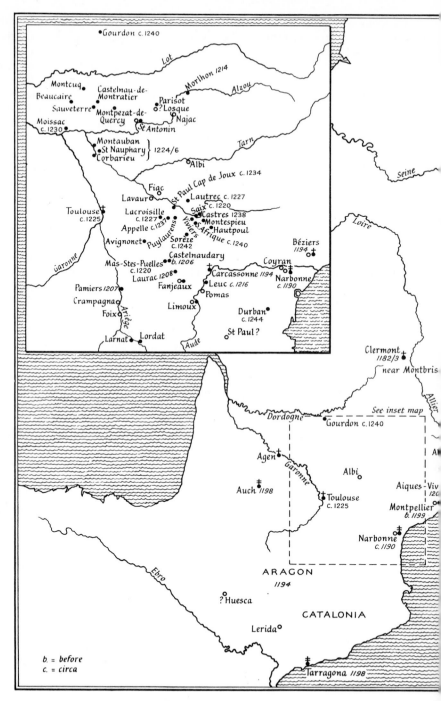

Map Two The Waldensians (1177–1277)

? Liège *1202/3*

Rhine

Moselle

Mainz 1233

Main

? Trier 1231

Regensburg c.1262

Metz *1199/1200*

? Schwäbisch Hall 1248

Danube

Toul *1192*

? Strasburg *1211/2*

Jonvelle c.1218

Rhine

Inn

Saône

Besançon 1248

Rhône

Dongo

Gruaro

Lyon *1177*

? Seregno

Bergamo *1218*

Verona *1199*

Vienne *1198*

Legnano

Milan b. *1206*

Cerea b. *1203*

Valence c. 1235

Pavia

Ronco

Montélimar

Turin *1210*

Piacenza c. *1192/7*

Po

llène

Pinerolo 1220?

Modena

nols

Embrun *1198*

Genoa

Orange

Sisteron

Faenza *1206*

Carpentras

Avignon

c.1204

Florence *1206*

s *1198*

Aix *1198*

Antibes

? Ramatuelle

Rome *1179*

0 _____ 250 *Miles*

0 _____ 400 *Km*

o *Places of origin of Waldensians*   ‡ *Seat of Archbishop*
• *Places of residence of Waldensians*   † *Seat of Bishop*
1206 Earliest dated evidence of the appearance of Waldensians before 1218
1237 Earliest dated evidence of the appearance of Waldensians after 1218

te. The Waldensians of Austria, detected in an inquisition of *c.* 1266, will be found
Map 6 (p. 159).

In Languedoc they seem to have been attracted by the frailty of the hierarchy's control of the religious scene, which enabled them to preach without interference in many places, and showed themselves eager to take advantage of the opportunity to show both the injustice of their excommunication and the orthodoxy of their beliefs by preaching against the Cathars and opposing them in debates. From Lyons they passed over to northeast France and into the German-speaking regions on the Rhine and beyond.[28]

Their appeal at first cut across class divisions. In the early days, companions of Valdes are described as giving up their goods and bestowing them on the poor, a fact which shows they were of some substance. Laymen formed a majority, but there were also fugitive monks and nuns, and some priests and *litterati*. Some support came from higher ranks in society, though it was less than the Cathars enjoyed; members of the class of ministeriales, lesser nobility in the service of the Empire, were noticed, for example, as adherents in the diocese of Metz.[29] The influence which preaching had on women was observed with a hostile eye by Catholic writers. Women thought suitable had the right to preach on terms of equality with the men, which may well have made the movement seem attractive to certain temperaments, dissatisfied with the circumscribed opportunities for religious service for women within orthodoxy.[30]

The Development of Waldensian Organization and Tenets

No rule for the new association has come down to us from the hand of Valdes or his contemporaries, but the regulations of the Poor Catholics, the group of reconciled Waldensians who carried on their way of life with the approval of the Church in the early thirteenth century, combined with incidental references by both Waldensians and their opponents, are sufficient to provide a reconstruction of the life of the group as it developed over the decades following *Ad abolendam*.[31] The leaders in the movement were the preachers, known as the *pauperes spiritu, fratres, sorores*, and later in Lombardy and German-speaking lands, *magistri, magistrae*, 'apostles', 'lords' (*Herren*); they travelled two by two in accord with the gospel texts, wearing simple, apostolic dress, at first apparently barefoot, but seen in sandals of a particular sort that came to serve as a sign of their special status. The granting of the right to wear the sandals accompanied the right to preach. Catholic writers sometimes called them the *Insabbatati* (from the word *sabot*) because of this.[32] Like Valdes, they had to renounce the world and give up their goods before they could become preachers. But though authentically part of the twelfth-century movement of wandering preachers, poverty did not have the same

[28]Ibid., pp. 288–93.

[29]*RB*, pp. 161–4, Selge, vol. cit., pp. 266–9, Böhmer, in *RPTK*, xx, col 809. G. Koch, *Frauenfrage und Ketzertum im Mittelalter* (Berlin, 1962) (Marxist survey, not always conventional, underestimated in the West; review by E. Delaruelle in *RHE*, LX (1965), pp. 159–61), pp. 156–7. Koch is one-sided on class, but notes shortage of early sources. I express here my regret at Dr Koch's tragically early death. For class structure post-1250, see below, pp. 158–61.

[30]Koch, *Frauenfrage*, pp. 158–9.

[31]Böhmer, in *RPTK*, xx, cols 811–2; survey of life and ideas on cols 811–19.

[32]Ibid., cols 806, 812, 813; Selge, vol. cit., p. 270, n. 118.

passionate force among them that it had had among the hermits of western France, or that it was to have in the future among the Franciscans. Valdes, after making a similar break with the world of property as St Francis of Assisi, and influenced like him by the tension between the Christian conscience and the business world, thereafter did not feel the same need to strive perpetually for the highest possible form of renunciation.[33] Austerity rather than destitution was the keynote of the Waldensians.

Preaching consisted of simple exhortation, the call to repentance, and the criticism of sins, both in the individual and in the Church, together with the repetition of many texts of Scripture, learned by heart in the schools of the movement, often in astonishing quantities.[34] The training necessary for the preacher, which on the French side of the Alps came later to be some five or six years, and on the Lombard side one or two,[35] was particularly devoted to the direct study and memorization of the bare text of Scripture in vernacular translation. Only after selection and training, together with the renunciation of goods and of marriage, could the preacher begin his mission. Thus, in a sense, he was as marked off from the rest of society as any Catholic priest. The difference was that in the association no episcopal ordination was considered necessary; women might be granted the right to preach; and no distinction was made between those who happened to be in priest's orders and the others who were laymen.

Preaching helped to recruit more members for the office of preacher. Moved by exhortations, the hearer might then receive spiritual counsel to go and undo the injustices that he had committed and from this he might progress to the status of the 'recently converted', who in a kind of novitiate were tested and instructed in preparation for mission.[36] Others remained in the world, and were known as 'friends' (*amici*), who supported the preachers by their alms and participated in the study of the vernacular Scriptures. Their task was to see to the bodily needs of the preachers, to collect a kind of tax among the supporters, later known as the *talea* in Italy, and to maintain the schools of the association, generally held in private houses.[37] Like the preachers, their knowledge of the Bible was often remarkable. Children began to learn the gospels and the epistles. It was not unknown for an illiterate supporter to know forty Sunday gospels by heart, and in Austria in the thirteenth century a relatively objective Catholic observer, the Passau Anonymous, recorded the case of a member who knew all the book of Job by heart.[38]

Attitudes of the Church towards vernacular translations (in so far as they were to be used by the common people) tended to be hostile, partly because of the use made of them in practice by heretical preachers. Waldensian

[33]For my dissent from Selge on the poverty issue, see Appendix C below.

[34]Böhmer, in *RPTK*, xx, col. 814.

[35]Ibid., col. 812.

[36]Preaching in Selge, vol. cit., pp. 95–127, 142–7; relation to confession (using Durand of Huesca), pp. 95–8.

[37]Böhmer, in *RPTK*, xx, cols 815, 829–30 (assuming later practice reflected earlier; evidence of the *talea* ibid., col. 830).

[38]Ibid., col. 815 and refs; on Passau Anonymous, see below, p. 154 n. 19.

translations were not rejected by ecclesiastical authority as of themselves inaccurate and, in a famous letter on the subject of the Waldensians taken at Metz, Innocent III commended the desire of understanding holy Scripture. But he went on to criticize the association of translations there with unauthorized preaching and 'secret conventicles', and to explain that 'the secret mysteries of the faith ought not . . . to be explained to all men in all places . . . For such is the depth of divine Scripture, that not only the simple and illiterate, but even the prudent and learned, are not fully sufficient to try to understand it.'[39] Here lay the nub of the matter. The study of Scriptures demanded training and skill; the use of it formed a part of the Church's teaching and could not be divorced from it. Scripture was to be mediated, as it were, to the faithful through authorized preachers; the bare text was not to be put into the hands of anyone who might misuse and misunderstand it. The Waldensians naturally rejected this viewpoint and were inclined to think that the authorities and the learned created needless obfuscation. They stressed the literal understanding of the text and the direct fulfilment in their own lives of Christ's demands.

There was a gradual slide deeper into heresy; as the original moderation of Valdes and the Lyons group was breached, the Waldensians spread and developed their teaching in fresh circumstances, and the split from the Church took a psychological toll. The process can be traced in the years between *Ad abolendam* and 1205, the time at which the French and Lombard wings of the movement divided.

Valdes's own influence was always exerted in favour of moderation, with an eye to the ultimate reconciliation with Rome that he seems never finally to have ruled out. He was supported by some of the clerical converts, for whom Durand of Huesca, the former priest, active in Languedoc against the Cathars, is the best spokesman. His *Liber antiheresis*, composed in the late eighties or early nineties, a handbook designed to equip former clergy who read Latin for controversy with both Catholics and Cathars, is proof of the surviving will to orthodoxy in some sections some years after the condemnation of *Ad abolendam*.[40]

Durand was fighting a battle on two fronts: against the orthodox controversialists, who objected that the Waldensians had no right to preach, and that they parasitically lived off their hearers when they ought to have earned their bread by their labour; and against the Cathars, with their own claim to observe the apostolic life, who objected that the Waldensians were not members of the Church because, unlike themselves, they did not have the orders of bishops, priests and deacons. In justifying Waldensians and arming his readers for attack on the weak points of Catharism, its dualism and the lack of austerity of its believer class, Durand keeps free of heresy for most of the time. The root of the matter, of course, was the right to preach, even after

---

[39]*Epistolae (PL,* ccxiv, cols 695–9); trans. by M. Deanesly in *The Lollard Bible* (Cambridge, 1920), p. 31 (a remarkably undated survey on attitudes to Bible reading in the West); ch. 2 has an introduction to the Waldensians; Böhmer in *RPTK,* xx, col. 815.

[40]Above, p. 67, n. 2; dating, Selge, *Waldenser,* ii, pp. xvii–xviii; purpose, ibid., i, p. 45; Thouzellier, *Catharisme et Valdéisme,* pp. 60, 271. Name Durand of Huesca (Aragon) and not Osca (ibid., pp. 213–4 of 2nd edn, correcting theory of Dossat).

authority had prohibited it, and the appeal which Durand makes to God's call to Valdes as justifying it. Here there was a direct challenge to Church authority. But Durand, a practical controversialist with a missionary aim, does not use the issues as a springboard for a developed heretical theology. He does slip into Pelagianism in his eagerness to refute Cathar teaching on predestination but as a whole, the simple biblically based piety of the *Liber antiheresis* is orthodox.[41]

Some made more radical inferences from the common Waldensian thesis of the prime responsibility of the individual for his destiny, and denied Catholic belief in the value of prayers for the dead, or went farther and rejected purgatory altogether. Others, setting out from the Waldensian desire for fidelity of the texts of the gospels, argued that the sayings of Jesus, such as His injunction, 'swear not at all', were to be taken literally, and that in consequence of this principle, all lies were to be treated as mortal sins, and oaths and shedding of blood forbidden in all circumstances. One group in Languedoc carried rigorism so far that they claimed that, as true disciples of Christ, they alone could baptize where neither the Cathars nor the Catholic clergy could. Valdes repudiated them about 1200, whereupon they seem to have formed themselves into a Church of their own, with a hierarchy of bishop, priests and deacons.[42]

There were many pressures working against early orthodoxy. Awareness of the moral need of the Church, which was a mainspring of the movement, easily inclined preachers to move on from a criticism of fallen clergy to a rejection of their sacraments. The study of the vernacular Scriptures could rouse fresh questions about contemporary belief in the minds of idealists. Initially, Scripture reading was buttressed and restrained by a concomitant study of the Church Fathers—Valdes's initial stock of translations included patristic texts[43]—but there were many simple men in the association, and the battle with the hierarchy over the legitimacy of their preaching constantly led Waldensians to appeal to the text of Scripture. From this the way led to a more clearly Biblicist attitude, in which whatever was not justified in the text of Scripture alone was not legitimate. The battle with the Cathars also tended to move them away from orthodoxy because it put pressure on them, as they wrestled for the souls of the people, not to seem less faithful to the words of Scripture than their opponents and not to appear mere collaborators with the stained Catholic Church. The Cathars wholly rejected lies, oaths and the shedding of blood: could the Waldensians afford to seem less Biblicist on these issues than the Cathars were? The stress on doing penance in the movement led to an increased use of confession which could hardly be met by clergy accustomed to hearing confessions at most once a year. Low estimates of the character of the Catholic priesthood also inhibited recourse to them, and so confession to laymen within the Waldensian circle emerged as a substitute. A similar motive, of concern for the pastoral needs of their adherents, led the

---

[41]Prologue to *Liber*, Selge, *Waldenser* II, 8. discussion, ibid., I, ch. I; for Durand on predestination, see Thouzellier, *Catharisme et Valdéisme*, p. 75; K. V. Selge, 'Discussions sur l'Apostolicité entre Vaudois, Catholiques, et Cathares', in *CF*, II, pp. 143–62.

[42]For this para., Selge, vol. cit., ch. 2; comment by Grundmann in *DA*, XXIV (1968), pp. 572–3.

[43]Etienne de Bourbon in Lecoy de la Marche, *Anecdotes Historiques*, p. 290; Selge, vol. cit., p. 152, n. 73.

Waldensians to celebrate the eucharist themselves in regions where it was not readily available from the hands of Catholic priests.[44] When the former Waldensian, Bernard Prim, was received back into the Church in 1210, it was conceded that honourable motives were at work among Waldensians who did this.[45] But the move was dangerous because it opened the way to a rival Church and organization, with its own 'pure' sacraments, in contrast to the 'impure' ones of the sinful priests in the Church.

Spontaneous moves farther from the Roman Church were aided by the geographical diffusion of the movement away from its original nucleus. More radical views emerge among the Waldensians found at Metz in 1199. Though not yet formally Donatist, they are highly critical of the clergy, and tend to be exclusive in their attitudes to their own preachers and translations: they give the impression of a group on the verge of forming a counter-church.[46] The Waldensians who crossed the Alps to Italy grew more extreme. Ardizzo's report on them in Piacenza in the last decade of the century describes how they broke up marriages in gaining recruits, took nuns from nunneries, and taught that only with them was salvation to be found.[47] The Humiliati affected the newcomers in another way, influencing them to adopt their own static life of manual labour, even for preachers, in place of the primitive wandering. To Valdes this was quite unacceptable: the gospel texts were mandatory for the preacher class, who were obliged to live from their hearers rather than by their own efforts.

Another source of dissension lay in the Lombard group's selection of ministers for the duty of administering the sacraments, in contrast to the purely temporary *ad hoc* arrangements normal on the French side of the Alps. The decision had a symbolic importance: where Valdes still thought in terms of reconciliation with Rome, and he and those like him saw a Waldensian administration of the sacraments as merely an occasional bowing to necessity, the Lombards wanted to make a permanent arrangement, and were indifferent to the effects that this might have on their relations with Rome.

A third factor precipitating crisis was the election of John de Ronco as provost, opposed bitterly by Valdes on the grounds that the only leader of the association could be Christ. Personalities played some part. The Lombards detected despotic tendencies in Valdes; John de Ronco seems to have been a raw personality, and a later report from the Catholic controversialist Salvo Burci accused him of being *idiota* and unlettered.[48] The election brought about a split in 1205; despite attempts at reunion, it was never healed, and the Waldensians for the rest of the Middle Ages remained divided into the Lyonist group, who remained faithful to Valdes and the Poor Lombards,[49] as they

[44]Selge, *Waldenser*, I, pp. 155–7 (reaction to Cathars), 146–9 (confession), 159–63 (eucharist).

[45]Ibid., p. 159; Innocent III, *Epistolae*, xiii, 94 (*PL*, CCXVI, col. 291); on Prim, see Thouzellier, *Catharisme*, pp. 232–7, 262–7.

[46]*PL*, CCXIV, cols 695–9 (above, p. 78, n. 39); Selge, vol. cit., pp. 290–3.

[47]Letter of Ardizzo, bishop of Piacenza, ed. Dondaine, in *AFP*, XXIX (1959), pp. 273–4 (article cited below, p. 98, n. 14).

[48]*WEH*, p. 273.

[49]Causes of split, Selge, vol, cit., pp. 172–88; for prime source, see below, p. 97.

were called, with their stronghold in Northern Italy. After 1205 the latter drew away still further, and became more explicitly Donatist.

The Italian split was one element in a general process of alienation of Waldensians from the Church. From the first refusal of the prohibition of preaching at Lyons in the early 1180s there had been a gradual decline from schism to heresy proper. The authorities had had the worst of both worlds, for prohibition had not greatly inhibited the spread of the movement yet it had contributed to its deterioration. The hope of reconciliation could not be deferred too long; even ineffective persecution increased Waldensian hostility to the Church; the breach from Catholic instruction and aid inevitably opened the way to popular heresies inside the movement. A natural impression is that the papacy and the bishops had wholly underestimated the strength of feeling which lay behind the Waldensian demands, and that .a heresy had emerged largely out of the attitudes of the Church.

The Speronists

While the Waldensians slipped out of orthodoxy into the world of the sects, another heretical group was forming in Lombardy, the Speronists.[50] They resemble the Waldensians in one thing: they were a group founded by a layman—something for which we have no earlier precedent, if we except the followers of Eon de l'Étoile as too like a robber band to be properly discussed.

Speroni was a jurist, a one-time friend of the great legal authority Vacarius, to whose refutation of Speroni's heresy we owe nearly all our information about the sect. Consul in Piacenza in 1164, 1165 and 1171, Speroni between the years 1177 and 1185 fomented a movement against the Church which lasted fifty years. Piacenza was and remained its centre. A probable starting-point can be seen in Speroni's involvement in the long conflict over the rights of the monastery of S. Giulia in Piacenza, in which he and other protagonists of Piacenza met papal opposition.

The heresy represented an extreme rejection of all Church authority, which spread well in Piacenza because the anticlerical spirit of the town favoured any movement of opposition to the Church. Priesthood itself was jettisoned. Here Speroni differed in approach from Arnold of Brescia, whose denial of the place of the priesthood sprang from a rejection of their vices: because they had sinned so deeply, their acts had lost validity; and because the Roman Church had become involved in property, it had lost its right to confer sacramental powers. Speroni was much more radical. No doubt his views were born out of a reaction against a power-loving priesthood, but his understanding of religion left no place for a priesthood *ab initio* and on principle. They simply had no function left, for Speroni condemned all the sacraments—especially baptism, the mass and penance— as their stupid inventions. All formal acts of worship and exterior observances represented an idolatrous materialization of spiritual religion; they were quite simply an obstacle. Arnoldists, or followers of the wandering preachers, might well have

---

[50]Ilarino da Milano, *L'Eresia di Ugo Speroni nella confutazione del Maestro Vacario, Studi e Testi*, cxv, (Vaticano, 1945); analysis of heresy and Vacarius's polemic: text, pp. 483–583; see esp. on Speroni (pp.37–75) reconstruction of core of heresy (pp. 411–22); place on Italian scene (pp. 423–69); extract in *WEH*, pp. 152–8.

broken into overt acts of violence—Petrobrusians, for example, felt so deeply about the distortions of the contemporary Church that they rejected them in dramatic scenes, burning crosses or eating meat ostentatiously at forbidden times. For the Speronists all this was unnecessary. Their members had already the consciousness of union with the Word; in Speroni's phrases, they had the Holy Spirit, the Spirit of Jesus and of wisdom, and were in union of faith and love with Jesus. They could therefore quietly attend mass while their minds were elsewhere, pursuing the interior calm and justice that lay at the heart of their beliefs, *alieno mente.*

The centre of their religion was a kind of interior baptism, a spritual communion with God. It was not an ascetic movement, and had nothing in common with the twelfth-century striving after apostolic life[51]—on the contrary, Speroni and his followers rejected ascetic practices, the good works and moral activity of the individual, in favour of a total devotion to interior sanctification. All that mattered was the inner life of the individual. Speroni denied that there was original sin, but argued for two categories of humanity, the predestined and the foreknown. The foreknown were doomed to damnation; by contrast the predestined soul remained holy even when, from the point of view of exterior justice, it was leading a life of sin.

Such a theology could hardly be the basis of an effective organization, and Speroni had no predilection for preaching. Yet his following lasted. One major reason, we may assume, was the Speronists' consciousness of their predestination. Speroni's liking was for a ministry of the written word, and we may suspect that he drew a following from the better educated. Certainly they outlasted his death, though they never became a dynamic feature on the Italian scene. The *Liber supra stella*, written by Salvo Burci in 1235, also a citizen of Piacenza, is evidence that some fifty years later they were still in existence.[52]

The Crisis Areas

The Speronists were odd men out in their century, but not in their locality. Lombardy, and to a lesser extent, central Italy in these decades was rapidly attaining the distinction of being the land of heresy *par excellence,* rivalled only by Languedoc. The causes were embedded in the development, economic, social and political, of all those regions where the semi-independent commune had established itself as a determining factor. A burgeoning economic life, in advance of developments anywhere else in Europe, put everything into the melting pot. There was an extraordinary mobility of classes, with peasants from the *contado* moving into the towns or transferring from one part of the *contado* to another, lords from the countryside coming into the towns and joining in the social struggles within them, while fortunes were made from commerce and industry. New classes of artisans, notaries and petty businessmen were formed, and the communes defied outside authority and started to battle for control of their own regions. Social change and mobility,

[51]Ilarino da Milano, *Eresia,* p. 435.

[52]Ilarino da Milano, 'Il "Liber supra stella" del piacentino Salvo Burci contro i Catari e altre Correnti ereticali', *Aevum* XVI (1942), pp. 272–319; XVII (1943), pp. 90–146, XIX (1945), pp. 218–341; see his *Eresia,* p. 42.

Violante has suggested, made men ready to break with tradition in religion and opened their minds to unorthodox ideas.[53] The vivid economic life of Italy fostered reaction against the business world and the practice of usury bound up with it, and led some idealists into the heretical groups who practised poverty, or stimulated them into violent reaction against a hierarchy who officially denounced usury and were leaders of a Church based on a gospel which called for renunciation, yet were themselves deeply involved in moneymaking. The continuance of a lay educational tradition in Italy, and the intellectual agility sustained by the commercial life and political intensity within the communes, opened the way to protests against a bureaucratic Church with a limited place for its laity, and aided the growth of heretical groups which gave a place to the laity for preaching, Scripture reading and spiritual direction. The same agility and the questing spirit which accompanied it was also a seed-ground for those elements of plain disbelief which intertwined with other causes of dissent to create heresy. Orthodox enthusiasms, like the flight to eremitism or the increase of itinerant preachers, blended with economic forces to create a flux which shook the power of traditional ecclesiastical forms and organization to hold the faithful. Exchanges of view were facilitated by the heterogeneous character of the travellers, not so much on the great international routes, but on the lesser roads where the pace was less hot, and lower clergy, pedlars, itinerant artisans and pilgrims were thrown into informal contact.[54] The geographical position of Italy and the opening of routes through commerce facilitated both the entry of missionaries and the flight of refugees from persecution elsewhere. Movement itself created a psychological climate in which it was easier to step outside orthodoxy.

The politics of communal struggles aided heresy because they weakened the authority of the natural guardians of faith, the bishops, and confused the contest between orthodoxy and heresy with the battle for independence of the communes from episcopal and papal power. The investiture controversies had destroyed the control of the bishop over his town. He remained a considerable figure because of his high birth and connections with ruling families, as well as the lands and rights of his bishopric; but his interest had become only one political force among a series of others, and he had no power any more to ensure that the rule of faith was maintained and heresies put down by force. So heretical groups might be tolerated in communes, not because they had a hold on a major portion of the populace, but because they demonstrated independence from episcopal control.

Similar effects flowed from the popes' struggle against the temporal claims of the emperors in Italy. There was a natural alliance between heretics and the Ghibellines, the factions which existed in the cities based on local and family groupings and interests, but owning a general allegiance to the Empire. Heresy was a stick with which imperial supporters could beat the papacy, disliked for its political rather than its religious claims. Ghibellinism, then, provided the favourable milieu in which heretics could swim. At the same

[53]*HS*, pp. 171–98; Italian background in Volpe, *Movimenti religiosi*; attempted refutation by Morghen in *Medioevo Cristiano*, pp. 204–81.

[54]Violante, *La Pataria Milanese*, 1 (Rome, 1955), pp. 103–25.

time the efforts which popes made to raise money, levy troops and exert pressure in these contests made them easy targets for the classic contrast drawn by the preacher between a worldly and wealthy Church involved in the infighting of Italian politics and the simple band of Apostles gathered round Jesus or depicted in action in the Acts of the Apostles.[55] Too often the clergy in Italy appeared in the guise of politicians, tax gatherers or warriors rather than as pastors. It is the political involvement of the popes in Italy which explains the apparent paradox that in the Middle Ages heresy flourished most readily in lands that lay closest to the seat of the Papacy.

An upward movement in the graph of heresy over all Western Europe, placed by Wakefield about mid-century,[56] was followed in the sixties by an intense struggle between Alexander III and the emperor Frederick Barbarossa over Italy. This had the effect of distracting the popes from the problem of heresy, and of delaying attempts to grapple with it. *Ad abolendam* followed on the reconciliation of pope and emperor and was a first fruit of the new peace. While the contest was on, there was much destruction in Italy; the fighting and schism in the papacy fomented by Barbarossa disrupted religious life, and contributed to the weakness of ecclesiastical authority on which Italian heresy flourished. Most suggestive is the transmutation which took place in the term 'Patarene' between its origin in the eleventh century, as a term for supporters of the orthodox if radical reform in Milan favoured by the papacy, and its reappearance in the third Lateran Council of 1179, and then in *Ad abolendam*, long after the Pataria had died away, as a technical term for Italian heretics, most often applied to the Cathars.[57] It was an indication of the loss by later twelfth-century popes of the leadership of popular religious sentiment, now tending to flow out of the Church rather than into it.

Two examples, one of partial success, the other of defeat for the forces of orthodoxy in the last decades of the century, may suffice to show how the situation then lay in Italy. In Milan St Galdinus, consecrated archbishop in exile during Barbarossa's wars, began in 1167 to restore the fortunes of his see and, towards the end of his pontificate, to preach against the Cathars who were then spreading in the city.[58] His *Vita* attributes much success to his efforts, and to the effects of his campaign we may perhaps assign the conversion of the heretical teacher Bonacursus, who proceeded in his *Manifestatio* to describe the heresy he had left.[59] The significant feature of the *Vita* is the vagueness with which the heresy is mentioned, a sign that at this time Catholics were not very well informed about their enemy, and the fact that St Galdinus had no other weapon but exhortation. Evidently he could not coerce the citizens to drop Catharism. He checked the rise of heresy, but only temporarily. In the first decade of the thirteenth century James of Vitry said, with a moralist's exaggeration, that Milan was a pit of heretics.[60] In fact

[55]Volpe, *Movimenti religiosi,* pp. 38–48, Morghen, *Medioevo Cristiano,* pp. 275–81.

[56]*WEH,* p. 28.

[57]See above, p. 40 n. 4; for heretical nomenclature, see Thouzellier, *Hérésie et Hérétiques*; and on Patarines, pp. 204–21.

[58]*Acta sanctorum,* April 18, II, p. 591; *WEH,* p. 151.

[59]Ilarino da Milano, 'La manifestatio heresis catarorum quam fecit Bonacursus', *Aevum,* XII (1938), pp. 281–333; *WEH,* pp. 170–3.

[60]*Lettres de Jacques de Vitry,* ed. R. B. C. Huygens (Leiden, 1960), pp. 72–3.

they were minorities, divided and disputing among themselves, but they were energetic, and each group seems to have had more supporters there than anywhere else.

The other example is that of Orvieto, where Catharism first appeared a little after mid-century, to make but modest progress till about 1170, when the arrival of two preachers from Florence began to raise the temperature. In the end a territorial dispute with the Papacy caused Innocent III to put Orvieto under interdict; the bishop withdrew, Catharism made inroads in his absence. Innocent's action had an effect opposite to the one intended: while the city still lay under the ban, an heretical teacher from Viterbo began to preach and drew many after him.[61] When the Catholics of the town rallied and appointed Pietro Parenzo to restore order, he was assassinated. In the reaction and the proliferation of miracles which followed on instant popular veneration of the dead Pietro, Catharism went underground. But it still survived, and the story had lessons, *mutatis mutandis*, for the treatment of heresy in all the Italy of the communes. Catharism and the evangelical heresies, some of which had been in part stimulated into existence by the menace of the Cathars, had made a place for themselves within many of the towns. Responsibility for their progress or repression lay heavily with the laity, as the case of Orvieto shows. The popes and the bishops could not count on support to put them down. This loss of authority over heresy and the evident failure of *Ad abolendam* produced in Italy a state very like crisis by the end of the century.

In the other major area of disquiet, Languedoc, the conditions which fostered heresy were unlike those in Italy,[62] though the end result in the emergence of small but tenacious heretical minorities, and a loss of power by churchmen to control them, was much the same. The resistant forces were not primarily the towns, which were smaller than those of Northern Italy and lacked their independence, but elements of the petty nobility in the countryside. St Gilles and Toulouse had international trade connections, and there were common linguistic and cultural links along the Mediterranean littoral into northern Italy; yet commerce in the Midi was smaller in scale than in Lombardy. Industry produced for a regional market, by and large, and was stable. The flux in social classes which followed on the exceptional economic vitality of Italy, as well as the intellectual agility and the higher standards of lay education, were missing.

The precondition for the success of heresy in the affected regions of Languedoc was the chronic political anarchy caused by the gradual decomposition of the authority of the counts of Toulouse since the time of the journey to the first crusade of count Raymond IV,[63] and the disequilibrium

[61]V. Natalini, *S. Pietro Parenzo: la Leggenda scritta dal maestro Giovanni canonico di Orvieto* (Rome, 1936), pp. 155–6; quoted in Manselli, *Eresia*, p. 186. See *MBPH*, pp. 127–32.

[62]W. L. Wakefield, *Heresy, Crusade and Inquisition in Southern France 1100–1250* (London, 1974) (concise survey with translation of documents), ch. 3 and bibl.; P. Wolff *et al.*, *Histoire du Languedoc* (Toulouse, 1967); J. R. Strayer, *The Albigensian Crusades* (New York, 1971) (lucid on politics and war, but out-of-date on heresy); P. Wolff, 'France du Nord, France du Midi. Les Luttes sociales dans les Villes du Midi français', *Annales*, ii (1947), pp. 443–54. Definition of Languedoc and other geographical terms in Wakefield, *Heresy, Crusade*, p. 50, Strayer, *Albigensian Crusades*, ch. 1.

[63]A. Dupont, *Les Cités de la Narbonnaise première depuis les Invasions germaniques jusqu'a l'Apparition du Consulat* (Nîmes, 1942), pp. 686–7.

created by the rival, undecided claims to suzerainty of three powers, the kings of France, the kings of England and the counts of Barcelona, followed by their heirs the kings of Aragon. Local conditions also militated against the establishment of any one overriding political authority; the existence of partible inheritance by females created a fatal subdivision of rights in land, and hampered the raising of armies by feudal means. Mercenaries were widely employed in consequence; and churchmen, denouncing the spread of heresy, simultaneously deplored the ravages of these *routiers*.[64] Chronic war disrupted Church life and handicapped bishops who might be interested in an active oversight of the rural parishes where heresy first established itself. It also created a condition of lawlessness, with plundering of Church property by secular lords and much petty friction, which tended to devalue the influence of churchmen in purely religious matters, and correspondingly increase the popularity of a profoundly anticlerical heresy which rejected all Church authority. Disorder inhibited the great local lords when the call came to put down heresy: they lacked the power to do so, and in the uncertain conditions could not afford to alienate any subjects.

The petty nobility in the rural areas enjoyed a large measure of independence from their suzerains, but no very secure economic position. The subdivision of inheritance led to the appearance of large numbers of knights, with resources insufficient to support them and little outlet but in waging of war. Usurpation of tithes by these men was widespread. Rural clergy were poor for this reason, and heavily dependent on local nobles; the latter had a commitment against doing justice to the legitimate claims of churchmen, and a predilection for anticlerical heresy which taught that the payment of tithes could not rightly be demanded by the Church from the laity. As in Italy, anticlericalism formed the favourable ambience for heresy proper, but it was an anticlericalism focussed more closely on local rights and less concerned with high political claims. Within this anticlerical atmosphere, men in the early stages were more often patrons, fautors of heresy or fringe members, the women the true converts. As they joined the ranks of Cathar perfect or gave wholehearted support to their preachers, the heresy began to settle in. In a second generation more menfolk made the renunciations demanded for admission to the leading class of perfect or, at least, became believers; under the umbrella of noble protection the heresy was preached to lower classes. Both then and earlier the heresy made its impact in some of the towns, especially Toulouse, where it secured some men of influence, though the surest support for it always remained in the countryside.[65]

The clergy of the Midi lacked either the will, the ability or the resources to put effective obstacles in the way of the heretical preachers.[66] The higher

[64]Griffe, *Débuts*, pp. 7–14, 117–24; M-H. Vicaire, ' "L'Affaire de Paix et de Foi" du Midi de la France', in *CF*, IV, pp. 102–27.

[65]Griffe, *Débuts*, ch. 7 (comment, p. 182, n. 14). For social context, see C. P. Bru 'Éléments pour une Interpretation sociologique du Catharisme occitan', in *Spititualité de l'Hérésie: le Catharisme*, ed. R. Nelli (Paris, 1953), pp. 23–59 (clarifying survey, arguing that Catharism was not specifically urban (p. 36). Koch, *Frauenfrage*, ch. 1, s. 1, overstresses towns and textile workers (but pp. 26–8 presages Griffe's hypothesis; see discussion of motivation p. 31); J. H. Mundy, *Europe in the High Middle Ages* (London, 1973), pp. 534–49, is perceptive.

[66]Y. Dossat, 'Le Clergé méridional à la Veille de la Croisade albigeoise', *RHL*, I (1944), pp.

clergy were also affected by the disorders, and were often not on good terms with their secular counterparts. They had their share of unworthy prelates— the archbishop of Narbonne from 1190 to 1212 was an ineffectual absentee— and the best of them were competent rather than inspiring. Before Fulk of Toulouse (appointed in 1206), none of them was able to inspire the laity in their charge to fervour against the heresy. Clergy most in contact with the heretics were hampered by poverty which, because it was not voluntary, had no spiritual benefit, and was merely a handicap. As far as we know, the lower clergy were no worse morally, than, say, the lower clergy of Normandy, where there was no heresy;[67] but they were poorly educated and demoralized by their treatment at the hands of the laity. They made a feeble showing in contrast to the dedicated ascetics who represented the heresy, and they lived in a region not distinguished for the quality of Catholic intellectual development.[68]

The Midi's achievement in the cultural sphere lay in the study of Roman law and its troubadour literature, sponsored by the courts of leading aristocrats and especially by noble ladies. It was not heretical, though it did share in the prevailing anticlerical atmosphere; its influence was confined to a small class, and it was irrelevant to the heresy question.[69] In the religious sphere the land was underdeveloped: it lacked the schools which gave lustre to Northern France and provided the sinews for intellectual defence against heresy and, though there had been orthodox preaching missions and a special association with the crusading ideal, no major reforms had affected Church life. As elsewhere, a demand for apostolic life in poor wandering preaching was met, not by the orthodox, but by heretics.

One feature of the region was its toleration of different views and races. Jews were well treated,[70] so were heretics; Waldensians as well as Cathars moved freely.[71] Given the inability of local forces to contain the situation, intervention from outside the Midi might well seem the only answer; it was attempted, following an appeal to Louis VII of France and a letter to the Cistercians sent by Raymond V, count of Toulouse, in 1177, but it was not pressed home, and the results were superficial.[72] A projected expedition by the

---

263–78, 'La Répression de l'Hérésie par les Évêques', in *CF*, VI, pp. 217–51; H. Vidal, *Episcopatus et Pouvoir épiscopal à Béziers à la Veille de la Croisade albigeoise, 1152–1209* (Montpellier, 1951); R. W. Emery, *Heresy and Inquisition in Narbonne* (New York, 1941); E. Delaruelle, 'Le Catharisme en Languedoc vers 1200: une Enquête, *AM*, LXXII (1960), pp. 149–67 (stimulating set of queries); review of C. E. Smith, *The University of Toulouse in the Middle Ages* (Milwaukee, 1958) in *AM*, LXXIII (1961), pp. 234–5; on learning, see *CF*, V; Wakefield, *Heresy, Crusade*, ch. 4 (surveys Church; discussion of numbers of heretics, pp. 68–71); on relation of reform to heresy, cf. Griffe, *Débuts*, pp. 16–19, correcting Fliche, in *Histoire de l'Eglise*, ed. Fliche and Martin, IX, 91. See below, p. 100, n. 22.

[67]Strayer, *Albigensian Crusades*, p. 18.
[68]Bibl. in P. Ourliac, 'La Société languedocienne du XIIIᵉ Siècle et le Droit romain', *CF*, VI, pp. 199–216.
[69]D. Zorzi, *Valori religiosi nella Letteratura provenzale. La Spiritualità trinitaria* (Milan, 1954); Koch, *Frauenfrage*, pp. 139–44.
[70]B. Smalley, reviewing the 2nd edn. of Thouzellier, *Catharisme* (*JEH*, XXI (1970), pp. 184–6).
[71]Above, p. 76.
[72]Gervase of Canterbury, *Chronicon*, ed. W. Stubbs, LXXIII, i (*RS*) (London, 1879), pp. 270–1; date of Raymond's appeal, Thouzellier, *Catharisme*, 2nd edn., p. 19, n.23; letters, *PL*, CCIV, cols. 235–42; CXCIX, cols. 1120–4.

kings of France and England came to nothing. A legatine mission scored some success by securing condemnation of a rich heretic, Pierre Maurand, in Toulouse and bringing two leaders of heresy, one probably the Cathar bishop of Toulouse, to a public discussion in the city. But the two came under safe conduct, and left freely at the end, excommunicate but not otherwise punished.[73] In 1181 an armed expedition to Lavaur put pressure on the Trencavel viscount of Béziers, implicated with heresy, and enforced the handing over of the two heretics who had gone free in 1178. They duly confessed.[74] But such short-term expeditions only scratched the problem, and were handicapped by lack of local knowledge.

There was a vicious circle here. Churchmen in the Midi were not tackling the problem; churchmen outside could not well understand the area. More lay below the surface, probably, than the legates understood. Raymond V's appeal may be interpreted as an attempt to call in fresh forces in the ancient quarrel with the viscounts of Béziers.[75] There is a suspicion that Maurand's emergence as the major suspect in Toulouse owed something to social tensions there and his own successful career in business.[76]

The legates did what they could. Of Henri de Marcy, the conscientious Cistercian who was member of the first mission and leader of the second, one could not reasonably expect that he be another Bernard of Clairvaux. He did not greatly like the Midi, and turned down an offer of the bishopric of Toulouse.[77] After he left the scene this phase of intervention ended. Alexander III especially had given attention to the problem after the easing of the crisis with the Empire. From the fall of Jerusalem in 1187, however, the papacy was preoccupied elsewhere. For the cure of the affected region of Languedoc, probably some lever was needed against the aristocrats who declined to use force against heresy; what was certainly necessary was prolonged preaching by churchmen who knew the language and the locality, and this the region did not have.

In the absence of fresh intervention, the situation grew worse rather than better. Not all the south was seriously affected. The heresy noticed in Gascony did not become a problem. The Mediterranean seaboard was scantily affected. The crucial region lay, rather, to the west and inland, in the eastern Toulousain, the Carcassès and the eastern Albigeois and in their leading towns.[78] In certain places within these lands, because of the attitudes of some members of the nobility, by the end of the century the Cathars had come near to displacing the Catholic Church, rendering parish clergy impotent, preventing the administration of the sacraments and securing in practice a right of open preaching for themselves. In Toulouse and other towns they were a known but unmolested minority, and included men of influence. The leading aristocracy were still not effective persecutors and Raymond VI, who

---

[73]Sources, trans. of Roger of Hoveden, *WEH*, pp. 194–200; similar text trans., *MBPH*, pp. 113–16.

[74]Narrative 1173–81, Griffe, *Débuts*, chs. 4 and 5; on Lavaur, pp. 126–32.

[75]Wakefield, *Heresy, Crusade*, p. 83.

[76]J. H. Mundy, *Liberty and Political Power in Toulouse, 1050–1230* (New York, 1954), pp. 60–2 (links between heresy and social tension, pp. 74–84); and his *Europe*, p. 304.

[77]Griffe, *Débuts*, pp. 113–4, 137–9.

[78]Ibid., pp. 176–7; (see also map on endpapers).

succeeded his father as count of Toulouse in 1194, was more equivocal in his attitude to heresy than his predecessor.[79] In many *castra*, the fortified settlements of the countryside, the Cathars' leading class was installed in houses, directing men and women in austere lives, preaching and giving counsel, even receiving the payments normally due to the parish clergy. Waldensians, officially under the ban of the Church, were in practice little hampered.

Conclusion

To survey the regions of Italy and Languedoc, where the Church's authority to impose submission to its doctrines had broken down, makes a fitting conclusion to a chapter on heresy in the twelfth century, because it is a story of lost opportunities and of only partially successful repression: by the end of the century the balance in the battle between heretical minorities and ecclesiastical authority had definitely swung against the Church. One should be chary of giving literal credence to the preachers and reformers who so loudly proclaimed the sins and weakness of the Church; the medieval Church retained great vitality together with its scandals and defects, and was ever capable of comprehending in one organization extremes of devotion and of wickedness. Nowhere could one justly speak of a mass apostasy, and only the ambiguous character of the anticlerical ambience in which heresy proper moved could lead one to think it was likely to happen. The will to heresy has to be distinguished from faint-hearted orthodoxy and a desire to impede any increase in the secular power of the Church; and the number of committed heretics, by all indications, was still not very great.

None the less an anxious situation did exist, the more so because the hierarchy seemed not to have ideas for meeting the challenge. The tragedy had been that so much enthusiasm had already slipped away, condemned to the twilight world of the sects. With few exceptions, the heretical groups of the century were still not mounting a profound doctrinal challenge to the Church. Their appeal was emphatically to Christian life, and they drew converts above all because of the attractive power of the earnest and dedicated lives of many of their teachers and the force of their exhortation to moral living in their hearers.

No doubt because of the utterly changed circumstances in which the heresies of the high Middle Ages expanded as contrasted with those of the late Roman world, we miss the intellectual heresy based on the teaching of some distinguished mind that formed the stuff of the classical heresies condemned in the early centuries. The intellectual appeal of the heretical leaders in the twelfth century is very limited and, though they are often men in orders, they do not include anyone of strong academic background. The common ground between many of them was the appeal to an apostolic life based on wandering preaching in poverty and, where this was practised, crowds could be drawn to listen and follow.

Sometimes it seems almost a matter of chance whether the following collected will remain orthodox or form a sect. Instruction was not adequate to

[79]Ibid., p. 207.

D *

guard the faithful against deviations of belief, and the situation remained fluid. Leaders of heretical groups were not always clear themselves where their ideas were leading them. In these circumstances, the decisions of authority were particularly potent: elements within the dissident religious movements were susceptible to a recall to the Church, provided outlets could be found for their enthusiasms. The desire to hear preaching and to preach was a recurrent theme. So was the yearning for simplicity, sometimes an illusory simplicity of the romanticized early Church and an impatience with sophisticated explanations. Certain texts from the gospels struck their leaders, and demanded a direct and literal observance. There was a will to understand directly what lay in the gospels. Asceticism had an appeal *per se*, irrespective of the motivation and the doctrinal substructure. Anticlericalism was generally the stimulus for heresy, as well as being its protection. The most common heretical tenets were concerned with the powers of the priesthood and the demands of conscience—with the validity of sacraments administered by unworthy clergy and the value of infant baptism, as opposed to the willing acceptance of belief by the adult. Involved with the deviations from orthodoxy were social tensions hinted at rather than clearly revealed in the sources, associated with the lack of outlets for religious women, struggles for power in the towns, poverty and wealth.

That reform in the lives of the clergy would have taken much of the sting out of twelfth-century heresy is a commonplace. Part of the difficulty lay in the rising expectations of the laity and the stimulus imparted by Gregorian reforms. The corollary of the way of thinking that laid such stress on the sacred character of the priest's office was that the priest's life must be worthy of so high a calling. The solution, given the problems of the recruitment or supervision of clergy, their training, and the standards of the higher clergy in many areas, remained bafflingly difficult.

What was clear was, that to meet the challenge of heresy, it would not be enough to maintain the old ways. On the lowest level, the episcopal inquisition was not adequate for the searching out of offenders, and its operations were too dependent on the energy, or lack of it, of the individual diocesan. Understanding of the tenets of the heretics, though it had grown through the century, especially with the appearance of full-scale summaries of unorthodox beliefs after 1160, still had far to go. Parts of Languedoc and much of northern and central Italy plainly presented peculiar difficulties because of the widespread fautorship and patronage of heresy. At a higher level, the demands and enthusiasms of the popular movement for preaching and the apostolic life, though they conflicted with much precedent and canon law and upset interested parties, were not of themselves heretical at all. Doors closed at Lyons and Verona could be reopened. More could be done to separate off misled enthusiasm from the recalcitrant elements, to bring into focus the alien inspiration of Catharism, and draw away from it adherents unaware of the implications of dualism. The lines between heresy and orthodoxy altogether could be drawn more clearly.

There was not much time. The sects had grown since the beginning of the century in cohesion and durability. In the early decades they barely outlast the deaths of their founders, and are obviously profoundly dependent on the force of the individual charismatic personality. Then Catharism develops, a supranational heresy, no longer nearly so dependent for its existence on individual personalities, important though they may be, and capable of lasting because of its developed ritual and organization and the dogmatic envelope it gave to dissent. As the country wore on, the evangelical heresies seem also to last better, and Waldensianism appears, the culmination of the previous wandering preacher movements, strengthened by the novel element of vernacular translations of Scripture.

By the end of the century there was more heresy, it was more firmly embedded, and two crisis areas had emerged. It was this sombre scene which confronted the young Pope Innocent III on his elevation to the Papacy in 1198.

Part Three

Heresy and the Church

7

The Counter Attack: Innocent III to Innocent IV

With the advent of Innocent III the papacy was for the first time occupied by a churchman who made the treatment of heresy and the religious movement associated with it one of the prime occupations of his pontificate.[1] In the previous century Alexander III and Lucius III had both taken steps to deal with the problem; but in comparison to Innocent's subtle handling of the difficulties their solutions appear fumbling and incomplete. Moreover, Innocent was followed by three popes, Honorius III, Gregory IX and Innocent IV, who all gave attention to the counter-attack on heresy. The work of two saints, Dominic and Francis, and the emergence of the orders of mendicant friars, encouraged by Innocent and aided by his successors, had a powerful effect on thirteenth-century religious life, and provided trained personnel to preach against heresy and to pursue its recalcitrant adherents. More study of heresy and the application of scholastic methods to its refutation brought forth fruit in treatises and handbooks that classified heretical tenets, and made clearer where precisely the boundary between heresy and orthodoxy lay.[2] Under Gregory IX use of the overriding authority of the papacy brought into being a papal inquisition to supply the deficiencies of the episcopal prosecution of heresy, and to give new energy to the tracking and examining of offenders. By the mid-thirteenth century the guiding principles of the Church's counteraction were settled, and most of the machinery requisite for repression was in action, not to be altered in essentials for the rest of the Middle Ages.

Innocent's part in this upswing of orthodox fortunes was that of the initiator who set out the principles for future action. His approach was two-sided; he offered to enthusiasts who had strayed a means of returning to the Church, and diminished the dangers in the movement for wandering preaching in poverty by welcoming this form of apostolic life under safeguards within the Church; and at the same time he attempted to make the use of force against fautors and obstinate heretics more effective. His metaphor was that of the farmer who distinguishes carefully between wheat and tares in his field, taking precautions against uprooting the one with the other.[3] Proper handling of the heresy problem demanded precise and careful examination of what heretics

---

[1]*RB*, pp. 70–156; comment by E. Jordan in *RHE*, xxxii (1936), pp. 968–72. Cf. A. C. Shannon, *The Popes and Heresy in the Thirteenth Century*, (Villanova (Pa), 1949).

[2]Borst, *Katharer*, pp. 6–21.

[3]*PL*, ccxiv, cols 788–9; *RB*, p. 74 n. 5. Cp. *PL*, ccxv, cols 1246–8; and Bolton, in *SCH*, ix, p. 86.

believed and, above all, of their attitudes to authority. If they were willing to submit, then arrangements might be made to meet the needs of enthusiasts wherever they did not conflict directly with orthodox doctrine. If they were recalcitrant, then every kind of measure might be employed to bring them to justice and force those who patronized them to relinquish their support.

Innocent explored all the resources of canon law to find a place for popular religious associations that had hitherto lain on the margin of orthodoxy or beyond. Humiliati who wished for recognition were accepted, and given regulations that allowed the continuance of three branches with separate ways of life: one clerical, a second consisting of laymen and women living in communities, and a third consisting of married men living with their families, all according to existing legal norms.[4] A careful explanation showed them that there were legitimate occasions when oaths had to be sworn, but they were allowed to avoid any that were not strictly necessary, and to retain other special features of their apostolic way of life as they had observed them while under the ban of the Church. The wholesale refusal of the right to preach that had helped the Humiliati into heresy after the third Lateran Council was breached with a fine distinction: members of the third, the married group, who were 'wise in faith and expert in religion' might preach, provided that they confined themselves to moral exhortation and eschewed the preaching of doctrine—that was properly the province of the clergy.[5]

Durand of Huesca, converted after a colloquy with the representatives of orthodoxy at Pamiers in 1207, was given, together with the colleagues who came over with him, the right to lead a life of wandering preaching without property, engaging in mission against heresy, exactly as he had done while a Waldensian, provided that he accepted Catholic authority and repudiated errors such as Donatism, which had been current among some Waldensians. He and his group were given the technical status of penitents in the Church, living under three vows of poverty, chastity and obedience, and styled 'the Catholic poor'.[6] Bernard Prim, also a Waldensian from Languedoc who came over in 1210, was given similarly sympathetic treatment. As with Durand's group, the basis for his reconciliation with the Church was the profession of faith which Henri de Marcy had imposed on Valdes, with the addition of certain points on the sacraments and the repudiation of the right of women to preach.[7] The important difference with the case of Valdes was that, the repudiation of errors once completed, preaching was permitted. Durand and Prim, after they had submitted, were allowed to continue essentially the same way of life as poor wandering preachers.

These decisions in effect detached a small group of moderates from the movement of Waldensian preachers and rescued many Humiliati for the

---

[4]M. Maccarrone, 'Riforma e Sviluppo della Vita Religiosa con Innocenzo III' *RSCI*, xvi (1962), pp. 29–72; and Bolton, in *SCH*, viii, p. 78.

[5]Tiraboschi, *Vetera monumenta*, ii, pp. 133–4; *RB*, p. 81, n. 24, trans. of phrase, Bolton in *SCH*, viii, p. 77. But would they stop short at moral exhortation, in fact? (Miss Bolton, in a private letter, noting their rate of literacy.) For aristocratic Humiliati, see Bolton, in *SCH*, viii, p. 79; and for income, her unpublished 'The Poverty of the Humiliati'.

[6]*EFV*, pp. 129–36; *WEH*, pp. 222–6, Selge, *Waldenser*, i, pp. 193–225; Thouzellier, *Catharisme et Valdéisme*, 2nd edn, pp. 215–26; for status, cf. Maccarrone, in *RSCI* xvi (1962), pp. 29–72.

[7]*EFV*, pp. 136–40; Thouzellier, *Catharisme*, pp. 232–7; Selge, *Waldenser*, i, pp. 188–93.

Church. For a moment it might well have seemed that Innocent's policy was going to have more far-reaching effects, as a hundred Waldensian preachers in Italy after Durand's conversion asked, under conditions, for acceptance by the Church;[8] but we do not know what happened to them, and after 1212 we hear no more of such requests. Innocent's sympathetic approach could only work if reconciling moves came from the Waldensians themselves: the bulk of the movement made no further approaches to Rome, but attempted to recover unity amongst themselves.

At first, in the aftermath of the Waldensian split of 1205,[9] the situation remained confused. Donatist views gained ground amongst the Poor Lombards, who were in a strong majority in Italy; yet members of the Lyonist wing, who were faithful to the tradition of Valdes, did not disappear altogether. A reaction amongst some of the Italian membership in the direction of moderation took place after a council of the Lombards in the period 1208–9, when a hen upset the chalice as John de Ronco celebrated the eucharist, and women trampled on the spilt wine. There was a split. Some indignant brothers declared, in reaction against such disorder, that the sacrament should only be administered by Roman priests.[10]

Contacts between Lombards and Lyonists over the Alps were not totally severed. In time the deaths of John de Ronco and Valdes appeared to remove personal obstacles to reunion, and a last attempt, possibly emanating from the Waldensians then feeling the effects of persecution in Languedoc, was made to bring the two wings together. Six representatives from each side met in conference near Bergamo in 1218 to thrash out their differences. The Lyonists were ready to make generous concessions on the issues which had kept them apart, allowing provosts and ministers for the sacrament to be appointed for life if the Lombards insisted, and dropping Valdes's rigid opposition to their arrangements on manual labour. The conference broke on the Lombards' Donatism, and the issue, subordinate but of high emotional significance, of the salvation of Valdes and his companion Vivet. The Lyonists insisted that they were in paradise; the Lombards answered coldly that they would be if they had satisfied God for their sins before their deaths. Eucharistic beliefs formed the doctrinal breaking point, the Lombards making merit, not office, the crucial question for the validity of the sacrament and, in our source for the conference, a letter of information to adherents of the Poor Lombards in Germany, massing authorities in Scripture and the Fathers for their point of view, their opponents standing on the Catholic belief that the sacrament was valid only if the celebrant were a priest, whatever his life might be.[11]

Two rival traditions had evolved. The Lyonist wing supporting Valdes in 1218 had still not broken irrevocably with the Church. They stood firm on the belief that their preachers had a direct mission from God, and they rejected the Church's excommunication. They did not press on, as the Lombards did,

---

[8]Ibid., pp. 204–5.
[9]Above, p. 80.
[10]Selge, vol. cit., p. 307.
[11]*EFV*, pp. 169–83, trans. *WEH*, pp. 278–89; Selge, vol cit., pp. 305–12, Böhmer, in *RPTK*, xx, cols 810–11. I accept Germany as the destination, on the evidence of the title subsequently added to the document.

to subject all practices of the Church to stern examination in the light of
Scripture and the pattern of the early Church. If critical of the Roman
hierarchy and priesthood, they had still not unchurched them. The
Lombards had, and pressed the others to do the same.

The wings never came together again after the failure at Bergamo, though
some sporadic and not wholly hostile relations between them continued,
aided perhaps by the fact that the missionary endeavours of the two wings
tended to lie in different regions.[12] The moderates did not return to the
Church, and voluntary reconciliations, such as those of Durand and Prim, are
not recorded again; instead, persecution encouraged more out-and-out
opposition. The chance of reunion with the Church seemed to have
disappeared.

The success of the Waldensian groups who returned to the Church was
partial. Prim's group brought to the service of the Church an apostolate based
on a poor life, with exhortation and some recourse to manual labour; the Poor
Catholics under Durand pursued a more learned mission, with a hospice at
Elne in Roussillon which also formed a centre for the production of
antiheretical writings.[13] Durand, a precise polemist who painstakingly
followed the convolutions of developing dualist doctrine and over-matched
his opponents in knowledge of Scripture, worked on, growing in stature
between his Waldensian *Liber antiheresis* and his Catholic *Contra Manicheos*.[14]
Both groups had the advantage over heretics of realizing in their own persons
the apostolic life of poor preaching; but they were unable to break down the
hostility of the bishops or to gain a major popular success, and in the
perspective of thirteenth-century Church history they appear as imperfect
sketches of the successful mendicant orders. The reconciled Humiliati earned
the praise of James of Vitry in 1216 for their preaching against heresy in
Milan; he knew of some 150 houses of theirs.[15] Their success was of its time;
the Humiliati remained exclusively Italian, and they did not go on to form an
order of first-class importance. The breakthrough for the harnessing of the
apostolic life of poor, wandering preaching to the mission of the Church came
only when two saints were able to make use of the fertile climate of opinion
and Innocent's will to experiment.

In Languedoc in 1206, when a mission of Cistercians, earnest but
hampered by official status and entourage, failed to make progress in a
preaching drive, the Castilian bishop Diego of Osma and his subprior
Dominic hit on the idea of preaching in poverty in accord with the gospel
texts, and on terms of equality with their enemies the Cathars. Dominic,
constantly encouraged and aided by Innocent, established himself in
Fanjeaux, in the centre of the Cathar country, and founded a house nearby at

---

[12]Ibid., col. 811.

[13]Elne, in Roussillon, then ruled by the kings of Aragon, diocese in province of Narbonne. On
the school, see Thouzellier, pp. 269–84 and references.

[14]*Liber*, text, Selge, II; analysis, Thouzellier, pp. 60–79, implications, Selge, I, ch. 1; *Contra
Manicheos*, in Thouzellier, *Un Somme anti-Cathare: le 'Liber contra Manicheos' de Durand de Huesca*
(Louvain, 1964); reviewed by J. Jolivet in *RHR*, CLXIX (1966), pp. 77–80; analysis in Thouzellier,
Catharisme, pp. 303–73 (authorities cited on pp. 375–424). Pioneer study, including other themes,
A. Dondaine, 'Durand de Huesca et la Polémique anti-Cathare', *AFP*, XXIX (1959), pp. 228–76.

[15]*Lettres*, ed. Huygens, p. 73 ('CL congregationes conventuales').

Prouille for women and girls rescued from the Cathars.[16] In 1215 he moved to Toulouse; in 1216–17 he obtained recognition for his order of preachers, known to history as Dominican friars—in effect a special development of the way of life of the Augustinian canons to whom Dominic belonged. Meeting a widespread demand, they rapidly grew into a large international order dedicated to the preaching of the faith, and including in its aims the confutation of heresy.[17] They affected the whole religious landscape, setting new standards in preaching, entering the universities and playing a major part in the development of scholasticism, bringing their piety and zeal to bear on the towns short of pastoral care, where heresy found adherents, and deploying against Cathars and Waldensians the silent but most effective argument of their own observance of apostolic life. Determined papal support, good planning by Dominic and his successors, and the Languedoc emergency all helped the young order to avoid suffocation by conservatism, though opposition by the secular clergy to the rights of the friars to preach, to hear confessions and to intervene in the parishes long remained a factor in Church life.

Five years before the fourth Lateran Council, at which St Dominic's plans were discussed, St Francis of Assisi, with eleven companions, asked at Rome for confirmation of a way of life of the most extreme poverty blended with preaching based on the gospels, especially the account of the sending of the Seventy.[18] Francis's first rule consisted largely of texts, and was not based on an existing rule at all; moreover, the renunciations he asked for seemed beyond human powers. The pope seems to have hesitated, but was persuaded by the argument that to turn down Francis's request would be tantamount to saying that the Gospel itself could not be observed. He met the request by the unprecedented course of giving Francis's way of life an oral confirmation; a right to preach was granted to Francis, and through him to his followers, on terms resembling those given to the Humiliati. The group, at first a lay association, was allowed to preach penance—to engage in moral exhortation rather than the preaching of doctrine that was reserved to clergy. Rapid growth in numbers, contemporary needs and papal policies soon turned them into a great international order of friars, clerical and often learned, with full rights of preaching, and many resemblances to the Dominicans.

St Francis himself hardly referred to heresy at all. His Testament has an observation on binding suspect members of the order so as to bring them safely to the cardinal protector. Étienne de Bourbon records a meeting with a heretic who complained to him of the misdeeds of a concubinary priest. Francis's response was simply to kiss the priest's hand in token of reverence for his office.[19] Preaching for him was a spontaneous overflow of the interior life; unlike Dominic, he had no aim of confuting heresy specifically, but thought of his order as auxiliaries to the priesthood, preaching penance and thereby, no

[16]Vicaire, *St Dominic; CF,* 1; J. Guiraud, *Cartulaire de Notre Dame de Prouille, précedé d'une Étude sur l'Albigéisme languedocien au XIIe et XIIIe siècles,* 1–11 (Paris, 1907).

[17]For introduction, see D. Knowles, *Religious Orders in England,* 1 (Cambridge, 1950), pp. 146–62.

[18]*Ibid.,* pp. 114–26; Matt. 10. 7–13. See below, ch. 12.

[19]L. Lemmens, *Testimonia Minora s.XIII de S. Francisco Assisi* (Quaracchi, 1926), pp. 93–4. I owe the ref. to Dr R. B. Brooke.

doubt, recalling men from error. Circumstances changed this, and the Franciscans came to play an important part directly against heresy through preaching, the intellectual refutation of error, the writing of treatises, and a full apostolate in the towns, made more effective through the institution of the third order. But their most distinctive contribution lay in the revolution they helped to bring about in popular piety through their stress on the incidents of Christ's life and His sufferings, and their acceptance of the created world and joy in nature. It was the indirect answer to Cathar rejection of the world and their non-human Jesus.[20]

In the problem area of Languedoc, the centres of heresy once discerned, Innocent characteristically began seeking solutions at two levels simultaneously. One was the fostering of religious revival through preaching, as shown in his advice to his Cistercian legates 'to proceed in such a way that the simplicity of your attitude is clear to the eyes of all',[21] and in his encouragement of the mission of Diego and St Dominic; the other was the application of pressure to the unwilling episcopate of the region and the leading nobles who would not put heresy down. The second came to dominate the first after his legate, Pierre de Castelnau, was assassinated in 1208 in circumstances which threw suspicion on count Raymond VI of Toulouse. Innocent called a crusade, and so put into the field north French barons eager for Raymond's lands.[22] At the end of the pontificate Raymond stood dispossessed of nearly all his holdings apart from those in Provence, and the bulk of the episcopate had been deposed and replaced by others who, Innocent hoped, would be more fervent against heresy. Yet the effects of the war were to ally, for the moment, local patriotism and interests entirely with the cause of heresy. Innocent gave a full legal justification for the crusade, based especially on his own decretal of 1199, *Vergentis in senium*, with its assimilation of heresy to the crime in Roman law of lèse-majesté, with concomitant penalties of confiscation of goods;[23] but he was unable to keep control once the crusade was launched, or to maintain canonical procedure. The lands of Raymond VI were confiscated without any trial taking place, and other southern nobles were arbitrarily dispossessed. The war had its own momentum. The champion of the Church, Simon de Montfort, was a fine general who lacked the gifts of a politician. Innocent was not master of the spirits he had conjured up.

In the long term the Crusade helped to create a new political situation dominated by the north French, in which effective persecution became

[20]E. Delaruelle 'L'influence de saint François d'Assise sur la piété populaire,' in *Relazioni*, III, pp. 449–66; Manselli, *Eresia*, p. 270.

[21]*PL*, CCXV, col. 360; trans. Vicaire, *St Dominic*, p. 87

[22]M. Julien, 'Pierre de Castelnau: un Légat autoritaire', *CEC*, IX (1958–9), pp. 195–202, Wakefield *Heresy, Crusade*, ch. 6, and bibl., Strayer, *Albigensian Crusades*; P. Belperron, *La Croisade contre les Albigeois et l'Union du Languedoc á la France (1209–1249)* (Paris, 1942) (North French bias); A. P. Evans, 'The Albigensian Crusade', in K. M. Setton, *A History of the Crusades*, II: *The Later Crusades, 1189–1311*, ed. R. M. Wolff and H. W. Hazard (Philadelphia, 1962), pp. 277–324; *CF*, IV (esp. for ideas); comment in Thouzellier, *Catharisme*, p. 269, n. 1, B. Hamilton, *The Albigensian Crusade* (London, 1974) (Historical Association pamphlet G. 85).

[23]Maisonneuve, *Études*, pp. 156–8, R. Foreville, 'Innocent III et la Croisade des Albigeois', in *CF*, IV, pp. 184–217, Thouzellier, *Catharisme*, pp. 136, 146, 155–6.

possible. But there were side effects. Crusade was a blunt instrument. When it was used again to eradicate dualists in Bosnia in the pontificate of Gregory IX, it actually increased their security in the land.[24] The bishop of Bremen called a Crusade in 1234 against the *Stedinger*, peasants who opposed his rule and refused tithes, as though they were heretics, and in so doing showed how easily the mechanism could be corrupted.[25] Moreover, it will always be open to doubt whether such an application of force to the situation in Languedoc was required, and whether Innocent, distant from the scene, was misled on the true character and extent of heresy in the Midi, especially by the authoritarian Pierre de Castelnau.[26] Not many years were given to preaching. Dominic had few helpers and only the one religious house at Prouille in the early days.

The active pontificate of Innocent III left a body of case-law, precedent and legislation for dealing with heresy which supplemented and improved, but did not fundamentally change, the episcopal inquisition as prescribed by *Ad abolendam*. Exhortation, the use of legates with overriding powers—even deposition of unworthy bishops, as in Languedoc—gingered up episcopal prosecution of heresy, or alternatively tempered its crudities. At the end, in the fourth Lateran Council canons summed up existing legislation, and a dogmatic constitution, mainly anti-Cathar and based closely on the profession of faith presented by Henri de Marcy to Valdes, gave a concise picture of the errors to be suppressed.[27]

An intellectual heresy, the trinitarian views of a Calabrian abbot, Joachim of Fiore, was also condemned at the council, albeit with a stress on Joachim's own submission to the papacy in his lifetime.[28] Joachim's error was contained in a *libellus*, now lost, in which he attacked the trinitarian teaching of Peter Lombard, author of the authoritative textbook, the 'Sentences', and a leading influence at the Paris theological school, to which Innocent himself had belonged. Joachim's own major literary activity, in which he applied traditional methods of exegesis to Scripture in order to understand the patterns of history and to foresee the future, was not condemned, although, amongst much that was orthodox, it contained a potentially subversive notion of a coming third age of the Holy Spirit, that would in some sense supersede the arrangements of the present Age of the Son.[29] A group of supporters of Amaury of Bène, a Paris master who died in about 1206, had been condemned in 1210, some to death, others to perpetual imprisonment.[30]

[24] See below, pp. 142–50; J. V. A. Fine, jr, 'Was the Bosnia Banate subjected to Hungary in the Second Half of the Thirteenth Century?' *EEQ*, III (1969), pp. 167–77.

[25] Grundmann, *Ketzergeschichte*, p. 39; Lea, *Inquisition*, III, pp. 182–6.

[26] Delaruelle, in *AM*, LXXII (1960), pp. 149–67; contrast contemporary plea for force in treatise attributed to Ermengaud de Béziers, ed. Dondaine, *AFP*, XXIX (1959), 271, *WEH*, pp. 230–5; analysis, Thouzellier, *Catharisme*, pp. 284–92.

[27] Mansi, XXII, col 982, *EFV*, 158–63; trans., in *DTC*, I, pp. 683–6; Dondaine, in *AFP*, XVI (1946), pp. 191–235.

[28] Mansi, XXII, cols 982–6, M. Reeves, *The Influence of Prophecy in the later Middle Ages, A study in Joachimism* (Oxford, 1969) (the fundamental study of Joachim and his influence), pp. 28–36.

[29] Definitive exposition is in Reeves, *Prophecy*, pp. 16–27, 135–44; cf. an illuminating analysis by the same writer, 'The *Liber Figurarum* of Joachim of Fiore', *MRS*, II (1950), pp. 57–81.

[30] *RB*, pp. 355–73, M. Th. d'Alverny, 'Un Fragment du Procès des Amauriciens', *AHDLMA*, XXVI (1951), pp. 325–36, sources trans. in *WEH*, pp. 258–63. Bène (sometimes Bènes or Bena) was a parish in the diocese of Chartres.

Amaury had been influenced in a pantheistic direction by his reading of John Scotus Erigena, the ninth-century theologian, and elements in his teaching had created scandal during his lifetime. These views, mediated through clergy with pastoral duties and misunderstood by them, passed on to a group of laity, especially women, in dioceses round Paris to create a sect of Amaurians or Amalriciani; these made crude inferences from Pauline texts, believed that the Holy Ghost was incarnate in them and that they had attained a state of sinlessness, in which they were no longer in need of the Church and its sacraments. 'All things are one,' they were quoted as saying, 'for whatever is, is God',[31] Even the *Pater Noster* was bowdlerized to eliminate discrepancies with their extravagant views.[32] It was a classic case of distortion of intellectual teaching by those unfitted to understand it. The curious feature about the Amalriciani is their belief that an Age of the Spirit was at hand, of which they were the forerunners, when all men would become 'spiritual', as they were: it sounds like a crude version of Joachim's Age of the Spirit.[33]

The pantheistic views of Amaury were condemned in the same canon of the council as Joachim's trinitarian exposition; on some other occasion in the pontificate Ortlieb of Strasburg was also condemned for having taught that man must keep himself from all external things and only follow the Spirit in him,[34] and in 1210 a work of David of Dinant imbued with pantheism was also burnt. From the evidence we have there appears to have been some efflorescence of 'spiritualizing' heresy cut short under Innocent. Of Joachim, however, more was to be heard.[35]

Innocent's successor Honorius III, at once less resolute and less original, nevertheless continued to build up anti-heretical legislation by ensuring that laws on the duties of secular powers to repress heresy and aid Church authorities were made part of secular codes. The Emperor Frederick II made such laws part of imperial legislation—it was originally his *quid pro quo* for coronation by the pope—and made burning the punishment for the recalcitrant.[36]

But the major innovation came under Gregory IX when, after some experiments with various procedures and after realizing the inadequacies of episcopal inquisitions, he resorted to special agents equipped with full powers from the papacy to hunt out heretics. In 1233–4 he made arrangements for a

---

[31]*Chartularium universitatis Parisiensis*, ed. H. Denifle and E. Chatelain, I (Paris, 1889), p. 71, quoted in *RB*, p. 363, n. 18.

[32]'Beau Pere qui estes in celz et en la terre, confermez vestre nom en nos cors; denez nes vostre regne; vestre volente seit faite en terre si come au cel; denez nos que mesters nos est a chascun et chascun jer aus armes; pardonez nos nos mesfez si com nos pardonom a austrui; gardez nos des enginz au de de (able?); delivrez nos de toz maus.' D'Alverny, *AHDLMA*, (loc. cit.) Here we may detect a pantheistic note ('in celz et en la terre'), the replacement of material bread by vague needs, the transformation of Evil into accidental evils. See, further, *AHDLMA*, loc. cit.

[33]Grundmann's judgement in *RB*, p. 365, and *Ketzergeschichte*, p. 43.

[34]W. Preger, *Geschichte der deutschen Mystik*, I (Leipzig, 1874), p. 468, l. 78. On Ortliebians, see Grundmann, *Ketzergeschichte*, p. 45. See Leff, *Heresy*, II, p. 309; on all these episodes, cf. Grundmann, *Ketzergeschichte*, pp. 41–2; Neoplatonic background in G. Leff, *Medieval Thought* (London, 1958).

[35]Below, pp. 186–93.

[36]Maisonneuve, *Études*, pp. 243–57.

staff of such agents to be given powers in Languedoc[37]. They showed themselves so much more efficient than the bishops that their inquisition became the normal means of extirpating heresy. The episcopal inquisition tended in most lands affected by heresy to become of secondary significance. So the papal inquisition of the Middle Ages was born.

It was the last move required to implement all the existing laws against heresy. The agents so appointed supplied the deficiencies of the bishops, for they were appointed for the one purpose of putting down heresy, and were not distracted by other business. Their commissions to act as inquisitors were of long duration, appointees could thus build up knowledge and gain a professional's expertise. Most commonly Dominicans were appointed to the office by arrangement with their superiors: they brought to the task the dedication of men under vows belonging to a highly trained order with a special vocation against heresy. Franciscans, more rarely appointed, had similar dedication. Continuity of record was established. Each inquisitor kept registers, with the depositions of suspects, which could be handed on to his successors or used as a a basis for further inquiries at a later date. The records were a threat to everyone who had once been interrogated, and even to the relatives and descendants of suspects, against whom a record of conviction or complicity could be invoked. With such data at his disposal a medieval inquisitor had resources comparable to that of a modern policeman, ever ready to check and cross-check information. One full confession by a heretic of wide acquaintance could uncover a multiplicity of leads to his fellows; the practice of granting a period of grace at the beginning of an inquisition in which punishments were waived for those who gave information, and the insistence that only full confession of all available facts gave proof of repentance were calculated to produce a free flow of incriminating details. An international body, the inquisition could link up actions against heresy in different lands, and try to prevent the escape of refugees; flight at an early stage of proceedings or while awaiting trial remained one of the few effective means of avoiding successful prosecution.

As the customs and procedures of the inquisitors developed, so in time a class of writing often known as 'inquisitors' handbooks' came into existence, assembling past experience on heretics and their beliefs, and giving information on the customs inquisitors used and the regulations under which they worked.[38] In Languedoc a working knowledge of Catharism under a few simple heads had become the common knowledge of clergy habitually in contact with the heretics, and this knowledge passed over to the thirteenth-century inquisitors; in Italy, ever more sophisticated, inquisitors tended to

---

[37]Y. Dossat, *Les Crises de l'Inquisition toulousaine au XIIIe Siècle (1233–1273)* (Bordeaux, 1959), ch. 5, see review, B. Guillemain, *AM*, LXXIII (1961), pp. 106–111; Lea, *Inquisition*, I, ch. 7 *et passim* (still of value); chs. 7–14 reprinted, with introduction by W. Ullmann, in H. C. Lea, *The Inquisition of the Middle Ages: its Organization and Operation* (London, 1963). Further bibliography below, p. 169, n. 1.

[38]A. Dondaine, 'Le Manuel de l'Inquisiteur (1230–1330)', *AFP*, XVII (1947), pp. 85–194, Borst, *Katharer*, pp. 21–7. Polemical literature (see below, p. 170) in Dondaine, 'Nouvelles Sources de l'Histoire doctrinale du Néo-Manichéisme au Moyen Âge, *RSPT*, XXVIII (1939), pp. 465–88; W. L. Wakefield, 'Notes on Some Antiheretical Writings of the Thirteenth Century', *FS*, XXVII (1967), pp. 285–321 (demonstrates extent of casual plagiarizing).

have a more speculative interest in the origins and nature of the heresies they were dealing with. There was in any case a general rise in the number and standards of the treatises which described and refuted heresy, a product of the new scholasticism and of the concern of churchmen over the problem; these contributed to the pool of information available to the inquisition; in turn, further treatises were also influenced by the habits of mind of the inquisitors themselves.

The inquisitor was the heir to the body of legislation against heretics and their supporters which reached back to *Ad abolendam* as well as to the enactments passed after 1233 in his favour. It was a formidable structure. The procedure of inquisition was ideally suited for the uncovering of heresy, which was an elusive crime. Under it any suspect could be summoned and put under oath to declare his participation in forbidden rites and meetings, his contacts with heretics, or any relevant information at all about his beliefs and his movements; from 1252 by a decision of Innocent IV, who improved the detailed workings of the inquisition, torture might be used on him.[39] It was intended that the instruments should be applied by the secular power, and not the inquisitor's staff; but four years after Innocent's bull his successor, Alexander IV, permitted inquisitors to evade the restriction. The subject could thus be compelled to incriminate himself. Heavy penalties compelled suspects or witnesses to appear and to answer; others enforced the aid of the secular power, whenever required, to ensure his attendance and to assist with, or be responsible for his or her punishment if convicted. Rights to the property of convicted heretics also helped to secure the willing support of the secular power. Fautorship of heresy was a grave crime, and penalties could be incurred by a mere obstruction of the inquisitor in his duty.

In the determination that nothing should stand in the way of speedy and efficient action against heresy, the checks designed in canon law to ensure fair trial, the validity of evidence, and the impartiality of the judge were all set aside. In the last resort the inquisitor, who combined the role of judge and of priest dealing with a penitent, held near-unfettered powers over the suspects who came before him. At his discretion—and the scrutiny of his sentences required under the regulations tended to be slight and formal—was an array of penalties stretching from fines, pilgrimages and the wearing of yellow crosses on the clothing, to imprisonment up to and including life and burning, as well as sentences of confiscation, destruction of dwellings, and attendant disqualifications from office-holding affecting descendants.[40]

If the clergy and secular authorities did give wholehearted support to the inquisition, and its agents were given time to conduct thorough and repeated investigations, it was difficult to see that, armed with these powers, they could fail to eliminate a popular heresy.

---

[39]Maisonneuve, *Études*, p. 312. Use of torture in secular courts, mentioned by Innocent IV to justify use by inquisition, developed as the ordeal became discredited, R. C. Van Caenegem, *La Preuve dans le Droit du Moyen Age occidental. Rapport de Synthèse* (Brussels, 1965) (*Recueils de la Société Jean Bodin*, XVII), p. 739 and n. I owe the ref. to Dr A. V. Murray.

[40]See Lea *Inquisition*, I, chs 12, 13; Dossat, *Crises*, pp. 247–68; articles in *CF*, VI. I have been unable to consult W. Ullmann, 'The defence of the Accused in the medieval Inquisition', *Irish Ecclesiastical Record*, 5th ser., LXXIII (1950), pp. 481–9; on it, however, see Wakefield, *Heresy, Crusade*, p. 192.

The innovations of these decades permanently altered the circumstances under which the Church met the challenge of heresy. The initiative passed to the Church. The enclaves of orthodox Europe, where in practice heresy had enjoyed a measure of toleration through ecclesiastical inertia or the anticlericalism of the secular power, were gradually eliminated. The decisions taken early in the century marked an end for the view, still sporadically expressed earlier on, that gave precedence to peaceful conversion and counter-preaching over repression. It was accepted that force was the correct answer, to be applied vigorously, and an apparatus was now in existence that legitimized its use and defined the offences against which it was to be employed. The phase of uncertainty that had characterized the eleventh and twelfth centuries now finally came to an end.

The counteraction of the Church affected the manifestations of heresy. In place of the open preaching and agitation of the twelfth century, we meet more secret missionizing and underground conspiracy. The emergence of the friars met for a time the demand for poverty and wandering preaching in an orthodox context. The development of theology and the diffusion of information about heresy enabled the seeker after truth to know better where he stood. The distinction between heretical sects and Catholic orders grew clearer.

Yet all was not progress: counter-attack against heresy was not the same thing as fundamental reform. Innocent III had always stressed the intimate connection between heresy and the failings of the clergy, and in some ways it was easier to welcome innovations in the religious life and to legislate for more efficient repression of heresy than to make reform prevail against deep-seated abuses or deficiencies in the Church. Grave problems connected with the numbers, selection and training of the clergy remained. The difficulty of the wealth of the Church continued, and was basic. The reforms initiated at the fourth Lateran Council had but limited success; response to legislation varied widely in different lands, stretching all the way from the English Church, where the council was the prelude to something of a golden age with a plethora of scholars and saints on the episcopal bench, to the churches of Spain, obsessed with the crusade in the Iberian peninsula, where the effect was non-existent. Innocent's own will to experiment with forms of dedicated life met an apparent check in canon thirteen of the council, which forbade new religious orders. Although its meaning was less restrictive than has been assumed,[41] nevertheless, given episcopal conservatism and the decisions of later popes and councils, the net effect was to make it harder for the Church to accept fresh religious movements in the future, and Innocent's immediate notion of communities of clergy for preaching and ministry under the direction of bishops was stillborn.

In the political sphere, Innocent's design for a settlement of the old problem of papal-imperial relations and the security of papal lands in Italy failed to hold: a subsequent struggle for power with Frederick II overshadowed the pontificates of Gregory IX and Innocent IV, began to tarnish a traditional focus for lay piety through the misuse of crusades launched against the Hohenstaufen, and led the very popes who did much to

[41] Leff, *Heresy*, i, p. 15, needs to be modified by Maccarrone, in *RSCI*, xvi (1962), pp. 29–72.

raise the efficiency of prosecution of heresy, as we have seen, to restrain their agents wherever disturbances caused by the pursuit of heretics led to the risk of losing allies against Frederick.

The heavy conflict with the Cathars was not brought to a successful conclusion until the early fourteenth century.[42] Friars, inquisition, lay confraternities, the development of Catholic piety, and rising standards of education, together with the internal dissensions of the heretics, combined to bring them down, but only after great efforts had been expended. The Waldensians, though by and large less hard pressed than the Cathars, came under heavy fire in the lands of their origin on each side of the Alps, but compensated in some degree for their losses by wide extension of missions in German-speaking lands to the east and by finding refuge from persecution, both geographically and psychologically, through the erection of a camouflage of subterfuge.[43] These heretics lasted beyond the thirteenth century into the age of the Reformation. Cathars and Waldensians, the most notable of the surviving twelfth-century heretics, now demand separate treatment, and will be discussed in chapters of their own, with the intention of showing both the attractions of their life and beliefs that gave them vitality and drew in recruits, and also how each of the heresies fared under the stiffer pressures of a resurgent Catholicism.

New developments in Church life did not, however, bring a final solution to the problem of heresy. Reform by means of centralization and the growth of canon law raised standards in the Church; but, carried on against a background of inadequate communications and central bureaucracy, coupled with the strain of papal taxation and the Italian conflicts, it created simultaneously a ground swell of opposition, the potential seedbed of heresy. Above all, stress on law, when it was unfertilized by religious sentiment, aided the growth of formalism. It was no chance that 'spiritualizing' heresies, with varied roots but having in common a claim that their adherents were more 'spiritual' than their fellows and a desire for escape from the routine of the medieval Church, its hierarchy and sacraments, grew more common as the thirteenth century wore on. What is noteworthy is that the heresies sprang more commonly from inner circles of Church life, and were not the heresies of 'outsiders', as were those of the Cathars and Waldensians.[44]

The very instruments of the Catholic resurgence that won back the initiative for the Church began to create heresy. The Franciscan friars, subjected to great pressures in their swift development from a small brotherhood to a large and powerful order with a leading intellectual role, fell into difficulties, growing in intensity from the time of the council of Lyons in 1274 and issuing, first, in internal rebellion and then in true heresy, which was spread to the laity through the third order.[45] The inquisition's techniques,

---

[42]Below, ch. 8, s. 2.

[43]Below, ch. 9.

[44]Compare the analysis of social class among Cathar adherents below (pp. 114–19) and among the Waldensians (pp. 158–61). There were few clergy among the Cathars, and hardly any of high rank. From the later thirteenth century Waldensianism is pre-eminently the religion of the small man.

[45]Below, ch. 12.

directed by the papacy and higher churchmen, could and did make heresy where none existed, imposing beliefs on victims who did not hold them, or, through interrogations under torture, exaggerating and distorting the unorthodox views they in fact held. So some disquieting features in lay mysticism and the views of a few deviant individuals, handled with prejudice, were blown up into the supposed heresy of the Free Spirit in the early fourteenth century.[46]

How these new heresies came into existence or were artificially created will be discussed after an analysis of the position of the Cathars and Waldensians.

[46]Below, ch. 11, s. 2.

8

The Cathars[1]

Catharism appeared to be the most powerful heresy of the thirteenth century. Reaction against it by leading churchmen helped to change patterns of Church life. More than any other group, the Cathar heretics inspired alarm and hostility, and they stimulated the development of the inquisition; not only bishops, but also popular movements that were themselves under suspicion, the Waldensians and the Humiliati, felt the need to check their influence. A description has already been given of the factors in twelfth-century popular religion that favoured Cathar proselytism, and of the means whereby Bogomil missionaries, who had been unable to make a lasting impact in the West in the eleventh century, found a platform for spreading their beliefs in the twelfth, blending their ascetic life with an existing movement for wandering preaching in poverty. A narrative account of twelfth century heresy has described, in effect, the external reasons for the growth of the heresy of Catharism. It should now be balanced by an analytic account, intended to examine more closely internal reasons for its success, taking evidence without strict attention to chronology from varying points in time after the end of the first missionary phase in the early 1160s. Italy and Languedoc will be the prime sources for examples, since they were the regions where Catharism was most strongly established and where evidence is readily available; though it should not be forgotten that Cathars were apparently well represented in Germany until the persecutions there of the second and third decades of the thirteenth century.

1 The Appeal of Catharism.

The Status of the 'Perfect' and the Rites of the Sect.

Any attempt to explain the attractions of Catharism must take the 'perfect' as

[1]The authoritative survey is Borst, *Katharer*, with historiography to 1950, pp. 1–58 (reviews by H. Grundmann *HZ*, CLIII (1955) pp. 541–6), E. Dupré Theseider (*RSI*, LXVII (1955), pp. 574–81), H. Sproemberg (*DLZ*, Jhrg. 78, XII (1957), pp. 1095–1104), R. W. Emery (*Speculum* XXIX (1954), pp. 537–8), E. Werner (*Byzantinoslavica*, XVI (1955), pp. 135–44) and W. Ullmann (*JEH*, VII (1956), pp. 103–4); doctrinal analysis from standpoint of comparative religion in H. Söderberg, *La Religion des Cathares: Etudes sur le gnosticisme de la basse antiquité et du Moyen Âge* (Uppsala, 1949) (a pioneer work, still with valuable historical references); C. Schmidt, *Histoire et Doctrine de la Secte des Cathares ou Albigeois*, I–II (Paris 1849); bibliography to 1963 in Grundmann, *Ketzergeschichte*, pp. 22–8; speculative survey in Manselli, *Eresia*; many documents (badly edited) in Döllinger, *Beiträge*, II, translations from good texts in *WEH*, with analysis (the best single achievement of the book), summary, pp. 41–50; for relationship to Bogomils, cf. Puech-Vaillant, *Traité* and ch. 2 above; for Balkan dualism generally, see A. Schmaus, 'Der Neumanichäismus auf dem Balkan', *Saeculum*, II (1951), pp. 271–99. For Loos, *Dualist Heresy* (not available at the time of writing), see above, p. 10, n. 11.

a central theme. Numerically, these men and women, the adepts, were a small élite. Although in the time of prosperity for the Cathars in parts of Languedoc, when whole families became deeply committed and young adolescents adopted the status, there could be quite heavy concentrations of the perfect, as for example at Mirepoix, where there were fifty houses of them,[2] it was still true that the perfect were few in comparison with the other classes of adherents, the believers and the more loosely attached sympathizers. On this small body of the perfect in normal health the drawing power of the movement depended and, when they fell both in numbers and in calibre, it was doomed.

Entry to the status was conferred by the ceremony known as the *consolamentum*,[3] which derived from the rite whereby the Bogomils admitted their adepts.[4] A first part of the ritual, the delivery of the prayer, possibly once corresponding to the *baptisma* of the Byzantine Bogomils, granted the candidate the right to say the Lord's Prayer, the rank and file supporter, being still in the domain of Satan, having no right to call his God 'Father' at all. A second part of the ritual (or separate rite),[5] corresponding to the Byzantine *teleiosis*, forgave the candidate's sins, and did away with the consequences for him or her of the fall of the angels from heaven and their imprisonment in bodies by Satan. At the Fall, it was believed, the angel that formed the soul of a man had left behind his spirit in heaven; with the *consolamentum* soul and spirit were reunited, and the soul passed out of the power of Satan.

The preliminaries to attaining the status were usually arduous. The candidate had to be approved by other perfect and have shown fitness to undertake the life by a year's probation, in which he fulfilled the fasts of the perfect on every Monday, Wednesday and Friday as well as during three penitential seasons—all on bread and water—and at all times observed the prohibition of the products of coition: meat, milk, eggs, cheese. In effect both candidate and perfect observed the dietary regime, made more rigorous by days and weeks of bread and water, of the modern vegan who declines any aid to life from the animal kingdom at all. The one exception to the rigour of this rule was the consumption of fish, which the Cathars, in common with many orthodox, believed to be the product, not of coition, but of water itself.[6] Naturally all sexual contact was forbidden and, especially in the last days of the movement, even the most harmless physical contact between man and

[2]Griffe, *Le Languedoc*, p. 150. 'usque ad quinquaginta'—a rhetorical phrase.

[3]For the *consolamentum* and other rituals, see Borst, *Katharer*, pp. 190–202, Söderberg, *Religion*, pp. 218–37, 250–6 (standpoint of comparative religion, not fully critical of individual sources); M. Cazeaux-Varagnac, 'Exposé sur la Doctrine des Cathares', *Revue de Synthèse* n.s., XXII, XXIII (1948), pp. 9–14 (underlying principles); introduction to J. Guiraud, *Cartulaire*, I (lucid and still helpful, safer to use than his hurriedly written *Histoire de l'Inquisition*, I–II (Paris 1935); on the distractions of Guiraud's career, see Y. Dossat's commemoration address (*CF*, II, pp. 275–89). Latin text of *consolamentum* in A. Dondaine, *Un Traité neo-manichéen du XIIIe Siècle: Le Liber de duobus principiis, suivi d'un Fragment de Rituel cathare* (Rome 1939), pp. 151–65; Provençal in L. Clédat, *Le Nouveau Testament traduit au XIIIe Siècle en Langue provençale, suivi d'un Rituel cathare* (Paris, 1887), pp. ix–xxvi; comparison in Dondaine, *op. cit.*, pp. 34–9 trans. with other rites in *WEH*, pp. 465–96.

[4]Above, pp. 19–22.

[5]*WEH*, pp. 465, 776, n.4.

[6]Borst, p. 184.

woman was rigorously excluded.[7] If married, a candidate had to abandon his or her partner; if not, lifelong celibacy was the rule.

Sexuality formed part of Satan's creation. The angels imprisoned were sexless; in one of the most affecting of the dualist myths they wept when they found that the bodies in which Satan had thrust them were sexually differentiated.[8]

Once having received the *consolamentum*—or, in the contemporary phrase, 'having been consoled'—the newly fledged perfect faced a lifetime of rigid observance of the precepts of his life, made more exacting than the analogous life of the most ascetic orders in Catholicism by the incongruity with Cathar theology of any device for meeting lapses, such as the Catholic confession, contrition and penance. Every month the perfect of a community or locality held a meeting for the public confession of sins amongst themselves, the *apparellamentum*;[9] but this was reserved for minor faults, such as failure to say the requisite number of *Pater Nosters,* and was an occasion for mutual encouragement in the tense battle for perfection in their way of life. It was not used for breaches of the code of abstinence which formed the backbone of Cathar morality. These all ranked the same: it was equally serious, say, to fall by eating an egg as to indulge in theft or commit a murder;[10] any breach of the code involved the sinner once more in Satan's world, and lost him the *consolamentum.* It is not quite clear what did happen in the early days to one who had lapsed. Later a form was used for re-consoling a sinner; but it was a ceremony held in private, without the presence of the mass of supporters, and it was only allowed after substantial penance.[11] Standards were long maintained. James Capelli, the Franciscan controversialist from Milan, carries conviction when he describes the short shrift given to a fornicating perfect: either he was ejected, or only re-consoled after a heavy penance.[12]

Breach of the code entailed loss of the *consolamentum* both for the sinner and for all those who had in turn been consoled by the sinning perfect. One fall could entail a chain-reaction. Sacconi comments, 'all Cathars labour under very great doubt and danger of soul.'[13] The reason was that no one could tell if a minister of the *consolamentum* had committed a secret sin. There was, in consequence, much anxious re-consoling as rumours of faults of these men reached their followers. All in all, the perfect in the heyday of Catharism walked a tightrope, carefully, even obsessively, maintaining a way of life that was intended as far as possible to eliminate outlets for the natural instincts, taking care not to eat the forbidden grease, ensuring that the proper gulf was

---

[7]Koch, *Frauenfrage,* pp. 108–9.

[8]*Interrogatio Johannis* (originally Bogomil), in R. Reitzenstein, *Die Vorgeschichte der christlichen Taufe* (Leipzig & Berlin, 1929), pp. 297–311; trans.*WEH,* pp. 458–65, at p. 460.

[9]Ibid., p. 466; Borst, pp. 199–200.

[10]Sacconni's *Summa,* ii; Dondaine, *Un Traité,* pp. 64–78, D. Kniewald, in *Rad Jugoslavenske akademije znanosti i umjetnosti,* CCLXX (1949), p. 104, ff; *WEH,* pp. 329–46, at p. 320; *MBPH,* pp. 132–45.

[11]Borst, pp. 178–96.

[12]*WEH,* pp. 301–6 (trans. and comm.), at p. 305. I have not consulted the original text (ed. D. Bazzocchi (1920) but as amended in *WEH.*

[13]Dondaine, *Un Traité,* pp. 69–70 *WEH,* pp. 329–46; at p. 336.

maintained between the sexes,[14] repeating over and over his chains of *Pater Nosters*, the prayer of the sect.

Yet this harsh way of life had its attractions. There was the sense of common endeavour among the perfect of a community. Capelli writes of the spirit which prevailed among the deacons of the sect in Italy and the Cathars who came to their hospices 'linked to each other by a bond of affection.'[15] There was, too, the appeal of being able to carry the burden; the analogy is with the monks of the Egyptian desert, competing like athletes of Christ in their austerities. There was the appeal of exclusiveness itself. Only the *consolamentum* saved; it was the sole means of escape from Satan's power. The perfect had received it, and, provided that he could maintain his footing on the tightrope and the minister who had given it to him did not lapse, he was assured of his return at death to heaven, or at least of progress on the chain of being towards it.

In the world, moreover, there were immediate compensations. The perfect, except in time of persecution, seem never to have been withdrawn from society. If he held office he was continually on the move, preaching, administering the *consolamentum*, encouraging his fellow perfect. Thinness and pallor through fasting, the black robe put on at the *consolamentum*, were the outward signs and the uniform of his state of perfection; they revealed him publicly as it were for the admiration of all. If he or she did not hold office, then a house would be their normal seat, where sympathizers would visit them, for at least as long as the time of security for the perfect lasted. Their struggle for perfection was played out against a background of public respect and adoration; even in the underground years after the inquisition had got a hold, as perfect moved about secretly, they were still sustained by the devotion of a believer class who saw in them a race of restored angels, the one tangible presence of the divine in Satan's world.

Ritual and instructions for daily living brought perfect and adherents into contact on terms which highlighted the status of the former. The *melioramentum*, the greeting to the perfect which was often the first overt sign of involvement in Catharism and which the inquisition called 'adoration', conveyed the gulf between the categories and the aspiration of the adherent to be one day consoled. It was supposed to be given on all occasions of meeting, at services, or on entry to a house of perfect. Threefold genuflections and greetings to the perfect with replies culminated in the exchange—from the adherent, 'Pray God for me, a sinner, that he may make me a good Christian and lead me to a good end', and from the perfect, 'May God be prayed that he may make you a good Christian.'[16] This had special meaning; to be a good Christian, or a Christian at all, in Cathar belief was to become a perfect. To come to a good end was to die in possession of the *consolamentum*, not having forfeited it by lapse. In the exchange and the genuflection perfect and adherent reminded each other of their status, the one waiting, not yet freed from Satan, the other outside his power, in a unique position.

[14]Manselli, *Eresia*, pp. 226–31.

[15]*WEH*, p. 303.

[16]Borst, p. 198 and refs. given. I follow Borst's version; compare the exchange in Bernard Gui, *Manuel de l'Inquisiteur*, ed. G. Mollat, 1 (Paris, 1926), p. 20.

The breaking of bread, the ceremony preceding a meal, again gave the key-role to the perfect. The senior present held bread, wrapped in a white cloth, while the *Pater Noster* was said, blessed it and distributed it to all. Variously explained as an allegory recalling the supersubstantial bread of the Cathar version of the *Pater Noster* or as an imitation of the Catholic *eulogia*, a distribution of blessed bread, the act served to bring perfect and adherents together.[17] The bread was a reminder to the rank and file of the presence of the perfect; in times of persecution the fragments of the blessed bread were carefully preserved by adherents for later use.

Instructions for the saying of the *Pater Noster* kept the gulf between adherent and perfect. The Provençal ritual, one of the two texts of their ceremonies to emanate from the Cathars, refuses all place to the rank and file adherent: 'The office . . . of saying the Prayer should not be confided to a layman', it says.[18] Their role was quite passive; they would merely listen as the perfect said the *Pater Noster*. So the formal ceremonies supported the perfect in his way of life: entry to the status was hard, and preserving it inviolate harder still; but the consciousness of a unique position in mankind, reinforced by the attention of the outer supporters of his sect, would often hold him to his austerities.

The appeal of the position of an adherent in the sect was of a quite different type. The great majority of the ordinary sympathizers would never go forward to receive the *consolamentum* in full health and so endure the *abstinentia*, the period of probation, or the restrictions of the perfect's life, though these were features which attracted them to the sect in the first place. Their attachment to Catharism was marked by attendance at sermons and by the performance of the *melioramentum*. A little deeper attachment might involve attendance at the breaking of bread and a more active share in the maintenance of the perfect.

The status of believer was something more. It is still not clear whether a formal ceremony was needed to attain the status. The Provençal ritual speaks of a believer who has had the Prayer administered to him, and the rite which precedes the administration of the consolamentum proper is styled the ministration of the Prayer. Was the believer, the *credens* of the inquisition sources, one who had passed through special training and had the right to say the *Pater Noster* though he had not yet received the consolamentum and was not one of the perfect, or was he or she simply a heavily involved supporter of the sect?[19] In the dark days for Catharism the inquisition classed believers according to their functions: of collectors, for the expenses of the perfect, of receivers, who gave them refuge, or of the guides, for the perfect making their way over the country in secrecy.[20] The matter is not clear.

But whatever the truth of the position with regard to the believer, it is apparent that all who were not perfect, whether fringe sympathizer or committed believer, had very limited functions in the sect, and could not have

[17]Ibid., p. 201 (*eulogia*); Manselli, *Eresia*, p. 233 (allegory).

[18]*WEH*, p. 491, Clédat, *Nouveau Testament*, p. xxi.

[19]Ibid., pp. xi, xxi; *WEH*, pp. 485, 491. I am indebted to Professor W. L. Wakefield for information.

[20]Y. Dossat, 'Les Cathares d'après les documents de l'inquisition,' in *CF*, III, pp. 71–104 (the latest, concise survey), at p. 89.

more so long as they were still attached to Satan's creation. In practice they seem to have lived in no way greatly different from their orthodox contemporaries, were married, engaged in war, and worked in various ways for their living. Logically, however, Catharism had no morality for them at all so long as they remained without the *consolamentum*. From this probably sprang the assumption of most Catholic polemists that their morals were low, especially that they tended to sexual depravity and had usurers among them, who were unrestrained by Cathar teaching. No very clear evidence for this has yet been adduced. Cathars sometimes did retain wealth even as perfect, but they found few adherents amongst the leading businessmen of their time, and in Languedoc they were not active in the biggest commercial centres.[21]

All accusations of sexual depravity in the Middle Ages need to be treated with care. Like any other group whose activities were secret, Cathars tended to be the butt of accusations that meetings were occasions for orgies, even when, in the case of the perfect, it seems least probable. So, *mutatis mutandis*, with the adherents. No doubt it was logical for them, sharing Cathar beliefs, to regard any sexual activity that did not issue in procreation as at least one stage better than bringing more souls into the power of Satan through childbirth: whether in fact they acted on their assumption on this point has yet to be proved. They may well have lived like the Catholics—or better.

One action was crucial for all categories of adherents: the reception of the *consolamentum*. The Provençal ritual, a late thirteenth-century text as it stands, includes a formula for consoling the sick.[22] The ministers are to inquire how the candidate has behaved to the Church and whether he owes it money; he is to be clothed and helped to sit up in bed. The rites of the delivery of the Prayer and the laying-on of hands are there, but shortened and run together; all that the sick man or woman has to do is to make the responses and promise abstinence; the absolute minimum is to be conscious enough to say the *Pater Noster*. It became part of the art of the ministers of the sect to time the administration well, so that the candidate could speak, but death would soon follow.[23] If there was recovery, the Provençal ritual required another administration of the *consolamentum*. For the dying the austerities they promised were of little moment; the reward in escape from Satan was no less great than that of the perfect who were consoled in full health. Many more received the *consolamentum* in this way than through the ceremony reserved for those who had passed through the period of probation. The austerities of the way of life of the perfect were so great that it could never have been undertaken by the mass of the membership, and the deathbed *consolamentum* was the solution to the problem.

[21]Compare Borst, pp. 105–6, and R. W. Emery's review in *Speculum*, xxix (1954), pp. 537–8. 'Catharism in southern France ... cut across class lines. But in so far as we can identify the followers of the sect, they appear to have been rather significantly concentrated outside of the more advanced districts economically ... usurers themselves were—we must suppose—relatively hard-headed men, little likely to risk everything by identifying themselves with an outlaw and suspected group ...' (Professor Emery in a private letter). See also J. H. Mundy, *Liberty and Political Power in Toulouse, 1050–1230* (New York, 1954) (the standard account). For sexual accusations, see Wakefield in *WEH*, pp. 46–7; Manselli, *Eresia*, p. 201; cp. Borst, *Katharer*, pp. 180–3 On sexual morality of perfect, see below, p. 131.

[22]Clédat, *Nouveau Testament*, pp. xxii–xxvi; *WEH*, pp. 492–4.

[23]Dossat, in *CF*, iii, p. 83.

E

The Social Context

Certain social factors intertwined with the religious influences to keep the élite in being and to draw in sympathizers. These can most easily be studied in Languedoc because there a systematic investigation by the inquisition from the fourth decade of the thirteenth century onwards elicited series of confessions[24] from most of the key affected areas which go right back to the decades before the Albigensian Crusade when the heresy settled in. Italy is more problematical because really effective action by the inquisition came so much later in most cities, and thus the evidence does not relate in the same way to the time of the implanting of heresy in the last thirty years of the twelfth century. Moreover, the history of heresy in Italy tends to be more disparate. Each city has its own story.[25] Nevertheless, certain generalizations emerge for Italy and may be used as points of contrast.

In Languedoc favour by the rural nobility provided the matrix for Catharism. In the first generation of the implantation period men were more often the patrons, while their womenfolk seem to have been drawn towards the position of perfect in rather larger numbers. In the Niort family,[26] for example, the men began as patrons, and took to the *consolamentum* only in the course of the thirteenth century. A comparatively small number of supporters and actual perfect high in the social categories gave prestige to the movement; lesser nobility were thickly involved, and all classes participated. Certain areas of the countryside were most heavily affected but there was no gulf between town and country and movements of population carried heresy from one to the other and vice versa. Family influence is the most important single social factor, and here the initial impact of the Cathar missionaries on women in the *castra* of the countryside was decisive. Inquisition records build up a vivid picture of houses of women perfect, often only with a mere handful of inmates, but densely distributed across the affected regions in many of the villages where candidates for the *consolamentum* were trained, sermons were delivered to any of the locality who were willing to hear and common meals were held. From them the deacons and officers of the sect went out on their pastoral duties. A widow might receive the *consolamentum* and then be joined by others in her own house, which thus became a natural centre for the sect, or a single woman might be aided by her family; in other cases women left their husbands to undergo the probation. A good example of a noble lady setting up as a perfect is the case of Blanche de Laurac, whose husband Sicard had been one of the major figures in the rural nobility.[27] She received the *consolamentum*, and made her home a house of perfect; one boy and four daughters were brought up in heresy, three daughters marrying and thus diffusing Catharism at the adherents' level; another became a perfect and the son, after first

---

[24]Esp. used by E. Griffe, *Le Languedoc cathare de 1190 à 1210* (Paris, 1971). See also M. Roquebert, *L'Épopée cathare, 1198–1212: l'Invasion* (Toulouse, 1970); earlier summary by C. P. Bru, 'Éléments pour une Interpretation sociologique du Catharisme occitan', in *Spiritualité de l'Hérésie: le Catharisme*, ed. R. Nelli (Paris, 1953), pp. 23–59.

[25]E. Dupré Theseider, 'Gli Eretici nel Mondo Comunale Italiano', *BSSV*, LXXIII (1963) pp. 3–23.

[26]W. L. Wakefield, 'The Family of Niort in the Albigensian Crusade and before the Inquisition', *Names*, XVIII (1970), pp. 97–117, 286–303.

[27]Griffe, *Languedoc*, pp. 109–13; Roquebert, *Épopée*, p. 114.

supporting Simon de Montfort, went to defend his sister at Lavaur and was hanged for breaking faith with the crusaders. Blanche's grandson remembered living with her and eating bread blessed by the perfect. In about the year 1200 almost all the population of Laurac turned out to hear preaching and give the *melioramentum* to the perfect.

Houses of men perfect were formed in the same way, as in the case of the knight Pierre Raymond de Cuq, who was consoled in his house at Auriac and lived there with other men perfect.[28] But, although the houses for men were also of some importance, one may suspect that the quiet diffusion and implanting of heresy in families was naturally a woman's work, and that men perfect played their most effective role as the mobile ministers of the sect, bishops, bishops' auxiliaries, deacons, preaching, visiting, administering the *consolamentum* and, above all, calling on the dying to administer their *consolamentum*, which came to take the place of the Catholic extreme unction.[29] A territorial basis existed for their organization. Bishops took titles in an impudent imitation of Catholicism, but in Languedoc resided at rural places where they were sure of the protection of the local nobility, and not in the towns of their title. The *filius maior* and the *filius minor* were vicars of the bishops, and succeeded them at their deaths; Deacons had their spheres of influence and regular residences. But all these ministers must often have been on the move.

Noble or humble, a perfect lived cheaply, for the way of life demanded so little expenditure. But whereas the noble woman could live on her own money, together with gifts of adherents or family, those lower in society had to work, and so some houses of perfect engaged in cottage industry or trade: at Mirepoix they had a shoemaker's shop, at Les Cassès and Montmaur they made shirts and footwear.[30] Heretical influence was then diffused at the place of work or, as in the case of Pierre de Gramazie, who went to work in his childhood in workshops owned by the heretics at Fanjeaux, imbibed with apprenticeship.[31]

The influence of heretics on children helped to make Catharism part of the background of life; Bernard Mir remembered as a child going in to a house of perfect at Saint-Martin-la-Lande and being given nuts to eat and taught to bend his knees to ask for a blessing, so being trained in the *melioramentum*.[32] Hospitality made contacts. At Puylaurens the mother of Sicard de Puylaurens lived with two of her sisters and another noble lady, all perfect, and men and women came and ate fruit from their hands. Families tolerated widely different views. In the Arrufat family at Castelnaudary the head of the household left his wife free to welcome both Cathars and Waldensians. Pelfort de Rabastens, lord of the settlement there, had a mother and sister who had been consoled. A witness described the easy contact between the family and its heretical members, as Pelfort's wife visited the heretic ladies; yet the same

[28]Griffe, p. 99.

[29]Dossat, in *CF*, ii pp. 71–104; correcting and supplementing Guiraud. *Inquisition*, esp. i, ch. 7.

[30]Griffe, p. 189. For example at Cordes, see Koch, *Frauenfrage*, p. 18n., correcting Grundmann in *Relazioni*, iii p. 399n, Schmidt, *Histoire*, i, p. 289.

[31]Griffe, p. 189.

[32]Ibid, pp. 125–6 and foll. refs; p. 95 (Puylaurens), pp. 122–3 (Castelnaudary), pp. 65–8 (Rabastens).

noble house produced Raymond de Rabastens, archdeacon of Agen and, briefly, bishop of Toulouse.

In a few places Cathar influence reached a peak. At Cambiac, for example, the curé complained that he considered all his parishioners bar four to be Cathar believers,[33] at Caraman, Lanta and Verfeil about 1215 few died without the *consolamentum*, although as well as the heavily affected villages there were others where Cathars were a minority. The perfect often enough occupied in practice the position of the Roman clergy, being exempt from certain impositions and receiving goods at the death of their faithful. The creation of an atmosphere in which adherence to heresy was nothing abnormal, in which custom reinforced devotion, was a considerable achievement, and its effects were long lasting.

We may ask how far non-religious factors were at work in producing this result. Koch, the East German Marxist historian, puts his finger on one factor when he describes the social and economic forces influencing the women in Languedoc. The houses of women perfect, Koch points out, occupied the place of beguinages elsewhere in western Europe, providing outlets more cheaply than nunneries for widows and other surplus women.[34] Poor girls were left with perfect women. Jordan of Saxony, the Dominican, complained of the way in which parents put daughters into these houses of perfect to be supported— and so, inevitably, to be drawn into heresy. For the nobility, Roman laws of inheritance gave a place to women that they did not have in many other parts of Europe, and so made it easier for widows and heiresses to set up houses of the perfect. The life of the perfect might give meaning to the surplus woman's existence, just because of its rigid duties of prayer and fasting; so might the use of her residence as a focus for missionary work and hospitality.

In ritual and status, Catharism offered certain advantages to women not to be found in Catholicism. No position in Catholicism, not even that of abbess, offered the status which accrued to a woman who received the *consolamentum*. The woman perfect, no less than the man, possessed the spirit. If she was debarred by her sex from holding office and could never be deacon or bishop, she took precedence in any gathering over all supporters who were not perfect, whether man or woman. If no man perfect was present, she would lead the prayers. She was entitled to the *melioramentum* from all. It would seem that members of the nobility tended to avoid giving it to a woman, but no doubt those lower in the social scale did not.[35]

Sometimes a religious passion is the only possible explanation for a woman maintaing the perfect's life, as in the case of Furneria, wife of Guillaume-Roger de Mirepoix, who apparently left her husband to live in a house of perfect women, went to Lavelanet, returned to take her daughter away, induced her to be consoled and finally fled before the crusaders to the fortress at Montségur.[36]

---

[33]Ibid., p. 91, and following refs, (Caraman, Lanta, Verfeil). On numbers, see Wakefield, *Heresy, Inquisition*, pp. 68–70.

[34]*Frauenfrage*, chs 1, 3; comments on motives, pp. 14, 31; following refs, Jordan of Saxony, p. 28 (see *Libellus de principiis ordinis praedicatorum* in *MOPH*, xvi (Rome, 1935), p. 39); ritual, *Frauenfrage*, ch. 7.

[35]Comment of Professor W. L. Wakefield, in conversation.

[36]Griffe, pp. 148–9.

In Italy family links seem to have been of lesser importance, though all our early generalizations are weakened by a lack of broad-based evidence for the years of initial infiltration. Certainly there Catharism had a less firmly territorial base. Whereas in Languedoc the historian can draw a line on the map—say from Marmande in the Agenais in the north down to the foothills of the Pyrenees in the south, and from Toulouse in the west to Béziers in the east—and be sure that he has included much the greatest part of the heretical activity in the Midi, and that all the heaviest concentrations within the outline are directly contiguous to each other,[37] in Italy Catharism had its supporters scattered in a multitude of cities, especially Milan, Piacenza, Cremona, Brescia, Bergamo, Vicenza, Verona, Ferrara, Rimini, Florence and Orvieto, in the countryside and along the routes which led from southern France to Lombardy.[38] Bishops, deacons and supporters kept in touch with each other through the network of communications established in the developed areas in the north and centre where Catharism largely settled, but the nexus was, in geographical terms, much looser than in Languedoc. Bishoprics, which in Languedoc were delimited territorially, in Italy generally were not. Instead, the dividing lines were differences of belief, which sprang out of Italian contentiousness and ingenuity and the greater proximity of Italy to the cradles of dualism in the East.[39] Personalities counted for more, and disputes were exacerbated by them. Bishops and deacons ruled adherents scattered over sprawling territories, with duplicate organizations at enmity with each other exercising oversight in the same cities.

Mobility was a keynote of the lives of many of those involved in Catharism, more so in Italy than in Languedoc. The merchant class, of greater weight because of the Italian economic development, was of its nature given to travel. Catharism had a hold amongst them and, to judge by the statistics of the goods confiscated by the inquisition in the course of the thirteenth century, some wealthy individuals were found among them.[40] Many of the lesser men in the sect, the artisans and pedlars, were also forced to travel by the nature of their occupation, and weavers and other cloth and leather workers were often enough footloose people.[41] Dupré Theseider has uncovered significant links in the late thirteenth century between Catharism and the trade of pursemaking at Bologna.[42] The workers travelled from house to house and town to town making and selling their wares and at the same time making heretical contacts. Inns, workshops and mills were casual meeting places for supporters. At Modena certain mills were known in the late twelfth century as 'the mills of the Patarenes' (which by this time meant Cathars).[43] In other cases certain houses were known to be safe refuges for perfect who travelled about on their pastoral duties. Armanno Pungilupo of

[37]Ibid., pp. 18–22.

[38]Dupré Theseider, in *BSSV*, LXXXIII (1963), p. 11.

[39]Below, pp. 126–33.

[40]Dupré Theseider, *BSSV*, loc. cit. p. 17n.

[41]C. Violante 'Hérésies urbaines et Hérésies rurales en Italie du 11ᵉ au 13ᵉ Siècle', in *HS*, pp. 171–98, s. 3.

[42]L'Eresia a Bologna nei Tempi di Dante', in *Studi storici in onore di G. Volpe* (Firenze, 1958), I, pp. 383–444.

[43]Dupré Theseider, in *BSSV*, (loc. cit.) p. 16; L. A. Muratori, *Antiquitates Italicae Medii Aevi*, v, pp. 86–7.

Ferrara said that signs were used which made it possible to recognize houses of the Cathars.[44] Evidence given to the inquisitors provides us with glimpses of the blend of family influence and upbringing, casual contact and proselytism in which heresy existed, much on the lines of Languedoc. In Ferrara, for example, a maker of sacks had brought up his son and daughter to be supporters of the sect; they received instructions at home and in a neighbouring house, and were visited by a number of perfect. Aristocratic dwellings in the *contado* of various cities formed safe hiding-places for leading Cathars under pressure in the cities.

Aristocratic patronage was important—the support, based on hostility to the Church, of Ezzelino da Romano and the marquis Oberto Pelavicino, for example, was of great value for the spread of Catharism in the regions of the March of Treviso and the Po valley that they controlled[45]—and developed into deeper involvement in a number of cases, such as those of Stefano Confalonieri in Milan,[46] Conrado da Venosta in the Valtellina,[47] and the Uberti of Florence.[48] But the carrying class, as it were, of Italian Catharism seems to have been the artisans and lesser traders. Two modern authorities, Violante and Dupré Theseider, concur in this generalization. Although Cathars did exist among the major bourgeoisie, by and large the leading businessmen tended, as in Languedoc, to be conventional in religion. Members of the *arti minori*, minor commercial operators and artisans, were those most persuaded by Catharism, and the reserve areas of support in the cities seem to have been the suburban areas between the old walls and the new ring, built to accommodate the population growth of the twelfth and thirteenth centuries.[49] Here the Humiliati and the friars installed themselves, and here, above all, the battle was fought out between heresy and orthodoxy in the thirteenth century.[50] The most insecure and dependent were not members in any great numbers; both perfect and adherent tend to be those who had at least a small competence. The unskilled labourers and the flotsam and jetsam of the cities were not numerically significant. Nor were peasants. Whereas in Languedoc the peasants were early drawn in, albeit in small numbers, by the patronage of the rural nobility, and then became more and more important later in the history of the sect, in Italy this class was missing from the membership, or from the records, throughout.[51]

The sect had limited intellectual appeal: it could capture the half-educated and have some attraction for those of some general culture, but not for those with any theological education. So we will not expect to find learned

[44]Violante, in *HS*, p. 186. (see also foll. ref. to Ferrara).

[45]Guiraud, *Inquisition*, II, pp. 447–51, 472–3, 534–8, 543, 545–50.

[46]For the organizer of the plot against St Peter Martyr, see Guiraud, *Inquisition*, II, pp. 496–8, 542–3, and Violante, in *HS*, p. 181 (note survey of Catharism in cities, pp. 179–84).

[47]Ibid., p. 181; see Manselli, 'Les Hérétiques dans la Société italienne du 13ᵉ Siècle', in *HS*, pp. 199–202.

[48]See J. N. Stephens, 'Heresy in Medieval and Renaissance Florence', *PP* LIV (1972), pp. 25–60.

[49]Violante, in *HS*, p. 184.

[50]A. V. Murray, 'Piety and Impiety in Thirteenth-century Italy', in *SCH*, VIII, pp. 83–106; at p. 86.

[51]Violante, in *HS*, pp. 184–5. Materials for class analysis with exposition, brilliantly precise but schematic, on the history of the Cathars, in Borst, *Katharer*.

members of the clergy or those of university background. There seems to have been some particular appeal for notaries and physicians[52]—men of skill, but not well based in theology. This is as high an intellectual calibre of adherent as one would expect Catharism to attract.

One may ask how far it was the status of the perfect which appealed to the artisan and to those of lower class generally. The Cathar conception of perfection, attained through a set of tangible measures of abstinence and by repetition of prayers, appealed to the individual's sense of achievement.[53] Ascetic life was not, as in an informed Catholicism, a means to perfection; it was the sole means of salvation. The Cathar teacher could say without reserve to his neophyte, 'Do this; receive the *consolamentum* and you will be saved.' It was a part of the strength of the movement's appeal. How far did the rise in status, achieved by the individual's own efforts at self-mortification, entitling him to the *melioramentum* from members of all social classes and to a veneration from all adherents, appeal to those whose occupation kept them low in the social scale? Was this a factor which helped to hold to the way of life the apostles of Cathar Italy, Mark the gravedigger and his humble companions?

Teaching

In all areas methods of missioning followed the pattern of the Bogomils: there was a pedagogic progression from the generalities, which seemed to blend easily into the contemporary religious environment, to the inner mysteries, reserved for the perfect or for believers of long standing.[54] The approach, natural to all sects influenced by Gnosticism, had the effect of concealing the profoundly heretical nature of Catharism from the neophyte until he was sufficiently detached from the influence of orthodox belief.

Much proselytism was done informally, and in this all the perfect and believers played their part. Formal preaching, whether in houses, on ritual occasions or in the days of prosperity openly in public places in Italian cities and the villages of Languedoc, was more commonly a duty of those who held office in the sect.

But because of the overriding importance of the class of the perfect, from whose number alone the officers could be chosen, no duty was ever reserved entirely to these officers, and rank and file perfect sometimes preached— women among them, though never so much as Waldensian women preachers—their most likely audience being a gathering of adherents, not other perfect.

The nature of these sermons can be gleaned from chronicle and other accounts, from extant Cathar treatises, and to some extent from the texts of the rituals. Two principal objectives in the open preaching seem to have been to detach casual sympathizers from the influence of the Church, by playing on the sins of the clergy in contrast to the standards set down for Christian living in the gospels and epistles, and by using a particular Cathar exegesis of Scripture, together with unwelcome natural phenomena, to inculcate the belief that the visible world was evil; thunder, earthquakes, the existence of

[52]Ibid., p.125 and refs.
[53]E. Werner, reviewing Borst, in *Byzantinoslavica*, XVI (1955), pp. 135–44.
[54]Manselli, *Eresia*, pp. 223–31.

worms, toads and fleas, for example, were cited to show that the world could not have been the work of a good God.[55] Many of the world-renouncing texts of Scripture were pressed into service to show how the teaching of Christ and his apostles rejected material things. No attention was paid to the rules of exegesis: texts were wrenched out of context, and no hint was given of the precise meaning of 'the world' to the New Testament writers.[56] But the audience for a Cathar sermon would not be familiar with the rules of exegesis, and they would hear what would seem to them an exhortation by good men based on the words of the founder of Christianity and of his followers. Preaching was heavily larded with texts—at least, this seems a fair inference from the surviving Cathar treatises, a good part of which consist of Scriptural references and quotations.[57]

Much Cathar exhortation was, of itself, wholly orthodox and dwelt on the need for patience under persecution, a moral life and fidelity to Christ. Outwardly, the perfect were not readily to be distinguished from good monks or nuns. In a *cause célèbre* which dragged on until 1301 Armanno Pungilupo, of ascetic reputation, who had been buried with honour in the cathedral of Ferrara in 1269, was finally proved to have been guilty of heresy and posthumously condemned.[58] Near Toulouse in 1234 when an old woman near her end desired the *consolamentum* the Catholic bishop got wind of it: he came in and spoke to her of the contempt of the world and of earthly things. Hearing him, she believed he was a Cathar, and confessed her heresy. The bishop had her burned.[59]

At a number of points orthodoxy and Catharism converged, and the likenesses readily deceived the unwary. Some dualist teaching on Satan would have sounded like Catholic doctrine. The *consolamentum* administered to the dying must have seemed like Catholic extreme unction. In orthodoxy, it was not unusual for a dying man to be carried to a monastery before his end, and there take the habit: the practice of taking the dying to a house of perfect, which occurred in Languedoc, would have appeared much the same. The language of orthodox ascetic writers, discussing the nature of the world or the inferiority of the female sex, often came quite close to dualism. Even the practice of the perfect of saying chains of *Pater Nosters* was not unknown to thirteenth-century piety. The perfect honestly thought that they were the only true Christians, that the clergy were servants of Satan's Church; and that Cathar teaching presented a stream of pure underground Christianity, often persecuted, but always surviving and reaching back to the days of the

---

[55]Manselli, in *CF*, III, p. 169.

[56]See, e.g. C. Thouzellier, *Un Traité cathare inédit du Début du XIIIe Siècle d'après le Liber contra Manicheos de Durand de Huesca*, (Louvain, 1961), (reviewed by E. Delaruelle in *RHE* LX (1965), pp. 524–8), pp. 90–5, *WEH*, pp. 498–500.

[57](i) Thouzellier, *Traité*; (ii) *Liber de duobus principiis*; first ed. in Dondaine, *Un Traité*; latest ed., intro., trans., in Thouzellier, *Livre des deux Principes*, (Paris, 1973), earlier analysed by Borst (pp. 254–318). Partial trans. of Dondaine text in *WEH*, pp. 511–91; (iii) *A Vindication of the Church of God* and a separate gloss on the *Pater Noster* in T. Venckeleer, 'Un Recueil cathare: Le manuscrit A.6.10 de la Collection vaudoise de Dublin, I: une Apologie; II: une Glose sur le Pater', *RBPH* XXXVIII (1960), pp. 820–31; XXXIX (1961), pp. 762–85, trans. *WEH*, pp. 592–606.

[58]Guiraud, *Inquisition*, II, pp. 587–90.

[59]Dossat, in *CF*, III, pp. 101–2.

Apostles.[60] By a strange chance the rite of the *consolamentum* that appears in the thirteenth-century texts does seem to have been based on a rite for baptism and on practices connected with the catechumenate much earlier than the contemporary Catholic rites of baptism or ordination.[61] The adherent who witnessed these ceremonies was exposed to much that was wholly edifying and orthodox. Little wonder that many in the days of the growth of the sect were deceived.

One other element in proselytism is at first sight surprising in a sect whose inner mysteries made considerable demands on the credulity of followers. This was the appeal to raw scepticism. We have seen this in action in the Rhineland, where Cathars appealed to materialist arguments to deny orthodox views of the mass.[62] Heresy did not create this scepticism, which was of spontaneous growth,[63] but it latched on to it to deny this or that doctrine or practice of the Church. Catharism benefited from doubts cast on the validity of the Church's teaching, just as Bogomilism had done.

Introduction to the hidden revelation of Catharism came after the neophyte had received a grounding in dualism, and through rites and practices had had impressed upon him the vital importance of the *consolamentum*. The period of *abstinentia* before receiving the *consolamentum* was also a period of instruction when, if not earlier, the candidate was given more specific information on positive beliefs of the sect and acquainted with their mythology. Doctrines held in the inner circle of the perfect were sometimes denied altogether, as in the response of two perfect to Bernard de Montesquieu of Puylaurens in 1273, who was told, contrary to fact, that they did not believe that the devil created man's body.[64] For most candidates, entry on the *abstinentia* would have brought an end to this concealment: they could then feel the attractions of the secret revelation, placed, they would believe, in the position of the Apostles, to whom Christ had said, 'it is given unto you to know the mysteries of the kingdom of heaven'[65].

These secrets were concerned pre-eminently with finding explanations for the presence of good in a world which the neophyte had already been taught to regard as evil. How had the soul, which was the work of a good God, found its way into a body created by Satan? Many of the answers given by teachers in the sect followed, with variations, the pattern of the Bogomils.[66] Satan was a good angel, or a son of God, who fell and carried other angels with him, then created the visible world and with it bodies into which he beguiled the fallen angels.

A second set of explanations, however was based on quite different

[60]Dondaine, *Un Traité*, p. 159, ll. 22–4; *WEH* p. 477.

[61]Guiraud, *Cartulaire*, I, pp. clxii–clxv; *Inquisition*, I, ch. 4.

[62]Above, p. 63.

[63]For the thirteenth century, see Murray, in *SCH* VIII, pp. 83–106; note case cited by Dossat in *CF*, III, p. 78. I have benefitted from conversation with Professor W. L. Wakefield on this point and from his unpublished article on records of an inquisition held at Toulouse 1270–3, with evidence of spontaneous scepticism. Compare English Lollardy (below, pp. 266, 268–9).

[64]Dossat, in *CF*, III, p. 38.

[65]Matt. 13.11.

[66]Borst, pp. 143–56; myths discussed in Söderberg, *Religion*; R. Manselli, 'Églises et Théologies cathares' in *CF*, III, pp. 129–76 (sketch with psychological insight).

E*

assumptions: that there was an evil God, co-eternal and of equal powers with the good God, and that the Fall and imprisonment of the angels in bodies was caused by an invasion of heaven, which captured good angels and imprisoned them in bodies of the evil creation against their will. In this version the evil principle and his creation would never come to an end, although the good angels would be released from their prison; in the older Bogomil version, as in orthodoxy, Satan in the end was subject to the power of God; his evil creation would in the Last Days be consumed. The crucial difference between these views—the first moderate dualist, the second radical dualist—lay in the status of evil: did it originate with a fallen spirit or an eternal evil principle? Both views evolved in Balkan and Byzantine dualism, and were then transferred to Western soil. The first was the dualism described in Bulgaria by Cosmas the Priest and, with variations, in Byzantium by Euthymius of Peribleptos and Zigabenus;[67] the exact origins of the second view are still obscure, and all that we know with certainty is that it was brought into the West from Constantinople by Nicetas, the most influential of medieval dualist missionaries, in the late 1160s or a little afterwards.

Despite their profound differences, both views rested on the same conviction of the utter incompatibility of the body and soul. Both set the struggle between matter and spirit, good and evil, on which the candidate for the *consolamentum* was already engaged, within a cosmic frame. Belief in the truth of Cathar teaching rested on personal experience of this struggle, and the exemplification of it in the perfect; the myths came to add colour and literary force, to give a sense of space to the daily struggle of the candidate or perfect, and to provide fantastic narratives for the adherents.

The Stories

The raw material for the stories about the Fall and its consequences derived from a mixture of Scriptural reminiscence, names and anecdotes, with much apocryphal matter, part from Jewish apocalyptic literature, part from ancient extra-canonical Christian legends still circulating in the Middle Ages, combined with the sheer imaginative power of certain teachers. Legendary material played a considerable part in medieval popular religion; thus the use of apocryphal material was nothing strange in itself. Scriptural fragments, incorporated arbitrarily to authenticate the stories, maintained contact with the central Christian tradition. The Apocalypse was a storehouse of images; the story of war in heaven and the fall of Satan[68] was familiar in the orthodox tradition. The teacher embroidered further on these themes with a dualistic bias. One direct importation was the *Interrogation of John*, or Secret Supper, brought from the Bogomils in Bulgaria who composed it by Nazarius, bishop of the Italian church of Concorezzo, about 1190.[69]

What the stories have in common, whether exemplifying moderate or radical dualism, is literary force, a tendency to gross materialization, an interest in sexual themes, and a strong vein of fantasy. The *Interrogation of John*, describing how Satan solved the problem of inducing Adam and Eve, angels imprisoned in clay bodies, to have sexual intercourse, depicts him planting a

[67]Above, pp. 13–22.
[68]Rev. 12. 7–9.
[69]Reitzenstein, *Vorgeschichte*, p. 293; *WEH*, p. 465.

bed of reeds in Paradise, making a serpent of his own saliva, then entering the serpent and emerging from the reeds to have intercourse with Eve with its tail.[70] The story echoes part of the narrative of Genesis, but embellishes it with some powerful carnal imagery.

The same literary quality and free play of storytelling emerges from stories of the Fall current in a last phase of Catharism in Languedoc. In these[71] Satan stood outside the gate of heaven for thirty-two years hoping to entice the good angels; once inside, he tempted them with the greater joys he said he had to offer in his own kingdom, including a most beautiful woman. Curious to see a woman, something quite unknown to them, the angels fell into Satan's trap, were inflamed with lust, and in crowds followed him out of heaven, until God closed the gap through which they fell. Satan then created a heaven of glass for them; but God broke it and the angels found themselves despoiled of their splendour, and deceived. They repented, and sang songs of Sion; to take away memories of their past, Satan shut them up in human bodies.

In some accounts the battle between Satan and his seduced angels and the forces of the good God in heaven took pride of place;[72] there were vivid descriptions of the flow of blood, the destruction of the seduced angels' bodies, and the fall of their souls from heaven. The sufferings of the children of Israel in Psalm 78 were taken as an allegory of this battle.

Sometimes a wild fantasy takes charge, as in the explanation, cited by St Peter Martyr and probably derived from an Italian group, of the Cathar prohibition of flesh-eating.[73] Beasts and birds, it was said, were of human flesh—the foetuses of pregnant women which fell from heaven onto the earth after they had miscarried during the battle between the forces of God and Satan. The prohibition of eating their flesh thus amounted to a prohibition of cannibalism.

Together with the stories of the Fall in all their variations, there was a vision of heaven not substantially different from that of orthodox popular religion, but sharpened by the utter contrast in dualist belief between earth and the heaven of the good. We have an example of its consolatory power in the case of a perfect from Languedoc related by a witness before the inquisition at Pamiers in 1321, who had been troubled by doubts about Catharism, and was rewarded by a vision, in which he mounted on the shoulder of an angel through the seven heavens to the presence of the Father, who asked him whence he had come. 'From the land of tribulations', was the answer. He wanted to stay, but the Father told him that he could not do so, 'since flesh born of corruption could not remain there', but must descend to the land of tribulations and preach the faith. The vision was of a southerner's heaven. He saw 'great brilliance, many angels, beautiful groves and singing birds . . . most moderate temperatures.'[74] The model for his journey through the

[70]Reitzenstein, *Vorgeschichte*, pp. 301–2; *WEH*, p. 460.

[71]Summary by Söderberg, *Religion*, p. 73, based on versions as related to inquisition by Döllinger (*Beiträge*, II, pp. 149–51, 173, 176, 186, 203–5, 213–5, etc.).

[72]Borst, pp. 145–6.

[73]T. Kaeppeli, 'Une Somme contre les Hérétiques de S. Pierre Martyr(?)' *AFP*, XVII (1947), pp. 295–335; at p. 330; Manselli, *Eresia*, pp. 226–7.

[74]Döllinger, *Beiträge*, II, pp. 166–7; *WEH*, pp. 456–8. See Vaillant, in *RES*, XLII (1963), pp. 109–21.

heavens was an *apocryphon* of the early Christian centuries, the *Vision of Isaiah*, much used by the Bogomils. Such images were an especial aid in persecution, which was made more tolerable by the certainty of entry to heaven, provided only that a valid *consolamentum* was retained.

The stories obviously played a major role in Catharism, for members of the sect devoted much attention to retailing them and weaving new ones out of the mass of available material; a kaleidoscope of these poetic narratives, continuously developing through the history of the sect, has been bequeathed to us. Variations are accounted for by the different nuances of dualism, stretching all the way from the frail Satan of the Bulgarian *apocryphon*, the *Interrogation of John* (which influenced the moderates), powerless to act except at the will of the Father,[75] to the eternal evil principle of the Italian teacher John of Lugio.[76] Adjustments in the stories met the needs of different schools of dualism, developed within the Cathar movement by leading personalities.

Flexibility of myth was also a consequence of the sovereign power of the perfect in the field of religious belief. Inventiveness in the teacher was apparently prized. The language of the stories was that of revelation: Cathars listened to a teacher expounding mysteries that he knew, which were guaranteed by his personality and status, and which they were disposed to accept. The stories evidently met an emotional need—for legendary narrative *per se*; for an expression, it may be, of disgust with organic life registered in the sequences of coarse imagery of the stories; for a transposed sexuality, for an outlet for poetic imagination. Most simply, they met the needs of those who lacked much logical and critical sense, who were satisfied with the flimsy, partial argumentation of Cathars handling sacred texts, and who loved good stories.[77]

The liking for myths was the common possession of radical and moderate dualists alike; but radicals differed so much from all the schools of moderates that it is reasonable to assume that the attractions of Catharism were for them somewhat different, requiring a little separate treatment.[78] Radicals were dualists who were prepared to rewrite the traditional tenets of Bogomilism in order to iron out the logical contradiction they saw in the appearance of good in an evil world. Moderates, they believed, did not solve the problem of the origins of evil by their stories of the fall of Satan and his ordering of the world on the basis of an initial creation by God, but only pushed it, so to speak, one stage further back. The dilemma remained: How was evil compatible with the creation of a good God? To satisfy themselves, they postulated two creations, wholly distinct and equally eternal, and bravely followed out the consequences of their belief—two heavens, two earths, for example, or a life of Christ in another world, judgement already passed, hell identified *tout court* with this earth. There were still confusions, and all was affected by the atmosphere of uncritical myth-making characteristic of the whole movement. The pressures of Catholic teaching and polemic showed up their contradictions, and led them deeper into difficulties, especially on the nature

---

[75]Reitzenstein, *Vorgeschichte*, p. 300; *WEH*, p. 459.
[76]Below, p. 132.
[77]See Manselli's comments (*Eresia*, pp. 212–3).
[78]Borst, pp. 143–74 (fundamental), Manselli, in *CF*, iii, pp. 129–76.

of Christ.[79] But in so far as the radicals were faithful to their principles, there were important differences of psychology and belief between them and the moderates. Radicals had to be determinists. Evil is not born of an act of free will, as the moderates and the orthodox believed. Satan, no longer the officer of God who sins by pride, is the agent of the evil God who penetrates the good creation. The good angels are incapable of sin; Satan deceives or forces them.[80] If radicals still made use of the myth of the seduction of the angels, this was an illogicality, inherited from moderate Bogomilism.

The appropriate myth for the radicals is that of battle in heaven and conquest by Satan. Captured in Satan's bodies, radicals could not tell whether they were the angels conquered by Satan but bound to return to the good creation, or the devils of the evil creation who would stay below in the hell which was earthly existence; only at death would they know. Yet, as is common in such cases, this did not prevent their enthusiastic adherents from sacrificing themselves and clinging zealously to their *consolamentum*. Unconsoled, the angel trapped in the body of a sympathizer moved on in a chain of existence. Souls wandered from body to body, stretching back to humble creatures and forward to distinguished and noble men, till they arrived at a body of a perfect. If indeed the soul was an angel, then in possession of the valid *consolamentum* after death, it returned at once to the heaven of the good creation. A sympathizer, on the other hand, was in effect rewarded by a step up in the chain; he would next be incarnate in a more attractive being. So, as a stimulant, transmigration of souls had a similar function to the orthodox doctrine of purgatory; penance must yet be done, but there was ultimate hope. Cathars speculated with pleasure on their previous incarnations. In Languedoc a perfect related how he had been a horse, and conveniently found a shoe by the road that he said he had cast in his previous life.[81]

For an evil life, however, there was the penalty of slipping back on the chain to a lower creature. For the devils there was the prospect of endless punishment in different bodies as the evil God and his servant Satan imposed through sexuality their penalty of life on earth. It was a picture of stark force, more gaunt and at the same time more logical than that of the moderates.[82]

It is obvious how deeply Catharism distorted Christian belief, for all the appeal to the Scriptures, made more effective by the vernacular translations kept by the perfect, for all the Christian language of their ritual and the texts which decked their mythology. As Guiraud long ago pointed out,[83] the true affinities of the perfect lay with the ascetic teachers of the East, the bonzes and fakirs of China or India, the adepts of the Orphic mysteries, or the teachers of Gnosticism. Cathar belief, just like Bogomilism, to which it was heir, upset the structure of sacramental life in favour of one rite of supreme importance, the *consolamentum*; replaced a Christian morality by a compulsory asceticism,

---

[79]See Dondaine, intro. to *Un Traité* and extracts from John of Lugio in *WEH*, pp. 511-91; Borst, p. 122.

[80]*CF*, III, p. 147.

[81]Ibid., p. 142.

[82]Emotions best conveyed by Manselli (*CF*, III, pp. 129-76).

[83]*Cartulaire*, I, pp. ccxxii-ccxxiii.

which made faults consist rather in a soiling by matter than an act of will;[84] eliminated redemption by refusing to admit the saving power of the Crucifixion; and rejected the Trinity in favour of a subordination of two persons to the Father. Cathars could not admit that Christ was God—an angel, perhaps, or a son of God, but still not equal with the Father. Nor could they logically admit that he was man, with a body like that of other men. So the hinge of Christian belief, the Incarnation, was destroyed. Radical dualism went still further in its destruction of the pillars of Christian belief, and can hardly be regarded even as extreme Christian heresy. With its belief in two gods and two creations, it might almost be described as another religion altogether.

Yet these distortions of Christian belief would not necessarily repel the uninstructed Catholics, who largely formed the audiences of heretical preachers; the divergences from orthodoxy in all probability would not be apparent to them. The positive drawing power of the heresy lay above all in the life of the perfect and the status of the *consolamentum*; we have seen how the allure of these two drew sympathizers into the heresy or, less reputably, kept them in a kind of vacuum waiting for a death-bed *consolamentum*, and how the social context in Languedoc and Italy supported an heretical church organization. Dogmatic instruction followed on a process of assimilation of the sympathizer to the heretic's way of life, which excited his zeal and interest while detaching him from the residual influence of the Church, damned from the start as the Church of Satan. Myths entranced those of poetic imagination and limited critical sense. As churchmen generally complained, a committed Cathar had great immunity to the preaching and teaching which pointed out the difficulties and contradictions of his position. So Cathars were made and retained for their faith.

2. Divisions and Decline.

The fall of Catharism was as dramatic as its rise. From appearing to be a major threat to the Church in the early thirteenth century, it sank to a small, persecuted minority and disappeared altogether in the course of the fourteenth. To account for this we need to bring together the history of the Western Church and the internal development of the sect itself. To some extent this will mean holding up the members of the sect to another kind of mirror to that employed in the previous section in order to show, in place of their attractions, the defects and weaknesses of their position. It will also mean a shift in emphasis amongst the sources, making greater use of Catholic anti-Cathar treatises and summaries in addition to the information from chronicles, inquisitors' interrogations and the works and rituals of the sectaries chiefly used above.

We should look first at the history of organizational and doctrinal dispute within Catharism, which followed speedily on its emergence in the West.

Missionaries, refugees or traders, the dualists of the East who carried their beliefs into the heart of Catholic Europe and began the Cathar movement, also carried with them the religious and personal conflicts which beset them at

[84]As in Bogomilism; see Puech-Vaillant, p. 261.

home.[85] The enterprise which built up Catharism made itself felt in the West in the 1140s; in 1166 or shortly after Nicetas, bishop of a radical dualist Church in Constantinople, arrived in Lombardy to confront Mark the gravedigger and the youthful Cathar mission, thus sowing the seed of dissensions there which ended only when the inquisition destroyed the Cathar Churches of Italy. Two sources inform us of the encounter. One is the work of a Catholic observer in Lombardy writing before 1214–15, who had access to details of the doctrinal history of the Italian Cathars,[86] the other is the account of Anselm of Alessandria written some fifty years later, reflecting the tradition of the sect, which reached him in his capacity as inquisitor, no doubt via interrogations.[87] Differing in detail, they agree in the importance they attach to Nicetas's visit.

The message of Nicetas to Mark and his friends was quite simple: the Church order on which they based their status was faulty. The earlier source makes extensive use of the Catholic term *ordo*,[88] which seems to mean the authentic tradition both of the *consolamentum* and of the orders of bishop and deacon in the organization, on the analogy of the apostolic succession in the Catholic Church. It was of profound importance, for without the true order Mark's *consolamentum* and that of his group was void, and they were lost. Mark heard the stranger from Constantinople with attention, and decided to accept his order, that of Dragowitsa[89] or Drugonthia[90], in place of his own, which was that of Bulgaria.[91] The Lombard group were reconsoled, and Mark received the gratification of episcopal orders from the hands of Nicetas, so becoming the first Cathar bishop of Italy.

More was involved in the reconsoling than a change of order. Subsequent history shows that with the order came the doctrines of radical dualism. The location of Dragowitsa (probably the original of Drugonthia and other forms) is obscure: the name may possibly have derived from the river Dragovitsa in the region of Philippopolis in Thrace, long a stronghold of the Paulicians. Bulgaria is clear enough. This was the cradle of Bogomilism, and its order represented the traditional, early Bogomil belief represented by Cosmas and

[85]For Eastern dualists, see above, ch. 2; D. Obolensky, *Bogomils;* Puech-Vaillant (esp. for nuances of dualism).

[86]*DHC; WEH*, pp. 159–67; *MBPH*, pp. 122–7.

[87]*TDH; WEH*, pp. 167–70, see also pp. 361–73; *MBPH*, pp. 145–54.

[88]*DHC: AFP*, xix (1949); p. 306, l.5, l.6, l.8, l.9, l.12, l.17; p. 306, l.1; p. 308, l.9, l.11; p. 309, l.1; p. 310, l.8, l.10; p. 312, l.7 (*ordo*); p. 306, l.16 (*ordo episcopi*); p. 307, l.1, l.6 (*episcopalis officio*); p. 308, l.9 (*episcopatus officium*); p. 308 l.31 (*ordo episcopatus*). *TDH*, by contrast, though its narrative carries the same implications about the vital role of *ordo* barely uses the term: see *AFP*, xx (1950), '... Marchus ... voluit ire ultra mare ut reciperet ordinem episcopalem ab episcopo de Bulgaria.' For diaconate, see *TDH*, in *AFP*, xx (1950), p. 309, l.2, '... factus est Marchus diaconus.' For vicars of bishops, *filius maior, filius minor*, see Borst, p. 211.

[89]Identification (hypothetical) and all other Balkan church sites, F. Šanjek, 'Le Rassemblement de St-Félix de Caraman et les Églises cathares au XIIe Siècle', *RHE*, LXVII (1972), pp. 767–99; map and commentary in M. D. Lambert, 'Die katharischen Bistümer und die Verbreitung des "schismas" von Osten nach Westen', in *Atlas zur Kirchengeschichte*, ed. Jedin and others, pp. 56–7.

[90]'Drugonthia' (*DHC*); 'Drugontia' (*TDH*); 'Drogometia' (acts of council of S. Félix (*Act. Fel.*, below, n.92)), 'Dugunthia' (Sacconi; see Dondaine, *Un Traité*, p. 70), taken as corruptions of Dragowitsa.

[91]B. Primov, 'Medieval Bulgaria and the Dualistic Heresies in Western Europe', *Études historiques à l'Occasion du XIe Congrès International des Sciences Historiques* (Stockholm & Sofia, 1960), pp. 79–102.

the moderate dualism of the mission phase of Cathar history before Nicetas.

From Italy, Nicetas and Mark are said to have passed on to Languedoc. The journey is not mentioned in the Italian sources, but the presence of both men is attested by one controversial document, the Cathar record of a council held at S. Félix de Caraman, a village in the Lauragais, in 1167 or, less probably, in 1172.[92] It was a mighty gathering, attended by the chiefs of the Cathars in the Midi, 'a great multitude' of all their followers, and a leader from Northern France. All listened to Nicetas and, we must assume, his attack on the legitimacy of the order of Bulgaria, to which they had hitherto belonged, and were reconsoled under the order of Dragowitsa. Nicetas spoke of the tranquillity which prevailed among the dualist Churches of Byzantium and the Balkans, and of the virtues of a territorial delimitation; he urged the Cathars of the Midi to follow their example. They did, and the document records their decisions. One bishopric at Albi already existed; three more were set up for Toulouse, Carcassonne and, by a plausible modern hypothesis, Agen,[93] with the North French leader as bishop of their Church. After candidates had been elected, they all received their episcopal orders from the hand of Nicetas. With Mark and Nicetas, there were then seven bishops present, symbolizing the seven Churches of Asia in the Apocalypse, of which Nicetas spoke.

No word was said in the text of doctrine but the sporadic evidence of the teaching of the Cathars after this date shows that they were radical dualists accepting the two-god doctrine.[94] Nicetas returned to the East, having achieved a notable victory for his Church and teaching.[95]

After some years another visitor from the East arrived in Italy with disquieting news. Petracius of the Church of Bulgaria came to tell the Lombard Cathars that Simon, who had administered the *consolamentum* to Nicetas (presumably somewhere in the East) had been guilty of moral lapses including suspect contact with a woman.[96] If this minister of the *consolamentum* fell, so did all he had consoled; and again the Lombard dualists were lost.

[92]Controversial document (*Act. Fel.*) rehabilitated by Dondaine (*Miscellanea Giovanni Mercati,* v (Rome, 1946), pp. 324–55); accepted by Borst (p. 99), Griffe (*Débuts;* trans. pp. 81–3), Šanjek (*RHE,* LXVII (1972))—on basis of place-name identifications but are they ever compelling? Rejected by Y. Dossat 'Remarques sur un prétendu Evêque cathare du Val d'Aran en 1167', in *Bulletin Philogique et Historique du Comité des Travaux Historiques et Scientifiques, Années 1955 et 1956* (Paris, 1957), pp. 339–47; 'À propos du concile cathare de Saint-Félix: les Milingues', in *CF,* III, pp. 201–14 and R. I. Moore 'Nicétas, Émissaire de Dragovitch, a-t-il traversé les Alpes?,' *AM* LXXXV (1973), pp. 85–90. I believe arguments for authenticity to be not decisive, and the question still open.

[93]Dossat in *Bulletin Philologique* (above, n. 92); Thouzellier, *Catharisme et Valdéisme,* p. 14, n. 7. (against *Act Fel.* reading of 'aranensis'); on Albi, see M. Becamel, 'Le Catharisme dans le Diocèse d'Albi', in *CF,* III, pp. 237–52.

[94]For Languedoc, there is the *Manifestatio* attributed to Ermengaud de Béziers, (ed. Dondaine, in *AFP,* XXIX (1959), pp. 268–71), written before the crusade (radical dualism, but moderate dualism then reappearing: 'Est autem quedam heresis que de novo prosilivit . . .' (p. 271)); see also Dondaine, in *Miscellanea* v, p. 354, and Moore, in *AM,* LXXXV (1973), p. 88. For Italy, analyses by contemporaries in *DHC* and *TDH.*

[95]A victory in Italy, even if *Act. Fel.* is not authentic. The significance of Nicetas's journey is a key-theme of Borst (pp. 98, 108, 142). It is a victory, Borst believed, with seeds of defeat, for it began a phase of greater concentration on dualism in Catharism, which in the end repelled Western Christians. Compare Dondaine in *Miscellanea,* v, p. 354.

[96]'inventus in conclavi cum quadam' (*DHC,* in *AFP,* XIX (1949), p. 306, ll. 13–14).

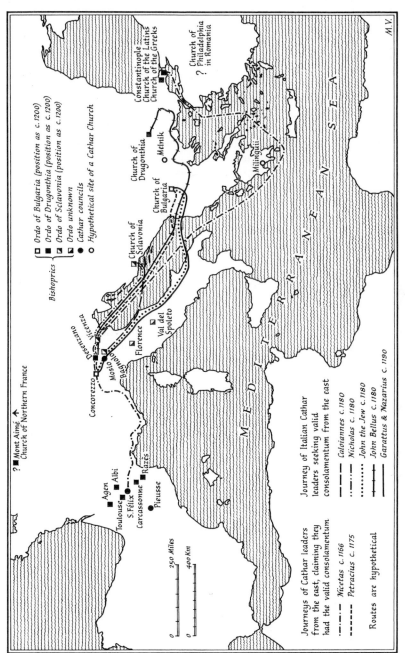

Bishoprics
□ Ordo of Bulgaria (position as c.1200)
■ Ordo of Drugonthia (position as c.1200)
◩ Ordo of Sclavonia (position as c.1200)
◪ Ordo unknown
● Cathar councils
○ Hypothetical site of a Cathar Church

Journeys of Cathar leaders
from the east, claiming they
had the valid consolamentum.
—·—·— Nicetas c. 1166
— — — Petracius c. 1175

Journey of Italian Cathar
leaders seeking valid
consolamentum from the east
—·—·— Caloiannes c.1180
—··—··— Nicholas c. 1180
·········· John the Jew c.1180
—+—+— John Bellus c.1180
———— Garattus & Nazarius c. 1190

Routes are hypothetical

Map Three
Dualist Churches and the Spread of Dissension

M.V.

This time there was no unified response: some supported Petracius, others vacillated. Accounts differ a little:[97] in Anselm of Alessandria the coming of Petracius shortly preceded the death of Mark the first bishop and the succession of Judeus (John the Jew). When Judeus took office, Nicholas of the March, ambitious to be bishop himself, raised a fresh doubt: had Mark himself made a good end? Were the others of Judeus valid? For the anonymous writer of the early thirteenth century, it was simply Petracius's story that troubled the consciences of the Lombards and resulted in the formation of two parties: that for Judeus and that against him, led by a certain Peter of Florence.

The Cathars yet felt their need of unity, and after a time sought advice from a Cathar bishop outside Italy, who recommended reconciliation by election and the drawing of lots: each party should choose a candidate from the other, and chance should then decide between them.[98] At Mosio, between Mantua and Cremona, they held a council, and Garattus emerged as the bishop accepted by all. But, according to the anonymous writer, just as Garattus was preparing to go in search of an undoubted *consolamentum* from the church of Bulgaria and collection was being made for his expenses, he was discovered in reprehensible circumstances with a woman.[99] With that, all attempt at unity foundered.

Now others were despatched to find a foolproof *consolamentum*. From the Church of Bagnolo, with its centre in or near Mantua, Caloiannes went to the Church of Sclavonia, a group of moderate dualists in the predominantly Catholic coastal strip of Dalmatia converted to heresy by merchants trading from Constantinople;[100] from Vicenza Nicholas went to the same destination. Judeus, who had humbly resigned office before Mosio to create unity, was next persuaded to take office again as bishop of the Church based on Mark's birthplace at Concorezzo near Milan and to go himself to Bulgaria as a necessary preliminary to get a valid order. Garattus, though at first subdued, remained a force to be reckoned with and about 1190 seems to have made his own pilgrimage to Bulgaria, accompanied by Nazarius of the Church of Concorezzo, who also brought back with him the Bogomil *apocryphon*, the *Interrogation of John*.[101] Other Churches came into existence at Florence and the Val del Spoleto; here and probably elsewhere local patriotisms played a part.

Thus on the ruins of Mark's original mission there emerged six separate

---

[97]Compare *DHC*, p. 306; *TDH*, in *AFP*, xx (1950), p. 309. *DHC* generally preferred as source nearer to events and more circumstantial on Italian Cathar Churches. It lacks legendary opening on Manes in *TDH* (*AFP*, xx (1950), p. 308).

[98]*DHC*, in *AFP*, xix (1949), p. 306 l.22—p. 307, l.3. Emissaries are sent 'ad quemdam episcopum ultra montes.' But is this not likely to be a Cathar bishop in Languedoc? He recommends that the successful candidate should go to Bulgaria to get his episcopal orders ('ut . . . iret in bulgariam ordinem episcopatus suscipere . . .'), i.e. to a moderate dualist church. If *Act. Fel.* is authentic and Languedoc radical dualist, Moore asks, how is this possible? (*AM*, LXXXV (1973), p. 87). See below, p. 131, n. 106.

[99]'. . . garattus . . . duobus testibus astantibus, reprehensibilis, causa unius mulieris, habitus est' (*DHC*, in *AFP* xix (1949), p. 307, ll. 35–6).

[100]Identification of Sclavonia in *TDH* (*AFP*, xx (1950), p. 308 ll. 11–14; for Prior Suibert of Hungary in 1259, see Gerard of Fracheto, *Vitae Fratrum*, ed. B. M. Reichert, (Louvain 1896), pp. 305–8; literature above, p. 127 n. 89.

[101]Above, p. 122, n. 69.

Cathar Churches in Italy, with competing adherents scattered widely, but generally linked together by common belief and order; map 3 shows the distribution of their geographical centres as well as the journeys which fostered or accompanied their growth, from east to west the fateful movements of Nicetas and Petracius, from west to east the quest of western Cathars for the authentic *consolamentum*.

Accounts of the Italian conflicts are retailed to us by hostile witnesses who were not displeased at the discomfiture of the heretics. It is difficult to know what to make of the sexual scandals which punctuate this history. Libertinism was an element in Gnostic heresy; from the tenet that all matter is evil and contact with it, including sexual relations, is to be condemned, it is possible to adopt another position, that for the elect, who have freed themselves from the taint of matter, it has become wholly indifferent whether they engage in sexual relations or not. They are, so to speak, beyond sin, and the rules which must be observed by neophytes no longer apply to them. This was the teaching of the Byzantine heresy of the Messalians, who believed that their initiates, after training and self-denial and the expulsion of the demon in every man's heart, could indulge or not as they pleased, wholly without sin in either case.[102] But there is little sign of libertinism on principle in the Cathars, to judge by the testimony of the inquisition or the evidence of the response to congregations at this stage to news of the fall of this or that perfect. Philip, bishop of Desenzano, was said by Anselm of Alessandria to have disseminated the maxim that there was no sin for man or woman below the girdle, and to have gained followers on the strength of it.[103] The story may have been slander. More significant was the statement of Sacconi from his own experience that perfect regretted not having taken more advantage of the sexual freedom of the believer before they received the *consolamentum*.[104] In the last resort, however, we need assume no more than the commonsense view, that some perfect did fall, as did many among the Catholic clergy, and that the hypersensitivity and rigidity of the Cathars over the *consolamentum* tended to exaggerate any genuine failing, and may even have led to the invention of others. The libertine in the days of vitality of the sect was very much the exception.[105]

Personal conflicts, anxiety over the *consolamentum* and local patriotism all made the Italians a prey to dissensions imported from the East. Their intellectual activity perpetuated the doctrinal divisions and created others; differences of belief continued a disunity, in contrast to the stability of the territorially based and less speculative Church of Languedoc. The Cathars of the Midi adopted the radical dualism of Nicetas,[106] and long kept it with a minor strand of moderate dualism. Finally there was a more general swing, it would seem, to moderate dualism, all without breaking the structure of the organization or engendering personal ill-feeling. Dossat finds only one

[102]Obolensky, *Bogomils*, pp. 48–52.

[103]*TDH*, in *AFP* xx (1950), p. 310, l.3–4; cited as hearsay ('dicitur').

[104]Dondaine, *Traité*, p. 66.

[105]See Capelli's evidence, above, p. 110 and n.12.

[106]If we assume *Act. Fel.* is authentic. Evidence for radical dualism in Languedoc is independent of *Act. Fel.* (Moore, in *AM* LXXXV (1973), p. 88, above, p. 128, n.92) M.-H. Vicaire, 'Les Cathares albigeois vus par les Polémistes', in *CF*, III, pp. 105–28 is helpful.

instance of an adherent in Languedoc refusing contact with another because of a doctrinal difference.[107]

In Italy the doctrinal quarrels continued after the disintegration into separate Churches, fed by the struggles of leading perfect against each other, and by the pressures of rational reflection or of the example and polemic of the orthodox. The most profound division was that which lay between the radical dualists of Desenzano and the moderates; the Churches which accepted the orders of Sclavonia occupied a middle ground between them and the traditional Bogomilism of Bulgaria. Especially significant are the efforts in the thirteenth century of two Cathars on opposite wings of the movement to put their beliefs on a more rational footing. Desiderius, *filius major* of the Church of Concorezzo, tried to do away with the influence of the *apocrypha*, and taught that the texts of Scripture on marriage were to be interpreted literally for the adherents of the sect, so providing them with a conventional sexual framework.[108] He acknowledged that Christ did have a human body. John of Lugio, probably originally of the Church of Desenzano, and his followers took the opposite view and taught that dualism of the moderate kind could not be defended, any more than Catholicism, and that the only logical answer to the problem of evil was a thoroughgoing radical dualism, given philosophical justification in the Book of Two Principles from their school, the most considerable intellectual achievement of any Cathar. Repetitious, ultimately wearying, as its first editor Dondaine justly noted[109], it was a sign that Italian Cathars were beginning to feel the force of Catholic polemic.

The evidence suggests that the Cathars began with a stress on evangelical life in the twelfth century, and came in time to devote more and more attention to dualist beliefs, which at first had remained in the background. Catholic counter-attack constantly stressed dualism, aiming to show the wavering faithful that Catharism, so far from being a movement of reform and asceticism, was in fact a heresy which denied fundamental doctrines of Christianity: their polemic forced the Cathars to think more about their dualism, and drew it out of the shadows.[110]

Both John of Lugio and Desiderius were attempting in their different ways to update Catharism in response to new needs and more effective attacks. Neither could impart a new direction to the heresy, though both attracted followers. Desiderius battled against his bishop Nazarius, a weaver of fantasies of the old school, and split the Church of Concorezzo; John of Lugio could not move older adherents but did reach some members of the younger generation of Cathars. The majority of the Italian Cathars were not deeply interested: they liked their *apocrypha* and their myths, for all their internal contradictions.[111] But where Desiderius and John of Lugio and their disciples had been impelled to rethink their position by the force of a revived and better informed Catholicism, we may assume others outside Catharism had been

[107]*CF*, III, 79.

[108]*TDH*, in *AFP* xx (1950), pp. 310–12, trans. in *WEH*, pp. 362–4, *MPBH*, p. 149. Borst, p. 122.

[109]*Un Traité*, p. 22; on the author, see Thouzellier, *Le Livre* (latest ed, above, p. 120, n. 57), pp. 33–46.

[110]Vicaire, in *CF*, III, pp. 105–28.

[111]On this I prefer Manselli (*Eresia*, p. 272 and n.41) to Dondaine (*AFP*, xx, p. 274).

influenced against the movement altogether. Orthodox polemic and the preaching and argument based on it would not necessarily detach existing adherents[112] but it warned others against being drawn in to heresy. Borst is surely right to see in the work of these two a symptom of decline.

In the thirteenth century in Languedoc as well as in Italy, a conventional pattern of Church life built up in Catharism; obedience, order and hierarchy came to outweigh the earlier stress on morality. A Latin ritual for the *consolamentum*, based on an original Provençal text, came to be written in Italy, thus sacrificing the freshness and immediacy of contact of the vernacular for dignity and solemnity on the Catholic pattern.[113] Borst sees in the development of rituals for lesser occasions an imitation of the sacramental structure of Catholicism.[114] An important step was taken when it was admitted that a perfect who had fallen could be reconsoled, and a procedure for doing so emerged.

The Cathars attempted to prove that they had seven orders, just as the Catholics.[115] The constitutional position could never be quite the same as in Catholicism because of the status of the perfect. In the Latin rite of the *consolamentum*, however obedience by the candidate to his superiors was given greater emphasis.[116] The rights of election of the whole body of perfect diminished in practice; it became usual to feel that the bishop could only be consecrated by another bishop, as in Catholic practice. The more the *consolamentum* was administered on the deathbed, the more importance attached to the ministers of the sect, especially the deacons, who undertook this duty. The increasing prominence of the hierarchy tended to depress the status of the women perfect, who were debarred from these offices; myths were affected by practice, Koch believes, and the fundamental early tenet of equality of the sexes after the administration of the *consolamentum* was obscured by narratives which stressed woman's secondary creation or her evil role as a tool of Satan.[117] *Verkirchlichung*, the development of a conventional Church structure and life outlined for us by Borst,[118] represents both a natural stage in the history of religious movements and, especially in Italy, an effect of the peaceful competition with the Church; but it diminished the force of Catharism's challenge to orthodoxy.

Meanwhile, repression of heresy, first in Languedoc, then in Italy, grew more effective. The political situation decided the extent to which legislation against heresy was actually effective. In Languedoc, Innocent III's crusade at first threw the Cathars into disarray and scattered their communities. Numbers of perfect were killed as a byproduct of operations, but the organization re-formed and continued to work, albeit with diminished

[112]Implied in Manselli, *Eresia*, ch. 9 (characterization of Cathar supporters, pp. 210–3); compare Vicaire, *CF*, III, pp. 122–3. Contemporary polemists and modern historians may have exaggerated the significance of nuances of dualism for rank and file Cathars. See above, p. 124.

[113]Above, p. 109, n. 3; dating, *WEH*, p. 465.

[114]*Katharer*, p. 121.

[115]Ibid., p. 212, n.34 and refs.

[116]Ibid., p. 282.

[117]Koch, *Frauenfrage*, pp. 71–8.

[118]A good working hypothesis, which nevertheless cannot be fully secure until we have more exact dating of developments in Cathar rites and practice. Mr R. I. Moore reminds me that Garattus was rehabilitated and that the story of Nicetas's mission shows concern for consecration of bishops by other bishops.

numbers. In 1225, indeed, they held a council at Pieusse and decided to set up a new diocese at Razès.[119] Even in the thirties, after the settlement at Paris in 1229, Count Raymond VII of Toulouse, in whose lands some of the most obstinately Cathar regions lay, was still acting equivocally, and his servants gave only partial support to the inquisitors;[120] in 1238, anxious to detach Raymond from support of Frederick II, Gregory IX met his wishes and virtually suspended the tribunal based on Toulouse for three years.

The years 1241 to 1243 were the turning-point.[121] Two vain revolts showed the southern nobles that they would never regain independence by force; and the killing of a party of inquisitors at Avignonet aroused determination to scotch the heresy. The murder had been organized from Montségur, a castle in the foothills of the Pyrenees long a refuge for perfect and their supporters; an army under a royal seneschal besieged and took it and handed over to the Church two hundred or more perfect, including the bishops of Toulouse and Razès. The Cathars of the south never recovered from the loss of so many of the élite. At the same time Raymond abandoned his policy of equivocal support, and began to persecute. In 1249, with less discrimination than the inquisitors, he burnt eighty suspects at Agen in one day. His successor Alphonse of Poitiers, brother of king Louis IX and a cold zealot, was unusually energetic in persecution.

In fact, for the majority of the southern higher nobility, the Cathars had always been negotiable. The wars had been fought over the control of the south, not over heresy, and Raymond VII was characteristic of most of the higher nobility in being ready to throw the heretics over when it was politically expedient to do so. Once the struggle for control of Languedoc was decided, the heretics found few important defenders. There were great conspiracies, both of silence and of action, including a plot to steal inquisition records at Carcassonne and the murder of inquisitors' assistants at Caunes.[122] The last Cathar was burnt in Languedoc as late as 1330.[123] Nevertheless, from 1243, the writing was on the wall.

Why, given the final defeat of the indigenous baronage of Languedoc, this should have been so may be illustrated by examining the inquisitors of the region at the top of their form in the inquiries of Bernard de Caux and his aides in the region of the Lauragais and the neighbourhood of Lavaur in 1245-6.[124] In these investigations 5,471 persons in two archdeaconries were interrogated. Questions were of the police-court type, concerned with the external acts such as adoration, which revealed complicity with heresy; only marginally did they deal with belief. Each adult in the communities shown on map 4 was compelled to answer. If a suspect broke down under interrogation, others would follow; lies were uncovered by cross-checking. Five more

[119]But note Wakefield's comment (*Heresy, Crusade*, p. 132); sequence of events described in chs 7, 8, 9.
[120]On Raymond, see Dossat, *Crises*, pp. 271-5, and Wakefield, *Heresy, Crusade*, pp. 148-50.
[121]Ibid., ch. 10 (bibl. on Montségur given on p. 191, n. 3).
[122]Plot at Carcassonne described in Guiraud, *L'Inquisition*, II, chap. 11; and murder at Caunes by Wakefield (*Heresy, Crusade*, p. 187). See also the latter's 'Friar Ferrier, Inquisition at Caunes, and Escapes from Prison at Carcassonne', *CHR*, LVIII (1972), pp. 220-37.
[123]Borst, *Katharer*, p. 136.
[124]Dossat, *Crises*, chs 2, 3, pp. 226-44 (map, pp. 228-9; table of sentences, pp. 258-9).

St Lieux-les-Lavaur

Agout

Girou

Lavaur   Places of origin of heretics
sentenced March–July 1246

Lavaur

Massac

St Sauveur

St Paul-
Cap-de-Joux

Guitalens

Gauré

Drémil

Valesvilles

Veilhes

Maurens

Cambon

Saussens

St Anatoly

Lanta

Prunet

Puylaurens

Saix

Viviers-les-
Montagnes

Montespieu

Saune

Ste Foy d'Aigrefeuille

Odars

Préserville

Auriac

Fourquevaux

Tarabel

Cambiac

Nogaret

Labastide-de-Beauvoir

Varennes

St Julia

Montégut

Montgiscard

Maurémont

St Germier

Maurens

Roumens

Baziège

Goudourville

Juzes

Villenouvelle

Trebons

Montgaillard

St Félix

Dreuilhe

Les Cassés

Vaudreuille

Montesquieu

Lavelanet

St Paulet

La Pomarède

Gardouch

Barelles

Folcarde

Montmaur

Labécède

Renneville

Pechbertier

Montferrand

Issel

Verdun

Avignonet

Airoux

Villemagne

Lagarde

Beauteville

St Michel-de-Lanès

Baraigne

Castelnaudary

Gibel

Cumiès

Le Mas-
Saintes-Puelles

St Martin-la-Lande

Lasbordes

Villepinte

Montauriol

Villeneuve-
la-Comtal

Pexiora

Fresquel

Peyrefitte

Mireval-
Lauragais

Bram

Mayreville

Laurac

Villesiscle

Generville

Cazalrenoux

Gaja-la-Selve

Fanjeaux

Hers mort

Hers vif

Ariège

Blazens

Plaigne

Barsa

Vixiège

Vendinelle

M.V.

Map Four
Inquisition Versus Catharism: The Enquiries of 1245–6

inquiries were launched in this region. In 1260 the record of the original investigation was recopied.

Sentences of Bernard De Caux, 1246

Community	Prison	Crosses and other penances	Community	Prison	Crosses and other penances
Airoux	0	1	Le Mas-Saintes-Puelles	0	8
Auriac	0	4	Les Cassés	1	3
Avignonet	0	11	Montauriol	0	1
Baraigne	0	3	Montégut	0	3
Barelles	3	3	Montesquieu-Lauragais	0	7
Beauteville	0	2	Montgiscard	1	4
Bram	0	3	Montmaur	0	2
Cambiac	1	4	Odars	0	1
Cambon	0	4	Pexiora	0	5
Castelnaudary	0	8	Prunet	0	1
Drémil	0	1	Roumens	1	4
Fanjeaux	3	25	Saint-Germier	0	1
Gaja-le-Selve	0	1	Saint-Julia	0	1
Gibel	0	1	Saint Martin-la-Lande	7	19
Goudourville	1	2	Saint-Paul-Cap-de-Joux	0	1
Juzes	0	2	Saint-Paulet	1	1
Lanta	0	1	Villeneuve-la-Comtal	0	7
Laurac	2	28	Villepinte	0	3
Lavaur	1	5	Villesiscle	0	3
Lavelanet	1	0			

The table of sentences, derived from the close study of Dossat, covers those pronounced by Bernard de Caux between 18 March and 22 July 1246, and gives us as fair a picture of the extent of heresy in this region in 1245–6 as we are likely to get. As Dossat warns, it is still not wholly accurate as a picture of heresy uncovered in these enquiries, as the manuscripts on which he based the table are not necessarily comprehensive, but it is unlikely to be gravely misleading. Heretics were a minority, but a tenacious one, and they were widespread, as the thirty-nine localities in the table shows. A wide, if rather thin, scattering seems a fair inference, although we may notice some concentration in the southwest corner of the region, in, for example, Fanjeaux, Laurac and St Martin-la-Lande.

However, tenacity on the part of the heretics, was matched by tenacity on the part of the inquisitors. The sequence of enquiries shows that in this region the connections with heresy of the whole population were searched out by blanket interrogation, then rechecked over the years, gradually rooting out the guilty. Sentencing was not unusually harsh. The table lists 207 sentences; twenty-three were of imprisonment, and the rest consisted of lighter penalties, such as compulsory pilgrimages or crosses worn on the clothing. Burning was not included in the records Dossat surveys, but we know from other evidence that its incidence was quite light.[125] The essence of the method was persistence and long memory: terror was maintained as much by the threat as by the reality of prison or fire. No minority religious movement could continue

[125]Wakefield, *Heresy, Crusade*, pp. 184–5, 193, n.10.

indefinitely in the face of pressure of this kind. So far we need not spend much time on the internal contradictions of Catharism or the innovations of Catholicism to understand why the heresy disappeared in Languedoc.[126] No doubt the friars had a contribution to make quite independently of their inquisitorial activities, but it is not clear that any major improvement in the standards of the regular clergy did occur: Olivi's evidence for the late thirteenth century suggests it did not. The Cathars of Languedoc were eliminated primarily by efficient police work.

Signs of decline were apparent from the forties onwards. The life of the perfect changed character,[127] and secrecy grew. The black robe was exchanged for a girdle worn next to the skin, and individual perfect moved from houses known to the public to huts and cabins. Chances of proselytism lessened and, as far as the women were concerned, the popularity of Dominic's foundation at Prouille seems to have grown. Women perfect were in retreat, while about mid-century Prouille had fifty nuns. Emigration of Cathars to their colleagues in Italy began.[128] By about 1250 Sacconi calculated that the old Cathar Churches of Toulouse, Albi, Carcassonne and Agen had less than 200 perfect between them;[129] perhaps, though, as an inquisitor and a former perfect he tended to exaggerate the extent of the Church's success by that stage.[130]

Still there was adaptation to circumstances. The range of contacts, which extended as far as a North French immigrant, of the Cathar deacon Pagès in his long career from 1269 to 1284 in Cabardès and neighbouring lands, shows how heresy could live on in these late days.[131] Under pressure, leaders authorized the perfect to shed blood;[132] the *convenenza*, a pact between a perfect who would administer the *consolamentum* and a candidate, to be fulfilled at a moment of necessity when death was at hand and the candidate could no longer speak, was evolved to meet more desperate circumstances. The *endura*, a form of suicide, occasionally by violent means, but usually by taking to bed and refusing food, passing from life secure in the possession of the *consolamentum* on a diet of sugared water, became an occasional feature;[133] it had always been a logical end for those who believed that life itself was an imprisonment under Satan, and a possible psychological effect of the obsessive and perfectionist life of the perfect, but its early incidence is rare and a little ambiguous. Never at all frequent, its incidence increased in late Catharism, when after 1295 one commanding personality, the radical dualist Pierre

[126]In relation to Languedoc, I here differ from Dondaine (*AFP*, xx (1950), p. 274) and Borst (p. 133). I am still moved by Borst's powerful book, but believe he underestimates force, esp. in Languedoc, to some degree in Italy and overestimates the destructive effect of radical dualism. See above, p. 131.

[127]Koch, *Frauenfrage*, chs 4,9; Dossat, in *CF* iii, p. 74.

[128]Dupré Theseider, in *CF*, iii, pp. 299–313.

[129]Dondaine, *Traité*, p. 70; *WEH*, p. 337.

[130]Comment of Professor C.N.L. Brooke.

[131]Guiraud, *Inquisition*, ii, pp. 277–8.

[132]For this and what follows, see Y. Dossat, 'L'Évolution des Rituels cathares', *Revue de Synthèse* n.s. xxii–xxiii (1948), pp. 27–30.

[133]Dossat (*CF*, iii, pp. 85–7) corrects and supplements C. Molinier 'L'Endura: Coutûme religieuse des derniers Sectaires albigeois', *Annales de la Faculté des Lettres de Bourdeaux*, 1ʳ ser., iii (1881), pp. 282–99.

Autier, led a revival; for him the *endura* could be a convenient means of removing followers who knew too much when the inquisition was on their track.

But gradually, as repression continued and thorough investigations eliminated this or that circle of contacts, heresy died out. Autier, a notary from Ax at the edge of the Pyrenees, showed the beliefs still had appeal when he returned from exile in Italy in 1295 to raise some hundreds of adherents in a career of underground preaching that lasted until his capture and burning in 1310.[134] But the bulk of his followers were poor peasants and artisans, and the creed he taught one of desperation. With the career of Belibasta, a perfect who kept a concubine and sold the *consolamentum*, we encounter mere decadence.[135]

The turn of the Italians to suffer the force of the inquisition came later. While the churches of Languedoc crumbled, Italy was a relatively safe place of refuge; during the siege of Montségur a Cathar bishop in Cremona sent through a fraternal letter to the bishop of Toulouse with an offer of asylum, which he refused.[136] Guides and hospices by the way facilitated the emigration of heretics from Languedoc, probably for the sake of secrecy along the most difficult route by the Alpes Maritimes, Nice, the Col de Tende and so via Roccavione to the plain of Cuneo.[137] A trickle of perfect came back on return missions to give pastoral care or the *consolamentum* to the fragments of the Churches of Languedoc in the dark days, and at Asti the greatest of the exiles, Autier, received his heretical ordination. Sacconi noted that the remains of the North French Church, amounting to some 150 perfect in mid-century, had found refuge in Verona and Lombardy, generally.[138] This security was, however, based on no firm foundations, since Cathars in Italy were being tolerated by communal authorities, not so much for their own sake as for the sake of the autonomy of the cities or anticlerical and antipapal feeling, and when, for one reason or another, opinion tilted against the heretics, they had no reliable defenders.

Local sentiment was volatile. As we have seen, Catholic reation in Orvieto brought Pietro Parenzo into power;[139] his assassination instantly aroused popular feeling in sympathy. Yet in 1239 the Dominican convent in the city was sacked.[140] In Florence there was violence against a Ghibelline *podestà* in 1245 because of his failure to take action against the Cathar Barone del Barone. On the other hand, the inquisitor St Peter Martyr was assassinated in 1252 because of his prosecution of heretics in the country outside Milan, and seven years later there was protest in the city against the work of his subordinate and successor Sacconi.

So matters swung to and fro. What generally preserved the quasi-immunity

---

[134] J.M. Vidal, 'Les derniers Ministres de l'Albigéisme en Languedoc: leurs Doctrines', *RQH*, LXXIX (1906), pp. 57–107; 'Doctrine et Morale des derniers Ministres albigeois', *RQH*, LXXXV (1909), pp. 357–409, LXXXVI (1909), pp. 5–48; Koch, *Frauenfrage*, pp. 82, 87–8; differing emphasis by Wakefield in *Heresy, Crusade*, p. 189.

[135] Borst, p. 136. On one village in Languedoc, see E. Le Roy Ladurie, *Montaillon* (Paris, 1976).

[136] Manselli, *Eresia*, p. 221.

[137] Guiraud, *Inquisition*, II, ch. 9; Dupré Theseider, in *CF* III, pp. 299–316.

[138] Dondaine, *Un Traité*, p. 70; *WEH*, p. 337.

[139] Above, p. 85.

[140] For this and following episodes, see Manselli, *Eresia,* ch. 12, and Guiraud, *Inquisition*, II, ch.8.

of the heretics in the first half of the century was the struggle between Frederick II and the popes. Having secured the promulgation of antiheretical legislation by Frederick II and built up a corpus of law against heresy, the popes were unwilling to exert great pressure on the cities to implement this legislation for fear of losing allies. Suspicion in the communes of central authority was at first enough to prevent general acceptance of statutes of support for the introduction of the inquisition, and the popes lacked the leverage to insist. Frederick's own attitude was opportunist.[141] The reality of his concern was shown by his inaction towards heresy in the Regno: to take effective action would have meant introducing the friars to his kingdom, and he was unwilling to do this on political grounds. But he noticed the reluctance of Gregory IX to press the heresy issue so long as his own political requirements made it inconvenient, and used this as a point of criticism in his propaganda. His successor Manfred was a fautor of heretics.

The Cathars used any support that they could find. A natural conjunction of interest brought them into alliance with the Ghibellines. But the heretics never formed an independent force anywhere in communal politics; they generally tended to receive favour in times of interdict, but they were pawns in a political battle, and when the Ghibelline forces lost they were without support.

Till 1250 the association with Ghibellinism carried the heretics into a blind alley. While Frederick lived, relative security remained. They were not free of the risk of legal proceedings by any means; but they still had numerical strength. Sacconi, trying to reckon up the strength of the various Churches, assessed Concorezzo, the moderate dualists, as greatest with 1500 perfect; below that came Desenzano with 500 and a series of smaller ones at lower figures—Bagnolo at 200, Florence, Val del Spoleto and Vicenza at 100. The organization outlasted Sacconi, and the lists of bishops for the various Churches go on without interruption into the eighties.[142]

Nevertheless, the death of Frederick II and the decline of the imperial party in Italy, the victories of the papal champion Charles of Anjou against Frederick's successors, and the success of conservative Guelf parties in the cities tilted the balance against the dualists. Charles of Anjou's system had no room for the heretics; the popes, released from the anxiety over allies, could press the case for persecution. Patrons died, in Verona Oberto Pelavicino was succeeded by the Scaligeri, who were no longer willing to assist heresy.[143]. One by one, in a halting sequence which lasted through the rest of the century, cities allowed thorough inquisitorial proceedings. Flight to protectors in the *contado*, movement to other cities, and concealment delayed but could not prevent decline. In Florence a stage in this downward movement is marked by the numbers of perfect who submitted in the inquisition held in 1282 by brother Salomone da Lucca.[144] At Sirmione by

---

[141]Manselli, pp. 283–4.

[142]Borst, pp. 231–9.

[143]Manselli, *Eresia*, p. 285.

[144]Ibid., p. 218; confessions of converted perfect in Languedoc in H. Blaquière and Y. Dossat, 'Les Cathares au Jour le Jour: Confessions inédites de Cathares quercynois', in *CF*, III, pp. 259–316, see pp. 259–89.

Lake Garda an expedition captured 178 perfect, who were burnt in Verona in 1278, and dealt a terrible blow to the Church of Desenzano.[145] The repression still did not go easily; traditional suspicion of the inquisition remained, and some Cathars struck back—in the Valtellina an inquisitor was murdered, Parma sacked its Dominican convent in 1279[146]—but by the end of the century even Milan, the ancient capital of heresy, had been brought to order. The last major series of trials were held in Bologna from 1291 to 1309.[147] Cathar history thereafter is that of a remnant. The last bishop to be reported in western Europe was captured in Tuscany in 1321;[148] survivors continued for a time to find refuge, possibly in the Lombard countryside and in the Alps.[149]

A summary of the history of the inquisition in Italy, however, does not alone explain the decline of the heresy; the peaceful countermeasures of the Church and the internal difficulties of Catharism are also relevant. The inquisitors in Languedoc were very largely policemen; in Italy they were something more. St Peter Martyr, for example, as well as pursuing his legal duties, was the leader in a movement for setting up Catholic confraternities to deepen faith and erect barriers against heresy.[150] The intellectual level was higher than in Languedoc, and it is fair to assume therefore that the intellectual attack on heresy and the effect of the conflicts in Catharism mattered more. In Languedoc it is enough to point to police work to explain the fall of the heresy; in Italy police action was still needed to cut down the recalcitrant. But a general change in the atmosphere and a revived Catholicism inhibited the flow of recruits on the earlier scale; so the heresy was squeezed into its ultimate oblivion. One can speculate about economic factors, and argue that improvements in conditions drew men's minds from a creed which so relentlessly preached that the world was utterly in the power of Satan; but too many in easy circumstances participated in the heresy, and men's motives for adherence to a religious group are generally too complex for any simple correlation between poverty, injustice and Cathar recruitment, or between economic improvement and Cathar decline, to carry conviction. Catharism was in any case eclectic, a religion that absorbed ideas and practices sponge-like from various quarters, and so catered for varied needs, somewhat at the expense of consistency. Knowledge was expanding in the thirteenth century, and with the development of universities and of medical schools and the expansion of travel horizons widened. Catharism could not keep up.[151] Two developments on the Catholic side, however, were of especial importance for the change of outlook that inhibited this particular heresy.[152] One was the rise of a new piety, associated especially with the Franciscans,

---

[145]Guiraud, *Inquisition*, II, p. 573.

[146]Ibid., pp. 573 (Valtellina); 575 (Parma).

[147]Dupré Theseider, in *Studi storici in onore di G. Volpe*, I, pp. 383–444.

[148]Stephens in *PP*, LIV (1972), p. 30.

[149]Evidence on Catharism in the Alpine valleys in the late middle ages may be suspect: see below, p. 162.

[150]Guiraud, *Inquisition*, II, ch. 18; studies by G. G. Meersseman in *AFP*, XX (1950), pp. 5–113; XXI (1951), pp. 51–196; XXII (1952), pp. 5–176, cited Manselli, *Eresia*, p. 268.

[151]I am indebted for information on this to Dr A. V. Murray.

[152]Manselli, *Eresia*, p. 270 (Franciscans); 331 (Joachimism).

which focussed attention on the incidents of Christ's life. The Christmas crib, the vivid preaching about Christ's life, the devotions centred on the Crucifixion which led the worshipper to participate in the sufferings of Jesus were the enemy of the dualist faith. For most adherents the Cathar Christ was a wraith or a visiting angel, and not a man; he was venerated above all as the distant founder of a pure Church. He could not survive against the competition of the Catholic Christ, man and God, as realized in the piety of the thirteenth century. The positive sentiment concerning nature and creation had similar effects in dispelling, by experience rather than reason, the Cathar vision of all matter as evil.

Finally the appearance of Joachimism on the thirteenth-century scene contributed to popular religious feeling a set of myths that rivalled in their appeal the myths of the Cathars, and yet were more optimistic in tone. As in Cathar eschatology, there was to be a profound struggle with evil, but it would issue in a state of bliss here on earth, a foretaste, after spiritual warfare, of the pleasures of paradise. For those who had taste for such things, the myths were more positive; dualist myths of creation and the End faded in competition with them. All was not gain for the Catholics; there were dangers in Joachimism, and heresies fed on it.[153] But it was another factor against Catharism. In a word, Italian dualism was in part eradicated by force and in part simply outgrown.

The Decline of Bogomilism in Byzantium and the Balkans

In the cradle lands of Bogomil heresy in Byzantium and the Balkans, both the impact and the ultimate fate of dualism was less dramatic than in the West. In Byzantium persecution was sporadic. It was handicapped by the troubles of the failing Byzantine State, fragmented as it was after the fourth crusade of 1203-4 and still afflicted by problems of authority in its last phase, after the recapture of Constantinople from the Latins in 1261; the late Byzantine Church never uprooted the heretics.

In Constantinople itself radical dualism lived on after the persecutions of Alexius Comnenus early in the twelfth century, as the career of Nicetas in Italy testifies. A cluster of persecutions under Manuel Comnenus, which included activity by St Hilarion in his diocese of Moglena in Macedonia and even issued in the deposition of two bishops in Asia Minor, still did not bring Bogomilism to an end.[154] In the last decade of Manuel's reign (1170-80), Theodore Balsamon wrote, perhaps with gloomy exaggeration, of whole regions inhabited by Bogomils;[155] in the capital the heretics had vitality enough, it would seem to win converts among the Latin settlers on the ruins of the Empire in the thirteenth century, for a Church of the Latins as well as of the Greeks in Constantinople was recorded by Sacconi in his list of dualist Churches.[156] No source, however, for Byzantine Bogomilism after Euthymius Zigabenus is wholly satisfactory, and certainly none has the sensitivity to nuances in belief of the priest Cosmas for early Bulgarian heresy. The sources

---

[153]Below, pp. 186-93.
[154]Obolensky, *Bogomils*, pp. 220-6; on St Hilarion, see Puech-Vaillant, p. 134.
[155]Obolensky, *Bogomils*, p. 229.
[156]Dondaine, *Un Traité*, p. 70.

introduce Messalian elements into their accounts of the heresy; given the low calibre of these records, it is impossible to be sure whether Bogomilism came to blend Messalianism with its own traditions, or whether the sources have muddled the two heresies together.

In Bulgaria Bogomils lived on, playing their part in creating the dissensions of the Italian Cathars, and later, in 1211, attracting the attention of the tsar Boril. Here again, however, our source, the Synodicon of the tsar, is weak.[157] In the West, Sacconi knew and listed the dualist Churches of Byzantium and the Balkans in his time, and understood their importance as founts of orders; but he was not informed about their internal history, and put down an arbitrary round figure, below five hundred, for all the perfect included in their ranks.[158] Obscurity, both for Byzantium and Bulgaria, deepens in the course of the later thirteenth and the fourteenth centuries, and we lose track of the heresy in the development of Hesychasm in Byzantium, in Messalianism and in the confused beliefs of Bulgarian Church members, given to demonology and magic. The dualist heresy, killed off or outpaced by developments in Church life in the west, appears to have died away in Byzantium and the Balkans quietly and spontaneously.

Two attempts were made by Bogomil missionaries or refugees to conquer fresh territory, one partially successful, the other a failure. In Serbia in the second half of the twelfth century dualists were dealt with vigorously by Stephen Nemanja, who imposed execution, banishment and burning of books; his younger son St Sava, as archbishop at a council at Žica in 1221, banished Bogomils or forcibly baptized them. Cosmas was translated into Serbian, probably in the twelfth century, and legislation reintroduced after St Sava's time against Bogomils.[159] Conquest under the glorious reign of Stephen Dušan probably had the effect of including under Serbian rule populations in Macedonia and part of Bosnia infected by Bogomilism—penalties against these heretics are included in Dušan's law code of the mid-fourteenth century.[160] In Serbia, therefore, a Bogomil problem persisted; but the Serbian Church was autocephalous, not weakened by undue influence from the conquering power of Byzantium, as the Greek Orthodox Bulgarian Church had been in Cosmas's time, and it was able to act firmly.

In the wild lands of Bosnia infiltration was more successful.[161] Refugees fled

---

[157]Puech-Vaillant, p. 134, noting that it adds little to Cosmas; trans., pp. 344–6. V. S. Kiselkov, 'Borilovijat Sinodik kato istoričeski izvor', *IP*, xix (1963), p. 71 (in Bulgarian); cited by E. Werner (*SM*, iii, ser. 5 (1964), p. 680. But see now Werner's more optimistic research report, 'Ketzer und Weltverbesserer . . .' *SSAWL*, cxvi (1974), pp. 5–57, esp. pp. 5–26.

[158]Dondaine, *Un Traité*, p. 70. The Church of the Latins in Constantinople is assessed separately at less than 50 perfect.

[159]A. Solovjev, 'Svedočanstva pravoslavnih izvora o Bogomilstvu na Bakanu', *Godišnjak istoriskog društva Bosne i Hercegovine*, v (1953), pp. 1–103 (French summary, pp. 100–3) (helpful survey of Greek Orthodox sources on Bogomilism in Balkans; see esp. interesting note on Serbian Synodicon from Dečani text); on alleged pope of dualists in Bosnia, see correction by J. Šidak in *Zgodovinski časopis Organ Zgodovinskega društva LRS Ljubljana*, vi–vii (1952) (German summary, p. 285).

[160]Solovjev, loc. cit.

[161]Discussion of Bogomilism in Bosnia must involve the question of the heretical character of the indigenous Bosnian Church. Was it given over to dualism, or simply maligned by Western and other observers? Professor J. V. A. Fine, jr., promises a full treatment in English with the

there from the persecutions of the Catholic Archbishop of Split on the Dalmatian coast in the late twelfth century and, probably, from the actions of the Serbian Church.[162] Innocent III intervened, and his legate in 1203 secured agreement at Bilino Polje from a mysterious monastic group called *krstjani* to certain standards, to a refusal to receive Manichees or heretics and a renunciation of any possible heresy for themselves.[163] But the influence of Rome in this remote land was slight. The interior was habitually neglected by the Archbishop at Dubrovnik, in whose province it lay, and one native bishop was, apparently, wholly unworthy; in 1233 he was deposed and replaced by a German Dominican, who in turn was succeeded by another Dominican named Ponsa. Under this alien rule persecution of heresy began, only to be cut short by the effects of military action by Hungary, which campaigned, probably *c.* 1236–7, to bring the whole country under its rule.[164] The kings of Catholic Hungary claimed a suzerainty over the bans of Bosnia, and were perhaps inclined to treat accusations of heresy launched against Bosnians with great seriousness only when they coincided with their own territorial ambitions. Technically, the campaign was a crusade, preached under the auspices of Gregory IX; but it had the opposite effect to that intended. The reactions of the Bosnian nobility and the expulsion of the Hungarian conquerors brought about a cessation of all persecution and the removal of the Catholic bishop. Thereafter dualism was left in peace.

The heretical Church of Sclavonia, insecure in Dalmatia, seems to have

provisional title of *The 'Christians' of Medieval Bosnia,* in which he will argue that heresy was present in Bosnia but that the Bosnian Church itself was not heretical. Mrs Yvonne Burns plans to tackle all the documents afresh. Meanwhile, two leading Yugoslav scholars, S. Ćirković and J. Šidak accept that it was a heretical Church, and this is the prevailing judgement; for introduction, S. Ćirković, 'Die bosnische Kirche', in *Oriente cristiano*, pp. 547–75, is essential. I owe the ref. to Dr H. Lietzmann, and advice to Professor S. Ćirković. For J. Šidak's summary of his (revised) view on the Church, see his 'Das Problem des Bogomilismus in Bosnien', *Atti del X Congresso: riassunti delle communicazioni*, pp. 365–9; for research articles, cf. J. Tadić (ed.), *Dix Années d'Historiographie yougoslave, 1945–55* (Belgrade, 1955) and *Historiographie yougoslave, 1955–65,* (Belgrade, 1965), and esp. Šidak's "Ecclesia Sclavoniae" i misija dominikanaca u Bosni', *ŽFŽ*, III (1955), pp. 11–40 (German summary, p. 40). I owe advice to Professor J. Šidak. Details of Church life (based esp. on Latin sources and assumption of heretical character of Church) are in D. Kniewald, 'Hierarchie and Kultus bosnischer Christen', in *Oriente cristiano*, pp. 579–605; sidelights and historiography in M. Miletić, *I 'Krstjani' di Bosnia alla luce dei loro monumenti di pietra* (Rome, 1957) see esp. pp. 15–23. A collection of texts is in O. D. Mandić, *Bogomilska crkva bosanskih krstjana* (Chicago, 1962), pp. 435–51 (but note that his exposition is uncritical). Discussion with Mrs Burns has led me to question more closely the hypothesis of a heretical Church. I am indebted to Professor E. Werner for interesting me in the problem, and to the help of Mr and Mrs V. Sinčić. See also Dr fra L. P., [Petrović] *Kršćani Bosanske Cr'kve (Kr'stiani cr'kve Bos'nske)* (Sarajevo 1953) (*ex inf.* Professor Fine). (Available from Franciscan friary, Sarajevo). For Loos, *Dualist Heresy* see below, p. 389.

[162]Ćirković, *Oriente cristiano*, p. 548.

[163]Photograph of text in Mandić, *Bogomilska crkva*, p. 454, discussion by Ćirković, in *Oriente cristiano*, pp. 548–51, Kniewald, ibid., pp. 579–82, Miletić, *I 'Krstjani'*, pp. 49–66, 179–80, suggesting hypothesis of origins of *krstjani* among Basilian monks.

[164]Šidak, in *ŽFŽ*, III (1955), pp. 11–40. Moves towards a crusade took place in 1221; another campaign took place in approximately 1236–7; thereafter there was a swing against Hungary and Catholic persecution. By mid-century the Catholic bishop had his seat at Djakovo on land given by Duke Koloman, the Hungarian heir—a sign of the failure to win Bosnia for Catholicism.

made the Bosnian interior its home.[165] The papal curia believed that the old Bosnian Church, an isolated and idiosyncratic body, had itself been taken over by the dualists.[166] This may or may not have been true. Hungary believed in the heretical character of the Church, but had a perennial interest in gaining papal support for plans of reconquest. At the Catholic city of Dubrovnik *gosti*, apparently members of the hierarchy of the Bosnian Church, were regularly received as diplomatic emissaries of Bosnian rulers.[167] The men of Dubrovnik referred to them as Patarenes, a common name for Cathars, originating in Italy,[168] and observed that they would not swear oaths, although the Bosnian laity would.[169] A fifteenth-century Bosnian MS, contains a short sequence of prayers which has an interesting, if not wholly conclusive, resemblance to prayers used in a very similar sequence by Western Cathars.[170]

It was said that the Bosnian Church had a hierarchy of its own, with four ranks, that of *djed*, who was the head ('signor e padre spirituale de la glexia vostra di Bosna') *gost*, *starac* and *strojnik*.[171] By the institution of the *vjera gospodska* (the lord's word of faith, a mechanism designed to preserve the balance between ruler and nobles), a crucial role was reserved for members of the Bosnian Church. The ruler gave his guarantee for life and limb and property to the noble; the guarantee might not be broken save in case of a breach of faith, a *nevjera*, by the noble, and judgement as to whether a *nevjera* had indeed been committed was in the hands of commissions including nobles and churchmen, in which a place was often reserved for the *djed*.[172]

Gosti grew rich. The tomb of Gost Milutin (shown opposite), though crudities of carving and the ragged way the inscription is continued on the side and back of the pillar reveal low cultural standards, also shows the reality

[165]Above, n. 100. See *TDH*. Hypothesis of take-over of old Bosnian Church by dualists is Šidak's (revised) view, followed by Ćirković (*Oriente cristiano*, pp. 551–3). Mandić (*Bogomilska crkva* (for contents, see E. Werner, in *SM*, 3rd ser., v (1964), pp. 675–83)) supposes a heretical Bosnian Church in 1180: evidence (e.g. at Bilino Polje) does not support this theory.

[166]See Latin sources on Bosnia, D. Kniewald, *Vjerodostjnost latinskih izvora o bosanskim krstjanima* (Zagreb, 1949); reviewed by A. Vaillant, in *RES*, xxviii (1951), pp. 272–3.

[167]M. Dinić, *Iz Dubrovačkog arhiva*, iii (Belgrade, 1967), pp. 181–236 (Serbian edition, with texts in original languages), 'Jedan prilog za istoriju patarena u Bosni', *ZFB*, i. (1948), pp. 33–44 (French summary, p. 44). Sources from Dubrovnik have appealed to historians as not obviously subject to Hungary or Western bias. I am grateful to Professor S. Ćirković for generously sending me a copy of Dinić's book.

[168]Above pp. 72, 84.

[169]Dinić, *Iz Dubrovačkog arhiva*, iii, s. 2, no. 4, p. 183.

[170]Analysis of Radosav MS. in A. V. Solovjev, 'La Doctrine de l'Église de Bosnie', *ARBB,* 5th ser., xxiv (1948), pp. 481–533; see esp. pp. 522–8; an implicit correction of his treatment of 'Dignum et justum est' (*recte*. 'It is worthy and just') is to be found in *WEH*, p. 781. Solovjev was an ardent but sometimes undiscriminating supporter of the heretical character of the Bosnian Church, and his conclusions cannot be accepted without reservation; see e.g., J. Šidak on Bosnian gospels in *Slovo* (Zagreb), iv–v (1955), pp. 47–63 (French summary, pp. 61–2) and xvii (1967), pp. 113–24 (French summary, p. 124); but on Radosav MS. note Kniewald (*Oriente cristiano*, p. 599, n. 54).

[171]Latin source, Dinić, *Iz Dubrovačkog arhiva*, iii, s. 2, no. 31, p. 193; analysis of titles by Kniewald (*Oriente cristiano*, pp. 583–93) (on assumption of heretical character of Church); on *djed* as *padre spirituale*, see ibid., p. 585.

[172]S. Ćirković, ' "Verna služba" i "vjera gospodska" ', *ZFB*, vi (1962), pp. 101–12 (in Serbian) (summary in *Oriente cristiano*, pp. 565–6).

Plate One
Gost Milutin

INSCRIPTION:
In Thy Name, most pure Trinity. The stone tomb of the lord Gost Milutin, of the family of
Crničan. He perished otherwise than by the grace of god. Biography: I lived in the honour of the
Bosnian lords. I received gifts from great lords and suzerains and from the Greek lords. And all
this is known.

(from the French trans. by M. Vego)
(below, p. 146, n. 173)

of this wealth.[173] Milutin's remains lay on a walnut bier in a brocade robe adorned with lions and stars woven with threads of pure gold. Distant as such men were from the ascetic leaders of the early Bogomil and Cathar missions, Western churchmen believed that the Church over which they exercised authority had heretical beliefs. Remote and exotic, Bosnia, a land of heresy, appeared in reputation a little like Tibet to the eyes of nineteenth- and twentieth-century Western observers—a strange country where anything might happen.

In fact, it is not quite clear that the official Bosnian Church was dualist. One important piece of evidence, used by some to demonstrate that it did have heretical belief, is the language of the testament of Gost Radin, drawn up in Dubrovnik in 1466.[174] Radin, one of the last of the leading churchmen of the old Bosnian Church and an adviser of Duke Stephen Vukčić of St Sava, fled before the Turkish invasions to Dubrovnik, where he was given sanctuary in consideration of his long services to the city, and made his testament. Bequests of 300 ducats to members of the Bosnian Church appear to reveal peculiar categories, not directly resembling those of any other Church but having affinities with the Cathars and Bogomils. S. Ćirković, in a summary of research on the Bosnian Church in 1963, distinguished three categories of membership among Radin's legatees, the 'true Christians' (*pravi krstjani*), the 'baptised' (*kršteni*), 'those who do not love sins' (*koji greha ne ljube*) and the 'people who eat fat foods' (*mrsni ljudi*).[175] The crucial word in the testament is *mrsni*, translated by the document's first editor as 'meat-eating'; Ćirković's summary adopts a slightly variant translation. Meat-eating roused echoes in historians' minds of the renunciation of meat by dualist perfect in East and West, and led them to see analogies among the membership, in idiosyncratic Bosnian terms, to the *perfecti* and *credentes* of Western Catharism.

No linguist, apparently, has ever analysed this text. The fresh translation by Yvonne Burns in appendix E, reveals that the word *mrsni* is a misreading, and that these supposed categories of Church membership mentioned in the testament never existed. Radin spoke in an imprecise and rhetorical way[176] of the members of his own Church to whom alms were to be given. They are described (i) as baptized people of the true apostolic faith and as true Christians on the religious side, and on the secular side as *kmets*, i.e. peasants; (ii) as good people who do not love sin, whether male or female Christians on the religious side, and on the secular as old *kmets* and poor ones; (iii) as from 'our Law', on the religious side, and blind, crippled, weak, poor, unsightly, leprous people, blind, crippled, hungry and thirsty old men and women.

[173]M. Vego, *Zbornik srednjovjekovnih natpisa Bosne i Hercegovine*, III, (Sarajevo, 1964), pp. 52–3 (dating to 1318; Mme N. Miletić, of the Sarajevo Museum, queries in a private letter whether such precision is possible), analysis Miletić, *I 'Krstjani'*, pp. 122–78 (assuming orthodoxy of Church). I am grateful to Mme. N. Miletić for photographs.

[174]See the introduction to the fresh annotated translation below, appendix E.

[175]Example of interpretation taken from Ćirković (*Oriente cristiano*, p. 555) (translating the key phrase transcribed as *mrsni ljudi* as 'Leuten, die fette Speise geniessen'); French trans. of testament, with facts on Radin, in A. V. Solovjev, 'Le Testament du Gost Radin', in *Mandićev Zbornik* (Rome, 1965), pp. 141–56, reviewed by J. Šidak in *Slovo* (Zagreb) XVII (1967) pp. 195–9 (summarizes sequence of historians' interpretations). I am grateful for photocopies to the Director, Historiski arhiv, Dubrovnik.

[176]Below, p. 375. Cf. appendix E, n. 23.

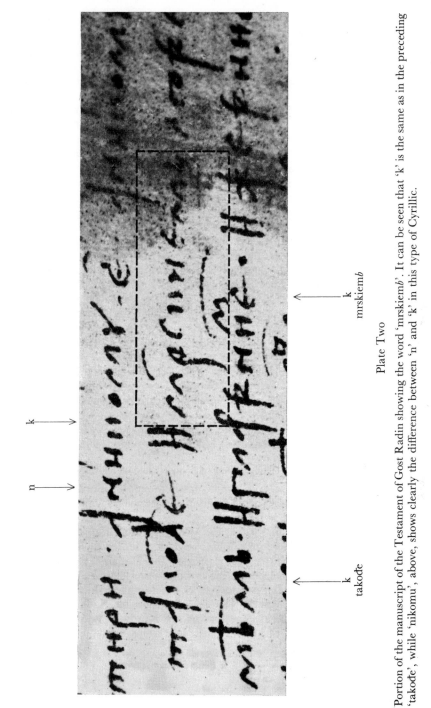

nikomu

n

k

takođe

k

mrskiem *b*

k

Plate Two

Portion of the manuscript of the Testament of Gost Radin showing the word 'mrskiem*b*'. It can be seen that 'k' is the same as in the preceding 'takođe', while 'nikomu', above, shows clearly the difference between 'n' and 'k' in this type of Cyrillic.

In other words in the three separate sentences dealing with these beneficiaries different terms are used to describe the same thing: membership of a separate Church, defined plainly in contradistinction to the Catholic Church (the Church of Dubrovnik) on the religious side, and on the secular side categories of need. These latter are defined in detail with increasing emphasis on distress—from the broad category of *kmets*, then the old and poor, and finally categories of even more severe affliction. A parallel to this mode of writing can be seen in the subsequent description of the needy of Dubrovnik to whom 300 ducats in alms are also to be given. Their service for Radin differs from that required of his Bosnian adherents. The latter are to say a godly prayer; the Catholics are to light candles in their churches.

The fresh translation leaves us with a repetitious, almost incantatory description of needy recipients of alms, firstly from among Bosnian Church members, secondly from among the Catholics of Dubrovnik. There is no implication here of dualism in the Bosnian Church, and that fact must sow fresh doubts about the heretical character of the official Church.

But, whether Bogomil heresy directly infected the Bosnian Church (which is uncertain) or merely existed freely in independence of it and unpersecuted (which is at the very least acceptable), it appears to have had little impact on the people. Dubrovnik courts came into contact with the 'custom of the Bosnians' among immigrants from the interior, who were accustomed to take wives on conditional terms, and might on occasion repel one in favour of another. It seems that this practice had no connection with dualist attitudes towards marriage; it suggests, rather, a lack of contact by the Bosnians with any Church.[177] The Franciscans who worked in Bosnia were obliged to put questions to the papacy about the baptism of adult converts, and Bosnian immigrants to Dubrovnik were regularly baptized there and given fresh names. The Bosnian Church, heretical or not, seems to have had limited impact: a Dubrovnik merchant said that the Patarenes (by which he meant the Bosnian Church) repelled the poor from their houses and received the rich.[178]

Meanwhile, the turn of events in the fourteenth and fifteenth centuries opened Bosnia to external forces. The development of mines in the interior brought in mining experts from Saxony via Slovakia and Hungary, and Catholic clergy to minister to them. A Franciscan vicariate of Bosnia was founded between 1340 and 1342, too small and with too wide an area of responsibility to make a major impact, but still unsullied by the overtones of Hungarian aggression which had damaged the Dominican mission of the previous century.[179] Expansion of the Bosnian State between 1373 and 1377 brought in ancient Serbian territory, and a well-embedded influence of the Serbian Orthodox Church.[180] The map (drawn for S. Ćirković on the assumption of the heretical character of the Bosnian Church) depicts the

---

[177]Ćirković, *Oriente cristiano*, p. 562. But contrast the conclusions of J. Šidak, 'Franjevačka "Dubia" iz g. 1372–3 kao izvor za povijest Bosne', *Istoriski Časopis*, v (1955), pp. 207–31 (in Serbian; German summary, p. 231).

[178]Ćirković, in *Oriente cristiano*, p. 567 and ref.

[179]Šidak, in *Istoriski Časopis*, v (1955), pp. 207–31.

[180]Ćirković, in *Oriente cristiano*, p. 563.

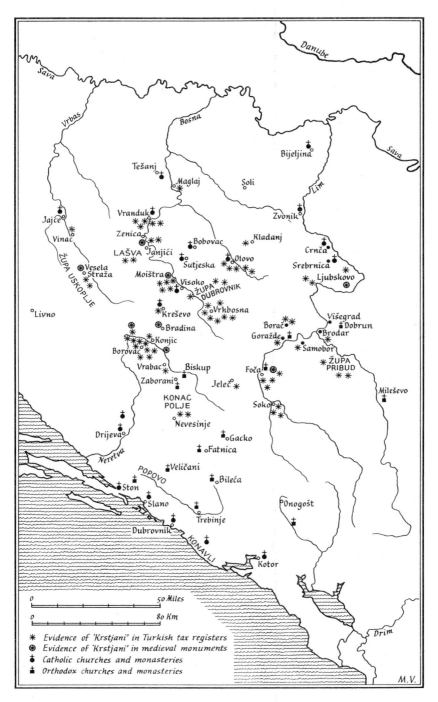

Map Five
The Bosnian Church and its enemies

progress of these forces.[181] Fresh late medieval missionary development is shown in the interior, west of the Drina and well south of the Sava river, in a belt of Catholic churches and convents, in part related to the new mining areas. On the coastal strip, marked by Catholic signs from Ston to Kotor, was Catholic territory; farther to the west lay the Catholic strongholds of Split and Trogir. Orthodox churches and monasteries are more evident in Herzegovina, in a belt lying between Bosnia proper and the coast; some lie in the lands conquered from Serbia in the late fourteenth century. They formed a basis for expansion of Orthodox influence.

The Bosnian Church is traced by two methods. One plots those few of the great number of memorial stones (known as *stećci*[182]) that have inscriptions recording the presence of their members, or employs other documentary evidence to site members of the Church. The other relies on the tax registers kept by the Ottoman Turks after their conquest of Bosnia, which distinguish Christians from Moslems under three titles, *kristian, gebr, kâfir*, and, it has been held, list the remnants of the Bosnian Church under the first name.[183] If Okiç's investigations are correct, they formed but a small remnant: only some 635 souls in registers extending from 1469 into the seventeenth century.

Till the last decades of the independence of the Bosnian State, the old Church kept a considerable place.[184] Diminished by Catholic and Orthodox competition, it yet had official status. In the end, the Western denunciations of the Church as heretical helped to bring both Church and State to an end, as King Stephen Thomas, in a vain attempt to bring in Latin aid against the encroaching Turks, turned against the Bosnian Church,[185] and certain of his subjects, indignant at the loss of their old Church, betrayed fortresses to the Moslems.

[181]S. Ćirković, *Istorija srednjovekovne Bosanske države* (Belgrade, 1964) (in Serbian), p. 284; reviewed J. V. A. Fine, jr, in *Speculum*, XLI (1966), p. 526–9.

[182]M. Wenzel, 'Bosnian and Herzogovinian tombstones: who made them and why', *Süd-Ost Forschungen*, XXI (1962), pp. 102–43; map, p. 117; and *Ukrasni Motivi na Stećima* [Decorated Tombstones from Medieval Bosnia and Surrounding Regions] (Sarajevo, 1965). O. Bihalji-Merin and A. Benac, *The Bogomils* (London, 1962) (for illustrations; see introduction by A. Benac).

[183]T. Okiç, 'Les Kristians (Bogomiles Parfaits) de Bosnie d'après des documents turcs inédits', *Süd-Ost Forschungen*, XIX (1960), pp. 108–33. A research team at the university of Sarajevo is at work on the registers.

[184]J. Šidak, 'O autentičnosti i značenju jedne isprave Bosanskog 'djeda' (1427)', *Slovo* (Zagreb), XV–XVI (1965), pp. 282–97 (German summary, pp. 296–7; argues for Church retaining its prestige until the 1440s, in some contrast to Ćirković (see below)).

[185]Ćirković, in *Oriente cristiano*, pp. 572–5 (note evidence of Orthodox hostility to the Bosnian Church, pp. 572–3). Loos, *Dualist Heresy*, p. 316, significantly notes the Serbian Synodicon which anathematizes Gost Radin in person.

9

The Waldensians after the Conference of Bergamo[1]

The Circumstances of Survival

Only one heresy of the twelfth century survived in unbroken continuity into the sixteenth, to emerge from its hiding-place and link hands with the Protestant Reformation. While Catharism disappeared, Waldensianism outlasted all the persecutions, albeit in remote places or in the lower ranks of society. One reason lay in the fact that Waldensianism stood closer to the central strand of Christian belief, and that the rising standards of education and more effective counter-preaching of the thirteenth century tended to expose the alien character of Catharism. More important, however, was the lower intensity of persecution to which Waldensianism was exposed. In most countries Catharism was the heresy *par excellence*; Waldensianism presented itself as a secondary enemy to the minds of the persecutors. Treatises, intended to convince and confute, had been written against them in the early days of the movement and, as works for and by inquisitors emerged, so Waldensians found a regular place among the enemies of the Church. But they were generally felt to be less dangerous than the Cathars.

Only in Germany could it be said that during much of the thirteenth century the Waldensian rather than the Cathar appeared as the principal target.[2] The progress of persecution was affected by the extraordinary career of Conrad of Marburg, given a special commission to seek out and punish heresy by Gregory IX. His activities resulted in mass executions of suspects

---

[1]The fullest general survey is still H. Böhmer, 'Die Waldenser', *RPTK*, 3rd edn. xx (Leipzig, 1908), cols 799–840; historiography in K. V. Selge, 'Die Erforschung der mittelalterlichen Waldensergeschichte', *TR*, Neue Folge, 33 Jhrg, iv (1968), pp. 281–343, a reference I owe to Dr. A. Patschovsky; Leff, *Heresy*, ii, pp. 452–85 (based esp. on Haupt with helpful bibliography; overstresses value of organization); briefly in Grundmann, *Ketzergeschichte*, pp. 32–4. Modern research surveyed by G. Gonnet, 'Waldensia', *RHPR*, xxxiii (1953), pp. 202–54, and 'Il movimento valdese in Europa secondo le piu recenti ricerche (secoli xii–xvi)', *BSSV*, lviii (1956), pp. 21–30; 'Un decennio di studi sulla eterodossia medioevale', *Protestantismo*, xvii (1962), pp. 209–39. A fresh edition of Waldensian documents is planned for the *MGH* by K. V. Selge and A. Patschovsky, of fourteenth-century Lombard-Austrian material by P. Biller in England, and of the Brandenburg-Pomerania trials by D. Kurze in West Berlin. For earlier Waldensian history see above, chapters 6 and 7. J. Gonnet and A. Molnár, *Les Vaudois au Moyen Age* (Turin, 1974) came to my notice after this chapter was written. It provides a much-needed synthesis. The earlier chapters assemble material from scattered articles by Gonnet; chapters 4 (on underground Waldensianism) and 8 (on theology) by Molnár demand special attention.

[2]H. Haupt, 'Waldenserthum und Inquisition im südöstlichen Deutschland bis zur Mitte des 14 Jahrhunderts', *DZG*, ii (1889), pp. 285–330, 337–411, (still fundamental); synthesis in A. Hauck, *Kirchengeschichte Deutschlands*, (Berlin & Leipzig, 1954), iv, pp. 896–906.

without adequate evidence, and his reign of terror was only ended by his murder in 1233. Clearly he affected innocent and guilty alike, and wasted the powers of his office on, for example, mythical adherents of the devil. He failed to winkle out all the Waldensians,[3] and they spread further as circumstances grew more propitious. Episcopal repression was, as generally, less pertinacious than that of papal inquisitors; and reaction against Conrad's excesses tended to inhibit persecution. Moreover, political conditions were long unfavourable; Church life was disturbed by the papal-imperial conflict under the Hohenstaufen and the long vacancy in central power which followed it. Antipapal propaganda gave a platform to Waldensian preachers, and they profited by the lack of intensity in persecution. The Germans, by the time of the failed conference at Bergamo, adhered to the Poor Lombards and their views, more radical and more hostile to the Church than those of the Lyonists, suited the changed circumstances of the thirteenth century.

So the Waldensians not only survived but also established missions farther east, in Austria and in parts of eastern Germany, in Thuringia, the Mark of Brandenburg, Pomerania and Neumark, following the waves of German emigration and passing into Bohemia, Moravia, Hungary and Poland.[4] These successes in eastern Europe were in some measure a compensation for losses in Waldensian cradle lands. Less effectively pursued than their brothers in Northern Italy, the Germans came regularly to their gatherings in Lombardy and helped to support them with many offerings.[5]

In time international links slackened. Though Austrian Waldensians in the sixth decade still looked to the Lombards for support in a crisis, the Germans generally ceased to send their representatives to the Lombard chapters in the fourteenth century; instead, they held their own annual gatherings, generally in the bigger towns on market days.[6] Occasional persecutions struck them without seriously damaging them. Inquisitors often slandered them, accusing them of sexual depravity, and confusing them with a wholly mythical sect of Luciferans.[7] Then, at the end of the century, a fierce co-ordinated attack in eastern and central Europe, associated especially with the name of the Celestinian Peter Zwicker, came near to driving them out of existence.[8]

In Languedoc, though they received somewhat softer handling than the Cathars, they were still affected by persecution, and had become much less active by the mid-thirteenth century.[9] In the Spanish kingdoms we lose track of the Waldensians in the course of the century.[10] In Northern Italy, when

[3]See Haupt on Waldensian survival generally (*DZG*, II (1889), p. 288). He argues that they had a greater religious appeal than the Cathars. But did they outlast Conrad better than the Cathars? It is not quite clear.

[4]Grundmann, *Ketzergeschichte*, p. 33.

[5]Böhmer on German-Lombard group, in *RPTK*, xx, cols 821–5; see col. 821.

[6]Ibid., col. 829.

[7]R. E. Lerner, *The Heresy of the Free Spirit* (Berkeley, 1972) pp. 25–34; D Kurze, 'Zur Ketzergeschichte der Mark Brandenburg und Pommerns vornehmlich im 14 Jahrhundert', *JGMO*, XVI-XVII (1968), pp. 50–94; esp. pp. 52–62.

[8]Haupt in *DZG*, III (1890), p. 46; Leff, *Heresy*, II, pp. 478–80; Kurze, loc. cit. (excellent trial analysis) describes proceedings launched by Zwicker.

[9]Wakefield, *Heresy, Crusade*, p. 188; Y. Dossat, 'Les Vaudois méridionaux d'après les Documents de l'Inquisition', in *CF*, II, pp. 207–26.

[10]Böhmer in *RPTK*, xx, col. 819.

Salvo Burci was writing his treatise in 1225, the time of more effective persecutions was just beginning.[11] It is significant that it was above all in inaccessible and mountainous regions, on both sides of the Alps, in Franche-Comté, in Dauphiné, long a stronghold, and distant parts of Provence and in the Cottian Alps on the Italian side, that the congregations lived on in the late Middle Ages, sporadically denounced by authority, and still more sporadically affected by active repression.[12] Here, as elsewhere, parish clergy were inclined to blink at evidence of Waldensian activity—for example, Austrian clergy in 1259 were threatened with loss of office if they did not denounce suspects[13]—and the impetus for episodes of persecution tended to originate from clergy of higher rank or from the papal inquisition. In the Cottian Alps, when they had a measure of independence before the great persecution of 1487–94, some of the rank and file as well as preachers absented themselves from mass.[14] However, this was a rare phenomenon, and generally the Waldensians survived by adapting themselves to an underground existence. In the mountains this meant adaptation to mountain conditions, with all that this implies in straitened circumstances and intellectual isolation. Outside the mountain valleys numbers in the later Middle Ages seem to have dropped. Bernard Gui, a very active inquisitor in Provence in the early decades of the fourteenth century, found Cathars and Beguins but dealt only with rather small batches of Waldensians.[15] In Italy they were to be found in the fifteenth century in Romagna and the central regions of the peninsula, even in Rome, and they are traceable in larger numbers from the fourteenth century onwards in Calabria, where repression appears to have been slack;[16] but their heartland lay in the Alpine fastnesses.

Waldensians survived narrowly, their heads kept down by repression or, alternatively, hemmed in in their remote valleys, courageous and tenacious, retaining their vernacular Scriptures and, often, their ethical way of life, but no longer capable of assuming the role of the movement of awakening in the Church envisaged by Valdes. When a new race of evangelical heretics arose from the Hussite movement in the fifteenth century, they looked with some veneration at these veteran opponents of the Roman Curch;[17] both Taborites and Bohemian Brothers were anxious to establish contact with them, and the dynamic influence of the Taborites may indeed have been responsible for a greater Waldensian vitality in the second half of the fifteenth century.[18] But

---

[11]Ibid., col. 821.

[12]Lea, *Inquisition*, ii, pp. 145–161, 195, 159–69 (old summary of facts for France and Italy; compare Böhmer in *RPTK*, xx, 819–23 on influence from Italy to France over the Alps.)

[13]Hauck, *Kirchengeschichte*, v, 399.

[14]Böhmer, in *RPTK*, xx, col. 830.

[15]Leff, *Heresy*, ii, pp. 481–2. That he treated Waldensians as Cathars (ibid., p. 482) is unlikely.

[16]Böhmer, loc. cit. Gonnet and Molnár, pp. 142–4 trace the origins of Waldensians in Southern Italy back to Angevin measures designed to support their rule. Charles the Lame (1285–1309) called in textile workers from Northern Italy to aid the economy. They included Waldensians.

[17]A. Molnár, 'Les Vaudois en Bohême avant la Révolution hussite', *BSSV*, cviii (1960), pp. 3–36; below, pp. 295–6.

[18]Selge, art. cit., p. 339; on disillusionment, see ibid., 339–41, Böhmer, col. 834, A. Molnár 'Luc de Prague et les Vaudois d'Italie', *BSSV*, lxx (1949), pp. 40–64; esp. p. 62. For Bohemian-Waldensian contacts, see now Gonnet and Molnár, ch. 5.

those who had contact with them often suffered some disillusionment at the evasiveness and subterfuges born of their sufferings and their inevitable lack of intellectual calibre. Life underground had exacted its toll.

Belief and Practice

The Passau Anonymous, a composite work on Jews, heresy and Antichrist sometimes described as an inquisitor's manual, the Waldensian section of which was based on the author's experience of an inquisition held in Austria in about 1266, gives us by implication or direct statement the reasons for the continuing attraction of the movement, even under persecution. It lay in the contrast between, on the one hand, a run-of-the-mill, fallible clergy, not too well instructed and with a tendency to superstition, and, on the other, the gathered few of the Waldensian movement, leading a high ethical life, studying Scripture, visited by ministers manifestly poor for the sake of the Gospel, a devoted underground élite confronting the mass of clergy and people.[19] The heretics were zealous. 'All Leonists', the Anonymous notes, 'men and women, adult and child, learn and teach unweariedly by day and night; the workman devotes the day to his work, the night to religious instruction, so that little time remains over for prayer; the newly-converted after a few days seek to draw others into the sect.'[20] The basis of the vernacular Scriptures was important, most of all because of the potency of Scripture itself, but also because of the opportunity for direct instruction and self-instruction through the plain text afforded by the Waldensian system for the laity, in contrast to their passive role at orthodox services. Scripture-reading or Scripture-learning was a religious outlet open to all, intelligent, partially educated and totally ignorant, and it kept knowledge of the text in being, even when texts ran low in persecution or had to be hidden.

Much of the heart of Waldensian belief lay in a cutting away of what was seen to be the excrescences of orthodox belief in purgatory, in images and in pilgrimages—in an insistence on good living, and the literal observance of the texts of Scripture. They would not take oaths, because they believed that the text, 'Swear not at all', must be taken literally; they would not lie; they would not accept judgements of blood—an attitude which had the more poignancy when executions of heretics took place. What they heard, no doubt initially from orthodox instruction based on Scripture, was to be observed to the letter, and not glossed away. Individual responsibility was stressed, and simplicity of belief. There were but two ways, Waldensians held: one to heaven and one to

---

[19]M. Nickson, 'The "Pseudo-Reinerius" Treatise: the Final Stage of a Thirteenth-Century Work on Heresy from the Diocese of Passau', *AHDLMA*, xxxiv (1967), pp. 255–314; extracts from the text, on heresy in the Passau diocese (pp. 291–303). Note the rustic flavour of the section on causes of heresy (pp. 291–3). The treatise is an abridged version of parts of the Passau Anonymous; on the relationship, see Nickson's introduction (pp. 255–60) and A. Patschovsky, *Der Passauer Anonymus: ein Sammelwerk über Ketzer, Juden, Antichrist aus der Mitte des 13 Jahrunderts* (Stuttgart, 1968). Dr Patschovsky is preparing a new edition of the Anonymous for *MGH*.

[20]Haupt's translation (*DZG*, 1 (1889), p. 301); extracts from the Anonymous by W. Preger, 'Beiträge zur Geschichte der Waldesier im Mittelalter', *ABAW*, xiii (1877), pp. 181–250; see pp. 234–45: for other extracts and editions, see Nickson, in *AHDLMA*, xxxiv (1967), pp. 256–7; cf. her text (*ibid.*, p. 292). 'Leonists' are the wing who remained faithful to Valdes, described in this book as Lyonists. These terms may be used loosely by contemporaries.

hell.[21] The Anonymous said that they could be detected just because they were better than their neighbours.[22] It was, in effect, the religion of the ordinary layman who had rejected his clergy for ministers of his own, like him in condition and in devotion, and who was sustained by his Scriptural knowledge. Wherever clerical abuse gave a hold to propaganda, wherever the need for better vernacular instruction was felt, the way was open to building congregations.

Secrecy helped. Étienne de Bourbon, the Dominican inquisitor who died in Lyons in 1261, described the extraordinary shifts in disguise to which the preacher class were reduced in order to remain undetected, notably in the case of one leader who carried with him the clothing of a set of trades, into which he might change as necessary, becoming at one moment a pilgrim, at another a penitent, or a jobbing bootmaker, or a barber, or a reaper.[23] Everywhere the woollen dress that was the badge of the preacher was given up, though at varying rates in different regions; passwords were invented, trades were taken, or the disguise of wandering tradespeople assumed; it seems to have become necessary for the preachers to arm themselves against betrayal. Trades provided natural contacts through which converts might be gained. The preachers were a small category numerically, though vital spiritually: mobility and skill in evasion kept them ahead of a persecution that was at best spasmodic.

At home the hearers of the preacher lived quietly, just as the orthodox did, attending mass and hearing their parish clergy, only seeking to avoid the actual reception of communion. The inquisitorial tradition marked them as insidious:[24] nothing need give away a careful adherent but the visits of the mobile preacher. Sacramental life within the sect became much diminished, sometimes almost non-existent, and the contact, for preaching and confessing, could be brief and secret. A striking example is the case of the Waldensians of Brandenburg and Pomerania in the late fourteenth century, who only saw their preachers on average once or twice a year, when they came in secrecy, known only by Christian names, to hear confessions, sometimes from countries as far away as Hungary or Poland. Followers, usually of a low cultural level, believed that these confessors went to paradise periodically to hear God's voice or to obtain power from Him, and that it was much more efficacious to confess to them than to local priests, who did not lead their pure lives.[25]

Rank and file in these prosecutions lacked the capacity to give a justification for their beliefs, which extended from a borderline position between Waldensianism and Catholicism to wholesale polemic against the

[21]Summary on beliefs by Böhmer, loc. cit., cols. 825–30; K. Müller, *Die Waldenser und ihre einzelne Gruppen bis zum Ausgang des 14 Jahrhunderts* (Gotha, 1886) still has value. See also Gonnet's work of 1967, below p. 163, n. 59.

[22]Haupt, in *DZG.* 1 (1889), p. 301.

[23]Étienne de Bourbon, *Tractatus de septem donis* (ed. Lecoy de la Marche, *Anecdotes historiques* (Paris, 1877)) c. 342; other refs. by Böhmer, col. 815.

[24]On this, note the agreement between the treatise of David of Augsburg (W. Preger, 'Der Traktat des David von Augsburg', *ABAW*, xiv (1879), pp. 181–235) (possibly originating in France; see Dondaine, in AFP, xvii (1947), pp. 180–3) and the Passau Anonymous.

[25]Kurze, 'Ketzergeschichte', pp. 77–8, 81, 82–3. On preaching secretly to small groups, between three and thirty in number, see ibid., p. 78.

Church. We meet the characteristic pungency of denunciation from an adherent who said that it was as senseless to pray for the dead as to give fodder to a dead horse;[26] but there was also an attachment to the cult of Our Lady co-existing illogically with other rejections of Church doctrine and practice. An impetus from literal understanding of Scripture has plainly been of prime importance for the existence of these Waldensians, as is witnessed in the insistence on the necessity of rejecting oaths because of the gospel texts; what kept them in being at the time of the prosecutions was above all a concern for leading a pure moral life, reinforced by the rare visits of their preachers.

The split between the Lyonists and the Lombards concerned the Waldensians less, as persecution affected them all. Though the split was not healed, limited relations persisted in individual cases, as in the case of the French Waldensians who about 1240 spent a long time studying in a school of the Lombards in Milan, and that of the French leader Joannes Lotaringius, who at the end of the thirteenth century journeyed through Italy.[27] Everywhere pressure welded together the rank and file, and transformed the earlier movement of awakening within the Church of Valdes's day into a heretical counter-Church. Catholic observers remained aware of the fundamental distinction often observable between the preachers, sometimes called the perfect, and the believers, disciples or friends who formed the rank and file; but they came to apply the term 'Waldenses' to them all. This was true of the Passau Anonymous and equally of a source of 1264 for Provence.[28] The shift of terminology corresponded to a gathering together of the committed adherents and their teachers in face of persecution.

In self-protection Waldensians evolved a version of their own history in order to give themselves a longer and more distinguished pedigree with which to confront the Catholic controversialists.[29] From letters exchanged on the occasion of the defection of two preachers in Austria, which led the local Waldensians both to seek comfort from the Lombards and to defend their own position against the defectors, we learn that the Austrians had worked into their history a commonplace of the poverty movement of Northern Italy, the defection of the Church at the time of Constantine through the acceptance of endowments:[30] as Pope Sylvester accepted the fatal gift, they said, an angel was heard crying, 'Today is poison poured out in the Church of God.' A companion of Sylvester, however, rejected the gifts, was excommunicated, and with his fellows endured persecution, thus maintaining through poverty the purity the Church had once had in the centuries before the Donation of Constantine. So, on this showing, there was a Waldensian movement before Valdes, who becomes, not the initiator, but, in their words, the 'repairer'[31] of

[26]Ibid., p. 84; cf. Müller, *Waldenser*, pp. 111, 112; on doctrines and Marian cult, see Kurze, pp. 83–6. Compare pungent phrases in Lollardy (below, pp. 268–9) and among some Hussites (p. 295, n. 35).

[27]Böhmer, col. 811; Lotaringius, in Döllinger, *Beiträge*, ii, p. 109.

[28]Böhmer, col. 812.

[29]G. Gonnet, 'I Valdesi d'Austria nella seconda Metà del Secolo xiv', *BSSV*, cxi (1962), pp. 5–41 (summary, pp. 27–9); trans. of letters in E. Comba, *Histoire des Vaudois.* i, *De Valdo à la Réforme* (Paris, etc., 1901, pp. 190–205); see Döllinger, *Beiträge*, ii, pp. 355–62.

[30]Gonnet, in *BSSV* cxi, p. 15; the story does not originate with Waldensians (as Leff, *Heresy*, i, p. 9, argues). Cf. Bonacursus on Cathars, (*WEH*, p. 173).

[31]Gonnet, loc. cit., p. 16.

the movement, stimulating it at a time of flagging zeal. Echoes of fact linger in the story that Valdes tried to convince the hierarchy of the justice of his case, but was excommunicated; the venue, however, has become Rome, and Valdes himself has suffered an extraordinary change, being described as a priest, and given the name Peter. The Waldensians thus met the embarrassing controversialist's question, 'Where were you before Valdes?' by evolving a version of Church history which made them from the outset the true Church, and the papal Church a false or malign one from the time of the Donation of Constantine, incidentally overturning the truth about Valdes—that he was a layman who claimed the right to preach—by putting him into priest's orders. The unhistorical name Peter recalls Peter in the gospels and in Acts as leader of the Apostles: it forms a kind of counterclaim to the papacy as successor of St Peter, and recalls the episode in Acts of Peter confronting the Sanhedrin and declaring that he would obey God rather than men[32]—just as the Waldensians claimed to do, rejecting human traditions and rites in favour of those alone they believed to be of divine origin. A Waldensian version of Church history was a comfort in time of trouble, for it showed alternations of shining life and decadence, like the phases of the moon, in which nonetheless a faithful remnant survived. In their phrase, although the new moon seemed to come to nothing, 'yet it is always the moon.'[33]

No one man ruled the whole Waldensian movement after Valdes. Amongst the Lombards an important role was played by the general chapters,[34] held once or twice a year, at which the vital decisions were taken about the spending of money, the reception of new brothers and sisters, appointments to office and missionary activity. The chapters held together the Lombards and the Germans in the thirteenth century, as we have seen,[35] although they did so somewhat loosely, for the German representation was slight; but by the fourteenth century that direct link had been lost. The friends formed a supporting class to the preachers, fulfilling a function not unlike that of the *credentes* of the Cathars of Languedoc, who aided the journeys of the perfect and gave financial and other support. In Italy they gathered the voluntary tax, the *talea*; in Germany, too, they were money collectors, and kept the treasure of the congregations. In Austria in the fourteenth century the leadership was reproached by a defecting master with the offence of having too much wealth and of having ceased to be adherents of apostolic poverty.[36]

The manner of life of the friends differed in various regions. In Lombardy, where the issue had been so significant at the conference of Bergamo, they probably joined the workers' associations on the pattern of the Humiliati, with set work places which were also centres of instruction and evangelization.[37] The nature of meeting places varied according to the pressures put on the movement, from a regular, known building, like the

[32]Acts 5.29.

[33]Döllinger, *Beiträge*, ıı, 354.

[34]Böhmer, cols 818, 821.

[35]Above, p. 152.

[36]Gonnet, in *BSSV*, cxı, p. 25; Marxist view in E. Werner, 'Ideologische Aspekte des deutsch-österreichen Waldensertums im 14 Jahrhundert', *SM*, 3rd ser., ıv (1963), pp. 218–37. On *talea* and money-collecting, see Böhmer, col. 830.

[37]Ibid., col. 815.

school which long existed in Milan, to individual houses of supporters, as in Brandenburg and Pomerania, visited fleetingly at night by the wandering preachers to give exhortation and absolution behind closed doors.

Women remained important, both as preachers or 'perfect', and as supporters, personally and financially.[38] Hospices existed, both for them and for mixed groups, in which the ascetic life was followed; the ceremony of reception had affinities with the conferring of the *consolamentum* in Catharism. Preaching by women, once a stumbling block to the orthodox hierarchy, continued, and was observable as late as the fifteenth century; women were still playing a considerable role in Piedmont in the later fourteenth century. But Koch is probably right when he argues that the position of women tended to deteriorate, conforming more to the general status of women in this period in the world outside the Waldensian heresy, *pari passu* with a loss of impetus in Waldensianism—especially in the South of France, where from the early fourteenth century it became more difficult for them to enter the preacher or perfect class. The *De vita et actibus* is witness that in the late thirteenth century they were being excluded from the chapters.[39]

Social origins of both adherents and preachers, where known, tended, after an initial phase stretching from the preaching of Valdes to about the middle of the thirteenth century, to be remarkably uniform. Above all, Waldensianism was the religion of the small man, whether in town or country.[40] At first, preachers both had gained recruits higher in society and themselves had been of higher rank; Valdes was a rich business man, and the same factors which drove him out of his business acted on others of similar station; and a group of former clerics existed among the preachers. In the diocese of Metz the heretics had support among *ministeriales*; in Strasburg in the 1220s they gained for their cause a burgher of high standing called Wann; in Bavaria for a time they held hopes of capturing for their cause a count, Otto II. But examples of higher adherence or patronage became rare as the century advances and, though in the later Middle Ages examples exist of well-off townsmen becoming involved, the lasting success of the movement lay lower in society; the core consisted of peasants and artisans. This, of course, does not tell us whether adherents were necessarily poor, for wide variations of wealth were possible in these classes.[41] What seems clear is that much support lay in the countryside; the Passau Anonymous lists forty-two places, scattered in rural localities, as affected by heresy in Austria about 1266; they are small places, forming the ecclesiastical administrative units from which the inquisition was directed, and heretics may well have been found in hamlets or farms round about the villages and small towns marked on the map. With minor variations, the names reappear in reports of the inquisition at Krems in 1315, as if heresy had continued there; but it is likely that the old list of *c.* 1266 was simply attached

[38]Koch, *Frauenfrage*, pp. 156–69.

[39]Ibid., p. 168.

[40]Summary in Grundmann, *Ketzergeschichte*, p. 33; for social origins, see Böhmer, cols 809 (early years), 824–5 (later Middle Ages), and see now Gonnet and Molnár, pp. 164–6.

[41]Kurze, pp. 88–91, esp. p. 89 (close analysis of one grouping; note disagreement with Werner (*SM*, 1963). For the higher classes represented in Mainz, Strasburg, Bavaria, see Hauck, *Kirchengeschichte*, IV, p. 903.

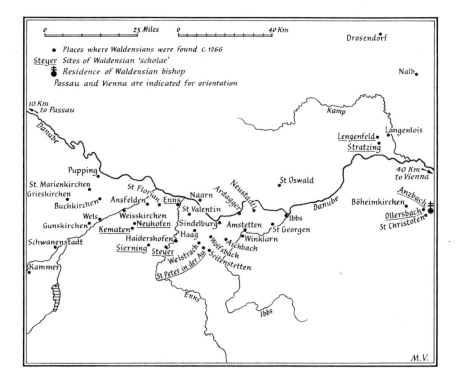

Map Six
The Waldensians in Austria

to the reports.[42] Ten places underlined are the *scholae* of the sect: either these were the instructional centres where formal teaching was given and the Scripture learnt, in a fashion similar to the English Lollards of the fifteenth century, or, as Nickson argues, they were simply 'heretical counterparts of orthodox congregations, visited by wandering ministers of the sect.'[43]

A precise analysis by Erbstösser for affected German-speaking regions of the second half of the fourteenth century again shows how rural the setting of heresy was.[44] Nuremburg is one exception where there was a continuity of heresy inside the town; Freiburg in Switzerland another at the end of the

[42]Preger, in *ABAW*, XIII (1877), pp. 241–2; identifications and discussion by Nickson, in *AHDLMA* XXXIV (1967), pp. 255–314 (esp. pp. 278, 280; on rise of Waldensianism in Austria, pp. 288–91). On the inquisition at Krems, see text in Nickson, p. 308 ('Ut autem' onwards), and Patschovsky, *Passauer Anonymus*, p. 139, n. 9. I owe illuminating comment to Dr M. Nickson and Dr A. Patschovsky. Compare rural distribution of Cathars in map 4 (above, p. 135).

[43]*AHDLMA*, XXXIV, p. 290.

[44]M. Erbstösser, *Sozialreligiöse Strömungen im späten Mittelalter* (Berlin, 1970). (Marxist survey of Flagellants, Waldensians, Free Spirit); see for helpful social and geographical observations, pp. 119–31.

Plate Three

Pra del Torno, Val d'Angrogna, a Waldensian redoubt in Piedmont as seen in 1827

period he surveys. Strasburg produced some good hauls of heretics; but it is by no means clear that it was a true centre of the movement, for some had evidently fled to the town as a refuge from persecution at the time of the Winkler outbreak of 1400. Austria clearly harboured a village movement; in Brandenburg and Pomerania at the end of the fourteenth century peasants and artisans were the supporters;[45] a list made by the inquisition in September 1391 of twelve 'rectors'—evidently preachers drawn from a wide area in Germany and neighbouring lands—showed that none of them came from a large town, and the majority had originated in a village; materials we have for Italian Waldensianism suggest a similar picture. When the movement was pressed back into places of refuge, support lay among the villagers, peasants and artisans. Pre-eminently humbler members of society were attracted by Waldensianism. It has the distinction of being the one international medieval heresy to attract wide support from the peasantry.

The Piedmontese valleys constitute a special case, for there deep poverty and isolation was the necessary background; a feeling of the distinctiveness of the valleys as contrasted to the life of the plains may have played a part in sustaining the movement. If we can believe the reports of the proceedings of inquisitions held in Piedmont at various times in the fourteenth and fifteenth centuries, the valleys also acted as refuge-points for heretics of another cast altogether, and formed a crucible for a Cathar-Waldensian syncretism which co-existed with the dominant strand of plain Waldensianism.[46] So we meet, beside the denials of purgatory and the invocation of the saints, the rejection of oaths, the Donatism and the belief in the superiority of confession to their own preachers, and an idiosyncratic logic: that Christ was not true God, since God could not die,[47] Cathar teaching on dualism and the *endura,* and the acceptance of sexual licence. We meet the extraordinary figure of Giacomo Bech, interrogated in 1388, who apparently had in his time been an adherent of the *fraticelli,* the Waldensians and Cathars of the mitigated dualist variety;[48] and Giovanni Freyra, who confessed in the preceding year to having adored the sun and moon, saying the *Pater Noster* and *Ave Maria.*[49] We also meet the hoary old *canard* in the interrogations of 1387–8 and 1451 of the secret sexual orgy, begun after one of the preacher class, the *barbi,* put out the light, saying, 'Qui ama, si tegna!'[50] The orgy story casts doubt on all the rest, for it was

[45]Above, n.40.

[46]G. Gonnet, 'Casi di sincretismo ereticale in Piemonte nei secoli XIV e XV', *BSSV,* CVIII (1960), pp. 3–36; for editions, see footnotes. A partial, faulty edition of 1387–8 proceedings is in Döllinger, II, pp. 251–73. An interesting, detailed analysis of the environment (accepting syncretism), G. G. Merlo, 'Distribuzione topografica e composizione sociale delle comunità valdesi in Piemonte nel basso medioevo', *BSSV* CXXXVI (1974), pp. 1–30, reached me after this chapter was written.

[47]Gonnet, 'Casi', p. 19; for oddities, see the belief in a dragon (ibid., p. 21).

[48]Ibid., pp. 22–4. There is even a fragment of immoralist Free Spirit Heresy, p. 34 (for Free Spirit, see below, pp. 173–81) Bech sounds to me like a verbal exhibitionist, and his evidence suspect.

[49]Ibid., p. 17.

[50]Ibid., p. 33. On the barbi (or barbae), sing, barba, see T. Pons, 'Barba, barbi e barbetti nel tempo e nello spazio', *BSSV,* LXXXVIII (1967), 47–76. The term was current in the fifteenth century. I owe the ref, and a note of its contents to Dr P. Biller.

quoted too frequently and too crudely by persecutors and chroniclers against various sects to carry credibility.

The first known source in the medieval West for stories of heretics participating in indiscriminate sexual intercourse in the dark is the account of the Orléans heresy of 1022 by the monk Paul of Saint-Père de Chartres.[51] Such practices were attributed to heretics in the twelfth century by Guibert de Nogent[52] and Walter Map;[53] Gregory IX issued a bull describing heretics of his day who so indulged,[54] and interrogators elicted confessions about orgies at various times from Templars and rebellious Franciscans.[55] We are bound to ask, 'If inquisitors, who have free use of torture to command, can elicit such slanderous testimony in these instances, what is the value of other, uncorroborated evidence drawn from those they questioned?' Persecution naturally tended to push together in a common underground Waldensians and their enemies, the Cathars. But how far there was a real influence of Catharism on Waldensianism[56] despite the chasm of belief between them; whether there was an influence which went beyond mere nomenclature; and how far persecutors on various occasions, and not only in Piedmont, lumped the two heresies arbitrarily together, are all questions that have yet to be satisfactorily answered.

The literature of the sect was of a character adapted to its membership:[57] it had a predominantly ethical character and was closely linked to Scripture. What vernacular biblical texts they possessed, and what their origin was, remains somewhat obscure. Valdes commissioned a Bible translation in the language or dialect of Dauphiné of the region of Grenoble, and German translations were in use before the end of the twelfth century; these, we may assume, continued to be used. Other texts may have derived from the Cathars, who were in existence before the Waldensians, and who used vernacular Scriptures. Scripture held a dominant place: it was the 'unique norm of teaching and living', and to it appeal on all disputed questions was made. Waldensian literature proper, or literature taken over by the Waldensians, served the purpose of opening or explaining the Scriptures and of confirming the membership in their ethical life. The best known piece, the *Nobla leycon*, was a poem dating in its present form from the fifteenth century

---

[51]Below, Appendix A. Gonnet ('Casi', pp. 33–6) accepts charges of immorality. I dissent.

[52]Guibert de Nogent, *Histoire de sa Vie (1053–1124)*, ed. G. Bourgin (Paris, 1907) III, xvii, pp. 212–3; discussion of orgy stories, M. Barber, 'Propaganda in the Middle Ages: the charges against the Templars', *NMS*, XVII (1973), pp. 42–57; see pp. 45–8.

[53]*De nugis*, ed. James, I, xxx, p. 47.

[54]*Epistolae saeculi XIII e regestis pontificum Romanorum*, ed. C. Rodenberg, *MGH* (Berlin, 1883). *Epistolae* I, no. 537, pp. 432–4; trans. by Barber, loc. cit., pp. 45–6.

[55]F. Ehrle, 'Die Spiritualen: ihr Verhältniss zum Franciscanerorden und zu den Fraticellen', in *ALKG* IV, pp. 1–190; at p. 137 (note discussion of *barilotto*; I dissent from Ehrle's judgment that orgies took place, find significant the use of torture on suspects, and consider popular suspicion poor evidence); also Templars in Barber (art. cit.), and below, pp. 172–3.

[56]Older summary by Müller (*Waldenser*, pp. 136–8) and Böhmer (col. 826). Answers must wait on fresh analysis of sources.

[57]Böhmer, cols 801–2, 827–8; M. Esposito, 'Sur quelques Manuscrits de l'ancienne Littérature religieuse du Vaudois du Piémont', *RHE*, XLVI (1951), pp. 127–59; Selge (*TR* (1968), pp. 335–6) notes absence of modern work on vernacular Waldensian texts. A valuable summary can now be found in Gonnet and Molnár, *Vaudois*.

which gives a survey of the whole Bible under the headings of the three laws of God; the law of nature, the law of Moses and the law of Christ. There was also simple catechetical material such as the seven articles of faith, and orthodox extracts such as a collection of sentences from the Fathers, and a work of Augustine on the virtues and vices, called 'the Thirty Stages'. This type of reading matter was not heretical at all, and reveals no trace of syncretism or corruption through the underground existence of the sect.

The nature of the hierarchy of the movement varied between the two wings, and fluctuated in the course of time;[58] the situation is also complicated by the possibility that hostile observers did not always grasp the details of the leadership. After the conference of Bergamo the Lombards, rather than the Lyonists, were more interested in having leaders for life; yet by the end of the thirteenth century the Lyonists were appointing a *maior minister* who was to hold office for a lifetime. The threefold orders of bishop, priest and deacon are often witnessed in the sources, but were not employed in precisely the manner of the Catholics. Nor are they continually in evidence; congregations held different views, some stressing the priesthood of all believers, others stressing more the distinction between 'perfect' and the rest. Rule and the episcopal *ordo* did not necessarily go together—men in bishop's orders were sometimes used for sacramental functions without exercising power. It was not always held that the threefold orders had an indelible character: they might be conferred for a time.

Such variations followed from the existence of the major split in the movement between Lyonists and Poor Lombards, from the scattered nature of the congregations and from the effect of Catholic pressure in keeping them apart. Most of all, differences flowed from the biblicism of Waldensians; all beliefs and practices were set against the word of Scripture, and different groups naturally formed different interpretations.[59] By the fifteenth century, for example, the German-Lombard group appear to have forgotten that there was a distinction between bishop and deacon. On the eucharist there were many variations. There were those who took a spiritualizing view; there were those who believed that the validity of the sacrament was conditioned, not only by the worthiness of the celebrant, but also of the communicant; there were Donatists and sacramentalists; there were those who believed that the eucharist should be celebrated once a year on Maundy Thursday, and those who believed that it should be celebrated every day during common meals.

Erbstösser rightly observes that the passage of time did not tighten Waldensian organization.[60] At Bergamo they were sufficiently close knit for both wings to be able to send representatives. But such a unity did not last. In the fourteenth century Bernard Gui, the Dominican inquisitor long active in the South of France whose work on the Waldensians is admittedly heavily

---

[58]G. Gonnet, 'Nature et Limites de l'Episcopat vaudois au Moyen Âge', *CV*, II (1959), pp. 311–21; Böhmer, cols. 816–9, 829–30.

[59]Doctrinal strands within the Waldensians best surveyed in G. Gonnet, *Le confessioni di fede valdesi prima della riforma* (Turin, 1967). Compare the variety of views on baptism and the Eucharist, and see also G. Scuderi 'Il Problema del Matrimonio nella Fede, nella Pietà e nella Teologia del Valdismo medioevale', *BSSV*, CVI (1959), 31–54.

[60]*Sozialreligiöse Strömungen*, p. 133.

derivative, described quite an elaborate organization with varied offices.[61] Germany, on the other hand, had no such structure, and the congregations of Peter Zwicker's persecution were held together by the simplest means; yet the Germans still had resilience, and outlasted a heavy persecution. That fact, coupled with the varieties of organization over the centuries, casts doubt on any hypothesis which lays weight on organization as such as a factor in survival. It was not the offices, or even the chapters, which counted in the last resort; it was the tenacity and mobility of the preachers visiting their flocks, the *barbi* of the Alpine valleys, the *Meister* in Germany. Educational standards were variable, duties quite simple, and the instruction dispensed of a quite lowly standard; but in quality of life and devotion the preachers with few exceptions continued to be pre-eminent. They kept Waldensianism alive till the Reformation.

[61]Leff, *Heresy*, II, pp. 463-4, citing Bernard Gui's *Manuel*, ed. Mollat, I, p. 52.

10

Tension and Insecurity:
Gregory X to John XXII

While the Cathars were being put down by persecution and by peaceful competition from the Church, and the Waldensians were driven deeper into obscurity, the popes faced grave problems, not directly connected with doctrinal unorthodoxy.[1] At first the search for security and independence in Italy lay at the heart of their troubles; they had fought for years to defend themselves against the menace of the Hohenstaufen dynasty holding simultaneously the Empire and the Regno, and threatening them in Rome. Under Innocent IV every means, fair and foul, was used to defeat Frederick II, and no small part of the papacy's reputation and sacral quality was sacrificed in the process. Later, in order to prevent Frederick's heirs again menacing the papcy's independence, a papal champion, Charles of Anjou, was employed to take and to defend the Regno. As we have seen, Charles's success had effect throughout the peninsula, and incidentally helped to create the conditions for the determined persecution of Cathars in Lombardy. The papacy achieved a major victory through the Angevin alliance, and eliminated the Hohenstaufen—only to find the power and ambitions of Charles, brother of Louis IX of France, and the strength of the Capetian dynasty to which Charles belonged profoundly disquieting.

The conflict with the Hohenstaufen had important side-effects: it tended to debase papal policy, and the search for a rival champion helped to create parties within the college of cardinals and to increase tensions between national groups. When in turn the dangers of Charles's power became apparent, one of the policies adopted was that of attempting to build up the papal states in central Italy as partial counterbalances by means of nepotistic appointments.[2] Successive popes sought security through promoting relatives; but pontificates were short, and the relatives of one pope might well be the enemies of another. The policy brought no long-term security and damaged papal reputations.

Charles's decline was due, not to papal policy, but the effects of his

---

[1] Summaries and bibliography in B. Moeller, *Spätmittelalter, Die Kirche in ihrer Geschichte*, ed. K. D. Schmidt and E. Wolf II, H, Pt. I (Göttingen, 1966) (exposition from 1250); F. Rapp, *L'Église et la Vie religieuse en Occident à la Fin du Moyen Âge* (Paris, 1971) (from 1303); reflections in R. W. Southern, *Western Society and the Church in the Middle Ages* (Harmondsworth, 1966), See J. K. Hyde, *Society and Politics in Medieval Italy* (London, 1973) for Italian background, and G. Barraclough, *The Medieval Papacy* (London, 1968) for papal history.

[2] Hyde, *Society*, p. 130.

misgovernment. A revolt in Sicily in 1282, aided by intrigue and bribes from his foreign enemies, gravely weakened his position. The Angevin menace was thereafter effectively removed, but the popes did not jettison the Angevin alliance. Instead, they backed the attempts of Charles and his heir to regain the island of Sicily and, over a period of two decades after the revolt of the Sicilian Vespers, committed papal money and prestige to the Angevin cause, declaring expeditions against their opponents to be crusades. In the end, despite these efforts, defeat had to be accepted at the Peace of Caltabellotta, to which the pope assented in 1303.

This was one beneficent event in the pontificate of Boniface VIII, a first-rate canon lawyer and capable diplomat who was also a gross nepotist and ruthless power politician. Under his highly controversial rule, a dispute with the king of France, Philip IV, escalated into a major conflict. Shortly after Boniface had issued the bull *Unam Sanctam* in 1302, the most extreme statement of the temporal claims of the papacy, he was attacked by Philip's servants in his residence at Anagni, and died shortly afterwards of shock. His fate and his doubtful reputation overshadowed the following two pontificates, for Philip used the threat of a charge of heresy against Boniface as a means of applying pressure. Clement V, elected after the short pontificate of Boniface's immediate successor, Gascon-born, settled at Avignon, partly because of his personal predilections, partly because of the convenience of being close at hand for negotiations with Philip. The temporary residence of the papacy there lasted, with one short interruption, till 1377. Temperamentally reluctant to take firm action, Clement, however he might manoeuvre, in the end felt himself compelled to accept Philip's will. At the Council of Vienne in 1312 he suppressed the order of Templars, earlier convicted of wholly imaginary offences at the instigation of Philip, who needed their goods in order to satisfy pressing economic needs. As if to underline the changed position of the clergy *vis à vis* the laity, the same council discussed the encroachments of the laity on ecclesiastical goods and jurisdictions without finding any effective defence against them. It was a melancholy contrast to Innocent's fourth Lateran Council a century earlier.

After a prolonged vacancy, John XXII was elected to succeed Clement in 1316. As trenchant as Clement had been vacillating, he at once set about restoring the papal position, and in an eighteen-year pontificate, aided by the waning of France's strength after the death of Philip IV, went far towards recreating independence. In place of his predecessor's debts he built up an unprecedented surplus. The curia was reorganized, and once again the papacy came to occupy a central position in international diplomacy; all spheres felt the impress of the pope's personality—energetic, authoritarian, inflexible. On issues of faith and heresy, his instinct was to back authority, to define and condemn, and to give work to the inquisition. The pontificate was marked by a series of definitions and proceedings aimed at suspect theologians and sectaries. Authoritarian methods roused opposition. Obstinate determination to make his own will prevail over the choice of emperor aroused a conflict with Lewis of Bavaria, who gave protection to Franciscan rebels and heretics as a weapon against the pope, and John failed to bring him down. At the end, lacking the suppleness of Innocent III and the essential aid of powerful reform movements within the Church and religious orders, he had been unable to stimulate profound or long-lasting changes to the benefit of the Church, and the methods whereby he rebuilt the papal position alienated opinion.

Over the clergy, in contrast to the laity, the papacy exerted an ever-increasing control during these difficult years. Centralization continued apace within the Church, and canonists erected a structure of thought which drew out the implications of the doctrine of the 'fullness of power' inherent in the papal office. A major impetus to centralization was, however, fiscal. Costly wars and foreign policy, and expanding bureaucracy demanded money and the growing papal power within the Church was more often directed towards stopgap solutions of immediate problems than the needs of reform. In form and theory, the place of the papacy within the Church expanded; in reality, popes suffered from a chronic insecurity and inability to match means to ends.

A changing society was becoming less amenable to papal leadership. Damaged by the papacy's own misuse, the attractions of the crusading ideal waned. One stage in its decay was reached by the time that Gregory X, a sincere crusading pope, summoned the council of Lyons of 1274. It was intended to heal the schism with the Greek Church, counter Charles of Anjou's designs on Byzantium, and act as a launching platform for an expedition to the Holy Land. Gregory's investigations at the time of the council revealed how far interest in crusades had waned; a traditional link between papacy and laity was gradually eroding.

The Empire was far less significant than it once had been: power had passed to the national kingdoms. The events of the pontificates of Boniface VIII and Clement V showed the difficulties which popes had in coming to terms with the shift in temporal power that had taken place.

Educational standards amongst the laity were rising, and new directions in lay piety were beginning to make themselves felt. The mystical way, formerly the preserve of the monastery or nunnery, was being opened to the laity and to the secular clergy, with the aid of the friars and their spirituality. It reflected a developing trend towards individualism in later medieval piety, not of itself hostile to the Church and the sacraments—indeed eucharistic fervour might be a feature of the pursuit of the mystical way—but stressing the soul's experience of God rather than the Church's mediation.

No movement arose on the scale of the Cistercians in the twelfth century or the friars in the early thirteenth to rouse the energies of the devout and give backing to any papal reforming designs; reform impulses were still there, but they found expression in piecemeal, local movements or in the lives of dedicated individuals. The Franciscans, so long a support of the papacy, showed signs of strain; at the council of Lyons earlier dissensions dating back to St Francis's lifetime began to emerge again in a form so acute as eventually to demand prolonged papal investigation.

Complexity, bureaucracy and worldliness produced a reaction. The popes faced difficulties that were not susceptible of swift, personalized solutions; but their position was rarely considered with sympathy, and from the early years of the fourteenth century we may detect something of the sense of betrayal which Leff rightly distinguishes as characteristic of late medieval opinion about Church leadership.[3]

Abuse of the inquisition's powers, the Free Spirit and the heresy associated with the Spiritual Franciscans, to be discussed in the following chapters, have to be set against this background of centralization, political pressure and change in the years between the council of Lyons and the death of John XXII in 1334, affecting both the men and women accused of heresy and their repressors.

[3]*Heresy*, I, p. 29.

I I

Inquisition and Abuse

1. The Problem of the Inquisition

The papal inquisition was founded by Gregory IX, building on the foundations of his predecessors, and its extraordinarily wide powers of investigation and punishment were granted in order to make an end of heresies already condemned by the Church, most notably Catharism.[1] Naturally new sects and heresies that arose fell within its purview and, equally naturally, the influence of those who were given inquisitional powers tended to be directed towards the tightening of the Church's law on heresy, in favour of condemnation rather than toleration of doubtful beliefs and practices. The desire of the inquisitor was for clear-cut condemnations and lists of erroneous beliefs that could be incorporated in handbooks and used as a basis for action in the field; his instinct was to widen the scope of his authority and to bring more activities into his sphere. So, for example, inquisitors attempted to bring sorcery under their jurisdiction after application to Alexander IV, whose ambiguous declaration that they might only do so if 'manifest heresy' were involved was used as a starting-point for an ultimate, if long delayed, assumption of authority in this sphere.[2] Higher churchmen who shared the inquisition mentality exercised their influence in similar ways, and were inclined to see heretical tendencies in movements and groups in the Church of which they disapproved. Bishops within their dioceses exercised wide powers and, if zealous, could give scope to their suspicions on the same lines as the inquisitors. The untramelled power of the inquisitor, the high penalties exacted or exactable for heresy and the opportunities in some cases of enrichment of interested parties in the wake of convictions made it inevitable that the unscrupulous would seek to take advantage of heresy charges to advance their own power, to ruin rivals or to feather their own nests.[3] Unjust accusations of heresy were not new, and there is little doubt that zealots with no pertinacious will to unorthodoxy were killed or ruined in the twelfth century, before the development of more advanced techniques of detection

[1]Above, pp. 102–5; survey in C. Thouzellier, 'La Répression de l'Hérésie', in *Histoire de l'Église*, ed. A. Fliche and V. Martin, x pp. 291–340; bibliography in E. van der Vekené, *Bibliographie der Inquisition: ein Versuch* (Hildesheim, 1963); short notes in Wakefield, *Heresy, Crusade*. A full account of the inquisition and its distortions is beyond the scope of this book.

[2]Lea, *Inquisition*, III, p. 434; see J. B. Russell, *Witchcraft in the Middle Ages* (Cornell, 1972); *WEH*, p. 251.

[3]Lea (I, chs. 7–14) is still of value: see above, ch. 7, n. 37.

and judgement. Confusion, then a major factor, was no longer so prevalent in the late thirteenth century; the new feature was the international character of persecution and its greater sophistication. On the one hand, the development of anti-heretical treatises, bulls of definition and inquisitorial handbooks helped to dispel the old ignorance;[4] on the other, if prejudice did once enter into these sources, they were disseminated much more widely, and the new character of persecution made possible what had not existed earlier—the manufacture of a whole artificial or semi-artificial heresy.

At the lowest level the office of inquisitor exposed its holder to temptation: it was the other side of the coin in the new efficiency of persecution which flowed from the commissions and legislation of Gregory IX and his successors. *Inquisitio* as a legal process confounded in one and the same person the offices of prosecutor and judge. The secrecy of proceedings, the wide powers of arrest and imprisonment, the lack of any obligation to inform the accused of charges against him or to name witnesses, the absence of defending counsel, and the extreme difficulty of appealing against decisions meant that the preservation of justice rested to a large extent on the integrity of the individual who conducted a case. There was scope for greed, political bias, the malice of neighbours, bullying and sadism. Weight was given to mere *fama*, the ill report of a suspect's orthodoxy in a neighbourhood. Some yielded to the temptations of their authority; others, especially in early days, remained zealous, hard-working bureaucrats, inclined to cut corners in their eagerness to get to grips with heresy, yet not gravely unfair to suspects.[5]

The most important danger, however, lay in misunderstanding and unconscious distortion, either through over-sophisticated questioning or over-rigid adherence to some preconceived pattern of heresy derived from treatise or handbook, then imposed by forceful interrogation on a cowed suspect. Bernard Gui, who completed his manual about 1322–3, gives us an example of the dangers of over-sophistication in his section on tricks of the Waldensians, in turn taken from a thirteenth-century work attributed to David of Augsburg.[6] The inquisitor questions his suspect on the articles of faith. He replies briskly, 'I firmly believe.' The inquisitor asks him about transubstantiation. He replies, 'Ought I not to believe this?' The inquisitor responds, 'I am not asking if you ought to believe it, but if in fact you do', and gets in turn the reply, 'I believe all that you and other good doctors order me to believe.' The inquisitor believes this is an evasion, and goes on, 'Those good doctors which you are willing to believe are the masters of your sect. If I think as they do, you will believe both me and them; if not, not'. So the two continue to wrestle until the wily Waldensian is finally broken down on the sensitive issue of oath-taking.

No doubt life underground did produce the Waldensian heretic experienced in such evasions, equivocating to save himself and his friends, and

---

[4]Above, p. 103.

[5]See, e.g., Y. Dossat, 'Une Figure d'Inquisiteur: Bernard de Caux,' in *CF*, VI, pp. 253–72. The career of the outrageous Conrad of Marburg (above, p. 151) shows how, even in the earliest days of these free-ranging commissions, power could be abused; see Wakefield, *Heresy, Crusade,* pp. 185–6, for sound comment.

[6]*Manuel,* ed. Mollat, I, p. 67; on authorship, see Dondaine, in *AFP*, XVII (1947), pp. 93–4, 180–3; Borst, *Katharer,* pp. 22, 25; and for comment, Patschovsky, *Passauer Anonymus,* pp. 135–6.

trying to avoid direct lying; but inquisitors would also meet simple Catholics, untrained on the limits of heresy and orthodoxy, nervously attempting to ingratiate themselves, and falling deeper in the mire. Behind interrogation lay torture, to be applied at the will of the inquisitor, who, if he felt he was never touching rock bottom belief in his suspect's answers, could use force in such a way as to compel incriminating answers, at least from most of common humanity. Confinement, fear and detachment from family and friends worked in the same way, and might lead to conviction by baseless, or scantily based, confession. The danger of a vicious circle was obvious, for inquisitors believed that in heresy they were fighting the work of the devil and were inclined to think that suspects were more subtle than they really were. Force, and the threat of force, could produce the guilty answers they felt they ought to be getting. The classic example is witchcraft, whose apparent popularity owed so much to the interest of inquisitors.[7]

More subtle distortion might spring from the use of leading questions based on handbooks' summaries of heretical tenets, obliterating an individual's personal variations of belief. Heresies changed, and handbooks did not necessarily keep pace with them; they tended to be based on a stereotype, and did not take adequate account of variations within heretical groups in different areas and times. Or the ethics of heretics might be slandered, and their tenets confused with those of other, more extreme heresies; we have seen the likelihood that this was the case in fourteenth and fifteenth-century Piedmont.[8]

Each set of records of proceedings and testimony needs to be examined closely, in order to see whether the inquisitor or the bishop's officers have, through their questioning, provided a fair and accurate picture of heresy or a heretical group. Sometimes there are signs of distortion of testimony or blind repetition of predetermined sentiments; sometimes idiosyncratic replies by suspects and the flavour of many-faceted heresy as it appears in real life will assure us of the substantial accuracy of what we read; sometimes the signs are that the beliefs of a group have remained fairly static, and our records are doing substantial justice to the accused. The historian making these assessments will take account of deterioration in accuracy and fairness among inquisitors in the later medieval centuries.

In the higher ranks of churchmen manipulation of heresy charges occurred. A grey area is revealed, for example, in the activities of Bernard de Castanet, bishop of Albi, who controlled the workings of the inquisition in his city, damping them down as long as the heresy-infected leading bourgeoisie were on his side in battles of jurisdiction against the king, unleashing them in a famous set of trials of 1299–1300, after leading citizens had broken the alliance, and had come to work with royal officials against his interests.[9] The convicted were indeed heretics, and the bishop, an ultramontane ecclesiastic

---

[7] Lea, III, p. 50; the approach tends to differ from that of Russell, *Witchcraft*. Earlier work in H. C. Lea, *Materials toward a History of Witchcraft*, ed. A. C. Howland (Philadelphia, 1939); J. Hansen, *Quellen und Untersuchungen zur Geschichte des Hexenwahns und der Hexenverfolgung im Mittelalter* (Bonn, 1901).

[8] Above, p. 161.

[9] J. L. Biget, 'Un Procès d'Inquisition à Albi en 1300', in *CF*, VI, pp. 273–341; G. W. Davis, *The Inquisition at Albi 1299–1300* (New York, 1948). I have accepted Biget's viewpoint.

of the stamp of Boniface VIII, no doubt was in any case little inclined to distinguish between the crime of heresy and attacks on his temporal power, especially when they were the work of the same persons; but the fact remained that those convicted were the partisans of the Albi oligarchy and the king against the bishop, and that the trials followed hard on the heels of another, apparently unsuccessful, attempt in 1297–9 to put pressure on hostile oligarchs through the bishop's temporal jurisdiction. The importance of city politics for the Albi inquisition was obvious.

The development of papalist canon law in the thirteenth century tended to reinforce autocracy, and to encourage the inclination to equate heresy with disobedience to the pope, in the temporal sphere as much as in the spiritual; strangely enough, Frederick II's imperial legislation, *mutatis mutandis*, tended to confound heretics and political offenders in a similar fashion. The vague use of heresy charges ran hand in hand with the debasement of the crusade to attain political ends for the popes within christendom, the accusations being a part of the propaganda against offending rulers and a justification for military action against them. So the Hohenstaufen were attacked in this way;[10] so Boniface VIII used the charge against his enemies in the Colonna family; so John XXII proclaimed his political enemies in Italy, the Visconti of Milan, the Esti, the Ghibellines of Umbria and the March, guilty of heresy, and declared the recalcitrant emperor Lewis of Bavaria to be a fautor.[11] As temporal opponents of the popes often favoured or tolerated heretics as pawns in their political game, or refused for reasons of security to allow the Inquisition to operate in their lands, accusations of fautorship of heresy were not wholly baseless. But contemporaries recognized that it was concern, not about unorthodoxy, but about papal rights and the balance of power in Italy that motivated these charges. A debasement of the concept of heresy was implicit in this type of action.

The Templars

The loose use of heresy charges could not be expected to remain a monopoly of churchmen, and Philip IV of France and his ministers made the most dramatic and unscrupulous use of them in the entire period in their actions against the Templars (1307–12). They had been preceded by charges against Boniface VIII, scion of a Campagna family, a man of scant tact and of easy manners, whose insensitive actions and pungent remarks brought him many enemies, and provided a fund of disturbing statements that, spiced with exaggeration and hearsay, had formed the pretext for charges of heresy and other malpractices brought by Philip the Fair and his servants.[12] The threat of a formal trial of Boniface acted as a blackmail on the insecure Clement V, and opened the way for the French crown's sudden assault on the Templars in

---

[10]For this example and others, Lea, III, ch. 4, 5; Grundmann bibliography in *HS*, pp. 448–50.

[11]F. Bock, 'Studien zum politischen Inquisitionsprozess Johanns XXII', *Quellen und Forschungen aus italienischen Archiven und Bibliotheken*, XXVI (1935–6), pp. 21–142; XXVII (1936–7), pp. 109–34; 'Der Este-Prozess von 1321', *AFP*, VII (1937), pp. 41–111, 'Processi di Giovanni XXII contro i Ghibellini italiani', *ADRSP*, LXIII (1940), pp. 129–43.

[12]T. S. R. Boase, *Boniface VIII* (London, 1933), pp. 355–79; articles in *HS* (Grundmann bibliography), p. 449, nos. 515–8.

1307.[13] Novel forces were arrayed against the papacy when an advanced secular monarchy, already blooded in the contest of wills with Boniface VIII, made uninhibited use of inquisitional techniques in order to gain the Templars' wealth. The inquisitor of France was the king's confessor; and the bishops of the kingdom were solid in support of the monarchy's cause; and the Templars were a rich secretive body that seemed to have lost its crusading *raison d'être* when the last foothold of the Christians in the Holy Land at Acre fell in 1291. Disappointment at the failure of Christendom to recover Jerusalem and the search for a scapegoat may have made some of Philip's subjects receptive to charges against the Templars; it does not seem that anyone outside France believed them, and no modern historian of repute will accept them as true. The Templars, it was said, imposed a denial of Christ and blasphemous rejection of the Cross on their novices, required them to kiss their receptor's posterior, told them that homosexuality was lawful, adored an idol, and had the custom of not consecrating the Host when priests in the order celebrated mass. To this extraordinary farrago of nonsense were added other variant tales—of eucharistic heresy, worshipping a cat, betraying the cause of Christendom to the Moslems, of laymen in the order hearing confessions and granting absolution, of unlawful gains and sinister secrecy in chapter meetings. Charges were skilfully selected to undermine popular confidence and had more than one echo of accusations customarily made against heretics.[14]

The vicious circle was operating with a set of accusations from tribunals directed by the episcopate and royal servants. Tortured or in other ways subjected to pressure, a sufficient number of Templars confessed, to provide 'evidence' for the case against them. The affair demonstrated that any string of accusations could be made effective, given the necessary zeal in interrogation and the employment of force; outside France, however, interrogation worked less well in providing evidence, because the necessary drive to produce confessions was lacking. But sufficient had been done to ruin the order's position. Clement was dogged by the threat of Boniface's memory, and too heavily involved to draw back; and at the Council of Vienne in 1312 the order was suppressed, and the French monarchy had gained the resources it urgently needed.

2. The Free Spirit and Heretical Mysticism

The Templar episode was the most naked case of the use of the machinery of persecution for pure slander; the treatment of the beguines, beghards and mystics in northern Europe was a more subtle case of misunderstanding, in which genuine grounds for disquiet combined with suspicious conservatism and the persecuting mentality to smear pious, unprotected groups.[15]

---

[13]Value still in Lea, III, pp. 238–334; up-to-date account, with literature in M. Barber, 'Propaganda in the Middle Ages: the Charges against the Templars', *NMS* XVII (1973), pp. 42–57, who plans to survey the whole subject in a book, *The Trial of the Templars*.

[14]Barber, *art. cit.,* pp. 45–8, 54.

[15]H. Grundmann, 'Ketzerverhöre des Spätmittelalters als quellenkritisches Problem', *DA*, XXI (1965), pp. 519–75 (fundamental reassessment of sources), R. E. Lerner, *The Heresy of the Free*

Beguines were religious women leading lives of chastity, generally grouped in convents, supporting themselves by manual work and engaging in prayer, but without any fixed rule, organization or final vows.[16] In the north *beguinus* as a term for a man was at first not usual; the male equivalent there was usually termed a beghard. He frequently lived by begging, but resembled the much more numerous female beguines in leading a religious life without fixed organization. The terms, however, were used rather imprecisely.[17]

The beguine movement in the north was a spontaneous, local outgrowth of the urge to apostolic life which moved zealous Christians in the twelfth century, and offered occupation for women, generally in comfortable circumstances, who could not expect to find a husband. The very institutional formlessness of the beguinages may have been an attraction, and their simplicity made foundation easy. They fitted naturally into urban life, met a need for women who could not find acceptance in established orders, and so continued an unobtrusive existence in large numbers in certain towns of Flanders, northern France and Germany. They also attracted devout women who preferred the role of the beguine on religious grounds to that of the nun.

The beguine and beghard occupied an ambiguous position. Rigorous interpretation of canon 13 of the fourth Lateran Council might put their position in question.[18] In status they lay somewhere between the orders and the parish clergy, subject to neither, and liable to be lookd at askance by both.[19] Beghards formed a suspect penumbra to the mendicant orders. Mystical works formed a stimulus to the piety of these groups, often aided by confessors and directors from the mendicants and distinguished by a stress, in the style of the friars, on the incidents of the lives of Christ and Mary in the gospels. Because of their lack of established status and organization, they were vulnerable to the accusation of heresy, and popular suspicion seems to have given them their name, beguine being most probably a corruption of Albigensis, the term for a Cathar of southern France. Both beguines and beghards came to enjoy a strangely mixed reputation, sometimes the butt of accusations of sexual immorality on no good grounds, sometimes accused of the hypocritical feigning of virtue, but also praised and given patronage by churchmen of influence. James of Vitry, inspired by Marie of Oignies, the

---

Spirit in the later Middle Ages, (Berkeley, 1972) (the standard critical account for northern lands); R. Guarnieri, 'Il movimento del Libero Spirito', *Archivio italiano per la storia della pietà*, IV (1965), pp. 351–708 (quarry for material, value for work on Porete's *Mirror*). I am indebted to Professor R. E. Lerner for information, and for his work, extensively used in this section.

[16]Older literature, sometimes superseded, in Grundmann, *Ketzergeschichte*, pp. 52–8 (written before his 1965 article); background in E. W. McDonnell, *The Beguines and Beghards in Medieval Culture, with Special Emphasis on the Belgian Scene* (New Brunswick, 1954); reflections by Southern *Western Society*, pp. 318–31. *RB*, (pp. 170–318) discusses the problem of women and the religious life, and beguines (pp. 319–54), but some conclusions are upset by the important revision, based on German evidence, of J. B. Freed ('Urban development and the *cura monialium* in thirteenth-century Germany', *Viator*, III (1972), pp. 312–27. I owe this ref. and comment to Miss B. Bolton; see her 'Mulieres sanctae', in *SCH*, x, pp. 77–95.

[17]Lerner, *Free Spirit*, pp. 35–7. The Beguins of southern France (below, pp. 197–203) form part of a different movement, linked closely to the Spiritual Franciscans, principally in the Franciscan province of Provence.

[18]Above, p. 105.

[19]Lerner, *Free Spirit,* ch. 2, is helpful.

pivot of a movement of female piety in the diocese of Liège, gave them help;[20] Fulk, bishop of Toulouse, thought that beguines might be used as a bulwark against Cathar influence;[21] in the mid-thirteenth century Robert Grosseteste placed their way of life, poor but self-supporting through manual labour, on a higher level even than the mendicancy of the friars.[22]

But by the time of the council of Lyons in 1274, the earlier suspicion that had dogged them had again risen to the surface. It was a time of growing friction and tension in Church life, and beguines and beghards tended to be Aunt Sallies.[23] The mendicants, conscious of their waning popularity, struck out at groups close to them in their attitudes yet precarious in status, and made them scapegoats; on the other side, forces hostile to the friars used them as stalking horses for attacks in reality directed against the friars. Self-interested hostility there had always been, in the resentment of relatives or would-be husbands at the loss of their women to the beguine life. At the time of Lyons pamphlets appeared against the beguine movement; the Franciscan Gilbert of Tournai complained that beguines had unauthorized vernacular translations of the Scriptures containing heresies (which he did not specify), and that they read these in public places; Bruno of Olmütz proposed bluntly that they should be told to marry or enter one of the established orders. Canon 13 of the fourth Lateran Council was reiterated and, by the decision of the Council, became a barrier *tout court* to all new forms of religious life: no new order was to be founded, and those that had come into existence despite the canon were to be suppressed. Without leading to any direct action, this obviously made the situation of beguines and beghards more precarious. Nothing occurred in the following decades to refurbish their image. Instead, synodal decrees in Germany witnessed to irritation at beghards as unauthorized preachers; arrests for heresy occurred at Colmar and Basle of both beguines and beghards in 1290; and the Franciscan chapter at Colmar, faced with a procession of three hundred beghards begging for bread, warned their members against associating with these suspect competitors.

The beguines entered the crucial early decades of the fourteenth century vulnerable, their reputation damaged by accusations against their beliefs and behaviour, although they were not, as yet, the butt of any precise charge of heresy. The mystical movement generally had begun to occasion some suspicion: in an ill-recorded episode, the scholastic Albertus Magnus reported in the 1270s on a set of opinions emanating from the Swabian Ries that contained pantheistic and immoral beliefs—the outflow of speculation, it may be, on the state of mystical adepts.[24] But no evidence connects the mystics of the Ries with the beguines and the opinions, extant only as isolated fragments of testimony, are too inconsistent with each other and too unrelated to a historical or literary context to provide clear evidence of the reality of a heresy in Swabia at that date.

All that can be inferred safely from Albertus's judgement is that anxiety was

[20]McDonnell, *Beguines*, p. 20.
[21]*RB*, p. 172.
[22]Ibid., p. 322.
[23]Lerner, *Free Spirit*, pp. 45–6.
[24]Grundmann, *Ketzergeschichte*, pp. 45–6; Lerner, *Free Sprit*, pp. 13–19.

stirring in the Church in his time about the pursuit of the mystical life. It was a consequence of a growing vogue for mystical reading in the vernacular, made possible by the greater leisure and resources of aristocracy and bourgeoisie and their higher educational standards, and an increased democratization of the mystical way. Once the province of the monk and nun, often in enclosed orders, the mystical way had become more accessible to those outside, to the beguine and to the pious layman. The possible dangers in the pursuit of mysticism, the absence of firm control through an institutional framework over those who now pursued it, and the very fact that profound theological matters were being presented in the vernacular, appeared as an anxiety to authority. The beguines heavily involved in the mystical movement were accused of harbouring a sect of heretical mystics, named as adherents of the Free Spirit.

Soon the popes began to concern themselves with antinomian heresy. In 1296 Boniface VIII issued a bull against a sect who prayed in the nude, and in 1311 Clement V was writing to the bishop of Cremona to require the uprooting of a sect of the Free Spirit of Italy, claiming freedom of action because of the inspiration of the Holy Spirit in them.[25] In 1307 an authoritarian archbishop of Cologne, Henry of Virneburg, included in decrees for his diocese, as well as complaints of a traditional style against beghards (of both sexes; he apparently preferred not to use the term beguine for the females) for defying the canons against new orders, preaching and interrupting friars' sermons, a charge of heretical mysticism. Then, between 1306 and 1308, a beguine named Marguerite Porete of Hainault, one of whose books had already been burnt by the bishop of Cambrai, was arrested for spreading heresy 'among simple people and beghards' through another book, and was sent to Paris. There she refused to respond to interrogation, and was convicted of heresy on the strength of some extracts taken from this book, submitted for judgement to a commission of theologians. Her earlier conviction meant that she was guilty of relapse, and she was burnt in Paris in 1310.

The charge was again heretical mysticism, but in this instance we have the heretic's own work with which to check the veracity of the accusations made against her. By chance, the treatise which caused her conviction and burning, the *Mirror of Simple Souls*, survived, to circulate anonymously in monasteries and nunneries, in the original and in translation, from the fourteenth century to the present.[26] So little obvious was the heresy in it that hardly any of its readers over the centuries questioned its orthodoxy; or if they did they came down eventually on the side of the *Mirror*, like the Middle English translator

[25] Ibid., pp. 78–84 (also for Henry of Virneburg); L. Oliger, *De secta spiritus libertatis in Umbria saec. XIV; disquisitio et documenta* (Rome, 1943) (accepts genuineness of accusations).

[26] Lerner, *Free Spirit*, pp. 68–78, text of *Mirror* ed. Guarnieri in *Archivio Italiano per la storia della pietà*, IV (1965), pp. 513–635; for account of case, see under appropriate years in her chronology of heresy; trans. of Middle English version in C. Kirchberger, *The Mirror of Simple Souls* (London & New York, 1927). For the way in which suspicion came to play on the mystical language sometimes used in impeccable sources, see Lerner, 'The Image of Mixed Liquids in Late Medieval Mystical Thought', *CH*, XXX (1971), pp. 397–411. An account of Middle English texts is given by E. Colledge, 'The Treatise of Perfection of the Sons of God: a fifteenth-century English Ruysbroeck translation', *English Studies*, XXIII (1952), pp. 49–66.

who felt some disquiet but concluded that it was written of 'high divine maters and of highe goostli felynges and kerningli and ful mystili it is spoken.'[27] Indeed it was, using an extensive vocabulary, and drawing on what was plainly deep personal experience to describe in dialogue form the progress of the soul through seven states of grace, the greater part of it being both traditional and edifying.

The danger lay in the fifth and sixth states, the highest that could be attained in this life, when the 'annihilated' or 'liberated' soul is unified with God. Here, in Lerner's judgement,[28] Marguerite Porete went beyond traditional masters, applying, for example, the similes used by St Bernard of Clairvaux for the state of the soul in paradise to its condition in an advanced mystical state here below. There were some extravagant thoughts: the soul, still in the body, is described as being united with the Trinity, or as finding God in itself without searching. There is much about the soul's farewell to the virtues, which could lead to misunderstanding by those who failed to observe Marguerite's reasons for saying it, that the virtues are always with the liberated soul in any case. There is a definite anticlerical taint in the contrast repeatedly drawn between the liberated soul and those at earlier stages who require traditional aids and disciplines, and between 'Holy Church the Little', under reason, and 'Holy Church the Great', ruled by divine love. Finally, there is something disquieting in Marguerite's description of the passivity of the liberated soul: it 'does not seek God by penance, nor by any sacrament of the Holy Church, nor by thought, words or works.'[29] Marguerite was aware of the dangers of *doubles mots*, and remarked that 'simple minds might misunderstand them at their peril.'[30] She was treating of esoteric matters, and it was not a book for the many, although obviously designed for reading aloud in the vernacular. Two factors seem to have weighed in her condemnation: her pertinacity, shown in the repeated dissemination of her views and her refusal to respond to interrogation, and the alleged publicity given to the *Mirror* among simple people. What might have been possible in an established nunnery, without publicity, appeared not to be allowed to a beguine who wanted to propagate her work. Her views were not fairly represented. The *Mirror* is very doubtful on the passivity of the liberated soul and on its lack of any need for the sacraments, and presumptuous on the state of union with God in the fifth and sixth states; on the other hand, it is not libertine. Porete's enemies argued that it was, quoting a phrase of the *Mirror* on the liberated soul giving 'to nature, without remorse, all that it asks';[31] they omitted Porete's covering explanation, that in the liberated state nature 'does not demand anything prohibited.'

Heresy, then, in this case, if it existed at all, was of a specialized character, concerned solely with the condition of mystical adepts at an advanced stage of perfection; there was no advocacy of libertinism and disregard of the moral

[27]Quoted, Lerner, *Free Spirit*, p. 74, from text, ed. M. Doiron, in *Archivio . . . pietà*, v (1968), p. 247.

[28]*Free Spirit*, pp. 200–8.

[29]Ibid., p. 205; Lerner's translation from Guarnieri text on p. 586.

[30]Lerner, p. 208; Guarnieri text, pp. 533, 537.

[31]Lerner, p. 76; Guarnieri text, p. 527. Here and elsewhere I have found Lerner's judgement convincing. Other views on the *Mirror* are in Lerner, p. 201, n. 3.

G

law for anyone; and the accusations against Porete gave an unfair picture of her views. Doubts about her case are only reinforced when we realize that the inquisitor of France directing the final moves against her was also responsible for accusations against the Templars.

Hard on the heels both of the Porete case and of the statutes of the council of Mainz in 1310, witnessing to a continuing concern in the Rhineland about beghards and heresy, came the decision of the general council of Vienne in 1312, in *Ad nostrum*, that there was a heresy of the Free Spirit amongst the beguines and beghards of Germany;[32] it was called an 'abominable sect'. Beliefs were set out in eight clauses. All were concerned with the belief that those who had attained a lofty state of perfection, such as the adepts who reached the fifth and sixth states of the *Mirror of Simple Souls*, could then escape the trammels of ordinary men. The opinions that those in this category had become incapable of sinning or of surpassing their present state of grace, that they did not need to fast or pray since they had obtained such control over their senses that they could afford to them complete freedom, and that they were not subject to obedience, because 'where the spirit of the Lord is, there is liberty',[33] were all condemned. Five other clauses dealt with further consequences or aspects of the condition of sinless freedom, condemning the view that it was possible to attain final blessedness in this life; that the divine light of glory was not needed to enjoy the vision of God; that acts of virtue were only necessary for imperfect men, and that the perfect soul no longer needs them; that sexual intercourse was not a sin when nature demands it; that it was not necessary to rise at the elevation of the Host, since this meant descending from the heights of contemplation. The sect who held these views was to be rooted out.

But did such a sect ever exist? The surprising answer, after so much research has been carried out on a supposed heresy of the Free Spirit, is that in the medieval inquisitor's usual sense it did not. There was no organized sect at all, with a teaching programme hostile to the Church, like the Cathars or the later Waldensians. All that really existed were individual mystics in communication with like-minded friends and followers on an informal basis, some of whom wrote or said some dangerous or extravagant things. *Ad nostrum* took a set of these statements that looked heretical or immoral when quoted out of context, and wove together a heresy and a sect from them.[34]

---

[32]P. Fredericq, *Corpus documentorum inquisitionis haereticae pravitatis Neerlandicae*, i (Ghent, 1889), no. 172, pp. 168–9, partial trans. in Leff, *Heresy*, i, pp. 314–5 (Leff's exposition of the Free Spirit (ch. 4) cannot be recommended; see Grundmann, in *DA*, xxiv (1968), pp. 284–6; Offler, in *EHR*, lxxxiv (1969), pp. 572–6; Lerner, p. 8). A Patschovsky, 'Strassburger Beginenverfolgungen im 14 Jahrhundert', *DA*, xxx (1974), pp. 56–198 (clarification of beguine and beghard trials in Strasburg with new ms. evidence); see p. 117, n. 153. He regards concern about heresy in the Rhineland episcopate as the major impetus leading to *Ad nostrum*; see also his warning about elements of genuine heresy in some Free Spirit accusations (pp. 98–9). For Council of Mainz, see ibid., pp. 96, 141–2.

[33]2 Cor. 3.17.

[34]The central theme of Lerner, *Free Spirit*; compare Grundmann, in *DA*, xxi (1965), pp. 519–75; contrast Leff, *Heresy*, i, ch. 4 and M. Erbstösser and E. Werner, *Ideologische Probleme des mittelalterlichen Plebejertums. Die freigeistige Häresie und ihre sozialen Wurzeln*, (Berlin, 1960), who offer differing explanations of the Free Spirit (see extract trans. by Russell, *Religious Dissent*, pp.

The council of Vienne took its decision in an atmosphere of intense hostility to the beguines. We know from another of the bulls decided on at Vienne, *Cum de quibusdam*, that the fathers of the council had seriously considered suppressing the beguines outright.[35] The bull opens by decreeing suppression, and draws back from doing so only in an escape clause at the end, either the fruit of Vienne's second thoughts or of a subsequent revision. The perils of beguines discussing high theological matters, disputing on the Trinity, the divine essence and the sacraments, were mentioned in the bull as ground for suppression.

On top of this general hostility arrived the reports of antinomian heresy abroad in the Church. Much of the documentation of the Council of Vienne has vanished, making exact reconstruction of the historical context of *Ad nostrum* impossible; but Marguerite Porete's *Mirror* gives us an essential clue as to how the council came to attribute antinomian heresy to the mystics, for there we have the opportunity to put side by side some of the charges against a mystical suspect and the actual statements from which they are derived. The *Mirror* was a quarry for certain suspect statements condemned in *Ad nostrum*: clause six of the bull, on the perfect soul having no need of the virtues, is derived from Porete's work but, significantly, without the justification that the fuller context of the statement in the *Mirror* would give. Other clauses on rising at the elevation of the Host, on attitudes to prayer and fasting, and to sexual intercourse, have analogies to statements in the *Mirror*, or can be derived from misunderstanding of statements there.[36] Mystics, of whom Porete is a fair, though not distinguished, example, were describing rare states and treating great mysteries, that lay near the limits of ordinary language: they used paradoxical, even shocking, phrases in trying to convey their meaning. These were taken up, rawly and literally, by the council, and fashioned into a heresy.

Definitions in *Ad nostrum* helped to create heretics to match the bull. When it was issued early in John XXII's reign, it became part of the apparatus for fashioning interrogations by inquisitors and other churchmen who believed themselves to be on the trail of the Free Spirit. Faced with the suspect beghard or beguine, or what they believed to be a heretical mystic, they took him or her through the clauses of *Ad nostrum*, and in successful cases elicited the appropriate, self-convicting answers. Preliminary questions—Was the suspect 'free in spirit'? Did he believe he was sinless?—answered affirmatively, could open the way to a systematic interrogation based on the clauses of the bull, taken one by one. Answers as given by suspects in the records sometimes reproduce almost word for word the expositions of *Ad nostrum*.[37]

Testimony appeared to show that those who held the views condemned in *Ad nostrum* did practise libertinism. There were stories of orgies, of aberrant

143–7), but are alike in accepting the existence of a sect; discussion on these assumptions also in Erbstösser, *Sozialreligiöse Strömungen*, pp. 84–119.

[35]Fredericq, *Corpus* I, no. 171, pp.167–8; partial trans. in McDonnell, p. 524.

[36]Lerner, *Free Spirit*, pp. 82–3.

[37]Grundmann first brought out the vital relationship between *Ad nostrum* and the interrogations of suspects (*DA*, XXI (1965), pp. 519–75). See esp. the interrogation of Konrad Kannler at Eichstätt in 1381.

sexual practices, outrageous statements like that of Johann Hartmann in 1367, that the free in spirit could have intercourse with sister or mother, even on the altar.[38] It is all suspect; Hartmann was probably a verbal exhibitionist. Other testimony sprang from envious gossip, inquisitorial imagination, or distortions of the paradoxical statements of true mystics.[39] The accusations consort uneasily with the hard evidence of poor, ascetic lives among beguines and other followers of mysticism. Magnetic rogues of the Rasputin variety, combining libertinism and religion, cannot be excluded; but they were surely a small proportion of those interrogated. Similar scepticism should be applied to talk of other breaches of the ethical code, theft, murder, disobedience; such offences have not been proved.

What in fact did the Free Spirit amount to? For a century and a half after *Ad nostrum* cases of the heresy were turned up. Suspicion of the kind that issued in the bull played round other, greater figures. The leaders of the vernacular mystical movement had to exercise vigilance in their teaching to avoid the suggestion of complicity with the Free Spirit. Meister Eckhart himself fell victim to the same Henry of Virneburg, who had launched accusations against the Cologne beguines; he was accused of heresy, and had twenty-eight propositions from his work condemned in 1329 after his death. Beguines and beghards went on suffering from suspicion; as a movement they were saved from total shipwreck by the hesitation in *Cum de quibusdam*, and in 1318 by John XXII's defence in *Racio recta* of 'good' beguines who led stable lives and did not dispute on high theological matters.[40] But the Free Spirit affair damaged them, and so long as the zeal against the Free Spirit lasted, which seems to have been for about a century after *Ad nostrum*, they were at peril from investigations. Suspicion of heresy combined with disciplinary proceedings to help to regulate them, cutting down the number of individual beguines and small groups and driving them into larger beguinages; at the same time the impetus to the beguine life tended to fade. Their greatest days were over by the mid-fourteenth century.

Meanwhile, the Free Spirit investigations trawled up odd cases, usually in the towns of Germany. The sources in the north are resistant to much positive analysis. A thorough sceptical analysis on the lines of Lerner's work has yet to be undertaken for the supposed cases in the southern lands; an analysis may turn out to give different results from the north. But what peeps through the distortions seems to be this. There was a movement of radical mysticism, running *pari passu* with the writings of the best-known masters such as Eckhart, and feared by them. It was not libertinist or immoral, but went at least to the limits of orthodoxy in its views on the possibility of union with God in this life, and was indifferent, if not hostile to the sacraments and to the mediating role of the Church. Apart from this core of somewhat perilous belief and practice was a miscellaneous assemblage of suspects, suggestible women liable to say what interrogators wanted, some eccentrics, even madmen who

---

[38]Testimony in Erbstösser and Werner, *Ideologische Probleme*, pp. 136–53, comment, Lerner, *Free Spirit*, pp. 135–9.

[39]As above, pp. 177–8.

[40]Fredericq, *Corpus*, II, no. 44, pp. 72–4, McDonnell, *Beguines*, p. 536. For a note on subsequent history, see below, pp. 204–5.

might have remained untroubled but for investigating zeal, some religious individualists, perhaps touched by mysticism but having odd views of their own—anti-sacerdotal, for example, possibly Amaurian, or rigorist on sexual ethics. Free Spirit suspects were not necessarily beguines or beghards at all, and there was a good deal of slander.

12

Spiritual Franciscans and Heretical Joachimites

The Franciscan Problem

The origins of the Franciscan problem run back deep into the thirteenth century and are inseparable from the ideals and personality of St Francis himself.[1] Utterly dedicated to the ideal of poverty which he saw in Christ's commands in the gospels, above all in the account of the sending of the Seventy, Francis bequeathed to his followers the belief that the Franciscan way of life reincarnated that of Christ and the Apostles. His way of living was extraordinarily hard, harder to bear than that of the most ascetic monastic orders, for Francis aimed to renounce not only individual but also common property, the normal background of collective security for even the most austere individual monk. Moreover, Francis intended that for many of his followers an extraordinarily harsh standard of poverty should be combined with a pastoral activity in the world. From early days the two objectives tended to run counter to each other; yet the very combination of harsh poverty and pastoral activity gave a spiritual force to the early Franciscans which drew in recruits at a prodigious rate whose presence and needs soon begin to distort the original ideal. Troubles occurred in Francis's own lifetime: at the end, after years of semi-eremitical life in resignation from active government of the order, Francis dictated a last Testament in which he looked back with nostalgia to the simple early days of his brotherhood and, by implication or direct statement, condemned many of the developments then taking place which mitigated the old poverty and simplicity, and tended to give his order a privileged place within the Church.[2] It was his deathbed statement, and to this day it cannot be read without emotion.

[1]M. D. Lambert, *Franciscan Poverty: the Doctrine of the Absolute Poverty of Christ and the Apostles in the Franciscan Order, 1210–1323* (London, 1961), esp. chs 1 and 2, (see review by L. Hardick in *Franziskanische Studien*, XLIV (1962), pp. 124–8), Leff, *Heresy* I, pp. 51–255 (esp. helpful for intellectual aspect and bulls of John XXII), J. R. H. Moorman, *A History of the Franciscan Order from its Origins to the Year 1517* (Oxford, 1968) (comprehensive survey), R. B. Brooke, *Early Franciscan Government, Elias to Bonaventure* (Cambridge, 1959) (constitutional history, personal insights); documents in H. Böhmer, *Analekten zur Geschichte des Franciscus von Assisi*, 3rd edn, (Tübingen, 1961); *Scripta Leonis et Angeli Sociorum S. Francisci*, ed. R. B. Brooke (Oxford, 1970) (see intro.), D. Knowles, *Religious Orders in England*, I (Cambridge, 1948), ch. 11 (short intro.). R. B. Brooke, *The Coming of the Friars* (London, 1975) (docs on early Franciscans, background of preachers and heretics, with comment). References hereafter curtailed in view of accessibility of histories in English.

[2]Text and analysis in K. Esser, *Das Testament des heiligen Franziskus von Assisi* (Münster-i-W., 1949).

Constitutionally Francis had no right to bind his successors; yet he ordered this Testament to be kept with the rule and read with it, and his command, legally invalid as it was declared to be,[3] carried all the emotional weight of the dying speech of a beloved founder. More than any single document, the Testament was the stimulus to subsequent internal dissention.

The majority of friars were either not fully aware of the distinction between Francis's personal wishes and the existing way of life in the order, or felt that change was positively desirable. Transformation still retained a considerable degree of poverty, more than that of the older monastic orders; yet it enabled the order to fulfil a major role in the life of the Church which would have been impossible if the numbers and conditions of Francis's own time had continued unchanged. Papal policy favoured change, and a series of clarifications of the rule from the popes legitimized the process. How far this adaptation of the order's life was right or wise must always remain controversial; the historian of heresy must observe that the transformation, by deploying so much disinterested zeal in the service of the Church and diffusing Franciscan preaching and piety, went far to aid the defeat of Catharism.

Dissatisfaction with the transformation of the life of the order to fit the needs of a clerical body with a place in the universities, developed techniques of preaching, and privileges to take up all the duties of the secular clergy, and the mitigation of the old poverty which this entailed, found only occasional outlet, both in Francis's lifetime and for years afterwards. The nucleus for this disquiet lay in a body of simple early companions, generally with a taste for the eremitical life, who could not approve of the influx of learning and the great place which the Franciscans gained in the Church: these men handed on the traditions, filtered through their own minds, of Francis's life and sayings, especially in the last years, and kept alive the memory of the Testament.

A transformation so great and so rapid imposed strains on tender consciences. Were the friars in fact being faithful to the literal words of the rule which they professed when they followed the mitigated way of life of the bulk of the order? Were they in fact in breach of their vow? Was it honourable to continue to claim the highest poverty and a peculiar fidelity to the life of Christ and the Apostles, when in practice they used money, which Francis had forbidden, and enjoyed the fruits of property, which Francis had excluded? Such questions were disturbing, and not only to rigorists. The most passive plea for freedom to follow a primitive observance implied a criticism of the majority's way of life and, as the practitioners of *satyagraha* in Gandhi's campaign against the salt-tax found, passive disobedience can stimulate violent response. Hence the ferocity of punishment with which recalcitrant rigorists were treated by some superiors, and the casual violence apparent, for example, in the burning of the Testament over the head of a friar by some exasperated minister.[4]

The Disputes in the South of France
The dispute over the rightfulness of the observance of poverty in the order had all the makings of a profound conflict. Yet a true crisis did not begin to emerge

[3] By *Quo elongati (BF,* Epitome, pp. 229a–231b).
[4] Lambert, *Poverty,* p. 84.

until the time of the council of Lyons in 1274 and the following years. This was almost certainly due to the fact that friars in considerable numbers would not be moved, so long as the order did maintain the substance of its mitigated way of life. After 1274, though much zeal remained, the Franciscans had passed the peak of their early enthusiasm,, and in various provinces were no longer keeping adequately even to the mitigated way of life. Worldliness rather than gross abuse was the problem, together with the difficulty of holding firmly to a rule glossed and 'clarified' in various ways; but it was enough to stimulate a more widespread call to return to an earlier standard. Italian provinces— Umbria, Tuscany and the March of Ancona—were affected, partly because a living tradition of Francis's wishes existed there, and partly because of the existence of a strong eremitical tradition which tended to rigour over poverty, and in the case of Tuscany because of the influence of one teacher, Petrus Johannis Olivi, a native of the South of France and for some years lector in Florence, and of his fervent supporter Ubertino da Casale.[5] In the Franciscan province of Provence, geographically wider than the title would imply and including a substantial part of the Midi, a special situation existed.[6] Subsequent history must lead us to conclude that ministers in that area were both relaxed in their attitudes to poverty and harsh in enforcing discipline. Abuse stimulated rigour, and the province became deeply divided between defenders of the *status quo* (and worse), generally called 'Conventuals', and the rigorist Spirituals.

The situation was made more complicated and more acute by the abilities of Olivi, a friar from the convent of Narbonne; he was the dominating mind among the Spirituals and, independently of the poverty issue, a thinker of the front rank at a time of unusual disturbance and confusion in the history of scholasticism.[7] His achievement for the Spirituals was to work out a doctrine of the *usus pauper*. This firmly associated sustained and serious infringements of austerity in the use of goods with breach of the vow of poverty; repeated and gross deviations without justification, so that the 'use' of goods by a friar was to be considered rich rather than poor, involved the offender in mortal sin. Friars who became bishops could not be dispensed from this obligation to the 'poor use'. This doctrine focussed the order's attention on their actual, day to day, observance as opposed to their formal (and often rather hollowly juridical) renunciation of property rights. The years of transformation had issued in a theory of Franciscan poverty whereby the order held no property at all, all rights over the goods they used being by a legal fiction retained by the papacy.[8] Earnest but moderate friars, of whom the greatest was St Bonaventure, minister-general 1257–74, were not satisfied with renunciation of property rights as summing up Franciscan poverty; they accepted the papal ownership, but still struggled against practical relaxation in the use of goods.

[5]On Olivi, see below, n. 9; on Ubertino, Godefroy, 'Ubertin de Casale', *DTC* xv, cols 2020–34 and, a fine sketch, L. Oliger, 'Spirituels', *DTC*, xiv, cols 2522–49.

[6]R. Manselli, *Spirituali e Beghini in Provenza* (Rome, 1959); cf. his *La 'Lectura super Apocalipsim' di Pietro di Giovanni Olivi* (Rome, 1955).

[7]Leff, *Heresy* 1, pp. 100–62.

[8]Lambert, *Poverty*, chs 3–6.

At a time of deteriorating observance, the Olivi doctrine appeared to strengthen such earnest superiors.

But there were difficulties. No aspect of Franciscan life was so vulnerable to changes as day to day poverty; powers of dispensation and the discretion of superiors were needed if Franciscans were to maintain their duties in the world, and consciences were not to be overloaded. The *usus pauper* could be held unduly to infringe these rights of superiors. Behind Olivi lay poverty fanatics; it was not clear what they might make of the *usus pauper* as an obligation, so there were some grounds for considering Olivi's doctrine as 'perilous', in the words of one censure.[9] Controversy grew over this issue, strengthened by the Spirituals' honest reaction to abuses in the province, and by the chance that Olivi was a bold speculative thinker who in his scholastic writing threw off views which, in part following the way which led to Ockham, alarmed some other Franciscans.[10] Often inferior minds did not grasp what Olivi as an academic thinker intended; his views on poverty and points of doubt in his scholastic writing became bound together in an internal struggle in which superiors and other scholastics pressed charges of heresy and error over almost two decades before his death in 1298, and thereafter till the council of Vienne in 1312, without ever succeeding in pinning a definitive condemnation on him. Much of this was unfair: though at one stage rehabilitated and sent to Florence, Olivi in consequence of the dissensions did not achieve the academic recognition which his talents deserved and ended his career as no more than *lector* in Narbonne. Academic controversy, with serious undertones springing from the state of the order and the nature of Olivi's influence, had much the same effect on a smaller scale as conflicts at Prague over Wyclif had in the early fifteenth century:[11] issues, too long undecided, roused bitterly divided parties, and turned an academic conflict into a popular fight. Dissension amongst the Franciscans of the first order easily spilled over into the lay world through the institution of the third order: in the Italian provinces this does not seem to have happened on any scale, but in the Midi tertiaries from the towns were drawn in.

One reason lay in the existence of a tradition blending rigorist views on poverty and Joachimite speculation in a lay circle which went back to Hugues de Digne, Olivi's religious ancestor in the area, who can be glimpsed in mid-century pondering Joachimite prophecy with laymen, notaries and others at Hyères.[12] Olivi himself had magnetic qualities, not fully discernible to us in his extant writings, and endured harassment with courage: he acted as a focus for the religious sentiments of tertiaries under the influence of Spiritual friars who met to hear mass, to be encouraged in their personal life by the hearing of

[9]D. Laberge, 'Fr. Petri Joannis Olivi, o.f.m.: tria scripta sui ipsius apologetica annorum 1283 et 1285', *AFH* xxviii (1935), pp. 115–55, 374–407; xxix (1936), pp. 98–141, 365–95; note esp. xxviii, p. 382, lines 7–8.

[10]Leff, *Heresy*, i, pp. 107–11; but see also A. Maier, 'Zu einigen Problemen der Ockhamforschung', *AFH*, xlvi (1953), pp. 174–81.

[11]Below, pp. 281–7, 290–301.

[12]Lambert, *Poverty*, p. 178. For a sidelight on Hugues de Digne and his influence on the fate of the Brethren of the Sack, see K. Elm, 'Ausbreitung, Wirksamkeit und Ende der provençalischen Sackbrüder ... in Deutschland und den Niederlanden' in *Francia: Forschungen zur westeuropäischen Geschichte*, i (Munich, 1973), pp. 257–324. I owe the ref. to Dr A. V. Murray.

sermons and vernacular treatises in which Spiritual beliefs played a great part, and who became convinced both that Olivi was a martyr to unjust persecution and that the conflicts about poverty in the order were the prelude to the Last Times. Without understanding the academic issues, these tertiaries or more casual sympathizers, known as Beguins, were quite clear in their minds about the practical issues of poverty under discussion, the pressure that Spiritual friars were under, and the heroic virtue of Olivi. Joachimism, misunderstood or adapted for the Franciscan situation, heightened the tension in these Spiritual-directed lay circles, and was the most dangerous single element in an amalgam of doctrines forming in the eighties and nineties in the heat of persecution and conflict in the Midi.

Joachimism and the Development of Heresy

The exact nature of Olivi's influence and of his own thinking about the Last Things remains the most suspect and elusive aspect of his work. One great stimulus to his eschatological interest lay in Joachim of Fiore, the Calabrian prophetic writer who died in Innocent III's pontificate after a lifetime spent pondering the patterns of history discernible through meditation on the Scriptures.[13] Three popes, Lucius III, Urban III and Clement III, had encouraged him in his exegetical writing[14] and, though his influence received a blow in the condemnation of a trinitarian *libellus* at the fourth Lateran Council, his ideas on history and the future were quite uncondemned, and had great potency, directly and indirectly, throughout the thirteenth century.

Joachim's ideas on a coming third age of the Holy Spirit had a special appeal to members of religious orders. Ever scholarly, reluctant to fix precisely on a date for the end of the present order of things or to describe closely the conditions of life in the third age of the Spirit, Joachim nonetheless lived in a state of constant expectancy—'I suspect all times and all places,' he said—and through his writings bequeathed to the clerical world a persuasive set of metaphors, symbols and Scriptural parallels for apocalyptic speculation.[15] His diagram of the sequence of history, produced by him personally or under his influence in the *Liber figurarum* (*c.* 1200), may better convey the nature of his appeal than a more detailed exposition.[16] In the centre is the trumpet of the Apocalypse ('I was in the Spirit . . . and heard behind me a great voice, as of a trumpet saying, "I am Alpha and

[13]Above, p. 101.

[14]Reeves, *Prophecy*, p. 28.

[15]I follow here Reeves, *Prophecy* (with full literature, cited above, p. 101, n. 28), and in *MRS*, II (1950), pp. 57–81, work which I admire. For the broad context, see R. W. Southern, 'Aspects of the European Tradition of Historical Writing; 3. History as Prophecy', *TRHS*, 5th ser., XXII (1972), pp. 159–80, esp. pp. 173–7; orientation in H. Grundmann, *Studien über Joachim von Floris* (Leipzig, 1927); *Neue Forschungen über Joachim von Floris* (Marburg, 1950); discussion in relation to heresy in Leff, *Heresy*, I, pp. 68–83; reflections in F. Seibt, 'Utopie im Mittelalter', *HZ*, CCVIII (1969), pp. 555–94.

[16]*Il libro delle figure dell' Abate Gioacchino da Fiore*, ed. L. Tondelli, M. Reeves and B. Hirsch-Reich, 2nd edn. (Turin, 1953), II tavola 18ab; Reeves and Hirsch-Reich, *The Figurae of Joachim of Fiore* (Oxford, 1972), pl. 9, and discussion (note two versions), pp. 120–9; on authenticity of *Liber figurarum*, pp. 75–98.

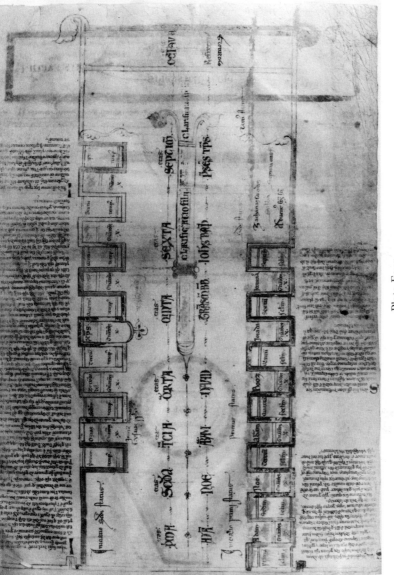

Plate Four

The Third Age of the Spirit: the Seven *Etates* of the World

Omega . . ." '[17]). It speaks in the third age of the Holy spirit, given below the trumpet as *tercius status*, and provides the spiritual understanding which characterizes the age of the Spirit. The history of mankind is flowing into the state of illumination which is the culmination of life on earth. There is a *status* corresponding to the first person of the Trinity, beginning on the far left of the diagram with the *initiatio primi status* marked by Adam, characterized by married men; then a second *status* corresponding to the second person of the Trinity, beginning on the upper left of the diagram with the *initiatio secundi status* marked by the reign of Uzziah ('Ozias'), in which the prophet Isaiah appeared, and characterized by the clergy. Mankind is on the eve of the dawning of the third age, characterized by a new order of monks—the words *presens tempus* can be seen below the bell-joint of the trumpet, still in the age of the clarification of the Son (*clarificatio filii* in the diagram). The *status* are not rigidly divided; they are seen by Joachim rather as relay runners in a race: at one point the runner gets ready to hand over the baton and the two runners run along side by side before finally making the change-over.[18] A herald, as it were, of the third age had already appeared in St Benedict of Nursia, founder of monasticism; a new order of monks, yet to come, would characterize the third age, and would be agents of the new spiritual understanding.

Joachim did not exactly know what this order would be: in the phrase of his modern interpreter Marjorie Reeves, like Moses he viewed the promised land, but could not enter it himself.[19] To be a member of that new order had a powerful attraction, and it is little surprise that religious of various kinds after Joachim's day believed that the spiritual understanding of the new age was to be bestowed on their institution. The friars, with their consciousness of innovation, were natural candidates, and the legend grew that Joachim had in fact forecast not one order but two, and that he had sketched the habits of the two major orders, the Dominicans and the Franciscans.[20] But of all the groups to whom Joachim appealed, the Franciscans were affected most deeply.[21]

Some of the reasons for the attraction of Joachim's ideas can be glimpsed from the diagram. One is the perennial attraction of the approaching end, seen in the proximity of the bell of the trumpet to the culmination of history, to be seen beyond the line on the right of the trumpet. To the ever-fascinating task of attempting to calculate the time of the Last Things, Joachim brought distinction of mind and a method familiar to all Scripture students of the day. That the Old Testament provided parallels and prophecies of the New was a commonplace; Joachim's method involved extending this use of parallels, natural in a time in which the inner meaning, as opposed to the literal sense, of Scripture was of such dominant importance, to provide a key to the time after the New Testament. As there was a concordance between the pattern of

[17]Rev. I. 10–11.

[18]See intro to *Il libro* by L. Tondelli (*Il libro* I (Turin, 1953)), pp. 86–9; Reeves, *Prophecy*, p. 138; Reeves et al., *Figurae*, pp. 122–3. Note Reeves's summary (*MRS*, II (1950), p. 77), 'The third *status* describes the emergence of a new plane of spiritual existence rather than the appearance of a new set of institutions. . .'

[19]*Prophecy*, p. 146.

[20]Ibid., pp. 72–3.

[21]Ibid., pp. 135–292.

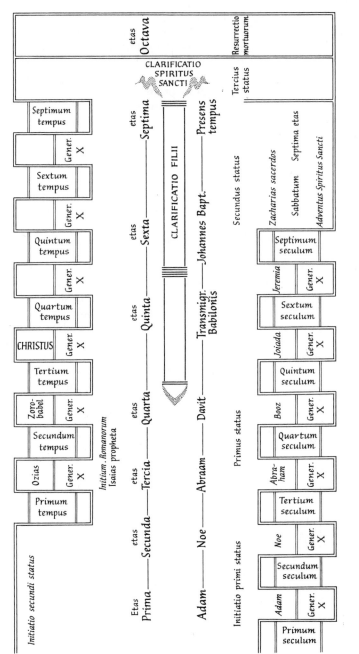

The Third Age of the Spirit: the Seven *Etates* of the World (from *Il libro*, ed. Tondelli, Reeves, Hirsch-Reich)

events in the Old and New Testaments, so there would be a concordance between the events described in Scripture and those that took place after the writing of the New Testament, and Joachim worked indefatigably on traditional exegetical principles[22] to solve the riddle of the future.

The essence of the technique lay in recognizing the key events and personalities, in their numerical sequence, which provided the parallels, mapped out time and marked the approach to the end of the world. As is familiar in such speculations, each disappointment in forecasting can readily be overcome; the basis of calculation may be altered, while the principle remains intact, and the reader of prophecies prepared for some new date.[23] So one such date, 1260, marked by an extraordinary outburst of flagellating penitential processions in Italy, spreading over the Alps to Germany and Poland, passed by with no supernatural event.[24] The focus of expectation moved on, and 1290 became the date, with subsequent transferences right through the Middle Ages, so long as Joachimite techniques remained as basis for prophecy.

The Franciscans' Scriptural training and their preaching, with its taste for vivid symbolism and anecdote, opened the way for interest in Joachim's rich store of parallels and symbols; the high importance that all friars attached to Francis, and the early sense that something new, blessed by God, had appeared in the order, contributed to the spread of Joachimism in various forms and to the loose assimilation of the Franciscans by some writers to the role of the new order of the third age. An identification of Francis with the angel of the sixth seal in the Apocalypse, who in the Joachimite hypothesis was the herald of the new age, became a commonplace among Franciscan writers.[25] Attachment to Joachimism stretched all the way from a loose use of his symbols, as a kind of decorative *jeu d'esprit*, to a profound involvement in versions of his ideas which acted as a mainspring to religious life.

In the process Joachim's own views were remodelled. He had said very little about poverty for his new order in the third age; that aspect of religious life was crucial for Franciscans, and in their versions it became the decisive mark of the new order. Joachim had anticipated an intensification of persecutions as an immediate prelude to the dawning of the third age. There were to be two Antichrists, one shortly before the third age, the other at its end, as part of the persecutions which would herald the second coming and the end of human history.[26] The success of Islam under Saladin gave him one clue that his third age was not far off: it represented the requisite increase of pressure on the Church. But it was a characteristic of Joachim as an

[22]Reeves stresses the basis of Joachim's thought in traditional exegesis; see e.g. *Prophecy*, pp. 10, 16–17.

[23]Southern, 'Aspects of European Tradition', p. 177.

[24]Reeves, *Prophecy*, pp. 54–5; R. Manselli, 'L'Anno 1260 fu Anno Gioachimito?', in *Il movimento dei disciplinati nel settimo centenario dal suo inizio* (Perugia, 1962), pp. 99–108 (composite work, fundamental on Flagellants).

[25]Reeves, *Prophecy*, p. 176; S. Bihel, 'S. Franciscus, fuitne angelus sexti sigilli (Apoc. 7.2)?', *Antonianum*, II (1927), pp. 59–90.

[26]Reeves, *Prophecy*, pp. 295–392; H. M. Schaller, 'Endzeiterwartung und Antichrist Vorstellungen im 13. Jahrhundert', in *Festschrift für Hermann Heimpel* (ed. mitarbeitern des Max-Planck-Instituts für Geschichte), II (Göttingen, 1972), pp. 924–47.

Plate Five
The Seven-headed Dragon

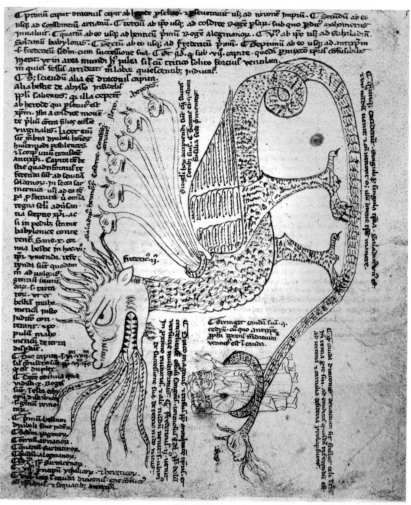

Plate Six
A Debased Dragon

apocalyptic writer that he set the events of his own time in the full context of history, and so in the diagram of the dragon of the Apocalypse in the *Liber figurarum* (Plate 5) Saladin features as one head in a sequence going back to Herod; the other, pseudo-Joachimite diagram (Plate 6) demonstrates both the process of adaptation and the diminishing of Joachimite prophecy to serve the preoccupations of one context in time.[27] The dragon in this example has turned into a bird of prey; the Holy Roman emperors assume a more important place on the side of evil, with both Henry I and Frederick II among

[27] *Il libro*, ed. Tondelli et al., II, tavola 26, fig. 2; analysis in Reeves and Hirsch-Reich, *Figurae*, pp. 269, 274 (p. 147, for manifestation of Antichrist; index, for discussion of Antichrist and Gog and Magog).

the heads, the seventh, larger than all the rest, being that of Frederick. The text refers plainly to Frederick II and his heirs (*cum successione sua*) as Antichrist; the great struggle of the papacy with the Hohenstaufen is thus seen as the prelude to the coming of the third age. By contrast, the genuine Joachimite drawing leaves the last head anonymous—this is the Antichrist of Joachim's writings, yet to appear in history. The diagram gives only one mild form of adaptation—it may be allowed to stand for a wide variety of use and abuse of Jochimite ideas.

Guglielma and Dolcino

Worse distortions of Joachim appeared outside the Franciscan order, in unlearned milieux where ideas were passed on from original Joachimite and pseudo-Joachimite texts, it would seem, by oral transmission. In Milan the bones of a certain Guglielma, who had died in 1281, were dug up and burned by the inquisition in 1300, when it appeared that a circle of her initiates in Milan revered her as an incarnation of the Holy Spirit.[28] The relatively harmless but simplistic idea of the angelic pope,[29] shortly to come to cleanse the Church, took on an unusual guise in the hands of this circle, perhaps no more than thirty in number, including some wealthy adherents, who had come to believe that a woman from their midst, Manfreda, would be the pope, who would convert the Jews and Saracens and usher in a new age. She would be accompanied by women cardinals. The existing gospels would be superseded by four new ones, written under the guidance of the Holy Spirit.

Guglielma's heirs were not difficult to uproot; the Apostolic Brethren, however, founded by Gerard Segarelli in Parma in 1260, the year of the Flagellant outbreak and one of the key dates of Joachimite prophecy, were more resilient and had a surprisingly wide circle of influence.[30] Segarelli, according to Salimbene the chronicler, had been refused admission to the Franciscans at Parma; a simple, unlearned man who must nevertheless have had some force of personality, he gathered a group who, like him, practised the most direct and literal imitation of the life of the Apostles, to the embarrassment of the Franciscans, as Salimbene's hostility reveals. Quite literally, they lived for the day, begged only necessities of life which were consumed on the spot, had only one habit where the Franciscan rule allowed two, engaged in demonstrations whereby they stripped off their clothing and divided it afresh amongst themselves, so as to show their utter detachment from individual ownership, and called themselves, not *minores*, as the official order did, but *minimi*.[31] They lasted, and gained popular approbation, because they followed the Franciscan ideal with a rigour, even to excess and fetichism, in a way that the majority of the friars of the later thirteenth century

[28]Reeves, *Prophecy*, pp. 248–50.

[29]Ibid. (see index); F. Baethgen, *Der Engelpapst* (Halle, 1933); see B. Töpfer, *Das kommende Reich des Friedens* (Berlin, 1964) (survey of prophecies, esp. in 12th and 13th cents, subtly related to economic and political background; Marxist assumptions).

[30]Reeves, *Prophecy*, pp. 242–8, with sources; Leff, *Heresy*, I, pp. 191–5; I have made greatest use of Töpfer, *Reich*, pp. 280–324, illuminating in its comparisons of Dolcino's views with other prophecies.

[31]Ibid., pp. 284–6, 292. Töpfer notes that the term *apostoli* was used rather by outsiders than the group itself.

did not. Parma supported them; the bishop in early years did not move against them. But the council of Lyons in 1274 banned unauthorized orders; in 1285 Honorius IV banned them explicitly; in the 1290s proceedings for heresy were taken against some members. Segarelli, first condemned to imprisonment, was burned in 1300. Inquisition proceedings of 1299 in Bologna give us a glimpse of a group, not as yet violently opposed to the Church[32] but justifying disobedience through their own attainment of the state of perfection of the primitive Church by the practice of poverty. Popes of the post-Constantinian Church (that had abandoned the poverty of the primitive Church), they argued, had no right to force them to give up their way of life.

With the replacement of Segarelli in the leadership by Dolcino, the bastard son of a priest from the diocese of Novara, who had picked up some learning, the sect grew more strongly heretical, and responded with violence to the pressures of the inquisition. Dolcino issued a manifesto in 1300, in which he claimed direct inspiration by the Holy Spirit for himself and a crucial role in the imminent coming of a new age for the Apostolics he led. Instead of the three *status* of the Joachimites he postulated four—one, of the patriarchs and prophets of the Old Testament, a second, initiated by Christ and the Apostles and lasting till the time of Constantine, a third, just nearing its close, from Constantine, and a fourth, about to come, in which the true apostolic life of his group would prevail, and, side by side with the *status*, four *mutationes*, of which the fourth had been initiated by Gerard Segarelli. The conviction of the overriding value of the apostolic life, as observed by Dolcino's group in contrast to all others, led logically to the insertion in Joachim's scheme of a fourth *status* to accommodate it.[33] Even Francis's position is dimmed in comparison with that of the leaders of the Apostolics. He is not actually given the place of a 'forerunner' of the new *status*, shortly to come, and the way of life of the Apostolics, because of its stricter poverty, is taken as superior to that of St Francis and St Dominic. The fate foretold for the existing Church at the coming of the new age was dramatic: pope, prelates, clergy and monks, except for a repentant remnant, were to be exterminated within three years by a new emperor, Frederick, the king of Sicily, who had successfully defied Papal and Angevin expeditions against him; then the holy pope would appear, and all the benefits of the new age would follow. This extravagant picture was rounded off by a passage in which Dolcino described a pattern of history in terms of the seven angels and seven Churches of the Apocalypse, in which Segarelli was the angel of Smyrna and he was the angel of Thyatira. In a second manifesto of December 1303 prophecies, unfulfilled, were brought up to date, and again in a manifesto at the end of 1304 which has not come down to us.

But there was no waning of confidence; some even alleged that Dolcino himself was to be the pope of the new age. He took to the mountains between Vercelli and Novara in 1304, and recruits followed him, both local peasants and Apostolics from farther afield, who supported him in plundering raids

---

[32]Töpfer's interpretation.
[33]Töpfer, p.299, following R. Kestenberg-Gladstein, 'The "Third Reich"; a Fifteenth-century Polemic against Joachimism and its Background', *JWCI*, xviii (1955), pp. 242–95; at p. 251.

and violent resistance of Church forces. Ghibelline leaders, with whom he had mysterious contacts,[34] may have emboldened him, and no doubt the inquisition's repression stimulated a violent response; the poverty of peasants near his mountain refuge made them susceptible to his teaching. But the rapid development under Dolcino of an extravagant but not profoundly dangerous movement[35] into a violent rebellion is pre-eminently a tribute to the heady influence, in appropriate hands, of pseudo-Joachimite ideas of the new age. It took more than one expedition and an application of the crusading indulgence before Dolcino was taken and burnt in 1307 and his following destroyed; even then adherents outlasted the leader and the failure of his prophecies.

In the Franciscan order itself, well before these events, one scandal, that of the Eternal Gospel in 1254, served to reveal the dangers of the third *status*. The question about Joachim's construction always was: What was the significance of the transition between the second and third *status*? Did it imply supersession of the present hierarchy and sacraments, in the same fashion as the coming of Christ and his founding of the Christian Church superseded the Synagogue and the Old Law? For Joachim this was never so. With talents rather poetic and artistic than dialectical, he saw the Scriptural parallels and precedents in terms of a constantly-moving kaleidoscope of images. The patterns of three, with their dangers, were always accompanied by patterns of two, standing for the two dispensations of the Law and Grace, of the two eons, before and after Christ which would last to the end of time.[36] In the *Liber figurarum*, the words 'end of the New Testament' in diagrams are never associated with the transition from the second to the third *status*, only with the consummation of the orthodox patterns of twos. The changed conditions of life in the third *status* represented a fructification of trends in the second *status*, but not revolutionary institutional change. And yet, whatever Joachim's intentions, the whole tenor of his treatment of the third *status*, with it emphasis on 'spiritual men' and new spiritual understanding, tended easily to subvert faith in the present, visible order, with its hierarchy, laws and sacraments.

In 1254 a crude adaptation of Joachim by Gerard of Borgo San Donnino, who taught that Joachim's three principal works were the gospel of a new age, superseding the Old and New Testaments, revealed to all just what the dangers were.[37] His condemnation ended the phase of relatively carefree use of Joachim, and was followed by refutations of the three-age theory, but not the complete jettisoning of Joachimism. There was much more in Joachim than the three *status*, whose sinister potential had often not been recognized in early years, and various quite orthodox writers continued to make discriminating use of his symbols and categories. The Spirituals, however, held firmly to him, and wedded their doctrine of poverty to a version of

[34]Töpfer, pp. 314–6.

[35]I have not been able to examine evidence of aberrant views on sexual activities; they are discussed by Töpfer (pp. 292–3).

[36]Reeves, in *MRS*, II (1950), pp. 74–6. I find the description of Joachim as a poet helpful. See discussion of Joachim's orthodoxy by Reeves (*Prophecy*, pp. 126–32).

[37]Lambert, *Poverty*, pp. 107–9; Reeves, *Prophecy*, pp. 59–70; B. Töpfer, 'Eine Handschrift des Evangelium aeternum des Gerardino von Borgo San Donnino', *ZG*, VII (1960), pp. 156–63.

Joachim's apocalyptic speculations, more subtle than that of the simple-minded Gerard, but still tending ultimately to the subversion of the contemporary Church.

No authentic text of Joachimite work has come down to us from the Spiritual Franciscans' leaders in mid-century, John of Parma and Hugues de Digne, but in Olivi's *Lectura super Apocalipsim* we have a major Joachimite text that give us a clue to the nature of his influence in the South of France.[38] The work, completed late in life and, no doubt, the fruit of reflection on his sufferings and that of the Spirituals, adapts Joachim wholeheartedly to his own time. As in Joachim's own work, mankind was on the eve of great events, but they were seen pre-eminently in terms of current Franciscan history. It was St Francis who was the initiator of a new age, and his rule was its gospel; full spiritual understanding would come to Francis's true disciples, (i.e. the Spirituals), but only after the persecutions of the carnal Church, made up of all the evil forces in the visible Church, and especially the enemies of poverty and the advocates of pagan learning, the false doctors. A deepening of suffering, and the falling away of many in the Church, would be followed by the joys of the new age, described in terms very like Joachim's. So the struggle between Spirituals and Conventuals in the South of France was invested with a cosmic significance. Joachim gave the groundwork for this scheme, but his fluctuating symbolisms had been given a precise, historical meaning. The dangers implicit in a third age were still there and intensified by being given a more definite historical setting. The problem, as with other Joachimites, lay in the relationship between a hypothetical new epoch shortly to dawn, and the institutions and laws of the contemporary Church and, although on this issue Olivi was careful, in controversy with his own sympathizers, to urge adherence to the commands of lawful authority in the Church and to distinguish in the *Lectura* between the carnal Church as a set of evil forces inside the Church and the visible Church as a whole, his teaching in the work very easily gave rise to revolt and heresy.

A similar subversive effect followed from the transposition of the Franciscan crisis, apparent here and elsewhere, into Joachimite terms. Spirituals, anxious about the undermining of the observance in the order through papal bulls and the glossing of the rule, harked back to Francis's Testament, called for literal observance and looked askance at papal 'clarification'. But what if the rule was the gospel of a new epoch, and if Francis and his disciples, with the rule and the Testament had taken the mantle of Christ as at the beginning of the Christian epoch? Was the rule in fact above all papal clarification and glossing? What if the persecutors of the Spirituals, their superiors and the false doctors were followers of Antichrist? Might not resistance *à l'outrance* to them be justifiable? Thoughts of this kind helped to raise a disciplinary dispute inside a religious order to the plane of doctrinal conflict. Moreover, Joachimism gave a purpose to the Spirituals' troubled lives. The sense of certainty of their victory gave them both courage and obstinacy, and helps to account for a certain extravagance and recklessness in their actions which

---

[38]Manselli, *Lectura*; criticism in Leff, *Heresy*, I, pp. 122–39, esp. p. 139. See E. Pásztor, 'Le polemiche sulla "Lectura super Apocalipsim" di Pietro di Giovanni Olivi fino all sua condanna', *BISIAM*, LXX (1958), pp. 365–424.

tended to make the split between Spirituals and many of their superiors irreconcilable. So with the development from Joachim to Olivi: though heresy proper has not been reached, we stand on its verge. With the development of Joachimism and Spiritual ideas on poverty amongst simpler friars and Midi tertiaries behind Olivi we do reach heresy.

The Beguins and Popular Heresy

In his *Lectura* Olivi inferred nothing more from the prophecies of approaching persecution than the necessity for the Spirituals to show patience in their sufferings. His comments on the Apocalypse were presented with caution, as possible but not certain interpretations of the future and, though he strongly developed Joachim's sentiment that the mystical Antichrist would be found within the Church and referred to the coming of a pseudo-pope, he never made personal identifications of living people as key figures in the prophecies. In his popular works of edification, recently edited by Manselli,[39] he exhorts his followers to virtuous life on traditional lines of Franciscan piety; only mentions of the need for vigilance as the last times approach betray his special interests.

When a local adherent, the friar Matthew de Bosicis, who went to Rome in 1299 with five Beguins and thirteen women taking with him the works of Olivi, made a confession of faith at a date between 1299 and 1304, no doubt in consequence of the suspicion then spreading of the Spiritual movement, his words showed a simple adherence both to Olivi and his teaching and to wholly orthodox tenets on the need for obedience and the nature of the visible Church.[40] But was Matthew exercising 'economy' in his confession, and not revealing all his thoughts?[41] That there were grounds for disquiet in Olivi's oral contacts with his followers emerges from the ostensibly trivial point of the moment at which the spear pierced Christ on the cross. This occurred, Olivi said, before rather than after death; but that was not what the Vulgate text said. Olivi's ground for change, amongst other things, was the vision of a contemporary, which he alleged against Scripture. With the *usus pauper*, the spear-wound tenet was treated by followers as the teaching of a master, to be

---

[39]*Spirituali*, pp. 267–90. See now the remarkable ch. 3 in B. Tierney, *Origins of Papal Infallibility, 1150–1350* (Leiden, 1972), in which it is argued that Olivi's doctrine of infallibility was developed in order to meet the utterances of a pseudo-pope. Olivi's concern was to buttress the papal decrees already issued on the Franciscan way of life. Tierney repays reading and re-reading.

[40]Tierney, pp. 42–6.

[41]Compare the declaration of Cathars at Lombers 1165, above, p.64; see M. D. Lambert, 'The Franciscan Crisis under John XXII', *FS*, xxxii (1972), pp. 123–43, at p. 131n. Manselli, in the tradition of Morghen, tends to stress the importance of the actions of ecclesiastical authority in 'creating' heresy in the province of Provence, especially after the burnings of 1318. To demonstrate this he must argue for the orthodoxy of Spirituals and Beguins there before the major persecutions of 1318 and the following years, when documentation is sparser and the point is very difficult to prove. I argue for a doctrinally unsound oral influence by Olivi before his death in 1298 and am not convinced that the persecutions of the eighties and nineties were motivated by prejudice alone, though I accept that long-term mental and physical pressures on the Spirituals stimulated excesses. Compare C. Schmitt, in *AFH*, liii (1960), pp. 330–2.

received with veneration. The affair gives us a glimpse of another more cloudy and visionary Olivi, not usually revealed in his writings.[42]

Authorities believed that his popular influence was baleful. Preoccupied with the prime battle over Olivi's scholastic views and the *usus pauper*, they did nevertheless periodically advert to the popular background in the province. In 1285 he was accused of being the head of a 'superstitious sect'; in 1299 a provincial council warned against extravagences; there was an investigation of his work on the Apocalypse, and a complaint about it in 1311.

The tragedy of the Spiritual movement was that its settlement was so long delayed. Treatment by the usual procedures of disciplinary action within the order could not work, because superiors who attempted to carry them out were self-interested and stained with abuses, especially in the Midi. There was yet too much idealism amongst the friars, and too much sympathy among outside sympathizers, churchmen and laymen, for a local repression to be carried out without complaint or publicity. The Spirituals, for all their faults, carried the authentic note of the passion for poverty; and this both united them to St Francis, and ever won them some hearts. At the same time, grounds for disquiet on doctrinal grounds did exist, both in Italy and in the Midi, in the influence of Joachimite thought, the rigidity and lack of balance of Spiritual views on poverty, and the exaggerated place that the rigorists gave to their heroes, above all to Olivi. So neither side could achieve victory for their views, which tended through combat to become more extreme; and as the disputes dragged on, first inside the order, then at the papal court and at the council of Vienne, patience waned, and the Spirituals and Beguins became more deeply involved in Joachimite extravagance. Clement V, sympathetic but weak, never grasped the nettle: he removed some of the worst superiors from office, and stopped persecution, but did not make a viable settlement.[43] Then the whole landscape darkened for the Spirituals, as the chance of a double vacancy in both the papacy and the generalate from 1314 to 1316 removed central control, and allowed a resumption of persecution. The raising, then the dashing of hopes, and the renewal of persecution, was the stimulus to rank heresy; the identification of the carnal Church with the whole visible Church, that seemed to have turned against them, transformed individual popes and churchmen into the evil figures of Joachimite prophecy.

The distinctions in Olivi's work on the Apocalypse were finely drawn: it was not to be expected that untrained tertiaries would go on making them and stay within orthodoxy as they found Olivi's reputation attacked and heard of the cruelties of Conventual superiors. Olivi's death in 1298 did not help; equivocal as his teaching was, he did restrain the wilder spirits. Dead, his tenets became the centre for the *cultus* of an unauthorized saint, his death-day celebrated as a feast, pilgrimage to his tomb stimulating conversions to the Spiritual way, Joachimite interpretation turning him into the angel of the seventh seal, whose face shone as the sun.[44] Joachimism heightened

---

[42]Lambert, *Poverty*, pp. 172–3; for all controversies, see chs 7, 8; fuller account, esp. valuable on Olivi's treatises and thought, Leff. *Heresy*, I, pp. 100–63.

[43]Leff, *Heresy*, I, pp. 155–6, Lambert, *Poverty*, pp. 198–201; Manselli, *Spirituali*, p. 109, is interesting.

[44]Rev. 10. 1, from Catalan *De statibus ecclesie*, dated by Manselli to 1318 (*Spirituali*, pp. 164–7).

expectations and stimulated a sense of crisis. Extravagance reached great heights: at the end of the chain of persecution, in 1325, a weaver, William Ademarii, a Beguin from Narbonne, told an inquisitor that Olivi had made a work on the Apocalypse that was admirable, and such that, if all the heads of men were reunited into one sole head, it could not have composed such a work if it had not been made by the Holy Ghost, and that it would convert the Saracens to the faith of the Roman Church—one of the events, in fact, that was to mark the start of a new epoch.[45]

Thus a popular heresy was in the process of formation in the Midi in the first two decades of the fourteenth century, fanning out from Spiritual friars to tertiaries under their influence to sympathetic secular clergy and lay patrons in the towns. The area affected abutted on, and to some degree corresponded with, old Cathar-infected regions, but the inspiration was quite different. Olivi and his followers were firm in their opposition to both the Cathars and the Waldensians, whom they saw as members of Antichrist, and there are hardly any signs of interpenetration of doctrine between Catharism and the Spiritual heresy.[46] Furthermore, the old centres of Catharism lay farther to the east, whereas the Spiritual heresy had its centres in two towns less important in Catharism and nearer the coast: Narbonne because of Olivi's memory, and Béziers because of the patronage of the devoted lay supporter Pierre Trancavel, and also because the two convents had been taken over by Spirituals during the interregnum in the papacy and generalate. The area of diffusion stretched at its maximum extent from the coastal line of Perpignan to Nice and, inland, from Toulouse to Avignon.[47] There was a thinner band of support over the Pyrenees, in more developed regions of the kingdom of Aragon. The core lay in the towns: workers in the country were not affected and neither was the layer of immigrant Northern Frenchmen, lay or clerical.[48] It was a Languedocian heresy, and may even have owed something to local feeling against authority. Towns backed the Spirituals and appealed on their behalf partly because they were opposed to the activity of the inquisition and its implications in secular politics, and adherents may well have been attracted by a movement which came to denounce wealthy upper clergy, because of their own experience of the clergy in Languedoc.

The Cathar crisis does not seem to have brought a major change in spiritual quality in the higher clergy; a more effective juridical activity can be observed, and the restoration of tithes opened the way to a major church building programme in the century between 1250 and 1350 but this was not the same as spiritual revival.[49] Franciscan rigorists, in their obvious

---

It is fair to add that the general trend of Manselli's exposition (chs 2–4) differs from mine and, using esp. minor works of the Spirituals and supporters, stresses their relative orthodoxy before 1318 and the arbitrary nature of persecution.

[45]Ibid., pp. 181–2.
[46]Ibid., p. 264; for a possible exception, see p. 221.
[47]Ibid., p. 256; for Cathars' sites, see above, p. 117.
[48]Ibid., pp. 258–63.
[49]See J. H. Mundy, 'Charity and social work in Toulouse, 1100–1250', *Traditio*, XXII (1966), pp. 203–87, esp. p. 206; Wakefield, *Heresy Crusade*, p. 130 and n. For a case of the Church benefiting from an individual accused of heresy, see Wakefield, in *Names*, XVIII (1970), pp. 294–5. I owe refs to Professor W. L. Wakefield.

destitution, were not, in externals, wholly unlike the perfect; and the interrogations of the inquisition show how Beguins were attracted by the poor life of their leaders.[50] In each case, it was the ethics of the dedicated individual which formed a major appeal. Rich as well as poor laymen were involved but there were numbers of poor tradesmen of modest culture, butchers, weavers and the like, whose attitudes to the rich and powerful who, they believed formed the carnal Church, were surely in part shaped by their social position and the gulf which separated them from the wealthy. Nevertheless the heresy sprang mainly from a religious motive: it was the belief of élite groups, devoted if unsubtle rank and file Franciscans, and dedicated laity. Numbers were fairly small—120 members of the first order who took over the convents of Narbonne and Béziers, smaller numbers of friars in Italian provinces. When the inquisition set about destroying the popular base of the heresy in the Midi, they were working on groups linked by geography, family or individual personalities that did not usually number more than twenty and were often less. There was no popular involvement in terms of adherents or patrons on anything like the scale of Catharism.

Paradoxically, John XXII,[51] the dynamic administrator whose election in 1316 ended the long vacancy after Clement V, was at one and the same time responsible for cutting short the movement of Spirituals and Beguins and so safeguarding orthodoxy and for putting the finishing touches to the development of full-blown heresy within the movement. One hardly knows whether to wonder more at the energy and efficiency which John brought to the task of repression or the recklessness and haste which he demonstrated in his handling of the doctrinal problems of the Franciscans.

For him, a native of Cahors, who had worked in regions neighbour to the Spirituals' catchment area in the south and came informed to the problem, the question was not whether the movement was dangerous or unorthodox but how it might most effectively be put down. Leading Spirituals who had patrons were removed from the scene without punishment, the rebellion in Narbonne and Béziers ended, Olivi's teaching on the Apocalypse again subjected to academic examination, recalcitrant Italians pursued. His neatest stroke was to take down the previous bull of clarification on the rule, Clement V's *Exivi de Paradiso*, extract two clauses, on the wearing of poor clothing and the prohibition of granaries and cellars, which Clement had concluded were points of obligation for the friars yet should be subject to the individual discretion of superiors, and to reiterate them in a bull of his own, *Quorumdam exigit*, insisting on the power of superiors to decide what was poverty (*vilitas*) in clothing and when it was right to have the security of food storage through using cellars and granaries.[52]

Quorumdam was used to sort sheep from goats. An inquisitor presented it to

---

[50] See Manselli's comments (*Spirituali*, chapters 7, 8, *passim* (most valuable section)), and Leff, *Heresy*, I, pp. 212–30.

[51] For John and the Franciscans, see Leff, *Heresy*, I, pp. 157–66, 206–11, 230–3, 238–55 (see characterization of John (pp. 206–7) and analysis of his terminology, using *Quia vir reprobus*); Lambert, *Poverty*, chap. 10, and in *FS*, xxxii (1972). pp. 123–43; Tierney, ch. 5, is illuminating on the theory of papal power. Note his correction (p. 188) of Leff, *Heresy*, I, pp. 241, 246, 249, on John and the key of knowledge.

[52] *BF*, v (Rome, 1898), no. 289, pp. 128–30.

suspect friars and put to them two questions. Would they obey the precepts contained in *Quorumdam exigit?* Did they believe that the pope had the power to make such precepts as were contained in *Quorumdam exigit?* The questions touched on a nerve-centre, for to say 'yes' meant giving up the patched, dramatically poor habits that recalled Francis's dying words about his early life in the Testament, and served as a party badge and, against the tenor of the rule, allowing the foresight for the morrow, implied in the keeping of cellars and granaries. To return to obedience to superiors on these issues meant giving up the distinctive Spiritual position and admitting that, as John said, poverty was great but 'unity was greater';[53] to admit the Pope's power of dispensation over the rule was to abandon the view, forged by the Spirituals in the battle over the observance, that the Franciscan rule, written under divine inspiration, was like the Gospel and not subject to alteration by any human hand.

Four friars were obdurate in refusing assent and, after a high-ranking commission had reported that to refuse the Papal right to make the precepts contained in *Quorumdam exigit* was tantamount to heresy, were burnt at Marseilles in May 1318.[54] Armed with *Quorumdam* and this decision, plus a bull which condemned unauthorized groups of friars and tertiaries (*fraticelli, fratres de paupere vita, bizzochi* or *beghini*),[55] the inquisition was equipped to roll up the movement in the South of France. Another bull, with a somewhat arbitrary list of errors, was issued primarily against Spirituals in Tuscany.[56] Meanwhile, a commission reported adversely—and with some injustice—on Olivi's work on the Apocalypse, and theologians condemned a more definitely heretical Catalan work on the ages of the Church. Olivi's *Lectura* was not definitively condemned till 1326; but his tomb was destroyed early in the pontificate, and possession of his books was treated as incriminating.

Over some seven or eight years inquisitors destroyed the core of the heresy, catching the members of the first order who escaped the net spread by John and the Conventuals in 1317, moving against the patrons who helped fugitives and the Beguins who were the chief lay supporters. Condemnation to crosses, pilgrimages and burnings, and the usual pressures to produce recantations whittled support away, providing occasional small batches for the pyre, beside the Cathars and Waldensians, who still required attention in this region.[57] By 1326–7, when the inquisition laid by the heels Pierre Trancavel of Béziers and his daughter, who used his resources to aid refugees, and Bernardo Maurini, the secular priest of Narbonne who gave valuable exhortation and encouragement to the cause, the back of the movement was broken.[58] Thereafter, although there was still an aftermath in Languedoc and

[53]Ibid., p. 130b.
[54]For event and significance, see Manselli, *Spirituali*, pp. 150–78, 190.
[55]*Sancta Romana* (*BF*, v, no. 297, pp. 134–5).
[56]*Gloriosam ecclesiam* (ibid., no. 302, pp. 137–42).
[57]See Bernard Gui's first-hand account in *Practica inquisitionis heretice pravitatis, auctore Bernadone Guidonis,* ed. C. Douais (Paris, 1886); G. Mollat, *Manuel de l'Inquisiteur* (Paris, 1926) (abridged, with Fr. trans.); further materials in P. Limborch, *Historia Inquisitionis,* (Amsterdam, 1692); account of sources in Manselli, *Spirituali*, ch. 1.
[58]Manselli, pp. 234–7.

cases turned up in Majorca and elsewhere,[59] the Spirituals had lost their most significant territorial base.

So the crisis in the south ended. Yet John, who did most to destroy the movement, also played a part in pushing it deeper into heresy. The four friars who stood firm at Marseilles were regarded as martyrs, and interrogations after 1318 tell us of the shock that the news of the deaths gave to the fugitive friars and Beguins. Surely this blow was one of the persecutions that heralded the opening of the seventh seal of the Apocalypse and the new epoch in history? The decision against the rule, as they saw it, helped to confirm identification of John XXII with the mystical Antichrist who, it was prophesied, would strike against Francis and his true followers. When John, nothing if not thorough, turned his attention in 1322–3 to the contemporary doctrine of poverty of the whole Franciscan order, and made a dogmatic decision on the poverty of Christ and the Apostles in an anti-Franciscan sense,[60] that only strengthened their conviction of his true position, as the enemy of the elect. Was not persecution the mark of those who would enter on the Sabbath age of quiet and contemplation? The ashes of those who burned were gathered up and venerated as relics. Gagliarda, wife of the notary Bernardo Fabri, confessed in a human touch that she had said over such relics kept at their home, 'If you are the bones of saints, help me.'[61] Others were firmer in their convictions. The *sermo generalis* before burning, at which the errors of the heretic were described and denounced, and the actual execution could and did have the effect sometimes of actually spreading heresy. At times of burnings the priest Peirotas was busy in the localities, using the occasion to exhort fellow-believers, by the example of courage in martyrdom, to persevere in belief.[62] There was a chain-reaction, stiffening Beguins and others in their beliefs. The decisions of John strengthened the view that he was Antichrist, and precipitated discussion of the place of present events in the approach to the seventh age of the Church. Eschatological hopes made adherents more determined to be faithful to their beliefs; *Quorumdam exigit* decided them not to yield on habits and granaries; burnings provided more saints, nucleus of a spiritual Church opposed to the carnal Church of pope and prelates. But the effects could not last; the persistence of the inquisition soon swept the recalcitrant few away, and forced the others into recantation.

John's settlement was effective but undiscriminating.[63] An artificiality hangs round the decisions in *Quorumdam exigit*, leaving the impression that heresy had come to consist in opposition to the orders of the pope. The authoritarian approach to problems of doctrine was characteristic of John. An impatient administrator, he produced a decision that provided a convenient basis for inquisition action. Later, when involved in controversy with the whole Franciscan order, he produced decisions about poverty that were careless, easily open to attack and which failed to grapple with the real

[59]See D. Douie, *The Nature and the Effect of the Heresy of the Fraticelli* (Manchester, 1932).
[60]*Cum inter nonnullos* (*BF*, v, no. 518, pp. 256–9).
[61]Manselli, *Spirituali*, p. 221, n. 3.
[62]Ibid., pp. 218, 315–8.
[63]Contrast John's handling of the Dominicans; see E. Hillebrand, 'Kurie und Generalkapitel des Predigerordens unter Johannes XXII', in *Adel und Kirche: Festschrift für G. Tellenbach* (Freiburg, 1968), pp. 499–515. I owe the ref. to Dr A. V. Murray.

issue—the place of poverty in the religious life and its relation to Christian perfection. His lack of care helped to cause another revolt of Franciscans, so that by the end of his reign there were not only *fraticelli de paupere vita*, the first-order heirs of the old Spirituals, but also *fraticelli de opinione*, former members of the official order, who opposed his decisions on the poverty of Christ.

Yet heresy there was, 'uncreated' as well as created, for a long incubation lay behind the views of the Beguins. John unwittingly stimulated certain excesses; but he did not bring the heresy as a whole into being.[64] Its essence lay in exaggeration. From earliest days poverty had been a prime occupation of the Franciscans, but it was transmuted by the simpler Spiritual friars and Beguins into the one crucial issue before the Church—a very different position from that of St Francis. The cumulative effect of the disputes, the repressions and the anxieties of rigorists about their views was to go far towards overturning the basis of Christian ethics,[65] and making it consist simply in renunciation of goods and destitution in daily living. Joachimism and the imminent expectation of cosmic change heightened the distortion. The intensified struggle between good and evil on the eve of the end of the world (or, as in Joachim's view, of the present epoch) tended to narrow down to the battle over the observance of poverty. A sectarianism made the writings of one devoted friar with a talent for speculative thinking and a taste for the Apocalypse into a teacher on a par with Paul, or with the Four Doctors of the Church; and turned the Franciscan rule, on which a divine inspiration had played, into a writing that stood on a level with the gospels themselves. The battle over obedience, first in the order, then with ecclesiastical superiors at large, led on to a viewpoint which rejected the whole visible Church, equated the pope with the mystical Antichrist, and waited confidently for the supersession of the hierarchy.

Earlier generations were inclined to shrug off dangers in prophecy. If they were false, events would prove them so.[66] The Midi heresy showed again the flaws in this view. Exaggerations of poverty showed up elements of unhealthy thinking in the whole Franciscan order, and through the Johannine crisis brought the Franciscans to their lowest ebb in the fourteenth century. It was a tragedy for the Church. The events of the early fourteenth century revealed how a popular heresy could emerge within the very citadel of the Church. It was the enemy within.

By the end of John XXII's pontificate in 1334 the roll-call of popular heresies and movements of religious dissent had swelled—the Apostolics, Dolcino's rebels, the extremist Spiritual Franciscans, and their outflow in the tertiaries and Beguins of Southern France and the fraticelli of Italy, the heretical mystics, and the adherents of the Free Spirit in Germany, Silesia and Bohemia. The combative old man was busy to the last with the aftermath of his settlement of the problems of the Franciscans, writing at length in 1329 to refute the members of the order under the former minister-general Michael of Cesena, who could not accept his decisions on the poverty of Christ and had

[64]There is a difference of emphasis between my judgement and that of Manselli and Leff.
[65]Knowles, *Religious Orders*, II, p. 93.
[66]This explains the long toleration of doubtful pseudo-Joachimite speculation.

broken into revolt in the previous year,[67] then embroiling himself in his last years in a controversy over his own doctrine of the Beatific Vision,[68] first evolved in reaction against Olivi's treatment of the issue. The Vision affair, however, remained personal: no theological judgement was issued and John's successor, Benedict XII, sensibly regulated the matter in his bull *Benedictus Deus* of 1336.

Under Benedict the pace of activity died down. Time and periodic persecutions whittled away the heretics. Dolcino and the Apostolics had been a one-for-all outbreak. The Beguins of Southern France had been exposed to intensive inquisition activity in the 1320s; they gave scant trouble afterwards. The intellectual Franciscans under Michael of Cesena, secure in their refuge with Lewis of Bavaria in Munich, having only an intellectual challenge and no popular appeal through austerity of life, faded with the deaths of their founders about mid-century. In Italy, especially in the south, and in tiny groups elsewhere the *fraticelli* who would not accept John's settlement and regarded him as a heretic continued an existence in the half-light.[69] Sectarian to the last, they disputed among themselves as to who would be the Saviour to usher in a new age. Most commonly, they unchurched all who gave obedience to John XXII and his successors, on the grounds that his decisions on poverty were heretical and the practices of the Church and Franciscan order unfaithful to Christ's precepts. But they advanced no new arguments, living on with the themes of their attack on John XXII unchanged, supported by a popular reverence for the austerities of their life. In Florence they had a particularly long influence.[70]. It took the determination of the saints of the Franciscan Observance in the fifteenth century, Capistrano and James of the March, who blended a life of true poverty with orthodoxy, to roll up the last remnants of the rebellion. The last of them disappear from recorded history with a trial at Rome in 1466.

Prosecutions of supposed adherents of the Free Spirit fluctuated according to individual interests, and tended to run down as the vitality of the mystical movement in the beguinages faded. At Strasburg repeated persecutions are recorded, in 1317–19, 1365, 1368–9, 1374 and 1404.[71] In the first instance, in 1317, bishop John I was pursuing heresy, pre-eminently among the males, the

---

[67]*Quia vir reprobus* (*BF*, v, no. 820, pp. 408–49); Leff, *Heresy*, I pp. 238–55; B. Töpfer, 'Die Anschauungen des Papstes Johannes XXII über das Dominium in der Bulle "Quia Vir Reprobus" ', in *Folia Diplomatica* (Brno, 1971), pp. 295–306.

[68]Knowles, *Religious Orders*, I, pp. 248–52; Pásztor, in *BISIAM*, LXX (1958), pp. 365–424 and 'Una Raccolta di Sermoni di Giovanni XXII', *Bullettino dell' Archivio Paleografico Italiano*, n.s., II–III (1956–7), pp. 265–89; D. L. Douie, 'John XXII and the Beatific Vision', *Dominican Studies*, III (1950), pp. 154–74; M. Dykmans, *Les Sermons de Jean XXII sur la Vision béatifique* (Rome, 1973). (Review by B. Smalley, in *MA*, XLIII (1974). pp. 52–3).

[69]Leff, *Heresy*, I, pp. 230–8, Douie, *Fraticelli*, pp. 209–47, documents ed. F. Ehrle, in *ALKG*, IV, pp. 63–180, with discussion of term *fraticelli* (pp. 138–80) (see esp. remarks on *fraticelli* unconnected with Spirituals (pp. 168–78)). Summary by Oliger in *DTC*, XIV, cols 2522–49; F. Vernet, ibid., VI, cols 770–84, s.v.

[70]Stephens, in *PP*, LIV (1972), pp. 36–53.

[71]Patschovsky, in *DA* XXX (1974), pp. 56–198. Not all persecutions are well-recorded; date of 1365 is a hypothesis (ibid., p. 113). Summary (partially modified by Patschovsky) by Lerner (*Free Spirit*, pp. 85–105); see case of Malkaw (ibid., pp. 101–3) for a classic case of slander.

beghards;[72] later, probably from the pontificate of Urban V in the sixth decade of the century, the curia, rather than the bishop, seems to have provided the major impetus; later still, an individual inquisitor had greatest weight. A strand of genuine heresy and disobedience cannot be discounted as a factor behind these persecutions, but one major recurring source of trouble lay in the resentments of the secular clergy in the city against the popular influence of mendicants who were intimately linked with the beguine movement.[73] Targets of the persecutions varied, including beghards, anticlericals and individualists, deviant mystics, beguines in convents, pious women, tertiaries: the effects of the troubles were to drive the beguine movement more than ever towards the mendicants, obviously for protection. Prejudice played a considerable role, and later persecutions produce less good evidence for doctrinal deviations.

In Germany, Silesia and Bohemia prosecutions were affected by the will of the ruler, being inhibited in Germany for the duration of the contest between John and Lewis of Bavaria, but supported in Silesia and Bohemia by the Margrave Charles, later king, and again given free scope in Germany when the pro-Church Charles reigned as Emperor Charles IV.[74] They revealed numbers of individual enthusiasts of varying orthodoxy, not necessarily adherents of the Free Spirit, together with Waldensians, who were the most resilient heretics of these regions. In one interesting case at Schweidnitz in Silesia the inhabitants of a beguinage were shown to be followers of a fiercely ascetic life, with much flagellation, fasting and hard work, believers in their superiority, despite outward humility, and despising church attendance, for which they were inclined to substitute their own prayers. Free Spirit beliefs in union with God did exist among them, but not libertinism, though they were accused of it.[75] The wave of persecution in the Empire led by Martin of Prague, Peter Zwicker and Eylard Schoenveld towards the end of the fourteenth century and in the early years of the fifteenth,[76] though mainly directed against the Waldensians, carried beguines, beghards and supposed heretical mystics into the inquisition's net, but by the time of the Council of Constance in 1414–18 the stream ran thinly. At the Council, the beguines, shrunken in number, were defended against attack: *Ad nostrum's* influence had waned: few more cases turned up in the fifteenth century, although the pursuit of the mystical way still had its hazards. The last well-recorded case of Free Spirit heresy north of the Alps is that of Hans Becker of Mainz, burned in 1458.[77]

The heresies that emanated from the Franciscans, the mystics and the imaginations of churchmen were disquieting, not so much because they

---

[72]Ibid., p. 96; on decision of Council of Mainz 1310, see ibid., pp. 141–2. On name of John I (incorrectly given as 'of Dürbheim' in Lerner, *Free Spirit*), see Patschovsky, art. cit., p. 94 n. 82.

[73]See Patschovsky's summary (pp. 116–8). Breaches of discipline play an important role, and the terms beguine and beghard are loose ones.

[74]Lerner, *Free Spirit*, pp. 107, 131.

[75]Ibid., pp. 112–9.

[76]Ibid., pp. 145–6; for proceedings of Zwicker in Brandenburg and Pomerania, above, p. 152 n.7.

[77]Lerner, *Free Spirit*, pp. 177–81.

represented *per se* an important direct threat, but because they were symptomatic of failings in the late medieval Church.

Though the Spiritual Franciscans had some powerful patrons, notably in southern royal houses, their case was not one that of its nature would stimulate a serious revolt against the Church. The practice of poverty, rather than the whole structure of belief woven round the Spirituals' protest, formed the basis of their popularity. *Fraticelli* met a real need which orthodoxy did not. The tragedy of the disputes, so trenchantly resolved after 1316, was that they lost to the sects idealists who were sorely needed. Probably the heresy of the Languedocian Beguins and the *fraticelli* would not have come into existence if the order before the fourteenth century had been able to contain and give outlets to its zealots; after they had gone and the controversies had had their enervating effect, the order was the weaker, and the way to needful reform made harder by being associated with heresy.

Still less than the Franciscans were the adherents of the Free Spirit capable of mounting an assault on the established system. At worst, they were isolated, individual deviants: moreover, as we have seen, there was a great deal of artificiality about this heresy. What the Free Spirit episode did show was the inability of authority at the time of Vienne and afterwards to come to terms with the beguine movement and to provide guidelines for its life, satisfactory to all parties in the Church. The cases after *Ad nostrum* also show us evidence of an anticlericalism both more widespread and more significant in the history of the Church than the Free Spirit.

Part Four

Evangelical Heresy in the Late Middle Ages

13

Church and Society: Benedict XII to Eugenius IV

With the death of John XXII the most sustained effort of the popes at Avignon to recover their erstwhile power and independence came to an end; John's successors lacked his exceptional talents, and their problems grew.[1] The most significant legacy from John lay in the development of administration and the increased sophistication of papal fiscal machinery; under his successors the process of reserving benefices for papal provision went on developing, primarily for fiscal reasons; the volume of papal business grew, and itself created a demand for more finance. The popes, whether efficient or not, austere or luxurious, were caught in an inflationary spiral[2] in which their real power was in no way increased, while the activity of their officials grew and the oportunities for true reform, if anything, diminished. There was a quantity of self-interested protest at a high level about the growth of papal intervention and the 'sinful city' of Avignon, coexisting with what could fairly be called informal concordats[3] between the papacy and secular governments, with growing bureaucracies that needed rewards, hard-pressed for resources at a time of economic regression, and anxious to benefit from the treasures of the Church. A system had come into being, based on detailed compromises, which met the needs of various interests in Church and State, however much complaint was made about it; in practice, in the underlying alliance between Church and State, it was the State's power which was now uppermost.

At the same time, papal centralization and defects in its administration excited popular disapproval, reinforced by the feeling of the devout that the proper place for the popes was at the tombs of Peter and Paul. Within the college of cardinals there were signs of the growth of an oligarchy, seeking to assert the powers of electors and put shackles on individual popes. Much valuable day-to-day business transacted at the curia, and a certain sophistication within the bureaucracy could not weigh in the scales against the general loss of prestige and leadership suffered at Avignon.

In 1378, shortly after the return from Avignon to Rome, disaster occurred. The conclave elected an unsuitable candidate, the aggressive and wilful Urban VI. A genuine reaction against the man they had chosen, combined with divisions among the cardinals, oligarchical sentiment and national

[1]See p. 165 above, n. 1; also M. E. Aston, *The Fifteenth Century: the Prospect of Europe* (London, 1968).
[2]Southern, *Western Society*, p. 133.
[3]I owe the phrase to Dr A. V. Antonovics.

feeling, created a schism. All existing problems were vastly accentuated. Thenceforward two popes existed, one with a seat at Avignon under Clement VII and his successors, and the other at Rome under Urban VI and his successors, excommunicating each other and their rivals' supporters, and deploying all available resources to unseat their opponents. Conflicts between states had helped to create the Great Schism, and now kept it in being; all the abuses for which the papacy had been held responsible in the past were sharply increased, as electors on the rival sides chose men of war and diplomacy rather than reformers, and the popes sacrificed all higher considerations to the search for victory.

Need stimulated response, and a conciliar movement developed, primarily in order to end the Great Schism, but secondarily, however, to reform Papacy and Church, and in some cases to check a papal headship that appeared unworthy by leadership through general councils. The way to these objectives proved hard. At the council of Pisa in 1409, the adherents of the conciliar party introduced a third claimant to the tiara, reigning as Alexander V, who was intended to end the conflict, but failed to obtain the withdrawal of his rivals. His existence only made matters worse, as did that of his successor, John XXIII, elected in 1410. Not till 1417 at the council of Constance did one man, Martin V, emerge as a generally acceptable candidate. Weakened by the schism and by the advantages the kingdoms had gained during it, the papacy under Martin V trod warily and slowly regained ground. Both Martin and his successor, Eugenius IV, had to face tenacious resistance from supporters of the conciliar party, who wanted reform on their own terms, and they could only be said to have effectively outridden opposition from this quarter by about 1439, after Eugenius had succeeded in splitting the movement by transferring the council of Basle first to Ferrara and then to Florence, and scoring the triumph of securing union between the Greek and Latin Churches.

Throughout the fourteenth century, the schism and the days of vitality of the conciliar movement, reform was constantly discussed, proposals put forward, and sermons preached, often in the most violent terms and by holders of high clerical office, denouncing abuses without bringing about any major reforming action. The need for reform tended to become a cliché. Naturally circumstances, especially after 1378, focussed attention on the need for reform at the head. But how was it to be effected? Different voices recommended different means, and wished to carry measures of varying degrees of vigour. If there was to be reform in the head, should it not be in the members also? And yet bishops and cardinals were in various ways beneficiaries of the system to be reformed, and there were secular interests to be considered also. Meanwhile, the immediate need was to end the schism. After it was over, more profound reform remained on the agenda, as it had done on so many occasions in the past, but it tended to be driven into the background by the struggle between papalists and conciliarists, and so was never realized.

A concomitant, and to some degree a result, of these events, was a feeling of mistrust towards ecclesiastical institutions, especially those on a large scale; it was reinforced by the Great Schism, but is discernible earlier. It underlies the loss of vitality of the major orders, and helps to explain the earlier success of the beguine movement, till it was checked by official disapproval and the heresy accusations. While all the high level disturbances in the leadership of the international Church continued, a popular religion blossomed in the towns, in the parish churches, and in the confraternities which became so popular, and which assembled various social groups for the practice of their religion. A great vogue existed for works of popular devotion in the vernacular, and there was some dissemination of scriptural versions in the form, not of the bare text of the original, but in compilations and meditations linked predominantly to the mystical movement of the late Middle Ages. The practice of pilgrimage flourished and the cult of saints developed, sometimes to extravagance. In the wealthy towns a merchant class spent heavily on the building and decoration of churches; preachers readily drew large crowds, and the individual prophetic figure characteristic of the time, the mystic or the reformer, attracted reverence.

Anticlericalism was the natural accompaniment to the major failures in leadership and to the abuses. It was not always the case that the state of the clergy was worse in the fourteenth and fifteenth centuries than it had been earlier, but their deficiencies were attracting a more impatient response from the laity.[4] The relationship between clergy and laity had undergone a change, due to the widening horizons, the spread of lay education and an increasing lay self-consciousness and independence which become apparent at about the turn of the thirteenth and fourteenth centuries north of the Alps. Italy had long been a special case because of the higher standards of education attained by the laity there in an earlier age. Congregations were less ready to accept a clerical leadership *per se*; they were more questioning, and their expectations were higher. A low opinion of the clergy was fostered in this period by elements in the clergy themselves, through denunciatory sermons; though one has to note the existence of a literary, satirical anticlerical tradition, of clerks making jokes about clerks, which is as old as Walter Map in the twelfth century.[5]

One difference between the late Middle Ages and earlier centuries was that anticlerical ideas were more likely to be put into effect in the latter period, and Erastianism was both more possible and more widespread. The clerical profession had always been a net holding all manner of fish, and it continued to be so; ordinations were on a considerable scale, and investigation of suitability merely formal; the bishop was generally a remote figure, appointed for political or social rather than religious reasons, unable, even if he willed, to break through the barriers of custom effectively to discipline or unite the clergy of his diocese; there were many avenues of promotion open to the talented priest, and a parochial post was not necessarily rewarding or attractive. It was at the level of the parish clergy, despite some efforts at reform and some improvements, that the late medieval Church proved least effective, and it was here that some of the greatest stimuli to anticlericalism existed.

[4] See Rapp, *L'Église*, ch. 9, and on Italy, D. Hay, *Italian Clergy and Italian Culture in the Fifteenth Century* (London, 1973). Society for Renaissance Studies. Occasional papers no. 1)
[5] I owe comment to Professor C. N. L. Brooke.

Extremism was a characteristic of the time. It links to political events and to economic troubles. The Hundred Years' War between England and France, which broke out in 1337, initiated a long sequence of conflicts, produced devastation over wide areas of France, and had a baleful effect on Church life; we have seen the part which it played in the outbreak and continuation of the Great Schism. Secular governments had their own problems of authority, made worse by economic pressures and by the effects of warfare. The Black Death in 1348–51 was a catastrophic event, removing at a blow more than a third of the population, and sparking off a great outburst of penitential flagellation, intended to assuage God's wrath and expiate the sins of the individual penitent; renewed visitations, though less disastrous, had important demographic effects and elicited similar, if not so violent emotional responses.[6]

Processions of men, initially well organized, walking two by two, with a precise ritual to follow, of the saying of *Pater Nosters* and *Aves* and of flagellation accompanied by chants and songs, passed through Austria (probably their place of origin), Hungary, Germany, Bohemia, the Low Countries and Picardy, summoning the citizens of the towns to which they came to join them and scourging themselves in some public spot, generally the market-place.

The most striking feature lies in the strength of the emotions which lay behind these painful and repeated self-chosen penances, a reminder of the violence of feeling still latent in popular spirituality, comparable to the early crusade impulse, the Alleluia preachings in thirteenth-century Italy, or the outbreak of flagellation in 1260, coupled with the self-control often apparent in a movement that appears to be quite spontaneous, uncontrolled by any existing authority, and in the hands of the laity. There would-be flagellant took an oath to carry out his flagellation for thirty-three and a half days, recalling the years of Christ's earthly life, confessed to the masters of the movement, and undertook to pay his debts or make restitution for past wrongs. Within the procession he followed a strict ritual and obeyed the masters, flagellating twice a day in public and once at night; after the conclusion of the pilgrimage he promised to flagellate on Good Fridays for the rest of his life. Unbeneficed clergy joined, but the great bulk of penitents were laymen.

The attitudes of ecclesiastical authority varied. In the Low Countries, for example, the Bishop of Thérouanne formally authorized them; at Tournai a rule which the Bruges flagellants had adopted was presented to the chapter; but the author of the *Annales Flandriae* thought that they were beghards, and attacked their belief that all sins would be remitted after their penance. The

---

[6]E. Delaruelle, 'Les grands Processions de Pénitents de 1349 et 1399', *Il movimento dei disciplinati nel settimo centenario del suo inizio* (Perugia, 1962), pp. 109–45 (on Netherlands, but with general refs); G. Székely, 'Le mouvement des Flagellants au 14ᵉ Siècle, son Caractère et ses Causes', in *HS*, pp. 229–38, Erbstösser, *Strömungen*, pp. 10–69 (Marxist analysis, with hypothesis of penetration of the movement in Thuringia by Free Spirit), R. Kiekhefer, 'Radical Tendencies in the Flagellant Movement of the Mid-fourteenth Century', *JMRS*, IV (1974), pp. 157–76 (re-examination of sources, with critique of Erbstösser); English account in Leff, *Heresy*, II, pp. 485–93. Dr J. V. Fearns is working on a comprehensive analysis. See his map and notes, (*Atlas zur Kirchengeschichte*, ed. Jedin et. al. pp. 48, 65).

fear was of a lay movement without clerical control that had undertaken mass penance without authorization and without receiving the sacrament of penance from the priesthood. Moreover, there were extravagances. A Dominican preacher, for example, said that the blood of the flagellants was more precious than any since Christ's. In certain areas, notably Thuringia and Franconia, they tended to become more violent and anticlerical. Conceivably this was the case more often when their arrival preceded, rather than followed, the plague. Before the arrival of the Death, flagellation was one of the few outlets open to a fear-ridden population; after it had arrived, the worst could be seen, and there were practical tasks, such as burying the dead, available to dampen emotions.[7]

In the end, Clement VI condemned them in 1349. As the stimulus of mass mortality faded, so the movement waned, although there were recrudescences, in some cases associated with much more overt antisacerdotalism and heresy proper. The use of the scourge, long a traditional monastic discipline, had been taken up by the laity in a crisis on a mass scale, quite independently of the hierarchy, and by some of them turned into a kind of supreme sacrament.

The Death, a unique catastrophe for contemporaries, sparked off a religious response of unusual intensity; other long-term changes in the economy and society, still imperfectly understood, and the effects of warfare produced tensions and uprisings in town and country. The roots of these disturbances lay in the major changes in the Western economy which made themselves felt from almost the beginning of the fourteenth century in certain regions, affecting class relationships, the internal life of towns, and the condition of peasants. In towns a major factor lay in the rigidity of government by closed circles of wealthy bourgeois, directing affairs to their own profit, and arousing the hostility of artisans eager to share in the new wealth. Before the Death, the increase in town populations in advanced areas to an unprecedented size accentuated this hostility, as small groups of families were seen to regulate the destinies of so many; after the massive fall in population tension continued, as the rich in a contracted economy attempted to hold on to every source of wealth.

Troubles had begun in the late thirteenth century in the Low Countries, and continued during the following century; there were sporadic crises elsewhere and widespread disorder in western Europe at various times between the spring of 1378 and the early months of 1383.[8] In France anger was turned against royal officials, tax collectors and moneyers; generally at the time of the Black Death the fear of mortality issued in pogroms of Jews, who were accused of responsibility for the epidemic; in England there were periodic xenophobic outbreaks.

In the countryside lords who were under heavy economic pressure attempted to enforce ancient rights over the peasants and, after the fall in population, to prevent free movement for better wages or conditions at a time of labour shortage. In France, one of the most violent peasant uprisings, the Jacquerie, took place in 1358; in England, the Peasants' Revolt of 1381 led to

[7]Kieckhefer's hypothesis.

[8]M. Mollat and P. Wolff, *The Popular Revolutions of the late Middle Ages*, London, 1973.

the death of Simon of Sudbury, archbishop of Canterbury; the mob attacked officials and destroyed records, and briefly held the south-east of the country in fear. A combination of grievances came to a head with the imposition of a poll tax for an unsuccessful war; the underlying factor was the irritation of a comparatively prosperous peasantry with out-of-date restrictions which lords were attempting to impose on them. Further visitations of the plague, on a smaller scale, in the later fourteenth century and in the fifteenth added to the tension of life, sometimes inducing flight to penance, as in the Flagellant episode. Man's mortality was unusually vivid in the years following 1348.

Thought was marked by a tendency to take issues to extremes, and by a mistrust of reason.[9] The great system-building of the thirteenth century was over. The synthesis between faith and reason of St Thomas Aquinas had fallen under heavy attack almost as soon as it was launched. The wholesale condemnation of theses, some of St Thomas, some of others, by Bishop Étienne Tempier of Paris in 1277 marked the turning point; thereafter different groups of scholastics separated, debating among one another individual issues; the effect of the Tempier condemnations was first to create confusion, and, then, in the long run, to facilitate a division between the spheres of faith and reason.

New ideas appeared with great rapidity; Duns Scotus, the Scottish Franciscan who died in 1308, both subjected traditional Aristotelian and Augustinian views to effective criticism and launched forth on a structure of thought of his own, inventing novel technical terms to do so. William of Ockham, an English Franciscan who had his career in a university cut short when he joined Michael of Cesena's revolt against John XXII's decisions on poverty, was the fountain head of a powerful current of thought often referred to, somewhat inaccurately, as nominalism. This school had in common with some thinkers of the eleventh and twelfth centuries a stress on the particular in the traditional debate about universals.[10] But discussion was being carried on in the fourteenth century in a quite different atmosphere from that of earlier centuries. Where Aquinas and other thirteenth-century thinkers had been concerned to demonstrate how far natural reason supported the truths of faith, the trend in Scotus, Ockham and other contemporaries was to stress the contingent and limited nature of man's knowledge. Ockham went farther than Scotus on this road; moreover, his expositions on the absolute freedom and overriding power of God, buttressed by a series of brilliant paradoxes, set a gulf between man and the unknowable God and appeared to sap the traditional bases of moral theology. Reason could not support faith, which rested on revelation and authority.

The separation thus effected had beneficial effects in one sphere, for it opened the way to advances in natural science; on the other hand, it undermined traditional supports for faith and moral behaviour, and issued in a fashion both for scepticism and for fideism; if reason could not support faith,

---

[9] G. Leff, *Medieval Thought from St Augustine to Ockham* (Harmondsworth, 1958), part 3; for debate on Ockhamism and its effects (with recent literature), see Rapp, *L'Église*, pp. 332–46, and for more recent work by Leff, below, p. 219, n. 4.

[10] For explanation, see Leff, *Thought*, pp. 104–14, 259–60; and on terminology, Rapp, *L'Église*, p. 337 and my comment below (p. 220 n. 8).

it could be argued, then neither could it disprove it, and beliefs, even if they seemed improbable, could be accepted on external authority alone. How far Ockham has been adequately understood by modern writers, and how far he was responsible for some of the effects attributed to his teaching, is currently the subject of debate; responsibility for some of the more extreme positions of fourteenth-century intellectuals may well lie with other, lesser contemporaries or successors of his. Whatever the ultimate origins of Ockhamism and the so-called nominalist school, it provoked a reaction against this *via moderna*, notably by Thomas Bradwardine, archbishop of Canterbury, who died in 1349, during the Black Death, reasserting traditional doctrine and in metaphysics taking up the opposite position to the Ockhamists, that of realism.[11] Characteristically, however, this reaction too was often marked by the extremism that we must expect of the age.

The more critical climate of opinion, the currents of thought stemming from Ockhamism in the earlier fourteenth century, and the weakening of clerical authority and prestige in the age of the Avignonese papacy and the Great Schism are essential background for the study of the evangelical heresies of the late Middle Ages, stemming from Wyclif, the English Lollards[12] and the Bohemian Hussites. The existence of so much high-level dissent, the reiteration at all levels of the need for reform, and the widespread doubt and uncertainty about the true nature of the Church and the authority of the pope gave opportunities and stimuli unknown to the heresies of the past. Wyclif, co-founder with his early preachers of the English Lollards and part-inspiration of the Bohemian Hussites, was one of the leading academic figures of his day; his progress into heresy in his last years, ignoring the verdict of authority, then deliberately disseminating his views, was something novel in a scholastic of his eminence. An academic could speak to academics, and sparks of Wyclifite heresy blew about in the university world, taking fire here and there among scholars, and passing from them more widely into society.

The widespread criticism of authority, the consciousness of abuse and the scandals of the schism both gave cover to and stimulated Wyclif's attacks. So his heresy gained, for a little time, a base in the university of Oxford, and, because of Wyclif's academic reputation, found its way to the university of Prague. Certain ideas of Wyclif on disendowment and clerical jurisdiction had a natural appeal to rulers and nobility—the potential was there to build upper-class patronage on a scale not achieved by any previous heresy. Heretical doctrine and practical politics could work together. Moreover, the heresies of Wyclif, the Lollards and the Bohemian preachers all lay within the main stream of Christian doctrine and appealed to discontents which were of common concern; the ground for support was wider than the appeal of the Spiritual Franciscans could be, and lacked the alien, exotic quality in Catharism, ultimately repugnant to informed Western Christians. Three factors—the initial base in universities, the potential for gaining upper-class support, and the wide appeal of their teachings—made the new evangelical

[11]Leff, *Thought*, pp. 296–9; for explanation of realism and the reaction against scepticism, see literature below (p. 220, n. 7; p. 221 n. 13).

[12]The best explanation of the origin of the name is in D. Kurze, 'Die festländischen Lollarden', *AKG*, xlvii (1965), pp. 48–76.

heretics more dangerous to the papacy and hierarchy than any earlier movement.

And yet, although Wyclif and his fellows gave expression, often in radical form, to widespread discontents, and worked within an existing intellectual and spiritual tradition, to which they were deeply indebted, their teachings and heresies only struck deep root in two countries, England and Bohemia, both of them a little on the margin of Europe. England had been immune from popular heresy earlier, while Bohemia had been the scene of some Waldensian persecutions, probably not very serious, and little else. Wyclifite and Hussite heresies of various kinds were disseminated, and found some echoes, in Scotland, France, Poland, Hungary, Austria and other German-speaking lands, even in Dalmatia, but provoked no long-lasting response. Lands earlier moved by heresy were, on this occasion, not especially fertile. The machinery of repression moved against the heretics; Wyclif, Hus and the rest formed only a section amongst the many voices raised in favour of reform; there were still deep reserves of feeling behind orthodox doctrine and traditional practice; there was no printing to spread heresy rapidly from one country to the next; precisely the factors which built up Hussitism in the lands of the Bohemian crown acted to cut back support in neighbouring countries. So there was no breakthrough for the new heresies. But still the Wyclif affair and the rise of Lollardy was a major event in English Church history, and the long Hussite crisis formed a turning-point in the Bohemian lands.

14

John Wyclif

1. The English Church in the Fourteenth Century

England produced no significant heresy before the late fourteenth century. Orthodox movements, whether it was the developing interest in the canon law, the new monasticism of the twelfth century, or the orders of friars in the thirteenth, passed into England. Contacts with Europe culturally and ecclesiastically remained close. Commercial and economic links with the towns of Flanders, once a fertile ground for religious dissidence, remained active through the wool trade. Yet heresy from the continent made no impact, and there was no native growth of it[1] before Wyclif fired an old store of combustible anticlericalism and untapped religious zeal in the late fourteenth century.

One reason for this lay in the tight-knit, close-governed nature of the English Church. By continental standards, the control of the ruler over the Church remained very close. The investiture controversy in England was a very brief one, and ended in a compromise that left the substance of power in the matter of appointment to high ecclesiastical office in the hands of the Crown.

England was never the scene of the most spectacular scandals in appointments, which on the continent were most often associated with areas of aristocratic dominance. Royal influence over episcopal appointments tended to be consistent with a fair standard, sometimes, indeed, a distinguished one, as the episcopate of the thirteenth century shows. Ecclesiastical abuse, that first stimulus to heresy, was not notably apparent in England before the fourteenth century. The Franciscans, whose decline on the continent brought a new heresy to birth in the sect of the *fraticelli*, kept their purity and combined good life and learning longer in England than perhaps in any other province. Finally, the effective administration of the country kept a check on the ports, and care was taken to filter the ideas which might pass into the country. Cathars who came in from the continent under Henry II were swiftly rounded up and sentenced.[2] In 1224 the first Franciscan missionaries were kept in Dover castle till they were able to prove their innocence of unorthodoxy.[3] Through the thirteenth century there is evident a

---

[1]For the rare exceptions, see below, p. 269.

[2]Above, p. 65.

[3]*Chronica de Lanercost*, ed. J. Stevenson (Edinburgh, 1839), p. 30. I owe the ref. to Dr R. B. Brooke.

care to supervise merchants from France and elsewhere who might be tainted with heresy.

By the latter half of the fourteenth century, the position of the Church had quietly and undramatically worsened. The episcopate was not unworthy, but it generally lacked the exceptional quality of the previous century. As in Europe generally, no new movement of note had arisen to fill the gap left by the decline of the friars as a source of the most disinterested zeal. There was still vitality in the religious scene, but it was a vitality that could easily lead away from orthodoxy. The English mystics, writing their treatises in the vernacular, making their own direct ascent to God, were no doubt read by few, but they may well be symptomatic of a wider feeling that was not fully content with the official channels of worship and organization. By the end of the century official sources were taking note of the existence of a new man, the literate layman; some action was taken to make a place for him, but not enough. The sermon literature of the time reveals the readiness of the churchmen to denounce abuses; it also reveals, by its repeated mention of abuses over the years, a failure to uproot them. Certain old failings remained throughout the later Middle Ages: an excess overall of clergy, an excess of ill-paid unbeneficed clergy who formed a reservoir of discontent, a monasticism that could not be fairly called decadent but had ceased to be a motive force, a certain canonists' petrefaction in the machinery of the Church, too formal in its procedures easily to allow reform to be effective.

Against this background the period of war strain and ineffectual government which followed on the renewal of the Hundred Years' War in 1369 becomes significant. The failures in the French war and the taxation necessary to pursue campaigns that were in fact beyond the powers of the English kingdom created a cry for disendowment. The size of ecclesiastical endowments gave obvious occasion to this agitation; it was made popular by the desire of the Commons to do something to shift a burden of taxation that, ineptly imposed, helped to spark off the Peasants' Revolt in 1381. Unconnected with reforms as it was, the agitation against the Church gave special opportunities to radical preachers. It favoured the mendicants, with their old complaints against the endowed possessioners, and it gave a brief popular platform to John Wyclif. It favoured anticlericalism, not specially strong in England, but at this time given an exceptional outlet by John of Gaunt and other soldiers and politicians. Ineffectual government in the dotage of Edward III and the minority of Richard II facilitated the rise of extremism and the struggles of factions, some of whom turned to attack the Church as part of their internal struggles.

When a native heresy appeared and was carried rapidly about England, the Church was unprepared. Lack of familiarity with heresy inside the country cut off English churchmen from the developments that had led to the rise of the papal inquisition on the continent. The inquisition came to England only in the one exceptional case of the Templars, and, once the alarm was raised, the episcopate adopted cumbersome procedures in an attempt to stamp out the infection. Though they achieved the essential task of preventing Lollardy from coming to power, they had neither the experience nor the personnel to prevent a rapid expansion of adherents on the eve of the

Peasant's Revolt, or to cut the sect off totally in the aftermath of Oldcastle's revolt early in the fifteenth century. Orthodoxy was never able fully to erase the effects of the agitation of the 1370s and the years immediately following, in which Wyclif's heretical ideas were formulated and the first Lollard preachers began to spread their message along the roads of England. But, before we examine the origins of Lollardy proper, it will be necessary first of all to outline Wyclif's career, and attempt some answer to the long controversial question, Why and how did Wyclif come to hold his heretical views?

2. The Development of Wyclif's Heresy

Early Career

No exact parallel to Wyclif's career can be found in the history of medieval heresies. His is a unique case of a university master turned heresiarch, who inspired a popular movement against the Church. A heresy charge was a recognized hazard in the intellectual contests of the Schools, and not necessarily of great import; deliberate defiance of the Church, such as Wyclif came to make in his last years, was another matter altogether. Two thinkers in the fourteenth century, Marsiglio of Padua and William of Ockham, had made such a defiance and developed lines of thought which show affinities to Wyclif's;[4] but neither is truly comparable. Ockham founded no movement— he joined the schism of Michael of Cesena and developed his views of the Church from the safety of Lewis of Bavaria's court at Munich, and his influence remained intellectual. The same is true of Marsiglio, an astonishingly secular-minded writer but a lone voice, political theorist rather than theologian, without a reputation or depth of learning like that of Wyclif. He too inspired no popular movement.

On the other side, the leaders or founders of popular heresies had not hitherto been men of intellectual standing. They had most frequently been preachers and agitators like Henry the Monk, Valdes or the Bogomil missionaries of the twelfth century. Arnold of Brescia had an intellectual training, but his heresy owed all to his eloquence and powers of personal leadership.[5] Even Petrus Johannis Olivi offers no clear parallel, for, although he was of intellectual calibre to be mentioned in company with Wyclif and was the major inspiration of a popular heretical movement, he was in no sense the founder of the Spiritual Franciscans, which without him would certainly have existed, though they would have been less dangerous.[6]

Wyclif's heresy owed nothing to any pre-existing heretical movement. Its popular adherents, the English Lollards, came in the end to resemble the Waldensians, but they did so quite independently of any continental influence. They owed the germ of their beliefs, simplified and adapted as they were, to Wyclif himself. Wyclif's radical ideas were powerful enough to

---

[4]Leff, *Heresy*, II, pp. 411–444 *passim*, and 'The Changing Pattern of Thought in the Earlier Fourteenth Century', *BJRL*, XLIII (1961), pp. 354–72; see Offler's comment on Leff's treatment of Ockham (*EHR*, LXXXIV (1969), p. 574).

[5]Above p. 59.

[6]Above p. 184.

inspire a movement which outlasted persecution for over a hundred years, produced a literature of its own and a line of martyrs and devoted missionaries right up to the time of the Reformation, without their originator ever apparently having displayed any outstanding powers of personal leadership or even any very direct interest in the practicalities of building up a new religious group. The spontaneous incubation of so dangerous a heresy in intellectual circles, Wyclif's readiness to break with tradition and to defy ecclesiastical authority, and the ambiguities of his relationship as a scholar with a movement of popular preachers, all lend special interest to the study of his life.

Wyclif was a product of the intellectual environment of Oxford, where by far the greater part of his life was passed, from the time of his entry to the university as a young man to his enforced departure at roughly fifty years of age in 1380.[7] His dabbling in politics in the 1370s took him away on occasional missions, and the last years of his life (after 1380) were spent in retirement in the rectory at Lutterworth. Otherwise he remained, in the usual and necessary fashion of the day, an absentee from the benefices whose revenues made possible his academic work at Oxford. His experience was very largely academic, and much less either pastoral or political.

Oxford marked him deeply, whether by direct influence or by provoking violent reactions. As a young man, he fell under the influence of the nominalism then fashionable, which had developed from the writings of William of Ockham and his school, and was marked by a mistrust of the power of reason to demonstrate the truths of faith.[8] Nominalism, and the scepticism and fideism which accompanied it, are fundamental for the understanding of the fourteenth-century intellectual scene, arousing deep conflicts, and opening the way for a series of radical or extremist thinkers to put forward their views. The anti-intellectual tone of moralists of the time and the development of the English school of mystics represent one kind of hostile reaction to this prevailing mode of thought;[9] the maturer Wyclif represents another reaction. In place of the distrust of reason introduced by the nominalists, he put forward, as Beryl Smalley shows, what he saw as a better way of reasoning.[10]

A strong reaction against nominalism at Oxford was, in itself, nothing new. Both Bradwardine and Fitzralph, for example, had earlier written against this

---

[7]H. B. Workman, *John Wyclif: a Study of the English Medieval Church*, I–II, (Oxford, 1926) is an old-style compendium still valuable for facts. A helpful survey of thought is in Leff, *Heresy*, II, pp. 494–558; a vital corrective to Workman on political side, frailer on religious aspect, is K. B. McFarlane, *John Wycliffe and the Beginnings of English Nonconformity* (London, 1952); see also M. J. Wilks, '*Reformatio regni*: Wyclif and Hus as Leaders of Religious Protest Movements', in *SCH*, IX, pp. 109–30. I am indebted for the account of Wyclif here to Leff and, above all, to the illuminating article of B. Smalley, 'The Bible and Eternity: John Wyclif's Dilemma', *JWCI*, XXVII (1964), pp. 73–89. I have also benefited from attendance at her unpublished lectures on Wyclif.

[8]'Terminism' is felt by some historians to be a more accurate label. I have here used 'nominalism' simply because it is more familiar.

[9]Smalley, loc. cit., p. 73.

[10]Ibid.; note comparison between Plotinus and Wyclif. For summary of background, see pp. 73–7.

school.[11] Like Wyclif they were Augustinians. The major thinker, Bradwardine, attacked the Ockhamist school not without effect, and probably some of the philosophical realism he had defended survived in the background. He and Fitzralph provide occasional parallels to Wyclif, who came to admire them; he adapted one of his best known theses, on dominion and grace, from Fitzralph.[12] The work of Thomas Buckingham *c.* 1350 shows that Bradwardine's great work against the nominalists, the *De causa Dei*, was still being discussed; this would make it natural for Wyclif to develop an interest in analogous problems. But when Wyclif's own metaphysical position had been fully formed and came under hostile criticism, no-one suggested that anyone else was responsible for it. His final position was too individual and idiosyncratic to have been borrowed: he had worked out an answer for himself, which differed drastically from the ideas of his youth.

From nominalism he swung round to the opposite extreme—to ultra-realism. Research has shown scattered through his writings, phrases in which he looks back on his past 'sophistries' in something of the same manner and tone that a spiritual writer might use in bewailing the sins of his youth.[13] The violence of the reaction was something analogous to a conversion, and he plainly had quasi-religious feelings about the philosophical position that he had come to adopt. Speaking of realism ('the knowledge of universals') he once said, 'A knowledge of universals is the pre-eminent step on the ladder of wisdom by which we search out hidden truth; and this, I believe, is the reason why God does not permit the school of universals utterly to fail.'[14] The element of personal conversion involved in the adoption of realism helps to explain the obstinacy with which he later clung to his metaphysics. In the end, when it became clear that the consequences of his philosophical position would be a direct clash with the doctrine of the Church, it was the doctrine of the Church which had to go, and not Wyclif's philosophy.

The intellectual environment of the Oxford in which he grew to maturity is a necessary background both for the high reputation he came to hold and for some of the idiosyncratic features of his thought. It is generally agreed that between *c.* 1350 and 1370, the time of his initiation into academic studies, there was a lack of outstanding thinkers.[15] Wyclif spoke contemptuously of the thinkers of his age, and looked back behind them to Bradwardine and Fitzralph, as we have seen, and still further to Grosseteste in the thirteenth century.[16] At the time his metaphysic was formed, he needed the dicipline of effective controversy to check the extremism to which he was naturally

[11]J. A. Robson, *Wyclif and the Oxford Schools* (Cambridge, 1961), chapters 2, 3 (graceful introduction, fundamental for Wyclif's early philosophy).

[12]A.Gwynn, *The English Austin Friars in the Time of Wyclif*, (Oxford, 1940), pp. 35–59.

[13]Robson, *Wyclif*, p. 145, more forcefully by B. Smalley reviewing Robson, (*MA*, xxx (1961), p. 202) and 'Bible and Eternity' pp. 77–81; another view in M. J. Wilks, 'The Early Oxford Wyclif: Papalist or Nominalist', *SCH* v, pp. 69–98.

[14]Smalley's translation (*JWCI*, xxvii (1964), p. 81); for text, see Robson, *Wyclif*, p. 154, n. 1.

[15]Ibid., pp. 97–112, S. H. Thomson, in *Speculum*, xxxviii (1963), pp. 497–9, J. M. Fletcher, in *HJ* lxi (1962–3), pp. 179–80.

[16]B. Smalley, 'The Biblical Scholar', in *Robert Grosseteste, Scholar and Bishop*, ed. D. A. Callus (Oxford, 1955), esp. pp. 70, 83, 95–7; Robson, *Wyclif*, pp. 26–9, 186, Smalley, in *MA*, xxx (1961), pp. 202–3.

prone[17] and he did not get it. Because of this relative vacuum of leading figures, he seemed to overpower his contemporaries. Those who later became his enemies witness to the great effect he had. Thomas Netter of Walden, whose *Doctrinale* was the most effective reply to Wyclif's academic supporters, said that at first he was 'astounded by his sweeping assertions, by the authorities cited, and by the vehemence of his reasoning.'[18]

But most of all, he influenced contemporaries because, in contrast to the sceptics, he offered certainty of knowledge. The example of Scripture may be taken to illustrate this. Wyclif was troubled that the sceptics were criticizing Scripture. An important quotation came from Augustine's *De doctrina Christiana*, 'Faith will waver if the authority of Holy Scripture should fail. If faith wavers, then charity weakens . . .'[19] It was nominalism which he felt was undermining faith in Scripture; already he believed, the supporters of nominalism were leading the laity into error.[20] His answer flowed from a metaphysic based on the indestructibility of universals. Scripture became a divine exemplar conceived in the mind of God before creation, and before the material Scriptures were written down. Because it was a divine idea, every word of it was true, and every part as authoritative as the other.[21] Ultrarealism led directly to a fundamentalism which, on philosophical grounds, put Scripture beyond the reach of doubt.

It was a bold thesis, which at first sight might seem to bowl over the opposition. Yet the certainty was purchased at a high price, and the philosophical position Wyclif adopted had unorthodox implications, notably on time and being and the eucharist. John Kenningham, who was in debate with Wyclif in 1372–4 had seen that Wyclif's ultrarealism made impossible an acceptance of the orthodox doctrine of transubstantiation, with its concomitant annihilation of substance. As Wyclif moved from philosophical to doctrinal works, the awkward consequences of his metaphysics became ever more apparent.[22]

At an early phase of the development of his thought, Wyclif became involved in politics. His entry into royal service took place probably in either 1371 or 1372. In 1374 he was describing himself as 'in a special sense the king's clerk.'[23] The invitation came either from the Black Prince or John of Gaunt; in either case the motive was plain. Wyclif was already known for his anticlerical views, and he was being engaged because it was felt that his opinions on disendowment and the necessity of reform of the Church by the State could be

---

[17]Leff, *Heresy*, II, p. 500.

[18]Robson's translation (*Wyclif*, pp. 203–4).

[19]Smalley's translation 'Bible and Eternity', p. 75; the original, ibid., n. 10, and in Wyclif's *De veritate sacrae scripturae*, ed. R. Buddensieg, (*WS*), I, pp. 157–389.

[20]Smalley, loc cit., p. 77; the Middle English poem *Pearl* makes significant assumptions about the laity's interest in theology (Robson, p. 33).

[21]Robson, pp. 163–4. I am indebted to Professor M. Deanesly for showing me the importance of this.

[22]Leff, II, pp. 500–12, making the Kenningham affair basis for analysis. Note comment on Wyclif (p. 505): '. . . he had an inexhaustible supply of logical devices which hid an impoverished and inflexible mode of thought.' See Robson, *Wyclif*, pp. 162–70, Smalley, 'Bible and Eternity', pp. 86–7. For Wyclif on Scripture, see Leff, II, pp. 511–45.

[23]Workman, I, pp. 231–9; dating approximate.

a useful counterweight to the more traditional views of clerical speakers.[24] Wyclif's known service was relatively limited. In 1371 he may have sat silent in parliament, while two Augustinian friars were arguing for the legitimacy of taxing the Church's wealth in time of war—the evidence is uncertain;[25] in 1374 he was a diplomatic agent in negotiations with the papacy; in 1377 he gave an opinion in the government interest on the export of bullion to Avignon; and in 1378 he defended, in effect, the actions of royal servants in a *cause célèbre* on the violation of sanctuary.[26] But these episodes had an importance out of proportion to their intrinsic weight, for they secured to Wyclif the protection of great men, who headed off ecclesiastical authority's attempts to silence him. In two hearings, one in St Paul's in 1377, the other in Lambeth palace chapel in 1378, when the bishops tried to take action, the protection, first of John of Gaunt, then of the Black Prince's widow, was decisive.[27]

The residual loyalty of Wyclif's former employers, together with the effect of the Great Schism on the freedom of papal action, preserved Wyclif from any personal judicial proceedings in the last years of his life, thus enabling him to produce his most radical treatises. Royal service coincided roughly with the time in which his interests turned to the doctrine of the Church. In the *Postilla super totam bibliam* (finished 1375–6), he can be seen stressing the poverty and humility of the early Church, and beginning to use Scripture as a standard of criticism for the Church of his own time.[28] The need for poverty is again stressed, though still with moderation, in the *De civili dominio* (1376–8).[29] By the time we reach the *De ecclesia* (1378) Wyclif is defending a quite revolutionary doctrine of the Church which would overturn the established order.[30] This was the year of decision in his work as well as the year of the Great Schism.

It is difficult to think that there was no interaction between the two sides of his career. When Wyclif put himself in the service of anticlerical politicians,[31] he could think, however unrealistically, that he was helping to

[24]McFarlane, pp. 58–60.

[25]Mr J. W. Sherborne draws my attention to an ambiguity on this point.

[26]Workman, I pp. 240–6, 302–4, 313–24; perspective in McFarlane, chs 2 and 3; see esp. his summary on Wyclif's motives, pp. 84–5.

[27]Workman, I, pp. 284–8, 307–9.

[28]B. Smalley, 'Wyclif's Postilla on the Old Testament and his Principium', in *Oxford Studies presented to Daniel Callus* (Oxford, 1964) Oxford Historical Society, n.s., XVI, for 1959–60, 253–97 and analysis in G. A. Benrath, *Wyclifs Bibelkommentar*, Berlin, 1966; review by J. Crompton in *JEH*, XVIII (1967), pp. 263–6.

[29]Workman, I, pp. 257–66; Leff, II, pp. 529–30. See below, p. 228, n. 52.

[30]Workman, I, pp. 6–20; challenge of his ecclesiology best seen in Leff, II, 516–45.

[31]His biographers deprecate this, Workman mildly (I, p. 279; cf. p. 282), McFarlane more fiercely (p. 70). Both quote the chronicler's phrase, 'running about from church to church', on his preaching in the London diocese in the autumn of 1376 (see T. Walsingham, *Chronicon Angliae*, ed. E. M. Thompson (*RS*) (London, 1876), pp. 115–6; McFarlane's dating); McFarlane believes that in this he was acting the part of Gaunt's 'clerical hireling', by stirring up public opinion against his enemy William of Wykeham, then bishop of London. Benrath, (p. 336, n. 137) sounds a warning against this interpretation. The chronicler is not favourable to Wyclif. If W. Mallard's dating is correct (*MH*, XVII (1966), p. 99), we have six examples of sermons from the autumn of 1376, concerned with moral and spiritual instruction or a movement of renewal in the Church. They are not aimed at Wykeham.

hasten the time when the State would bring about the reform of the Church by force according to his own prescriptions. At the same time, the effects of this experience together with the increasing pressure of controversy as the true nature of his views became apparent, helped to make him more bitter and violent. From 1378, the tone of his works tended to change for the worse; he was inclined to quote himself more, and abused his enemies more violently; his theology becomes more radical, and his denunciations more repetitive. Personal disappointment may have played a part in the sharpening of his attacks on the Church and contemporary churchmen. Certainly he could have hoped for more than he got from his high patrons, and we can readily understand the violence of his attacks on the endowed monastic orders when we examine the case of Canterbury Hall, intended to put monks and seculars into one foundation of which he was appointed warden. He actually occupied the post for two years, only to find himself turned out by a monk archbishop of Canterbury in 1367.[32]

Yet personal experience was no more than a contributory factor. His doctrine of the Church was closely allied to his metaphysics. An early citation may suggest how his view of the Church was influenced by his ultrarealism. He wrote, 'I consider that the Church ordains nothing, unless there is an underlying reason; on account of which there is rational cause that it *is* so before it be ordained by man.'[33] So clearly did he have the archetypal reality of the Church before his eyes that he came to reject in its favour the visible Church of the fourteenth century.[34] Just as in the case of Scripture, the Church had existed from eternity; Wyclif denied the doctrine that it had come into being with the Incarnation. In comparison with this eternal Church, the visible Church steadily lost authority in Wyclif's writings till it became in the end simply the dwelling of Antichrist. An adaptation of the Augustinian doctrine of predestination had the effect of voiding the visible Church of authority. Elect and foreknown were rigidly divided in this world. The elect were immune from the consequences of mortal sin: their grace of predestination stood, even with mortal sin. Conversely, the ministrations of the foreknown, however high they stood in the ecclesiastical hierarchy, were void of effect. The result was to remove the necessity of a priesthood, since every one of the elect was necessarily more priest than layman as a member of the Church.[35]

The heretical implications of Wyclif's doctrine need no underlining. Nor does the breach with traditional teaching in his doctrine of Scripture. He never made the text of the Bible alone the standard of judgement for all doctrine and conduct, for he always retained the need for an established interpreter—the Fathers as a shield against heresy, above all Augustine.[36] But

[32]Workman, I, pp. 171–94; McFarlane, pp. 27–30. The decision against Wyclif was taken in 1367; he was finally deprived by 1371.

[33]Smalley's translation is in 'Bible and Eternity', p. 83; text, amended by her, in footnote.

[34]See esp Leff, II, pp. 515–6; on the external factors in Wyclif's progression to heresy, see p. 499.

[35]On the vital importance of metaphysics for Wyclif's view of the Church, see Leff, II, p. 511; analogous stress for doctrine of Scripture is in Benrath, ch. 5.

[36]On Wyclif's use of Scripture as an authority, M. Deanesly, *The Significance of the Lollard Bible* (London, 1951); P. De Vooght, *Les Sources de la Doctrine chrétienne d'après les Theologiens du XIVe Siècle et du Debut du XVe* (Paris, 1954) (a defence of Wyclif); M. Hurley, ' "Scriptura Sola": Wyclif

towards the end of his life, he did come to say that everything that was not in Scripture directly or by implication was Antichrist, and in practice Scripture more and more came to be an exclusive measuring-rod.

This attitude amounted to a radical innovation, for fourteenth-century theologians had not made a distinction between Scripture, tradition, and the laws of the Church, which were understood to harmonize. Thomas Netter of Walden perceived this when he said, 'What chiefly fills me with dismay is that Wyclif in all his proofs halves the Christian faith: he accepts, so he pretends, the faith of Scripture; but beyond the written faith he disregards and sets aside that faith of the whole church which Christ and also Paul the Apostle handed down, though not in writing.'[37]

As for the Church of Wyclif's day, by his death it had been stripped in his writings of all claim to belief. It had been stigmatized as the Church of Antichrist; the hierarchy had been rejected; the papacy, subjected to an historical analysis, had been shown to have no justification.[38] In detail, Scripture properly interpreted and described as 'God's law', had replaced canon law.

The indestructibility of universals and the consequences which Wyclif drew from it also involved him from early days in an inconsistency—he could not both accept transubstantiation and maintain his metaphysics. In Kenningham's time he had evaded the issue; it remained an unsolved question till 1379, when, with the publication of *De apostasia* and *De eucharistia*, he faced up to the long delayed consequences of his philosophy and denied the doctrine held by the Church. Thereafter he continued to write on the subject, making clear his opposition to the annihilation of substance, but not arriving at a fully defined position of his own. The metaphysics mattered; in the end they were decisive; but on this issue Wyclif took a long time before he drew all the consequences.[39]

The eucharistic heresy had great historical importance because it led to the parting of the ways with the last of the Oxford supporters outside his own proto-Lollard group, and to his departure from Oxford. In mid-winter 1380–1, the chancellor, William Barton, one of Wyclif's opponents, summoned a commission of twelve doctors, which by a narrow majority condemned his eucharistic views. There is no ground for thinking that the commission was packed or manipulated by outside ecclesiastical authority: it fairly represented a growing disquiet within the university about the development of Wyclif's views.[40] It mattered more than the condemnation of the theses on dominion and disendowment sent to Gregory XI at Avignon in

and his critics', *Traditio*, xvi (1960), pp. 275–352; re-issued separately (New York, 1960) (corrects De Vooght); review by B. Smalley, in *EHR*, LXXVIII (1963), pp. 161–2 (best short summary).

[37]Quoted by Hurley, in *Traditio*, xvi (1960), p. 329.

[38]Leff, II, pp. 534–41; Workman, II, pp. 73–82 (stresses effects of schism and Spenser's crusade); McFarlane, p. 95.

[39]Robson, pp. 187–95; Leff, II, pp. 549–57; M. E. Aston, 'John Wycliffe's Reformation reputation,' *PP* xxx (1965) pp. 40–1 for contrast between Wyclif's views on the eucharist and the Reformers' notion of them; Crompton's summary in *JEH*, xviii (1967) pp. 263–6.

[40]McFarlane, pp. 97–9 corrects Workman, II, pp. 140–8; note also Leff's summary (*Heresy*, II, p. 554, n. 8) on Workman's treatment earlier (pp. 30–41) of Wyclif's eucharistic doctrine.

1377,[41] for the beginning of the Great Schism in the following year eliminated the papacy's further interest, and on these issues Wyclif knew he could count on the support of his lay patrons as well as some academics. On the eucharist he lacked support. When in the *Confession* of May 1381 he reiterated his denial of transubstantiation he was defying his fellows. Soon afterwards, he withdrew from the university and retired to the rectory at Lutterworth.

Wyclif and Lollardy

Wyclif had kept university supporters surprisingly late. There were a number of reasons why he should have had a strong influence. The most important has already been mentioned: in an age when the fashion in theology was doubt, he offered certainties. He was a bold dialectician and an able debater. His use of Scripture and the completion of his *Postilla super totam bibliam* in 1375–6, the first commentary on the whole Bible since the days of Stephen Langton, helped to bring back the Bible to the centre of studies. His anti-intellectual and Christocentric piety, the appeal for reform and the denunciation of abuses, all corresponded to strands of contemporary thinking, and could call forth suitable echoes.[42] For the arts faculty, in their conflicts with law, he would gain popularity by his trenchant attacks on canon law.[43] His stress on the need for poverty in the Church and his attacks on the possessioner orders made him a natural ally of the friars, above all the Augustinians, who kept on terms with him longer than any other group. In 1377 four doctors from the mendicant friars were ready to defend Wyclif in St Paul's.[44] An Augustinian, Adam Stocton, described Wyclif on his copy of the *De potestate papae* as *venerabilis doctor*; only later was this crossed off in favour of *execrabilis seductor*.[45] It was only with the eucharistic heresy that he was abandoned by the friars.

Finally, Wyclif in his ultrarealism was in the van of a European movement of reaction against early fourteenth-century nominalism. This kept alive a respect for him independent of his late heresies, evidenced for us, for instance, in the acephalous and anonymous manuscripts in which his philosophical works were being collected in Oxford in the fifteenth century, or the reaction by university masters to Arundel's heavy-handed visitation in 1411; they were clearly not Wyclifites, but nevertheless valued university independence and thought Wyclif's views might still be at least the subject of argument.[46] The reputation of Wyclif was accepted in some surprising quarters. Archbishop Arundel himself acknowledged the justice of the Lollard William Thorpe's remarks when he was standing trial in 1407. 'Sir,' Thorpe said, 'Master John

[41]Workman, pp. 292–9; McFarlane, pp. 79–81; for place of English Benedictines in stimulating papal intervention, see D. Knowles, *Religious Orders in England*, II, (Cambridge, 1957), pp. 98ff.

[42]Benrath, *Wyclifs Bibelkommentar;* Crompton in *JEH*, XVIII (1967), pp. 263–6; De Vooght (*Sources*) notices how much more Wyclif quotes Scripture than was usual among contemporary commentators; see the discussion (favourable to Wyclif) on pp. 168–200.

[43]J. Fines, 'Studies in the Lollard Heresy' (unpublished Ph.D. thesis, University of Sheffield, 1964), pp. 18–19. I am indebted to the author for generously allowing me to use his thesis.

[44]Workman, I, p. 286; McFarlane, pp. 74–5.

[45]Gwynn, *Austin Friars*, pp. 238–9. J. E. Crompton (*JEH*, XII (1961) p. 163) warns against considering the Carmelites generally as *quondam* allies.

[46]Robson, 240–6; review by J. M. Fletcher in *HJ*, LXI (1962–3), pp. 179–80; E. F. Jacob, 'Reynold Pecock, Bishop of Chichester' *PBA* XXXVII (1951), pp. 121–53.

Wycliffe was holden of full many men the greatest Clerk that they knew then living; and therewith he was named a passing ruely [virtuous] man, and an innocent in his living.' Arundel acknowledged that, 'Wyclif your author [founder] was a great Clerk', and that 'many men held him a perfect liver.'[47]

This reputation drew essential support for the heresy. As the condemnations of Wyclif's work became effective, particularly after the Council of 1382 and Courtenay's visitation of Oxford, the more superficial supporters in the university fell away.[48] But a distinguished and controversial career had gathered enough varied strands of patronage and interest for a residue of scholars to remain committed supporters. The existence of this circle was vital to the development of English Lollardy, for it provided the popularizers who mediated Wyclif's thought to a wider public.

Vital, too, were Wyclif's views on the relations between Church and State and the necessity for some measure of ecclesiastical disendowment, for it was obviously these which attracted the attention of great men, involved him in politics and gave him a wider public notoriety. Wyclif's remedy for the abuses of the Church lay in forcible reform by the secular power. The low moral standards of the Church were, he believed, caused by an excess of property— the State would help to bring about change by some measure of disappropriation. The clergy would be left a sufficiency. Tithes they might have, since they were permitted by the Old Testament; but even this concession was subject to good behaviour—they could be witheld by parishioners from a sinful clergy.[49]

As early as 1370–1 Wyclif had been expressing his ideas on possession; but it was not until the *De civili dominio* of 1376–8 that he put them in written form.[50] A doctrine of dominion and grace such as he developed there had a considerable lineage. It had once been used in an ultramontane sense by the Augustinian Giles of Rome, who had argued that dominion could only be justly held through the Roman Church; all outside it, heathen or excommunicate, forfeited thereby lawful rights of possession and authority. Fitzralph turned the argument against the friars, his *bêtes noires*, by arguing more generally that all rights of authority and possession derived from God, and were thus dependent on the holder being in a state of grace; the friars, who were not, thus did not justly exercise the rights which they held within the Church. Wyclif simply took over this argument, and developed it to cover the whole Church. It linked, of course, with his fierce attacks on clerical abuses: plainly many of the clergy were not in a state of grace, could not justly hold dominion, and might be deprived of their possessions. As a theory, it obviously

[47]Quoted by McFarlane, p. 35, from Thorpe's *Examinacion* (*STC* 24045); modern edn by H. Christmas for Parker Soc. (Cambridge, 1849); see A. W. Pollard, *Fifteenth-Century Prose and Verse* (London, 1903) pp. 118–20, and J. Fines, 'William Thorpe: an Early Lollard', *History Today*, XVIII (1968), pp. 495–503.

[48]McFarlane, pp. 106–15; Workman, II, pp. 246–93.

[49]For Wyclif's attitude to property and government, see M. E. Aston, 'Lollardy and Sedition, 1381–1431', *PP*, xvii (1960), pp. 1–44; Leff, II, pp. 527–31; Smalley, 'Bible and Eternity', pp. 87–9. Wyclif's doctrine on the conditional nature of the clergy's right to tithes was among the Twenty-four Conclusions condemned in 1382; see Leff's comment (II, p. 529). I am indebted to Mrs Aston for answering my queries.

[50]McFarlane, p. 60; relation to predecessors in Gwynn, *Austin Friars*, pp. 59–73.

commended itself to lay lords who, in a time of unsuccessful war and weak government finance, were seeking for some new means of financing the war effort. Wyclif attracted interest because of the virtually uninhibited place he gave to the secular power as disappropriators and reformers of the Church.

At first sight the theory of dominion and grace might seem to have dangerous and anarchical implications for lay lords as well as churchmen. Might they not also fail to be in the state of grace necessary to hold lawful dominion, and might they not also be open to disappropriation? In practice, that awkward conclusion did not have to be drawn: in the *De officio regis* (1379) Wyclif provided an answer in his thorough-going Erastianism. The king was God's vicar. He and secular lords could not lawfully be resisted. Even tyrants must be accepted. Sin did not invalidate their authority—only that of churchmen.[51]

It is now becoming clearer that the doctrine of dominion and grace, which became so famous in Wyclifian historiography, never had the importance that older writers tended to give it in the structure of Wyclif's thought. It was overshadowed by the much more fundamental attack on the authority of the visible Church contained in Wyclif's predestinarian views and in the consequences he drew from them.[52] Yet its historical importance was considerable.

One of the first to be alarmed by Wyclif's views were the monks, a prime target in the attack on Church wealth. It was they who early engaged Wyclif in controversy on this subject, and it was they who sent propositions from the *De civili dominio* to Avignon to be censored by the Pope in 1377.[53] Amongst the views which Gregory XI condemned were opinions which appeared to put all civil dominion into uncertainty, and thus affected lay lords as well.[54] When other controversialists took up their pen against Wyclif and the Lollards, they were naturally not slow to point out the dangers of anarchy for the secular power, which, as they saw it, were embedded in the doctrine of dominion and grace; William Wodeford the Franciscan, for example, argued that the upshot of Wyclif's views on dominion was that he legitimized a popular disappropriation of 'kings, dukes and their lay superiors whenever they habitually offended.'[55]

This was to misunderstand Wyclif. When the peasants in 1381 did engage in forcible disappropriation, they earned Wyclif's firm condemnation in the *De blasphemia*, together with a note that the overtaxing which had caused the revolt would not have been necessary if his remedy of a measure of ecclesiastical disendowment by the State had been put into practice.[56] Wyclif

---

[51]Description of *De officio regis* in Workman, II, pp. 20–30; on significance, see Leff, II, pp. 543–5.

[52]I follow Leff, II, pp. 546–9. He differs from M. J. Wilks, 'Predestination, Property and Power: Wyclif's Theory of Dominion and Grace', in *SCH,* II, pp. 220–36 (see Leff, II, p. 546, n.2). Yet both dethrone the doctrine of dominion from its former position within the totality of Wyclif's beliefs. Contrast Workman, I, pp. 262–3.

[53]Above, p. 226, n. 41.

[54]Texts in Workman, I, p. 293, n. 5. For Lollard sources generally, see *FZ*; and for account of origins, J. Crompton, 'Fasciculi Zizaniorum', *JEH,* XII (1961), pp. 35–45, 155–66.

[55]Aston, 'Lollardy and Sedition', p. 9.

[56]Ibid., pp. 3, 36, n.5.

never lost faith in lay lords as potential reformers and thus, somewhat oddly, at the end of his life combined a stark ecclesiastical egalitarianism with a profound belief in the just authority of the civil power. In his scheme of things, a sinful pope might be deposed, a sinful or tyrannous king not; the orders of soceity remained sacrosanct. In secular politics, Wyclif remained profoundly conservative; in ecclesiastical matters he became a near anarchist. This juxtaposition of viewpoints might well be criticized as unrealistic, for few would agree that the abuses of the late fourteenth century sprang so exclusively from the ecclesiastical side.[57]

Wyclif's ideas on disendowment drew him into political affairs, and seemed for a moment to open the way to reform on the lines he desired: in the event, the checks in Wyclif's writings against civil anarchy tended to be forgotten, as circumstances, the actions of some of his followers, the fortuitous event of the Peasants' Revolt, and the skill of his opponents all combined to give him and the movement he inspired the reputation of being political anarchists.[58]

Yet while Wyclif was losing support among the upper classes and in the universities, the movement of preachers was already getting under way; this carried his beliefs to a wider public, and partially compensated for these losses by embedding Lollardy among a section of the artisan class. Wyclif's connection with this process of evangelization has always been an uncertain one. We know relatively little of his life once the breach with Oxford had been made. At Lutterworth he had as companion his secretary, John Purvey, who began the work of popularization.[59] We can infer from the unbroken flow of controversial Latin treatises in his last years that he spent his time writing. These works break no new ground: they continue to spell out, with increasing acrimony and radicalism after he had lost all official support including that of the friars, the implications of his doctrines of Scripture, the Church and the eucharist. The composing of them would have filled his time.[60]

Vernacular work from his own hand can have been at most a marginal activity, peripheral to the central one of defending and expounding against the controversialists who, to the last, pressed so hard upon him. A host of English treatises was once attributed to him;[61] but a dogmatic comparison, an examination of style or of probable dates of authorship on internal evidence, make it clear that some cannot be his work, but were written by his followers after his death under his name. In any case, we must reconcile their existence with Wyclif's explicit caveat, repeated in one of his last works, the *Opus evangelicum*, against the discussion of theological problems before the common

[57]See Smalley's comment ('Bible and Eternity', p. 88).

[58]Aston, loc. cit., p. 5.

[59]M. Deanesly, *The Lollard Bible and other medieval Biblical versions*, Cambridge 1920 (still best general survey on popular attitudes to Bible reading; ch. 9, pp. 225–51, on Wyclif as instigator of a vernacular Bible; value also for Lollard history (1384–1408), if read beside McFarlane); see esp. her reflections on his recantation, pp. 283–5; pungent comment in McFarlane, pp. 119–20, 152–3.

[60]McFarlane, p. 118; Workman, II, p. 307.

[61]*Select English Works of Wyclif*, ed. T. Arnold, I–III (Oxford, 1869–71); *The English Works of Wyclif hitherto Unprinted*, ed. F. D. Matthew (London, 1880) *EETS*, o.s., LXXIV); *Wyclif: Select English Writings*, ed. H. E. Winn (Oxford, 1929).

people.[62] The bulk, probably the overwhelming bulk, of this literature comes from the followers rather than the master.[63]

On the other hand, there is no doubt that the greatest achievement of these years, the vernacular translation of the Bible, sprang immediately from his inspiration; it is inconceivable that the early translator could have embarked on such a mammoth task without an impetus from the master. A vernacular translation was a natural outcome of Wyclif's doctrinal position. If the visible Church had lost its authority to mediate salvation to the people, then the word of God, properly interpreted, was the one remaining certainty.[64] The novel relationship set up by Wyclif between Bible and Church demanded wider access to the Scriptures. If it was God's law, which should be asserted over the accretions of canon law that had usurped its place, then it should be known to those, clergy or laity, who had the duty of seeing that it was observed in England. The reform Wyclif envisaged was to take place on the basis of Scripture; it should then be known to the secular powers, who were to compel the clergy to reform, and to those elements among the existing clergy who were ready to heed the call to repent. Hence the phrases which occur in the *Opus evangelicum*, arguing that there was 'no man so rude a scholar but that he may learn the words of the gospel according to his simplicity';[65] or earlier, in the *De veritate sacrae scripturae*, that 'all Christians, especially secular lords, ought to know and defend the holy scriptures.'[66] He stresses the guidance of

---

[62]Smalley, in *MA*, xxx (1961), p. 203, comparing *Johannis Wyclif De ente: librorum duorum excerpta*, ed. M. H. Dziewicki, (*WS*; London, 1909), p. 131 with *Opus evangelicum*, ed. J. Loserth, 1 (*WS*; London, 1895), p. 367; original phraseology in Robson, *Wyclif*, p. 217; contrasted with Valdes in Deanesly, *Lollard Bible*, p. 245. On the practicability of Wyclif's position in his last year, note Smalley's comment: 'By that time he resembled a man who sets fire to a skyscraper and hopes that only the right people will notice.' (loc. cit.).

[63]New work on the MSS will transform knowledge of popular Lollard writing, as A. Hudson ('Some aspects of Lollard book production', in *SCH*, IX, pp. 147–69) demonstrates. I had not used this when I wrote my text; I am grateful to Dr J. A. F. Thomson for the ref. Miss Hudson argues against Wyclif's authorship of any English works (p. 152); McFarlane (p. 118) and Aston (*PP*, xxx (1965), p. 40 (refs ibid., n. 40)) see it as unproven; Deanesly (*Lollard Bible*, pp. 268–70) makes the case for the tract *The holy prophet David saith* (text, pp. 445–56); Workman (I, pp. 329–32; II, pp. 175–7) accepts the sermons and nine other pieces—surely far too much. Aston on the *Wicket* (*PP*, xxx (1965), pp. 37–8) shows how one Lollard work, which differs in its thinking from Wyclif, may yet have 'parallels from Wyclif's Latin works for certain of its arguments.' A. Hudson ('A Lollard compilation and the dissemination of Wycliffite thought', *JTS*, xxiii (1972), pp. 65–81) suggests on the evidence of language, that links between Wyclif and poor priests may be closer than has been thought. For a new article on the Wyclifite Bible, see below, p. 391.

[64]Leff, II, ch. 7; see esp. p. 524.

[65]Ed. J. Loserth, 1 (*WS*; London, 1895), p. 92; translated Deanesly, *Lollard Bible*, p. 246. New work on the Lollard Bible is in S. L. Fristedt, *The Wycliffe Bible* 1 (Stockholm, 1953) (review by L. Muir in *Speculum*, xxxiii (1958); comments by C. Lindberg in *MS. Bodley 959: Genesis–Baruch 3.20 in the Earlier Version of the Wycliffite Bible* (Stockholm, 1959–73, 6 vols). Developing hypotheses are in the introductory notes to each of Lindberg's volumes, with conclusions in the fifth (1969): authorship, pp. 90–7, summary, pp. 97–8. A further summary is given in the final volume (pp. 66–70). I am indebted to Dr A. B. Cottle for drawing my attention to this work. On commentaries, there is H. Hargreaves, 'The marginal glosses to the Wycliffite New Testament', *Studia Neophilologica*, xxiii (1961), pp. 285–300. Fristedt (*Wycliffe Bible*, II (1969)) edits the Latin text and English translation of a treatise by Augustine of Hippo (*De salutaribus documentis*) to demonstrate the principles of translation adopted in revising the EV and argues vigorously for Wyclif's participation; see op. cit., I and II, bibliography.

[66]Ed. R. Buddensieg, (*WS*) I, London, 1905, p. 136; trans. Deanesly, *Lollard Bible*, p. 243.

the Holy Spirit on those of good life, but not necessarily of much learning, who seek to understand.[67] In thoughts such as these lay a starting-point for later Lollard thinking.

The first translation, however, did not go so far. It was a painfully literal crib of the Vulgate, with past participles rendered direct into English and a Latin word-order imposed rigidly on the English sentence.[68] It was not intended for indiscriminate dissemination; one purpose may well have been to aid preachers who, basing themselves on the Scriptural text on Wyclifite principles, would need to read out translations in their sermons. A translation of the whole Bible would give them a work of reference. Elements of Latin they might already possess; a crib to the Vulgate would be an ideal aid for them. More ambitiously, the translation could serve in a lord's household, where the newly literate upper-class laity might read the text and expound it to their subordinates.[69] The literalness of the version expressed a continuing reverence for the Vulgate; if the written Scripture expressed God's Word, then it might be dangerous to make free with the word sequence. Moreover, a rigid following of the Latin word-order facilitated the insertion of glosses phrase by phrase in a similar fashion to Richard Rolle's orthodox translation of the Psalter.[70]

Versions of the Bible for the laity were not wholly unprecedented. Certain vernacular versions existed in orthodox circles in various European countries, intended for the use only of rulers and the highest nobility. Wyclif cited them in defence of English translations. If Anne of Bohemia could have versions in Czech and German, he argued, then why were English versions to be judged heretical?[71] The precedent was only a partial one, for these Bibles circulated in a highly restricted milieu, where every check existed against misunderstandings of the text. They were expensive devotional toys. Even the first Wyclifite version would have had a wider diffusion. Copies were

---

[67]See esp. trans. from *De veritate sacrae scripturae* (Workman, ii, p. 151).

[68]Compare the Vulgate of Gen. 1.3 (Dixitque deus, fiat lux, et facta est lux') with the translation in MS. Bodley 959 ('And God said/be made light/And made is light' (spelling modernized) (Lindberg, *MS Bodley 959*; see p. 74). For this early version, see *The Holy Bible . . . in the Earliest English Versions*, ed. J. Forshall and F. Madden (Oxford, 1850); the edn is criticized by Fristedt (*Wycliffe Bible*, i), who notes that they left over eighty MSS. uncollated, and argues that they have not arrived at the ultimate originals of either EV or LV. His work is followed up by Lindberg in his edn of MS. Bodley 959, the incomplete copy of the OT in the EV which ends at Baruch 3. 20, and argues that this MS. of *c.* 1400 represents the earliest extant version, in fact an original copy of an English prototype, both being revised and corrected. Fristedt suggested that the regular use of northern and north-west midland dialect in some of the earliest MSS, and especially the treatment of the Yorkshire 'and(e)', revealed Wyclif's hand in correction, and possibly also in trans. of EV. Lindberg rejects this, believing that, though Wyclif, with or without helpers, did translate the NT, the dialect mixture in MS. Bodley 959 points to Nicholas of Hereford as the supervisor of the OT translation, and its crudities of translation exclude the possibility of Wyclif's direct participation. S. L. Fristedt ('The dating of the earliest manuscript of the Wycliffite Bible', in *Stockholm Studies in Modern Philology*, n.s., i (Stockholm, 1960), pp. 79–85, at p. 80) suggests that Hereford's origins were in Yorkshire. The same writer gives a polemical discussion at pp. xlvii–lxvii of volume two of his *Wycliffe Bible*. For new work, below, p. 391.

[69]Deanesly, *Lollard Bible*, p. 245.

[70]Ibid., pp. 144–7.

[71]*De triplici vinculo amoris*, in *Polemical Works in Latin*, ed. R. Buddensieg, i (*WS*; London, 1883), p. 168; Deanesly, *Lollard Bible*, p. 248. See also M. J. Wilks, *art. cit.* below, p. 391, at p. 155, n. 34.

multiplied, and could be expected to pass freely into the hands of well-disposed laity at a level below that of the court circle.

In contrast to Rolle's psalter, the Wyclifite version presented all who cared to read with a bare text, not merely of the psalms, which because of their use in worship presented a special case, but also of those parts of the Bible which contained the most abstruse expositions of doctrine. Even in its clumsy early version, the Wyclifite translation had begun to break with medieval tradition, which saw Scripture as a whole as a difficult text to be assimilated by a trained clergy through the means of handbooks and expositions, and mediated to the faithful perhaps by gospel harmonies, but not under any circumstances to be placed raw in their hands without check and supervision.[72] The translation made vivid indeed Wyclif's innovation of separating Scripture from the whole body of tradition and the deposit of faith and making it stand starkly on its own. The early literal version was, of course, only a beginning: it had none of the driving force of the free translation which came out after Wyclif's death. But it was Wyclif's most important bequest to the Lollard movement.

On preaching, Wyclif's contribution to the rise of Lollardy is most ambiguous. Certainly the duty of preaching had a high place in his revolutionary concept of Church life, for it was the principal means of conveying the truths of Scripture to ordinary men. His late works are scattered with references to 'poor priests' who were to hear and spread true doctrine, and in one of his *Sermones quadragintae* we note Wyclif's feeling that he is speaking to members of a 'recognizable movement.'[73] But there is no evidence that Wyclif sent out priests himself.[74] If he had been active in the development of preaching campaigns, then one would have expected Lutterworth to have been a centre of popular Lollardy. Yet it produced no single Lollard in all the record of heresy trials. Walsingham's picture of Wyclif sending out preachers in russet mantles is not confirmed by the other chronicler of early Lollardy, Henry Knighton, who shows Wyclif in a passive role, attracting acolytes by his academic reputation and his skill in disputation.[75] William Thorpe's account in the record of his trial conveys a similar picture when he speaks of those who 'commoned [communed] oft with him, and . . . loved so much his learning that they writ it, and busily enforced them to rule themselves thereafter.'[76] Walsingham wrote of ordinations of Lollards in Salisbury diocese, and there was indeed a case of a William Ramsbury being tonsured by a certain Thomas Fishburn, and invested with a russet habit to go and preach the heresy.[77] The chronicler assumed that Wyclif did the same. In fact, Wyclif was not the organizer of the heresy: his legacy to his followers lay in the realm of ideas.

That it was an explosive legacy will be apparent if one considers the doctrinal positions which Wyclif had reached in the course of his intellectual odyssey. He left the Lollards a set of ideas with all the potential to build an

[72]Ibid., p. 239; compare Innocent III's views (above, p. 78).

[73]Mallard, in *MH*, XVII (1966), p. 99.

[74]Workman (II, pp. 201ff.) requires correction. McFarlane, (p. 101) brings good sense to bear.

[75]Knighton, ed. Lumby (*RS*), II, p. 186.

[76]A. W. Pollard, *Fifteenth-Century Prose and Verse*, p. 119.

[77]Aston, 'Lollardy and Sedition', p. 13. See below, p. 239, n. 23.

effective sect. His predestinarianism did away with the authority of the visible Church; his doctrine of Scripture armed his followers with an inexhaustible arsenal of criticism against it. He came near to a doctrine of the priesthood of all believers; he did away with a hierarchy in the Church and, by his stress on the poor priests against the Caesarean clergy, appealed to a pre-existing cleft within the Church of his day. Finally, the literal translation of the Bible took the first step towards putting the bare text, with all its dangerous heresy-making potential, into the hands of any man who cared to read for himself or attend a Lollard conventicle.

15

The English Lollards

1. From Wyclif to Oldcastle's Revolt

The Early Evangelists

The reactions in Oxford to Wyclif's eucharistic heresy, the Peasants' Revolt, and Courtenay's purge of 1382 were all in their different ways blows to Wyclif's ideas and following; yet they were not fatal. Religious feeling, leaning in Wyclif's direction, obviously lay close to the surface, and could easily be mobilized, while counteraction came a little too late, when Wyclif's following was already at work. So Lollardy spread quickly, in Knighton's view, 'like the overwhelming multiplication of seedlings.'[1]

A small group of academically trained men—we may call them 'proto-Lollards'—mediated the master's late, radical ideas to a popular audience. Of these the best-known are Nicholas Hereford, Philip Repton, John Aston and John Purvey, Wyclif's secretary in his last years. The first three had been attracted to Wyclif's ideas in Oxford; the fourth was evidently a man of education and, one assumes, of university training, but details are lacking. Repton was an Austin canon; the others were secular clerks. Their position was a little equivocal, for all at one time or another recanted or submitted to ecclesiastical censure, and two (Hereford and Repton) finally abandoned support of Lollardy for ever. No doubt their academic standing is relevant: they were men who desired reform, and had been swept away by Wyclifite ideas; counter-argument, more mature reflection and, perhaps, realization of the consequences of persistence in heresy detached them from their new beliefs. Even so, the first enthusiasm had kept its hold for one, perhaps two, of them, who returned to Lollardy; and in any case submission came too late to obviate the effects of their work. Martyrdom was not essential for the growth of Lollardy.

Hereford,[2] a man of academic calibre, an Oxford master of arts, was believed by Knighton to have been the first leader of Lollardy, and there is evidence that he played a significant part in the writing of the first Bible.[3] He

---

[1]*Chronicon Henrici Knighton*, ed. J. R. Lumby, *RS*, II (1895), p. 183; Fines, *Studies*, p. 33 ('quasi germinantes multiplicati sunt nimis').

[2]Workman, *Wyclif*, II, pp. 131–7, Deanesly, *Lollard Bible*, pp. 232–6, 276, 377 (but with no sound evidence of Leicester canonry), McFarlane, *Wycliffe*, pp. 102, 107–12, 115, 118, 126–9, 137.

[3]Certain MSS of EV break off at Baruch 3.20; Bodl. MS Douce 369, part 1, gives Hereford as translator to that point; Cambr. Univ. Lib. MS Ee. i. 10 (overleaf) notes, 'Here endith the

Plate Seven

The Lollard Bible: the Early Version breaking off at Baruch 3, 20 (cf. p. 234, n. 3 with the note of the break, 'Here endith . . .' 7 lines from the bottom in the right hand column in the illustration.)

was a natural radical, who supposedly once preached a sermon arguing that archbishop Sudbury, who was lynched in the Peasants' Revolt, had deserved his fate and a man of curious optimism, who responded to Courtenay's excommunication of him by travelling to Rome to appeal to Urban VI in person. After escape from Rome and a period underground, he was arrested. Eventually he recanted some time before 1391, and not only recanted, but spoke against Lollardy.

translacioun of Her. and now bigynneth the translacioun of J. and of othere men' (spelling slightly modernized). See Lindberg, *MS. Bodley 959*, v, pp. 90–7, who argues that the break was caused by Hereford's final recantation, not by his flight to Rome in 1382; contrast Deanesly, *Lollard Bible*, p. 254. MS. Bodley 959 breaks off at the same point without comment. Fristedt (*Wycliffe Bible*, II, p. xlvii) observes that the break 'simply marks the point at the bottom of the last recto column . . . where the scribe waited for the ink to dry.'

Repton, the Austin canon of St Mary-in-the-Fields, Leicester, recanted before Hereford, and rose to be abbot of his house and finally bishop of Lincoln, where he had to pursue Lollards. As bishop he worked hard as a reformer within the Church.[4] Lollardy for a time had seemed to him a key to reform; then he dropped it. But an underlying zeal remained.

Aston was originally of the diocese of Worcester, and perhaps a principal evangelist for the West Country. Like the rest, he also recanted; but later he returned to Lollard evangelism, and seems to have died in the heresy about 1388.[5]

Of all the academic Lollards,[6] John Purvey, Wyclif's secretary, lasted longest, and may well have been the most important, for he appears to carry the greatest responsibility for producing a popular Lollard literature.[7] Very likely it was he who directed the second, free translation, and thus launched the Bible of the mass of humble Lollards. There is no doubt of his devotion. The long adherence of Bristol to heresy can probably first be attributed to his evangelizing. If he was responsible for supervising the second translation, then he was both zealous and scholarly, for it is a careful piece of academic work. His zeal for learning is further shown by his work on a heavy apparatus of glosses intended to accompany an English text of the gospels. When he was at last laid by the heels and recanted in 1401, it was a heavy blow. Yet even so, though he was considerately treated, and put on probation by being given the benefice of West Hythe, conveniently near the archbishop's castle at Saltwood, he held it for only three years before he resigned and disappeared from history, driven back, perhaps, by his true feelings to Lollard evangelism.

Recantations could not break the movement. Hereford had a career as an evangelist before and after the abortive journey to Rome; Repton seems to have had time to introduce Lollardy to the Leicester area; Aston had some years of activity before his death; and Purvey was hardly molested in a career as Lollard lasting some twenty years. All this left a considerable body of converts and writings behind.

In addition to the principal academic Lollards, there were others, less notable but still academically trained, who took to evangelizing. The two best known are Richard Wyche, a priest of the diocese of Hereford, who was active during the late fourteenth century in the north, had contacts with Sir John Oldcastle, and was burnt in London in 1440 after a long and indefatigable career as an evangelist.[8] He would have been too young to know Wyclif

---

[4]Workman, II, pp. 138, 162–3, 252, 282–9, 335–6; Deanesly, pp. 121–3, McFarlane, pp. 102–3, 108–15, M. Archer, 'Philip Repington, Bishop of Lincoln, and his Cathedral Chapter', *UBHJ*, IV (1954), pp. 81–97.

[5]Workman, II, pp. 138, 162–3, 252, 282–9, 335–6; Deanesly, pp. 135–6, 276, 445; McFarlane, pp. 102, 109–11, 113–4, 122, 126–8.

[6]Academic in contrast to the simple Lollards of the type of Smith and Swinderby; there is still no direct evidence that Purvey was at Oxford.

[7]Sympathetic account in Deanesly, pp. 233–8 and chs 10, 11 *passim* (judgement on recantation, pp. 283–5, hypothesis of authorship of General Prologue and LV, pp. 376–81). McFarlane, pp. 119–20, 149, 152–3, Workman, II, pp. 137, 162–70 (requires correction on alleged final imprisonment), 177–8, 390–5. Leff, *Heresy*, II, pp. 578–83 analyses Lavenham's compilation of his heretical theses.

[8]F. D. Matthew, 'The Trial of Richard Wyche' *EHR*, V (1890), pp. 530–44; M. G. Snape, 'Some Evidence of Lollard Activity in the Diocese of Durham in the early Fifteenth Century',

personally, but he argued so skilfully with the assessors of the bishop of Durham, and was so familiar with Wyclif's views, that he must have had an academic background. William Thorpe, who travelled round England in a threadbare blue gown, preaching and talking with well-disposed clergy, for nearly twenty years before he was brought before Archbishop Arundel in 1407, claimed to have known Wyclif personally, and talked of the master's career as an academic;[9] it seems likely that he also had had academic training. Others, like Thomas Turk, fellow of Exeter, or William James of Merton, are examples of academics at Oxford of the early generation who were tainted with Lollardy, and whose careers are only faintly known.[10] In a movement whose evangelists are only revealed to us through charges of heresy or unlicensed preaching, there were more of the early Oxford generation who adapted Wyclif's views for the mass of population who were either never caught or whose interrogations have not survived. It was very likely an Oxford Lollard who introduced Wyclif's work into an alphabetical theological commonplace book[11] and another who included both Wyclif and Lollard sermon material in a similar compilation.[12] Smuggling in Wyclifite material in this fashion made a pro-Lollard writer harder to detect than if he preached openly. Medieval Oxford had a large clientele of clerks who left without proceeding to a degree; as Fines points out,[13] they also might have absorbed some of Wyclif's ideas without having the equipment to understand them adequately: they would then be a natural source for the early debasement of his doctrine.

A second category of early Lollard evangelists consisted of chaplains, unbeneficed priests and lower clergy generally. Here Lollard tenets fell on fertile soil. The proportion of unbeneficed to beneficed clergy seems to have risen in the later Middle Ages. They had little in common with a wealthy upper clergy.[14] In the Peasants' Revolt the lower clergy were active as agitators and sometimes associated with the most violent episodes. Some may indeed already have been wandering anticlerical agitators, as John Ball had been for years before the revolt broke out. Doctrines which rejected a hierarchy in the Church, wished to redistribute Church wealth and sharply criticized the religious orders and the upper clergy, would find willing hearers in this

Archaeologia Aeliana, 4th ser., xxxix (1961), pp. 355–61; J. A. F. Thomson, *The Later Lollards, 1414–1520* (Oxford, 1965) (standard account of Lollard trials, see below p. 253, n. 89), pp. 15, 148–50, 177, 192; McFarlane, p. 162; letter to Hus in *The Letters of John Hus*, trans. H. B. Workman and R. M. Pope (London, 1904), pp. 30–4; *Responsio* in *FZ*, 370–82.

[9] Text of Thorpe's account of his trial in A. W. Pollard, *Fifteenth-Century Prose*, pp. 107–67; J. Fines, in *History Today*, xviii (1968), pp. 495–503, esp. p. 497.

[10] A. B. Emden, *A Biographical Register of the University of Oxford to A.D. 1500* (Oxford, 1957–9), s.v.; Fines, *Studies*, p. 22.

[11] A. Hudson, 'A Lollard Compilation and the Dissemination of Wyclifite Thought', *JTS*, xxiii (1972), pp. 65–81.

[12] E. W. Talbot, 'A Fifteenth-Century Lollard Sermon Cycle', in *University of Texas Studies in English*, xix (1939), pp. 5–30. I have been unable to consult this personally.

[13] *Studies*, p. 22.

[14] A straw in the wind is the drawing apart of higher and lower clergy in convocation during the second half of the fourteenth century. Attitudes to taxation differed. Dr J. R. L. Highfield, to whom I am indebted, tells me that 'usually the hierarchy joined the king in bullying the lower clergy', and that Courtenay's intervention as bishop of London on behalf of lower clergy was exceptional.

category. Often such clergy were close to the laity and would make some common cause with them. Chaplains were frequently the sons of craftsmen.[15] As Lollardy put down roots among the craftsmen, so chaplains and the unbeneficed clergy would find themselves talking to their own kind. Their class and their economic background made them more effective and dangerous evangelists. Training was hardly thorough. They were thus open to the influence of new doctrines and, by lack of education, shielded from the academic treatises in which Wyclif's opponents sought to refute his views.[16] In their hands, together with lay helpers, Lollardy both spread widely in the country and began to lose its academic basis.

The case of Swinderby at Leicester is a good example of the way in which this happened.[17] The first seed was most likely planted by Philip Repton, with his strong local connections. It flowered in a nucleus round the chapel of St John the Baptist outside the walls of the town, where a chaplain called Waytestathe and a craftsman, William Smith, became active in preaching and the production of tracts. The most notable member of the group, however, was William Swinderby, who had had a career as a revivalist before Lollardy appeared on the scene, travelling round the country from a base in a cell at the abbey of S. Mary-in-the-Fields, or living as a hermit in the woods outside the town. Lollardy gave him a congenial set of tenets to preach; to Lollardy he brought gifts of denunciation and rhetoric that remind us of Henry the Monk in the twelfth century, who, like him, came to heresy only after a previous career as an orthodox preacher.[18] The errors which he abjured before the bishop of Lincoln will illustrate the progress from Wyclif's tenets to Lollardy. He had taught, among other things, the rightfulness of parishioners withholding tithes from an incontinent parish priest, the illegitimacy of imprisonment for debt, or of a prelate excommunicating except where he knows the sinner to be already excommunicate by God. The priest in mortal sin who says mass 'rather commits idolatry than makes the body of God.'[19]

Swinderby was one of the most effective of all the evangelists. He planted heresy in Leicester and some of the market towns round about, then in Coventry, and finally in western Herefordshire, where the gentry gave him protection against the bishop. He almost certainly converted the young Oldcastle, the future military leader of Lollardy. Only in 1392 did his career come to an end, when he disappeared with a faithful companion into Wales.

---

[15]Deanesly, p. 189.

[16]Convocation was using the vernacular in the seventies. (J. R. L. Highfield, 'A Note on the Introduction of English into the Proceedings of the Convocation of Canterbury', *MA*, XLX (1950), pp. 60–3). Were clergy who had to be addressed in English more likely to accept a sect stressing the vernacular? (Dr Highfield in a private letter.) Anti-Lollard academic work is discussed in Knowles, *Religious Orders,* II (see index s.v. Wyclif). Popular antidotes are rarer; see Fines, *Studies,* p. 41, n. 3, p. 119; for anti-Lollard sermons of Henry V's reign, R. M. Haines, ' "Wild Wittes and Wilfulnes": John Swetstock's Attack on those "Poyswunmongeres", the Lollards', in *SCH,* VIII, pp. 143–53.

[17]McFarlane, pp. 103–5, 121–5, 127–36, 150, 174.

[18]Above, p. 49.

[19]Swinderby's abjuration is in *FZ,* pp. 337–9; McFarlane (p. 124) notes omission of specific abjuration of the denial of transubstantiation, despite the fact that this was once an accusation against him.

Others, too, had considerable achievements. In the early fifteenth century William, the parish priest of Thaxted, nurtured a whole series of Lollard groups in Essex. In one circle at Colchester a Franciscan, John Brettenham, joined in the reading of tracts and translations.[20] Similarly, heresy in the north Midlands owed much to the chaplain William Ederick from Aston-on-Trent.[21] William Sawtry, the first Lollard to be burnt, had been a chaplain in Norfolk, and had an unknown period of Lollard preaching behind him when , he was first apprehended in 1399.[22] William Ramsbury is an interesting case of a Lollard layman being ordained by one of the sect and then wandering for four years before 1389 spreading his beliefs in the Salisbury diocese. He held some radical views, notably on marriage, with sentiments that sound oddly like those attributed to the adherents of the Free Spirit; yet he had not emancipated himself from the mass, which he said according to the Sarum use with vestments, allowing himself a few omissions.[23]

The Laity

A heresy which preached the equality of laity and priesthood might be expected to find lay evangelists also. William Smith was an example, often to be repeated in fifteenth-century Lollardy, of the self-taught craftsman disseminating heresy. A conversion to vegetarianism and teetotalism after he had been jilted was in turn followed by service to the Lollard group. He taught himself to read and, when Swinderby had left the scene, continued with the work of producing tracts based on Scripture and the Fathers. Practical issues of worship and religious practice rather than highly academic heresy took chief place: when he and his fellow Lollards of Leicester were denounced in 1389, the accusations related to lay preaching, indulgences, auricular confession, tithes and the veneration of images.[24] Doubtful views on transubstantiation may have been unjustly attributed to the Leicester group.[25] Smith's career was cut short by a visitation in 1389 from Courtenay, who saw to it that the tracts were surrendered and he did penance.

In Herefordshire, Walter Brute, an esquire of very small landed resources, of Welsh background and some dialectical and rhetorical gifts with a bias to the Apocalypse, was aide to Swinderby.[26] His appeal would have been to the submerged Welsh of the region. Northampton harboured a Lollard group in 1392–3, apparently first brought to life by a mercer's apprentice from

[20]McFarlane, pp. 173, 178.

[21]Ibid., pp. 174–5, 178.

[22]Ibid., pp. 150–2.

[23]A. Hudson, 'A Lollard Mass', *JTS*, xxiii (1972), pp. 407–19; on the Free Spirit, see esp. article 14 alleged against Ramsbury and the writer's argument from the conjunction of articles 7, 10, 13, 14, of influence on Ramsbury of the 'contemporary sect' of the Free Spirit. I do not believe this sect existed (see above, pp. 178–81), though aberrant inferences from mystical experience were made by individuals (as this article observes, on the basis of English texts); and I suggest the starting-point for Ramsbury's views lay in dislike of clerical and monastic celibacy (note article 9), and had a practical rather than mystical keynote (note stress on procreation in article 10). There may have been actual promiscuity (article 14), or accusations may have slandered him, working a heresy out of a preacher's denunciatory hyperbole.

[24]McFarlane, p. 140.

[25]Ibid, pp. 124, 131, 133.

[26]Ibid., pp. 136–8.

London, then carried forward by the mayor. Here vanity and self-display were as much in evidence as righteous living, with William Northwold 'in Northampton amongst the Lollards and misbelievers reputed a prophet speaking with the tongue of an angel', laying false claim to a doctorate of divinity, and preachers dressing themselves in hoods and gowns to which they had no right.[27]

Thomas Compworth, an esquire of Kidlington in Oxfordshire, is an uncommon example of a follower higher in society who was more than a mere fautor of heresy, having indulged in lay preaching and got himself into trouble by refusing tithes to the abbot of Osney.[28] In general, however, the laity were not public preachers. Their role was that of a supporting layer, encouraging their clergy and forming reading circles. Claydon, the prosperous tanner from London burnt in 1415, invited friends to join him in readings and brought his servants into the heresy.[29] Adherents in the stationers' trade were especially useful for the distribution of tracts. Included among the heretics denounced at Leicester in 1389 were a parchmener and a scrivener. Oldcastle had connections with the stationers' trade in London: heretical tracts of his were discovered in an illuminator's shop in Paternoster Row in 1413, and after his rescue from the Tower his refuge was in the house of a London stationer, William Fisher.[30]

An appeal to the individual to search out the truths of Scripture for himself was part of the drawing power of Lollardy: it was most effective for the self-taught, for those who had lately become literate and for those in a trade which required literacy.[31] The craftsmen and bourgeoisie who in Leicester, Northampton, London and elsewhere took to Lollard doctrines were not necessarily poor men; through their skills they often finally acquired a competence, or sometimes even more. The successful among them would be aware that they had succeeded largely by their own efforts. For most of them the late fourteenth century was a period of prosperity. In Bristol and its hinterland, where the efforts of Purvey and his successors bedded down Lollardy in the class of skilled artisans, the textile industry which supported many of them was doing well. Such people would not have taken to a faith which preached wild millenarianism; this was more likely to appeal to the genuinely poor.

Craftsmen and lower clergy predominate among the Lollards; but there were exceptions. Swinderby in the Welsh March touched the gentry class; they protected him against the bishop of Hereford. From this area came Sir John Oldcastle, one of the converts of high rank, being a baron through marriage. There are other isolated examples.

The most interesting of all is the group knowns as the Lollard knights.[32] Differing lists of names of men of gentle birth involved with heresy are given

[27]Ibid., pp. 140–4, quotation from McFarlane's version of the original.
[28]Ibid., pp. 141, 143, 178.
[29]Thomson, *Later Lollards*, pp. 140–2.
[30]McFarlane, pp. 163, 166.
[31]Ibid., p. 180.
[32]W. T. Waugh, 'The Lollard Knights' *SHR* xi (1913), pp. 55–92 (pioneer study); K. B. McFarlane, *Lancastrian Kings and Lollard Knights* (Oxford, 1972), pp. 139–232. (Lectures, ed. J. R. L. Highfield, superseding all previous work.) Note contrast in tone (esp. pp. 139, 221–6) to

for us independently by two chroniclers, Knighton and Walsingham,[33] amounting to ten names in all. Further research confirms that something genuine lay behind the accusations. Walsingham called them 'the hooded knights' because they would not uncover in the presence of the Host. K. B. McFarlane, giving a verdict of 'not proven' on three of the ten cases, provides a detailed analysis of the lives of seven, all professional soldiers, all in the court circle, all in service to Richard II by the early 1380s. Several were linked either to the Black Prince or his widow. One knight of Lollard sympathies, Sir John Cheyne, may have been a lapsed priest. They were all known to each other, and the chance that the chroniclers, with the mass of gentry and aristocracy of England to choose from, should have picked on a group of men with lands in different parts of England, but nonetheless linked by personal ties, has long appeared to be an *a priori* argument in favour of their accusations.

The Lollard knights included three who demonstrably gave help to the movement. Sir John Montagu was sufficiently committed to remove the images from his chapel at Shenley and to harbour Lollard preachers. Sir Thomas Latimer made his seat at Braybrooke, in Northamptonshire, a Lollard centre, and was summoned before the council in 1388 at the time of the Merciless Parliament to answer for the possession of heretical books. That was a party move by the Apellants' faction, striking at a king's man by means of the heresy accusation. Latimer felt sufficiently secure, however, to continue to back heresy. At Chipping Warden, a small market town in the same county of which he was lord, the bishop of Lincoln had extreme difficulty in getting a writ served in 1388-9 on a chaplain accused of Lollard preaching. Latimer even brought a suit before the king's justices against the bishop's summoner. At the time of Hereford's arrest in 1387, Sir William Nevill petitioned for the prisoner to be delivered to his keeping as constable of Nottingham castle, 'because of the honesty of his person'—a strange description of a Lollard preacher on the run and betraying Nevill's sympathies, as McFarlane observes.[34] A sudden glimpse in the records such as this reveals attachments hitherto unproved; it is fair to surmise that some other cases of high-born sympathy never reached our records.

Sir John Clanvow, a great friend of Nevill, who died on an expedition with him near Constantinople, wrote in the last year of his life (1391) a vernacular religious treatise on the broad and narrow way, which reveals an ardent piety, nourished by a contemplation of the sufferings of Christ and marked by a concern for preserving an ethical life amongst the temptations of the world.[35] There is no breath of overt heresy in it, and it lacks the astringent criticisms of

---

Wycliffe on Lollardy's potential. (Further research led a notable historian to change his mind. Did he change too far?)

[33]*Knighton*, II, p. 181; *Thomae Walsingham historia Anglicana*, ed. H. T. Riley, *RS*, II, (1864), pp. 159, 216; see also *Chronicon Angliae RS*, p. 377.

[34]*Lancastrian Kings*, p. 199.

[35]V. J. Scattergood, ' "The Two Ways": an Unpublished Religious Treatise by Sir John Clanvowe', *English Philological Studies*, x (1967), pp. 33-56; see passage on Christ's sufferings (pp. 53-4). I am indebted to Dr V. J. Scattergood and Dr A. B. Cottle for information. Contrast McFarlane's characterization (*Lancastrian Kings*, pp. 200-6, esp. p. 201).

the Church to be found in Lollard work; yet it is easy to see a platform for some interest in Lollardy in the direct and practical tone of this work, its scriptural basis and its moral earnestness. If Clanvow ever had a connection with Lollardy, he entered into it, we may say from this evidence, out of religious faith.

For others among the knights, we have no such direct evidence of their mind. Some may have been anticlericals; certainly the proportion of professional soldiers among them, and links with the Black Prince, have led to conjectures that it was a liking for disendowment proposals as a means of raising war finance that led them to flirt with the heresy, and the interest of some members of the group in the lands of alien priories, taken into the king's hands during the wars with France, may be a pointer in this direction.[36] But the group included some whose interests were not confined to war: Montagu was a man of cultivated taste; Sir Richard Sturry had a copy of the *Roman de la Rose*, and was acquainted with Chaucer and Froissart; Clanvow and Sir Lewis Clifford both knew Chaucer, and Clifford bought ballads from Deschamps; V. J. Scattergood has given reasons for identifying Clanvow as the author of the poem *The Boke of Cupide*.[37] If Lollardy could find adherents such as these, we should be wary of underestimating the danger presented to the Church. No bishop could act uninhibitedly against these men when they were of such rank and stood so high in royal favour. They, and probably some others like them, formed small bulwarks of protection for Lollard evangelists in the twilight period after 1382.

Yet the group did not develop. No great issue comparable in its effect to the breach of Hus's safe conduct to Constance for Bohemian nobility emerged to swing noble opinion behind heresy.[38] It has even been suggested on the evidence of the wills of Latimer, Clifford and Cheyne, where they describe themselves as 'false' or 'traitor' to God, that they abandoned any attachment to heresy they may have had before their deaths.[39] Apparent acceptance of the doctrine of purgatory or going on crusade were actions of some members of the group that argue in the same direction. The wills, however, may easily mislead, and their language reveal a religious sentiment shared by some Lollards and other wholly orthodox contemporaries. Lollard beliefs are too fluid at this stage and Lollards too often inconsistent for their support of crusades or belief in purgatory to be taken as indicating abandonment of all patronage of heresy. Even if the Lollard knights never wholly gave up their interest—and we shall probably never know with certainty—on the other hand they do not seem directly to have won many more recruits, or to have succeeded in changing the climate after 1382 in Lollardy's favour.

The Appeal of Lollardy

Lollard tracts invited their readers, as it were, to teach themselves; implicit in

[36]McFarlane, *Lancastrian Kings*, pp. 190–2.

[37]'The Authorship of "The Boke of Cupide"', *Anglia*, LXXXII (1964), pp. 137–49. On Clanvow, Clifford and Sturry, cf. *Chaucer Life-records*, ed. M. M. Crow and C. C. Olson (Oxford, 1966), index, s.v.

[38]Below, pp. 297–301.

[39]Originally Waugh's suggestion ('Lollard Knights', pp. 63, 72, 86, 88); more subtle analysis by McFarlane (*Lancastrian Kings*, pp. 207–20).

the process was the direct relationship between the reader and the Holy Spirit, who would inspire those of good life.[40] Preaching remained the first means of gathering converts; the tracts and the vernacular Scriptures came second. They provided ammunition for the preachers, and confirmed the converts in their beliefs after they had joined the reading circles. After preaching came the informal dissemination of beliefs, at work, in taverns, in the family circle, through trade connections.

From an early period the Lollards were reproducing books of the Bible in translation for instructional purposes: we have a glimpse of the process at work at Leicester in 1384, when William Smith was copying translations of the Lollard epistles and gospels.[41] But the Early Version, pedantic and unlovely, was an imperfect instrument for a popular movement. With the appearance of the Late Version, (the graceful and free-flowing translation of John Purvey and his team) the situation began to change. It was completed by about 1395–7[42] and the fact that many manuscripts of it are extant, especially from the first forty years of its existence, shows that it met a real need in the population. Viewed through the eyes of Lollard clergy or lay evangelists, the text could point the way to heresy; the epistles and gospels, for example, could be used to stress the contrast between the simplicity of the early Church and the formalism of the contemporary ecclesiastical scene,[43] and the readings which came to form the staple activity of the sect, could draw out the absence of overt warrant in the scriptural text for such doctrines as purgatory or transubstantiation.

Lollardy's appeal to independent judgement has to be set against the background of ordinary Church life, where laity and clergy were set apart, and the laity still had a relatively passive role. Books of devotion, like the *Lay Folk's Mass Book*, assume that two sets of devotions will be proceeding simultaneously, one for priest, one for laity. The laity hearing the gospel in Latin was compared in a contemporary judgement to an adder which is affected by a charm said over it, even though it cannot understand the words.[44] In fact orthodoxy, despite the issue of vernacular works of instruction and the development of a literature of devotion, had not fully adapted itself to the needs of an age of increasing literacy. This gave a heresy based so much on the written text its great opportunity.

One of the most vital features of late medieval English religious life was its devotional movement. It is enshrined permanently for us in the apparatus of worship of the late medieval English parish church. This movement was not imposed from above—the records of the time allow us to see that the adornment of the parish church, using every device of the craftsman to heighten the sense of the numinous, was a popular matter, and that ordinary

[40]Deanesly, p. 269; see transcript of Lollard tract (p. 452).

[41]Ibid., p. 278.

[42]I follow Deanesly's views (op. cit., pp. 252–67) on date and authorship of LV. Compare Fristedt, *Wycliffe Bible,* II, p. lxiv: 'probably . . . halfway between 1388 and 1396.'

[43]See J. Fines, in *JEH,* XIV (1963), p. 165.

[44]B. L. Manning, *The People's Faith in the Time of Wyclif,* (Cambridge, 1919), pp. 7–9 (outdated on preaching and Biblical translations, but retains value for citations from contemporary edifying texts). See C. Wordsworth and H. Littlehales, *The Old Service-books of the English Church* (London, 1904), pp. 284–6.

parishioners readily subscribed. The Lollards had no sympathy for this; for example, Smith and Waytestathe at Leicester were accused of chopping up an image for firewood, and Smith of calling images of Our Lady at Walsingham and Lincoln 'the witch of Walsingham' and 'the witch of Lincoln'.[45] Thorpe represents himself in his trial by Arundel as attacking all paintings and images in church, pleading against this the second commandment.[46] The Lollards disliked symbolism and mystery—it seemed to them merely to obscure essential truths. In this way, on a lower level, they were following the lines of Wyclif himself, who laid such stress on the rational approach to faith.

The rational approach in their hands often came to mean a minimal approach to credal statements. Wyclif's consubstantiation, based as it was on a philosophical realism, came to be accepted by them on the basis of mere common sense. The bread could still be seen after the words of consecration; therefore it was plain that the substance of bread still remained. Sometimes, we may deduce, Lollard preachers appealed to a pre-existing doubt about the more difficult doctrinal demands of the Church. Richard Wyche before the Bishop of Durham represented himself as appealing to the laity who were onlookers to confirm his own 'minimal' approach to transubstantiation—he was too honest not to admit that in this instance they did not support him, but one sees the way in which he would as a preacher have approached the laity in this matter.[47] Lollardy provided an outlet for certain kinds of scepticism, about saints and their miracles, pilgrimages, wonder-working images and, above all, the central miracle of the mass.

Anticlericalism played a strong part. It must have been the most usual springboard into heresy, which commonly began in an alienation from the Church, caused by dissatisfaction with the clergy. The frequently expressed Donatist view that a state of sin in the celebrant invalidated the sacrament, or the plan of reform that would turn the clergy into salaried officials would have had little point if there had not been a dissatisfaction with the state of life of the clergy. When an approach was made to secular authority, Lollards were always ready to play their anticlerical card, appealing to the layman's suspicion of Church wealth, or, as in the Twelve Conclusions of 1395, attacking clerical celibacy.[48]

Lollardy often issued from an outraged Puritan conscience. Lollard writers and preachers could denounce the failings of the visible Church, often with considerable literary skill, because they had themselves felt them so deeply. We may consider Purvey's tract as a case in point, where a faint-hearted adherent is brought to full conversion by a sarcastic narration of the easygoing ways of the ordinary parishioner, enjoying his 'theatres, wrestlers, bucklerplayers . . . dancers and singers', dining and drinking by night and going to church afterwards, with the good ale rising into his brain and preventing him from noticing the false doctrine of the sermon.[49]

[45]McFarlane, *Wycliffe*, p. 140.

[46]Pollard, pp. 133–7; general comment in E. F. Jacob, *The Fifteenth Century* (Oxford, 1961), pp. 282–3.

[47]*EHR*, v (1890), p. 532.

[48]*FZ*, pp. 360–9; on unchastity, no. 3 (p. 361).

[49]Deanesly, p. 274.

Lollards had a sharp consciousness of sin. Swinderby's appeal to the king's justices in parliament, with its references to the ghostly enemy and the approaching end, gives us some inkling of whence this preacher drew his power.[50] The *Lantern of Light* gives much space to a stern warning against sin in general. It is in the first instance a call to repentance.[51] The revivalist element in Lollardy could readily deceive the unequipped parishioner. Owst has long shown us how fiercely the sermon and devotional literature of the time could attack clerical abuses.[52] Lollard denunciation might at first sight be believed to correspond with the sermons of orthodoxy, and there is some evidence that this is what happened. Thomas Beeby, a Leicester mercer, in 1382 left money in his will both to Swinderby and to the Franciscans, who were then the firm enemies of Lollardy.[53] Thomas Netter noticed how the audiences of the Lollards were liable to doubt whether they really were heretics.[54]

The entry of Lollard ideas was the easier because of the existence of a desire for quite radical reform within orthodoxy. A tract licensed by the official of St Albans for general reading said that a priest was to be obeyed only 'in as myche as he techith goddis law.'[55] *Dives and Pauper*, a popular manual for the laity, at least opened the question of the potential ill-effects of some popular devotions and admitted, for example, that men might use images simply to win money.[56] Lollards were aware of these tendencies within orthodoxy and they were also anxious to link themselves with pre-existing popular religious literature. Certain MSS of the English Psalter and the *Ancren Riwle*, which were ascribed to the orthodox mystic Richard Rolle, have been subjected to Lollard interpolations, no doubt with the aim of suggesting that Lollardy was not a novelty, but that such views had earlier had the support of an accepted devotional author who himself wrote in the vernacular.[57] The interpolated English version of the orthodox *Lay Folk's Catechism* served a straightforward propagandizing purpose, and did it rather crudely, for the Lollard sections

[50]McFarlane, *Wycliffe*, p. 133.

[51]*The Lanterne of Light*, ed. L. M. Swinburne (London, 1917) (*EETS*, o.s., CLI), written in the era of Oldcastle's revolt. Ch. 13 is repr. from 1831 edn in *Medieval Culture and Society*, ed. D. Herlihy (London & New York, 1968), pp. 404–10. Heresy lies in rejection of papacy and hierarchy for the company of the elect and in attitude to Scripture (pp. 15, 16, 25, 31); the author shares the Lollard rejection of images and pilgrimages (pp. 37–8, 84–5) and claims right of free preaching (pp. 11–12). But he accepts priesthood (p. 34) and has reverence for sacraments (p. 59), and there is no Donatism or rejection of transubstantiation in his work. For ethical concern, note denunciation of oppression of rich (pp. 69–71), Sabbatarianism (p. 91), attitudes to bribery (pp. 112–4) and selling suffrages (as he sees it) for money (p. 93). Ch. 12 is a commentary on the Ten Commandments.

[52]E.g., G. R. Owst, *Preaching in Medieval England* (Cambridge, 1926), pp. 292–4; Fines, *Studies*, p. 21.

[53]McFarlane, *Wycliffe*, pp, 124–5.

[54]*Thomae Waldensis Carmelitae Anglici doctrinale antiquitatum fidei catholicae ecclesiae*, ed. F. Bonaventura Blanciotti, I (Venice, 1757), cols 20–1; Fines, *Studies*, p. 34, n. 2.

[55]Owst, pp. 292–4.

[56]Manning, *People's Faith*, p. 101. *Dives and Pauper* (*STC* 19212–14) was completed between 1405 and 1410. A new edition by P. H. Barnum is planned for publication as *EETS*, o.s., CCLXXV.

[57]Deanesly, p. 304; E. Colledge, ' "The Recluse"—a Lollard Interpolated Version of the "Ancren Riwle" ', *Review of English Studies*, XV (1939), pp. 1–15, 129–45; H. E. Allen, *Writings ascribed to Richard Rolle*, (New York & London, 1927).

exist in strange proximity to Archbishop Thoresby's offer of indulgences to readers—something wholly against Lollard views, which the interpolators had nevertheless not removed.[58] Similarly, in about 1411 Wyclifite Sunday gospel sermons were being smuggled into an orthodox sermon cycle.[59]

The Strands of Belief

Variety of belief in the early days was a consequence of the development of the preaching strata in the movement from the proto-Lollards of academic circles to the simpler chaplains and laymen, and it was implicit in a theology which urged every man to seek his own guidance in the open Scriptures. Gradually a more academic Lollardy faded, as it was no longer reinforced by graduate recruits, and the simpler Donatism and anticlericalism of the less educated preachers took its place. Fundamental to the movement were the ideas of the relationship between Scripture and the Church which went back to Wyclif; inevitably, even among the proto-Lollards, the initial nuances were lost. The need to do battle with opponents and press on with an aggressive missioning may also have helped to radicalize Lollard thinking; this, Deanesly suggests, was the effect on the naturally scholarly and moderate Purvey, which helps to explain the discrepancies between his pre-1401 treatises[60] and the errors he abjured in 1401,[61] and the tract *Sixteen points putten by bishops ordinarily upon men which they clepen Lollards*, written after 1401, when he was no longer under the same pressures.[62] Direct contradictions between different Lollard authors are not lacking. The Twelve Conclusions of 1395 was pacifist,[63] the *Lantern of Light* of 1409–15 accepted the necessity of 'righteous smiting'.[64] The *Lantern* contained no eucharistic heresy, and was altogether moderate on the sacraments;[65] yet both Sawtry (burned in 1401) and the tailor Badby (burned in 1410) went to the stake in part because of their rejection of transubstantiation.[66] The *Lantern* expressed no Donatist views; yet the evidence of enquiries of the period shows that this was a relatively frequent heresy.[67] No doubt a full analysis of the tracts and judicial records together,

[58]Ed. T. F. Simmons, H. E. Nolloth (London, 1901) (*EETS*, o.s., cxviii) (see esp. pp. 102, 103, 106); Workman, ii, pp. 158–60, correcting Nolloth. See Wordsworth and Littlehales, *Service-books*, p. 262.

[59]Above, p. 237, n. 12.

[60]Theses extracted therefrom by the Carmelite Lavenham in *FZ*, pp. 383–99; see Workman, ii, pp. 165–7, Leff, *Heresy*, ii, pp. 578–83, for analysis of relation to Wyclif's thought. But note that Leff is using Lavenham, not Purvey's confession.

[61]*FZ*, pp. 400–7; the first five topics of Lavenham's compilation appear as topics of the abjuration.

[62]Text in Deanesly, pp. 462–7; dating follows Deanesly's hypothesis (pp. 461–2; discussion on pp. 284–5). Note difference between views on priesthood in Lavenham's treatise, pp. 387–9 (distinguished from Wyclif's by Leff, ii, p. 580) and those in the Sixteen points (Deanesly, p. 465).

[63]See *FZ*, pp. 366–7; discussion of texts in Workman, ii, p. 391, n. 2; H. S. Cronin, 'The Twelve Conclusions of the Lollards', *EHR*, xxii (1907), pp. 292–304.

[64]Ed. Swinburn, p. 99.

[65]Ibid., pp. xv (intro.), 59.

[66]*FZ*, 410, 411; Foxe, *Acts and Monuments*, ed. S. R. Cattley, iii (London, 1837), p. 221–9 esp. 222 (Sawtry); 235–9 (Badby); McFarlane, *Wycliffe*, pp. 150–2, 154–5. On Foxe, see J. A. F. Thomson, 'John Foxe and some Sources for Lollard History: Notes for a Critical Appraisal', in *SCH*, ii, pp. 251–7.

[67]Above, n. 51.

one of the major *desiderata* of Lollard studies, would show further discrepancies. Lollardy was as much a mood as a formal body of doctrines, and for a long time distinct strands of belief co-existed.

The doctrinal relation of Lollardy to Wyclif is complicated. The exigencies of evangelization meant that Wyclif's conclusions were adopted without the arguments that he used to reach them.[68] For many the philosophical background to his thinking soon faded, and the moral stress of Wyclif tended to assume the centre of the stage. No major Lollard treatise, it would seem, took up the implications of dominion by grace for civil possession, though occasional suspects expressed views on the point.[69] Most revealing of all is the change which Wyclif's eucharistic beliefs underwent in the hands of the Lollards. His positive views, as we have seen, can most fairly be said to have corresponded at the end of his life with consubstantiation; but the *Wicket*, put out under his name, possibly as late as c.1470, preached that the eucharist was a simple commemoration meal.[70] In this way Wyclif was simplified and at times distorted, detached from his contemporary academic setting and used as figurehead for a movement that had grown away from him. Yet he could certainly have recognized some of the tenets of late Lollardy. The effect of his explosive ideas on Scripture and the body of the elect are traceable throughout Lollard history.

The Actions of Authority

From one point of view, the reactions of Church leaders were eminently successful. By sounding the alarm, achieving a clear condemnation of some Wyclifite tenets, and purging Oxford in 1382, Courtenay checked the heresy's potential for rising in society and maintaining its intellectual base.[71] The Peasants' Revolt in the previous year was a stroke of luck. Wyclif's own reactions to it were plainly hostile;[72] nevertheless, it was widely believed that Lollards had some responsibility, and the belief influenced authority's reactions.[73] Its immediate sequel was a statute restraining the activities of preachers. Already eucharistic heresy was beginning to frighten away the more opportunistic anticlerical supporters; the belief that Lollardy meant sedition helped the process on. When Hereford and Repton sought out Gaunt as a shield in 1382, after coming under fire from Courtenay, they met with a refusal, symptomatic of the change in atmosphere that had taken place.[74]

On the other hand, the failure of bishops to follow Courtenay's vigorous lead and the absence of a fully co-ordinated machinery of repression was equally decisive for the continued existence of Lollardy. The preachers were

[68]See Leff's comment on the Twenty-five points: *Heresy*, ii, p. 576.

[69]See Thomson, *Later Lollards*, pp. 29, 145.

[70]Aston, in *PP*, xxx (1965), pp. 37–8; also her 'Lollardy and the Reformation: Survival or Revival', *History*, xlix (1964), pp. 149–70.

[71]Courtenay's vital role was first noticed by McFarlane in his *Wycliffe*: Courtenay, not Wyclif, is the true hero of the book.

[72]Above, p. 228.

[73]The most helpful article on this is M. E. Aston; 'Lollardy and Sedition'; I am much indebted to it. See also H. G. Richardson, 'Heresy and the Lay Power under Richard II', *EHR*, li (1936), pp. 1–28.

[74]Workman, ii, p. 282; McFarlane, *Wycliffe*, p. 110.

not adequately checked; bishops did not react quickly; Buckingham was not notably speedy in dealing with the Leicester outbreak; Trefnant, bishop of Hereford, was slow and, in his action against Walter Brute, somewhat easily satisfied by a generalized confession of orthodoxy.[75] Erastian bishops tended not to be keen heresy-hunters; it has been suggested that they were aware of some sympathy in high places.[76] Concern for justice and for the soul of the Lollard also tended to outweigh the practical merits of draconian measures. The long delays allowed to Oldcastle before condemnation were, admittedly, due to the personal wishes of the young Henry V; but the reluctance to burn in the case of the insignificant tailor Badby can only have sprung from humanity and a care for souls.

England was slow to follow continental example, and in some matters retained her individual customs. Torture was not used; time for reflection in an episcopal prison was usually effective enough in inducing confessions. Great stress was laid on the need to convert the prisoner from his heresy. Richard Wyche spent some three months in the bishop of Durham's prison, during which time he was subjected to six hearings before the bishop or his advisers, as well as two visits to him by individuals seeking to influence his mind, before the two formal sessions in which he was excommunicated and sent back to prison.[77] The rewards for recantation were generous: Purvey received a benefice after he had given in, and the anchoress Matilda at Leicester found that after she had been brought back to orthodoxy the archbishop offered indulgences to those who gave her gifts.[78]

This restraint helped to keep preachers in the field after they could have been laid by the heels. William Taylor, the academic Lollard, is the classic example. He was cited twice by Arundel, in 1406 and 1410, and on both occasions did not appear. He was taken to court in the Worcester diocese in 1417, and in 1420 came before Archbishop Chichele, when he recanted. Six months later he was arrested in Bristol and sentenced to life imprisonment, but he was released, and only burnt when he had been caught yet again.[79] Wyche is a similar example; his career as a missionary could have been brought to an end long before 1440 by keeping him under some surveillance.

The laity were most moved by the fear of rebellion, and action was most likely when their political interests were involved. Thus Courtenay pressed home his attack on Lollardy in the period of reaction which followed the Peasants' Revolt of 1381; the action of the Cambridge parliament of 1388, setting up new commissions of laymen as well as churchmen to deal with Lollardy, was in part an outcome of the Appellants' wish to maintain order in the secular as much as in the ecclesiastical sphere; when burning was introduced by the statute *De heretico comburendo* in 1401, the Church had been able to take advantage of political events. A usurper king needed all the help he could get from the clergy, and he may well have thought that the measures

---

[75]Ibid., pp. 121–4, 135–7. For lack of zeal by Wakefield of Worcester, see *SCH*, XI, pp. 143–4.

[76]McFarlane, *Lancastrian Kings*, pp. 225–6. For Buckingham, see *SCH* IX, pp. 131–45.

[77]Wyche's own account is in *EHR*, v (1890), pp. 530–44; on torture, note the dark phrase about Hereford and Purvey attributed to Arundel in Pollard, p. 165. But there is no general evidence for torture; see Thomson, *Later Lollards*, p. 230.

[78]Fines, *Studies*, p. 40.

[79]Thomson, *Later Lollards*, pp. 24–6.

intended to deal with unauthorized preachers could also be useful in checking the growth of political conspiracies and conventicles.[80]

At other times the attitude of the laity was somewhat changeable. In 1384 Nassington's translation of the *Speculum vitae,* an entirely orthodox work of piety, was submitted to the chancellor of Cambridge for a learned judgement for fear that it was heretical.[81] Yet the careers of the great evangelists, such as Thorpe, Wyche and Purvey, would have been quite impossible if the overwhelming majority of their hearers had not declined to betray them to authority. In the Commons conflicting emotions decided the approach to heresy; on the one side, the laity were unwilling to put more power into the hands of churchmen; on the other, they could be spurred on by the belief that State and property were being threatened by Lollardy. Anticlerical sentiment, a taste for the vernacular, and an unwillingness to be ruled overmuch by ecclesiastics accounts for some of the unwillingness to press home the repression of Lollardy.

Finally, Lollard attitudes to the secular power were affected by the course of events. They had inherited from Wyclif the belief that the secular authorities should be the instrument to reform the Church,[82] and the last two decades of the fourteenth century saw a series of attempts to persuade the State to take action. Only after long disappointment did a section abandon persuasion in favour of a *coup d'état.* After the *coup* failed, the general tendency was to leave the reform of the Church in the hands of God, and wait quietly for better times. Wyclif himself constantly appealed to the State; Swinderby to the justices in parliament. Tracts were written with an eye to influencing the upper classes, and in 1395 a Lollard bill demanding reform was put on the doors of Westminster Hall and St Paul's when parliament was in session.[83] As late as 1410 a proposal came before parliament to disendow the possessioners; but it gained no support at all in the quarters where it mattered most—with the king and the prince of Wales.[84]

Oldcastle's Revolt

The immediate occasion for the resort to force by Lollardy was the imprisonment of their most distinguished secular leader, Sir John Oldcastle.[85] Oldcastle was, like some of the Lollard knights, a man who made his way through the profession of arms, rising from a modest family background in Herefordshire: there is a parallel between his military service to the future Henry V when prince of Wales and the service of some Lollard knights to the Black Prince.[86] But times had changed. Henry V was a man of devout

[80]Aston, 'Lollardy and Sedition', pp. 32–3.

[81]Deanesly, pp. 215–6.

[82]For Wyclif's attitudes, see Leff, II, pp. 543–5.

[83]Correction of Deanesly (*Lollard Bible,* p. 283) on 1395 episode in McFarlane, *Wycliffe,* p. 147; see Aston, 'Lollardy and Sedition', p. 17.

[84]Aston, loc. cit.

[85]For what follows, see W. T. Waugh, 'Sir John Oldcastle', *EHR,* xx (1905), pp. 434–56, 637–58; and succinctly, with additional evidence on Oldcastle's rebellion, in McFarlane, *Wycliffe,* pp. 160–83.

[86]Above, p. 242; McFarlane, 'The Origins of the Lollard Movement', in *Relazioni,* VII, pp. 216–7 (earlier stage of his research into Lollard knights).

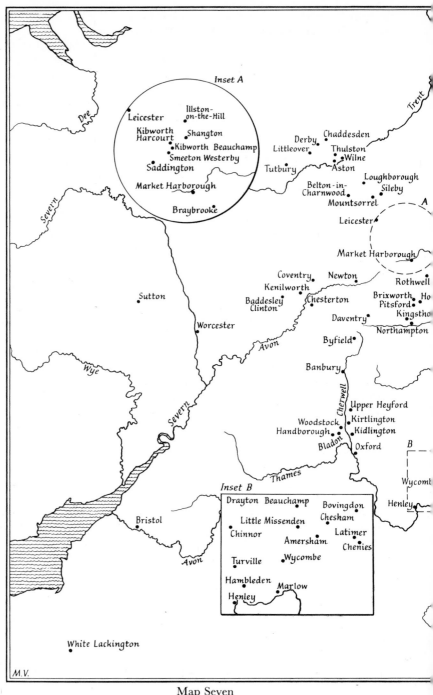

Inset A

Leicester
Illston-on-the-Hill
Kibworth Harcourt
Shangton
Kibworth Beauchamp
Smeeton Westerby
Saddington
Market Harborough
Braybrooke

Dee

Trent

Derby
Chaddesden
Littleover
Thulston
Wilne
Tutbury
Aston
Loughborough
Belton-in-Charnwood
Sileby
Mountsorrel
Leicester

Severn

A

Market Harborough

Sutton

Coventry
Newton
Rothwell
Kenilworth
Brixworth
Ho
Baddesley Clinton
Chesterton
Pitsford
Kingstho
Daventry
Northampton

Worcester

Avon

Byfield

Wye

Banbury

Severn

Cherwell

Upper Heyford
Woodstock
Kirtlington
Handborough
Kidlington
Bladon
Oxford

B

Wycomb

Thames

Henley

Inset B

Drayton Beauchamp
Bovingdon
Little Missenden
Chesham
Chinnor
Latimer
Amersham
Chenies
Turville
Wycombe
Hambleden
Marlow
Henley

Bristol

Avon

White Lackington

M.V.

Map Seven
Oldcastle's Rebellion

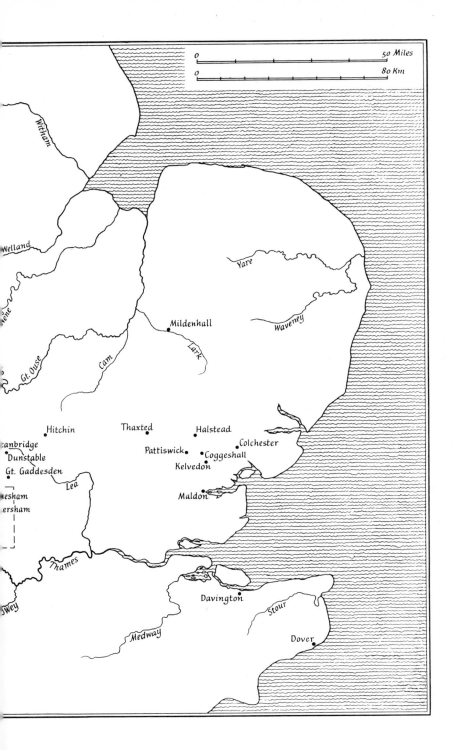

0   50 Miles

0   80 Km

Witham

Welland

Nene

Gt. Ouse

Cam

Lark

Yare

Waveney

Mildenhall

Hitchin

Thaxted

Halstead

Colchester

canbridge

Dunstable

Pattiswick

Coggeshall

Gt. Gaddesden

Kelvedon

Lea

esham

ersham

Maldon

Thames

Wey

Medway

Davington

Stour

Dover

character, and a determined opponent of heresy; Oldcastle was a fully committed Lollard. The only wonder is that he should have been left at liberty for so long. Probably a principal reason was his station in society. Though a clear abetter of Lollardy, twice brought before the council to answer charges relating to heresy, he was subjected to no punishment. In the end, however, he was unable to withstand the evidence of association with Lollard chaplains and the distribution of their tracts. In 1413 he was arrested. At his trial in St. Paul's he defied Arundel, declared his heresy on the eucharist and the Church, and was condemned. During the forty days respite which he was allowed by special grace of the king to reconsider his position, he was rescued from the Tower, and he proceeded to raise his followers in rebellion. The aim has never been clarified; the royal view expressed in proclamations was that Oldcastle intended to kill the royal family, nobility and upper clergy, and to dispossess the Church. We may assume that Oldcastle intended to enforce a Lollard reform. It was a wild scheme. The revolt should be seen as a gambler's throw that never had any realistic chances of success. The plot was betrayed, and the rebels rounded up before they could inflict damage.

It should impress us that a prisoner on the run could rouse rebellion from scattered Lollard congregations and self-seekers scattered as far west as Bristol and as far north as Derby. Map 7 plots the results of McFarlane's researches into the judicial records of the investigations into the revolt.[87] A shrewd judge, he estimated that our picture of the extent of the rebellion may not be far from the truth, for the attempt at revolution, even including the assassination of the king, plainly roused both officials and the populace to counteraction.

Rebellion was one result of the Lollard missionizing of the previous decades. Areas where the bishops had found Lollards to prosecute tend to coincide with those which sent men to join Oldcastle's last throw. Bristol, the old Lollard centre, sent the largest contingent, some forty craftsmen setting out under the leadership of six chaplains; the Leicestershire villages' participation reveals that, even if Leicester itself was not so deeply involved, the heresy was still embedded in the surrounding countryside. Yet some Lollard-influenced areas were mute on this occasion—Swinderby's old preaching-ground in Herefordshire and on the Welsh border generally, East Anglia, that we know to have given evidence of heretical activity, Oldcastle's area of influence in Kent.

Sometimes the depositions enable us to pick out a decisive leader who has roused a region. Such were William the chaplain of Thaxted, the evangelist of Essex; Walter Gilbert alias Kibworth, who had influenced both the Leicestershire villages near Kibworth Harcourt and the Derby area; and, in Derby and its surrounds, another chaplain, William Ederick; in Oxfordshire William Brown alias Davy, a glover of Woodstock. The patrons of heresy in higher classes also had their part to play—at Drayton Beauchamp in Buckinghamshire, the Cheynes; at Smeeton Westerby, among the Leicestershire villages, the most committed of the Lollard knights, Sir Thomas Latimer, its lord; in the lower valley of the Cherwell in Oxfordshire, Thomas Compworth.

[87]It follows closely McFarlane, *Wycliffe*, pp, 172–80.

Yet the map only presents a partial picture of the extent of Lollard sympathies in Henry V's reign, despite the energy of the commissioners in collecting evidence. The total numbers involved were very small. Three hundred is a maximum. Some may well have declined Oldcastle's call on principle; others may not have been able to come in time, because of their geographical isolation from London. The rebellion attracted the seditious and adventurers who had no unorthodox religious affiliations, but were merely out for the tangible rewards of a successful rebellion, as in the case of the rich brewer of Dunstable who bought gilt spurs in anticipation of the knighthood that was to reward his participation. The proof of the participation of non-Lollards lies in the actions of the government. Of those sentenced to be executed, a majority was condemned to be hanged. The bodies of the genuine Lollards were burnt after they had been hanged; this was an action adopted only in a small proportion of the total cases. Numbers of rebels and sympathizers were treated mercifully, and in these cases many were released after a term of imprisonment without being handed over to an ecclesiastical court—another indication that opportunists predominated over those of religious conviction.

The revolt marked a turning point in the relation between Lollardy and the State. It finally demonstrated to the country that the suspicion that heresy and sedition went together had good grounds.[88] Little hope as Lollardy had of gaining wide support before 1414, the revolt finally condemned it to the underground existence of a small minority.

2. Lollardy Underground

The Prosecutions after 1414[89]
In the surge of anxiety following the revolt plots were discovered linking Lollards with England's enemies—the Scots, the Welsh, the false Richard II—and emotions against the sectaries ran high.[90] The somewhat eccentric

---

[88]See Aston, 'Lollardy and Sedition', p. 35.

[89]For comprehensive survey based on episcopal registers and other evidence, see Thomson, *Later Lollards*, maps, pp. 52, 118, 172; (reviews by M. Deanesly, in *JEH*, XVII (1966), pp. 265–6; S. H. Thomson, in *Speculum*, XLI (1966), pp. 774–5, M. McKisack, in *JTS*, XVII (1966), pp. 505–6, R. B. Dobson, in *SHR*, XLVI (1967) pp. 63–4). For intensive study of select dioceses, exploiting esp. Westminster Cathedral MS. on Norwich prosecutions 1428, Lichfield heresy court book (discovered by Fines) for Lichfield prosecutions 1511–12, see Fines, *Studies*; maps pp. 60, 167; analysis of Westminster Cathedral MS. in appendix 2; insights in ch. of conclusions. Best short account of Lollard trial is J. Fines, 'Heresy Trials in the Diocese of Coventry and Lichfield, 1511–12', *JEH*, XIV (1963), pp. 160–74; for prosecution records also his 'The Post-mortem Condemnation for Heresy of Richard Hunne', *EHR*, LXXVIII (1963), pp. 528–31, and Thomson, *Later Lollards*, pp. 223–4. Documents are in *EHD*, IV, ed A. R. Myers, (London 1969), pp. 837–78. I am indebted for generous help to Dr Thomson and Dr Fines. For Tudor Lollards, see A. G. Dickens, *Lollards and Protestants in the Diocese of York* (Oxford, 1959) (great value for popular religious attitudes, less convincing on actual Lollardy in the north) and his overall survey in 'Heresy and the Origins of English Protestantism', in *Britain and the Netherlands*, II ed. J. S. Bromley, E. H. Kossmann, (Groningen, 1964), pp. 47–66. Sermons and literary evidence have yet to be fully exploited, but see E. F. Jacob, 'Reynold Pecock, Bishop of Chichester', *PBA*, XXXVII (1953), pp. 121–53, and V. H. H. Green, *Bishop Reginald Pecock* (Cambridge, 1945).

[90]Thomson, *Later Lollards*, pp. 8–18, Aston, 'Lollardy and Sedition', pp. 20–3.

but orthodox English mystic, Margery Kempe, being taken through Beverley under arrest, was confronted by local housewives, who ran out of their houses shaking their distaffs and crying out, 'Brennith this fals heretyk'.[91] Because of the revolt, public opinion turned decisively against the Lollards; there was natural indignation at the bloody details of the plot, and all the warnings of the bishops in the earlier decades seemed amply confirmed. In this phase of high emotion, detection and prosecution had every assistance. Oldcastle, hidden by sympathizers, was nonetheless rounded up and executed. Through the effects of the revolt and the state of opinion, the limited support of those of gentle birth for Lollardy faded out, and the congregations lower down the social scale were put under heavy pressure.

Yet such intensity of feeling could not last. Groups of Lollards, the majority quite unconnected with the revolt, rode out the storm. Surviving pro-Lollard clergy and other evangelists helped to keep the movement in being. Secular interest waned; the impetus to detection passed back again to ecclesiastical authorities. In 1428 Archbishop Chichele was apparently calling for fair copies of prosecution records to be deposited at Lambeth, with a view to making persecution more effective by co-ordinating information.[92] Stiff drives against heresy launched in Canterbury and Norwich dioceses showed that the Lollards were still in existence, and in considerable numbers;[93] in the Norwich diocese 101 came before the courts between 1424 and 1431.[94]

Then in 1431 another revolt was launched, but feebly, in circumstances that made it almost a caricature of that in 1414; though it resembled the Oldcastle rebellion in aiming at disendowment and the removal of the king and aristocracy, its leaders, William Perkins, a former bailiff of Abingdon with a record of conviction for non-religious offences, and John Russell, former associate of Richard Gurmyn the Lollard baker, in the London textile industry, once engaged in false moneying, were a far cry from Oldcastle, and the action fizzled out in the scattering of handbills in London, an assembly at East Hendred to march on Abingdon abbey, and a similar abortive attempt on Salisbury cathedral.[95] Only in Coventry, where there were executions, and in Leicester did something more serious occur. The link with Lollardy was tenuous—Perkins and Russell seem more like opportunists than members of Scripture-reading circles. Clergy had hardly any share, and we hear nothing of the doctrinal unorthodoxy of participants.

Thereafter no violent movement labelled as Lollard again gathered support over even as wide an area as the 1431 plot had done. *Pari passu*, as far

---

[91]Thomson, *Later Lollards*, p. 195.

[92]Fines, *Studies*, appendix 2, and *EHR*, LXXVIII (1963), pp. 528–31.

[93]For incidence of prosecutions, see table in Thomson, *Later Lollards*, pp. 237–8.

[94]Fines, *Studies*, p. 245.

[95]Fullest account by Aston, 'Lollardy and Sedition', pp. 24–30 (note valuable footnotes); Mrs Aston kindly informs me she would now modify some of the views in her article. I have followed the approach of Thomson (*Later Lollards*, pp. 58–62, 102, 146–8), minimizing the seriousness of the affair. Note doubts on Lollard participation (p. 61), and see his 'A Lollard Rising in Kent, 1431 or 1438', *BIHR* xxxvii (1964), pp. 100–2. Humphrey, Duke of Gloucester, made enquiries after the rising in Leicester and Coventry. There were also enquiries of various kinds in Wilts., Som., Cambs., Kent and in Hertford, and Sir John Cheyne, of Drayton Beauchamp (Bucks.), and his brother Thomas were arrested.

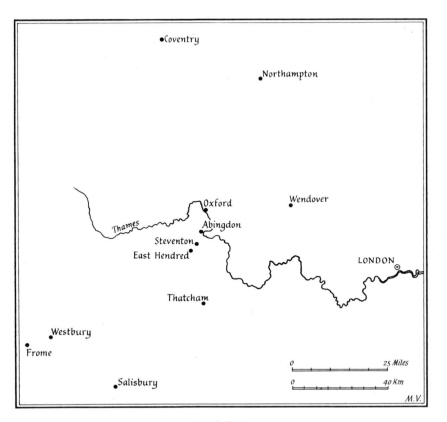

Map Eight
The Revolt of 1431

as our records are concerned, incidence of prosecutions drops away in the following decades. Apart from an action under Bishop Chedworth in the Chilterns in 1462–4, we meet few cases about mid-century.

Recorded prosecutions form a kind of parabola over the course of the fifteenth century—higher in number in the earlier decades, descending in the centre of the period, then rising again in a curve from 1486, when there was an important action in Coventry and Lichfield diocese, to the eve of the Reformation, when Protestantism from the Continent comes in to add another dimension to local heresy, and to complicate the task of the historian of Lollardy.

From 1486 prosecutions started to occur more frequently, and in certain areas they involved a greater number of abjurations— 74 in Coventry and Lichfield in 1511–12,[96] 96 in Salisbury diocese between 1491 and 1521, 300 in Lincoln between 1511 and 1521. The diocese of London, which included Essex as well as the capital, was strongly affected: a high figure may be given for the prosecution there in 1511,[97] 50 for the prosecutions of Fitzjames in 1518, over

[96]Fines, in *JEH*, XIV (1963), p. 161.
[97]For this estimate and the other figures, see Fines, *Studies*, p. 245.

200 (when Protestantism from abroad was already in the field) between 1527 and 1532.[98] If the mid-century lull in our records corresponds to a real lull in prosecutions, we can reconstruct what happened. Pressure from the bishops lessened in the middle years, so Lollardy revived and made more converts; an increased tempo of prosecution was the response, which nonetheless failed to stamp out the heresy.[99] Still a small minority, Lollardy was a tough one. It survived to merge with the new Protestantism.

The Reasons for Survival

Two reasons may be given for this survival, one linked to the interests of the English episcopate, the other to the indigenous qualities of the heresy and the nature of its adherents. Bishops, as we have seen on the Continent, tended to have a less sustained interest in the pursuit of heresy than inquisitors had; in England at this time they had multifarious duties and political commitments; some were absentees. It is therefore not surprising that only a proportion of them took active steps against Lollardy. Moreover, the proceedings that they did take were not of the drastically efficient, repeated kind that could uproot a heretical group altogether, without leaving a remnant that would start to evangelize once the pressure was lifted.

The individual, truly thorough investigations occasionally recorded throw into relief the deficiencies of the majority of episcopal prosecutions. At Norwich Bishop Alnwick kept at his task from 1428 to 1431, ensured that the forceful leader of the Norwich heresy, William White, was captured and burnt, and saw to it that those who abjured each had a copy of their abjuration to take home with them as a reminder of penalties that might occur for relapse.[100] Other members of the episcopate did not proceed with the same thoroughness. One wonders whether the efficiency at Norwich is responsible for the fact that we hear no more of heresy there after Alnwick's action. In Coventry the well-conducted investigation of 1511–12 brought 74 before the court, of whom only 45 were sufficiently deeply involved to be mentioned by name.[101] Coventry was a strong centre; but it also looks as if a thorough drive was uncovering the connections of heresy in a way that was not usual elsewhere.

For a series of prosecutions in England, our records give us only a trickle of abjurations, probably pruning some, but never all, of the branches of a local grouping, and so leaving a residue to grow again. Mercy as well as inefficiency kept heresy alive, maintaining an English distinction between relapse *vere* and *ficte*, which put off the final penalty and helped to keep missionaries in the field.[102] Heresy tended to be uncovered by chance. The routine of archidiaconal visitations of Kentish textile villages in the years before 1511

[98]A. G. Dickens, *Lollards and Protestants,* p. 8, and in his survey, 'Heresy and Origins', pp. 55–6; cf. Thomson, *Later Lollards,* pp. 137–8, 170–1.

[99]Fines's hypothesis (*JEH,* xiv (1963), p. 160); support for a comparable view in J. F. Davis, 'Lollards, Reformers and St Thomas of Canterbury', *UBHJ,* ix (1963), pp. 1–15, at p. 6; verdict of 'not proven' by Thomson, *Later Lollards,* p. 3.

[100]Fines, *Studies,* pp. 74–9, 83–6, Thomson, *Later Lollards,* pp. 131–2.

[101]Fines, in *JEH,* xiv (1963), p. 161; Thomson (*Later Lollards,* p. 109) shows there were more guilty than this.

[102]J. F. Davis, loc. cit.

give no hint that there was heresy there at all; yet, when a drive was launched in 1511, it became clear that it was rife among them.[103] Perhaps the inclusion of heresy among the commissions of vicars-general at the end of the fifteenth century improved the situation; in general, however, the launching of prosecutions remained quite fitful and spasmodic for most of the period.

The other factor preserving Lollardy was its appeal to the craftsman, the skilled artisan and his family who, the residual upper class support cut off, became the carrying class of the sect in its terminal phase. A Lollard community was above all a reading community, basing its common life on the public and private reading of the Scriptures and of Lollard tracts. At Coventry the sect came together for readings, either in twos, with a teacher helping a new convert, or in small groups.[104] In the Norwich group Margery Baxter had her husband read aloud to her in bed at night 'from a book of the law of Christ.[105] Lollard schools gave specific instruction, perhaps inculcating the aphorisms which conveyed beliefs to neophytes and illiterates.[106] Copying and distribution kept the Scriptures and the heretical literature in being, a jump ahead of authority, which tried but never succeeded in gathering it all in. The inner membership conducted their activities in an atmosphere of earnest study—which was exactly what would attract a type of recruit frequent among the skilled artisans. A reading sect had a natural appeal to a class in which literacy was incipient, and which included hard-working, independent people anxious to learn and to form judgements for themselves.

Conditions of work for the skilled man, who in order to gain an apprenticeship and earn a living was forced to move about, helped evangelization by person-to-person contact and kept loose links between the major Lollard areas; for example, John Jonson, the Birmingham cutler caught in 1511 in the ordinary course of pursuing his craft, had moved from his birthplace near York to London to be apprenticed, then migrated in turn to Coventry, Gloucester, Bristol, Taunton and other places, then to London, Maidstone and finally back to Coventry and Birmingham.[107] Lollard meetings could easily be disguised as trade contacts.[108] In one interesting example, industry itself formed the matrix of heresy, when Thomas Moon of Loddon, a glover, used his workplace to influence employees. There Lollardy passed from the laity to the clergy, as John Pert, a reader in the school built up at Loddon under Moon's influence, in turn initiated Hugh Pie, chaplain at Loddon.[109] Mobility imposed itself on a veteran evangelist, helping him to keep ahead of persecution, while at the same time possession of a skill helped him to move round the country. So James Willis the weaver, burnt in 1462,

---

[103]Thomson, *Later Lollards*, p. 190; on vicars-general and heresy, see Davis, ibid., p. 3.
[104]Fines, ibid., p. 166.
[105]Thomson, *Later Lollards*, p. 130.
[106]Fines's hypothesis (ibid., p. 167).
[107]Fines, ibid., p. 163.
[108]Does this explain the prominence of skilled men in underground movements? See J. F. Davis, 'Lollard Survival and the Textile Industry in the South-East of England', in *SCH*, III, pp. 191–201, at p. 196, citing analogy of skilled men in popular radicalism in eighteenth-century Austria.
[109]Fines, *Studies*, p. 54.

long eluded capture by changing his residence from one Lollard centre to another, from Bristol to London and finally to the Chilterns, confessing in Lent and taking communion at Easter, all the while instructing followers and keeping his copies of Lollard literature.[110] A few dedicated men of this kind were a mainstay of the movement at the end, whose vitality rested on the determined missionary.

Lollard beliefs might descend in great secrecy, as in the Morden family at Chesham in the Chilterns, where Richard Ashford, son-in-law of John Morden, knew nothing of his father-in-law's hidden beliefs till the old man opened his heart to him on his death-bed, initiating Ashford in a heresy he retained till his capture in 1521.[111] In another case in Coventry, a daughter was brought by her mother to the heretical household of the Laudesdales to be read to from a large book; years later she brought her husband to the same house to receive instruction.[112] Such family affiliations might keep the heresy going. Leading personalities, however, were needed to make converts in larger numbers and to efface the effects of anti-heresy drives. Occasionally we catch glimpses of these key men in action: for example, William White in East Anglia, tackling the problems of a congregation of limited literacy by vivid demonstration, employing a layman to celebrate the eucharist at Easter in place of himself, despite the fact that he was in orders, or quasi-ceremonially eating cold sausages with his followers on Good Friday to defy the Church's ordinance on fasting.[113] What must have been a personal charisma is now lost to us but implicit in results, in the case of Thomas Man, long resident in the Chilterns, who claimed that he and his wife had converted between five and seven hundred followers. No doubt he exaggerated, but there was a core of truth, for a witness at his second trial in 1518 said that he had instructed followers at Amersham, Billericay, Chelmsford, Stratford Langthorne, Uxbridge, Burnley, Burnham, Henley, Newbury and London, as well as in Suffolk and Norfolk.[114]

Whether the psychology of the convert was affected by the circumstances of his work it is now impossible to say. Where the records allow us to check occupations, they lie most frequently in the textile industry, this being the biggest employer of skilled workers in England.[115] Weavers as such are not specially prominent. As the master clothier emerged, employing his own labour and depressing the status of the once-independent worker to that of a wage-earner subject to dismissal, so circumstances of work for many deteriorated. The sources do not allow us to say whether many Lollards were seeking a psychological refuge from a disadvantageous economic position in

[110]Thomson, *Later Lollards*, pp. 34, 68–71, 152, 236n, 242. He abjured at the end, when he could not have hoped this would save his life.

[111]Ibid., pp. 90–1.

[112]Ibid., p. 110; Fines, in *JEH*, xiv (1963), pp. 165–7, 171.

[113]'Cold sausages' is Fines's translation (*Studies*, p. 54); aphorisms mentioned as teaching aid in *JEH*, xiv (1963), pp. 166–7.

[114]Thomson, *Later Lollards*, pp. 170–1, Dickens, 'Heresy and Origins', p. 58.

[115]The most determined attempt at statistics by Davis in *SCH* iii, pp. 191–201. I owe advice to Mr H. B. Clark. Skilled artisans in East Anglia 1428–31 in Fines, *Studies*, p. 60; in Coventry 1511–12, Fines, in *JEH*, xiv (1963), p. 162. Occupations are not necessarily given in sources.

an underground religion preaching religious equality;[116] we have no positive hint that this was so, though the possibility cannot be excluded. The number of prominent Lollards who had servants points against this view; more significant is the evidence that, broadly speaking, Lollardy survived in regions where it had already laid down support before 1414, at a time of greater prosperity for textile workers. A living tradition of Lollardy went on attracting recruits, whether work circumstances changed or not. The assumptions and outlook of the craftsman,[117] which made a minority susceptible to the Lollard mission, were what counted.

Class Structure and Distribution

The attractions of Lollardy to the artisan class worked in two ways. On the one hand, they gave it endurance within the Scripture-reading circle after the disaster of 1414; on the other, they made it more difficult for the heresy ever again to climb higher in the social scale. Adaptation to the needs of artisan circles accompanied, and was a consequence of, the diminution of the academic leadership. Oxford had been purged originally by Courtenay, then again by Archbishop Arundel in 1411, and the doors to academic recruitment thereby closed. Academically-trained men of an older generation who stayed in the field were whittled away in time. Peter Payne, an academic latecomer of considerable talents, left for Bohemia after he had been cited for heresy in the reaction after Oldcastle;[118] his logic pupil, Ralph Mungyn, worked on till he was condemned to life imprisonment in 1428;[119] the veteran Wyche was burnt in 1440.[120] By mid-century, though occasional conversion from within the religious orders brought in trained men, leadership was in the hands of unbeneficed clergy, generally of limited learning, and laymen, self-taught or instructed in Lollard schools. These could speak to their own kind; but they could not compose, and so new Lollard texts did not emerge, the only exceptions in the present state of knowledge being the lost tracts of William White from the 1420s and Wyclif's *Wicket*, for which a date of 1470 has been suggested.[121] Nor could they easily carry the heresy higher in the social scale. The association between Lollardy and sedition kept those of gentle blood away, and fresh recruits in that class were not made.[122] Wealthier business circles were not touched outside London, on the eve of the Reformation where

[116]This forms one of the explanations of Lollard survival discussed by Davis, *SCH* III: see esp., pp. 198–201.

[117]Dickens brings out the significance of artisan membership: see intro. to his *Lollards and Protestants*. In 'Heresy and Origins' he comments on 'cranks and individualists' (p.48), artisan mobility (p. 57), 'increasing . . . mental independence' (p. 64).

[118]Below, p. 330, Emden, *Biographical Register, Oxford*. R. R. Betts, *Essays in Czech History* (London, 1969), pp. 236–46.

[119]Thomson, *Later Lollards*, pp. 143–5.

[120]Ibid., pp. 148–50.

[121]Perspective given in M. E. Aston, 'Lollardy and the Reformation', and on *Wicket*, see her remarks in *PP* xxx (1965), pp. 37–8; on White's tracts, see Fines, *Studies*, p. 52.

[122]That is, in England. Some thirty persons in the late fifteenth century in Kyle and Cunningham, Ayrshire, including gentry and members of the court circle, were accused of Lollardy (Thomson, *Later Lollards*, pp. 204–7). Scotland did not undergo the experience of Oldcastle's revolt. But were the accusations justified? Early Lollard history in Scotland is obscure. Linguistic barriers existed, but there would have been points of entry for influences from England in the ports of the east coast and the universities. I owe information to Mr D. V. Murdoch.

M.V.

Inset A

Ashley Green
Princes Risborough
Missenden
Chesham
Little Missenden
Chesham Bois
Chinnor
Amersham
Hughenden
Stoken-church
West Wycombe
Turville
Wycombe
Penn
Beaconsfield
Harrow
Hedgerley
Hambleden
Great Marlow
Denham
Bisham
Cookham
Uxbridge
Henley
Burnham Abbey
Maidenhead
Iver
Bray
Dorney
Chalvey
Fifield
Windsor
Ankerwick

Ashbourne

Trent

Wigginton

Leicest

Birmingham

Coventry

Alcester

Worcester

Byfield

Almeley
Eardisley

Avon

Wye

Staunton

Walford
Norton Underhill
Hasleton
Micheldean
Gloucester
Windrush
Kidlington
Burford
Asthall
Severn
Witney
Thame
Lydney
Lechlade
Buscot
Faringdon
Steventon
Aylburton
Coxwell
W.Hendred
E.Hendred
Brightw
Pembroke
Woolaston
Wantage
Wallingfor
Letcombe Basset
Letcombe Regis
He

Portishead
Avon
Bristol
Turleigh
Broughton
Gifford
Hungerford
Speen
Rea
Bath
Bradford
Newbury
Wrington
Devizes
Marden
Pewsey
Woodhay
Hinton
Keevil
Wilsford
Norton St Philip
Rode
Steeple
Chirton
Dogmersf
Leigh
Beckington
Ashton
Odiha
Wells
Holcombe
Netheravon
Cror
Marston Bigot

Test

Salisbury
Winchester

Taunton
Meonstoke

0 ————————————— 50 Miles
0 ————————————— 80 Km

Wrington• *Heretics detected*
Taunton• *Heretics with suspect English books*

Map Nine
Lollardy Underground
(For gazetteer and notes, see appendix D section 2)

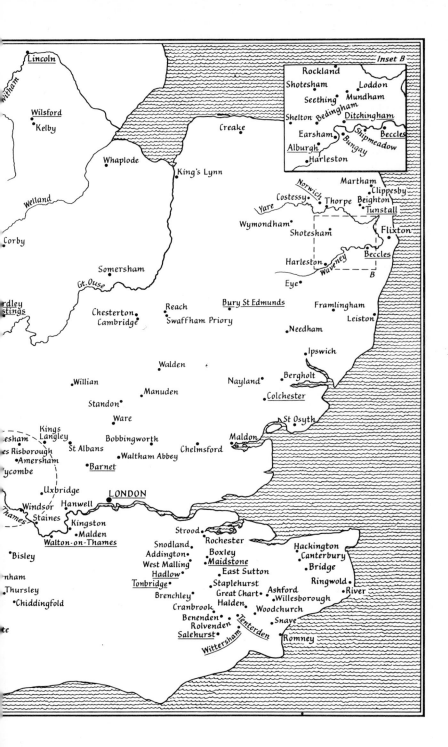

Rockland
Shotesham
Loddon
Seething
Mundham
Shelton
Bedingham
Ditchingham
Earsham
Shipmeadow
Beccles
Alburgh
Bungay
Harleston

B

Lincoln

Wilsford
Kelby

Creake

Whaplode
King's Lynn

Welland

Martham
Clippesby
Norwich
Costessy
Thorpe
Beighton
Yare
Tunstall
Wymondham
Flixton
Shotesham

Corby

Harleston
Waveney
Beccles

Somersham
B
Gt. Ouse
Eye

rdley
stings

Reach
Bury St Edmunds
Framlingham
Chesterton
Swaffham Priory
Leiston
Cambridge
Needham

Ipswich

Walden

Willian
Berghost
Nayland
Manuden
Colchester
Standon
Ware
St Osyth

Kings
Langley
Maldon
esham
Bobbingworth
s Risborough
St Albans
Chelmsford
Amersham
Waltham Abbey
ycombe
Barnet

Uxbridge
LONDON
Windsor
Hanwell
Staines
Kingston
Thames
Malden
Strood
Walton-on-Thames
Rochester
Snodland
Hackington
Bisley
Addington
Boxley
Canterbury
West Malling
Maidstone
Bridge
nham
Hadlow
East Sutton
Thursley
Tonbridge
Staplehurst
Ringwold
Chiddingfold
Brenchley
Great Chart
Ashford
River
Cranbrook
Halden
Willesborough
Benenden
Woodchurch
te
Rolvenden
Tenterden
Snave
Salehurst
Romney
Wittersham

the city's perennial financial quarrels with the Church helped to create the ambience for Lollardy,[123] and to a lesser degree in Coventry, where some richer men's interest can be dimly glimpsed about the time of the 1511–12 trials.[124] The overall picture is of a sect able both to survive and to grow at a certain level of society, but not able to break much fresh ground, socially or intellectually.

Map 9, which plots prosecutions for heresy between 1414 and 1522, illustrates this underground phase of Lollard history. Three inferences may be made from it. One is that Lollardy survived, broadly, in the same regions where it had lodged before 1414, and did not, it would seem, open up new ones. As Thomson has shown, Lollardy after 1414 was to be found in seven regional groupings, based in Kent, London, the Chilterns and the mid-Thames Valley, Bristol and the West Country, the Midlands, especially Coventry, Essex and East Anglia, with lesser clusters in Hampshire, and the Forest of Dean. As far as we can see, it was a southern survival. We know that at the time of Richard Wyche's trial in 1403 a community existed in the Newcastle area.[125] So many northern registers for the period have disappeared that it is impossible to say whether it lived on or not, and whether heresy was so exclusively a southern phenomenon. Oldcastle's revolt, for reasons of geography if nothing else, had no northern participants; it too was a southern phenomenon, and its rebel-bearing regions correspond fairly to those of Lollard survivial after 1414: London, the Chilterns and mid-Thames valley, Bristol, the Midlands and Essex all sent rebels to Oldcastle and produced heretics after that date. One oddity is Kent, almost blank for the rebellion, although Oldcastle should have had a local following through the Cobham estates he held there, and it was fertile for heresy later. The other is East Anglia, which contained heresy on some scale in the 1420s; it may be blank for the rebellion merely because of its isolation from London.[126] In sum, however, there is a geographical correspondence between the rebellion and the post-1414 heresy.

Examination of the gazetteer to the map, which lists the dates of prosecutions, as recorded in registers and court books, against the heretics' places of origin, demonstrates further how continuity was maintained until the Reformation. Within the seven regions prosecutions continued to be launched at varying intervals through the period; only in East Anglia do they come more or less to a stop. Persecution, in other words, was ineffective in eliminating heresy from at any rate six of the seven major regions.

Sometimes there are long periods between drives; the area of the Chilterns was only investigated vigorously on three occasions, by Chedworth in 1462–4, Smith in 1511, and Longland in 1521–2, yet it produced substantial hauls of heretics every time; from the well-documented prosecutions of 1462–4 and

[123]Dickens, 'Heresy and Origins', pp. 54–6; for earlier cases in London, see Thomson, *Later Lollards*, pp. 85–6, 156–7 (I prefer 'rich' as translation of *locupletes* (p. 85n.); background given in J. A. F. Thomson, 'Tithe disputes in later medieval London', *EHR*, LXXVII (1963), pp. 1–17.
[124]I. Luxton, 'The Lichfield Court Book: a Postscript', *BIHR*, XLIV (1971), pp. 120–5. I owe this ref. to Dr. J. A. F. Thomson. See also C. Cross in *SCH* XI (below, p. 391).
[125]M. G. Snape, 'Some Evidence of Lollard Activity in the Diocese of Durham in the Early Fifteenth Century', *Archaeologia Aeliana*, 4th ser., XXXIX (1961), pp. 355–61.
[126]McFarlane, *Wycliffe*, p. 173.

1521–2 we can distinguish a number of places as fertile in heresy in the last prosecution as in the first, despite the intervening lapse of time.[127] Often individual towns and villages have but one or two prosecutions recorded. This, however, can be somewhat deceptive. Episcopal registers, the staple source of evidence, tend to give places of origin less profusely than the rarer heresy court books. So if we must use registers alone, our source may give us, for example, only a selection of principal places and omit to mention lesser villages. The evidence, dependent as it is on the chances of detection and the survival of judicial records, is fragmentary and discontinuous; so the gazetteer, based on this evidence, necessarily tends to underestimate the degree of continuity of prosecutions in localities.

Certain notorious centres of heresy emerge nonetheless from the evidence we have: London at the top of the list, partly because it was the focal point of a large diocese and refugees from elsewhere fled to anonymity there;[128] Bristol, with a striking continuity and evidence of survival in certain districts, especially the Redcliffe area;[129] Tenterden, the Kentish textile village where White probably laid down a tradition;[130] Coventry, active in heresy and in the revolt of 1431.[131]

Another inference to be drawn from the map is that prosecutions in the seven regions of survival were generally launched against individuals or groups involved in Lollardy rather than against anticlericals or isolated heretics unconnected with the movement.[132] Heresy drives give us for a moment, it is true, a glimpse of the religious sentiments in an area, not all of which fall neatly into the rival categories of Lollardy or orthodoxy. Endemic anticlericalism was the milieu in which Lollardy floated and a convert passed through personal contact with a committed member from anti-Church views of an uncoordinated kind into a deeper involvement. The laconic entries of the episcopal register do not always enable us to draw this line, which in reality must often have been ambiguous.

One criterion of high reliability does exist, however, and has been noticed on the map. When prosecutions record the presence of suspect vernacular books in a locality, we can feel a measure of confidence that we are on the trail of a Lollard reading-circle, for these books were most commonly the tracts and Scriptures of the heretics rather than innocent vernacular works of piety such as *Nicodemus* or *Dives and Pauper*. Records of the presence of these books

---

[127]Fines, *Studies*, pp. 102–9, 157–205; Thomson, *Later Lollards*, ch. 3.

[128]Thomson, ibid., pp. 139, 155, 236.

[129]Ibid., pp. 22, 25, 26, 28, 33, 34 (see also 35), 39, 44, 46, 47; compare entries for 1448 and 1511–12 (a group active c. 1505–6) and note evidence of a continuity over half a century in the Redcliffe area; note also that the longest gap in prosecutions lies between 1457 and 1476, a time of general slackening of prosecution in England. Social composition in Bristol (according to Thomson) is as follows: 1420 2 priests; 1423 one of the same priests (William Taylor); 1448 weaver (unnamed), smith; 1476 three men (no details); 1511–12 (a group active c. 1505–6) carpetmaker, wiredrawer and others, no information for 1429, 1441, 1448 (case of William Fuer of Gloucester), 1457, 1499.

[130]Ibid., pp. 173, 174, 175–6, 178 (somewhat tentatively), 180, 187–9.

[131]Ibid., pp. 101 (John Grace, called a 'false prophet', but not a Lollard): see Aston, 'Lollardy and Sedition'. p. 14 and n. 70, 104–6, 107–16, for 1489 prosecution, see Fines, *Studies*, p. 129, and for 1511–12, *JEH*, xiv (1963), pp. 160–74.

[132]For cases of individual heresy in the fourteenth century, see below, p. 269.

are to be found in every one of the seven major regions in which Lollardy survived; in some they lie thickly, and prosecutions of suspects with books, as the gazetteer reveals, occur repeatedly over the years in the same places. True Lollardy formed the core of the cases in these regions up to the eve of the Reformation.

One further inference may be that Lollardy, by and large, survived in artisan circles, for the map demonstrates that the clusters of heresy-bearing localities lie in the areas of high population where industry had been developed. Only two regions significant in the development of the textile industry, York and the south Cotswolds, are either omitted or scantily represented; the gap in the former region may be due to *lacunae* in the surviving records, and in the latter to the lack of prosecuting zeal of the bishops of Worcester.

Together, map and gazetteer tend to underestimate the extent of the Lollard survival. No doubt, despite some sifting of the sources, the prosecutions still include some of mere sceptics, anticlericals and idiosyncratic heretics, but the exaggeration of the survival of true Lollardy which ensues must be more than offset by the contrary effects of defective source material. Many episcopal registers have been lost; others list no heresy, not because it did not exist, but because bishops and their officers did not detect, and perhaps were uninterested in pursuing it. There are curious blanks. Wales, into which Swinderby and Brute disappeared, has but two cases: of a priest and a layman at Pembroke in 1486 and 1488.[133] Was this due to absence of heresy, aided by the linguistic barrier over part of the region, or to ecclesiastical disorganization? One cannot say. The Welsh March is another puzzling area, for the region that included Oldcastle's seat and had once been Swinderby's campaigning ground might have been expected to have a later history of Lollardy, yet it is mute in the revolt of 1414 and has evidence of only two subsequent prosecutions: one at Almeley in Oldcastle's estates in 1433, and another at Eardisley in 1505,[134] both revealing the presence of suspect books. The border area was later of importance in the history of Nonconformity,[135] and registers for crucial periods are missing: there is a presumption that there was more Lollardy in the March than the map reveals.

It must be emphasized that the map is simply a pictorial record of the evidence of prosecutions of Lollards and other religious dissidents in the extant registers and court-books; used with care, it gives us a blurred outline of the heresy underground, but never the complete picture. A map of the Marian martyrs, compiled exclusively from Foxe's record of their sufferings,[136] is included here for purposes of comparison; it shows the major

[133]Thomson, *Lollards*, pp. 44–5, The priest was Irish.

[134]Ibid., pp. 31–2, 48.

[135]W. T. Morgan, 'The Prosecution of Nonconformists in the Consistory Courts of St Davids, 1661–88' *Journal of the Historical Society of the Church in Wales*, xii (1962), pp. 28–53; on Herefordshire parishes, pp. 30–1; note how Nonconformists, like Lollards earlier (Thomson, *Lollards*, pp. 1–2), tended to live near boundaries of jurisdiction. I owe information to Mr W. T. Morgan.

[136]See Appendix D, s. 3. I owe the idea of making the comparison to Mr D. Bethell, and the work of compiling it to my wife. I am indebted to Dr D. M. Loades for information.

difference between Marian and late medieval persecution and between the conduct of Marian and earlier Lollard suspects. The persecution was much more intense; according to Foxe 285 people were burnt in this short reign, between 1553 and 1558, and the intensity of activity is still greater than these facts would suggest, for there were no executions for religious opinions in the first nineteen months of the reign, to 3 February 1555.[137] The map is concerned solely with burnings, crammed into a space of three years and nine months and concentrated in London and the home counties, its victims being largely of humbler classes. There is no equivalent of this in the long Lollard history for, although a series of executions followed Oldcastle's revolt, these were primarily for armed rebellion rather than heresy, and no individual Lollard prosecution produced anything like such totals of executions in so short a time. The will of individual bishops such as Foxe's 'Dick of Dover' or local gentry to pursue suspects affected the incidence of prosecution in localities; but behind the operation as a whole lay the determination of Mary and her clerical advisers, reared in Spanish Counter-Reformation Catholicism, to uproot Protestantism. There was less inclination to mercy or leniency by judges than in the case of Lollards, and less inclination by the suspects, gathered in organized churches of their own,[138] to recant as the Lollards had done.

Late Lollard Beliefs

Life underground and the disillusionment of 1414, perhaps of 1431 also, largely stripped the sedition from Lollardy. Willy nilly, Lollards found themselves in some opposition to the State as it backed the demands on them of the Church, but they mostly gave up conspiracy. An apocalyptic tradition, one strand among the beliefs, though not a dominant one,[139] comforted some with the expectation of change in their favour; this was especially the case in a group at Newbury, uncovered in 1490–1.[140] In 1448 William Fuer of Gloucester expected war with the Catholics but, being pacifist, would not participate himself.[141] Lollards no longer planned to bring about conflict on behalf of their faith. There was no one left to call the regional groupings together, which existed without much knowledge of each other; individual contacts there were, and an evangelist might keep in contact with two, even three, regions, but nobody any longer knew them all. Survival, rather than military or political victory, was the immediate concern.

Late Lollards were not very conscious of Wyclif, but his legacy still helped them. The concept of the Scriptures as a divine exemplar, existing before the creation, had worked on the minds of the early Lollards and clerical

[137]For details of burnings and policy, see J. H. Blunt, *The Reformation of the Church of England 1547–1662*, II (London, 1882), ch. 5; modern analysis in A. G. Dickens, *The English Reformation*, (London, 1964), pp. 264–72.

[138]P. Collinson, *The Elizabethan Puritan Movement*, (London, 1967), p. 24.

[139]Cf. Davis, in *SCH* III, p. 200; Thomson, *Lollards*, pp. 240–1.

[140]Thomson, ibid., p. 78; note reference to prophecy of Lollard victory in a book known in East Anglia, p. 131.

[141]Ibid., p. 36.

Map Ten A
The Marian Martyrs in England

missionaries;[142] the effect of this belief in the final phase, however little
ordinary followers could have grappled with the realist philosophy which
underlay it, was to provide comfort in persecution. Its effect was to substitute
for the authority of the Church the infallibility of Scripture; Wyclif's doctrine
of the Church acted in a similar fashion. The visible and hierarchical Church
which persecuted the Lollards was the Church of Antichrist; the true Church
became the congregation of true believers.

Investigatory procedure made Lollardy sound very negative. An
interrogator subjected the suspect to a series of standard questions, negative
replies on orthodox points being recorded to be used as the basis for
convictions.[143] Three denials of Catholic belief and practice recur: on the
veneration of images, on pilgrimages, and on the mass.[144] The basis for the
denials often lay in a simple logic. John Morden of Chesham in

[142]I am indebted to Professor M. Deanesly for this comment in a private letter; see also her view
in *JEH*, XVII (1966), p. 266.
[143]Thomson, *Lollards*, pp. 224–6, 228–9; on Coventry, a typical case, Fines, in *JEH*, XIV (1963),
pp. 169–71. For trial records, see A. Hudson, 'The Examination of Lollards,' *BIHR*, XLVI (1973),
pp. 145–59.
[144]Thomson, ibid., p. 91 (note comment, p. 126).

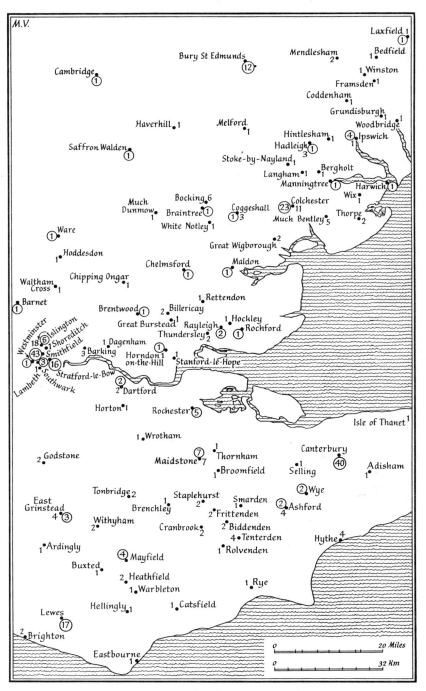

M.V.

Laxfield 1
Mendlesham 2
Bedfield 1
Bury St Edmunds (12)
Winston 1
Framsden 1
Coddenham 1
Cambridge (1)
Grundisburgh 1
Woodbridge 1
Haverhill 1
Melford 1
Hintlesham 1
Ipswich (4)
Hadleigh 3
Saffron Walden (1)
Stoke-by-Nayland 1
Bergholt 1
Langham 1
Manningtree (1)
Harwich (1)
Much Dunmow 1
Bocking 6
Wix 1
Braintree (1)
Coggeshall (1) 3
Colchester (23) 11
Thorpe 2
White Notley 1
Much Bentley 5
Ware (1)
Great Wigborough 2
Hoddesdon 1
Chelmsford (1)
Maldon (1)
Waltham Cross 1
Chipping Ongar 1
Barnet (1)
Rettendon 1
Westminster
18 (6) Islington
Shoreditch
Brentwood (1)
Billericay 2
Hockley 1
43 Smithfield
Great Burstead 1
Rayleigh (1)
Rochford
(1) (3) (16)
1 Dagenham
Thundersley 2
(2)
Lambeth Southwark
3 Barking
Horndon on-the-Hill 1
Stanford-le-Hope 1
Stratford-le-Bow
(2)
2 Dartford
Horton 1
Rochester (5)
Isle of Thanet 1
Wrotham 1
Godstone 2
Maidstone (7) 7
Thornham 1
Canterbury
Broomfield 1
Selling 1
(40)
Adisham 1
Tonbridge 2
Staplehurst 2
Smarden 1
Wye (2)
East Grinstead 4 (3)
Brenchley 1
Frittenden 2
Ashford (2) 4
Withyham 2
Cranbrook 2
Biddenden 2
Tenterden 4
Hythe 4
Ardingly 1
Rolvenden 1
Mayfield (4)
Buxted 1
Heathfield 2
Warbleton 1
Rye 1
Hellingly 1
Catsfield 1
Lewes (17)
Brighton 2
Eastbourne 1

0 ————————————— 20 Miles
0 ————————————— 32 Km

Map Ten B
The Marian Martyrs in England (Detail)
(For gazetteer and notes, see appendix D, section 3)

Buckinghamshire, explaining his beliefs about the mass to his still orthodox son-in-law, said, 'Thou are deceived, for it can nothing profit thee; for it is but bread and wine; and so it is when the priest began with it at mass, and so it is when the mass is ended.'[145] Alice Rowley at Coventry seized on the priests' gain from mass offerings to call the service a 'pretty falsehood' of the priests which enabled them to buy the bread for the Hosts and then to sell it at a higher price.[146] In East Anglia Margery Baxter resorted to a coarse *reductio ad absurdum* to attack transubstantiation.[147]

Morden's statement on images was similar to his view of the mass. 'They are but stocks and stones,' he said. 'for they cannot help themselves, how can they help thee? And the worshipping of them is but idolatry.'[148] On images the appeal to the unvarnished text of Scripture was potent. John Burell, of the East Anglian Lollards, appealed to the decalogue to dismiss the medieval practice of veneration.[149] Dislike of pilgrimages was bound up with the attack on this veneration, since representations and relics of the saints were the customary goal of the pilgrim's journey. In East Anglia the crucifix was attacked in terms oddly reminiscent of the Bogomils; 'no more credence should be done to the crucifix', it was said, 'than to the gallows which thieves be hanged on.'[150] At Coventry the focus for discontent lay in a particular image of Our Lady.[151] Pilgrimage centres received sarcastic names: among the East Anglian group Canterbury became 'Cankerbury'.[152] James Willis disapproved of church music and bellringing; in East Anglia church bells were described as 'Antichrist's horns'.[153] There is a recurrent feeling that the Church's demands on the faithful were unnecessary, a mumbo jumbo dictated by the desire of priests to get money or gain their own ends. Pilgrimages were rejected on the grounds that they involved waste of money.[154]

Beyond the three best-known denials, different Lollards attacked various other sacraments. In East Anglia during Alnwick's prosecutions, and again in London in 1499, marriage as a ceremony was rejected as superfluous: the basis lay in the belief that the will of the two parties was sufficient, without the presence of priest or any formal ceremony.[155] Dislike of ceremonies and mortuary fees lay behind the rejection of the need for burial in consecrated ground, implicit in the statement of Thomas Whyte of Ringwold in Kent in 1473, that it was as good for his soul if his body were buried in a marsh as in a cemetery.[156] Objections to the practice of baptism by a priest in church were

---

[145]Ibid., p. 91, spelling modernized, as in later quotations.

[146]Fines, in *JEH*, XIV (1963), p. 166.

[147]False gods eaten by the priests, who later 'emittunt eosdem per posteriores in sepibus turpibus sedentes' (Fines, *Studies*, p. 67, n. 3).

[148]Thomson, *Lollards*, p. 91.

[149]Ibid., p. 126.

[150]Fines, *Studies*, p. 63; above p. 17.

[151]Thomson, *Lollards*, pp. 104, 112.

[152]Ibid., p. 126.

[153]Ibid., p. 69; Fines, *Studies*, p. 63.

[154]See Fines's comment (*Studies*, p. 250).

[155]Thomson, *Lollards*, pp. 127, 159. Is there any analogy to this in the case of Ramsbury (above, p. 239)?

[156]Ibid., p. 183.

expressed by two men from Lydney in 1470, who said it could be done as well in a ditch as in a font.[157] This was an aphorism with a long history, for it is met in the confession of James Willis at his last trial in 1462, and in the confession of William Bull, the Dewsbury shearman, in 1543.[158] In a sense this was not heresy, but rather an objection to a canonical practice. A rejection of baptism altogether occurs in the East Anglian group, always one of the most radical, on the grounds that a child was redeemed in any case by Christ's blood;[159] rejection of sacraments or ceremonies of the Church was the message of the aphorisms of the sect, couched in terms that would be familiar to workers, in towns or on the land. For a Dewsbury shearman the font was a 'stinking tarn';[160] for a Lollard at Steeple Ashton in Wiltshire in 1488 it would be better to be sprinkled with lake water than holy water if the priest was a sinner;[161] for another at Kevill (Keevil) in 1506, Ball the carpenter could make as good images as those which were worshipped.[162] The 'better than' or 'as good as' of these comparisons is characteristic of the wry, sardonic religious egalitarianism of the typical heretic.

The appeal to reason could have odd results. Beside the standard views, we meet now and again quite idiosyncratic beliefs, such as that of John Edward in the Newbury area, who believed that Our Lady conceived and bore another son after Christ's ascension; or that of John Wodeward of Wigginton, near Tamworth, who was against baptism because there was no baptism before the time of Christ.[163] Such ideas can hardly have been inculcated in the reading sessions of the movement. Sometimes the opening of the Scriptures led to the development of odd personal views; sometimes an eccentric parishioner was attracted to the Lollard circle. Or concern with heresy alerted authority to doctrinal deviations unconnected with Lollardy which existed under the surface. Heresy did exist in England before Lollardy and some twelve cases, of scepticism, idiosyncratic belief, perhaps mental unbalance, not connected with any organization, have been uncovered in published records between 1300 and 1370.[164] Then there was no need for a doctrinal alert; after Wyclif and the turn to active persecution, more of such casual cases might come to light.

The tone of Lollardy, sceptical, ironical, highly suspicious of emotion, kept the members of congregations from exaggerated eschatological views.[165] Unlike the frontier Protestants of the American mid-west, the Lollards read their Scriptures within an orthodox ambience however much they kicked

[157]Ibid., p. 41.

[158]Ibid., p. 69; Dickens, *Lollards and Protestants*, p. 48.

[159]Thomson, *Lollards*, p. 127; Fines, *Studies*, p. 66.

[160]Dickens, *Lollards and Protestants*, p. 69.

[161]Thomson, *Lollards*, p. 45.

[162]Ibid., p. 83.

[163]Ibid., pp. 76–7, 104. Comment in K. Thomas, *Religion and the Decline of Magic* (London, 1961), p. 168.

[164]J. Fines's calculation (*Studies*, pp. 8–16). F. Makower, *The Constitutional History and Constitution of the Church of England* (London, 1895), pp. 183–94. See cases of Margaret Syward in I. J. Churchill, *Canterbury Administration* (London, 1933), I, pp. 313–4; Ralph Tremur, in *Exeter Episcopal Registers: Register John de Grandisson*, ed. F. C. Hingeston–Randolph II (London, 1897), pp. 1147–9, 1179–81; summary in Manning, p. 70.

[165]Thomson, *Lollards*, p. 249. It is one of Thomson's services to have clarified this point.

against it; they did not have the Bible and no other culture or background at all, as did the American pioneers, and so were not inclined, as they were, to arrogate to themselves the rights and obligations of Moses and the Old Testament prophets.[166] There is no sign of the gathering of artisans round a teacher claiming special divine inspiration.[167] or of the wildness, springing from an obsessive concern for the biblical text, such as apparently led the Presbyterians of Halmadary near Strathnaver in the Scottish highlands close to performing human sacrifice about 1740 in imitation of Abraham and Isaac.[168] Persecution did not produce the state of exaltation which Manselli rightly distinguishes in the later stages of the proceedings against Olivi's followers.[169] Accusations of sexual immorality, frequently launched against Continental heretics, were hardly ever made in England.

Pushed up against orthodox parish life and its ceremonies, which many of them dare not evade, and lacking strong intellectual leadership, it was natural that fifteenth-century Lollards should express their religious feelings in explosive negatives. We hear very little of rites of their own: occasional celebrations of the eucharist, some confessing to each other. Perhaps a ceremony lies behind the Coventry password, 'For we shall all drink of a cuppe'.[170] Whatever Lollard rites did exist, they were not important. The strongest positive part of their life was the reading, the mutual exhortation and the earnest practice of the virtues. The core of their belief lay in the direct contact of the praying, reading adherent with God, based on Scripture and unencumbered by any sort of intermediaries. It was a simple, radical sort of belief, with a spiritualizing view of the sacraments.

Anticlericalism grew stronger. Recourse to the Fathers became less and less feasible; they may even be attacked. The more strictly academic and doctrinal concerns faded. *Scriptura sola* became the norm; the ethical concern, always important, became dominant. Lollardy had adapted to the circumstances of its followers. The swing in Lollard opinion, moving farther away from its founder as time went on, made similarities to Waldensians, especially of the more radical kind, ever more apparent, despite the lack of contact with them and the different origins of English Lollardy. Though Lollards had less explicit doctrine of their own than any other movement to set against the Church, and they lacked any formal distinction between preacher and rank and file, with the special obligations and celibacy of the preachers, yet they had in common with the Waldensians an ethical stress, an emphasis on word rather than sacrament, Biblical translation, and an appeal to artisan membership. Both movements had the power to inspire a line of dedicated evangelists and pastors, more inclined to bow to persecution, so

[166]I owe this comparison to Professor M. Deanesly. Note, however, the contrast between the stable Scripture reading Lollard circles and the effects of Scripture within the Taborite movement (below, pp. 310–11, 315–7, 322–4).

[167]See above, p. 55.

[168]J. MacInnes, *The Evangelical Movement in the Highlands of Scotland, 1688 to 1800* (Aberdeen, 1951), pp. 103–4. I owe the ref. to Mrs T. Maley.

[169]Above, p. 202.

[170]Aston, 'Lollardy and Sedition', p. 13 and notes; Fines (*Studies*, p. 251) argues that most believed in the priesthood of all believers. For eucharistic beliefs, see Thomson, *Lollards*, pp. 82n., 112, 246–7; Fines, in *JEH*, XIV (1963), p. 167.

that they might live to fight another day, than many of the Cathar perfect, but quite as tenacious. On these few men both movements to a large degree rested. Other contributory factors in the survival are the relative leniency of the English tradition of persecution after the reaction to the Oldcastle revolt was spent, and the sporadic character of Waldensian persecution. Possibly, too, the fact that Waldensians rejected the oath and the shedding of blood, and thus were prohibited from entry to the leading classes of medieval society, meant that nobility had no reason to be jealous of them or to covet the lands which could be taken from them after conviction for heresy.

There is much to be said, however, for the view that both late Lollardy and Waldensianism of the Poor Lombard variety were the heresies of the Middle Ages *par excellence*, the perennial religion of the layman from lower classes, who painfully acquired some booklearning or learnt by rote passages of Scripture and passed on by word of mouth his anticlerical, Donatist views, mixed with an earthy scepticism about facets of Catholicism. Even in radical Hussitism, whose history, as we shall see, was so much briefer and more dynamic than that of the Lollards or Waldensians, we meet similar wry aphorisms. Perhaps the durability of both the English and the Continental heresy was due in the last resort to its appeal to this submerged reasoning piety, the beliefs of laymen who had their own devotional life and their own doubts about individual points of doctrine. A Valdes or a Wyclif and their followers could appeal to these sentiments. But they did not call them into being, and, among the multifarious causes of heresy, this body of largely hidden sentiment has been one of the underestimated forces in medieval Church history.

16

The Bohemian Reform Movement

Introduction

At almost the same time that English Lollardy as a political force went down to defeat in Oldcastle's rebellion, a comparable movement of religious dissent, in part stimulated by Wyclif's writings, was shaking the bonds of the distant kingdom of Bohemia. The dramatic but desperate revolt of Oldcastle was the last throw of the native English movement; after it, as we have seen, a residue of Lollards lived on underground by dint of their own tenacity and by courtesy of the lack of determination in persecution of some members of the episcopate. In Bohemia reform and heresy went a great deal farther. Disputes, in which Wyclif's name figured prominently, shook the university of Prague; agitation reached the Bohemian court and the international Church assembled at the council of Constance. At the moment when Henry V's soldiers were hunting down Oldcastle's conspirators, many of the Bohemian nobles were displaying their solidarity with the cause of their native reform leader, Jan Hus. Four or five years later, when Lollardy was reduced to a few of the clergy and some hardy artisan circles in England, its basis in the nobility and merchant classes almost wholly vanished, Hussite supporters were intimidating their opponents and preparing to do battle for their beliefs.

All was not Wyclif in the Bohemian movement—indeed it would be a misnomer to describe Hussitism *tout court* as his child. Nevertheless his ideas played a significant part in the complex of factors underlying the Hussite movement, and some of the religious enthusiasts given free play by the events leading to the revolution shared the ideas of the English Lollards.

The most remarkable feature of Hussitism was its repudiation of the close control of the papacy in doctrinal matters, and its establishment, however briefly and imperfectly, of a measure of religious toleration.

For some seventeen years, between the Defenestration of Prague in 1419 and the acceptance of Sigismund at Jihlava in 1436, and to a lesser degree in the years of struggle before 1419, the older unity of doctrine and canon law in the West under the papacy was, first in practice, then in open defiance, broken in pieces in this one country, and a remarkable range of belief unfolded. The Hussites and their supporters went farther than any other popular religious movement labelled as heresy before the Reformation in shaking the old order, and for this reason demand extended study. The history of their struggle, a failure in the end yet, relatively speaking, the most successful of them all, forms a natural conclusion to a study of the major heretical movements of the Middle Ages.

The Setting[1]

Bohemia was a latecomer to the circle of advanced nations. Under the first Přemyslid rulers it had been hardly more than a frontier province, on the fringe of the Holy Roman Empire; then under the last rulers of the dynasty it advanced more rapidly, aided by the influx of colonists and the growth of the indigenous population, to achieve under the Luxemburgs, above all Charles IV (king, 1346–78), a remarkable flowering of economic, cultural and political life. Charles had been administrator of the country on behalf of his absentee father John; then from 1346 he ruled both as king in Bohemia and as Holy Roman emperor till his death in 1378, and sought to make the country a focal point in his revised conception of the old Empire. With his father, he succeeded in securing the elevation of the see of Prague to metropolitical status; in 1348 he founded the university of Prague as an intellectual centre and training ground for administrators within the Empire; by his addition of the New Town he added greatly to the size and economic significance of his capital; finally, by his summons to the Austrian Augustinian canon Waldhauser to come and preach in his lands, he gave impetus to an indigenous movement of Church reform, the platform from which emerged, after decades of agitation, the Hussite revolution of the fifteenth century.[2]

His own part in sponsoring reform and opening the way for Hussitism is equivocal. On the one hand, many features in Bohemian Church and intellectual life which aided the progress of the movement had their roots in, or were affected by, the policies of his brilliant reign; on the other, his own piety, sincere as it was, remained relatively conventional. He, and the forerunners of Hussitism, whom he sometimes sponsored, did not favour heresy: he was the author of stern decrees against beghards and in favour of the inquisition. Religious feeling and economic interest combined to make him one of the great relic-collectors, and Prague a centre for saint cults and rich churches—features vividly attacked for their associated abuses by early preachers of the reform. The opening of Bohemia as a centre for the Empire involved also the opening of the Bohemian Church to the inroads of Avignonese fiscality, and appointment to high office became a matter of agreement between him and the popes.[3] His appointments to episcopal sees

[1] F. Seibt, 'Die Zeit der Luxemburger und der hussitischen Revolution', in *Handbuch der Geschichte der böhmischen Länder*, ed. K. Bosl, I (Stuttgart, 1967), pp. 351–536 (comprehensive, with bibliography; insufficiently known in England); F. Seibt, 'Bohemica, Probleme und Literatur seit 1945', in *HZ*, Sonderheft IV (1970), esp. pp. 49–99 (introduction to post-war work on Bohemia, with comments; valuable for Czech literature). I am indebted to Professor F. Seibt for comment and information. In English, K. Krofta, 'Bohemia in the Fourteenth Century', in *CMH*, VII, pp. 155–181 (now old); S. H. Thomson, 'Learning at the Court of Charles IV', *Speculum*, XXV (1950), pp. 1–20; R. R. Betts, *Essays in Czech History*, (London, 1969), omitting ch. 3 (pp. 29–41) (on this, cf. Leff, *Heresy* II, p. 632n.), H. Kaminsky, *A History of the Hussite Revolution* (Berkeley & Los Angeles, 1967) (fundamental and detailed study of history of ideas in relation to politics up to 1424, with distinguished knowledge of doctrinal sources); bibliography, pp. 551–3; on Charles IV, pp. 7–8. Names are given in the Czech forms here, except where a German or anglicized form is likely to be more familiar to the English reader.

[2] There is no satisfactory biography of Charles IV.

[3] J. Eršil, 'Les Rapports administratifs et financiers de la Papauté avignonaise avec les Pays de la Couronne de Bohême entre 1352 et 1378', *Rozpravy Československá Akademie Věd*, LXIX, (1959), p. 130 (summary of Czech article); R. E. Weltsch, *Archbishop John of Jenstein (1348–1400)* (The Hague & Paris, 1968), pp. 40–9.

were generally wise, but biased in favour of his friends and servants; he secured the persons he wished, while the papacy was given exceptional opportunities to obtain cash and benefits from the kingdom.

The nobility were the losers by such arrangements. They were beneficiaries from the traditional *Eigenkirche,* with its heavy lay control, and in this distant area the *Eigenkirche* style of Church government lasted on well after its supersession in more advanced lands. Reform ideas on Gregorian lines were only beginning to make their impact in the thirteenth century, when free election was secured for the sees of Prague and Olomouc, and Andrew of Prague led his campaign for freedom from lay control. For a long time papal intervention was slight and hesitant: for the whole period 1221–1316 Jaroslav Eršil has uncovered only twelve papal provisions relating to Bohemia.[4]

It was the absence at the curia of the bishop of Prague, John of Dražice, between 1318 and 1329 that opened the way for the introduction of papal provisions on an extensive scale; when it came, it came with a rush. Under Charles, all bishoprics and an increasing number of abbacies fell within papal rights of provision—at least theoretically—while in ten years of Clement VI's pontificate 300 bulls sent to Bohemia were concerned with lesser benefices.[5] Many of these provisions concerned appointments of foreigners, especially Germans. There was a comparatively small gap in time between the old, lay-controlled *Eigenkirche* and the late medieval type of informal concordat between pope and ruler for the distribution of office. This had important consequences, for the nobility retained a strong memory of their rights under the *Eigenkirche* and were, not wholly unjustly, inclined to see papal provisions as a system for rewarding foreigners. The course of events created a natural interest group, stronger than its opposite numbers in England, that had in practice seen rather more of late medieval papalism at work at the financial level and rather less of reforming Gregorianism, and was ready to swing its support behind a movement which advocated disappropriation and an implicit return to the rights of lay patrons.[6] The whole issue, like most others in Bohemia, was complicated by the existence of an incipient division in language and culture between German and Czech peoples.[7]

Much of the early development of Bohemia was due to the entry of German colonists. The early Bohemian towns tended to be German-dominated, and the mining areas, especially centring on Kutná Hora (Kuttenberg) and Jihlava (Iglau), which brought so much wealth to the Bohemian crown, were largely in the hands of German immigrants. The indigenous Slav peoples at first followed a German lead, their peasants adopting the settlement rights of the Germans because they were so successful, and their nobility, through the clergy, adopting the knightly culture of the German-speaking lands. But by the turn of the fourteenth century the flow of German immigration had passed

[4] Eršil, 'Rapports', p. 131; for general background, see F. Mildenberger, 'Die böhmischen Länder im Früh-und Hochmittelalter', Bosl, *Handbuch,* 1, pp. 165–347.

[5] Ibid., p. 132. Dr A. V. Antonovics in a private letter notes that there are problems of evidence.

[6] Seibt 'Die Zeit', p. 440.

[7] K. Bittner, *Deutsche und Tschechen. Zur Geistesgeschichte des böhmischen Raumes* (Brünn, etc., 1936).

its peak,[8]and signs appeared of an increasing self-consciousness in the Czechs of the Bohemian lands, with a greater interest in their language. The number of translations begins sharply to increase: the knightly literature of the preceding era is translated from German, by the end of the thirteenth century a complete Czech psalter is in existence, there are creeds and prayers in Czech, and in the course of the fourteenth century a Czech translation of the *Historia scholastica* of Peter Comestor and a Czech life of Christ put together by a Dominican from the *Meditationes vitae Christi*.[9] First awareness of national and linguistic difference appeared among the clergy; it was complicated by the development of a local patriotism, supporting inhabitants of the kingdom, Czech or German, against inroads of foreigners.

Yet, wherever social tensions existed in fourteenth-century Bohemia, they could readily become associated with the linguistic distinction between Czech and German speakers, as in the case of the slow Czech penetration of towns, where Czech speakers might come to resent the dominance in local government of the wealthier Germans, or in the relations of Czech nobles with towns in their neighbourhood, where the national difference served to heighten class antagonism. In Church life the rising standards of the lower Czech nobility in education carried them more frequently into the ranks of the clergy, and caused resentment of the entrenchment of the Germans in high positions, the inevitable consequence of their earlier cultural lead. Under the Luxemburgs there were attempts to redress the balance, as in the founding of Roudnice (Raudnitz), a house of Augustinian canons for the sons of Czech-speaking parents, which became a centre for the vernacular religious tradition, or Charles IV's foundation of a house for Czech canons in the old imperial palace at Ingelheim, in the middle of a German cultural area.[10] What Charles wanted in Bohemia was a balance between races and languages; but he did not wholly succeed in getting it, and underlying antagonisms continued, witnessed for us by the abbot Ludolf of Sagan, who studied in Prague in the 1370s and spoke of the hostility of German and Czech as comparable to that between Jew and Samaritan.[11] Balance was harder to maintain after 1378, when the strong central direction of Charles was replaced by that of his son, Wenceslas IV (1378–1419), who, surrounded by grave political difficulties, was incapable of emulating his father's mastery of this problem, or indeed any other.

A third characteristic feature of the Bohemian kingdom lay in the existence from about 1350 of a movement described by Eduard Winter, its principal historian, as 'early humanism'. Its most striking, but also more superficial, feature was letter-writing in the new humanistic style and the literary contacts with Prague of Petrarch, who stayed in the capital, and of Cola di Rienzo. Of more lasting significance was the new piety referred to by Winter as a parallel

[8]Seibt, 'Die Zeit', p. 416.

[9]Ibid., pp. 458–60, E. Winter, *Frühhumanismus. Seine Entwicklung in Böhmen* (Berlin, 1964).

[10]F. Seibt, *Hussitica. Zur Struktur einer Revolution* (Köln, 1965) (essays often subtle and stimulating, based on textual analyses, see on nationalist issue, p. 62 (Roudnice), 63–4 (Ingelheim), reviews, A. Borst, *ZFK* i/ii (1967), 176–7; R. Kalivoda, 'Seibt's "Hussitica" und die hussitische Revolution', *Historica*, xiv (1967), pp. 225–46. E. Lemberg, *Geschichte des Nationalismus in Europa*, Stuttgart, 1950, pp. 135–44.

[11]Bittner, *Deutsche und Tschechen*, p. 11; see *Speculum*, xliv (1969), pp. 310–11.

and even forerunner of the better-known Netherlands *devotio moderna*. In Bohemia it was associated pre-eminently with the spread of houses of Augustinian canons, who arrived in Bohemia in 1350, and were favoured by two archbishops of Prague, by Charles IV and by a number of noble patrons. Their spirituality stressed the study of books, notably of Augustine and the Fathers, the inner religous life of the individual, typified for example in the influential constitutions of Roudnice by the division of the *dormitorium* into individual cells, and had a strong pastoral concern. Other religious houses contributed; the Cistercian Königsaal produced the devotional masterwork, the *Malogranatum,* translated during the century into both German and Czech, and the Premonstratensian house of Tepl played a part in Biblical translation. As Seibt has warned us,[12] the influence of these new ideas affected only a thin upper layer of society; the Augustinian canons were no direct protagonists of the Hussite movement, but rather its opponents and, after the revolution, often its victims. Yet at least the *devotio moderna* of Bohemia helped to create in some influential circles the atmosphere of moral earnestness and a certain caution towards the formal and external machinery of traditional religious life that made a propitious climate of opinion for Hussitism.

The Beginnings of the Bohemian Reform Movement

Some of these characteristics may be seen in the preaching of Conrad Waldhauser,[13] who from 1363 worked as a freelance preacher supported by a benefice in Leitmeritz, then operated from the chief church of the Old Town of Prague. Charles's invitation to him to preach, and his position as his confessor and court chaplain, gave him official status from the outset. A keynote of his preaching was the denunciation of the abuses of the clergy, especially of simony. Religious orders were a special target because of their avarice and laxity; parents were even warned against putting their children into the novitiates of the mendicant orders because of their failings. Waldhauser disliked the abuse of relics: he attacked the passing off of a relic of St Barbara carried in procession in Prague as the saint's own, when its original, as he believed, could only be in Prussia. Denunciation of clerical abuse, a strong ethical stress, and radical social criticism were mingled with apocalyptic denunciations of the pseudo-prophets that deceived the people. Soon clerical opponents complained of him, and he was forced to go to answer them at Avignon, where he died in 1369. But before his career thus ended, he had established a circle of hearers among the Prague townspeople and students, and helped to set the tone for what was to follow.

His successor and convert, Jan Milič of Kroměříž, once a notary in the imperial chancellery, then a canon at the cathedral, had been led by Bible-reading and the preaching of Waldhauser to turn his back on his old life. After a year of solitude he became a poor preacher of repentance in 1364, based on

[12]Seibt, 'Die Zeit', p. 447; note section on monasteries, pp. 444–9. I am indebted esp. to Seibt's survey for Bohemian background. On the Bible generally, see J. Kadlec, 'Die Bibel in mittelalterlichen Böhmen', *AHDLMA*, xxxvi (1964), pp. 89–109, a study comparable to Deanesly, *Lollard Bible*; but see, on the effects of Scripture within Tabor, below, ch. 17, esp. pp. 310–11, 315–7, 322–4.

[13]Leff, *Heresy*, ii, pp. 610–11; Seibt, 'Die Zeit', pp. 466–8.

the parish church of St Giles in Prague.[14] The style was reminiscent of the orthodox wandering preachers of the twelfth century:[15] we recognize the same fiery asceticism, the refusal of meat and wine, sleeping on the hard ground, long prayers and lack of rest, combined with a certain vein of eccentricity, demonstrated in his obsessive interest in the coming of Antichrist and his extraordinary denunciation of Charles IV, his journeyings to convince the pope of the evils confronting the Church, and finally his strong moral concern and his interest in the conversion of prostitutes, reminiscent of the activities of Henry the Monk. Success with his hearers gave him the opportunity to take over twenty-nine houses in the prostitutes' quarter of the city, which he renamed Jerusalem and turned into a house for reclaimed prostitutes together with a community of preachers living a common apostolic life. Success in preaching, the institution of a new kind of parish in Prague, fiery denunciation of the sins of the clergy on the lines of Waldhauser, perhaps the hint of the suspect beguine style of life being fostered in Jerusalem, led to his being compelled to answer accusations launched against him in 1373, and to go to Avignon to do so. After justifying himself, he died before he could return to Prague, and his enemies combined to destroy the experiment of Jerusalem.

De Vooght, with justice, calls him the father of the Czech reform,[16] for in him the movement took root in a native Bohemian. His preaching at St Giles, then at the Týn church in Prague, was in Latin and Czech—German he had to learn in order to reach another category of hearers. By the foundation of Jerusalem, however short-lived, he began the process of gathering a nucleus of the reform-minded around an institution within the capital, and, to judge by the twelve articles of complaint against him, such as the charge that he recommended daily communion to inmates at Jerusalem, and used the phrase *Sanctus est sacerdos*,[17] he pointed the way to future developments.

The third in the line of reformers in Prague was Matthias of Janov, the theoretician of the movement.[18] Milič had been no intellectual, but Matthias, his disciple, had studied in Paris (1375–81), to leave as a *magister artium*. In Prague he lived as a titular member of the cathedral chapter, supported by his patron Adalbertus Ranconis, then for the last five years of his life from 1389 with the aid of a benefice in Nova Ves outside Prague. With Matthias the reform movement gained its major written work, the *Regulae veteris et novi testamenti*, a set of twelve rules of conduct, four derived from the Old Testament and eight from the New, intended to defend the faithful from the insidious attacks of Antichrist, whose members Matthias saw as omnipresent in the body of the visible Church. The work was a loosely articulated set of treatises, designed to meet the emergency in which he

[14]P. De Vooght, *L'Hérésie de Jean Huss* (Louvain, 1960) (fundamental for theology of Hussites and opponents to 1415); see also his more detailed *Hussiana* (Louvain, 1960), pp. 7–21 (both reviewed by G. Miccoli, *SM*, 3 sér. III (1962), pp. 189–96). Kaminsky, *Revolution*, pp. 5–55, repays study.

[15]Above, ch. 4.

[16]*Hérésie*: cf. pp. 14, 20–1.

[17]Seibt 'Die Zeit', p. 468, noting controversy on what he did in fact say.

[18]Leff, *Heresy*, II, pp. 612–9 is helpful; see Dr Vooght, *Hérésie*, pp. 21–35, Kaminsky, *Revolution*, pp. 14–23 (quotations but frail psychological interpretation).

believed the Church lay. By a return to the evangelical law found *par excellence* in Scripture and by the adoption of frequent communion, the Christian would be armed spiritually against the hypocrisy and formalism of existing Church life. Matthias continued the tradition of castigating the sins of the clergy and the religious orders while reinforcing the apocalyptic consciousness of his predecessors.

The work is overshadowed by the developments subsequent to the outbreak of the Great Schism, which seemed to be bringing the scourges of Antichrist within the Church to a climax. Attacks on clerical disorders had been common enough in western Europe; in other countries, as in Bohemia, congregations who heard these attacks believed them, but did not act; then the shocking spectacle of two rival popes, at Rome and Avignon, excommunicating each other and their rival's supporters—with Christendom divided into two camps because of the papal schism, exacerbated by national disputes—gave a new urgency to consideration of the state of the Church. As the schism dragged on, its obvious damage to the Church greater than in earlier papal disputes of the kind, men became convinced of the need, not only to stop the conflict by restoring unity to the papacy, but also to see that abuses in the Church were ended. Circumstances focussed attention on the popes as the source of troubles, for, in the need to get and keep supporters and money, both sides positively fostered abuse.

The outbreak and continuance of the schism is essential background for the understanding of the development of the Bohemian reform, for it stimulated the fight for change, and forced churchmen to think more about the nature of the Church and the papacy's place in it. It also weakened the authority of the papacy for dealing with doctrinal dissent, as the reform in Bohemia began to pass into heresy.

The situation was made more difficult after 1378 by the problems of Wenceslas as ruler.[19] His accession coincided with the outbreak of the schism; his character and circumstances meant that he could never be relied on to back the suppression of heresy (or what was labelled as heresy) in his kingdom. Charles had divided the Luxemburg inheritance among six relatives and, though Wenceslas had the lion's share in the kingdom of Bohemia, and was simultaneously king of the Romans, he was frequently troubled by the disputes and needs of the Luxemburg heirs, and unable either to use Bohemia as a firm support-point to develop his policies in the Empire or to rely on his powers in Germany, enfeebled by a long course of development outside his control, to aid him in Bohemia. In his kingdom he faced many troubles with his nobility, exacerbated by his relatives, especially by his brother Sigismund, and even had to endure imprisonment at the hands of his own subjects. He never secured coronation as emperor, and in 1400 he was deposed as king of the Romans and replaced by his rival Rupert of the Palatinate. All this, together with the complexities of the politics of the Great Schism, distracted him from Church affairs in Bohemia, leaving neither time nor inclination either to co-operate with reform or to help other churchmen put down the Bohemian movement. Wenceslas's problems had not fully

[19]Seibt, 'Die Zeit', pp. 473–94.

unfolded at the time of Matthias's writing of his *Regulae*, but they are not irrelevant to it. Both the Church and Bohemia had entered on a time of troubles, and Matthias's work reflects this in the urgency of its writing.

A number of features were, admittedly, not wholly novel: his attack on the proliferation of regulations in canon law, and his yearning for a new simplicity, the implied appeal to an earlier, more primitive Church, the interest in distinguishing the true Christians from the members of Antichrist within the visible Church—all have parallels in a century of Church life confronted with problems calculated to stimulate theological thinking of this type. What, however, is most striking in Matthias of Janov is his insistence on the value of the eucharist. To it he devotes the great part of the first two and all of the fifth of a massive five-book work, and it inspires some of his most eloquent passages.[20] Just as the return to the Bible enables the faithful to find their way through the suffocating mass of regulations of human invention, so the practice of frequent, and preferably daily, communion enables them to avoid the distractions of needless formalism in worship, of false relics and miracles. It is this which sets off Matthias from other reformers of the time.[21]

The advocacy of frequent communion for the laity was the issue which attracted the hostile attention of authority. In 1388 and 1389 the decrees of the Prague synod against attacks on the veneration of images and against the receiving of communion more than once a month by the laity were aimed, among others, at Matthias's teaching. On both issues he recanted; but he was again in trouble in 1392, two years before his death. Such harassments hardly affected his influence, and, though disciplined by loss of his functions for six months, he suffered no major disabilities. His work was not heretical, but nevertheless, it enshrined in written form some of the essential views of Bohemian reformers. It was a preacher's exercise, and concerned with Christian practice rather than dogma; if the theology was correct, the whole trend was towards criticism of the actions of churchmen, and in the stress on the personal spiritual probity of the individual lay raw material for attacks on the Church and its leadership. The vehement attacks on abuses were now available in written form, and influential after Matthias's death, as well as in his lifetime.

Each of the major figures, Waldhauser, Milič and Matthias of Janov, had had to meet entrenched clerical opposition; none of them had allowed their course of action to be deflected by it. A proof of their influence with some of the laity lies in the case of Thomas of Štítné, the south Bohemian country gentleman who attended lectures at Prague university and issued a series of handbooks for family religion in the vernacular, quite orthodox and unoriginal, but inculcating the same wariness towards formalities and superstitions in popular religious life, the same caution about the calibre of life in the monastery, and the same stress on the Bible and frequent communion for the laity.[22]

[20]Leff, ii, p. 616.
[21]As Kaminsky observes, (*Revolution*, pp. 21–2).
[22]M. Spinka, *John Hus: a Biography* (Princeton, 1968), pp. 19–20 (by enthusiastic supporter of Hus, valuable for factual detail; review, P. De Vooght, in *RHE*, lxv (1970), pp. 183–5).

The influence of the new ideas was reinforced by the foundation of the Bethlehem chapel in Prague, opened for sermons in the Czech vernacular in 1394 and seating three thousand people.[23] Among the patrons was a German knight, Johannes von Mühleim, but it was predominantly a Czech enterprise: together with the burgomaster of the Old Town, three masters of the Bohemian nation at the university were to fill the preacher's benefice. Bethlehem was thus the successor to Milič's Jerusalem as a focal point for reform; the vernacular preaching for which it was founded helped to stress the Czech aspect of the movement.

Reform ideas were not confined to Bethlehem and the audiences of the popular preachers. They also made their way at university level[24] in the complaints of John of Dambach, a Dominican, pupil of Eckhart and teacher of theology in the early days of Prague, who contrasted the baleful effect of the interdict on Church life in Germany with Charles's relic-collecting at home— a theme characteristic of the dislike of Bohemian reformers of formalism at the expense of true pastoral care—and later in the theses of Henry Totting of Oyta and of his pupil Conrad of Soltau, who in 1377 expressed doubt about the administration of the sacraments by concubinaries. Henry of Bitterfeld, the German Dominican who held a chair at Prague, spoke for frequent communion, and expressed his unease about indulgences, helping to form a Prague tradition on which Hussites proper were to build.

Thus by the end of the century there was a breadth of base to the reform movement of the preachers in Prague, aided by the existence of the Bethlehem chapel and the popular support it brought, and some dissemination of innovating ideas in the university. Yet no parallel success was being achieved in the prime aim of the movement, the reform of the body of clergy in Bohemia.[25]

The wealth of the Bohemian Church fostered abuse. Superfluity in endowments attracted unworthy candidates for ordination, and inspired an unhealthy interest in Church goods on the part of the laity. It would also seem that there were simply too many clergy: Tomek calculated that in Prague towards the end of the century, a city of 35,000 to 40,000, there were 1,200 clergy, 200 of them at the cathedral.[26] There was not work enough for them to do, and a contemporary treatise complains of the plight of clergy who did not know how to live from the daily mass-stipend of a Prague *groschen*. So, added to the dangers of overendowment, Bohemia was saddled with a clerical proletariat, a source of dissension within the clerical body and of scandal to the laity. Surviving aristocratic influence had something to do with this: John IV of Dražice, bishop of Prague, the founder of Roudnice, struggled against the abuse of the *mercenarii*, priests paid only a portion of their stipend by aristocratic patrons who confiscated the remainder to their own use. Both the first archbishop of Prague, Ernest of Pardubice, John's successor and then, after him, Archbishop John Očko of Vlaším were able to carry out administrative reforms in co-operation with the lay ruler; neither was able to

[23]Ibid., pp. 47–51, Seibt 'Die Zeit', p. 501; see his whole summary on Hus (pp. 500–6).
[24]Ibid., pp. 462–5.
[25]Ibid., pp. 436–44; Weltsch, *Jenstein*.
[26]Cited by Seibt, 'Die Zeit', p. 439; see De Vooght, *Hérésie*, pp. 99–101.

make a substantial change in the situation. Between Avignonese centralism and the control of the royal power, the ecclesiastical head of the Bohemian Church had little room for manoeuvre and, although Charles IV was sympathetic to reform, he was not prepared to push it on to the detriment of a system of royal patronage that benefited his bureaucracy rather than Church interests.

Under Wenceslas hopes diminished. His archbishop, John of Jenstein, had a strong personal piety and an interest in reform, but lacked political finesse; under his regime friendly relations with the ruler broke down in the pressure of schism politics, as John remained firm on the Roman side, while Wenceslas veered, for his own ends, towards the Avignonese interest. The archiepiscopate was disturbed by disputes, with Wenceslas in 1393 claiming what a modern writer has described as a return to the old proprietary system.[27] Personal conflict culminated in the same year in the murder of John of Pomuk, the archbishop's official; finally, John resigned. It was the tragedy of his generation that John of Jenstein could not make his way through these conflicts, for he had some contact with Matthias of Janov, wrote treatises himself, and was in touch with devotional currents of the time.[28] In the event, perhaps not wholly willingly, by supporting the attack on Matthias's advocacy of frequent lay communion, he ranged himself with the opposition and his own attempt at administrative reform, in the visitation of Prague in 1379–80, was checked by legal action and not resumed. Jenstein claimed that it was the first such major visitation, and it revealed that in no less than sixteen out of thirty-nine churches the incumbents gave cause for scandal.[29] After Jenstein, neither of his successors, his nephew Olbram ze Škworce (1396–1402) and Zbyněk Zajíc of Hasenburg (1402–11), showed themselves equal to the demands of their position.

Abuse thus continued, intensified by such scandalous arrangements as that arrived at between Wenceslas and the Roman pope, Boniface IX, in 1393 whereby a jubilee indulgence was granted to pilgrims visiting four churches in Prague as if they had visited Rome, and a half of their offerings at the church of St Peter on Vyšehrad were granted to the king.[30] The result of the failure to reform was an impatience in some sections of the population with churchmen, and a new stridency among the reformers. Earlier preachers stressed individual piety and the Second Coming; reform was to come through spiritual renewal by holy men. Matthias lamented the schism, but did not propose constitutional mechanisms to end it, as members of the conciliar movement did.[31] Now that was beginning to change; the element of popular demonstration against ecclesiastical failings intensified; the use of force to institute necessary reform was becoming more prominent.

The Influence of Wyclif

A further novel factor was introduced by the appearance of Wyclifite ideas at

---

[27]Weltsch, *Jenstein*, p. 72; see his ch. 2 generally (pp. 40–78).
[28]Ibid., pp. 154–79.
[29]Ibid., p. 162.
[30]Ibid., p. 71.
[31]I am indebted to Professor Seibt for discussion on this point.

the Charles University in Prague. Although his theology was not wholly unknown in early days—for Nicholas Biceps, a Prague professor, was arguing against Wyclif's eucharistic beliefs while Wyclif was still alive,[32] it was the philosophical works which first attracted attention. Marginal comments in manuscripts of Wyclif's philosophical works, which by a coincidence were copied by the young Hus, earning to help his keep as a student, convey the atmosphere in which this interest in Wyclifite philosophy sprang up. One warns the reader that the treatise *De ideis* should not be recommended to *non intelligentibus*; another sounds a note of uneasy admiration: 'O Wycleff, Wycleff, more than one head you have turned.'[33] These two comments show members of the University reacting in a similar manner to the Oxford scholars who first heard Wyclif's ultra-realist philosophy. It was difficult, sometimes alarming, and it could bowl men over with its bold propositions.

Interest in the philosophical treatises soon led on to an interest in the theological; and in stages, aided by the visits of Bohemian scholars to England, Wyclif's more dangerous works arrived in Bohemia. Two of these scholars, bachelors of the university, seem to have established direct contact with English Lollards and to have stayed at Latimer's manor at Braybrooke. Together with the treatises, they took back with them a fragment of Wyclif's tomb. Thereafter, until Lollardy was forced irretrievably underground, the two movements in England and Bohemia remained in contact.[34]

Wyclif brought complications.[35] On the one hand, his works gave a much stronger intellectual framework to the ideas of reform that had long circulated in Bohemia, and, for those who accepted Wyclif's inspiration, it imparted a new aggressiveness to the drive for reform. At the university the entry of his thought ended the phase of disparate, even somewhat opportunistic, reform thinking, which coexisted in the last three decades of the century with the predominantly moral revivalist preaching associated with Waldhauser, Milič, Matthias of Janov and the priests at the Bethlehem chapel. On the other hand, it repelled some intellectuals who had been sympathetic to reform, and gave a new handle to its opponents inside Bohemia, who were able to tar reformers with Wyclif's heresy.

In contrast to England, local circumstances in Bohemia provided an additional reason for the popularity of Wyclif's writings. It lay in the hostility, mingled with envy, of the Czech masters for the Germans at the university of Prague. One of these manuscripts of Wyclif has in the margin the gloss, in another hand: 'Haha, Germans, haha, out, out.'[36] The manuscript is of a philosophical work: the comment expresses the pleasure of a Czech at finding a philosophical weapon against the prevailing nominalism of the German masters. Ultra-realism could bloom in Prague because it seemed to be an

---

[32] D. Trapp, 'Clm 27034. Unchristened Nominalism and Wycliffite Realism at Prague in 1381', *RTAM*, xxiv (1957), pp. 320–60; background in F. Šmahel, ' "Doctor evangelicus super omnes evangelistas": Wyclif's fortune in Hussite Bohemia', *BIHR*, xliii (1970), pp. 16–34 (succinct and illuminating). I owe this ref. to Dr C. D. Ross.

[33] Ibid., pp. 18–19 and 19 n. 2; incorrect attribution by Spinka (*Hus*, p. 38).

[34] Šmahel, 'Doctor Evangelicus', pp. 20, 25, for scholars' visits; Betts, *Essays*, pp. 132–59, for English-Bohemian contacts generally.

[35] Seibt, 'Die Zeit', pp. 501–2; intellectual landscape in Šmahel, *art. cit.*

[36] Cited by Šmahel (p. 20).

answer to the Ockhamist views of, probably, a majority of the teachers in the theological faculty, who hailed from German-speaking lands or sprang from the Germans within Bohemia.

In the first years of the university Czech students had been few in number. By Charles IV's foundation the university was divided, on the Parisian model, into four nations, described according to the points of the compass, as Bohemian, Polish (which in practice often meant German), Saxon, Bavarian.[37] At the outset the Czechs (who would be only a part of the Bohemian 'nation') formed an insignificant proportion. In time, internecine university disputes and the founding of new universities in German-speaking lands led to a fall in the proportions of Germans to Czechs overall. In the arts faculty during the 1380s twenty-five per cent of all graduates came from the Bohemian nation; by about 1400 the proportion had risen to thirty-six per cent. Where the Bohemian nation in early years had provided some ten per cent of the deans in the faculty—an elective office—they were providing almost forty per cent by the years 1391 to 1408. In theology their masters had not earlier been leading lights. As a body, they tended to adhere to a somewhat conservative Augustinian realist tradition, and to have some feelings of inferiority: to such Wyclif's ultra-realism, with its bold answers to Ockhamism, would appeal as a means of exalting their own intellectual position *vis-à-vis* the Germans. By reaction against this, Germans tended to be the initiators in attacks on the orthodoxy of Wyclif and those who defended him—though not exclusively, for there were cross-currents, not all Germans being nominalists, and some Czechs of a moderate realist position opposing the ultra-realism of the Wyclifites. Nevertheless, the Czech-German division added a new dimension to the study of Wyclif and controversy about him.

Jan Hus

Just as Wyclif's teaching had begun seriously to affect the university, Jan Hus was appointed rector of the Bethlehem chapel. The new strands now discernible in the Bohemian reform movement all met in him: Wyclif, the stress on a Czech reform, the new urgency against abuse. His academic training brought him to Wyclif: he was a member, though not the most prominent, of the new radical generation of Czech masters to whom Wyclif initially appealed.[38] Other Czech masters made the pace, and were deeper thinkers. Hus, in this resembling the older tradition of the fourteenth-century reformers, was first and foremost a preacher, agitator and spiritual writer. Some time before his ordination as priest in 1400, he underwent conversion and ceased to be, as he later confessed, a conventional clerical careerist.[39] He found himself at the Bethlehem chapel. Flajšhans, the editor of his sermons, estimates that he preached some three thousand sermons during the twelve years of his service at Bethlehem, normally twice on every Sunday and saint's

[37]For these and following details, see Seibt, 'Die Zeit', pp. 449–57; also Bittner, *Deutsche und Tschechen,* pp. 102–6; on the university with recent bibliography, see Betts, pp. 13–28.

[38]Early university career in Spinka, *Hus,* pp. 24–53; early theological work in De Vooght, *Hérésie,* pp. 54–64; note contrast of latter's judgement (*CV,* VIII (1965), p. 236) and that of F. M. Bartoš (*CV* IX (1966), 176–7).

[39]Spinka, pp. 28, 43–6.

day, to overflowing congregations.[40] Under him the Bethlehem chapel became the centre of the popular movement, as it had not been under his two predecessors, who had been distracted by other duties. The situation can be vividly reconstructed, for we have texts of his sermons, even down to notes for his own delivery, showing immediate emotional rapport with his audience,[41] 'and then, as the audience responds, speak against idolatry'; 'this is the judgement of the letter. And then amplify if the attitude of the people justifies it.'

The chapel was a large, plain building, a preaching-church somewhat in the style of the churches of the Franciscans. On the walls were pairs of pictures: the pope on horseback and in pomp, contrasted with Christ in poverty, carrying his cross; Constantine making his donation to the pope, contrasted with Christ, wearing a crown of thorns, before Pilate.[42] Sermons corresponded to the pictures—orthodox, but fiercely attacking the abuses of the modern Church, and repeating the contrast with the poverty and simplicity of the primitive Church. Hus never fell into the Donatist view, impugning the validity of the sacraments administered by the unworthy priest[43] but, a deeply emotional man and a committed reformer, he was touched to the heart by the abuses that he saw around him, and he communicated this indignation to his congregation.[44] The effect of his preaching was enhanced by his own good life and obvious lack of personal ambition—he never wished for higher office than that of rector of Bethlehem, and his sermons and letters have running through them a thread of pastoral concern for all ranks of Prague society.[45]

The congregations at the Bethlehem chapel were Czech-speaking. Hus did not continue the practice of the earlier reformers, of speaking in both the Czech and the German vernacular; he spoke only Czech. He had been born among free peasants in an area of rich German settlement in southern Bohemia, and was conscious of the national and linguistic differences, so apparent in a nationally mixed area. He believed that the Czechs should be first in the offices of the kingdom of Bohemia, 'as are the French in the kingdom of France and the Germans in their own lands.' With the elements of Czech nationalism came also a consciousness of their special religious responsibility. He derived Bohemia from the Slav *Bóh* ('God'), called the kingdom *christianissimum*, and wrote of the *verny Chechy*, the faithful Czechs.[46] At Bethlehem he extended the range of his congregation, appealing to some

[40]Ibid., p. 51.

[41]Kaminsky, *Revolution*, p. 40, n. 124.

[42]Spinka, pp. 48–9.

[43]Leff, ii, pp. 659–62; also his 'Wyclif and Hus: a doctrinal comparison', *BJRL*, LX (1968), pp. 387–410.

[44]See De Vooght's comment (*Hérésie*, pp. 71–4); also Kaminsky, *Revolution*, p. 40, and comment on De Vooght, (ibid., pp. 35–7).

[45]*The Letters of John Hus*, trans. M. Spinka (Manchester, 1972), and *John Hus at the Council of Constance*, (New York and London, 1965), Spinka's trans. of Peter of Mladoňovice's account of Hus's trial, with introduction (letters of Hus, pp. 237–98); for background on churchmen and social conditions, see P. Brock, *The Political and Social Doctrines of the Unity of Czech Brethren in the Fifteenth and Sixteenth Centuries* (The Hague, 1957), pp. 11–34; Weltsch, *Jenstein*, pp. 130–40.

[46]On Hussitism and nationalism, there is a subtle chapter in Seibt, *Hussitica*, pp. 58–124; on Hus, see pp. 87–9, 100.

artisans as well as the Czech-speaking middle class. But he did not reach the German-speaking middle class of the capital, and his tenure of the rectorate of Bethlehem tended to aid the polarization, gradually taking place in the early fifteenth century, between Czech reformers and German opposition.

The Attack on Wyclifites

This polarization was accelerated by the development of an attack on supporters of Wyclif by German masters, which began in 1403 with an appeal for action against Wyclif's works to the Prague diocesan authorities by Elias Hübner,[47] a Silesian from the university, continued with an attack on the Czech Wyclifite Stanislav of Znojmo's writing by John Štěkna, an *emigré* from Prague, and culminated in 1408 with an appeal to the curia by Ludolf Meistermann, a Saxon also from the university. Interest in Wyclif's philosophy often coexisted with membership of the reform movement, and attacks on him tended to be seen by reformers as covert attempts to stifle their movement. The fact that Germans were responsible for these attacks drew the Czechs together in defence, not necessarily of the substance of Wyclif's teaching, but of the right to read and teach him, whether or not they all as individuals shared Wyclif's views. In fact some certainly did not, and there was a spread of views from very moderate teachers who thought Wyclif could be used, to Stephen Páleč and to Stanislav of Znojmo, who actually taught the Wyclifite eucharistic doctrine of remanentism, thus denying transubstantiation, in his *De corpore Christi*. Both of these produced works so influenced by Wyclif that the Wyclif Society in the nineteenth century thought that they were Wyclif's own.[48] There were also Czechs such as Andrew of Brod, who did not defend the teaching of Wyclif in his last phase, and disliked the idea of remanentism spreading in Bohemia.[49]

The pro-Wyclif Czech party were lucky in that the archiepiscopate was then held by Zbyněk, a former soldier of high family, ill-equipped theologically yet sympathetic to reform, who was lenient to the Wyclifites, and took till 1408 to make up his mind that firm action against the spread of Wyclif's views was necessary. The contrast to Courtenay's resolution against Lollardy is obvious.[50] Zbyněk's benevolence delayed condemnation, for though the German masters were strong enough to secure a university decision against Wyclif, they needed the archbishop's backing to bring the Wyclifites down, and the prolonged debate on the issue, mediated to the populace by Czech students at the university, popularized radical tenets of Wyclif (or alleged tenets) in a way that nothing else could have done.

Hübner's original list of excerpts was an old one—the forty-five items included twenty-four from the English condemnation made at the Blackfriars Synod of 1382, and the remaining twenty-one probably came from an earlier condemnation[51]—and he was attempting to argue that Wyclif had already

---

[47]For doctrinal disputes, see De Vooght, *Hérésie*, pp. 75–118; Spinka, *Hus*, pp. 47–85.

[48]On varying influence of Wyclif, see De Vooght, op. cit., pp. 85–92; on the sincerity of Hus's rejection of remanentism, ibid., pp. 60–3, 96–7, 365–6, 473–4; *Hussiana*, pp. 263–91.

[49]Kaminsky, *Revolution*, pp. 38, 113, n. 54; Spinka, *Hus*, p. 71.

[50]Above, pp. 247–8.

[51]Kaminsky, *Revolution*, p. 24, n. 66.

been officially condemned, and that such condemnations should automatically be given effect in Bohemia. At the time this did not make much of an impression; but the excerpts were disseminated over the years in a way that Hübner and his colleagues never expected. They were cited out of their contexts, in short and pungent sentences that could not have been better adapted to act as the slogans of a popular movement.[52] They solved the problem of conveying ideas of Wyclif from the difficult setting of the master's prolix Latin treatises.

Such sentences are article 10 ('It is contrary to Scripture that churchmen should have possessions'), article 16 ('Temporal lords can at will take away temporal goods from the Church and possessioners who habitually offend') or article 14 ('Any deacon or priest can preach the word of God without the authority of the apostolic see and the Catholic bishop') had an immediate and subversive significance. In effect, the excerpts thus collected were such as to void the hierarchical and sacramental system of the Church, open the way to a reduction to apostolic poverty, and put her in the hands of the royal power and the temporal lords. Powerful heresies were represented: article 4, denying sacramental validity to the acts of a bishop or priest in mortal sin, was pure Donatism; article 5 denied Christ's institution of the mass; article 37 said that the Roman Church was a synagogue of Satan. Two excerpts, articles 7 and 11, by undermining both absolution and excommunication, much weakened the position of priesthood and episcopate. Bandied to and fro, the articles containing such sentiments passed out of university circles.

Meanwhile, in the university Wyclif remained a centre of debate. The questions would always arise, How much of Wyclif was to be assimilated? Was it to be the philosophy only? The reforming sentiments and the political ideas? The remanentism and the doctrine of the Church? The Czechs at the university continued to maintain a common front despite their individual differences. When Zbyněk started to put real pressure on them in 1408, they responded by agreeing as a body to forbid any defence of the forty-five articles 'in their heretical, erroneous and objectionable sense'[53] an action which preserved by implication a right to read Wyclif, but explicitly condemned only these specific articles, leaving open the question of their rightful attribution to Wyclif.

Yet the writing was on the wall when, ten days earlier, the master Matthew of Knín was tried in the archbishop's court and subsequently had to abjure remanentism, and there is little doubt that a full uprooting of Wyclif in Bohemia would still have been possible if Zbyněk had been able to follow up his first actions of the spring of 1408. The curia had backed Meistermann when he made his appeal: this turned the affair into an issue of authority, and made up the archbishop's mind for him. Gone were the days of the synodal decrees against abuse and the invitations to Hus to preach;[54] pressure from

---

[52]Šmahel, 'Doctor Evangelicus', p. 22, see also pp. 24–6. Text of 45 articles, M. Spinka, *John Hus' Concept of the Church* (Princeton, 1966) (useful summary, pro-Hus in tone; review by L. Nemek, in *CHR*, LV (1969), pp. 78–80), pp. 397–400; analysis in De Vooght, *Hérésie*, pp. 80–3).

[53]Trans., Spinka, *Hus*, p. 83.

[54]On Zbyněk's early favour to reformers and his change of mind, see Spinka, *Hus*, pp. 66–7, 69–71, 79, 83–7; and on his attitude to authority, De Vooght, *Hérésie*, pp. 95–6, 101; see below, p. 288.

abroad took Stanislav of Znojmo and Páleč away from Bohemia, to abandon Wyclif and become enemies of the movement they had once supported.[55] Implicated as they were in late Wyclifism, the Czech masters, as these events show, could yet have been deflected from defence of Wyclif, and popular dissemination of heresy could have been checked if Zbyněk had been able to keep up his counteraction.

What intervened was politics and the interests of Wenceslas in an emotional cause, which made it possible to build a party round the defence of reform, Jan Hus and the radical tenets of Wyclif, and created a new situation, without parallel in the history of Lollardy in England.

[55]Events outlined in De Vooght, pp. 105–6 subsequent views, below, pp. 290, 291, 294, 298, 301.

17

Politics and Hussitism, 1409–1419

The Decree of Kutná Hora

Schism politics interrupted Zbyněk's proceedings, and finally brought the effectiveness of his archiepiscopate to an end. Tired of the contest between the rival popes, a group of cardinals renounced allegiance to their masters, and proposed the election of a compromise candidate who should rally churchmen of both sides to end the schism. But their candidate, the conciliar pope Alexander V, was unable to do this, and so the move merely created three popes instead of two.

At the time, however, the conciliar proposal drew Wenceslas's favour. An agile, wavering politician,[1] he saw a chance to regain the office of king of the Romans he had lost in 1400, and to confront his rival Rupert of the Palatinate by shifting from the Roman to the conciliar interest, demanding support for his claim against Rupert as his price for doing so. This affected the Wyclif case, for it created a rupture with Zybněk, who in his soldierly fashion declined to break his oath to the Roman pope,[2] and suddenly made the Czech element in the Bohemian nation at the university seem a valuable source of support. To make his move to the council's party, Wenceslas needed the university on his side, and found that the German-dominated nations, Bavaria, Saxony, Poland, at the Charles University, obedient to Zybněk and mindful of the benefices they might one day wish to have in German-speaking lands of the Roman obedience, declined to change allegiance, while the Czechs generally, hoping for conciliar support for their reform and less interested in the lands following Rome outside Bohemia, were ready to follow their king's plan. To get the university's vote, despite the hostile nations, Wenceslas simply changed the voting system of the nations by the decree of Kutná Hora (Kuttenberg) on 18 January 1409, which henceforth allowed the Bohemian nation three votes instead of one, and reduced the three foreign nations to one vote overall.[3] The Czechs were the majority in the Bohemian nation by that time, so Wenceslas got the change of allegiance he wanted.

---

[1]Characterization, with reassessment, in Seibt, 'Die Zeit', p. 477.

[2]The oath is fundamental for Zbyněk's opposition to Wenceslas's decision for the conciliar party in January 1409; it is a good hypothesis that it also mattered in Zbyněk's turn against the reformers in 1408. See above, p. 286.

[3]Seibt, 'Die Zeit', pp. 490–1; Kaminsky, *Revolution*, pp. 56–75 (Kutná Hora and sequel, with insight into political motives); F. Seibt, 'Johannes Hus und der Abzug der deutschen Studenten aus Prag 1409', *AKG*, XXXIX (1957), pp. 63–80; analysis of decree in Seibt, *Hussitica*, pp. 65–7.

Kutná Hora and the secession of foreign masters and students to the number of seven or eight hundred, which followed their failure to reverse Wenceslas's decision, turned the Charles University into a regional university of a new pattern, and altered the balance of power broadly to the advantage of the reform party. Though not yet overall victors, the reformers had less opposition to conquer than before, since they no longer had to reckon with a concentration of opposition in the foreign nations. In the arts faculty Wyclif supporters now appeared to have a majority; in theology the situation was more complicated, since the philosophical ground of Wyclif's thinking was resisted by some Czech masters of the older tradition;[4] in any case the Bohemian nation included still the indigenous German masters, inclined against the reform party. Yet ground had been gained.

Most important was the re-alignment of political forces accompanying Kutná Hora. It had been won, in part, by skilful agitation under the direction of the lawyer John Jesenic[5] and the 'political intellectual' Jerome of Prague, the strange, stormy figure of the movement, a layman who was a theological teacher and a heavily committed realist.[6] Under their direction a link was forged between the ideas of the reform and the superior rights of the indigenous inhabitants of the kingdom. The association of this incipient feeling with Wyclif and reform was the distinctive feature of the Bohemian situation, which continued, despite vicissitudes, to hold and to grow in strength till older authorities broke down before it. The need to push Kutná Hora through helped the Bohemian reformers to become a political as well as an ecclesiastical party, allying with forces in the capital, and devising a propaganda that would appeal to native leaders. John Jesenic helped by creating a structure of theory, in part derived from Wyclif, justifying the supreme rights of the royal power in Bohemia in his work, the *Defensio mandatii*, thus influencing the king when he was uncertain whether to hold to his decision.[7] The notion of the Bohemian nation, chosen of God, faithful to its ideals, was launched by the Kutná Hora agitation.

In immediate terms, there was now a working alliance between king and reformers sufficient to prevent any legal action against the advocates of Wyclif, initiated abroad, from taking effect. The king hardly cared seriously one way or another about the cause of reform, but he was interested in scotching any foreign moves on doctrine that might disturb the peace of his kingdom, and he was inclined for the moment to see Zbyněk as the source of these disturbances. He and his magnates found useful the pleas made for apostolic poverty and against ecclesiastical authority, but this was about as far as his positive interest in the reform cause went; nevertheless, uncertain as he was as a long term Hussite ally, his attitude, coupled with the development of popular feeling, was quite sufficient to undermine Zbyněk's continued action against Wyclif supporters.

[4]See case of Blasius Vlk (Spinka, *Hus*, pp. 92–3).

[5]Kaminsky, *Revolution*, illuminates this.

[6]Betts, *Essays in Czech History*, pp. 195–235; interesting investigation of nationalism in Seibt, *Hussitica*, pp. 77–86; note summary on p. 86. See F. Šmahel, 'The Idea of the "Nation" in Hussite Bohemia', *Historica*, XVI (1969), pp. 143–247; XVII (1969), pp. 93–197.

[7]Kaminsky, pp. 67–70. Leff, *Heresy*, II, pp. 628–9, on Kutná Hora, requires amplification.

The archbishop called in Wyclif's works, excommunicated those who had held them, and proclaimed an interdict, without fundamentally altering the situation.[8] When he tried to bring the affair to a summary end by burning Wyclif's works in 1410, he encountered a popular agitation of university students and Prague citizens, who disrupted services, threatened priests, and invented a sarcastic ditty about the burning and Zbyněk's lack of theology. Popular opinion was influenced both ways, and the old theological battle over Wyclif came into the streets, with the opposition to Wyclif also taking to the pulpits, labelling the reform party Wyclifite,[9] and performing its parody of a reformer's mass. On the one hand, a party blocking the heresy case against Wyclif came into existence, blending learned university judgement, with its plea for free study of Wyclif and its varying mixtures of Wyclifite teaching and native reform, with political forces interested in Bohemian independence and royal power, supported at a much more uncivilized level by street agitation; on the other side were opponents, Czech and German, also capable of mounting popular agitation, with some strength in the capital but rather stronger in the provinces.

Hostility to his interdict finally forced Zbyněk out of office in July 1410; not long afterwards he died in exile. He was the last archbishop prepared to use all the canonical machinery to put down Wyclif's supporters. The king's physician, Albík of Uničov, his immediate successor, showed no eagerness in pursuit; Conrad of Vechta, archbishop from 1413, was equivocal in his attitude. In practice, a kind of Gallicanism,[10] facilitated by Wenceslas's policies, the enfeeblement of central authority in the Church, and Hussite pleas for the right of the kingdom to deal with its own affairs, was shielding Bohemia from the traditional pursuit of heresy. The tricky task of the pro-Wyclif party was to keep the king to this Gallican line.

Jan Hus and Nicholas of Dresden

In the aftermath of the Kutná Hora affair Hus rose to the position which he held until his death as the principal symbolic figure at the head of the movement.[11] He had not at first been a leader, but he had already become a target of the legal action against Wyclif's supporters; he was notorious to the conservatives because of the sharpness of his attacks on clerical abuse and, though his fame was most due to his popular oratory, he rose in intellectual pro-Wyclif circles as Páleč and Stanislav of Znjomo defected, and the departure of the foreign Germans gave chances for Czech scholars. In 1409 he was elected rector of the university. In 1410 he gained greater prominence through protesting against Zbyněk's burning of the books.

He was still not the most radical of the reform theologians; part of the case against him was that he provided a shield for preachers and agitators more

---

[8]Events to death of Zbyněk described in Spinka, *Hus*, pp. 100–20, 122–9; De Vooght, *Hérésie*, pp. 115–23, 128–43, 148–51; and motives in Kaminsky, pp. 70–5.

[9]Seibt, *Hussitica*, pp. 10–14. *Hussitae* was first used at time of Council of Constance (ibid., p. 11, n. 23). It was a term of abuse.

[10]See Kaminsky, p. 74.

[11]Perspective by Seibt, 'Die Zeit', pp. 500–6. See text of complaints against him by Prague clergy in Palacký, *Documenta*, pp. 153–5; interesting comment in Leff, II, p. 627.

clearly heretical than he was. This radical wing had certainly been in existence for some years; but its presence was felt more deeply because of the events of 1412.[12] In May an agent of John XXIII began to preach in Prague the crusade against Ladislas of Naples, and to offer indulgences to those who took the Cross. The crusade was a mere instrument of schism politics, and the use of indulgences unusually cynical. The king, however, was in favour of the crusade and gained some of the proceeds. Hus's denunciation of the practices employed in the indulgences trade offended him and broke the alliance with the royal power.

The year 1412, however, both coincided with the emergence of more Waldensian-type popular heresy among the reforming party and gave new chances for radicalism. Typical of the popular demonstrations was the procession led by Voksa of Valdštejn, in which a student, dressed as a prostitute with bare breasts hung with a mock papal bull, mimicked the hawking of indulgences. Chests intended for indulgence money were smeared with mud; at the cathedral the treasure chest received a pronouncement addressed sardonically to the disciples of the evil demon Asmodeus, Belial and Mammon. Jerome of Prague found himself in his element, composing, if we may believe his enemies, popular Czech songs, slapping a Franciscan who disagreed with him, intervening in a quarrel between an exhibitor of relics at St Mary of the Snows and a Hussite bystander, and snatching a sword to put friars to flight.[13] In July preachers of the indulgences were interrupted by young men in their sermons at the cathedral, Týn and St James's churches. The royal wrath was aroused by the indulgence agitation, and the magistrates ordered three offenders to be beheaded. Crowds followed their corpses to the Bethlehem chapel, and clothes were dipped in their blood. The Hussite movement had gained its first martyrs.

Increasing violence on the Hussite side touched off counter violence from the conservatives. In the cathedral, priests beat protesters in the sanctuary; a crowd from neighbouring parishes assembled to storm the Bethlehem chapel; Páleč preached in Czech at the St Gall church, denouncing Wyclif as the greatest and most astute of heretics.[14]

Naturally, at a time of bitter feelings, the pressures of academic politics and of mass audiences gave prominence to the most exaggerated opinions among the debaters. Znjomo and Páleč evolved the notion of the *ecclesiasticum et misticum compositum*, with the pope its head and the cardinals its body, which appeared to shrink the Church to pope and cardinals only. The phrase used for the description of Scripture, a *res inanimata*, till it was vivified by the decisions of the Church, so defined, particularly distressed Hus. Hussite views on the Church were a response, in part, to an extremist doctrine of their opponents. Both sides reacted to each other.

Late in 1411 or early in 1412 the Hussite radicals were reinforced by the arrival in Prague of a party of Germans from Dresden, former teachers who had mingled a radical theology with the normal grammar and the arts; the

---

[12]Events described in Spinka, *Hus*, pp. 130–64. and theology of Hus and opponents in De Vooght, *Hérésie*, pp. 183–204; *Hussiana*, pp. 303–62.

[13]Betts, *Essays*, pp. 216–8; Kaminsky, pp. 88–9, esp. n. 129.

[14]De Vooght, *Hérésie*, p. 219.

later confession of a pupil reveals that in their Dresden school they had taught the rejection of oaths, the right of all priests to preach freely without further authorization, the disendowment of the Church, the rejection of obedience to the Roman hierarchy and of the papal headship, and the inclusion of all necessary belief within the Bible.[15] It sounds Waldensian, and it remains controversial whether the beliefs of this group represent an autonomous outgrowth of Waldensianism in an intellectual environment, or merely a case of German Wyclifism, possibly formed initially among students at Prague who left after Kutná Hora.

Installed in Prague, the Dresden group were a radical influence. Most important was the master Nicholas of Dresden, who composed the *Tabule veteris et novi coloris* some time before October 1412. They can most naturally be associated with the phase of street agitation in the time of the indulgences crisis, for their natural setting was plainly processional placards, conveying in a striking visual form the contrast between the Churches of the popes and of the Apostles. Collections of authorities confront each other: on one side, the tables of the Old Colour, of the early Church; on the other, the tables of the New Colour, being texts and authorities which demonstrated the realities of the life of the papal Church as interpreted by Nicholas, forming a vivid and uninhibited attack on the whole apparatus of the law, hierarchy and endowment.

On the Prague streets the identification would have been plainer. A late Czech version of the *Tabule* illustrates the texts with pictures, and there is a high probability that the original was intended to be learned apparatus for a sequence of propaganda paintings, stretching from an early pattern of twos, contrasting Christ bearing his cross with the pope riding on a horse,[16] or Christ washing the feet of the disciples with the pope having his feet washed in the curia,[17] to the climax in which the Antichrist of Revelation is depicted in papal regalia surrounded by whores.[18] In Nicholas, we can see, the Hussite movement was passing from the theme of reform, however radical, within the existing framework of the Church, to an explicit rejection of it as the work of Antichrist.

Prague at this time gave special opportunities for men with a talent for street agitation. Before the end of the century it had attained the highest population figure for any city in central Europe.[19] Moreover, in the New Town of Charles IV there was an unusual concentration of manual workers: it was these men who formed the audiences for agitators such as Nicholas of Dresden and, later, Jan Želivský. F. Graus has produced calculations which suggest a high degree of poverty in Prague: 40 per cent of the population are classified by him as indigent.[20] Peasant immigration continually reinforced

[15]H. Kaminsky, 'Nicholas of Dresden and the Dresden School in Hussite Prague', in *Master Nicholas of Dresden: the Old Color and the New*, ed. H. Kaminsky and others (*TAPS*, n.s., LV, i) (Philadelphia, 1965), pp. 5–28, esp. 6–7.

[16]Table 1 (ibid., p. 38); Kaminsky, *Revolution*, pp. 40–9.

[17]Table 8 (ibid., pp. 60–1).

[18]Table 9 (ibid., p. 62); see heading ('What is said of the Antichrist applies to the Pope').

[19]Seibt 'Die Zeit', p. 431.

[20]Czech work, cited in J. Macek, 'Villes et Campagnes dans le Hussitisme', *HS*, pp. 243–56; at pp. 245, 250, nn. 12, 13; F. Seibt, in *HZ*, Sonderheft IV, ed. W. Kienast, pp. 65–7; general

the *chudina*, the town poor dependent on casual labour; poverty coexisted with great wealth in the nobility and the patriciate, and class divisions reinforced the radical preachers' appeal. For the hungry and the underemployed, reiterated denunciations of an over-endowed Church and simoniacal benefice-holders from the ranks of the patriciate held a special appeal. For the preachers the issues doubtless remained theological; for their hearers social and economic factors came powerfully into play.

The New Town was also unusual because of its governmental position. The struggle of the artisans against the patriciate for a place in town governments, a general feature in Bohemian towns in the second half of the fourteenth century, could most easily be won by the workers in their guilds in the New Town because of their strong numerical position. These guilds gave support to the Hussite movement; the German chronicler Andrew of Ratisbon noticed their importance. Yet the guilds of the New Town could hold together only so long as the conflict with the patriciate demanded unity. An earlier united adherence to reform broke down and, as revolutionary doctrine emerged from what had been initially a more moderate movement, part of the New Town support went over to the conservatives.[21] There remained as a rank and file for radical preachers the less established middle class and the true poor.

Meanwhile, news from Prague as it reached the curia painted the situation in the darkest colours and led to further action. In July 1412, as part of the case launched against the best-known reform supporter, a major excommunication was pronounced against Hus by Cardinal Stefaneschi, technically for non-appearance. An interdict on Prague forced Hus out of the city.

Exile from Prague, which lasted till Hus finally left Bohemia for Constance, gave Hus the opportunity to put his thinking onto a firmer theoretical basis. Controversy over Wyclifite issues with his opponents tended to cohere round the fundamental question of the nature of the Church. Politically, the cause of Bohemian reform tended to move into a dangerous impasse,[22] with intransigent conservatives and reformers still locked in conflict, foreign churchmen anxious over Bohemian heresy, and the king, who summoned in vain a commission to reconcile differences, unable to bridge the gap between the parties. Hus's appeal to Christ from the Church was effective writing, but made no change in the situation.[23] Meanwhile, the rival protagonists— Stanislav of Znjomo and Páleč on the one side, Hus on the other—continued a passionate debate about the Church, to which Hus's *De ecclesia*, published by being read in the Bethlehem chapel early in June 1413, was the most significant contribution.[24] It was a full scale answer to the doctrine of the

---

background, M. Malowist, 'The Problems of the Inequality of Economic Development in Europe and the Later Middle Ages', *Ec.HR*, 2nd ser., XIX (1966), pp. 15–28, esp., p. 21. I owe this ref. to Dr A. V. Antonovics.

[21]F. G. Heymann, *John Žižka and the Hussite Revolution* (Princeton, 1955), (detailed pro-Czech narrative from 1419) pp. 47–8.

[22]Seibt, 'Die Zeit', p. 503.

[23]De Vooght, *Hérésie*, pp. 224–9, discussion of appeal at Constance, p. 395, text trans. in Spinka, *John Hus at the Council*, pp. 237–40.

[24]Context in De Vooght, *Hérésie*, pp. 245–88; on Hus's doctrine of the Church, see *Hussiana*, pp. 124–69; most detailed account in Spinka, *Hus's Concept*; on Hus as thinker and his fate, see

Church implicit in the *consilium* of the conservative theologians at the synod of February. In contradiction to Páleč and Znjomo's notion of the *ecclesiasticum et misticum compositum*, Hus took as his starting-point the definition of the Church by Wyclif as 'the congregation of the predestinate'. Loserth long ago shook the early romantic tradition of Czech scholarship by demonstrating through simple textual comparison how deeply Hus plagiarized from Wyclif's writings;[25] his conclusion was that Hus was a puppet of Wyclif. Today, with a better understanding of the methods of scholasticism and a more realistic appreciation of Hus's intellectual powers, the discovery of widespread borrowing no longer shocks. Hus's relation to Wyclif was subtle. Wyclifian terminology was skilfully redeployed in the interests of a moderate and very largely orthodox theology.[26] Wyclif was valued as a reformer, while the full implications of his thought were not drawn out.[27]

Of course, such a proceeding was undertaken at the expense of fully systematic thought; but Hus was not a theological luminary of the first rank.[28] The structure of the *De ecclesia* makes this apparent. Part one was concerned with the nature of the Church, and discusses Wyclif's definition; part two deals with practical issues. In the first part Hus commits himself to the Wyclifite definition of the Church as the body of all the predestined, which, understood as Wyclif intended it, was heresy; yet in the second he fails to draw out the implications of the defintion. In Wyclif's writings his concept of the Church, with its vital distinction between the *presciti*,[29] foreknown to damnation, and the elect, logically led him to a denial of orthodox belief on the priesthood: no-one who was of the ranks of the *presciti* could be a true priest. In practice, priesthood in Wyclif's late writings has no obvious place. When we turn to part two of Hus's *De ecclesia*, we find he is ceasing to follow Wyclif: more at home in discussion of the practical issues confronting the Church, he veers towards the older and orthodox tradition in Matthias of Janov, of a distinction within the Church between the communion of the elect and the body of the faithful. The priesthood remains, even at the cost of logic. The turning back to Matthias is characteristic: it shows Hus in the last resort more the heir of the earlier Czech reformers than of the Wyclif he so venerated.[30]

Leff, *Heresy*, II, pp. 657–85, and his acute observation in *BJRL*, L (1968), pp. 387–410, stressing moral and practical character of his work. For the text, see *Magistri Johannis Hus tractatus De Ecclesia*, ed. S. H. Thomson (Cambridge, 1956). A still usable translation is that of D. S. Schaff, *De Ecclesia. The Church, by John Huss* (Westport (Conn.) 1915).

[25] J. Loserth, *Huss und Wiclif*, (München & Berlin, 1884; 2nd edn, 1925. Engl. trans., London, 1884); written in six weeks (Thomson, in *Speculum*, XXXVIII (1963), p. 118); see Kaminsky, pp. 36–7, Šmahel, in *BIHR*, XLIII (1970), pp. 26–7.

[26] A major theme of De Vooght, *Hérésie:* see esp. ch. 12 (review by S. H. Thomson, *Speculum*, XXXVIII (1963), pp. 116–21); F. M. Bartoš, 'Apologie de M. Jean Huss contre son Apologiste', *CV*, VIII (1965), pp. 65–74, controversy ibid., pp. 235–8, IX (1966), pp. 175–80; E. Werner, 'Der Kirchenbegriff bei Jan Hus, Jakoubek von Mies, Jan Želivský und den linken Taboriten', *SDAB, Klasse für Philosophie*, Jhrg. 1967, X, pp. 5–73; on Hus, pp. 9–26.

[27] Leff (*BJRL*, L (1968), pp. 387–410) brings a clear mind to bear.

[28] Leff and De Vooght have been preferred on this to F. M. Bartoš (as revealed in *CV*, VIII (1965), pp. 65–74).

[29] See Thomson's criticism of De Vooght's use of the term (*Speculum*, XXXVIII (1963), pp. 116–21).

[30] Leff, in *BJRL*, L (1968), p. 406.

In one issue his thought had moved during his career. In the *De ecclesia* he rejected the papacy as an institution of divine origin. The Petrine text referred only to Peter's confession of belief in the Son of God. The papacy, he believed, had originated with Constantine, and was dispensable. In his doctrine of the Church, therefore, Hus was unable to achieve the feat to which he attained elsewhere, of preserving Wyclif's words within a frame of orthodoxy: there, driven by his contemporary experience of the schism, he broke quite clearly with orthodoxy.[31]

Meanwhile, secure in aristocratic protection during his exile, he preached widely from his base in southern Bohemia, building up noble support in the countryside. When, in 1415, 452 of the nobility and gentry of Bohemia and Moravia put their seals to a protest to the Council of Constance against Hus's execution, a significant proportion of them, according to T. Č. Zelinka's calculations, sprang from this region, where Hus was active during his exile.[32] In this period he was at his most radical: 'he performed divine services, and preached at Kozí Hrádek in a barn . . . —he inveighed against the pope, bishops and canons, and constantly heaped abuse on the spiritual order.' The Czech chronicler goes on to describe activities at Kozí Hrádek (sited immediately south of Tabor on map 11) of a more violent character. 'Here', he said, 'the priest Věněk began to baptize children in a fishpond, and to slander the chrism and holy oil and holy water.'[33] He was describing the beginnings of Taborite radicalism in the countryside, a movement of which Hus could not have approved, but which he may have helped to stimulate by his rural sermons.

The Emergence of the Radicals

In the second decade of the fifteenth century the movement in the countryside rapidly took on a radical tinge: especially after the death of Hus and the introduction of Utraquism in 1415 as a Hussite Church began to form, parishes in the country were taken over by adherents of the reform, and radical priests inspired by the Hussite reform in Prague came out to conduct missions in the country. Some did not take benefices at all, and denounced those who did as 'priests of Pharaoh'.[34] These priests ostentatiously spurned all the apparatus of the late medieval Church, destroyed images, baptized, like Věněk, in ponds and streams, and celebrated mass in a 'purer', truncated liturgy in stables and barns. Their views were Donatist and anti-sacerdotal.

Spontaneously, this radical movement came to resemble post-1414 Lollardy, especially of the school of William White of Norwich,[35] or the Poor Lombard wing of the Waldensians.[36] To what extent the Hussite radicals were reinforced by a pre-existing underground Waldensianism in the

---

[31]De Vooght, *Hérésie*, pp. 466–8.

[32]Spinka, *Hus*, p. 180.

[33]Trans. by Kaminsky, *Revolution*, p. 165; on chronicler, see ibid., n. 78.

[34]Ibid., p. 201; narration generally on pp. 132, 141–70 (clarification of radicals' origins is a major service of Kaminsky; see also his 'Hussite Radicalism and the Origins of Tabor, 1415–1418', *MH*, x (1956), pp. 102–30).

[35]Compare the radicals' sayings (Kaminsky, *Revolution*, pp. 166–7) with the Lollard aphorisms (above, pp. 268–9).

[36]Above, pp. 79–81, 97–8.

countryside of southern Bohemia, finding an outlet as authority and the bonds of society were shaken by the Hussite movement, is still uncertain.[37] Evidence is often faulty. There is a presumption that Waldensianism was carried into Bohemia by the waves of German colonization.

In Austria, of forty-two places where Waldensianism was uncovered by an inquisition held in 1266, as recorded by the Passau Anonymous, six lay near the borders of Bohemia and Moravia. In 1315 fourteen heretics were burnt at Prague: the views attributed to them sound like a mixture of Cathar and Waldensian tenets, but there may be slander and muddle in our sources. In 1335 inquisitors were named by Benedict XII; about 1339 the Prague inquisitor was grappling with an outbreak centred on Jindřichův Hradec (Neuhaus), near the Austrian border, where apparently lapsed heretics attacked the local lord's castle and burned villages. But it has been suggested that the revolt may have been stimulated by the lord's excesses, and the accusation of heresy invented or exaggerated in order to bring in the inquisition. Sporadic references to inquisition activity thereafter demonstrate some continuity of heresy within Bohemia, but not necessarily a heresy with a strong numerical backing. Moreover, the heretics, when identifiable, appear generally to be Germans, and it is not clear how far heresy was able to leap over the linguistic barrier.[38] The evidence remains slender and uncertain, insufficient to support any hypothesis in which Waldensianism would assume a significant role in the development of popular heresy in Bohemia.

During Hus's exile, controversy made clear the impossibility of finding a formula to reconcile Hus with his opponents; Hus had become isolated from the king. In the capital the situation grew less favourable. The interdict imposed in 1412 represented perhaps the first success which the conservatives had had with public opinion since 1403. When in April 1413 Hus still lingered in Prague on one of his visits, and the parish clergy observed the interdict, there were diquieting signs that public opinion was being mobilized against him.[39] The king requested Hus to leave to avoid disturbances. His physical safety was still not in question, but the kingdom remained under pressure from abroad.

Hus at Constance

An initiative, born of Luxemburg family affairs, seemed to break the impasse. Sigismund, the brother of Wenceslas and often his enemy, had in 1410 been elected king of the Romans, by implication in rivalry to Wenceslas who would not accept that he had been deposed from this position. In 1411 the two

---

[37]A. Molnár, 'Les Vaudois en Bohême avant la Révolution hussite', *CV*, LXXXV (1964), cxvi, pp. 3–17, supersedes S. H. Thomson, 'Pre-Hussite Heresy in Bohemia', *EHR*, XLVIII (1933), pp. 23–42. See discussion, more positive on Waldensianism than Molnár, in Kaminsky, *Revolution*, pp. 171–9. Had Nicholas of Dresden and his school undergone Waldensian influence? See now Gonnet and Molnár, *Vaudois*, ch. 5.

[38]See Jerome of Prague's statement early in 1409 that heretics had been burnt in Prague within living memory—but not pure Bohemians (Seibt, *Hussitica*, p. 80). Were they Germans? Kaminsky discusses bilingualism (p. 178, n. 114). Further work on Bohemian Waldensianism is to be expected from Dr A. Patschovsky, who is editing a Bohemian inquisitor's handbook (Wolfenbüttel, MS. Helmstedt 311).

[39]De Vooght, *Hérésie*, pp. 262–3.

brothers sank their differences. Sigismund promised not to have himself crowned emperor so long as Wenceslas was alive. Then in 1414, if we can accept Bartoš's interpretation, the brothers struck another bargain.[40] Wenceslas agreed to the coronation of Sigismund on condition that Sigismund managed a settlement of his problem with Hus. The council which, largely through the initiative of Sigismund, had been summoned at Constance to settle the schism, offered a way out of the Hus issue. Hus should leave Bohemia to appear before the fathers of the council, thereby relieving Wenceslas of the external pressure on the kingdom, which he so much disliked.[41]

Probably neither of these lay rulers understood the intensity of feeling about Wyclifism. Hus hoped for more from the council than from the pope, and in optimistic moments believed that its members would join with him in reform. At Constance he had a sermon ready written but never delivered, calling on the council to put an end to the abuses.[42] He never completely trusted the safe conduct Sigismund offered—he wrote of the danger of death, and made his will before he left—but at the same time he was aware of the dangers to Bohemia if he stayed away from Constance. To go offered the chance of legitimizing the Bohemian movement and spreading it to the whole Church: bravely, and a little optimistically, he finally took the chance.[43]

When in October 1414 Hus left Bohemia on his journey to Constance, the movement for reform entered on a new phase. Long years of controversy within the kingdom had the effect that Hus, leaving for judgement at the curia, like Waldhauser and Milič before him, had behind him a much wider range of supporters and a much more thoroughly aroused public opinion.[44] A party that included clergy, skilful organizers, court officials and nobility followed with a passionate attention the twists and turns of a theological investigation which lasted from the end of the year, when Hus appeared first as an independent theologian freely come for learned discussion, to July 1415, when he was burnt as a heretic.[45] Stage by stage Hus's position worsened as, despite the initial compromise when John XXIII left him freedom of movement in return for the promise not to preach or appear at the formal ceremonies of the council, he was arrested and the safe conduct disregarded. Then in March, after John had fled from Constance, he was taken to be held incommunicado in the castle of the bishop of Constance at Gottlieben and finally brought back to be exposed to tumultuous public hearings and condemned. Weeks of well-meaning pressure to secure recantation, always firmly refused, ended in the ceremonies of degradation and public burning.

This dark story was described in the *Relatio* of Peter of Mladoňovice,

[40]For all the complications, Seibt, 'Die Zeit', pp. 476–93.

[41]*CV*, VIII (1965), pp. 69–70; Spinka, p. 222.

[42]Ibid., p. 226.

[43]Seibt 'Die Zeit', pp. 505–6, on safe-conduct, p. 504 and n. 40; will in *Letters of John Hus*, trans. H. B. Workman and R. M. Pope, pp. 149–51; see De Vooght, *Hérésie*, p. 316.

[44]Seibt's comment ('Die Zeit', p. 504).

[45]The best modern account is De Vooght, *Hérésie*, pp. 325–459; see also Spinka, pp. 219–90, comments in Kaminsky, pp. 52–5, 125, 133, 136–61; correction in P. De Vooght, 'Jean Huss et ses Juges', in *Das Konzil von Konstanz*, ed. A. Franzen and W. Müller, (Freiburg, etc., 1964), pp. 152–73.

secretary to Hus's noble supporter, John of Chlum, who observed the course of events in Constance.[46] His work was the Passion of a martyr, forming the classic picture for public opinion in Bohemia, its story of the death in chapter 5 becoming a set text for reading on the national day of Hus's suffering, 6 July. Sigismund, failing to stand by his safe conduct, was overheard acceding to Hus's burning, and thus played Judas; a party of native Bohemians, headed by the inveterate Czech enemy Páleč, the legal expert Michael de Causis, John Nas, the Prague canon of a German family, and Bishop John the Iron of Litomyšl, stood in the place of the Scribes and Pharisees at the trial of Jesus, and called for a hostile judgement. Hus, referred to as 'the Master', bore his martyrdom with patient dignity. The story, if written with *parti pris* by one of his supporters, followed the facts of the case, reproducing documents and quoting the participants with the pungency of an eyewitness. Hus himself, apart from the stay at Gottlieben, was never held so close that he could not receive visitors and write letters. The simple letters of exhortation to his friends written at Constance came to form a part of the devotional literature of a saint, suited to strengthen the faith of simpler followers who could not follow the complexities of the debates during the trial. For the nobles, and for humbler followers, the issue of honour, centring round the safe conduct Sigismund had given, became a key factor; for it was something instantly comprehended by them, when theological complexities passed them by. Hus and his followers believed their master was to have the chance to explain the principles of the Bohemian reform at the Council; the fathers at Constance had no such idea, and intended to investigate Hus like any other heretic. When it became clear that Hus was not going to receive anything other than the normal treatment of a heretic, the sense of shock and betrayal in Bohemia grew.

In October 1414 some leading nobles had written to Sigismund, drawing attention to Conrad of Vechta's certificate of Hus's orthodoxy, and urging him to ensure that Hus was not 'furtively abused, to the dishonour of our nationality and of the Bohemian land.'[47] That note, of the dishonouring of Bohemia by the council, continued to be struck. The nobles at home, informed by John of Chlum and his party and stimulated by a nucleus of committed Hussites, wrote letters of protest to Sigismund.[48] Sigismund had to consider Bohemian opinion; the childlessness of Wenceslas made it virtually certain that he would be the heir if anything occurred to remove Wenceslas from the throne. He was not prepared to commit himself *à l'outrance* to defend Hus from a council bent on prosecution of heresy; he did, however, use his influence to ensure that Hus was given a public hearing,[49] and d'Ailly and the directing forces of the council allowed Hus such hearings in order to satisfy Sigismund, despite the fact that by 7 June their own minds were made up against Hus.

The hearings gained virtually nothing for Hus and his cause—the hearing

---

[46]Text in Spinka, *John Hus at the Council*, pp. 89–234.
[47]Trans. Kaminsky, p. 138; on term trans. as 'nationality', see Seibt, *Hussitica*, pp. 102–17.
[48]Spinka, *John Hus at the Council*, pp. 153–4, 158–61; on feeling behind letters, see Seibt, *Hussitica*, pp. 102–17, on party organization, pp. 138–40.
[49]De Vooght, *Hérésie*, pp. 335, 385–6.

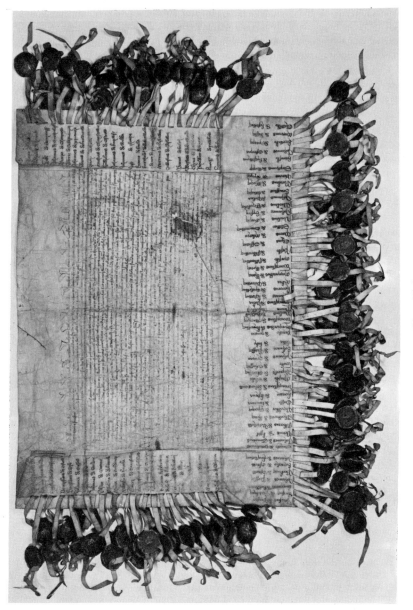

Plate Eight

The Protest of the Hussite Nobility, 1415.

of 7 June had to be adjourned because of disorder, and in two subsequent hearings Hus was interrupted too constantly to enable him to make an effective plea. Instead, they formed a part of the martyrdom: Peter headed his chapter on them in the *Relatio*, 'Here follow the so-called Hearings, but in Truth not Hearings but Jeerings and Vilifications.'[50] Towards the end, Sigismund became convinced that Hus was a heretic. Without following the theology with any attention, his interest then lay in urging Hus to recantation. Hus's scruples and his unwillingness to recant what he had not written Sigismund plainly did not understand. Then, when the final tragedy occurred and Hus was burnt, the resultant emotions in Bohemia blackened the council as an acceptable doctrinal authority, together with Sigismund as a ruler of honour, and fatally discredited the party of native Bohemians under Bishop John of Litomyšl, who had pressed for a condemnation and expected to go on to break the Hussites at home.

The protests of the nobility culminated in the letter of 2 September 1415 to the council, which baldly asserted that Hus was falsely burnt,[51] and amounted to a direct defiance of the proceedings of the council. In the eight copies which reached the council, 452 nobles of Bohemia and Moravia had put their seals to this defiance.[52] Such a rejection of an ecclesiastical decision on a matter of faith has no earlier parallel, certainly not in the patriotic support of an old Church, said to have been infected by heresy, in backward Bosnia,[53] or the mobilization of Languedocian patriotism and some religious feeling, part patronage, part true adherence, for the Cathars among the southern French baronage.[54] The actions of the council in 1415 had resulted in something new in the history of medieval heresy. A deeply emotional issue, rapidly comprehensible to all, in which religious sentiment blended with the defence of the honour of Bohemia, had assembled a wide segment of the nobility in the defence of a cause now branded as heresy.

Such a mobilization of opinion at home, it will be noticed, would not have been possible if Hus had been induced to abjure. The protesters were aware that Hus died *non convictus et non confessus*;[55] had this not been the case, many who were not directly committed to the cause of reform would not have been brought to join the protest of 2 September, and Hus's own party would have been left in disarray.

To Cardinal d'Ailly, Hus was just another case of heresy.[56] A nominalist, he believed that realism had the eucharistic heresy of remanentism as a consequence, and was not impressed by Hus's denials. For the body of the council, the reputation of Hus in Bohemia was decisive; if they wavered in

---

[50]Spinka, *John Hus at the Council*, p. 163.

[51]Kaminsky, pp. 143, 144 n. 9.

[52]See the distribution of protesters in map 11, pp. 302–3. For text and list of names, see F. Palacký, *Documenta J. Hus vitam illustrantia* (Prague, 1869), pp. 580–90. The Edinburgh MS. (P.C. 42), reproduced in illustration 8, contains 100 names, but one of the seals is missing. I owe information to Mr C. P. Finlayson, Keeper of MSS, Edinburgh University Library.

[53]Above, pp. 142–50.

[54]Above, pp. 100–1.

[55]Seibt, 'Die Zeit', pp. 505–6.

[56]Bartoš, in *CV*, IX (1966), pp. 175–6; see also *CV*, VIII (1965), pp. 72, 236; De Vooght, *Hérésie*, p. 389.

that view Páleč, John of Litomyšl and the rest were there to assure them.[57] Thus Hus's series of negative denials *nec tenui nec teneo* to the old Wyclifite forty-five articles made an impression, and his efforts at clarification had the result that the distorting forty-two articles of Páleč were finally whittled down to eleven; nevertheless, his own past defence of Wyclif dogged him. In part, the feeling of the council was comparable to that of inquisitors facing a simple heretic, who took the accused's denials for cunning evasions: repeatedly members of the council expressed the view that, though Hus might make sophistical denials, he continued to believe heresy with his heart. He was not allowed to examine the witnesses against him. While the extracting of articles from his works was supervised by the investigating commission with care, and did contain just, as well as unjust, attributions of doctrine, it was the testimony of witnesses that most obviously distorted Hus's views;[58] too many arrived at the council believing in Hus's guilt and the complexity of the evidence did not help them to shed their prejudice.

At the end, Hus refused to abjure, though to do so would have saved his life. He refused because of his utter unwillingness to abjure articles extracted from his works that he did believe and to recant articles that he claimed were not his own.[59] His courage helped to preserve the Bohemian movement. When on 31 August John of Litomyšl, following up the burning, received authorization to act against Hussites, he found a great barrier of sentiment interposed between Bohemia and the council decrees.

The Lay Chalice

Almost simultaneously the movement had acquired a symbol of its breach with the hierarchy assembled at Constance.[60] In the autumn of 1414 certain Hussites began to administer the chalice to the laity, and the practice spread. John complained to the council of irregularities accompanying the lay chalice; consecrated wine was carried about the country in flasks, and a woman who claimed the right of the laity to impose Utraquism snatched the chalice from the hands of a priest.[61] On 15 June 1415 the council prohibited the administration of the chalice to the laity. They admitted the facts of Christ's institution of the eucharist in both kinds and the precedent of the primitive Church, but argued that both the lay chalice and the reception of the eucharist after dinner had been discontinued for good reasons.[62] Hus had not initiated the chalice—'Go slow, Kubo,'[63] he was supposed to have said to his friend Jakoubek before he left—but he had favoured it in principle, and

[57]Kaminsky, pp. 37–40, 52, Leff, II, p. 648.

[58]De Vooght, *Hérésie*, pp. 334, 363, 388–90, 394, 410–1, 420–2.

[59]See comments in M. Creighton, *A History of the Papacy from the Great Schism to the Sack of Rome*, II (London, 1899), ch. 5. Trans. of thirty articles on which Hus was condemned in Spinka, *John Hus at . . . Constance*.

[60]On introduction of chalice and controversy on it, Kaminsky, pp. 98–126; F. Seibt, 'Die *Revelatio* des Jacobellus von Mies über die Kelchkommunion', *DA*, XXII (1967), pp. 618–24. On Jakoubek generally, see now P. De Vooght, *Jacobellus de Stříbro († 1429), premier Théologien du Hussitisme* (Louvain, 1972).

[61]Kaminsky, p. 132, and his section on 'The Utraquist Victory' (pp. 126–36).

[62]Ibid., p. 116.

[63]Ibid., pp. 133–4.

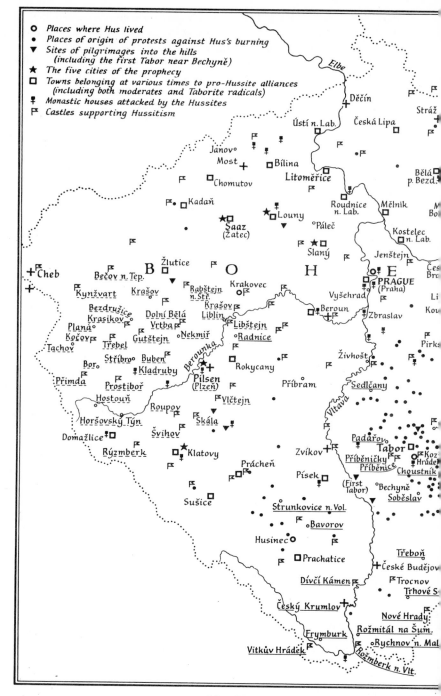

Legend

○ Places where Hus lived
● Places of origin of protests against Hus's burning
▼ Sites of pilgrimages into the hills
(including the first Tabor near Bechyně)
★ The five cities of the prophecy
□ Towns belonging at various times to pro-Hussite alliances
(including both moderates and Taborite radicals)
⚓ Monastic houses attacked by the Hussites
⚑ Castles supporting Hussitism

Elbe

Děčín
Stráž
Ústí n. Lab.
Česká Lipa

Jánov
Most
Bílina
Litoměřice
Bělá
p. Bezd.
Chomutov
Mělník
Mo
Roudnice
n. Lab.
Kadaň
Kostelec
n. Lab.
Šaaz
(Žatec)
Louny
Páleč
Jenštejn
Slaný
Čes
Bro
Žlutice

B   O   H   E
PRAGUE
(Praha)
Cheb
Bečov n. Tep.
Li
Krakovec
Vyšehrad
Kou
Kynžvart
Krašov
Rabštejn
n. Stř.
Beroun
Bezdružice
Krašov
Zbraslav
Krasíkov
Dolní Bělá
Liblin
Planá
Vrtba
Libštejn
Živhošt
Pirks
Kočov
Nekmíř
Tachov
Gutštejn
Radnice
Trebel
Bor
Stříbro
Buben
Rokycany
Sedlčany
Přímda
Kladruby
Pilsen
(Plzeň)
Příbram
Prostiboř
Hostouň
Vlčtejn
Roupov
Zvíkov
Padařov
Horšovský Týn
Skála
Tabor
Domažlice
Švihov
Příběničky
Koz
Hráde
Ryzmberk
Klatovy
Příběnice
Choustník
Prácheň
Písek
(First
Tabor)
Bechyně
Soběslav
Sušice
Strunkovice n. Vol.
Bavorov
Husinec
Třeboň
Prachatice
České Budějov
Dívčí Kámen
Trocnov
Trhové S
Český Krumlov
Nové Hrady
Rožmitál na Šum.
Frymburk
Rychnov n. Mal
Vitkův Hrádek
Rožmberk n. Vlt.

Map Eleven
The Hussite Movement in Bohemia and Moravia

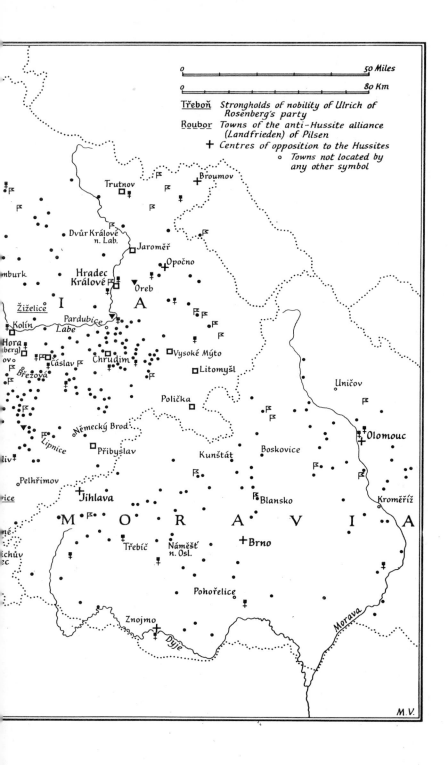

Třeboň   Strongholds of nobility of Ulrich of
        Rosenberg's party
Roubor   Towns of the anti-Hussite alliance
        (Landfrieden) of Pilsen
✝   Centres of opposition to the Hussites
○   Towns not located by
        any other symbol

50 Miles

80 Km

Trutnov

Broumov

Dvůr Králové
n. Lab.

Jaroměř

Opočno

Hradec
Králové

Oreb

Žiželice

Pardubice

Kolín

Labe

Hora
(berg)

Cáslav

Chrudim

Vysoké Mýto

ovo

Brežová

Litomyšl

Uničov

Polička

Olomouc

Německý Brod

Přibyslav

Kunštát

Boskovice

Lipnice

Pelhřimov

ice

Jihlava

Blansko

Kroměříž

M   O   R   A   V   I   A

né.

chův
ec

Třebíč

Náměšť
n. Osl.

Brno

Pohořelice

Znojmo

Dyje

Morava

M.V.

rejected the council's decree because it was a decision which went against Scripture.

Jakoubek, early defender of the lay chalice, spoke of the idea coming to him by *revelatio*, by which he meant the illumination which comes after prolonged consideration and study. Who exactly first raised the issue is still not clear. But it was a natural project to spring out of study of Matthias of Janov, who laid such stress on the importance of frequent communion, and to whom Jakoubek and others were so indebted. Over the centuries the laity had been excluded from the reception of the consecrated wine by a spontaneous development of the liturgy without any protest being made or the exclusion even being noticed: lack of interest in the issue was a natural concomitant of a situation in which the laity did not receive communion more than once a year.[64] Elsewhere in the fourteenth century, as in the case of the German mystical movement, stress on frequent communion did not lead to agitation for the restoration of the lay chalice. The Bohemian reform, however, was floated in an atmosphere of anticlericalism, which grew more intense in the early fifteenth century: in that atmosphere it is explicable that the withdrawal of the chalice should eventually have been seen as an unjust deprivation for which the clergy were responsible.

Paradoxically the Council's decree against the chalice actually fostered its spread. The decree of 15 June was followed by Hus's burning on 6 July: the two decisions tended to be lumped together in the minds of the Bohemians and Moravians, and the emotional reaction against the one buttressed the other.

Once the idea was launched, pre-existing Hussite thinking about the Church was brought into play in its defence. The chalice, at first sight a minor issue of eucharistic practice, renewed the debate over the whole nature of the Church and its *magisterium,* which had developed over Hus's *De ecclesia* and had been important at Constance.[65] Both sides were agreed that the body and blood of Christ were contained wholly in either the wine or the bread after consecration, yet the withdrawal by custom, despite the words of institution by Christ in the Last Supper, raised the question: what were the limits of the Church's power of decision over Scriptural precedents? The conservatives argued that the Church, having seen the benefits of communion in one kind, could rightly decide against the earlier precedents. For the Hussites that view was impossible, for the Church which decreed such alterations in early practice was the stained Church responsible for such evils in contemporary Christian life. They took their stand on such texts as John's, 'Except ye eat the flesh of the Son of Man and drink his blood, ye have no life in you.'[66]

The introduction of the chalice gained momentum as humbler members of the Hussite party among the clergy followed Jakoubek's lead, Hussite aristocrats sponsored the chalice, and local congregations eagerly responded. Passions were aroused. Prague, where the movement began, split into reformed congregations where the chalice was given, and traditional ones

---

[64]D. Girgensohn, *Peter von Pulkau und die Wiedereinführung des Laienkelches* (Göttingen, 1964) (reviewed by H. Kaminsky, *Speculum,* XLI (1966), pp. 132–4).

[65]Kaminsky, pp. 108–26 *passim.*

[66]John 6, 53.

where it was not. In April 1415 the town councillors prohibited either side calling each other heretics.[67] Utraquism touched every attender at mass in an immediate fashion; it forced the ordinary man to think out his relation to the Hussite movement before he took the step of going over to a congregation where the chalice was administered. The erosion of discipline brought about by the earlier conflicts over Wyclifism now enfeebled attempts to suppress the movement.

In November 1415 a further attempt to use coercion had the effect of bringing the victory of Utraquism. Conrad of Vechta, the cautious and opportunist royal servant, was induced to impose an interdict on Prague on the grounds that it gave residence to John Jesenic, who had long been excommunicate. As the support for the lay chalice, apart from Christian of Prachatice, lay among the unbeneficed clergy, the interdict made possible a takeover on a revolutionary scale.[68] Those who refused the chalice found themselves restricted to the suburban churches, where the interdict had not been imposed. A lifting of the interdict only brought the archbishop into difficulties with the council, still sitting at Constance; when it was re-imposed in 1416 lasting damage had already been done to the conservative position.

Giving the chalice to the laity involved more than a mere liturgical change. Where, as in Prague, the crowd pressed for the lay chalice, or, as elsewhere in the country, the noble patrons of livings wanted it, benefice-holders were presented with an ultimatum: in the last resort, to accept the chalice or to leave.[69] The same process operated in Moravia, where the canons of Olomouc complained to the council of the barons who maintained Utraquist priests.[70] Such actions necessarily involved a breach of the legal structure which gave the clergy tenure of their livings and rights to tithes and alms, and left decisions over their discipline to the bishops and the procedures of the canon law. Introducing the lay chalice by force was an actual demonstration of the superior powers of the laity over their clergy, whether it was exercised in the name of the lay patrons or of a local congregation, perhaps loosely represented by a Utraquist crowd. Utraquism could thus appeal to patrons among the nobility who hoped to recover the wider powers of patrons that they had held under the *Eigenkirche* system.[71] Wyclif, Hus and the Czech reforming party had taught the need for a poor Church, and Hus in his Czech work on simony had spoken of the rights of lay patrons and their duties to ensure spiritual care of a benefice:[72] Utraquism offered the opportunity to secure all these things.

Failure of Utraquists to impose their will in the parish churches also affected the situation. It tended to result in the formation of *ad hoc* congregations, for whom Hussite priests celebrated mass, in the words of one complaint, 'in fields and on casks, in barns on no consecrated altar'.[73] Such arrangements might begin, *faute de mieux*, because a consecrated altar for

[67]Kaminsky, pp. 156–7.

[68]Ibid., pp. 157–61; note general comment by Seibt (*Hussitica*, p. 129).

[69]Kaminsky, p. 160.

[70]Ibid., p. 163.

[71]Seibt, 'Die Zeit', pp. 512–13, early geographical distribution of Utraquists, p. 514; Kaminsky, pp. 151–6.

[72]Ibid., pp. 152–3.

[73]Trans. from letter of canons of Olomouc (ibid., p. 163).

L

Utraquist masses had been denied; they became demonstrations by the radical wing of the movement of their rejection of the apparatus of material aids to devotion and of the traditional ceremonial of the medieval Church. In congregations, Utraquism was one of a number of rejections, of the need for confession, for set forms of service, for law, even for priesthood with special powers.

Not all of these concomitants of Utraquism were desired by the nobility *en masse*; indeed, the Hussite league formed to defend Hussitism on 5 September 1415 by almost the same group of fifty-eight nobles who had sent the initial letter of protest about Hus's burning, never mentioned the lay chalice at all among the articles of their agreement.[74] The league stood for free preaching on Hussite lines without consideration for any technical issues of provision and appointment. The authority of bishops was not *per se* excluded: if accusations of error were made, the compact provided that a priest should be taken to his bishop for judgement, but that clause was subject to the important proviso that the error must be demonstrable by Holy Scripture and that, if the bishop attempted to punish a priest 'improperly, privately and without demonstration on the basis of Holy Scripture' the decision should be left in the hands of the university.

In effect, the league interposed a barrier between the kingdom and the operations of either the council or ecclesiastical authorities obedient to the council within the kingdom. The doctrinal authority of the international Church was replaced by that of the university,[75] and the jurisdiction of bishops made subject, in a way now characteristic of Hussite proceedings, to the private conscience of members of the league.

Nevertheless the league acted as a shield for the spread of the chalice, and inhibited the carrying out of hostile decrees of Constance through the vital years 1415–16. Citations to the council of all the 452 nobles who had put their names to the protest of September 1415 and proceedings against the magistrates and courtiers held responsible for allowing the spread of Utraquism were of no effect, since the league's membership was so weighty as to inhibit any Catholic reaction inside Bohemia from compelling obedience to these summons.[76]

The king remained passive. He carried neutrality towards the council almost beyond the limits of the possible. Alone of the kings of Western Europe, he sent no ambassadors to Constance. Probably his queen was more affected by the death of Hus than he was; his prevailing emotions seem to have been one of pique at the insult to his power, and suspicion of his brother's plans. Although he made no protest himself, he did nothing to prevent the protest letters of his nobility from being despatched. His whole position with regard to

---

[74]Trans. ibid., pp. 144–5; on background, pp. 141–61; see still E. Denis, *Huss et la guerre des Hussites* (Paris, 1878, 1930) (based on pioneer work of the great F. Palacký, yet has charm and perspective, and grows in value post 1415), pp. 177–9; J. Kejř, 'Zur Entstehungsgeschichte des Hussitentums', in *Die Welt zur Zeit des Konstanzer Konzils. Reichenau-Vorträge im Herbst 1964: Vorträge und Forschungen*, IX (Konstanz & Stuttgart, 1965), pp. 147–61.

[75]See Kejř, *Die Welt*, p. 53.

[76]Kaminsky, *Revolution*, pp. 149, 222–3; Denis, *Huss*, pp. 184–5.

his nobility was weak. Aristocratic powers in Bohemia were a problem of long standing.[77]

Seen from one point of view the division of the country into factions based on religious differences was nothing more than a continuation of earlier baronial dissidence[78] and Wenceslas's response, doing nothing and declaring that there was no heresy in Bohemia, a natural course of action for a ruler who lacked effective weapons against his nobles. The council, however, was not sympathetic to Wenceslas's difficulties, and had in their hands the threat of a crusade, a fact which probably influenced Wenceslas to attempt to act against the Hussites late in 1416. The reaction did not achieve very much;[79] it neither diminished the use of the lay chalice, nor brought about a return of the ecclesiastical property that had been seized in previous years, and the king soon gave it up.

In the country, Čeněk of Vartemberk, meeting the threat of a stifling of the Utraquist priesthood in the long run by the refusal of the hierarchy to ordain men of Utraquist views, compelled a suffragan bishop in the Prague diocese to ordain at his castle of Lipnic his own candidates, all Hussite and tending to be radical in their theology.[80] The university, threatened in the winter, emerged from stress as the active doctrinal authority of a Hussite Church which the league of September 1415 had envisaged.[81] They settled their internal disputes by declaring on 10 March 1417 that the chalice was beneficial to the salvation of all.

Radicals and Moderates within the Hussite Movement

Early in 1417 the university was engaged in defining its position towards its own Hussite radicals just as much as towards the council and its Catholic opponents. The gulf between the moderates of the stamp of Christian or Jesenic and the provincial radicals was already wide. The extremists, especially in the provinces, wanted drastic changes that entailed upsetting customary services. Rejecting purgatory involved the abolition of the chantries and the traditional masses for relatives and ancestors. Already a Czech version of the mass was in circulation, sponsored by Jakoubek;[82] provincial radicals wished to go beyond this and truncate the mass, turning it into a simple communion service with preaching closely based on the words of Scripture. They wanted to reject the intercession of saints. The radicals discussed in a letter of Christian Prachatice to Wenceslas Koranda, a provincial preacher, advocated that 'dubious relics of the saints should be thrown out on dung heaps.'[83] Koranda was actively destroying images. If the radicals had their way, the moderate Utraquists would find customary

---

[77]Seibt, 'Die Zeit', pp. 476–7, Heymann, *Žižka*, pp. 24–8, 37.

[78]Kaminsky, pp. 147–8. Sigismund, who hoped to inherit Bohemia, was probably sincere in his appeals for unity at this time.

[79]Ibid., pp. 223–7.

[80]Ibid., p. 242.

[81]Full context, ibid., ch. 5, an account which supersedes earlier narratives of events in 1417–18.

[82]Ibid., pp. 198, 257; cf. p. 194.

[83]Trans. ibid., p. 169. Note Kaminsky's reconstruction of the probable attitudes of Hussite lords to such actions (ibid., pp. 228–9).

patterns of Church life turned upside down. Moreover, there was an element of opposition to authority in the movement in the provinces: the driving-force came from certain lower clergy, but Christian also referred to unlearned laymen and women who were asserting their opinions.

The radicals were rejecting authority in the Church, whether of the bishop or of the university masters, in favour of the appeal to the text of Scripture. Their ideal was that of the gathered community centred on the chalice, using the power of magistrates to make the law of God prevail. From an attack on Hussite Church authority, there was an easy transition to the attack on secular authority, the rights of property, and the position of the nobility. Moderate Hussites, whose aims might be summed up in the desire for a measure of autonomy from the Roman Church and for the lay chalice, had every reason to be perturbed. The problem was not new in 1417. It followed from the cast of Hussite preaching before 1415, with its appeal to the law of Christ as overriding unjust decrees of the Church.[84]

Hussite theses opened the way to private judgement as the norm; the problem as the movement began to move sections of the populace was to know where to stop. At first the radicals, Nicholas of Dresden and Jakoubek, had worked together for the introduction of the lay chalice; probably in the autumn of 1415 they split, initially over the existence of purgatory. In the following year Nicholas left Prague and went to Meissen, where he was executed; Želivský, who took his place in 1418-19 as the radical preacher of the movement in Prague, believed that he had been pushed out by the university masters. Nicholas, in his sermon collection *Querite primum regnum*, was defending, in effect, Waldensian theses: he was rejecting all killing and oath-taking, and his discussion of the powers of the priesthood virtually eliminated the bishop. This was too much for the main body of Hussite masters, and for Jakoubek.[85]

Jakoubek's own position was unusual. As a leading radical among the masters and as the originator of the lay chalice, he held a certain responsibility for the extreme positions which were emerging in the provinces.[86] Clergy influenced by him went from Prague to preach in the country. Their violent destruction of images, so dangerous to unity, could find support in his writings; in 1414 in his *Sermo de confessione* he had rejected confession to a priest as inessential. A puritanical strain in his character, which led him to condemn singing and dancing, brought him closer to the radicals than to the moderate Prague leadership.

---

[84]See Werner, 'Der Kirchenbegriff', pp. 14-15, 21; A Molnár, 'Hus et son appel à Jésus-Christ' *CV*, viii (1965), pp. 95-104, De Vooght, *Hérésie*, pp. 151-3, 173, 176, 208-9, 226-7, 395, *lex Christi* in Prague 1408, pp. 89-92; for Jesenic on this issue, Kaminsky, *Revolution*, pp. 63-4. On the use of the term *lex evangelica* in pre-Hussite Bohemia, S. H. Thomson in *Speculum* xxxviii (1963), 116-21.

[85]Želivský's evidence in Kaminsky, *Revolution*, p. 219; *Querite*, ibid., pp. 207-13, death at Meissen, Kaminsky, 'Nicholas of Dresden', p. 12.

[86]For this and Jakoubek generally, Kaminsky, *Revolution*, is fundamental: see esp. pp. 180-204, synopsis in his 'Hussite Radicalism and the Origins of Tabor, 1415-1418', *MH*, x (1956), pp. 102-30; comments by De Vooght, in *RHE*, LXIII (1968), pp. 543-7, with deserved praise, but with some doubt whether Kaminsky sometimes explains theological opinion too much by the background of events and politics.

At the same time Jakoubek formed a part of the body of masters that were engaged in discussions intended to hold the often contradictory wings of the movement together. Because of his popularizing of the lay chalice, his simple and unworldly life, and his long connection with the reform party in the university, he occupied a position of leadership, and perhaps more than anyone helped to keep the wings together at a crucial stage.

The St Wenceslas synod of 28 September 1418 represented another attempt at a formula for unity, this time both more far-reaching and more inclined towards radicalism.[87] An assembly of masters and priests agreed on twenty-three articles, and laid down that in future no one was to teach any novelty without first submitting it for examination 'by the community of the brethren'. The articles rejected some key Waldensian-type theses, on the denial of purgatory, the refusal of the death penalty, Donatism and the right of laymen to consecrate at mass. The underlying principle of the extremists, that the explicit statements of Scripture constitute all that may be believed, was not allowed; yet, at the same time, the principle of the appeal to the primitive Church was preserved and, while a number of traditional Roman practices were allowed, they were suffered only under such qualifications as would still in fact allow for their abolition if the congregation so wished. The use of images, for example, was tolerated only if they were 'not wantonly or falsely adorned, in such a way as to seduce the eyes of communicants'[88] and provided it was not accompanied by outward acts of devotion, such as kneeling or the burning of candles. Latin was kept for the mass, but Czech was prescribed for the epistle and gospel, and all was subject to future change; ceremonies helpful to the law of God were to be kept 'unless something better is found'.[89] Infant communion, strongly disputed by John Jesenic and Simon of Tišnov, was allowed. The intention was to brake development on some issues, and to bring extremists under a Hussite synodal authority.

Unity among the Hussites from 1415 to 1418 was made easier by the rigid attitudes of the council. Having committed themselves in *Cum in nonnullis*, the fathers gave no sign thereafter till the end of the council in April 1418 that they were ready to negotiate the kind of compromise on the chalice that might have split moderate Hussites from extremists.[90] Those like Simon of Tišnov, who found the pace too hot, were offered no kind of halfway house between Hussitism as it was developing and complete submission to the other side. The election of Martin V as Pope in November 1417, who had had earlier, hostile experience of the Hus case[91] ensured the continuance of a firm line towards Bohemia. The project of a crusade was taken up again.[92] Early in 1419 the king determined on the only possible answer—the suppression of Hussitism. This, the last Catholic reaction of the reign, sparked off revolution.

[87]Kaminsky, *Revolution*, pp. 259–64.
[88]Kaminsky's trans. (ibid., p. 261).
[89]From Kaminsky's summary (ibid., p. 260).
[90]For conciliar attitudes, see J. Kejř, *Die Welt*, p. 60.
[91]Spinka, *Hus*, p. 114.
[92]For these and subsequent events, Denis, *Huss*, pp. 198–209 is still serviceable. Kaminsky, *Revolution*, pp. 266–96, blends narrative with analysis of motives of Želivský and incipient Taborites; his 'The Prague Insurrection of 30 July 1419', *MH*, XVII (1966), pp. 106–26, is the best account of the defenestration.

Tabor and Revolution

The king's major action was to decree the suppression of Utraquism in Prague and in the royal towns controlled by his officials. In the capital he yielded sufficiently to the entreaties of the magistrates and the burgomaster to allow three monastery churches to be left for the administration of the lay chalice. But all the others, apart from Christian of Prachatice's church, were re-occupied by Catholic incumbents.

The Catholics celebrated their victory provocatively. Churches and altars were ceremoniously reconsecrated, Hussite clergy forbidden to use the side altars of churches, Utraquists thrust out of office, and absolution refused to the sick who would not renounce the chalice. Parish schools provided a point of conflict within the capital. The Utraquists did not give them up; the returned incumbents opposed to the chalice thereupon established their own in bell-towers and in buildings belonging to their parish. Pupils of the rival schools exchanged blows and, as adults joined in, affrays developed in which men were killed. The forces of moderate Hussitism felt unable to react against their king in his desperation. It was left to the radicals to fight the repression, and thus to save the whole movement from oblivion.

In the provinces, the sudden prohibition of Utraquism in the churches drove out the zealous congregations wherever the royal order was obeyed. Automatically, initiative passed to the radical clergy. In southern Bohemia, the traditional radical area, chronicles describe the assembling of deprived Utraquists at about Easter time, when under the old order the annual communion of the laity was due.[93] A hill, probably Němějice near the castle of Bechyně, became a gathering point at which Utraquist congregations received the chalice and listened to sermons, and was renamed Tabor after the site in Galilee where Christ took his disciples for the Transfiguration;[94] it soon became the centre for a dramatic development of radical Hussitism. Persecution at this late stage fused scattered congregations and precipitated change. Tabor, from being an occasional meeting-place, became a settlement, with peasants from a distance abandoning their goods and setting off to the mountain for the services and the preaching; attempts by lords to prohibit their peasantry from attending helped to precipitate their flight. Other hills in southern Bohemia were taken as sites and given biblical names such as Horeb[95] and Olivet.[96] Congregations came together in great numbers in a kind of cycle of liturgical celebrations and open-air preaching missions, culminating in a meeting of 22 July which deeply impressed the chroniclers. They estimated the numbers present variously at forty and fifty thousand, and described contingents derived from the areas of Pilsen, Domažlice, Hradec Králové, Moravia and Prague.[97]

Preaching under the shadow of the imminent end of the lay chalice, a persecution which to the crowds at this time seemed to resemble those that

---

[93]Trans. of sources in Kaminsky, *Revolution*, pp. 278–80.

[94]Kaminsky, pp. 280–3 and notes. Fundamental Czech work on Tabor by J. Macek (Marxist) (reviewed, Seibt, *Bohemica*, p. 96 (and index s.v. Macek); discussed in Kaminsky, pp. 149n., 172n., 285n., 287–8, 320n., 341–2, 352n., 393, 398, 403–4, 422).

[95]Heymann, *Žižka*, pp. 131–3.

[96]Kaminsky, *Revolution*, p. 288, n. 84.

[97]Ibid., pp. 290–2.

presage the Last Things, aided the spread of chiliastic expectations. The renaming of Bohemian hills after the mountains in Scripture, as Molnár points out, would set up powerful echoes in the minds of the congregations— of the delivery of the Law to Moses on a mountain, of Christ's Sermon on the Mount, of the meeting of God and man in the transfiguration at Tabor.[98] Preaching and communion was followed by a meal, resembling the *agape* of the early Christians. Collections were taken to meet the costs of owners of fields damaged by the assemblies.[99] Food was shared equally, even to eggs and crusts of bread. Sermons were fiercely denunciatory of the clergy.[100] The climb up the hills intensified the feeling of withdrawal from a wicked world; a Taborite song stressed flight into mountains: 'Therefore do not resist evil,' it ran, 'but go out to the mountain, and here learn Truth; for so Christ commanded when he prophesied on the mountain and preached of the destruction of the temple.'[101] In a similar fashion the simple communism of the eating arrangements for poor peasants would mark the contrast between the charity of the mountain and the duties and obligations to their lords of the manorial world below from which they had come.[102]

In Prague the Taborite demonstrations in the countryside were paralleled by long processions of Utraquists to the churches where the lay chalice was still allowed. The king, on his way to mass, found himself surrounded by a crowd under the leadership of Nicholas of Hus, a petty nobleman of the radical party, demanding the re-granting of general permission for the lay chalice and infant communion;[103] he had Nicholas arrested. When the Utraquist councillors of the New Town intervened, he consented to banish him. Nicholas seems to have gone to agitate among the Taborites. Wenceslas dismissed the Utraquist councillors of the New Town on 6 July, replacing them by Catholics, who forcibly took over the remaining Utraquist parish schools, prohibited their processions, and probably imprisoned Utraquists.

At this juncture Jan Želivský, a former Premonstratensian who had abandoned his order and taken on the mantle of Nicholas of Dresden in Prague, took a hand in events.[104] There was much tension in the city as the king, characteristically moved by a personal episode in which he detected an insult to his power, seemed at long last to have decided to crush the Utraquists' movement. He was fearful of the Taborites: reports circulated that they were planning to depose him in favour of Nicholas of Hus. Želivský had arrived in Prague in about 1418, and had begun a career as a radical preacher based, in the days when Utraquism still flourished, on the church of St Stephen in the New Town. In the Catholic reaction early in 1419 he lost St

---

[98]Trans. from Czech, ibid., p. 283, n. 63. For A. Molnár's work, see Seibt, *Bohemica*, pp. 86, 91, 96, 97, 105. Original Czech form is Tábor.

[99]Denis, *Huss*, p. 203.

[100]Evidence of Lawrence of Březová (Kaminsky, *Revolution*, p. 284).

[101]Trans. in Kaminsky, p. 286.

[102]Macek's reflection cited ibid., p. 285.

[103]Denis, *Huss*, pp. 203–4; for development of opinion on Nicholas, cf. Denis, p. 224, Kaminsky, pp. 410–2, Heymann, p. 198.

[104]For Želivský as theologian, see Molnár, in *CV*, II (1959), pp. 324–34; as politician and military leader, see Kaminsky, *Revolution*, Heymann, *Žižka* (see index). Kaminsky uses Molnár's edition of sermons to reconstruct events of 1419.

Stephen; but was a preacher in one of the churches reserved for the Utraquists, Our Lady of the Snows. A large building, it housed a congregation of small artisans and poor people from the New Town. Želivský saw himself as their representative, describing himself in copies of his sermons there as 'Ž, preacher of the poor, unfortunate, miserable, oppressed'.[105] Powerful and eloquent preaching linked him intimately to his poor audiences. The Latin outlines for his vernacular sermons over a period from April to November 1419 survive, placing him in the radical tradition of Jakoubek, vividly contrasting Roman practice and the primitive Church, forceful in denunciation. A natural extremist, he was contemptuous of the university masters who had bowed to the king's will. The poor of his congregations helped to form the demonstrative processions of Utraquists in the capital; no doubt they sang the abusive songs about the rich lords and the clergy which have come down to us. The sermons dwell on the suffering of the true Christian, but not in any passive sense: suffering is linked with struggle.

On 30 July he used his congregation for a violent demonstration intended to destroy the new royal policy of suppressing the Utraquists.[106] After a sermon at Our Lady of the Snows, he took the consecrated Host in a monstrance, and led out his followers, some armed with pikes, swords and clubs, to his former church of St Stephen. Finding the Catholic priest had locked the doors against them, the congregation smashed them down and took over the building, which immediately was used for an Utraquist communion. From St Stephen, Želivský and the rest moved to the New Town Hall, where they found a number of the Catholic Czech councillors of the king's appointment. They demanded from them the release of the Utraquists held by them in prison. When the councillors refused, the angry crowd broke in, and threw some thirteen of them from the windows into the street below, where those who survived the fall were killed. Želivský's men then took over the New Town Hall, and summoned the residents to arms, electing four military captains and, later, new councillors to replace their victims. A force under the sub-chamberlain arrived at the Town Hall, but was too outnumbered to be able to restore the situation. The king, inflamed, yet persuaded of the need to compromise, was forced to confirm in office the New Town magistrates who had been thus intruded. Just over a fortnight later he died of apoplexy.

Inflamatory sermons, working on the imaginations of the poorest sections of the Prague population, had done their work. Želivský, however, was not only a scriptural preacher of great power, but was also a practical organizer and a politician. Kaminsky has given us attractive grounds for believing that the revolution of 30 July was a planned affair. Želivský planned a coup that would destroy the king's policy. His followers, if they broke out spontaneously against the councillors who shilly-shallied over delivering up the prisoners, were not so out of control as to loot the bodies of their victims;[107] the chains of office remained untouched on their corpses. The insurrectionaries proceeded

[105]Molnár in *CV*, II (1959), p. 327.
[106]Kaminsky, 'Hussite Radicalism', pp. 106–26; *Revolution*, pp. 289–96. Seibt ('Die Zeit', p. 515) notes that it was a conflict between Czechs, Hussite and Catholic.
[107]Kaminsky, 'Hussite Radicalism', p. 113.

at once to the business of electing captains and taking over control of the New Town. It is likely that Želivský did not stand alone but formed part of a conspiracy with members among the leaders of the Taborites.[108]

In a morning's action the radicals had gone far towards capturing Prague for their idea. The death of Wenceslas spoiled the plan, but could not put back their cause. With the defenestration they had brought off a successful rebellion against their king, and had wrecked the Catholic reaction most dangerous to them. Reform in Bohemia, which entered on a new phase with the enactment of the decree of Kutná Hora in 1409, culminated in 1419 in a revolution against the established order in the name of religion.

[108]Kaminsky's major hypothesis, attractive, not proved to the hilt. See also his attempt to relate the defenestration to Želivský's sermon (ibid., pp. 120–6: *Revolution*, pp. 292–3).

L*

18

Success and Failure: from the Defenestration to the Agreement at Jihlava

The Aftermath of Želivský's Coup

Wenceslas's death put the future of Hussitism into the melting-pot.[1] Sigismund, his brother, was the lawful heir, unacceptable to the radicals because of his record of complicity with the decisions of Constance, but still not wholly to be ruled out by the moderates. Moderate Hussites included in their ranks many attached to the principle of legitimacy, such as the university masters and the nobility, who would have found it difficult to reject Sigismund if only he had given some guarantees for a continued authorization of the lay chalice. Probably Ernest Denis was not wrong when he said that he could have taken the kingdom if he had moved at once. But he had other preoccupations, and the moment passed.

The Hussites united on a programme. At an assembly in late August or September, the barons and the towns set out their requirements.[2] They were, in effect, the conditions of acceptance for Sigismund. Though Utraquism was not treated as a necessity for all, the lay chalice was to be authorized, the traditional reservation of the chalice to the priest and Utraquism coexisting, if necessary, in the same church. Simony, widely interpreted, was to be put down, and priests were not to hold civil office. Bishops were to ordain candidates for orders without discriminating between Catholics and Utraquists and neither side was to call the other heretics. Utraquists were asking, not for victory, but for peaceful coexistence. They intended to hold on

[1] Denis, *Huss*, p. 212; still well-balanced narrative of events, 1419–36, ibid., pp. 211–454; to death of Žižka (1424), esp. for political and military aspects, cf. Heymann, *Žižka* (with final survey, 1424–36, pp. 456–83); lucid summaries in Creighton, *Papacy*, II. Seibt, 'Die Zeit', pp. 494–536, gives outline to 1436 with full literature. Kaminsky, *Revolution*, pp. 296–494 (often used here), is esp. valuable on Tabor and ideology, but stops in 1424; for brief analysis, see his 'The Religion of Hussite Tabor', in *The Czechoslovak Contribution to World Culture*, ed. M. Reichigl (The Hague, 1964), pp. 210–23. For concepts and nomenclature, see Seibt, *Hussitica* (sections on just war, *jazyk-linguagium*, *obec-communitas*); survey with perspective in F. Seibt, 'Die Hussitenzeit als Kulturepoche', *HZ*, CXCVI (1962), pp. 21–62, sources trans. (esp. on radicals, Taborites) pp. 253–329; Peter Chelčický's teaching (pp. 333–443) in *Das hussitische Denken im Lichte seiner Quellen*, ed. R. Kalivoda and A. Kolesnyk (Berlin, 1969), intro. by Kalivoda, with up-to-date Marxist interpretation and literature; broad comparison, F. G. Heymann, 'The Hussite Revolution and the German Peasants' War: an Historical Comparison', *MH*, n.s., I (1971), pp. 141–59.

[2] Kaminsky, *Revolution*, pp. 296–8; for general problem of communities, Estates, see Seibt, *Hussitica*, pp. 125–82, and cf. K. Hrubý, 'Senior Communitas—eine revolutionäre Institution der prager hussitischen Bürgerschaft', *Bohemia*, XIII (1972), pp. 19–43 (sociological approach).

to the gains of the past: the university was to remain the doctrinal authority; there was to be free preaching; papal decisions were to take effect in Bohemia only at the will of the king, council and barons. Yet there was still a desire for recognition within the international Church.

The nationalist demands were more far-reaching. The Czechs were to have the first voice in the kingdom. Judicial proceedings were to be held in the Czech language. Foreigners were not to take either civil or ecclesiastical office if capable Czechs were to be found to fill them. Thus, at the moment of crisis, the nationalist demands in Bohemia, which had grown contemporaneously with the religious, each supporting the other, reached their fullest expression. Other clauses reflected the interests of smaller groups. Prague had a special section of its own. The nobles had their particular interests: royal rights of taking escheats were to be restricted, Wenceslas's treasure was to be used in the interests of the kingdom, a hint that it should not be used to reward foreigners, such as the Germans and Hungarians of Sigismund's entourage, in preference to natives. The towns wanted an amnesty, the confirmation of their liberties, and laws against usurers and Jews.

The Rise of the Military Tabor

One group was hardly catered for: the radicals. The death of Wenceslas had been followed by disturbances in Prague and other towns where they had a strong following. A crowd led by Jan Žižka, a professional soldier in the royal service, sacked the Carthusian house at Smíchov outside the capital;[3] the inmates, largely Germans, had to be put in custody at the Old Town hall for their own safety. Inside Prague brothels were destroyed by zealots. In the provinces the great assemblies on the hills for communion and preaching continued unabated. Unaided, the New Town radicals under Žižka and Želivský took the fortress of Vyšehrad; in November a group which included pilgrims from the provinces took royalist positions in the Small Side.

Despite their protestations, the assemblies were a political force, and were undergoing a transformation into a fighting one. Queen Sophie and Čeněk of Vartemberk at the head of the council of regency saw the danger, and took counter-measures. In November the first pitched battle between the rival sides took place near Živhošť,[4] when a force of royalist nobility cut off a group from the south making their way to the November demonstration in Prague. In the capital the danger of a takeover by the radicals was most acute; but the combined forces of the New Town and the provincial zealots were unable to hold opinion on their side. The Vyšehrad was given up again to royalist troops, and the men from the provinces left Prague in disappointment, a mood which facilitated the swing to force.[5] Already at the 30 September assembly outside Prague, Wenceslas Koranda, leader of the Pilsen contingent, had said, 'The time to wander with the pilgrim's staff is over. Now we shall have to march, sword in hand.'[6] Koranda, with Nicholas of Hus,

---

[3]Heymann, *Žižka*, p. 69; background, ch. 4 generally.
[4]Kaminsky, p. 307.
[5]Best described, ibid., ch. 7.
[6]Heymann, *Žižka*, p. 80; for analysis of political situation in September-October 1419, see Kaminsky, pp. 301–6.

formed part of a small leading group engaged in the direction of the mass of pilgrims towards specific objectives, in the first instance political, then military.

Like the Waldensians, the radicals were initially believers in literal observance of the texts of the gospels prohibiting the shedding of blood; but even the Waldensians took up the sword in special circumstances, as for example, when their mountain refuges were attacked by troops under the inquisition.[7] There was an easy psychological transition from violent demonstrations, the image-breaking long usual in radical circles, the destruction of monasteries and brothels, on to the actual shedding of blood.

Preaching facilitated the process. In the winter of 1419–20, their leaders comforted the disillusioned with the prospect of the imminent end of the world. In a new coming of Christ their enemies would be destroyed; the remnant to be saved—which would come, of course, from the ranks of the radicals—were to flee to five cities in Bohemia,[8] where they would be saved from the wrath to come. Jakoubek and the main body of university masters reasoned against the radicals' use of texts and, in particular, against the necessity to flee to the cities of protection. On another side of the movement, Peter Chelčický, the nobleman of Waldensian views, stood apart from this development, and later wrote that he believed that the devil had deceived them into thinking that they were 'angels who had to eliminate all scandals from Christ's kingdom.'[9] Through all vicissitudes he clung to literal pacifism, and refused to have any contact with secular power. Nonetheless, the prophets had their way. Lawrence of Březová describes how peasants sold up their holdings, even at a low price, and with their wives and families came to the radicals' centres, throwing their money into a common fund.[10] The end did not come, and the mood of imminent expectation passed, but not before it had played its part in setting up a confederation of like-minded radical communities.

The five cities of the prophecy were all places where the radicals had made an early impact, and lay in western Bohemia: Pilsen, Saaz (Žatec), Louny, Slaný, Klatovy. Pilsen lay under the command of the fighting priest, Koranda, and was soon reinforced by Žižka, who brought a remarkable military expertise to canalize the energies of the dedicated men. Another area of refuge lay in south Bohemia, where Písek had a long tradition of extremism. Hradec Králové was yet another centre: here lay the rechristened Mount Horeb, with the Orebites under the priest Ambrose.[11] Both the southern and western centres were soon under attack. This intensified the religious emotions amongst the radical elect, but also led to losses. In a skirmish, Žižka for the first time demonstrated his skill in the use of artillery and war-wagons; but there was resistance to Koranda inside Pilsen, and disillusion when the projected date for the end of the world in mid-February 1420 passed. In

[7] Lea, *Inquisition*, II, pp. 259–60, 267.
[8] Kaminsky, p. 311ff.; Isa. 19, 18.
[9] Ibid., p. 321 (trans. Kaminsky).
[10] Ibid., p. 331.
[11] On these and all Hussite groupings against geographical background, see Seibt, 'Die Zeit', pp. 518–27.

March, after an armistice, Žižka and a party of the most determined followers left Pilsen to join the south Bohemian centre of resistance. There Pisek seems to have fallen to the royalists, probably in February; but the zealots who had had to leave the town made a surprise attack before dawn on Ash Wednesday on another nearby town, Ústi-nad-Lužnicí, which they took.[12]

Finally, moved by the needs of defence, they left Ústi for the abandoned fortress of Hradiště, on a near-impregnable site formed by a peninsula, with water defences on three sides from the rivers Lužnice and Tismenice. Ústi was burnt, and contact with the old and normal life was cut off. A rigorous communism was set up, with the holding of private property being taken as a mortal sin. Fortifications were put up at great speed, and the population divided into four groups for military and political purposes under captains. From the fortress parties went out to subdue the surrounding countryside. To this society Žižka brought his soldiers and his military genius. The fortress was renamed Tabor. To the old pilgrimage Tabor near Bechyně, there had succeeded a new military Tabor.

Much as Cromwell was able to develop his military innovations in the intense religious atmosphere of the New Model Army, so Žižka used the religious exaltation of the inmates of Tabor to mould them into an unusually well disciplined fighting force. Among the Taborites the failure of the end of the world to occur as anticipated did not lead to a slackening of zeal: to the prediction of the imminent and catastrophic end there succeeded the notion that Christ had already come, but secretly as a thief in the night;[13] his public advent was yet to be. Meanwhile, it was a time of vengeance. After fighting would come the reward: the elect who had fled to the mountains would possess the goods of the wicked. The nature of Tabor inevitably drew only the most dedicated of radicals from their homes and normal way of life. In an atmosphere of feverish religious activity, novel ideas were thrown up very rapidly. A hostile witness describes the priests telling their followers of the wealth they would have when the millenium dawned, when they would have an abundance of everything and would no longer have to pay rents to their lords.[14]

The violence of Tabor had religious roots; it also had a more practical cause, in the difficulties of supporting the zealots and their families; they needed the booty to be won in expeditions against their enemies. As the financial pressures made themselves felt, they were forced to impose the traditional lords' exaction of *holdy* on neighbouring peasants. This created disillusion; but the feeling of membership of the elect, the inspiration produced by the community in the fortress, the preachings, and the simple celebrations of the Utraquist communion, without regular altar, vestments or mass ritual, created a long-lasting momentum for Tabor that could ride out minor setbacks.[15]

Žižka's task was to improvise an army from the materials available to

---

[12]Events in Kaminsky, pp. 329–36; military aspect in Heymann, ch. 6.
[13]Kaminsky, p. 345.
[14]Trans. ibid., p. 340—surely significant for economic motivation.
[15]The atmosphere is reconstructed by Kaminsky in *The Czechoslovak Contribution*, ed. Reichigl, pp. 210–23.

peasants.[16] Threshing-flails, consisting of swipples studded with iron spikes, initially had to serve in place of conventional weapons; as their worth became apparent, they were deliberately manufactured. Peasant carts made do as transport: soon Žižka adapted them as war-wagons. They were improved for defence purposes by adding boards to protect both their occupants and the wheels, and places were made for hand-guns. Shields were developed to close gaps between wagons. Žižka had had experience of warfare against the Teutonic Knights in a campaign on behalf of the king of Poland, and may there have learnt something of the use of wagons; but the extension of their use from transport to a whole system of mobile defence seems to have been his innovation. The great virtue of Žižka's war wagons was that they enabled mobile columns to switch rapidly and effectively to defence against cavalry attack.

Sigismund and the Battle of Vitkov Hill

Meanwhile negotiations continued, spurred by the moderate Utraquists' fear of the excesses of the Taborites.[17] At a diet at Brno in December 1419 the Estates swore obedience to Sigismund, and Prague asked for forgiveness for its rebelliousness. It seemed as if he would allow a policy of toleration for the lay chalice, provided that his wishes were respected on other matters. Quietly he appointed two Catholic nobles as steward and chamberlain, with control of royal castles and towns, to outflank Čeněk of Vartemberk. Again a successful entry as ruler to Bohemia seemed eminently possible. But Sigismund spoiled his chances by dropping the mask of compromise.

Another diet at Breslau assembled the magnates of the Empire; in the atmosphere of power there, the direct military solution of the Bohemian problem seemed attractive. There were still centres of Catholic dominance in the country. At Kutná Hora the German population was engaged in a wholesale elimination of Hussites who, as the town's executioner became overburdened, were thrown into the abandoned shafts of silver mines. In south Bohemia the Hussites had been unable to eliminate the opposition of Ulrich of Rosenberg (Rožmberk). In February Sigismund decided for an expedition, declared a crusade by Martin V. In Breslau he demonstrated his new attitude to Bohemian heresy by assenting to the burning of a Hussite merchant from Prague. As far as recalcitrant towns were concerned, he marked the contrast between him and his vacillating brother by quashing Wenceslas's mild response to a revolt of workers' corporations against the town council in Breslau.

In the winter and spring 1419–20 the university masters debated the issues of war and peace.[18] In February Žižka submitted this theme to the university—an interesting demonstration of links, however frail, which still held between different wings of the movement. A little earlier two priests, one in favour of the radicals, the other more conservative, debated publicly the righteousness of war; the dispute was referred to Jakoubek and Christian of

---

[16]Heymann, pp. 97–101.

[17]Ibid., ch. 7; Denis, *Huss*, p. 233–7; Kaminsky, *Revolution*, pp. 361–5.

[18]Kaminsky, pp. 317–29; Seibt, *Hussitica*, ch. 2 (valuable for the intellectual origins of discussion).

Prachatice for judgement. They disliked the deductions being made by the provincial radicals from the imminence of the end of the world, but they allowed a right of resistance by Utraquist communities even against the will of the lords.

The necessities of the time were drawing university masters, as well as the Taborites, into the justification of revolution against the established order. In their discussions they moved, stage by stage, away from the traditional and much qualified support for Christian warfare to be found in Wyclif, and derived by him from Aquinas, to an acceptance of holy war, and even obligatory war, for the Bohemians who held to the cause of the chalice. Wyclif's exposition left no place for resistance against a lawful ruler; the Prague masters in their need boldly left him behind. As Seibt explains, their achievement was considerable.[19]

The crusade did what nothing else could do; it pushed into temporary unity the disparate forces of Hussitism.[20] In Prague, Old and New Town came together on 3 April 1420, and made an agreement setting up a form of military government under captains, with temporary powers overriding, though not superseding, those of the magistrates.[21] Želivský, who had been somewhat isolated during the phase of negotiation with Sigismund, regained influence. The citizens sent out a manifesto which struck the nationalist chord. Sigismund was to be repelled, as he had summoned a crusade and had called in the Germans, 'our natural enemies'. Responsibility for schism·did not lie with the Czechs: the Church, a malicious stepmother to them, had repelled them, despite the fact that they had only wanted to follow Christian law.[22] Čeněk, the weathercock of Hussitism, returning from Sigismund, joined the Prague citizens in their defiance, took over the Hradčany castle, and rallied the nobility. On 20 April the lords issued their manifesto, a formal *diffidatio* directed against Sigismund which enumerated his faults, from his complicity in the burning of Hus to the alienation of the Margravate of Brandenburg and the naming as bishop of Moravia of an 'enemy of the Slav race'.[23]

In both manifestos there was a similar theme of honour and nationality, defined in terms of language. The Czech keyword was *jazyk*, best translated as 'tongue'.[24] Its use links the manifestos of 1420 with the protests of the Bohemian and Moravian nobility in 1415. The later ones, which form a sequence of high rhetoric through the 1420s, almost certainly are the work of one hand, and reflect the interest of the Prague patriciate, university-educated, touched by humanism, and less orientated towards religion than secular concerns. Linguistic nationalism was a relatively sophisticated notion, but it was calculated to stir the emotions of Czechs far from university circles.[25]

---

[19]Seibt, *Hussitica*, p. 55; note comment, pp. 53, 57.

[20]Ibid., p. 17; note discussion of Hussites' lack of any self-devised term for all members of the reform movement, p. 14.

[21]Kaminsky, *Revolution*, p. 368.

[22]Denis, *Huss*, pp. 238–9.

[23]Ibid., p. 239.

[24]Seibt, *Hussitica*, pp. 102–9.

[25]In this and earlier sentences, I follow Seibt's research (*Hussitica*, ch. 3 (see p. 117); *HZ*, cxcvi (1962), pp. 21–62).

As the crusaders made their way into the country, national feeling was reinforced by stories of martyrdom, the *passiones* of humble Hussites, of which the best-known is the burning together of parish priest, peasants and children who refused to recant at Arnoštovice in July 1420 by the troops of the Duke of Austria.[26]

The manifesto of 3 April also included a formula for religious unity among the rival Hussite groups; modified, it reappeared on 20 April, and again on 27 May; decked with texts and authorities, it was translated and transmitted to Sigismund's army and to other towns. The formula became known as the Four Articles of Prague;[27] it was the minimum platform of Hussitism. The articles proclaimed Utraquism; the 'proper and free preaching of the word of God'; the necessity for all priests, from the pope downwards, to 'give up their pomp, avarice and improper lordship'; and for the Bohemian realm and nation to be cleansed both from public mortal sins and from slander. Different groups could read into it different meanings. The nobility on 20 April omitted the reference to public mortal sins; the radicals on the contrary, saw the same fourth article as an invitation to a revolutionary upheaval in the country. But the lay chalice united all.

Yet for many radicals it formed only a preliminary to a wholesale revision of the mass, which stripped it down to the decisive Scriptural texts, all translated into Czech, and it turned into a communion service bereft of traditional vestments and ceremonial.[28] Where the most moderate were satisfied with the concession of the lay chalice, and perhaps the translation of epistle and gospel into the vernacular, others went further, and treated the first article as giving them the right also to administer the chalice to infants. Modifications of the articles in different versions reflected the tensions beneath the surface. But the articles served their purpose: evolved under the pressure of invasion, they held together moderates and radicals for a common defence. They represented a minimum of what all would accept. They lasted long because no better formula could be found to reconcile the irreconcilable.

In the city of Prague the new common actions of April and May and the stress on the national interests of the Czechs in the manifestos led to a major emigration of Germans and Catholics, not to be reversed.[29] Houses, gardens and possessions were confiscated and redistributed, the community thus claiming a wholly revolutionary right of disposal. In this way the appeal of the manifestos to a linguistic nationalism issued speedily in action, and the flight of the Germans and the ruin of the German-Catholic patriciate with the takeover by Czechs created interest-groups irretrievably committed to resistance. The emigration of the late spring and early summer could be paralleled elsewhere. The reform still retained a supra-racial significance, and a line up of German Catholics inside and outside the kingdom versus Hussite Czechs was still far from automatic. Among the towns Pilsen, which unlike many Bohemian towns was exclusively administered in the Czech language, after a brief episode of radical dominance under Wenceslas

[26]Denis, *Huss*, p. 248.
[27]Kaminsky, pp. 369–75, Heymann, ch. 10.
[28]Discussed, Kaminsky, pp. 375–83.
[29]Denis, *Huss*, p. 261.

Koranda, stayed faithful to the conservative side, while on the other side Saaz, a town of mixed linguistic usage with a strong German population, stayed with the Taborites.[30] Nevertheless, the events of 1420 had gone far to unite Czech interests with the chalice. Even at this late stage, moderate Hussites and nobility again tried to treat with Sigismund; but, being rejected, reunited with the Taborites, who entered Prague in May.

The city's chances of surviving siege were not high, for Sigismund commanded a great force, and royalists held the fortresses of the Hradčany and Vyšehrad on two sides of Prague.[31] The weakness of the royalist position lay in the difficulty of supplying such an army, and, more than all else, the problem of morale, with native Bohemian Catholics fighting uneasily at the side of Sigismund's foreign subjects from Germany and Hungary. The battle of Vitkov Hill decided the issue. It was not a full-scale engagement, and the losses to Sigismund's army were not high; his troops failed by the narrowest of margins to secure the ridge of the Vitkov in a strategic position on the northeast of the city. The balance was turned by Žižka's eye for crucial ground and the fighting qualities of his Taborites.

In defeat, Sigismund listened to the advice of his Bohemian nobility, had himself crowned in the cathedral, then moved away from the city to the security of the Kutná Hora region, where he delayed through the rest of the summer and early autumn. Never wholehearted in military plans for long, he seems to have believed that his presence alone in the kingdom would in the end rally support for him as lawful ruler, and that the Hussites' unity would break down in internecine strife. But this was sadly to underestimate both the general suspicion of him as the betrayer of Hus, and the Czech national feeling against the Germans and Hungarians in his entourage. In November he came back too late to save the Vyšehrad fortress from going down to the assault of the Praguers, and in March 1421, after other conflicts, left Bohemia altogether with little accomplished. His hesitation and final departure were valuable to the Hussite cause, for they gave Žižka the chance later in 1420 and in 1421 to reduce towns and fortresses on the Catholic and royalist side, till Bohemia, though never wholly won for the chalice, formed a substantial bastion of Hussitism.[32]

Húska, the Adamites and the End of Želivský

Military success formed a shield for debate and organizational moves in which the Hussite parties defined their positions and eliminated their extremists. In the flush of victory after Vitkov, the Taborites attempted to swing Prague to their views, presenting a programme of Twelve Points to the community, demanding either instant action on clauses of the Four Articles, such as the disappropriation of priests or an interpretation of the clause on 'public sins', which would have imposed a puritanical regime on the city.[33] Their call for university masters to be subject to the 'divine law', which for the

---

[30]Seibt, in *HZ* cxcvi (1962), pp. 21–62; *Hussitica*, pp. 95–6.
[31]Heymann, ch. 9, for military details.
[32]This point is clarified by Heymann, (pp. 170–2, 174–5, 181–2, 199–208, 217–19).
[33]See trans. in Kaminsky, *Revolution*, pp. 376–7.

Taborites meant Scripture alone, would have destroyed the position of the university as the doctrinal authority of the Utraquists, and their demand that monasteries, 'unnecessary' churches, vestments and gold and silver chalices should be destroyed went far beyond the views of the moderate majority in the city. Destruction of the monastery at Zbraslav south of the city and desecration of the royal graves by a drunken contingent added disgust to the fear of Tabor of the moderates.[34] Repudiated, the Taborites left, and in September marked the doctrinal breach with Prague Hussitism by electing one of their preachers, Nicholas of Pelhřimov, as bishop. He was needed to ordain priests, to give status to Taborite preaching, and to organize it; the election marked a stage of definition within Tabor as well as against Prague, as the informal processes of the chiliast past gave way to more settled arrangements natural to a city-state, with dependent towns, craft industries developing, and peasants paying dues; by its disregard of apostolic succession, it also closed a door to reconciliation with the Utraquists.[35]

As a settled church developed in the towns of the Taborite lordship and their dependent populations, so problems of discipline arose. Martin Húska, one of the most eloquent Taborites and an 'ordainer' of Nicholas as bishop, led a party within Tabor that denied a real presence in the eucharist, and taught that the bread and wine should not be received kneeling but informally, in quantity rather than sacramentally, in love feasts reminiscent of the early Church.[36] The eucharist turned into a commemoration meal. Ardent as the Taborites were to strip down the mass to its Scriptural components, abolishing all pomp, vestments and accretions to the liturgy, pleading against their moderate Utraquist opponents that Christ did not dress in a chasuble, they were not prepared to follow Húska's inferences from Scripture and reason. The eucharist was a highly sensitive issue among all Hussites, and the Taborites, radical as they were, were yet the heirs of Matthias of Janov and the fourteenth-century reform; although they had moved from transubstantiation, nonetheless they were believers in a real presence, and the belief was of great emotional importance. Martin deployed the rationalist argument that the physical body of Christ was in heaven, and could not be in the eucharist,[37] and, pleading the Scriptural analogy of the Feeding of the Five Thousand, the people receiving seated on the ground, he contrasted the sacramental doses of wine and bread to the full banquet of the love-feast that he wished to introduce, while followers in the passionate fashion characteristic of Tabor proceeded to empty monstrances and trample on Hosts as a demonstration against traditional sacramental doctrine and practice.

Then Tabor exercised its authority to put down Húska's followers by force. As the new views evolved, Taborite leaders were engaged in discussion, centring on liturgical practice, with the moderate Utraquists of Prague, who had to be warned of the spread of the heresy, referred to as Pikartism, from

[34]Heymann, p. 168.

[35]Kaminsky, pp. 385–91.

[36]Subtle account, with full trans. of sources, ibid., pp. 397–433.

[37]Jakoubek's version (ibid., p. 424). Compare rationalist arguments on transubstantiation (above, pp. 63, 244, 268).

Pikart, a corruption of Beghard, and a loose term of abuse for a heretic.[38] Húska, imprisoned, then released, finally taken in the summer of 1421, was burnt in August with the concurrence of both wings of Hussitism.

The Húska heresy has been plausibly explained by Kaminsky as a development from the chiliast phase of the whole Taborite movement; Húska's group moved on from the point where their former fellows called a halt. The immediate issue of the laity's right to divide consecrated Hosts among themselves, on which Húska was first imprisoned early in 1421, was but the tip of a whole interpretation of Christian life that was out of accord with Tabor, and came to involve heresy still more profound than the eucharistic tenets. Fragmentary references make possible a reconstruction of Húska's teaching as based on a belief in the realisation of the kingdom among his Taborite group, in a way that made the law of Grace unnecessary. Paul's strictures on the Corinthians' confusion of the eucharist with indulgent feasts did not apply in Húska's view; his group believed it was right to make the eucharist a love-feast, in Peter Chelčický's description, 'meeting in love on the holy day, being diligent in the word of God, feasting and filling themselves up ..., and not growing thin on the little piece of bread of the popish and heretical supper.'[39] Chelčický found Húska's views drastic and disconcerting. Martin, he said, was 'not humble or at all willing to suffer for Christ.'[40] He quotes him as believing in a new kingdom of the saints on earth, in which the good would not suffer, and saying, 'If Christians were always to have to suffer so, I would not want to be a servant of God.'

It seems that some of the group came to believe that, because the kingdom had been realized in them, ordinary laws no longer applied. A heretical opening for the Lord's prayer, 'Our Father who art in us', was attributed to them by their opponents;[41] a section of Húska's followers, it was said, went so far as to act as if they were in the state of innocence before the Fall, men and women going naked, on the argument that clothes were a consequence of the Fall, and having sexual intercourse if they willed, and saying that it was no sin.[42] This extreme development followed on ejection from Tabor—the Adamites, as they were called, formed a strange community, defending themselves against attack from the main body, and having to be crushed by Žižka in battle, who had numbers of them burnt. Húska himself rejected the views of this group. Žižka, who sent a list of their evil doings to Prague,[43] believed that the community committed still worse acts, murder and sodomy included.

There is now no sure means of getting behind this testimony; one can only note the possiblity of slander, the undeniable fact that the group had aroused Žižka's ferocious anger, and the extraordinary hot-house atmosphere of Tabor in its early years, still, despite its greater anchoring in the economic

---

[38]Kaminsky, pp. 407–18. On beghards, see above, p. 174; Lerner, *Free Spirit*, pp. 36–44.

[39]Trans. in Kaminsky, p. 424. I follow Kaminsky's reconstruction of the development of Húska's views. Note criticism of Macek (ibid., pp. 403–4).

[40]Ibid., p. 400.

[41]Ibid., p. 427. Note the curious parallel with the Amalriciani (see above, pp. 101–2).

[42]Report of Lawrence of Březová, trans. Kaminsky (*Revolution*, p. 430; *FRB*, v, p. 475).

[43]*FRB*, v, pp. 517–20; trans. Kalivoda, *Das hussitische Denken*, pp. 327–9. Episode discussed by Lerner (*Free Spirit*, pp. 119–24).

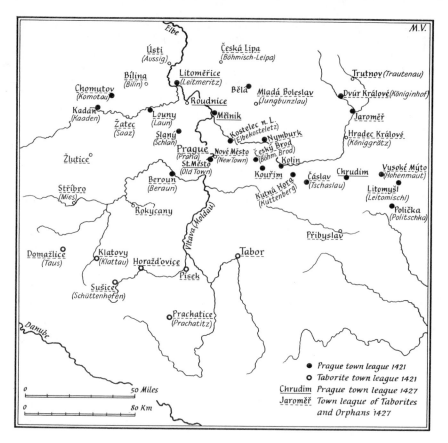

Map Twelve
Hussite Town Leagues in 1421 and 1427

world, relatively detached from ordinary living and dominated by the intense preaching of its priests and tireless discussion of Scripture. It was a setting in which every kind of dissident and novel belief was liable to come rapidly to life. Lawrence of Březová, the chronicler, attributed the start of the well-attested eucharistic heresy of Húska to the influence of a party of Pikarts and their families, possibly in fact Waldensians, who first came to Prague as refugees in 1418.[44] The fact may be relevant, but it is not a necessary postulate for the emergence of fresh heresy on the radical side in 1420–1. Taboritism itself was the great incubator of heresy.[45]

Prague came to the fore in the months after the fall of the Vyšehrad in November 1420.[46] The original centre for reform and revolution, it gained prestige from the military success won by its own forces, Tabor being sparsely

[44]*FRB*, v, p. 431; discussed Lerner, *Free Spirit*, pp. 121–3.
[45]My view. Lerner (loc. cit.) is more sceptical about sexual excesses; I think they may have developed spontaneously.
[46]F. Seibt, 'Communitas primogenita. Zur Prager Hegemonialpolitik in der hussitischen Revolution', *HJB*, LXXXI (1962), pp. 80–100.

represented at the assault; and in the spring it gathered under its hegemony a league of cities in mid- and western Bohemia. The adherence of Conrad of · Vechta to the Four Articles in April 1421, after long wavering, was also a gain for Prague as well as for the cause of Hussitism generally.[47] His adherence ensured that there would be a sufficient flow of ordinations to eliminate the risk of priesthood in Bohemia gradually dying out, and it gave a cover of legitimacy to Hussitism, however much this was repudiated by Sigismund and the ecclesiastics in the outside world. But at Čáslav, where in June 1421 a diet declared its adherence to the Four Articles, again rejected Sigismund, and attempted to gain Silesia and Lusatia for the movement, the composition of the government of twenty members, set up as a kind of oligarchic substitute for a ruler, showed by the limited place it gave to Prague's representatives that the capital's bid for leadership would not succeed.[48] Nevertheless, its capture by the radical forces would still have meant a fundamental change in the balance within Bohemia, and the year of Prague's bid for hegemony as a city was also the year of Želivský's boldest attempt to bring both Old and New Town under his dictatorship.[49]

The accidental death of Nicholas of Hus late in 1420 gave an opening for leadership, and the takeover of German and Catholic houses by Želivský's adherents in the aftermath of the emigration of spring 1421 strengthened the radicals' voting power. After Čáslav he felt strong enough to sack the administrators of the Old Town and declare the union of New and Old. For some months the city was ruled under the dictatorship of one of his radical supporters. But it was an uneasy success; Želivský always had the crowd with him to push forward his measures, but also the long-term opposition of the propertied classes, the moderate Utraquists and the Prague patriciate against him working on his administrators, so that political radicals appointed by him lost the edge of their zeal in face of conservative pressure. What finally broke him was the defeat of the Prague forces at Most and his failure to bring victory in the field to the city's forces in the way that Žižka had done for the Taborites. In February 1422 John Hvězda, his dictator, lost office; in March Hvězda's more conservative successor had him executed. His courageous death brought a reaction from the manual workers that formed his support, yet fatally weakened his party: Prague thereafter could be usually reckoned a a pillar of the moderate party, in religion and politics.

The clash of classes and the inability of the artisans and poor to prevail against the wealthier in Prague were the main reasons for Želivský's fall. Religion also played a part, for Želivský believed in *scriptura sola* as the authority for Hussitism, and was constantly attempting to upset the doctrinal position of the university masters and subject it to the 'divine law', as the Taborites did, while his party came to treat the mass as a bare communion service, in the manner of Tabor. Jakoubek and the university masters were firm against Želivský. 'Be diligent. Stop him'[50] were Jakoubek's words to the magistrates, two days before Želivský's murder.

[47]Heymann, pp. 220–1.
[48]Ibid., ch. 14; id., 'The National assembly of Čáslav', *MH*, VIII (1954), pp. 32–55.
[49]Kaminsky, *Revolution*, pp. 451–60; Heymann, pp. 241–53, 266–7, 272–3, 278–80, 307–18.
[50]Kaminsky, p. 460.

The Major Parties

As Prague and Tabor thus cut down their dissidents, debate still continued between the moderate centre of Utraquism, based in the capital, and the radical force of Taboritism. While they talked, searching for a way to unity, their own differences tended to clarify.[51] Tabor's supporters debated their eucharistic beliefs, and settled on a common doctrine, that Christ's body and blood were contained in the bread and wine 'in a sacramental or figurative sense'.[52] This divided Tabor from the believers in transubstantiation or consubstantiation on the moderate Utraquist side. Controversy over mass vestments continued; as usual in such conflicts, it was the visible sign of difference that attracted most attention, intensified by the focus of all Hussites on the eucharist, the natural consequence of their tradition and of the adoption of the lay chalice. Taborite ritual was now of the simplest—consisting of a common recitation of the Lord's Prayer, then the words of Christ at the Last Supper, pronounced in the vernacular on an unconsecrated altar, perhaps a table, the eucharistic vessels being ordinary cups and plates, and the church being bare of adornment. Priests wore no vestments, and were not distinguished from the laity. All received communion. Sermons, vernacular singing, and gospel-reading formed a part of what was a congregational service, with an emphasis very different from that of the traditional mass. When Taborites discussed the eucharistic celebrations of the Utraquist party, they attacked features of it as being useless to the people. The utility to the congregation is foremost. Fixed forms were inimical to the Taborite mode of life—readings of set portions of Scripture, for example, were dismissed because they would prevent the clergy from exposition 'according to the needs of the people and the time'.[53]

Divergences thus went so far between Utraquist and Taborite practice that it was difficult to see how any compromise formula could be worked out, though their representatives tried hard to do so. Moreover, beneath the liturgical differences lay a fundamental distinction of outlook which ran through all the issues dividing the parties. The Utraquists were reformers who desired changes where they saw a necessity for them; if there was not a positive reason for change in existing structures, on the whole they preferred to keep them. The Taborites were revolutionaries who insisted that all belief and practice must be brought to the touchstone of Scripture, the practice of the primitive Church, and common utility. It was *scriptura sola* at its starkest, set in the context of independent communities of peasants and artisans, wielding political and military power. Under its impetus, a series of components of traditional Catholicism, purgatory, the intercessory role of the saints and of Mary, the sacrifice of the mass, went down to destruction, leaving a religion of stark contrasts, between heaven and hell, God and Antichrist, Scripture and the Babylon of Rome.

One other feature of Tabor, which sprang from the residue of the eschatological expectation in which it was born, was the belief, helpfully

---

[51]Kaminsky, pp. 436–52, 460–81. For Tabor, I found his discussion in *The Czechoslovak Contribution*, pp. 210–23, esp. helpful.

[52]Ibid., p. 455.

[53]Ibid., p. 470. See description of Taborite eucharist (ibid., p. 444–5).

expounded by Kaminsky, that they were, not merely the imitators of the primitive Church, but that they in some way reincarnated that Church and possessed all its powers. This acceptance of a sovereign power of decision over all precedent and tradition emerges from Nicholas of Pelhřimov's discussion of the reliance to be placed on the Four Doctors and the Four Councils, a norm for the Utraquists. If by revelation . . . of Scripture', he said, 'God should today grant a more potent understanding to someone, that man would be more to be believed than those Doctors.'[54] *Scriptura sola*, the political independence and military power of the Taborite communities, and their belief in God's direct guidance on them, together made the Taborites the most dynamic sect of the Middle Ages. But it also made any form of accommodation with them extraordinarily hard.

Through the debates the two major parties were in fact drawing apart, for all the efforts at compromise. The effects of definition can be seen in the decisions of two synods, one held after the diet of Čáslav in 1421, the other almost a year later in 1422. The first, defining eucharistic belief in terms of the real presence, left open the way to compromise with Tabor; the second, by using the term 'corporeal substance', excluded their beliefs.[55] Within Tabor the departure of Žižka to join the Orebites removed an influence tending to restraint in religious matters; Tabor was allowed to become more radical, and compromise became yet more difficult.[56] Among the Utraquists the rise of John Příbram, a former adherent of Jakoubek, who still wanted the lay chalice, but in the context of reconciliation with Rome, and was prepared to cut away the other innovations of Hussitism to get an accommodation with the Church, sharpened the division with Tabor.[57] In 1422 and 1423 there were episodes of actual fighting between the two sides. The search for a substitute for Sigismund tended to weigh on the conservative side, for the candidate who arrived in Bohemia, Sigismund Korybut, nephew of Witold of Lithuania, first as governor-general for his uncle, then later as a claimant in his own right, favoured moderation in the reform.[58] His only chance, he came to see, of achieving acceptance in Europe as king in place of Sigismund was by making a reconciliation with the papacy, and so his influence was all on the side of Příbram's party. In any case, he was the candidate of the moderates, the nobles and bourgeois, who were uneasy at having no monarch. On the other side, Žižka originally tolerated Korybut. Tabor and the other radicals as a whole were indifferent, if not hostile, to monarchy.

It can be seen that almost every factor, the religious division, the conflict of class implicit behind it, and the differences in national policy, tended to keep Utraquists and Taborites apart. In favour of unity was the sense of common origin in the Bohemian reform, the symbol of the lay chalice, and the belief of many in both parties in the value of discussion. Tabor had a learned leadership, able and willing to engage in debate. There were experiments in

[54]Ibid., p. 469.
[55]Ibid., pp. 462–3.
[56]Heymann, pp. 354–6, 361–73.
[57]Kaminsky, *Revolution*, p. 461.
[58]Heymann, ch. 20, Kaminsky, *Revolution*, pp. 460–2; below, p. 329; on the Slav background, see Denis, *Huss*, pp. 308–25; later career of Korybut in Heymann and Denis.

toleration, but the Utraquists, though open to considerable deviation, were in the last resort unable to accept two such distinct sets of belief in Bohemia, while in Tabor there was too much that was irreconcilable. The gulf yawned.

One factor above all kept the two parties from civil war: the continuing pressure from the outside world. Sigismund had not given up the struggle when he withdrew in March 1421; he came again towards the end of the year with a formidable force, missed his chance of co-ordinating a two-pronged attack on the kingdom, but still had a numerical superiority over his opponents when Žižka soundly defeated him at Německý Brod early in 1422.[59] Vanquished, still attempting diplomatic moves against the Hussites, then distracted by his oriental schemes and the problem of the Turks, and not always on good terms with the imperial princes, he did not return for fourteen years to Bohemia. Nevertheless, there were other expeditions and pressures still, if not so formidable, Martin V remained an unyielding opponent and Ulrich of Rosenberg's party among the nobility supported conservatism.[60]

Every crusade—and there were such expeditions, given the crusade indulgence, in 1420, 1421, 1422, 1427 and 1431, as well as lesser forays—pushed the parties into unity to repel the invader. Bohemia was a beleaguered country; alone, the moderates could not be sure of defending it; they had to sink their differences with the radicals to keep native independence and the lay chalice in being. And yet military action, decisive as it was, only staved off the problem of the future of Hussitism. What was to happen next? Both Tabor and the moderates wanted in their different ways to spread their views to the outside world; they could, together, defend the bastion of Bohemia against any army that the Catholics were able to put against them, earning in the process such a reputation for Hussite troops that opposing forces sometimes dissolved at the mere sight of them; but they did not have anything like the same success in the peaceful process of disseminating their beliefs. From about 1423 at latest the support of Bohemia for Hussitism was reasonably secure, and the major parties settled in their divisions; their ultimate unity, aided by the need of defence, held, if precariously; but there was no major fresh advance made after that date for the chalice, or for either of the two parties.

Attempts at Spreading Hussitism

One plan that foundered sprang from the moderates, aiming at a reconciliation with the Church on terms that would preserve the chalice and their reform. Alliance with Slav powers to the east on a platform of resistance to Germans seemed to offer the chance of replacing Sigismund, bringing in a diplomatic counterweight to the emperor, and perhaps spreading Hussitism. Hence embassies offered the crown to the Slav rulers, Wladislav Jagiello, king of Poland, and his cousin Witold, grand duke of Lithuania. There were factors for the scheme in the Slav resurgence, which had led to the defeat of the Teutonic order at Tannenberg in 1410. Czechs had aided Poles on that occasion, and there was some common Slav feeling to build on. Sparks of

[59]Heymann, pp. 302–3.
[60]Narrative in Denis, *Huss*, chs 9, 10. I have been unable to use F. von Bezold, *König Sigmund und die Reichskriege gegen die Hussiten* (München, 1872–8), 3 v. See Seibt, 'Die Zeit', pp. 518–531; list of crusades, p. 525. See map 11 for Ulrich of Rosenberg's party.

Hussitism had reached Poland through native students attending the Charles University; Jerome of Prague had once stayed at the court of Witold; the reactions of Sigismund and the fears of Polish bishops suggest that a field for missionary activity did exist in these Slav lands.[61] Wladislav, however, though he would have welcomed a chance to strike at Sigismund, had too much to lose by acceptance. Witold, more committed against Sigismund, eager to win a crown, and at times enticed by the vision of a grand pan-Slav realm, maintained his interest longer; but the papacy's influence was insistent, and he fell away in 1423. His nephew Sigismund Korybut, originally his emissary, offered himself as candidate in 1424, and in effect, became leader after the death of Žižka. But he brought only himself and a few followers, not the support of another State, for Witold disowned him; when in power the military success of a Žižka generally eluded him, and he entered on secret negotiations with Martin V. When discovered, he was imprisoned in 1427, and sent home in 1428.[62] The affair discredited for the time John Přibram and his party. The plans for Slav alliance had not worked.

Peaceful missionizing in German-speaking lands was another means of spreading Hussitism; it produced sparks of response but no conflagration, and did not change the outlook for the Bohemian cause. There were no major conversions to swing a ruler or a whole region to the chalice, only quiet underground missionizing on the pattern of the Waldensians by individuals who become known to us when they eventually fall into the hands of the inquisition.[63] Perhaps the most notable of them was Friedrich Reiser of Donauwörth, who received episcopal consecration at Tabor and was active for a long period in south Germany and Alsace till his burning in 1458; he was succeeded in office by Stephen of Basle for a further ten years. But nothing of great significance came of this work. The Hussites worked to spread their views in popular propaganda: the Four Articles were speedily translated and spread, and vernacular manifestos were dispatched to explain their movement. Saaz, the German-speaking area attached to Hussitism in northern Bohemia, was especially active in the field of written propaganda. But, without the rapid and effective dissemination of views made possible by the printing-press in the sixteenth century, the whole enterprise remained necessarily small-scale. Luther sold some thirty thousand copies of his early works between 1517 and 1520; no comparable opportunity was available to the Hussites. Moreover, peaceful missionizing did not consort easily with military power, and the very success of the movement in Bohemia tended to work against its influence outside.[64] The decree of Kutná Hora, leading to the flight of German masters, created an interest block against Hussite theses in neighbouring universities; the flight of German Catholics later worked in the

[61]Heymann, pp. 30–1, Seibt, ibid., p. 532; Betts, *Essays*, pp. 219–20; Denis, *Huss*, p. 309. Seibt, *Hussitica*, pp. 82–3 is interesting.

[62]Heymann, pp. 456–7, 460–1.

[63]Seibt, 'Die Zeit', p. 532; *Hussitica*, pp. 94–5; H. Köpstein, 'Zu den Auswirkungen der hussitische-revolutionären Bewegung in Franken', *Aus 500 Jahren deutsch-tschechoslowakische Geschichte*, ed. K. Obermann, J. Polisensky (Berlin, 1958), pp. 16–20; id., 'Über den deutschen Hussiten Friedrich Reiser', *ZG*, vII (1959), pp. 1068–82. I owe these refs to Professor R. E. Lerner.

[64]This still seems a fair generalization, despite the evidence for German Hussitism given by Seibt ('Die Zeit', pp. 524–5, 529–30 (with full refs.)).

same direction. The association between the reform and Czech linguistic nationalism naturally weakened the international potential of Hussitism.

The Offensive Expeditions

Peaceful missionary work then, did not, perhaps could not, be expected to bring victory to the cause. There remained military power and negotiation at the highest level with ecclesiastical authority, to secure recognition for the Bohemian movement that would give it immediate security from attack in its own lands, with the possibility of spreading in Europe later. From 1426 to 1433 Procop the Shaven, the Taborite priest from southern Bohemia, heir in military skills to Žižka, though not quite his equal, led expeditions into neighbouring lands, with the aim of extorting by force from the Church this official recognition.[65] Procop led radical forces, and a secondary aim was to maintain *élan* in groups, still radical in religion, that had lost their revolutionary zeal in social matters, and were in danger of earning the hatred of the peasants for their exactions. Action abroad brought booty and prestige without damaging Bohemia. The old magic in fighting still worked, and Procop won great victories, conquering Silesia, winning tribute from the Germans round about, and taking his army to the Baltic in support of Poland. His actions and the sufferings of the lands round Bohemia, coupled with the fears of churchmen that Hussitism might spread if the situation were not defused, led to negotiation.

Negotiation and Settlement

One more crusade was mounted, then repulsed at Domažlice in 1431. In 1433 long preliminary negotiation ended in the entry of a party of Bohemians on reasonable terms to Basle to treat with the fathers of the council. This included all the major groups, Procop himself, John Rokycana, the skilful and learned representative of what might be called the middle Utraquist group, anxious for acceptance by the Church, but only in a manner that would preserve the substance of their wishes; Nicholas of Pelhřimov for the Taborites, and Peter Payne for the other radical group, the Orphans (Orebites, so called because of their loss by the death of Žižka).[66] Thus unity held as far as the negotiating table. On the other side, the leading spirit at the council, Cardinal Cesarini, who barely saved his life at Domažlice, had seen in practice the threat which Hussite power presented, and was convinced of the necessity to negotiate and to make reforms in the Church, more so than the hesitant pope, Eugenius IV, with whom the council was at odds.

Yet neither Cesarini nor his fellow members of the council intended that changes, even such as moderate Hussites wanted, should be imposed in the West; they desired to carry out reforms, indeed, on their own lines, but, most of all, to lead back the erring flock in Bohemia to the Church by gentle but temporary compromise and conciliation. Hussites cherished still the illusion that, if they were allowed to speak, the reasonableness of their case and the

[65]Heymann, pp. 457–63.

[66]Denis, *Huss*, ch. 11; E. F. Jacob, 'The Bohemians at the Council of Basel, 1433', in *Prague Essays*, ed. R. W. Seton-Watson (Oxford, 1948), pp. 81–123, Creighton, *Papacy*, II, chapters 5, 6; on Rokycana, see Heymann, 'John Rokycana: Church Reformer between Hus and Luther', *CH*, XXVIII (1959), pp. 3–43, on Payne, see above, p. 259, Betts, *Essays*, pp. 236–46.

necessity for the lay chalice would be seen by ecclesiastical authority. It was an idea that reached back to Hus, in his undelivered sermon on the evils in the Church for the fathers at Constance; and it was still held at Basle, remarkably enough, by Procop the Shaven. That illusion was broken; still, the negotiators were realistic enough to insist on a foolproof safe conduct for their party, and they tried hard to secure an imposition of the lay chalice on all in Bohemia, Catholics as well as Utraquists, and so obviate the dangers of civil war.

What weakened them was the profound desire for peace in Bohemia, through simple war-weariness, the sincere wish of Utraquists, who were not revolutionaries, for reconciliation, and the disunities behind the unified front of the negotiators. The legates, who came back to Prague to negotiate further, were aware of these divisions, and were instructed to play on them. At home, nobles who, whether Catholic or Utraquist, had gained heavily by the disappropriation of churches and monasteries, desired an end of war on terms that would allow them to keep these lands, and merchants who mourned lost prosperity wanted the country brought back into normal international relations. They pressed for peace. The longer that the negotiations dragged on, the more insistent the demands of the peace party became, the more the Hussite negotiators felt obliged to back down, and the more the tensions increased between radicals and moderates within Bohemia. The nobles mistrusted the military forces of the radicals, who had fought too long and now had too many adventurers and mercenaries in their ranks. The negotiations did not stop their expeditions, still winning victories in 1431, 1432 and 1433, yet showing signs of indiscipline. In 1433 the radicals tried to eliminate Pilsen and its region of southwest Bohemia, the last major support for Catholicism; a long blockade did not capture the city, troubles broke out, and Procop, insulted by some troops, laid down his command. Shortly afterwards, in 1434, a confederation of conservative forces, including Hussite, Moravian and Catholic nobility and the Old Town of Prague, met the radicals, Taborites, Orphans and New Town under Procop in battle at Lipany, and utterly defeated them. It marked the end of the military power of the radicals, and opened the way to acceptance of the Church's terms. The legates of the council had reported back that the lay chalice was one issue which would command wide support in the country; the council would have to make a concession of substance. In a confused scene in November 1433 at Prague representatives of both sides accepted a version of the Four Articles known as the Compactata of Basle.[67] Lipany enabled this to become the basis of a final settlement, after yet more negotiation, at Jihlava, when in 1436 the Bohemians promised peace and were reconciled to the Church.

The settlement did allow the lay chalice for all who wished it, but did not declare it to be holy and salutary, and did not impose it on the country. Division in Bohemia between Utraquists and Catholics thus remained. The council had merely granted permission for the chalice, but had not encouraged it, and had given no opening for the spread of the practice in the Church. The communion of infants, a valued Hussite practice, was not dealt with. The punishment of mortal sin was reserved to those 'whose office it is'; preaching was to be conducted by 'the priests of the Lord and by worthy

[67]Partial text in Denis, pp. 495–8.

deacons'.[68] Little here was to be seen of the radicals' zeal for righteousness in the kingdom, and the free preaching of laymen and women that they permitted. Priests were not to be owners of estates, and they were to administer faithfully the property of the Church. The last clause came nearest to the most substantial effect of the Hussite revolution: the widespread transfer of Church and monastic lands to the laity, whose secure ownership was guaranteed by Sigismund fifteen days after the ceremony at Jihlava.

With the reconciliation with the Church came also the return of the legitimate ruler. In the last years of the negotiations Sigismund had played a skilful role, promising more privately to the Hussites than the representatives of Basle would concede, till in the end they accepted a weak settlement on the security of Sigismund's word. They were deceived; once back in power, Sigismund in the short period before his death in 1437 initiated a Catholic reaction. Rokycana, elected archbishop of Prague by the estates in 1435, with an eye to thus providing a Utraquist whose presence in the archiepiscopate should act as a guarantee of the security of the Compactata, was never confirmed in his office, and the province was ruled administratively into the sixteenth century.[69] The cathedral, on the castle side of the Vltava, occupied by a Catholic chapter, never received him; in the eyes of the papacy the see had remained vacant from the death of Conrad of Vechta.

Rokycana's failure was symbolic of the rundown of the Hussite movement. It was said that the permission for the lay chalice was a concession for a time only, to contemporaries of the Compactata, and had no permanent status. The Compactata in any case were the work of the council of Basle, not the pope, and the papacy denied that it had ever accepted them. The Utraquists had once again to fight for their chalice, and never in fact won the lasting and secure recognition for which they had fought and negotiated, or succeeded in spreading their reform outside the lands of the Bohemian crown.

Between 1415 and 1436 the Hussites defied the Church, and were the first declared heretics to beat off a Catholic crusade. In these years they entirely changed the basis of the economic life of the Church in Bohemia, produced a new kind of clergy, and forced high ecclesiastical authority to treat with them on equal terms. Inside their country they undermined the centralized power of the Luxemburg monarchy, and produced a fighting force to terrorize Europe. Though they had no one to match the powerful, if flawed, intellect of Wyclif, they mobilized a remarkable variety of interest and talent before 1419, and threw up a series of notable personalities, from Hus himself to Jakoubek, with his advocacy of the chalice and his leadership in the university, Nicholas of Dresden as a popular agitator, Želivský as priest-politician, Žižka and Procop as field commanders. Their fatal weakness lay in the cleft dividing the radical from the moderate wing of Hussitism. Radicals, through Želivský, made the revolution, and, through Žižka and the Taborites, defended it. Moderates could not do without them, yet could not in the long run live with them. Beside the fighting, there were also quite novel episodes of toleration, a will on both sides to widen the bounds of discussion, and a perennial, sometimes naïve yet refreshing belief in the potency of

[68]Heymann, p. 471.
[69]G. H. Williams, *The Radical Reformation* (London, 1962), pp. 209–10.

discussion in religious affairs.[70] In the end, the division of parties destroyed much of the aims of the movement; war-weariness combined with the skills of Catholic representatives and of Sigismund to bring about a settlement unsatisfactory and insecure to the Bohemians.

Later Developments

In the years after Jihlava, the Utraquists showed their ability to fight for their reform against the pressures of Catholicism both inside and outside their country, but not to maintain the fervour of their religion.[71] Successful defence both against crusade armies, and internal dissidence under the leadership of George Poděbrady, then under the rule of Wladislav II, was followed by an agreement between Utraquists and Catholics within the country to live at peace. At the diet of Kutná Hora a measure of stabilization was achieved at home, checking attempts made in some quarters to intrigue with the papacy and accepting the Compactata. A diet in 1512 proclaimed the equality of the two religious groups; on the death of Wladislav in 1516 the government was in effect put into the hands of six directors, of whom three were Utraquists and three Catholics. The military threat of Tabor, irreparably damaged by the defeat at Lipany, was finally eliminated when Poděbrady took the town in 1452. So the moderate Hussites by force of arms won against the attempts of the papacy and its allies to undo the Compactata of Basle, and restore all Bohemia to the Roman obedience, ensured that the radicals would never again pose any military challenge to them, and contrived by peaceful means a working compromise with the large numbers of surviving Catholics. It was an achievement, but it was bought at a high price.

The lay chalice, albeit still a potent symbol, and the idiosyncratic eucharistic theology of Rokycana[72] proved insufficient to hold Utraquist supporters to their native tradition in face of the emotional and intellectual challenge of the new Protestantism of the sixteenth century. There was nothing in the views of moderate Hussites to match the power to change the Church implicit in the doctrine of justification by faith alone. Long wars and disorders, and the effects of the noble domination, which was the most lasting consequence of the Hussite revolution, left a Utraquist clergy that did not maintain the standards which their founders had desired. Perhaps, too, Utraquism itself was too moderate, too close to Rome, to have staying power, when the external pressures and fervours of the heroic age of Bohemian independence faded.

For Ernest Denis Utraquism was a compromise religion, ultimately unsatisfying because it did not follow to a logical end principles of the supremacy of Scripture and of the individual conscience, which, he believed, were implicit in the stand of the early Hussites. As the ideas of the sixteenth-century Protestant reformers made their way into the lands of the Bohemian crown, the position of the Hussite Church was eroded. The most moderate of the Utraquists, faced with the more drastic changes of the Reformation

[70]See Seibt, in *HZ*, cxcvi (1962), pp. 21–62.
[71]For Hussite history after Jihlava, see Denis, *Huss*, pp. 455–86; summaries on Utraquism and *Unitas Fratrum* in Williams, *Radical Reformation*, pp. 207–18; Seibt, 'Die Zeit', pp. 537–68; F. G. Heymann, *George of Bohemia, King of Heretics*, Princeton, 1965.
[72]Heymann, in *CH* xxviii (1959), pp. 3–43.

period, turned away to Catholicism; others went over to the Protestants. As early as 1520, Protestants had significant representation in the diet; in 1523 they formed a majority. What was distinctively Hussite fell away in face of the new, more powerful theology from Germany. The confession voted by the diet of 1575 was directly inspired by the confession of Augsburg; the cause of Bohemian independence, which still had to be fought for under different circumstances, lay in the hands of Protestants. The Utraquist priesthood faded away, and by the early seventeenth century was reduced to the merest remnant on the estates of certain nobles.

After so much warfare, diplomatic and high State action in the name of religion, it was hardly surprising that a pacifist group, foreswearing every exercise of power, and believing, like the Waldensians of fourteenth-century Austria, that poison entered into the Church with Constantine, should have kept a hold over men's minds long after the Utraquist Church had faded out. Peter Chelčický, a lay theologian and a prolific treatise writer, now identified as a nobleman called Peter of Záhorka, though he had much in common with Tabor, including a similar eucharistic doctrine, separated himself from them because of their acceptance of the rightfulness of shedding blood.[73] 'If power were supposed to be administered through Christ's faith by means of battles and punishments,' he asked, '. . . why would Christ have abolished the Jewish Law and established a different, spiritual one?'[74] Chelčický was uncompromising, by implication even rejecting the power that might be exercised by a Hussite king.[75] He stood apart from all the great events while maintaining contacts with the Hussite religious leaders. Rokycana admired him, and recommended him to his own nephew Gregory and other devout men who came together to form a community at Kunwald, a village in northeast Bohemia, in 1458. They led a strict life, practising poverty and community of goods; in 1467 at Lhotka, near Rychnov, they constituted themselves a separate Church, and took steps to obtain ordination from both a Catholic and a Waldensian source. Even converts from Utraquism had to be rebaptised on entry to the group, which called themselves first the Brethren of Christ's Gospel, then the *Unitas Fratrum*.

The movement, which remained small because of the strictness of its standards and its uncompromising rejection of power, attracted support from former Taborites, and entered into contacts with the Waldensians. Communities on the pattern of Kunwald grew. In time some rejected the rigidity of the separation from the world of the early Kunwald community, permitting members to take civic office and swear oaths, for example, and a division arose between moderates and rigorists, the Amosites. Nevertheless the movement flourished. Though, like the Utraquists, the *Unitas* felt the impact of the new Protestant theology in the sixteenth century, they were not overpowered by it, and maintained an individuality amongst the Protestant Churches, being known in modern times as the Moravian Brethren. Of all the forces unleashed by the Hussite revolution, they had the longest and most distinguished future.

[73]Brock, *Political and Social Doctrines*, ch. 1; Seibt, 'Die Zeit', pp. 533–4, 556–7.
[74]Kaminsky, *Hussite Revolution*, p. 322 (on relation to Tabor, see pp. 321–3, 391–7).
[75]Williams's reflection (op. cit., p. 210).

Epilogue

Medieval Heresies and the Reformation[1]

The Hussite defiance was the last major crisis of heresy before Luther's attack on indulgences. It shook authority, lay and ecclesiastical, but the crisis passed, and the seven decades which separate the Hussite acceptance of Sigismund at Jihlava in 1436 from the nailing up of Luther's theses at Wittenberg in 1517 saw no further major doctrinal challenge to the Western Church. The effect of Hussitism was to stimulate Waldensians who survived in secrecy; but the new movement could not undo the effects of an underground life on the old. Much the same might be said of the effects of the new Protestantism of the sixteenth century on the surviving popular heresies, Waldensianism, and English Lollardy. The supporters of these heresies had suffered too much, and either never had a powerful intellectual backing or, as in the case of Lollardy and Wyclif, had lost touch with what they once had. There are interesting cases of rapprochement between old and new; but the force and importance of the new exceeded the old, and the new movements did not owe a great deal to the old.

Joachimite ideas maintained a certain vogue in the cataclysms of the sixteenth century. Papal prophecies, especially those that stressed the evils of popes, attracted some reformers; Catholics countered by using Joachimite work to put in the foreground prophecies of holy popes who would in the future restore unity to the Church.[2] Certain Jesuits were attracted by the role of the 'new spiritual men' of a new age, just as the mendicant orders once had been, though they avoided the extravagances of the Spiritual Franciscans.[3] The heretical pseudo-Joachimite idea of the third age had a natural vogue amongst the revolutionaries of the Reformation; Thomas Müntzer drew on the pseudo-Joachimite *Super Heremiam*, and cast himself as an initiator of the new age, shortly to come. He said, 'The witness of Abbot Joachim has indeed counted greatly with me . . .' 'But', he went on in a characteristic phrase, 'my teaching is far higher than his.'[4]

[1] A precise account of the relationship of medieval heresy to the Reformation is beyond the scope of this book: all that is provided here is a glimpse of the problem. Williams gives summaries on Waldensians in the Alpine valleys and Italy (*Radical Reformation*, pp. 520–9). See, for all Waldensians, Böhmer in *RPTK* xx, cols 830–7; for Lollardy, Dickens, 'Heresy and Origins', pp. 47–66; M. E. Aston, 'Lollardy and the Reformation', pp. 149–70; and for recurring Joachimite ideas and themes, Reeves, *Prophecy*, pp. 274–90, 429–504.

[2] Reeves, pp. 453–62.

[3] Ibid., pp. 274–90.

[4] Ibid., pp. 490–1; Williams, *Radical Reformation*, p. 51 and n., quoted in A. G. Dickens, *Reformation and Society in Sixteenth-Century Europe* (London, 1966), p. 143.

Background influence may be postulated from older heresy, preparing popular opinion for change or acting as a seed bed for new sects, but no more. The fact was that the medieval Church had beaten most of its heretical movements: persecution, the isolation of supporters of heresy from intellectual life, the passage of time, and a changing religious climate eliminated them or pushed them to the margin of society. Late medieval currents of thought profoundly affected the Protestant reformers, of course; research has shown how much Luther owed to the medieval past, and we will recognize in the denunciations of sixteenth-century Protestants complaints familiar to us in the speech and writings of the condemned heretics of the Middle Ages. The abuses, especially in the lands where rulers could not, or did not, co-operate with indigenous reforming movements, remained the same. But the remedies now proposed differed from, and were more potent than, those offered by the supporters of medieval heretical movements.

Waldensians were moved by the events in Bohemia, and felt an affinity with the Taborites, with whom they had many beliefs in common. A group in Dauphiné in 1431 even made a collection for them.[5] Under persecution, adherents of the old heresy comforted themselves with the expectation of rescue by Hussite power. At Paesana in 1510 they said under interrogation that 'at the head of a great army, a king of the Bohemians would come . . . that he would kill all the clerics and take from them their temporal possessions, abolishing tolls and all sorts of exploitation . . .'[6] During the second half of the fifteenth century, Waldensianism took on a new vitality, roused, most likely, by the stimulus of the movements in the lands of the Bohemian crown.[7] Hussites of various shades felt a need for contact with them, as witnesses to the fact that opposition to Rome had existed long before the beginning of the Bohemian revolution; Chelčický mentions Valdes with Pope Sylvester, as hiding from Constantine: obviously he obtained the story from a Waldensian source.[8] Jakoubek knew Waldensians,[9] and the *Unitas* sought orders from them.[10] Luke of Prague, of their moderate wing, the Major Party, in the search for a true apostolic Church, entered into contacts with the Italian Waldensians.[11] Hussite preachers tried to use surviving Waldensian congregations as supports for their missionary enterprise in Germany.[12]

But the long underground existence had deeply marked the Waldensians. The *Unitas*, as they got into contact with the Italian membership, were disturbed at their power of deception, born of their secret life. Luke of Prague concluded that they needed instruction. Facing bloody expeditions in their Alpine redoubts, communities no longer followed their own prohibition of killing.[13] The presence of traitors and informers put strains on their morality. The *barbi* inevitably lacked intellectual contacts, and an atmosphere of magic

[5]Selge, in *TR*, 33. Jhrg, IV (1968), p. 339.
[6]Williams, p. 520.
[7]Böhmer, loc. cit, col. 831.
[8]Kaminsky, *Revolution*, p. 392.
[9]Ibid., p. 321.
[10]Williams, p. 211.
[11]A. Molnár, 'Luc de Prague et les Vaudois d'Italie', *BSSV*, LXX, x (1949), pp. 40–64.
[12]Seibt, 'Die Zeit', p. 532; Böhmer, cols 831–2.
[13]For late fifteenth-century persecutions, Lea, *Inquisition*, II, pp. 265–9 still has value.

and secrecy hung about them which disquieted some observers.[14] Yet they were survivors of a long resistance to Rome, believed by sixteenth-century contemporaries to stretch back to the days of Constantine, and their very existence demonstrated that Protestants had a history of their own, and had their forerunners and martyrs long before Luther and Calvin. So, as currents of Protestant influence began to reach the surviving Waldensians, each side had something to offer the other: the Protestants, their theology, and the protection of religious groups that had gained their independence; the Waldensians their history.

On the Waldensian side, new influences created parties for the *Unitas*, for Protestant influences from Saxony, for Zwingli, and for the French Swiss communities. The decisive moves were initiated by Guillaume Farel,[15] preaching in the Zwinglian tradition in 1523 in his homeland of Dauphiné. News of his work reached the neighbouring Cottian Alps; *barbi* came to visit him, and a body of support grew up within the Waldensian leadership. Contacts were opened with the Reformers Oecolampadius and Bucer, and in 1532 a great assembly of *barbi* at Chanforan in the Val d'Angrogna, to which Farel and other Protestants were invited, decided to accept, in substance, the theology of Farel, and to abandon most of their distinctively Waldensian traits, keeping, however, the position of the *barbi*, some of their practices, and pacifism. Money was set aside for the printing of a Bible, not in the Waldensian dialect, but in French, which became the first Bible of the French evangelical Church. A minority refused the decision to unite with the Protestants, appealing to the *Unitas* for support; elsewhere in Italy, groups in the Po valley, in Calabria and Apulia stood aside from the union. Loosely organized and subjected to pressures heavier than those suffered in the valleys, these Waldensians were open to a medley of influences. It has been conjectured that they formed a seed-ground for the development of an Italian anti-trinitarian anabaptism.[16] In Germany and Austria, in a somewhat similar fashion, surviving congregations have been said to act as a stimulus for the development of the anabaptist groups well known in early sixteenth-century history;[17] they had a considerable number of traits in common—the rejection of the oath, of war, of the holding of civic office and the uncompromising rejection of the world. The rejection of infant baptism or the practice of ordaining the preacher may, it is said, have acted as a first step towards the re-baptizing current in these sects. But these are only hypotheses, and much detailed research on the Waldensians in the sixteenth century has yet to be done. In any case, the congregations of Calabria and Apulia that had not accepted union were decimated by a persecution of 1560. Meanwhile, in the valleys the decision of Chanforan was gradually consummated over the years, especially through the work of French pastors from Lausanne. '

[14]G. Miolo, *Historia breve e vera de gl'affari de i Valdesi delle Valli*, ed. E. Balmas (Turin, 1971).

[15]For this account I follow Williams (with literature) and Böhmer (see n.1. above).

[16]The phrase and the theory in Williams, *Radical Reformation*, p. 528; general reflections on Italy are in Delio Cantimori, 'The Problem of Heresy', in *The Late Italian Renaissance, 1525–1630*, ed. E. Cochrane (London, 1970), pp. 211–25 (trans. of art. in *BSSV*, LXXVI (1957), pp. 29–38), with comment on the relations between Italian reform and medieval heresy; 'the field remains almost wholly unexplored' (p. 216).

[17]Böhmer in *RPTK* xx, col 832, using dogmatic comparison.

M

Waldensian history blends thereafter with that of the Protestant Reformation.

In England the meeting of the old Lollards and the new Protestants has affinities with the relationship between the continental reformers and the Waldensians; it is typified by the episode in which Lollards from Steeple Bumstead went up to London to show their ancient copies of the vernacular Scriptures, and found themselves sold a copy of the new version by Friar Barnes.[18] Inevitably the new theological learning from the Continent had a force lacking to the old traditions and texts of underground Lollardy.[19] The sect had behind it a great achievement; the missionaries of its underground phase had defied defeat, and had come near to re-founding Loilardy.[20] Its membership had endured long pressure and isolation while maintaining a certain sobriety of belief. They were not marked to any great degree by the extravagance or heightened eschatological expectations noted by the school of Morghen and Manselli as a characteristic effect of persecution. Nor were they often tainted by other underground beliefs: there are only rare cases of the practice of magic and adherence to Lollardy being combined, or at least taken up at differing times by one and the same suspect.[21]

The mere needs of survival, however, as in the case of the Waldensians, marked the sect in other ways, confining it very largely to men of limited education and social background. On the eve of the Reformation, despite evidence of rising numbers and of some foothold in middle class circles in London, it had not broken out of its confined circumstances; too long underground, it 'lacked the power of spiritual regeneration.'[22] Its services to the new Protestantism lay in the diffusion of the negatives of the sect outside its own Scripture-reading circles, contributing to the popular mood of lay independence, of sitting loose to the more petty demands of the Church, which formed a humus for the flowering of the new theology. Plain scepticism, as A. G. Dickens warns us, had a part to play, spreading outwards from the Lollards.[23]

Yet caution has to be observed on this thesis of 'diffused Lollardy'. Lollards were, so to speak, an extreme wing of the general anticlerical movement of opinion in the sixteenth century, always distinguished from anticlericalism proper by their Scripture-reading and their denial of transubstantiation, but always gaining recruits from this much wider spectrum of opinion. Anticlerical, rather than heretical, voices may be mainly responsible for this general climate of opinion, though there is little doubt Lollardy contributed. In the north of England, discussed in detail by Dickens, there is no very specific evidence of a Lollard survival beyond six cases in the records of York diocese between 1511 and 1534; of these one provides too little evidence to

---

[18]Thomson, *Later Lollards*, p. 138.

[19]Dickens, 'Heresy and Origins', pp. 63–4.

[20]See Fines, *Studies, passim*.

[21]Thomson, *Later Lollards*, pp. 71, 83, 179; possibly 67; K. Thomas, *Religion and the Decline of Magic* (London, 1971).

[22]Aston, 'Lollardy and the Reformation', p. 169. I find the perspective here convincing.

[23]A. G. Dickens, *Lollards and Protestants in the Diocese of York*, (Oxford, 1959), p. 13; for central theme of diffused Lollardy, summary, pp. 243–5. The quotation from Richard Flynte in 1542 is telling. I admire the book, but dissent from the northern Lollardy hypothesis; cf. Thomson, *Later Lollards*, p. 200.

support any hypothesis, another is the case of a Lollard who learnt his heresy in Lincoln, and another a Hull sailor with Lutheran contacts abroad, and three are Dutchmen. Indeed, they sound like Lollards rather than continental heretics; but, just as Free Spirit interrogatories based on *Ad nostrum* produce Free Spirit suspects,[24] so the usual English interrogatories based on experience with Lollardy tend to make those interrogated sound like Lollards. We are on safer ground if we speak of a diffusion of negative sentiments from the Lollards in London and the South; safer still if we concentrate on the secondary role of Lollards as smugglers of the continental Protestant literature and on the place of Lollard history and sufferings in propagandist writing, providing Foxe with a martyrology for the Protestants as the Waldensians did for the Church of Geneva.[25]

So, alike for Waldensians and Lollards, their role in the Reformation is a secondary one—as forerunners, as witnesses to the long history of doctrinal dissent, and as a background force, preparing the minds of ordinary people for the coming of Protestantism, or, in the case of the Waldensians, opening the way to the Anabaptists. Research has not said its last word on the question of background influence. Only detailed analysis, case by case and region by region, can disentangle the threads, distinguish between old heresy and new and, beside them, other less specifically religious influences on the English Reformation and the varieties of continental Protestantism. Neither the Waldensians nor the Lollards were of great significance for the development of the Reform. Utraquism, as we have seen, foundered in the changing climate of the sixteenth century; the other movements of the Middle Ages condemned as heretical were killed off or faded away before the Reformation.

---

[24]Above, pp. 179–81.
[25]Aston, 'Lollardy and the Reformation', should be read in conjunction with Crompton, *JEH*, XII (1961), pp. 35–45, 155–65. For Foxe, J. F. Mozley, *John Foxe and his Book*, (London, 1940); on his value as source, Dickens, 'Heresy and Origins', pp. 49–53; Thomson, 'John Foxe'.

Appendices

Appendix A

Sources for Eleventh-Century Heresy

1. Orléans 1022

Twelve sources record the episode, of which seven give information on the doctrines of the sectaries. These latter alone need concern us. They are:

(i) *Gesta synodi Aurelianensis*, extracted from the Vetus Agano of Saint-Père de Chartres (Bouquet, x, pp. 536–9);

(ii) *Johannis monachi Floriac ad Olibam Abbatem . . . epistola* (ibid., p. 498).

(iii) *Ex Historiae Francicae fragmento* (ibid., pp. 211–2).

(iv) Andreas of Fleury, *Vita Gauzlini abbatis Floriacensis*, in id., *Vie de Gauzlin, Abbé de Fleury*, ed. R.-H. Bautier et G. Labory (Paris, 1969), pp. 96–8 (w. trans.).

(vi) Raoul Glaber, *Les cinq livres de ses histoires* (900–1044), ed. M. Prou, iii, viii (Paris, 1886), pp. 74–81.

(v) Adémar of Chabannes, *Chronique*, iii, 59, ed. J. Chavanon (Paris, 1897), pp. 184–5.

(vii) Baldwin of Thérouanne, in J. Malbrancq Audomarensis, *De Morinis et Morinorum rebus*, ii (Tournai, 1647), pp. 661–3.

Source (i) had access to the recollections of the contemporary eyewitness Aréfast,[1] gives concrete detail, and sometimes appears to echo the words of the heretics in their trial.[2] In all points derived from Aréfast or the trial, the source may be taken as accurate. The story of nocturnal orgies and the confecting of a substance to be used as viaticum from the ashes of dead babies is not apparently so derived.[3] The author gives no source for it, and does not set it in a living context, as he does the other doctrines of his account. It should be excised as a digression, based on a literary model or popular slander.

Sources (ii) and (iii) summarize doctrines in words other than those of the heretics themselves. They appear reliable.

Source (iv) was written *c.* 1042;[4] it also gives a summary. Appended to it is an exhortation of Gauzlin closely based on the profession of faith by Gerbert of Aurillac. The difficulty here is that, where this source adds to the main outline of (ii) and (iii) (?denial of Trinity; ? denial of the Incarnation; ? heresy on the Virgin (or reference to inner-illumination)), the wording is inclined to be vague. The reference to Mary ('Filii Dei genetricem se habere similem et per omnia jactabant, cum nec similis visa sit nec habere sequentem') is especially obscure. Bautier and Labory translate, 'Ils se vantaient d'avoir une mère en tous points semblable à celle du Fils de Dieu, alors que celle-ci ne peut être tenue pour semblable à aucune autre femme et qu'elle ne peut avoir d'émule.' At this point the Latin echoes the liturgy;[5] it is hard to say whether it is an allusion to some heresy concerning Mary or to the heavenly guidance claimed by the heretics (taking metaphorically the translators' 'une mère'), and the matter needs

---

[1] On the author, see the introduction to *Cartulaire de l'Abbaye de Saint-Père de Chartres* in *Collection des Cartulaires de France*, i, in *Collection de Documents inédits sur l'Histoire de France*, ser.I: *Histoire Politique*, Paris, 1840, I, cclxvii-cclxxv.

[2] E.g. 'the fictions of carnal men . . . upon animal skins' (above, p. 27).

[3] Bouquet, x, p. 538. para. v.

[4] See *DTC*, s.v. 'André, moine de Fleury'; L. Delisle, 'Vie de Gauzlin, abbé de Fleuri', (*Memoires de la société archéologique de l'Orléanais*, ii (1853), pp. 257–322) and P. Ewald's edn (*Neues Archiv*, iii (1877), pp. 369–70) are superseded by Bautier and Labory. On relation to *Miracula*, see this edn (pp. 11–13).

[5] I owe information on this to Dr P. Meyvaert and hope to write more fully on Orléans heresy later.

(i) Paul of Saint-Père de Chartres	(ii) Jean of Fleury	(iii) *Historiae Francicae Fragmentum*	(iv) Andreas of Fleury
Rejection of Mass	Rejection of Mass		? Denial of Trinity
Denial of creation by Father?			? Denial of Incarnation
Docetism			? Heresy on the Virgin (or reference to inner illumination)
	Rejection of penance	Rejection of penance	Rejection of penance
Imposition of hands for initiation into sect		Rejection of imposition of hands by Catholic Church	Rejection of imposition of hands by Catholic Church
			Rejection of Church
Direct illumination by Holy Spirit for initiates	Rejection of marriage	Rejection of marriage	Rejection of marriage
			Rejection of bishops
Rejection of prayers to saints		Rejection of ordination	Rejection of ordination
Rejection of baptism	Rejection of baptism	Rejection of baptism	
	Rejection of flesh eating		
Viaticum from dead child			

(v) Adémar of Chabannes	(vi) Raoul Glaber	(vii) Baldwin of Thérouanne
	Denial of Trinity	
Secret rejection of Christ	Eternity of world	
	No punishment for lust	
	Denial of good works	
		Rejection of saints
		Rejection of baptism
		Flesh-eating allowed at any time
Adoration of devil		Rejection of cross
Viaticum from dead child		

M*

investigation. But we may note the literary cast of the phrases on the Trinity, the Incarnation and Mary, and the manner in which the whole paragraph summarizing the heretics begins with the Trinity, passes on to the Son of God and then to the Holy Spirit, and is rounded off by an allusion to Mary.

Source (v) has legendary overtones, refers to a *rusticus*[6]. as founding the sect in Orléans, and to the use of a dust made from dead boys (compare the viaticum in (i)).

Source (vi) summarizes doctrines cloudily in four sentences and confuses Héribert, the enthusiast from northern France, with Stephen, the indigenous leader in Orléans. There is no evidence for E. Sackur's supposition that the author was at the synod.[7]

Source (vii), Baldwin of Thérouanne, given in the compilation by the seventeenth-century Jesuit, Malbrancq, is not an original source. Malbrancq in part borrows *verbatim* from Glaber on Orléans, describes the spread of heresy in Aquitaine and Auvergne and Baldwin's fear that it might reach his own diocese. In passing, he characterizes the heresy in three phrases; but Malbrancq does not cite his source for this.

(i) is the principal source. The orgy story is readily excisable; without it the source gives a good account. (ii) and (iii) are lesser, but not untrustworthy sources; so is (iv), but it is marred by ambiguity of phrasing. (v)–(vii) are too shaky for their evidence to prevail over (i)–(iii).

The doctrines attributed to the group in the sources may be tabulated—(see pages 344–345).

The first three sources, which omit the orgy narrative, taken together, give us the following picture. Two elements are present, the one being a rejection of the rites and orders of the Catholic Church, the mass, penance, baptism, prayers to the saints, such as is common to many sects, and may readily arise by spontaneous generation from the soil of western Church life. The other consists of a number of features, not so readily classified as 'Western reform dissidence', which are features of the contemporaneous Bogomil heresy in Byzantine lands; they are the rejection of marriage, Docetism, the imposition of hands for initiation into the sect, and the rejection of flesh-eating.

J. B. Russell believes that the confusion of sources makes a dualist interpretation unlikely.[8] He cannot accept Jean of Fleury's attribution to them of a rejection of flesh-eating, on the grounds that it is contradicted by Baldwin of Thérouanne.[9] Baldwin is too frail a source to be used in this way. Jean of Fleury in fact says that the heretics 'a cibis quos Deus creavit, et adipe quam ab immunditiis abstinebant.'[10] The first phrase implies abstention from some whole category of food, the second adds as a further point that they abstained from animal fat as from things that were impure. There appear to be Bogomil echoes. The Bogomils rejected meat as part of the evil creation: Jean of Fleury's stress on foods as created by God is surely significant. But this is not strictly direct evidence of a rejection of flesh-eating as such, though that is a likely interpretation. Rejection of flesh-eating is a convenient short label on the table of doctrines, above, p. 344.

Secondly, Russell argues that the heretics' defence of their rejection of the virgin birth and of the Resurrection on rationalist grounds, because it was contrary to reason, or because they had not seen it with their own eyes, shows that the root of their heresy lay in an intellectual scepticism, born on Western soil, rather than in an importation of dualism.[11] But this is to suppose that such a scepticism did not act in East and West as a spur to heresy. It is a factor in the Bogomilism described by Cosmas.[12] In an interrogation one would expect heretics influenced by dualism to defend their views thus in the light of reason. The conclusion is that, while some further investigation is

---

[6]The addition 'from Périgord' (*Petragoricensi*) only appears in a twelfth-century MS. of Adémar, and Borst (*Katharer*, p. 75, n. 10) suggests it is an interpolation. See also *WEH*, p. 666.

[7]'Studien über Rodulfus Glaber', *Neues Archiv*, XIV (1889), p. 395.

[8]*Dissent*, p. 32. Compare Manselli, *Eresia*, pp. 128–9.

[9]*Dissent*, pp. 32–3.

[10]Bouquet, X, 498.

[11]*Dissent*, p. 34.

[12]Puech-Vaillant, *Traité*; text: pp. 58 (attitude to relics), 59 (on veneration of cross), 70 (on images), 75 (on origin of evil); see also p. 72 (possible echo of sneers at orthodox for venerating mere dust in the tomb) and p. 83, (on the miracles of Christ). Compare Thouzellier, *Un Traité inédit*, p. 73, on the Cathar use of reason.

needed, it is a good interim judgement that the Orléans sources, selected and analysed, provide us with a credible account of the doctrines of the sectaries there in 1022.

2. Gerard of Csanád

The relevant passage, as amended by Dr Silagi, is as follows:[13]

1   pro dolor, vero nunc multi pullulant in ecclesia, immo iam totum occupant orbem, et nemo est, qui talium ineptiis contradicat. o quantos sentio diaboli filios, quibus loqui non patior. hoc tempore omnes maledixerunt [apud nos] concitati zelo non solum divinis ritibus et aecclesie, et sacerdotibus,

5   quin etiam ipsi dei filio Jesu Christo, domino nostro. omnibus inaudita saeculi haereses repetere helemosinas pro animabus defunctorum Christianorum more expansas. non estimes, frater carissime, minorem persequutionem et heresem antiquioribus hanc esse. in fide et veritate fateor, quod vi compellabantur intolerabilia mendatia in dei expendere sacerdotes. diaboli autem iniquitas

10   unum, quod potuit, facit, nimirum quicquid ex lege dei noviter venientes ad beatissimam illuminationem docuimus, abstulit. omnes uno pene simul ore carnis negant resurrectionem, qua iniquitate nulla umquam in mundo maior iniquitas arbitranda. prohibemur iam loqui, et episcopi nominamur constituti etiam sub tributo, quibus totus committitur divino imperio mundus. nam

15   quorundam, nisi fallor, intentio est, quo ecclesiastica virtus, suffragantibus Methodianistis, atque dignitas apud nos circa hereticorum libitum tota quandoque infirmetur. quare hoc? nimirum dixi, quia filii diaboli, qui potestates sunt tenebrarum, ubique regnant et dominantur: Italia non consuevit hereses nutrire—ad praesens in quibusdam partibus heresium

20   fomentis habundare auditur. Gallia vero felix, que his munda peribetur, [Frantia] in multis claudicat, Gretia infelix, sine quibus numquam vivere voluit. Verona, urbium Italię nobilissima, his gravida redditur. illustris Ravenna et beata Venetia, que numquam inimicos dei passe sunt, ferre.

The 'apud nos' (l.3) is a marginal addition in the extant codex, and not necessarily in the original. The codex has been annotated after 'Gallia' (l.20), 'claudicat' has been inserted, and a second hand has added 'Frantia' in order to make the meaning plain. Finally, 'redditur' should be understood after 'ferre' (l.23).

Gerard's purpose is homiletic. He describes the virtues of the devil, in contradistinction to the virtues of God. Shortly before this passage, he writes, 'itaque omnes, qui Christo et sue ecclesie adversantur, diabolice virtutes dicendi.'[14] It is not part of his purpose to distinguish clearly the form taken by these *diabolice virtutes*.

Gerard before this passage refers to earlier heresies; then he turns to present threats to the Church. The term *haereses* is used four times, but *heretici* once. Unluckily Gerard uses these terms imprecisely. Demanding back money given for masses of the dead is 'inaudita . . . haereses' (ll.5–6); *haereses* are associated with *persequutio* (l.7) and with the loose phraseology of ll.8–9 (*intolerabilia mendatia* . . ., best translated as 'one is compelled to tell intolerable lies'). The threats and *haereses* he refers to in these early lines appear to be located in Hungary, for he suffers from them as bishop—i.e. during his Csanád episcopate, 1030–46. This follows from ll.13–14 ('prohibemur iam loqui et episcopi nominamur') and from the reference to the newly converted (ll.10–11: 'noviter venientes ad beatissimam illuminationem'). His description of *haereses* could fit Bogomilism, for he speaks of views which condemned the Church, its priesthood and rites, even Jesus Christ, rejected prayers for the dead, and denied the resurrection of the body; this last was a Bogomil tenet. The attack on Jesus Christ ('maledixerunt', l.3) is too vaguely described for certainty, but would hang satisfactorily with a Docetic Christology.

On the other hand, the demand for return of money given for masses may be

[13]Editions cited above, p. 35, n. 40. I am grateful to Dr Silagi for his advice. On Gerard's life, see Silagi, *Untersuchungen*, pp. 1–13.

[14]Batthyány, p. 97 (codex, ff. 45v–46r).

associated with plundering after a heathen reaction, and not linked to heresy in a strict sense at all; *persequutio* suggests heathen reaction quite as well as heresy, and so do the financial exactions (l.14: 'sub tributo'). The denial of the Resurrection could be a Bogomil tenet, but it is also the type of orthodox doctrine that heathen might jib at.[15]

Haereses, used again about France, Greece, Italy and certain towns in the last four sentences, cannot in this context mean heathen reaction. But the use is still imprecise. We have to note (a) that there is no necessary connection between the *haereses* apparently located in Hungary and those in Greece and Western Europe; (b) that in Gerard's mind the term might mean persecution of the Church ·or anticlericalism rather than doctrinal deviation. We cannot exclude Gerard's witness on Western Europe because of his Hungarian residence. He had studied in France, had been born in Venice, and visited Rome and Ravenna for Stephen of Hungary. His references to Italy and France sound contemporary and non-literary. The doctrinal description with regard to Hungary, the possibility of Bogomil influence spreading from Byzantium and the Balkans into Hungary, the reference to heresy in Greece (l.21) are all intriguing. Bogomilism as the *haereses* in Hungary and Western Europe is a possible hypothesis, but no more. The source is more subtle and elusive than Döllinger thought, and it is unlikely we can ever gain more precise information from it.

---

[15]See Silagi, *Untersuchungen*, p'. 31, n. 48, for titles of Hungarian articles of 1956 and 1965, the former arguing that Gerard is speaking of Bogomilism, the latter that by *heretici* Gerard means Christians who have returned to heathenism.

Appendix B

Johannes Von Walter and the Pauperes Christi

The major hypothesis in von Walter's *Die ersten Wanderprediger Frankreichs* was that, with the appearance of the wandering preachers in France, a new way of understanding the *apostolica vita* was born that led ultimately to the birth both of the Waldensians and of the Franciscans. Linked to this was a minor thesis: as this novel form of life developed, the old term *pauperes Christi*, hitherto used for the traditional monks and the poor that should be given alms by the faithful, took on a different meaning. It developed into something approaching a technical term for the wandering preachers and their followers. This second thesis was not a very important part of von Walter's work, and a refutation of it would hardly weaken his principal hypothesis. Nevertheless it is a mistaken thesis; the understanding of the term *pauperes Christi* in contemporary documents as a kind of touchstone for the presence of wandering preachers can lead historians into error.

Two recent examples of its mischief-making potential may be seen in K. Bosl's work on Regensburg,[1] and K. V. Selge's on the early Waldensians.[2] In the first a reference to *pauperes Christi* in a Regensburg deed of gift is taken as proof of the presence of wandering preachers in the town at a date between 1080 and 1088; while in the second a mention of *pauperes Christi* by Durand of Huesca in his *Liber antiheresis* is assumed to be an injunction to charity to Waldensian missionaries. In neither case is the inference justified. The *pauperes Christi* of Regensburg are simply traditional religious. The term has its old monastic connotation, and there is no proof that wandering preachers were ever active in Regensburg. In the *Liber antiheresis, pauperes Christi* has its primary meaning of 'the poor'. The poor wandering preachers of the Waldensian movement might have been subsumed under this heading; but there is no proof that this was so, and no indication that Durand has anything more specific in mind than an injunction to that charity to the poor in general which is the duty of all the faithful.

Such errors arise through assuming over-hastily that *pauperes Christi* in the twelfth century had taken on a precise meaning: of wandering preachers and their followers. Von Walter was over-bold in his views about *pauperes Christi*, and most of the evidence he adduces for this new meaning does not bear him out. *Pauperes Christi* continued above all to mean 'the poor', whether voluntary or involuntary. Von Walter's evidence and the use of his hypothesis by subsequent historians may now be examined.

Von Walter employed the sentence, 'quos alio nolebat censeri vocabulo, nisi pauperes Christi', in the *Vita* of Robert of Arbrissel by Baldrich of Dol,[3] where Robert is shown to call his followers *pauperes Christi*, to demonstrate that the term had come to have special significance. Adducing other examples, he commented, 'This name seems to have had a straightforward official meaning, since it appears in several sources: *pauperes Christi, pauperes Dei* and *pauperes fontis Ebraldi.*'[4] Later, while discussing the phrase *conversatio inter pauperes Christi* in its connection with Bernard of Thiron, he commented, 'It might be possible to conclude that Bernard, as well as Robert, called

[1]*Die Socialstruktur der mittelalterlichen Residenz-und Fernhandelstadt Regensburg* (München, 1966), pp. 34–5.
[2]*Die ersten Waldenser*, I (Berlin, 1967), pp. 124–5.
[3]*PL*, CLXII, col. 1053, para. 19.
[4]*Die ersten Wanderprediger Frankreichs*, I (Leipzig, 1903), p. 125, n. 4.

his followers *pauperes Christi*.'[5] Followers meant for von Walter the companions of the preaching tours, those who lived with the preachers as they followed the instructions of Christ at the sending of the Seventy, wandering, preaching and living off the alms of their hearers. In this interpretation he has been followed by later historians. H. Grundmann in the classic *Religiöse Bewegungen* commented, '. . . in Northern France the wandering preacher Robert of Arbrissel moved through the country barefoot, with flowing beard and hair and in wretched clothing, and gathered round him through his preaching the *pauperes Christi*, who have renounced all worldly goods and travel with their master in want and without fixed abode.'[6]

E. Werner took *Pauperes Christi* as the title of his book on the popular religious movements of the investiture period, and revealed that he understood it to be the new form of *apostolica vita*, conceived as wandering preaching in poverty, in the heading to his second chapter, 'Pauperes Christi: a type of religious life revived at the end of the eleventh and beginning of the twelfth centuries.'[7]

Von Walter was quite right to think that, in the *Vita* by Baldrich, Robert of Arbrissel calls his followers *pauperes Christi*; but an examination of the context shows that he was then referring, not to the companions of the preaching tours, but to the former companions who had been settled into the stable monastic life of his community at Fontevrault. The context shows who were the recipients of this title; the *Vita* describes how the numbers in Fontevrault increased and then, in passing, how the founder wanted to name them:

> Ipsius delibutum sermonibus, intantum peccatis abrenuntiantium crevit examen, ut numerus pene fuerit innumerus: quos alio nolebat censeri vocabulo, nisi pauperes Christi. Multi confluebant homines cujuslibet conditionis . . . Nec jam innumeram copiositatem praeparata capiebant tuguriola.[8]

Since they were to be accommodated in *tuguriola* ('huts'), they were plainly members of the settled community. *Pauperes Christi* is a term used by Robert out of his passion for humility in the community. It is on all fours with his own preference for the title of *magister* rather than *abbas*, and springs from a desire for modification of the traditional Benedictine monasticism of his time. The argument that *pauperes Christi* came to have an official meaning for Robert's followers, whether in Fontevrault or not, is hardly borne out by the instances von Walter cites. It appears in two, or at the most three, deeds of gift for Fontevrault out of the sixty-three published by Migne. Nor is there anything unusual in the way in which it is employed. One reference runs, 'Eleemosynas de nostris Christi pauperibus, ut ipsos apud summum judicem intercessores habeamus, erogemus',[9] and another, '. . . ego . . . cogitavi quidpiam misericordiae pauperibus Dei impendere.'[10] A third describes the nuns of Fontevrault simply as the *pauperes fontis Ebraldi*.[11] There is no difference of substance here from the sources of the ninth and tenth centuries, which commonly refer to monks and nuns as *pauperes*.[12]

Two references are made to *pauperes Christi* in the *Vita* of Bernard of Tiron, the second of the wandering preachers discussed by von Walter. One praises Bernard's contacts with the poor, 'Sed ego, fratres charissimi, quidquid sentiant alii, amplius admiror hujus gloriosissimi viri humilem inter pauperes Christi conversationem, quam sibi divinitus datam virtutem . . .'[13] The *pauperes Christi* are the involuntary poor; the source seems to be praising Bernard's equality with the poor in a manner reminiscent to us of the Franciscan age. The identification is made clearer three sentences later, where the *Vita* praises Bernard's charity to the sick, 'Sed quid non

[5]Op. cit., II (1906), p. 47, n. 2.
[6]*RB*, p. 17; cp. p. 40, n. 57.
[7]*Pauperes Christi* (Leipzig, 1956), p. 19.
[8]*PL*, CLXII, col. 1053, para. 19.
[9]Ibid., col. 1113, doc.xlv.
[10]Ibid., col. 1099, doc. x.
[11]Ibid., cols. 1113–14, doc. xlvii.
[12]M. von Dmitrewski, *Die christliche freiwillige Armut vom Ursprung der Kirche bis zum 12. Jahrhundert* (Berlin & Leipzig, 1913), p. 75; cited by Werner, *Pauperes Christi* p. 19.
[13]*PL*, CLXII, col. 1443, para. 134.

extorqueret a visceribus charitatis ejus, infirmorum et dolentium compassio?' The *infirmi* and *dolentes* are among the *pauperes Christi*. In the other references the hagiographer in a passage on Bernard's death praises him as being himself *pauper Christi*. '. . . membra, felici annositate confracta et incredibili parcimonia penitus emortua, quia charius pauper Christi non habuit, hereditario jure Tironensi ecclesiae credidit, coelitus sibi creditum, coelo spiritum reddidit . . .'[14]. Bernard is so poor that he can only bequeath body and soul—his body to the church of Tiron, his soul to heaven. He is as poor as the involuntary poor who have to depend on alms, and is thus a *pauper Christi*.

Only this second reference can be relevant for von Walter's interpretation. It is not concerned especially with Bernard's life as a wandering preacher, for the *Vita's* praise of his poverty relates to all the later period of his life, whether spent on the road or in the relative stability of the hermit settlement.

For two others of von Walter's wandering preachers, Girald of Salles and Vitalis of Savigny, the sources are meagre. Those for Girald yield no reference at all to *pauperes Christi*. For Vitalis we have only some lines in a poem in his necrology, praising both his own poverty and his care for the poor,

'Pauper, mendicus sibi vixit, largus egenis,
Pupillos, viduas, veste ciboque fovens . . .'
Eleven lines later we have,
'Nam, dum vixisti, Christo servire fuisti
Promptus, pauperibusque Dei victum tribuisti.'[15]
Pauperes Christi here means only the involuntary poor, whom he served.

The term does, however, occur more frequently in the sources cited by von Walter for Norbert of Xanten and his followers. The *Vita Norberti* (version known as *Vita* A), describing the action of the Englishman who joined Norbert's community and stole alms, refers to *pauperes Christi* among Norbert's followers, 'Sic ille plenus fraude pauperibus Christi, nichil mali suspiciantibus, paupertatem adauxit, intantum ut non remaneret eis, unde sumptus procurari posset diei unius.'[16] But the context shows that they were so described at a time after they were settled in a stable community at Prémontré. The phrases describing Norbert's services to his followers in the *Fundatio*, 'Ibi ergo pauper pauperibus Christi serviebat . . .'[17], and the count of Cappenberg's benefactions in his *Vita*, 'Ipse quoque . . . castrum suum Cappenberg et omnia sua Deo fideliter offerens . . . usibus ea pauperum Christi delegavit, tria videlicet exstruens coenobia . . .',[18] plainly have a similar connotation. A reference in the *Gesta archiepiscoporum Magdeburgensium* is more interesting, because it describes Norbert's followers as *pauperes Christi* at exactly the moment at which they were ceasing to be companions of the preaching tour, and were entering on a fixed settlement. 'Factum est autem, ut post multorum circuitus laborum deveniret cum discipulis suis pauperibus Christi in quoddam desertum Francia . . .'[19]

A clear reference to wandering preachers on the road as *pauperes Christi* is given in the description of the preaching journey of Norbert and Hugo, c. 1118, in the *Vita Norberti* (*Vita* B). Both forms of the *Vita* describe this journey, but only *Vita* B has the expression *pauperes Christi*.

'Erant enim veri pauperes Christi, laborem suum aliis gratuito impendentes, nihil a quoquam vel etiam in victu seu vestitu expetentes vel accipientes, nisi forte an missam eis oblatum fuisset: et hoc totum, quidquid illud erat, pauperibus erogabant . . .'[20]
We may compare the version in *Vita* A:
'Stupori erat novum in eo genus vitae, videlicet in terra degere et nil de terra quaerere. Iuxta mandatum namque evangelii neque peram neque calciamenta

---

[14]Ibid., col. 1438, para. 124.
[15]*Rouleaux des morts du IXe au XVe siècle*, ed. L. Delisle (Paris, 1866) p. 308.
[16]*MGH, Scriptores*, xii, p. 684.
[17]*MGH, Scriptores*, xx, p. 686.
[18]*MGH, Scriptores*, xii, p. 516.
[19]*MGH, Scriptores*, xiv, p. 142.
[20]*Acta Sanctorum*, June, i, p. 816, col. 27.

neque duas tunicas portebat, paucis solummodo libris et idumentis missae contentus . . . nichil a quoquam expetebat, sed si qua oblata fuissent, pauperibus et leprosis erogabat.'[21]

A re-examination of the position thus gives us only one case, from the *Vita* A, referring to Norbert and Hugo *c.* 1118, where *pauperes Christi* is applied to wandering preachers on mission; possibly one could add to this the reference to Norbert and his followers in the *Gesta archiepiscoporum Magdeburgensium.* This is not very much to show from all the source material for the wandering preachers that are discussed by von Walter. It is clearly quite insufficient to support any view which would make the employment of the term *pauperes Christi* a touchstone for the presence of wandering preachers.

It is surely significant that both sources on the preaching mission of Norbert and his companion speak of it as a novelty. *Vita* A speaks of 'veri pauperes Christi', *Vita* B of a 'novum genus vitae'. These terms will set up echoes in the mind of the description by Everwin of Steinfeld of the Cathars in Cologne in the fourth decade of the twelfth century:

> Dicunt apud se tantum ecclesiam esse, eo quod ipsi soli vestigiis Christi inhaerant; et apostolicae vitae veri sectatores permaneant . . . De se dicunt: Nos pauperes Christi, instabiles, de civitate in civitatem fugientes . . .[22]

Here heretical wandering preachers are claiming to be *apostolicae vitae veri sectatores* and *pauperes Christi.* The descriptions in *Vita* A and B of Norbert and in Everwin of Steinfeld of the Cologne Cathars, taken together, may give us a clue to what was occurring.

Ancient terms of honour, such as *pauperes Christi, pauperes, sectatores apostolicae vitae,* were popular in the twelfth century. *Pauperes Christi* went on being applied to the involuntary poor who needed the protection of the faithful, and to monks and nuns.[23] Canons laid claim to the title,[24] and so did Cistercians.[25] It was used for the followers of a wandering preacher after they had settled down to become monks.[26] The claim was made that wandering preachers, heretical and orthodox, were the 'true' *pauperes* or the true '*sectatores vitae apostolicae*'[27] The denudation of an unstable wandering life of poverty attracted a special popular reverence. But differing groups claimed, or were given, the title *pauperes Christi,* and none had a monopoly. It remained a popular term with a fluid variety of usage.

---

[21]*MGH, Scriptores,* xii, p. 675.

[22]*PL,* clxxxii, col. 676.

[23]For the eleventh century we may note that Gregory VII's reference to *pauperes Christi* in the *epistolae selectae* (*MG,* ii (Berlin, 1920)), ii, p. 188, clearly has this traditional sense. Another, (ibid., ix, p. 602) appears to denote the clergy in general. These references and others to the *epistolae selectae* given by Werner (*Pauperes Christi,* p. 17, n. 42) do not support his view that Gregory 'uses the concept in his letters and with it links together the revolutionary trends in Church reform, such as the Pataria and Hirsau.'

[24]Anselm of Havelberg, *Epistola apologetica* (*PL* clxxxviii, cols 1119, 1129, 1138; J. Mois, *Das Stift Rottenbuch* (München, 1953), p. 272; *Lotharii III Diplomata* (*MGH,* viii), no. 27, p. 43.

[25]St. Bernard, *Epistolae* (PL, clxxxii) cols 160–1.

[26]*Chronicon Affligemense, MGH, Scriptores,* ix p. 409. The foundation of the monastery took place in 1083. The chronicler wrote after 1122. The use of the term *pauperes Dei* for the monks is attributed to the bishop of Cambrai. I owe the ref. to Professor H. Grundmann.

[27]As new groups claimed to be *pauperes Christi,* so the old claimants, the monks, were put on the defensive. Compare to the *veri pauperes* of the *Vita* of Norbert and the *veri sectatores* of Everwin, the title of the work attributed to Rupert of Deutz, *De vita vere apostolica.* The issue is discussed by M. D. Chenu, 'Moines, Clercs, Laïcs au Carrefour de la Vie évangélique (XII Siècle)', *RHE,* xlix (1954), pp. 59–89.

Appendix C

K. V. Selge's Exposition of Waldensian Origins

The latest account of the early Waldensians is that of K. V. Selge, *Die ersten Waldenser* (Berlin, 1967), 2 vols, the first volume being an exposition, the second an edition of the *Liber antiheresis* of Durand of Huesca (here called Durand of Osca). Summaries by the author in French of his hypothesis will be found in *CF*, II, pp. 110–42; of the disputes on apostolicity between Cathars, Waldensians and Catholics on pp. 143–62, and of his view of the *Pauperes catholici* and *Pauperes reconciliati* on pp. 227–43. Selge's principal argument is that the majority of historians, with certain early exceptions, have given too high a place to poverty. In Waldensianism, he says, 'preaching is the real core, poverty the form of life of the apostolic preachers.'[1]

A principal support for his new hypothesis lies in Selge's inferences from Durand's silences and omissions in the chapter *De labore* of the *Liber*,[2] where he defends the rejection of manual work by Waldensian preachers, not out of a concept of *apostolica vita* understood as a means for the individual to attain perfection, but out of the need for the preacher to be freed from earthly cares, and from the appeal which he makes throughout the work to the need for preachers in the Church, as in the words of Scripture on sending labourers into the harvest;[3] Waldensian preaching aims first at the salvation of the hearer—'it is mission, and the *vita apostolica* with its value for perfection serves this primary mission.'[4]

To show that this was the primitive view, and not merely a development imposed on the Waldensians by the Church's refusal to allow the group a general right to preach, Selge then attempts to reinterpret the sources for Waldensian history[5] before the *Liber antiheresis*—Valdes's profession of faith made before Henri de Marcy, referred to as his *propositum*, and the conversion narratives in the Anonymous of Laon and Étienne de Bourbon. The *propositum*, Selge notes, makes no explicit mention of preaching; the sentences at the end concerned with the Waldensian way of life relate principally to poverty, and Geoffrey of Auxerre, who was present at the meeting in which Valdes accepted the *propositum*, later wrote that at the time Valdes swore that he would not preach.[6] Selge rejects Geoffrey's testimony as out of accord both with the tenor of the *propositum* and the importance which Valdes must have attached to preaching; he sees implied references to preaching in the last sentences of the *propositum*, where Valdes promises to observe the evangelical counsels as commands, and in his phrase about deviationist members of his group ('si forte contigerit aliquos venire ad vestras partes').[7]

In his discussion of the conversion narratives, he rejects an interpretation which would impose on Valdes a preliminary period of life in poverty lasting for years before he saw his duty to preach. He strongly prefers Étienne de Bourbon to the Anonymous of Laon, and argues that the commissioning of translations, which Étienne appears to place at the outset of his conversion, can only mean that he had already seen his duty to preach, and was assembling the material for the sermons of himself and his

---

[1] Selge, *Waldenser* I, p. 11; see also p. 17.
[2] *Op. cit.*, II, pp. 77–89.
[3] Matt. 9, 37f.; Lk. 10.2.
[4] *Waldenser*, I, p. 65.
[5] See above, pp. 67–9.
[6] *EFV*, pp. 46–7; *Waldenser*, I, pp. 26–9.
[7] *Waldenser*, II, p. 5.

companions.[8] As with Durand, so with Valdes: preaching was the primary aim, poverty merely its necessary concomitant.

Not all the inferences made from the sources are convincing. The argument from the abandonment of earthly care is an old one, and quite compatible with the twelfth-century understanding of *apostolica vita*. The reference to Waldensians reaching *vestras partes* in the *propositum* might spring from casual travel; it has no necessary implication of wandering preaching. To commission translations is not necessarily to make preparations for preaching. As Étienne de Bourbon describes Valdes's action, the desire to learn was a prime motive: 'audiens evangelia, cum non esset multum litteratus, curiosus intelligere quid dicerent, fecit pactum cum dictis sacerdotibus.'[9]

Particularly doubtful is the treatment of the Anonymous of Laon, the conversion narrative which most stresses zeal for poverty. Selge wishes to demote the Anonymous, making Étienne the prime source, the Anonymous being acceptable only in so far as it confirms the statements in Étienne and other sources.[10] He rejects as legendary *topoi* the story of the jongleur with the Alexius legend, Valdes's recourse to the master of theology for advice, the wife's appeal to Valdes before the bishop in the form of words given by the Anonymous, and, probably, the fact that Valdes was a converted usurer. His most positive point is illuminating: that the Anonymous account represents the fragments of a saint's Life that could not be completed because of Valdes's conflict with the Church.

But the rejection of the alleged *topoi* has no very clear basis outside an *a priori* conflict with the author's understanding of early Waldensianism. He argues, for example, that the Alexius legend does not correspond to the early characteristics of Waldensianism. On the contrary, a saint's Life which describes a unilateral breach with a wife for the sake of the Gospel and the conversion of a rich heir to a life of begging and almsgiving fits well with the facts of Valdes's own life which Selge will accept;[11] the Alexius legend with its approval of an enforced breach with a wife was later the subject of controversy by Catholic theologians; the rest of the Anonymous account and, in particular, the sending of the daughters to Fontevrault without Valdes's wife's knowledge seems to imply that Valdes's breach with his wife was indeed unilateral, and not approved by her. The fact that the vernacular form of the Alexius legend which Valdes would probably have heard served more for entertainment than edification does not alter the fact that it remained the story of a rich man who went and begged and suffered ridicule for the sake of the Gospel; and the fact that such jongleurs were frequently to be heard at this time makes the story surely not less, but more likely.[12] The recourse to the master of theology is not, in itself, improbable; it is compatible with the recourse to priests for translations, which is a prime theme of Étienne de Bourbon.

The appeal of the wife, grasping Valdes's clothing and begging him to consider the opportunity for her to do penance for her sins by giving him alms, i.e. by eating with her in preference to begging for his food from a friend, Selge sees as another pious *topos*. But one might expect that a wife, whether through a rejected affection or the will to avoid damage to her reputation, would try to persuade her husband to eat in her house rather than beg; and one would expect her to couch her request in religious terms when speaking with a man who was plainly gripped by a religious passion. The rejection of unjust gains was a normal accompaniment of conversion (compare the early story of the knights converted in the eleventh century by the wandering preacher Wedericus, who gave up 'sua omnia qua iniuste acquisierant').[13] Selge implies that the tradition deployed by the Anonymous made Valdes a usurer so as to blacken his character before conversion, thus making the conversion more vivid. Yet there is no proof that this did happen and, given the fact that Valdes was a rich man of business,

[8]Op. cit., I, p. 230.

[9]Trans. and edn above (p. 68, n. 4).

[10]*Waldenser*, I, p. 233, n. 19; compare W. Mohr, 'Waldes und das frühe Waldensertum', *Zeitschrift für Religions-und Geistesgeschichte*, IX (1957), pp. 337–63. For mild criticism of the Anonymous, see Gonnet, in *CF*, II, p. 93.

[11]*Waldenser*, I, p. 239.

[12]Ibid., p. 234, n. 23.

[13]*MGH, Scriptores*, IX, p. 407. I owe the ref. to Professor H. Grundmann. See his article on noble conversion, 'Adelsbekehrungen im Hochmittelalter', *Adel und Kirche*, ed. J. Fleckenstein and K. Schmid, (Freiburg, etc., 1968), pp. 325–45.

and that there was a time lag between business realities and the development of a popular moral theology which permitted interest, it is more likely than not that Valdes had practised what he believed to be usury, and had come to regret it.

The stress on poverty in the Anonymous is confirmed by other elements in the primitive documents. The chapter '*De usuris*' in the *Liber antiheresis* is insistent on the need for usurers to make reparation for their unjust gains to those they defrauded; the community formed at Elne by the *Pauperes Catholici* later on, in accord with early Waldensian aims, shows us the effects which the preaching might have on a rich man. It is exactly the pattern of thinking one might expect from a movement founded by a converted usurer. The importance of poverty is further shown by the reproaches levelled by Durand at the Cathars who had deserted it for *terrena negotia*. Selge, when he says baldly that Waldensianism was 'not a poverty movement',[14] is in fact referring simply to the relationship between poverty and preaching in his hypothesis; but as it stands it is a misleading description. Only a moderate conclusion on the poverty issue is here acceptable—that the Franciscans and Waldensians are too often loosely assimilated and that, though both movements were in part inspired by the same set of texts, they made different inferences from them, on the nature of begging, on manual work and on the necessity of preaching.[15]

Finally, one may doubt whether the distinctions which Selge seeks to make could have been apparent to Valdes, or whether the search for one authentic kernel to the movement is justified.[16] Even for Durand the evidence is somewhat precarious. It is simpler to maintain the traditional assimilation of the Waldensians to the poverty and preaching movements of the twelfth century. The Waldensians, like others, were moved by the texts of the sending of the Seventy, and sought a literal imitation: proof of this lies in Valdes's insistence, even at the price of schism in his movement, on preachers living from the gifts of their hearers, as Christ enjoined the Seventy to do, and in the choice of sandals as a kind of badge of office of the preacher in accord with Scripture.

The traditional view which Selge attacks in substance still holds the field. Yet even though the central hypothesis of Selge's book is untenable, the discussion which it entails is often incidentally illuminating, and the book represents a considerable contribution through its fresh analysis of early sources, the exposition of the content of the *Liber antiheresis,* and the synthesis of Waldensian history after 1184.

---

[14]See *CF,* II, p. 114, *TR,* Neue Folge, 23 Jhrg., no. 4 (1968) p. 330.
[15]Note illuminating contrast of Francis and Waldensians in *Waldenser,* I, p. 11.
[16]See the choice postulated, ibid., p. 229.

Appendix D

Gazetteers and Notes to Maps

1 Western Heretics and Eastern Dualists

Place	Date	Source	Type of Heresy	Social Composition	Notes
Acmonia	before 1025	Euthymius of Peribleptos	Bogomil	unknown	Diocese in Byzantine empire, scene of condemnation, presumably of proselytizing of John Tzurillas. (Obolensky, p. 174.)
Aĺovania	11th cent.	Gregory Magistros Aristakes of Lastivert	Paulician	(see notes)	District on N. frontier of Armenia, with part of population Paulician (T'ondrakeçi), supposedly Adoptionist, not dualist wing, but rejecting images, cross. Armenian Prince Vrver of Siri converted to heresy by Aĺovanian monk *c*. 1000. (Garsoïan, pp. 143–5.)
Aquitaine	*c.* 1018	Adémar of Chabannes	uncertain	*plebs*	'Exorti sunt per Aquitaniam Manichei, seducentes plebem' (Adémar). Manichei used too loosely to be taken as proof of dualism. Council of Charroux called by Duke William, 1027–8, to suppress heresies spread by 'Manichei'. (Borst, p. 74; Russell, pp. 35, 197).
Arras	1025	Letter of Gerard, bishop of Cambrai (*Gesta synodi Attrebatensis*)	Proto-dualist (see text)	illiterate, possibly manual workers	Origins in Italy, but *via* Liège. High valuation of manual labour possibly because they were workers (Manselli, *Eresia*, p. 132, n. 26). (Borst, pp. 76–7. Russell, pp. 21–7; also for dating, in *RHE*, LVII (1962), pp. 66–87.)
Belyatovo	1085–6	Anna Comnena	Paulician	warriors	Castle probably in mountains north of Philippopolis, whence Paulician Traulus, former servant of Alexius, carried on rebellion.

Place	Date	Source	Type of Heresy	Social Composition	Notes
Bulgaria	10th and 11th cents.	Cosmas the priest	Bogomil	peasants, clergy	Formerly extending from Adriatic to western shore of Black Sea; eastern lands annexed to Byzantium, 972, and remaining western portion, 1018. Place of origin of heresy conjecturally Macedonia and western Bulgaria (Obolensky, pp. 82, 151–67; D. Angelov, *Byzantinoslavica*, x (1949), pp. 303–12; new evidence by A. Solovjev, in *Godišnjak istoriskog društva Bosne i Hercegovine*, v (1953), pp. 100–3; I. Dujčev (*Medioevo Bizantino-slavica*, I, p. 2) dismisses Macedonian origin as 'pure hypothesis'.
Châlons-sur-Marne, village of Vertu	c. 1000	Raoul Glaber	Proto-dualist (see text)	peasant leaders, probable peasant following.	'. . . quibus etiam ipse persuasit, sicut sunt rustici mente labiles'; 'ad se traxit partem non modicam vulgi' (Glaber). (Borst, p. 73; Russell, pp. 111–13).
a part of diocese	c. 1046–8	Anselm, *Gesta episcoporum Tungrensium*, etc	uncertain	*rustici*	Information third-hand from introduction of Anselm to letter of Wazo, bishop of Liège, reporting letter of Roger, bishop of Châlons, asking for advice. Dualist-type doctrines, identification vitiated by literary contamination (i.e. 'Manichaei', Mani the Holy Ghost). (Borst, p. 79; Russell, pp. 38–41, 278–9).
Constantinople, monastery of Peribleptos	(see Ficker, above, p. 18 n. 63)	Euthymius of Peribleptos	Bogomil	monks	Note the monk who profaned the church of the Stenon (Obolensky, pp. 176–7; Puech-Vaillant, pp. 140–2).

Place	Date	Source	Type of Heresy	Social Composition	Notes
city, generally	c. 1110	Anna Comnena Euthymius Zigabenus	Bogomil	leader, doctor Basil; following, in aristocratic families.	'A very great cloud of heretics' (Anna Comnena). Basil had taught heresy for fifty-two years (Zigabenus); extent of organization implies activity in Constantinople well before 1110. (Obolensky, pp. 197–205; 275–6; Puech-Vaillant, pp. 136, 142–3.)
Csanád	1030–46	Gerard of Csanád	possibly Bogomil (see text)	unknown	Missionary bishopric in Hungary. Dating from words 'prohibemur iam loqui et episcopi nominamur' (*Deliberatio* of Gerard), implying contact with heresy during episcopate. (G. Silagi, *Untersuchungen zur Deliberatio ... des Gerhard von Csanád*, ch. 1. See Ravenna, Venice, Verona and appendix A, s.2).
Kčaw	end of 10th cent.	Gregory of Narek	Paulician	abbot	Armenian monastery, site not in fact identified, placed arbitrarily on the map for convenience, where abbot became Paulician (one of T'ondrakeçi, supposedly of Adoptionist, not dualist, wing, but rejecting images and Cross. (Garsoïan, pp. 96–7, 143).
Kibyrrhaeot Theme	first half of 11th cent.	Euthymius of Peribleptos	Bogomil	unknown	Administrative district of Byzantine Empire in southwest Asia Minor, near Gulf of Antalya. Euthymius first uses term 'Bogomil' of heretics there, existent at time of composition of *Epistola invectiva* (c. 1050). (Obolensky, p. 177; Puech-Vaillant, pp. 140–2.)

Place	Date	Source	Type of Heresy	Social Composition	Notes
Liège diocese	1010–24	Egbert of Liège	uncertain	unknown	Poem of Egbert, composed 1010–24, implies presence of heresy, brought from France; no details. (Russell, pp. 183–4, 303 (who first noticed poem)).
diocese	1025	letter of Gerard, bishop of Cambrai	Proto-dualist (see text under Arras)	illiterate, possibly manual workers	Heretics caught at Arras came via Liège on route from Italy (hypothesis of Russell, in *RHE*, LVII (1962), pp. 66–87).
diocese	c. 1048–50	letter of Théoduin, bishop of Liège	Protodualist	unknown	Berengarian (Théoduin). Docetism, rejection of marriage (provided we may take it as applying to all faithful or to all members of heretical organization) too distinctive to be spontaneously developed. Bogomil influence postulated, with Western heresy (doubts on infant baptism). See Russell, in *BSAHDL*, XLIV (1961), pp. 6–7 (but for rejection of his hypothesis about another source (letter of the faithful of Liège to Pope 'L'), also advanced in this article, see text above, p. 62, n. 56). (Russell, pp. 41, 307 (but note rejection of Russell's dating of the letter to Pope 'L' must modify his description of doctrines)).
Macedonia	10th and 11th cents.	see Bulgaria	Bogomil	see Bulgaria	W. Bulgaria. For Obolensky's hypothesis that it was cradle of Bogomilism, see under Bulgaria. On use of Macedonia, Bulgaria, Thrace as geographical descriptions, see Obolensky, p. 160 and n. 5.

Place	Date	Source	Type of Heresy	Social Composition	Notes
Mananał	early 11th cent.	Aristakes of Lastivert	Paulician	—	Border district of western Armenia in hands of Armenian, Prince Vrver of Širi, converted by Movanian monk to Paulicians (T'ondrakecʻi) supposedly of Adoptionist, not dualist, wing but rejecting images, Cross. 'A hotbed of heresy' (Garsoïan, p. 71, n. 165; pp. 143–4).
Monforte	c. 1028	Landulf Senior Raoul Glaber	Proto-dualist (see text)	countess, nobility, preaching to *rustici*, who came from Milan to the country.	Castle in Piedmont, site not identified; diocese of Asti (Glaber). Dated from Glaber's mention of coronation of Conrad. (Borst, pp. 77–8; Russell, pp. 35–8, 197–8, 201–2, 207–15).
Nevers	1075	*Annales Nivernenses*	uncertain	unknown	'1075. Hoc anno Belinus interfectus est hereticus, sociique eius morti traditi fuerunt' (*Annales*— chronicle of Cluniac house, St Stephen of Nevers). No other details. Belinus could have been a persecuted reformer like Ramihrdus of Cambrai; *socii* make genuine heresy more likely. Russell's discovery (p. 182).
Niš	1078	—	Paulician	warriors, general population	See Sofia. Town in east of independent Bulgaria annexed to Byzantium 972; site of rebellion led by Lecus, Greek Paulician from Philippopolis. (Obolensky, p. 189).

Place	Date	Source	Type of Heresy	Social Composition	Notes
Opsikion Theme	before 1025	Euthymius of Peribleptos	Bogomil	converts included most of villagers of Chilioi Kapnoi	Administrative district of Byzantine Empire in southwest Asia Minor; scene of proselytizing of John Tzurillas, where heretics were known as Phundagiagitae, derived from *funda* ('bag'). Obolensky, p. 177, disciple of Mani, Puech-Vaillant, p. 281, n. 3, see pp. 140–2. (Obolensky, pp. 175, 177.)
Orléans	1022	Paul of St Père de Chartres; Jean of Fleury; *Historiae Franciae fragmentum*; Andreas of Fleury; Raoul Glaber; Adémar of Chabannes; Baldwin of Thérouanne	Proto-dualist (see text and appendix A, s. 1	canons, nobility, a clerk, a nun	For five more sources on Orléans, which do not describe doctrines, see Ilarino da Milano, in *Studi Gregoriani*, ed. G. Borino, II, p. 52, n. 25. (Borst, pp. 74–6, Russell, pp. 27–35, 197, and interesting notes on pp. 276–7.)
Pelagonia	1096	*Gesta Francorum*; Peter Tudebodus; Robert the Monk; William of Tyre	Paulician	unknown	District in Macedonia round the towns of Bitolj and Prilep, where Bohemond and Normans bound for first crusade burnt a fortified town (*castrum*) inhabited by heretics, conjecturally Paulicians. 'Publicani' (William of Tyre). (Garsoïan, p. 15, n. 9; Obolensky, p. 163, n. 2).

Place	Date	Source	Type of Heresy	Social Composition	Notes
Philippopolis	late 10th, 11th cents.	Johannes Zonaras; George Kedrenos; Anna Comnena	Paulician	unknown	Town in Thrace (Plovdiv of modern Bulgaria); site of deportation of Paulicians from Syria in 978 by John I Tsimisces at request of patriarch of Antioch. In 1081 Paulicians from here fought for Alexius I against Normans. In twelfth century heretics a majority (Anna Comnena, who mentions Bogomils here). (Garsoïan, p. 130; Obolensky, pp. 146–7; 189, 190; Puech-Vaillant, pp. 317–8.)
Ravenna	1030–46	Gerard of Csanád	possibly Bogomil (see appendix A, s. 2)	unknown	See Csanád. Dating during Gerard's episcopate in Hungary. Words of *Deliberatio* may imply link between Ravenna, Verona, Venice, heresy in Greece, and possibly Bogomil heresy in Hungary. Gerard had knowledge of Italy as a former monk of S. Giorgio, Venice.
Sardinia	late 10th cent.	Raoul Glaber	uncertain	peasants	The grammarian Vilgard gained popular following for idolatrous enthusiasm for classics (Glaber). 'Classical' heresy must be rejected, but location of popular heresy in Sardinia, originally in Italy and at one stage spreading to Spain, may be correct. (Borst, p. 74, n. 6; Russell, pp. 110–11.)
Smyrna	before 1025	Euthymius of Peribleptos	Bogomil	unknown	Byzantine port; scene of proselytizing of John Tzurillas. (Puech-Vaillant, pp. 140–2, Obolensky, pp. 175, 177).
Sredets	1078	—	Paulician	warriors; general population	See Niš. Town in east of independent Bulgaria annexed to Byzantium, 972 (Sofia of modern Bulgaria); site of rebellion led by Lecus, a Greek Paulician from Philippopolis. (Obolensky, p. 189.)

Place	Date	Source	Type of Heresy	Social Composition	Notes
Thrace	mid-11th cent.	Michael Psellos	uncertain	unknown	District of Byzantine Empire, conjecturally site of heresy of Euchitae with Bogomil and Messalian elements. Siting of heresy accepted (following Obolensky, p. 184, n. 1), but not Psellos's description, due to literary contamination (following D. Angelov in Bulgarian—see E. Werner, *Studi Medievali*, ser. 3, III (1962). (Dujčev, *Medioevo Bizantino-Slavica*, I, p. 2, against Obolensky, pp. 183–8, and Werner, art. cit.; Puech-Vaillant, pp. 139–40.) For emendation of site of Tzurillas's proselytizing from Thrace to Thracesian Theme, see below.
Thracesian Theme	before 1025	Euthymius of Peribleptos	Bogomil	unknown	Administrative district of Byzantine Empire. Ficker amends Euthymius, *Epistola invectiva*, to place proselytizing of Tzurillas here rather than in Thrace. (Obolensky, pp. 175–6; Puech-Vaillant, p. 141).
T'ondrak	mid-11th cent.	Gregory Magistros	Paulician	unknown	District of Armenia, which gave name to T'ondrakeçi, Armenian branch of Paulicians from *c.* early 9th cent., supposedly of Adoptionist, not dualist views, but rejecting images and Cross. Here, as in other lands of ancient Mesopotamia, neighbouring Vaspurakan, and Taron, Gregory Magistros, Armenian noblemen and collaborator with Byzantium, pursued T'ondrakeçi. (Garsoïan, pp. 97–8, 144, 161, 227).

Place	Date	Source	Type of Heresy	Social Composition	Notes
Toulouse	c. 1022	Adémar of Chabannes	uncertain	unknown	'Manichei' destroyed at Toulouse. Dating by association with Orléans heretics. Adémar refers to spread of heresy: '. . . et per diversas Occidentis partes nuntii Antichristi exorti' Manichei used too loosely to be proof of dualism. (Borst, p. 74; Russell, pp. 35, 197.)
Upper Lorraine	1051	Lampert of Hersfeld	uncertain	unknown	Heretics discovered by Duke Godfrey II of Upper Lorraine brought to Goslar for judgement. Length of journey not obstacle to veracity of Lorraine origin; see analogy of Arnold of Brescia, brought from Bohemia 1146 to Pope at Viterbo. Evidence too slight to identify heresy. (Borst, p. 79; Russell, p. 42).
Venice	1030–46	Gerard of Csanád	possibly Bogomil	unknown	See Ravenna, Csanád.
Verona	1030–46	Gerard of Csanád	possibly Bogomil	unknown	See Ravenna, Csanád.

2 **Lollardy Underground** (Map 9)

The following gazetteer is intended to give further information on prosecutions for heresy in the period of English Lollardy's underground existence.

Dates given are those on which offenders came before the courts. Places given are normally those where the offender was resident at the time of prosecution and consequently where he gave vent to heretical sentiments or read suspect books. If, however, the reference is merely to the diocese in which the offender was tried, an x is appended to the date, e.g. Wells 1476x. London offers special problems: it is not always possible to say whether offenders came from the city or from some other part of the diocese, or whether they had taken refuge in England's largest city after incurring suspicion elsewhere.

Information is derived from J. A. F. Thomson, *The Later Lollards, 1414–1520*, (Oxford, 1965) and J. Fines, 'Studies in the Lollard Heresy' (unpublished Ph.D. thesis, University of Sheffield, 1964), but the timescale has been slightly altered. The intention is to show the Lollardy which survived underground after the disaster of Oldcastle's revolt. Prosecutions for participation in the revolt have not been included, nor have proceedings for heresy against non-participants which followed in the immediate aftermath and are primarily concerned with offences committed before 1414. The places of origin of participants in the revolts of 1414 and 1431 are plotted on maps 7 and 8. 1522 is the *terminus ad quem*. After this date it becomes difficult to distinguish with any certainty between Lollardy and the new heresies from the Continent. Prosecutions of 1521–2, reported in passing by Thomson, have been included whenever he refers to the places of origin of the offenders. An (F) by a place or a date indicates that the information has been taken from Fines alone.

Places where heretics were detected and prosecuted, as listed by Thomson and Fines, have been divided into three categories. A first category, where the alleged heresy appears *prima facie* to consist solely in anticlericalism or loose talk without any dogmatic basis, has been excluded from the map. A secondary category consists in those cases where offenders are accused of having suspect English books; places where heretics were found with such books have been underlined on the map and the dates of their prosecutions have been printed in italic in the gazetteer. The possession of books gives us an objective standard, even if not a totally watertight one, for the presence of Lollardy, as opposed to spontaneous heresy or anticlericalism. A third category consists of places where heretics were detected and brought to trial without mention of English books in the proceedings; in some of these there are other clear indications of the presence of Lollardy, such as expressions of reverence for Wyclif or evidence of contact with such well-known Lollard missionaries as William White or James Willis; in others, the brevity of information at our disposal prohibits certainty—one can only say that a balance of probabilities inclines to a judgement accepting the presence of heresy rather than anticlericalism. The possible connection of these cases with the Lollard movement might in some instances be determined by a close examination of the circumstances; in other instances it will always remain uncertain.

The list tends to underestimate rather than overestimate the extent of heresy. It is derived, of set purpose, from the two secondary authorities, Thomson and Fines. It is concerned solely with cases brought to trial. Incidental references show that other trials took place of which we knew nothing, and that heretics might escape the courts. There are also heretical outbreaks which cannot be dated and have therefore not been included.

	Addington	1426
	Aldburgh	*1428* ('Aldborough', Thomson; the suggested link with Hugh Pie makes likely the existence of suspect books.)
	Alcester	1428
	Aldborough	see Aldburgh
	Almeley	*1433*
	Amersham	1464 1511 1521
(F)	Ankerwick	1521
	Ashbourne	1488
	Ashford	1511

(F)	Ashley Green	1521
(F)	Asthall	1521
	Aylburton	1470 1472
	Barnet	*1427*
	Bath	*1418*
(F)	Beaconsfield	1521
	Beccles	*1430*
	Beckington	1476
(F)	Bedingham	1428
(F)	Beighton	1428
	Benenden	1425 1511(F)
(F)	Bergholt	1428
	Birmingham	1511
	Bisham	*1433* 1502
	Bisley	1514
	Bobbingworth	1468
	Boxley	1511
	Bradford-on	
	Avon	1518
	Bray	1507
	Brenchley	1431
	Bridge	1497
(F)	Brightwell	1521
	Bristol	1420 1423 1429x 1441 *1448* 1476 1499
	Broughton	
	Gifford	1518
	Bungay	1428(F) 1511
	Burford	1521
(F)	Burnham Abbey	1521
	Bury St	
	Edmunds	*1428*
	Buscot	1499
	Byfield	1416
	Cambridge	1457
	Canterbury	1469 1498 1511
(F)	Chalvey	1521
	Chelmsford	1430 1521
	Chesham	?1428 1464 1521(F)
(F)	Chesham Bois	1464
	Chesterton	1457
	Chiddingfold	1440
	Chinnor	1464
	Chirton	1514 1517
(F)	Clippesby	1428
	Colchester	*1428*(F) 1511 1518 1521
	Cookham	*1443* 1521
	Corby	1417
(F)	Costessy	1428
	Coventry	1424–5 *1486* 1489(F) *1511 1520* 1522
	Coxwell	1499
	Cranbrook	1425 1511(F)
(F)	Creake	1428
	Crondall	1440
(F)	Denham	1521
	Devizes	*1434* 1437
(F)	Ditchingham	*1424* 1428

| | Dogmersfield | *1513* |
| (F) | Dorney | 1521 |

	Eardisley	*1505*
	Earsham	1424(F) 1431
	East Hendred	1491 1521(F)
	East Sutton	1454
(F)	Eye	1428

	Faringdon	
	(Chipping Faringdon)	*1499*
	Farnham	1440
	Fifield	1504
(F)	Flixton	1428
(F)	Framlingham	1428

	Gloucester	*1448*
	Great Chart	1511
	Great Marlow	1464

	Hackington	1470
	Hadlow	*1431*
	Halden	1425
(F)	Hambleden	1464 1521
	Hanwell	1477
(F)	Harleston	1428
	Harrow	*c.* 1513 1521(F)
	Hasleton	1425
	Hedgerley	1428
	Henley	*1462* 1464 1521
	Hinton	1476 1486
	Holcombe	1518
	Hughenden	1464 1521(F)
	Hungerford	*1505* 1521(F)

| | Ipswich | 1428(F) 1521 |
| | Iver | *1521* |

	Keevil	1506 (probable identification)
	Kelby	1416
	Kevil	see Keevil
	Kidlington	1416
(F)	Kings Langley	1521
(F)	Kings Lynn	1428
	Kingston	*c.* 1513

(F)	Lechlade	1521
	Leicester	*1511*
	Leigh	1476
(F)	Leiston	1428
	Letcombe Basset	1499 *1508*
	Letcombe Regis	1508
	Little Missenden	1511 1521
	Lincoln	*1420–1431* 1428x
	Loddon	1424 1428
	London	*1415* 1417 1418 1421–2 *1428* 1430
		1433 1438 1440 1448 c.1450–6 1476
		1482 1494 1496 1499 1500 1508
		1509 1511 1512 *1518* 1521

	Lydney	1470 *1472* c.1499
	Maidenhead	1508
	Maidstone	1495 c.1499 *1511*
	Malden	1513
	Maldon	1430
	Manuden	1431
	Marden	1514
	Marlow	see Great Marlow
	Marston Bigot	1475
	Martham	1428
	Meonstoke	1496
	Merston Bicott	see Marston Bigot
	Micheldean	1511
(F)	Missenden	1521 (*see also* Little Missenden)
(F)	Mundham	1428
(F)	Nayland	1428
	Needham	1428–31 persecution (Thomson, p. 125)
	Netheravon	*1440*
	Newbury	*1491* c. 1502 *1504* 1521
	Norton St Philip	1460
	Norton Underhill	1420
	Norwich	*1428 (William White)* 1510
	Odiham	1440
	Pembroke	1486 1488 (not on map)
(F)	Penn	1521
	Pewsey	1514
	Portishead	1457
	Princes Risborough	1464
(F)	Reach	1457
	Reading	1416 1499 1508 1521(F)
	Ringwold	1473
	River	1511
	Rochester	1425
(F)	Rockland	1428
	Rode	1491
	Rogate	1470
	Rolvenden	1425 1511(F)
	Romney	1425
	Roode	see Rode
	Salehurst	*1438*
	Salisbury	1479x c.1504x 1518x
	St Albans	1427
	St Osyth	1506
(F)	Seething	1428
(F)	Shelton	1424
(F)	Shipmeadow	1428
(F)	Shotesham	1428
	Snave	1425
	Snodland	1516
	Somersham	1457
	Speen	1491
(F)	Staines	1521
	Standon	1453

N

	Staplehurst	1425 1512
(F)	Staunton	1464
	Steeple Ashton	1488
	Steventon	*1428* 1464 1491 1521
(F)	Stokenchurch	1464
	Strood	1436
	Swaffham Priory	1457
	Taunton	*1441*
	Tenterden	1422 1425 1428 1438 1450 *1511*
	Thame	1464
(F)	Thorpe	1428
	Thursley	1440
	Tonbridge	*1496*
(F)	Tunstall	*1428*
	Turleigh	1518
(F)	Turville	1464
(F)	Uxbridge	1521
	Walden	1467
	Walford	1472 1474
	Wallingford	*1443*
	Waltham Abbey	1493 1513
	Walton-on-Thames	*1521*
	Wantage	1521
	Ware	1477 1521(F)
	Wells	1476x *1491*x 1501
	West Hendred	1499(F) 1521
	West Malling	1425
	West Wycombe	1464 1521(F)
	Whaplode	1501
	Wigginton	1454
	Willesborough	1472
	Willian	1489
	Wilsford (Lincs)	*1416*
	Wilsford (Wilts)	1514
	Winchester	1428x 1454x 1491x(F)
(F)	Windrush	1521
	Windsor	1502 1521(F)
	Witney	1521
	Wittersham	1428 *1431* 1455
	Wrington	1476
	Woodchurch	1425
	Woodhay	1491
	Woolaston	1472 1511
	Worcester	1422 1448x
	Wycombe	1464 *c.* 1502
(F)	Wymondham	1428
	Yardley Hastings	*c. 1452*

3 The Marian Martyrs in England (Map 10)

According to Foxe, 285[1] people were burnt for heresy in Mary's reign, 233 men and 52 women among whom were 7[2] married couples, though they were rarely burnt together. Moreover 34[3] died in prison, 3 more as a result of their sufferings during persecution, and 1 was hanged, drawn and quartered. The occupations of those burnt are given in 151 cases.

There are 60 recorded places of burning, the four major centres, London (including for this purpose Southwark) Canterbury, Colchester and Lewes, accounting for 143 deaths, i.e. just over half the number of deaths by burning. In or near London, Smithfield saw 43 deaths, Stratford-le-Bow 16, Southwark 3, and Westminster 1.

There are 96[4] recorded places of origin or capture for 200 of those burnt, with the addition of Horsley (Essex), Wotton-under-Edge (Glos.), Stone (Kent) for 3 of those who died in prison. Of these 96, only London (19), Islington (18) and Colchester (11) produce more than seven victims.

In assessing the distribution of heresy, it has to be noted that the prosecutions of the Marian martyrs were compressed into the space of one short reign, while the prosecutions of the Lollards extended, in the map given, over more than a century. The incidence of Marian prosecutions depended heavily, as Dr D. M. Loades informs me, on the will of certain diocesans and members of the gentry who were intent on persecution. In a similar way, the incidence of Lollard prosecutions was greatly affected by the zeal of individual diocesans. Both maps, of Lollards and of Marian martyrs, record only a proportion of the adherents of their respective causes; nevertheless, it seems fair to assume, from the greater intensity of activity, that the Marian total does approach more closely to the true total of Protestants. It has to be noted that about 800 of Protestant opinion emigrated to avoid prosecution at the start of the reign. These were from higher classes. Another list of burnings giving figures under counties to a total of 288 is in J. Strype, *Ecclesiastical Memorials*, III, ii (Oxford, 1822), pp. 554–6. A. G. Dickens, *The English Reformation* (London, 1964), pp. 264–72 (2nd edn (1967), pp. 362–72) notes that a few cases are in neither Foxes nor Strype. A map of burnings is given in P. Hughes, *Reformation in England*, 5th edn (London, 1963), II, p. 263.

Places of Burning (60)

2	Ashford (Kent)	23	Colchester
1	Banbury (Oxon.)	3	Coventry
1	Barnet (Herts.)	2	Dartford (Kent)
3	Beccles (Suff.)	1	Derby
1	Braintree (Essex)	2	Ely
6	Brentford (Middx.)	1	Exeter
1	Brentwood (Essex)	3	East Grinstead (Sussex)
5	Bristol	3	Gloucester
12	Bury St Edmunds (Suff.)	1	Hadleigh
1	Cambridge	1	Harwich
40	Canterbury	1	Haverfordwest (Pemb.)
1	Cardiff	1	Horndon-on-the-Hill (Essex)
1	Carmarthen	4	Ipswich
1	Chelmsford (Essex)	6	Islington
2	Chester (includes 1 at Spittle-Boughton, just outside the city)	1	Laxfield (Suff.)
		2	Leicester
2	Chichester	17	Lewes (Sussex)
1	Coggeshall (Essex)	3	Lichfield

[1] Foxe presumed John Fortune, blacksmith of Hintlesham, Suffolk, condemned in the Norwich register (*Acts*, VIII, pp. 160, 163) and Richard Lush, condemned in the Bath and Wells register (pp. 377–8) to have been burnt, and they are therefore included in this total.

[2] Barbara Final could have been Nicholas Final's widow; cf. VIII, pp. 300, 326. Joan **Bradbridge** was very possibly Matthew Bradbridge's widow (ibid.), but these are not included in this total.

[3] Of these, three were women.

[4] In seven instances regions of origin only are given: Essex (VII, pp. 97, 781); Somerset (p. 381); **Wiltshire** (VIII, p. 250); Archdeaconry of Lewes (p. 430); diocese of London (p. 433); diocese of **Winchester**, (p. 490).

60 London (including Smithfield (43), Stratford-le-Bow (16), Westminster (1); see also Southwark (3)
7 Maidstone
1 Maldon (Essex)
1 Manningtree (Essex)
4 Mayfield (Sussex)
3 Newbury
2 Northampton
9 Norwich
3 Oxford
2 Rayleigh (Essex)
5 Rochester
1 Rochford (Essex)

1 Saffron Walden (Essex)
1 St Albans
3 Salisbury
3 Southwark
Spittle Boughton, see Chester
1 Steyning (Sussex)
1 Stratford
1 Thetford (Suff.)
3 Uxbridge (Middx.)
1 Walsingham (Norf.)
1 Ware (Herts.)
2 Wotton-under-Edge (Glos.)
2 Wye (Kent)
1 Yoxford (Suff.)

Places of Origin or Capture

1 Adisham (Kent)
1 Ardingly (Sussex)
4 Ashford (Kent)
1 Aylsham (Norf.)
3 Barking (Essex)
1 Bedfield (Suff.) (Foxe, VIII, p. 160; see p. 548)
1 Bergholt (Suff.)
2 Biddenden (Kent)
2 Billericay (Essex)
6 Bocking (Essex)
Bourne (Sussex). See Eastbourne (*probable identification*)
1 Brenchley (Kent)
2 Brighton
2 Bristol
1 *Broomfield (Kent) (Identification not certain)*
1 Buxted (Sussex)
1 Cardiff
1 Cattesfield (Sussex)
1 Chipping Ongar (Essex)
1 Coddenham (Suff.)
3 Coggeshall (Essex)
11 Colchester
1 Coventry
2 Cranbrook (Kent)
1 *Deane (Lancs.) (Identification not certain)*
1 Dagenham (Essex)
2 Dartford (Kent)
1 Derby
1 [East]bourne (Sussex)
4 East Grinstead (Sussex)
1 Framsden (Suff.)
2 Frittenden (Kent)
2 Godstone (Surrey)
1 Great Burstead (Essex)
1 Grundisburgh (Suff.)
3 Hadleigh (Suff.)
1 Haverhill (Suff.)

2 Heathfield (Sussex)
1 Hellingly (Sussex)
1 Hintlesham (Suff.)
1 Hockley (Essex)
1 Hoddesdon (Herts.)
1 Horndon-on-the-Hill (Essex)
1 Horton (Kent)
4 Hythe (Kent)
1 Ipswich
18 Islington
3 Keevil (Wilts.)
2 Kings Lynn (Norf.)
1 Lambeth
1 Langham (Essex)
1 Launceston (Corn.)
1 Laxfield (Suff.)
1 Leicester
19 London (including Shoreditch 1)
Lynn. See Kings Lynn
7 Maidstone (Kent)
2 *Mancetter* (in area between Coventry and Lichfield)
1 Melford (Suff.)
2 Mendlesham (Suff.)
5 Much Bentley (Essex)
1 Much Dunmow (Essex)
1 *Norgate (Kent). (Not identified)*
3 Norwich
2 Oxford
1 Reading
1 Rettendon (Essex)
1 Rolvenden (Kent)
1 Rye (Sussex)
1 St Davids (Pemb.)
1 Selling (Kent)
1 Smarden (Kent)
1 Stanford-le-Hope (Essex)
2 Staplehurst (Kent)
1 Stoke by Nayland (Suff.) (Foxe, VII, 382, but see n. 3)
1 Syresham (Northants)

4 Tenterden (Kent)
1 Thanet, Isle of, 'Calete', VII, p. 383, n.
   1.)
1 Thornham (Kent)
2 Thorp(e) (Essex)
2 Thundersley (Essex)
2 Tonbridge (Kent)
1 Waltham (Holy) Cross (Herts.)
1 Warbleton (Sussex)
1 Wells (Som.)
2 *West Barefold (Essex). (Not identified)*
1 White Notley (Essex?)

2 Wigborough the Great (Essex)
1 Winchester
1 Windsor
1 Winston (Suff.)
2 Wisbech (Cambs.)
1 Wix (Essex)
2 Withyham (Sussex)
1 Woodbridge (Suff.)
2 Woodmancote (Sussex)
1 Wrotham (Kent)
1 Wymondham (Norf.)

Occupations (Total given 151; unknown 134)

apothecary	1	hosier	2
artificer	2	husbandman	9
barber	1	husbandman's wife	2
barber's daughter	1	ironmaker	1
brewer	3	merchant & broker	1
brewer's wife	1	merchant tailor	1
bricklayer	2	miller	1 (& wife)
butcher	2	miller's wife	1
capper	1	painter	2
carpenter	3	pewterer	1
clergy	25	pewterer's wife	1
priest's widow	1	sawyer	3
constable	1	schoolmaster	1
cobbler	1 (& wife)	servant	7 (inc. 2 female)
cook	1	shearman	3
courtier	1	shoemaker	5
currier	1	shoemaker's wife	1
cutler's wife	1	smith	3
cutler's daughter	1	spinster	2
draper	1	tailor	3
fisherman	1	tallow chandler	1
fuller	4	apprentice	1
freemason	1	tanner	2
gentleman	8	turner	1
gentlewoman	1	upholsterer	1 (& wife)
glazier	1	weaver	12
glover	1	apprentice	1
labourer	7	weaver's wife	2
labourer's wife	1	wheelwright	1

The clergy include:
1 archbishop 1 archdeacon
4 bishops 1 ex-friar
1 ex-monk

Appendix E

The Testament of Gost Radin

Translation and Notes by Yvonne Burns

Introduction

This testament is to be found on the last four pages of the volume of testaments for the year 1466 in the Dubrovnik archives, where it was first noticed in 1910 by Dr Ćiro Truhelka, who published a facsimile and transcription in the Sarajevo journal *Glasnik zemalijskog muzeja u Bosni i Hercegovini*, XXIII, (1911). Other documents in the archives show that Radin had acted as the envoy of Duke Radosav Pavlović (who governed half the parish of Konavlie, the other half of which belonged to Dubrovnik) in 1422, 1423 and 1432, when he was referred to as *Krstjanin* Radin. In 1437, however, when his name next appears in the records, he is *Starac* Radin the envoy of Duke Stephen Vukčić, which title and office he still held in 1445. In 1450, although still in the duke's service, he had been given the title *gost*, which he retained until his death in 1467. (See Truhelka, ibid.).

These three titles were held by members of the Bosnian Church, which evidently preferred to use vernacular terms for these offices. These words are found in other areas also, *krstjanin* being a common form of the word for Christian in the western part of Yugoslavia, where it alternates with *krščanin*, while *starac* (lit. 'old man') is frequently found as a title in inscriptions on Orthodox Serbian manuscripts. It translates *presbyter* in the early Slavonic gospel codices Marianus and Miroslav's Gospel, etc. Both are found in the Glagolitic Old Church Slavonic MS Clozianus. *Gost* is of Common Slavonic origin, being cognate with *guest, gast, hostis,* the primary meaning being 'a person who is in another's house or in a foreign country'. In Old Russian texts the word has been translated 'merchant' although emissary would suit the contexts equally well. It is significant that Gost Radin acted as the trusted emissary of Duke Stephen, while the tombstone of Gost Milutin (see p. 145) states that he received gifts from great lords and rulers and from Greek lords. It seems very probable that his function had been similar to that of Gost Radin.

Yet other documents in the archives give details of how the bequests were collected by the beneficiaries, and one tells us that Radin's full name was Radin Butković, that is to say, Radin, son of Butko.

Gost Radin was not only the trusted emissary of Stephen Vukčić, but also a friend of Dubrovnik, using his influence with the duke on behalf of the city. Dubrovnik was grateful and in 1455 promised him a house, a pension and help to carry out anything he desired, whenever he wished to come there, an offer he was glad to accept when the duke died. He himself died within two years, before he could take advantage of the invitation to make his home in Venice, where he had sought sanctuary from the advancing Turks for himself and his followers.

The following translation was originally made from Truhelka's facsimile, but later the manuscripts themselves were studied in the Dubrovnik archives, with helpful results. The most important was the discovery that the word transcribed by Truhelka as *mrsni* ('meat-eating'), was in fact *mrski* ('unsightly'). The existence of another manuscript referring to the lighting of candles on the feast of St Nedelja was also important. (See n.18).

During the translation and during the subsequent investigation nothing was found in the Testament inconsistent with the Gost being a member of an independent Eastern Orthodox Church similar to the Serbian Church. If in his day there were heretics among the members of the Bosnian Church, then the evidence for it must be sought elsewhere than in the Testament of Gost Radin.

Translation
In the 1467th year of the Birth of Christ. . . .

This is the testament of Gost Radin, which . . .[1] two nephews[2] of Gost Radin, Vladisav Jurjević and Tvrtko Brajanović,[3] two of the heirs of the said Gost, who endorsed the testament in everything, and for themselves promised, both on their own behalf and on behalf of the other heirs, that all which is contained in it shall be to each one firm and unwavering without retraction.[4]

May it please the Almighty Lord God and be known to the self-governing and God-loving Dubrovnik principality[5] that I, Gost Radin, being by God's grace placed in my mind in every wholeness,[6] and in the true hope that it may be unchanging to me, both during my lifetime and after me, have deposited with Prince Tadioko Marojević and his nephew Maroje Naoković that which is contained and provided for in the writings and statements (one copy of which is with the notaries of the Dubrovnik principality and the other with me, Gost Radin), written by the hand of the same Prince Tadioko Marojević and under his authentic seal for this same trust.

Lest death should befall me, Gost Radin, either [by . . .][7] or by any other cause, there remains (and is with . . .[8]) that document which is contained and named[9] in the above mentioned writings and statements. Regarding this deposition, I have now decided how to arrange matters in a better and more correct manner than it was set out in the first document. This sequel to the first document we now make so that it contains all others, in order that my said property (which is to be found in the first document, mentioned above) shall be and must be ordered and disposed of according to the instructions in this document of me, Gost Radin, so that my bequests shall be made in full and in minted money to each relative, servant and friend of mine.

First of all, for my soul, for the soul of Gost Radin, let 600 golden ducats be given for the service of God.[10] Let these 600 ducats be given prudently and in the following manner:

300 ducats must and shall be given into the hand of my nephew,[11] Gost Radin of Seonica for him to apportion this sum with a true heart and in a good manner to baptized[12] people who are of the true apostolic faith,[13] to true Christian[14] peasants[15] (both men and women[16]), so that on every Great Day[17] and on the day of St Nedelja and on the day of St Petka,[18] they, bending their knees to the ground,[19] shall say a holy prayer for my soul that the Lord God shall free us from our sins and have mercy on us on the day of judgement for ever and ever. Especially let it be apportioned to those elderly peasants (both men and women) who are also poor but good people[20] who love not sin, of whatever sex they are[21] (whether male Christians or female Christians). My said nephew Radin must and shall distribute to them, to whomsoever he sees and thinks fit from our Law,[22] whether blind or crippled or weak or poor, to some 3 perpere, to some 4, to some 5, to some 6, to some 7 and to some 8, as he sees fit, and also to the unsightly[23] leprous[24] people and to the blind and to the crippled and to the hungry and to the thirsty and to the old men and to the old women it must and shall be given, as seems fit, on Great Feast days, and on the day of St Nedelja and on the day of St Petka; and especially on the day of the holy Birth of Christ and on the holy Annunciation and on the holy Resurrection of the Lord, and on the day of St George, my *slava*,[25] and on the day of the holy Ascension of our Lord, and on the day of St Peter and on the day of St Paul[26] and on the day of St Stephen the First Martyr and on the day of St Michael the Archangel, on the day of the holy Virgin Mary,[27] on the day of All Saints.[28] All that is designated above, as and how it is contained in this document, these 300 ducats—let Prince Tadioko Marojević, and his nephew Maroje Naoković, be obliged to give to the said Gost Radin for the sake of the faith that he believes and the fast that he keeps[29] that he cannot nor will not convey nor carry out less[30] than the above written and named 300 ducats, but will divide and apportion rightly and wholly and truly for my soul as and how it is designated above, if he does not desire to be fellow

to the disobeyer of God,[31] and if he does not desire his soul to be after death[32] before the Most High Lord God and before the holy indivisible Trinity. By this let him truly give peace to my soul, in so far as the almighty Lord God also wishes.

And also, in the same manner (word for word and letter by letter), in godly expectation, from these first 600 ducats I place a second 300 ducats under the jurisdiction and supervision of Prince Andruško Sorkočević[33] and Tadioko Marojević, that they be the sole arbiters of this, to divide and apportion the said chantry of me, Gost Radin, according to a true principle, to the wretched and poor, to the blind and crippled, to the orphans and widows. I have therefore detailed and entrusted my said chantry to them on account of their faith and the virtue of their nobility, so that they shall apportion it to whatever old or poor or distressed person they see fit, to some 3 dinars, to some 4 dinars and to some 5 and to some 6 and to some 7 and to some even 8 dinars, in order that candles shall be burnt for the soul of me, Gost Radin, in God's churches on those holy Great Days that are named above, and on each day of St Nedelja and St Petka.[34]

Over and above that chantry which has been put on one side for the service of God and of all saints, I, Gost Radin, not knowing the ending of my life, when or where or at what season, being sound in my mind, have ordered and arranged and set down the rest of my true property that my said property all stands completely mine, for me, in every way and in every circumstance completely and absolutely at my disposal. And should the death of me, Gost Radin, take place, I leave and dispose of the rest of my property as follows:

Firstly, to Vukava, Christian[35] (my cousin and Tvrtko's niece[36]), 150 ducats;[37] and to Gost Radin of Seonica, my nephew, 100 ducats;[38] and to the second Vukava, Christian (Vukna's youngest servant), 100 ducats;[39] to Stoisava, my youngest servant,[40] 600 ducats:[40] to Vukna, my sister, 60 ducats; to Vukna, my sister, 300 ducats;[41] and to Vučica, my niece, 200 ducats;[42] and to the three Christians who followed me, first of all let there be given to Vukša 60 ducats, and to Radoje 50 ducats. . . .[43] To Milisava, Christian, let there be given 20 ducats;[44] and to Radan, Christian, let there be given 60 ducats.[45]

And from the rest: first of all, let there be given to Pava, my sister-in-law,[46] with three sons, 2,000 ducats;[47] and to my niece Alinka, 100 ducats;[48] and to my nephew Vladisav, with two sons, 1,000 ducats;[49] and to my sister-in-law Ktava, 100 ducats.[50]

And to my servants who followed me, first of all to my Chamberlain Vukas, 100 ducats;[50] to Radosav and his brother Vukić Radilović, 60 ducats;[50] to Radovan Ostojić, 30 ducats;[51] and to the four Gojtanovići, Radivoj, Mihoje, Radosav and Obrad, to all of them, 70 ducats, so that there will be 30 ducats to Mihoje, and to all the other three 40 ducats;[52] to Radona Vukotić, 40 ducats;[53] to Vukić Vukašinović, 30 ducats;[54] to Obrad and Milica, Pava's servants, 10 ducats;[55] and to Gjuren and Ilija, 10 ducats.[56]

And to my friend, Prince Tadioko Marojević, 200 ducats[57] and my red fur-trimmed gown of six-stranded silk, trimmed with sable, which the Lord King Matijaš[58] gave me; and to Prince Andruško, 100 ducats;[59] and for the church and the sepulchre where my bones will be and lie, 140 ducats.[60]

And this statement Gost Radin makes so that those trusts which any person has placed with me may be made known, so that it be not lost to him nor come to less: First of all, let the 270 ducats of my cousin Gost Radivoj be given to him;[61] and to the child, the son of Božićko Milošević of Sěrčanica, let him be given 160 ducats.[62] and to Vuk, Gost of Uskoplje, 110 ducats.[63]

And the rest of my property, whether it is in plate or in any other form, let my four nephews, Vladisav, Tvrtko, Juraj and Radič, share it.[64] And the rest of my household goods and property is for Vukna, Vučica, Mihna, Tvrtko, Jurje and Radič, whether horses or my garments and bags or any kind of woven goods, excepting the fur-trimmed gown with gold, which is for Tvrtko.

All the above written and designated in God's hope, we have apportioned and ordered so that the above mentioned honest men and the above named rulers Prince Andruško Sorkočević and Prince Tadioko Marojević, and with them my two nephews Vladisav and Tvrtko will carry out the good method and allotment of all this.

Written in the year of our Lord 1466, in the month of January, on the 5th day, in Dubrovnik.

Notes

[1]At this point, and on the line above, the words cannot be deciphered.

[2]Brother's son.

[3]The parchment is very worn at this point, but knowing the names of the two nephews from other documents in the archives makes it possible to see that the indentations are consistent with this interpretation.

[4]Similar expressions are found in other texts published by Ljub. Stojanović in *Stare Srpske povelje i pisma*, (Beograd, 1929), I pp. 296, 305, II p. 33 hereafter referred to as *Lj. S.*

[5]Many other texts in *Lj. S.* contain stereotyped expressions using variations of the words used here. It is presumed that the same meaning is intended.

[6]Cf. Duke Stephen's testament: 'a u pameti moioi na punu krěpakʊ.' Gost Radin was present when the Duke's testament was written down by David, the metropolitan of Mileševo. Radin and David were the Duke's resident clerics and appear to have enjoyed equal status.

[7]Although there is no gap here, from the sense it seems that one or more possible causes of death may have been omitted by the copyist.

[8]The text seems to be corrupt here.

[9]A number of texts omit the first letter of a word if it is the same as the last letter of the preceding word. The translation given here assumes that this has been done.

[10]This is the term used for the liturgy in the Orthodox Eastern Church, as opposed to *misa* (mass) in the Slavonic speaking parts of the Western Church.

[11]Sister's son. He received the money on 15th July, 1467.

[12]*kršteniemb:* the normal word for baptized (here in the dative plural).

[13]This is the normal expression for orthodox Christianity. It was, for example, used by Justinian (*Corpus iuris civilis*, Nov. 132.).

[14]*krstjanin* is the form found in Bosnia, corresponding to *krščanin* in Croatia and *hrišćanin* in Serbia in modern times. Although writers on the Bosnian Church have taken this word to imply a member of a heretical Church, there is much linguistic evidence that this word is merely an early form of *krščanin*, in which the palatalization of *st* has not yet taken place. It has passed unremarked when found unconnected with Bosnia. A related word is the adjective *krstjanski*. See (a) Poljica Constitution of 1620 and 1688. No. 74: 'u svakoi crkvi ima se zvonit zdrava m(aria) za mrtvih na uru noći, u ko vrime virni *krstěani* imaju molit boga za iste mrtve.' No. 103: 'da iz nih na *krstěnski* puk nemu dan.' (b) Matija Divković (1563–1631), a Franciscan, wrote in 1609 in Sarajevo, 'Nauk *krstjanski* za narod slovinski' (Christian instruction for the Slavonic people). The work was printed in Venice in 1617. (c) JAZU Dictionary, s.v. '*počelo*' 'Dužan je svaki *krstjanin* misu slišati u svaku svetkovinu od počela do svrhe.' ned. 124. ('Each Christian is obliged to listen to the mass on every saint's day from beginning to end').

In this testament the same lack of palatalization is found in *neti* (nephew), genitive *netja*, dative *netju*. The modern form is *nećak*, in which tj > ć.

[15]*kmet* was the name given to a peasant who worked his lord's land. It was used with this meaning in Bosnia in Turkish times and afterwards. In Serbia, on the other hand, the word is used for the elected chief of a village.

[16]Both 'Christian' and 'peasant' have feminine forms, as is usual in the language when referring to living beings.

[17]Both Western and Eastern Orthodox Churches have certain feast days which are known as Great Feasts.

[18]This has until now been taken to mean Holy Sunday and Holy Friday. It has been said (Truhelka in *Wissenschaftliche Mitteilungen aus Bosnien und Herzegowinen*, XIII (1916), p. 69) that it could not mean St Nedelja and St Petka, and that the grammatical form *svetu petku* (accusative of *sveta petka*) was a mistake for *sveti petak* (accusative of *sveti petak*). However, the expression occurs three times in the text, and each time the form is *svetu petku*. It does not seem possible that such a mistake could have been made three times over in such a common word as a day of the week. These two saints often come in association; in Sofia two neighbouring churches are dedicated to them, while the same is true of two villages near Ohrid. Their cult spread to the Adriatic from Serbia, probably from the time, 1398, when the bones of St Petka were taken from Vidin to Belgrade. Earlier they had been in Trnovo, Bulgaria. These saints do not appear in the Roman calendar, and when certain areas passed from Serbian hands, missionaries from Rome changed

the names of the churches, thus making it more difficult to discover the extent of their cult. The bequests of Frančesko in *Lj. S.* I II, pp. 473–4, leaving money to the churches in Ston and Dubrovnik in 1485, confirm the interpretation given above. He wrote, 'I bequeath 2 perpere in honour of St Michael that 10 masses be said, and I bequeath 2 perpere in honour of St Nedelja that 10 masses be said, and I bequeath 2 perpere in honour of all saints (both male and female) . . .' Since the expressions used are the same in all three cases and the first and third are saints' days, it follows that the second must also be a saint's day. Ston had been a Serbian area, but had passed into the hands of Dubrovnik.

[19]In the Eastern Orthodox churches of Serbia and elsewhere the large trays of sand, in which one places the candles on entering, are arranged on two levels, the upper one for the living and one on the ground for the dead. When lighting a candle for the dead it is therefore necessary to bend the knees. This phrase may be an allusion to this.

[20]*dobri mužbje* has been interpreted by some as meaning the *boni homines* of heretical sects in the West. However, like *krstjanin*, the expression is well attested in many texts under circumstances where no one has suggested heresy.

[21]Literally, 'of whatever kind.'

[22]The expression 'of our law' is normally used by members of the Eastern and Western orthodox Churches alike when referring to a member of their own Church, while 'of his law' indicates that those referred to belong to the other. In the case of Gost Radin, 'our Law' must refer to the Eastern Orthodox Church, since his Law was clearly not that of either Dubrovnik or Venice and we know that these were adherents of Western orthodoxy. This is shown by two documents, one in Dubrovnik offering Gost Radin a house and a pension and an assurance that no pressure would be brought to bear to cause him to depart from the 'faith that he believed' (*Liber Privilegorum*, p. 115), the other in Venice agreeing to his request for sanctuary for himself and fifty or sixty members of his Law (Archivio di Stato, Venezia, Senato, Terra v, 151 10 March, 1466). The text of the latter is as follows (Marko Šunjić: 'Jedan novi podatak o gostu Radinu i njegovoj sekti,' *Godišnjak Istorijskog društva Bosne i Hercegovine*, XI, 1950):

> Quidam gost Radin principalis baronus et consiliarius domini duci(s) Stefani sancti Save cum maxima instantia petit a nostro dominio literas patentes et salvum conductum nostrum quo ei lecitum sit et valeat cum personis L in LX *ex suis legis et secte sue* cum facultatibus et bonis eorum se reducere sub umbram nostram et securi liberique ab omni molestia quae quoquomodo illis inferri possit stare, ire et redire. . . . De parte 60. De non 7. Non sinceri 15.

It will be noticed that Stephen was referred to as Duke of St Sava. St Sava was the founder of the independent Serbian Church, independent but still orthodox. The fact that Stephen's two clerics were Radin and David (the metropolitan of Mileševo where St Sava was buried) gives credence to the idea that there was parity between the Serbian and the Bosnian Churches. The words 'ex suis legis et secte sue' may be taken to mean 'of his section of the Eastern Orthodox Church,' i.e. the Bosnian Church.

[23]For historians who have used the testament as evidence for the heretical nature of the Bosnian Church, one of the key words is *mrsni*, which has been said to mean 'meat-eating' (a common use of the word in modern times). This was Truhelka's reading and translation, and on no other evidence than this word in this single document historians have maintained that the Bosnian Church consisted of two grades of members (albeit further subdivided), namely, those who eat meat and those who renounce it. However, 'meat-eating' is not the only meaning of *mrsni*. It also means unclean, and, in view of the fact that it was an adjective referring to lepers in the testament, that seemed a more feasible translation. In the event, it has become unnecessary to make a choice between these two meanings because a visit to the Dubrovnik archives the following year revealed that the word in question had been incorrectly transcribed by Truhelka, and is, in fact, *mrski*. The letter transcribed as 'n' by Truhelka consists of two very slightly curved vertical strokes, exactly the same as the letters he transcribed as 'k' in other parts of the testament. For it to have been an 'n' there would have to have been a third stroke linking the vertical strokes. A very thorough examination of the MS. was made with the aid of a magnifying glass and later in the strong light used to photograph the MSS. in the darkroom of the archives. The parchment is very clean and white in that place, and it is quite certain that no horizontal line has ever been inscribed to join the two upright lines. *Mrski* is the nominative plural of *mrzak* and the Academy Dictionary (Zagreb, 1911) pp. 96–7 gives many examples of its use under five headings. For the first the equivalents *exosus, odiosus, odio dignus, abbominato, abborrito, odiato, molestus* are quoted from various dictionaries, while the second groups together examples of its use as '*unpleasant.*' The third heading quotes *horridus, incultus, turpis, deformis, brutto, nauseabile, abbominevole, hässlich, garstig,* while the fourth quotes, among other examples, a phrase which corresponds to *injucundum esse aliquid alicui, pigere.* The fifth heading contains only one example, in which the meaning is '*disinclined*'. If the adjective refers to lepers alone, then probably '*unsightly*' is the most suitable translation. On the other hand, the translation '*unlucky*' or '*unfortunate*' would apply to all those people listed in this passage of the testament, which could then join the examples given in the dictionary under the fourth heading. On balance, however, considering it is preceded by the

word *i*, the former translation is to be preferred. One thing, however, is certain: Gost Radin was most definitely not referring to meat-eating people, but to every kind of unfortunate person who was not in a position to provide for himself. Conclusions reached on the basis of Truhelka's transcription *mrsni* must be rejected.

[24]The word used is the one found in early Slavonic gospel codices, such as Marianus and Miroslav's gospel, translating the Greek word for leper.

[25]Every Serb has his slava. It is the saint's day on which his ancestors accepted Christianity.

[26]Truhelka pointed out that the Western Church had a single festival for St Peter and Paul, but the Eastern Church celebrated separate festivals.

[27]The scribe originally wrote 'on the Day of St Nedelja', but *nedelja* was scored out before the words 'Virgin Mary'. It may have been due to the omission of several words, resulting in the need to omit yet another to obtain an understandable sentence. On the other hand it may have been due to a mistaken interpolation of the name 'Mary' after copying an original 'on the Day of St Nedelja, the Virgin.' In either case, it confirms the assumption that in this testament the words *sveta nedelja* mean St Nedelja and not 'Holy Sunday.'

[28]All the days mentioned are amongst the most important in the Byzantine Calendar.

[29]This injunction is made to Gost Radin, whose faith and fast are referred to.

[30]Cf. testament of Duke Stephen, *Lj. S.* I II, p. 89

[31]I.e., Judas Iscariot. Cf. *Lj. S.* I I, p. 301

[32]Two adjectives, meaning 'quiet' and 'peaceful', qualify '*soul*', referring euphemistically to the soul of Prince Tadioko after death.

[33]Prince Andruško was a member of a well-known Dubrovnik family. It is interesting to notice that, although Catholics in Catholic Dubrovnik, members of this family still consider themselves Serbs. This means that their origins were passed down from generation to generation. It accounts for the trust Gost Radin had in these particular friends in Dubrovnik.

[34]On 23 July 1472 Prince Andruško testified that the 100 ducats paid to him had been distributed to the poor, according to Gost Radin's wishes, while on 11 April, 1477 he testified that a further 50 ducats had been distributed. Nothing is known about the remaining 150 ducats.

[35]The female form of Christian (*krstjanica*).

[36]The word *kćerša* was incorrectly translated '*daughter*' by Truhelka. It is to be found in Poljica, as *ćerša*, ('niece'). (Franco Ivanišević: *Poljica. Narodni život i običaji, Zbornik za narodni život i običaje južnih slavena*, (Zagreb, 1904, IX p. 245). The people of Poljica say that their land was first settled by the three sons of Prince Miroslav of Bosnia, and later people came from Hungary and Bosnia for fear of the Turks (ibid, x, p. 302). Words used in Poljica may therefore prove useful when studying documents concerning Bosnia.

[37]Paid to Gost Radin of Seonica on her behalf on 15 July 1467.

[38]Paid on 15 July 1467.

[39]*Mlajša* ('youngest servant'), is found in Zlatarić's poetry.

[40]Paid to Gost Radin of Seonica on her behalf on 15 July 1467.

[41]It is strange to find two bequests of money to the same person, so there is probably a scribal error here.

[42]There is no note of this money being paid.

[43]Since only two names are given, it would appear that the scribe had omitted the third Christian. There is a hole in the parchment here. These legacies were not listed among those collected.

[44]Paid to Gost Radin of Seonica on her behalf on 15 July, 1467.

[45]There is no note of this money being paid.

[46]*Nevěsta* has various meanings, even in neighbouring villages. In this case it means '*brother's wife*,' as in Poljica (ibid, IX, p. 246). Truhelka thought it meant '*daughter-in-law*,' as it does in some parts of the country.

[47]Paid to her son Tvrtko Brajanović on 16 June 1470, on her behalf.

[48]Alinka, wife of Dragiša Vukšić and sister of Tvrtko Brajanović, with their consent, took her legacy on 27 November 1469.

[49]Paid to Vladislav Djurdjević on 16 June 1470.

[50]There is no note of this money being paid.

[51]Paid on 15 July 1467.

[52]There is no note of this money being paid.

[53]Paid on 16 June 1470.

[54]There is no note of this money being paid.

[55]Although these bequests are not specifically mentioned as having been paid, Tvrtko's statement on 16 June 1470 that all the money had been paid to him that was due as a result of the testament, may have included them, since the legatees were servants of his mother, whom he was representing.

[56]There is no note of this money being paid.

[57]Affirmation of this having been paid was made on 15 July 1467.

[58]Matthias Corvinus, king of Hungary, who gave a similar gown to Duke Stephen Vukčić. It is mentioned in the duke's testament.

[59]Affirmation of this having been paid was made on 15 July 1467.

[60]On 23 July 1472, Tvrtko Brajanović confirmed that he had received this.

[61]On 23 February 1470, Radivoj Priljubović Gost in Bijela, gave power of attorney to Tvrtko Brajanović and Cvjetko, a Christian, to obtain this, and it was obtained on 18 March 1470.

[62]This was handed to Vukić Milošević from Dračevica, on behalf of Nicola son of Božićko of Dračevica, on 15 July 1467.

[63]Paid to Tvrtko Brajanović, on behalf of Gost Vuk Radivojević, on 18 March 1470.

[64]Confirmation that this had been carried out was given on 16 June 1470.

NOTE

Italicised *b* signifies the Slavonic reduced vowel. It would not have been pronounced in this position.

Grateful thanks are due to the Yugoslav Government, the Hayter Fund and the Central Research Fund of the University of London for their contribution towards travel expenses, to Professor Svetozar Marković of the University of Sarajevo, and especially to the Director and staff of the Historiski arhiv, Dubrovnik, without whose help and cooperation the work could not have been completed.

Glossary of Heretics

Adamites. An heretical sect imitating nakedness of Adam, described first by Epiphanius and Augustine, then by Isidore of Seville; possibly originally to be identified with licentious Gnostic sect, the Carpocratians, but as organized, persisting sect in Middle Ages, wholly imaginary. Abusive term for a Hussite group. (p. 323.)

Albigenses, Albigensians. The term for Cathars in South of France, originally referring to adherents in the region of Albi.

Amalriciani. Pantheists; muddled followers of Amaury of Bène (condemned 1210).

Apostolics, Apostolic Brethren. Exaggerated imitation of the Franciscans, with heresies on poverty and perfection, founded by Gerard Segarelli in Parma 1260; broke into rebellion under Dolcino di Novara (burnt 1307). (pp. 193-5.)

Arnoldists. Followers of Arnold of Brescia (executed 1155), of Donatist and anticlerical views, attempting to impose apostolic poverty on the Church as an obligation; a North Italian movement or strand of thought. (pp. 57-9.)

beghards. Men leading a religious life without rule or vows, similarly to the female equivalent, the beguines, but more mobile, sometimes gaining a living by begging; accused of Free Spirit heresy in early fourteenth century. See beguines, Beguins, Free Spirit. (ch. 11, s. 2.)

beguines. Pious women leading a religious life without rule or vows, singly or in convents, often linked to the mendicant orders; popular from the early thirteenth century, but inhibited by prejudice and accusations of Free Spirit heresy in the fourteenth century. Name originally popular and pejorative, from Albigensis. (ch. 11, s. 2.) See also beghards, Beguins, Free Spirit.

Beguins. A pejorative term from the same root as beguine; applied to tertiaries and others of either sex associated with Olivi and other Spiritual Franciscans, chiefly in the Franciscan province of Provence, with exaggerated views on the place of poverty; suppressed after issue of *Quorumdam exigit* by John XXII in 1318; spelling with capital and no 'e' adopted for convenience in this book to mark distinction from the beguines. (ch. 12.) See also beguines, Fraticelli, Spiritual Franciscans.

Bogomils. An heretical movement, so called from the name (possibly a pseudonym) of a tenth-century Bulgarian village priest, preaching opposition to the Greek Church and teaching that all matter is evil; active in Byzantium and the Balkans; spread into Western Europe to form Cathar sect. (ch. 2.)

Bohemian Brethren. See Unitas Fratrum.

Calixtines. See Utraquists.

Cathars. Dualist heretics, teaching that all matter is evil. Derived originally from Bogomil influence and (possibly) Paulicians in Western Europe; foreshadowed in eleventh century Western heresy; active from twelfth to late thirteenth or early fourteenth centuries, esp. in parts of Lombardy and southern France. Term (Greek, 'pure ones') should properly be restricted to their leading class, the *perfecti*, but is commonly applied to the whole movement. (chs 3, 5, 6, 8.)

Flagellants. Movements, most commonly of laymen, engaging in mass flagellation in public as a form of penance; orthodox in origin; in 1260 stimulated in Italy by diffused Joachimite expectation of the end of the world; in 1349, by Black Death (term most commonly applied to participants in this episode), esp in the kingdom of Germany and neighbouring lands; condemned by Clement VI. (pp. 212–3.)

fraticelli (also fratricelli fraterculi). Spiritual Franciscans in Italy who broke away from the order to follow a literal observance; exaggerated place of poverty in religious life; condemned by John XXII in 1317; term (from the Italian *frate*) may also be used loosely for orthodox members of orders or hermits. (ch. 12.)

Free Spirit. Adherents of supposed sect of deviant mystics, esp. among beguines and beghards, accused of libertinism and autotheism after issue of *Ad nostrum* by Clement V in 1312; no organized heretical group in fact existed, and accusations were often imaginary, particularly when levelled against beguines. (ch. 11, s. 2.)

Henricians. Followers of Henry the Monk, preacher of penance, then heretic, influenced by Peter of Bruis, active in the first half of the twelfth century in French-speaking lands, who rejected the sacraments and the doctrine of original sin. (pp. 49–52.)

Horebites. See Orebites.

Humiliati. Loosely-organized congregations in northern Italian towns leading a penitential life with manual labour and preaching; refusal to laymen among them by Alexander III of the right to preach led to heresy, as in the case of the Waldensians; Innocent III gave regulations to Humiliati willing to return to the Church in 1201. (pp. 70–3, 96, 98.) See Poor Lombards.

Hussites. Generic term for Bohemian reform movement which challenged the papacy in the fifteenth century; originally a term of abuse; may be used in practice for the more moderate members of the movement. (chs 16–18.) See also Taborites, Unitas Fratrum, Utraquists.

Joachimites. The term used in this book for writers and others, both orthodox and heretical, seriously influenced by ideas and symbols emanating ultimately (but often in false and distorted versions) from the exegetical, prophetic works of Joachim of Fiore. (chs 7, 12.)

Lollards. (i) Imprecise popular term current in German-speaking lands, pejorative in origin and derived from *lollen, lullen* ('to sing'), applied to men leading a religious life without rule or vows; synonym of beghard.
(ii) in England relates to adherents of a popular evangelical heresy, given initial stimulus by teaching of John Wyclif, based on individual faith and supremacy of Scripture; apparently first applied in 1380 to followers of Wyclif's teaching (late in his life) in Oxford. (chs 14, 15.) See beghards.

Lyonists, Leonists. The moderate wing of the Waldensian movement, so called after the original centre at Lyons, that remained faithful to the tradition of Valdes and his early followers; separated from Poor Lombards from 1205; survived in France and its borderlands. (chs 6, 7, 9.)

Orebites. Radical Hussites from Hradec Králové (Königgrätz) in eastern Bohemia who formed a community and military force comparable to Tabor under the priest Ambrose, renaming their town after the Mt. Horeb of Scripture. (pp. 316, 327, 330.)

Passagians. A small group, possibly only found in Lombardy, who observed to the letter OT precepts, including circumcision; condemned by Lucius III in 1184. p. 72.)

Pataria. An eleventh-century reform movement in Milan, supported by the papacy; name probably derived from Milan rag-market. (ch. 4.)

Patarene. An Italian term for heretics, especially Cathars, current from third Lateran Council of 1179.

Paulicians. An heretical sect dating back to the early centuries; dualist by the ninth century and opposed by the Byzantine Church; a possible factor in the rise of Bogomilism and Catharism. (ch. 2.)

Petrobrusians. Adherents of Peter of Bruis, village priest originally from the Embrun region who preached in SW France *c.* 1119–*c.* 1140, rejecting all external forms of worship. (ch. 5.)

Pikarts. A loose term of abuse for heretics, derived from beghard. (pp. 322–3.)

Poor Lombards. Waldensians, based initially in Northern Italy, influenced by the Lombard climate of opinion to a more radical and anti-Church attitude; formed congregations supported by manual labour under influence of Humiliati, split from the Lyonists in 1205; active missionaries, esp. in German-speaking lands. (chs 6, 7, 9.)

Speronists. A minor sect, followers of Ugo Speroni of Piacenza, who disseminated a heretical predestinarian doctrine, and rejected the sacraments and belief in original sin; condemned by Lucius III in 1184. (pp. 81–2.)

Spiritual Franciscans. Rigorist members of the Franciscan order who struggled for a strict observance of the rule, esp. in poverty, and appealed to Francis's Testament; extremists among them provided the starting-point for *fraticelli* and other heretics condemned by John XXII in 1317 and subsequent years. (ch. 12.)

Taborites. Radical Hussites who began as a religious movement with eschatological expectations, later developing into a military and political organization, whose fighting powers were vital to Hussite success; major support for drastic religious changes in lands controlled by the Hussites; name of Tabor, with Scriptural echoes, given to fortress south of Prague in 1420, thereafter their base. (chs 17, 18.)

Unitas Fratrum (or **Bohemian Brethren**). A small, rigorist group within the Hussite movement influenced by pacifist ideas of Peter Chelčický, formally separated from Utraquist Church in 1467; ancestors of Moravian Brethren. (p. 334.)

Utraquists. Supporters of the lay chalice, who insisted that communion should be given to the laity in both kinds (*sub utraque specie*), i.e. bread and wine; the usage, initiated in Prague in 1414, was condemned by the council of Constance in 1415. The lay chalice became a symbol to the Hussite movement. (chs 17, 18.)

Vaudois. See Waldensians.

Waldensians. (or **Waldenses**). An evangelical heresy of the late twelfth century, springing from an orthodox poverty and preaching movement launched by Valdes, a former businessman of Lyons; fell into heresy following refusal of the right to preach and subsequent condemnation by Lucius III in 1184; split into a Lyonist and Poor Lombard wing, but continued in France, Germany, parts of Eastern Europe and Italy and survived into modern times. (chs 6, 7, 9.)

'Waldo, Peter'. Form for Valdes (Lat. Valdesius) employed esp. by older historians; Peter, though used by Waldensian controversialists in the fourteenth century, was not historically Valdes's name. See Waldensians (chs 6, 7, 9.)

Abbreviations

ABAW	*Abhandlungen der königlichen bayerischen Akademie der Wissenschaften (Historische Klasse)*
Act. Fel.	*Les Actes du Concile Albigeoise de Saint Félix de Caraman.* ed. A. Dondaine, *Miscellanea Giovanni Mercati,* v (*Studi e Testi,* cxxv) (Rome, 1946), pp. 324–55
ADRSP	*Archivio della Deputazione Romana di Storia Patria*
AFH	*Archivum Franciscanum Historicum*
AFP	*Archivum Fratrum Praedicatorum*
AHDLMA	*Archives d'Histoire doctrinale et Littéraire du Moyen Âge*
AKG	*Archiv für Kulturgeschichte*
ALKG	*Archiv für Literatur-und Kirchengeschichte des Mittelalters.* ed. H. Denifle and F. Ehrle
AM	*Annales du Midi*
ARBB	*Académie royale de Belgique, Bulletin de la Classe des Lettres et des Sciences morales et politiques*
BF	*Bullarium Franciscanum.* v, ed. C. Eubel (Rome, 1898). *Epitome,* ed. C. Eubel (Ad Claras Aquas, 1908)
BIHR	*Bulletin of the Institute of Historical Research*
BISIAM	*Bullettino dell'Istituto Storico Italiano per il Medio Evo e Archivio Muratoriano*
BJRL	*Bulletin of the John Rylands Library*
Bouquet	*Receuil des Historiens des Gaules et de la France,* ed. M. Bouquet
BS	*Balkan Studies*
BSAHDL	*Bulletin de la Société d'Art et d'Histoire du Diocèse de Liège*
BSSV	*Bollettino della Società di Studi Valdesi*
CCM	*Cahiers de Civilisation médiévale*
CEC	*Cahiers des Études Cathares*
CF	*Cahiers de Fanjeaux* (Toulouse):
	I *Saint Dominique en Languedoc.* (1966)
	II *Vaudois Languedociens et Pauvres Catholiques* (1967)
	III *Cathares en Languedoc* (1968)
	IV *Paix de Dieu et Guerre sainte en Languedoc au XIIIᵉ Siècle* (1969)
	V *Les Universités du Languedoc au XIII Siècle* (1970)
	VI *Le Credo, la Morale et l'Inquisition* (1971)
CH	*Church History*
CHR	*Catholic Historical Review*
CMH	*Cambridge Medieval History,* ed. J. R. Tanner, C. W. Previté-Orton and Z. N. Brooke (Cambridge, 1911–36). 8v.
CV	*Communio Viatorum*
DA	*Deutsches Archiv*
DHC	*De Heresi Catharorum in Lombardia.* ed. A. Dondaine, in 'La Hiérarchie Cathare en Italie', *AFP,* xix (1949), pp. 280–312
DHGE	*Dictionnaire d'Histoire et de Géographie ecclésiastiques*
DLZ	*Deutsche Literaturzeitung*

DTC	*Dictionnaire de Théologie Catholique*
DZG	*Deutsche Zeitschrift für Geschichtswissenschaft*
EC	*Études Carmelitaines*
EcHR	*Economic History Review*
EEQ	*Eastern European Quarterly*
EETS	*Early English Text Society* (London, 1864–; in progress). Original series (o.s.)
EFV	*Enchiridion Fontium Valdensium*, 1, ed. G. Gonnet (Torre Pellice, 1958)
EHD	*English Historical Documents*, ed. D. C. Douglas (London, 1953–; in progress). 13v.
EHR	*English Historical Review*
EV	Early Version of Wyclif Bible (see p. 231)
FF	*Forschungen und Fortschritte*
FRB	*Fontes Rerum Bohemicarum*, ed. J. Goll, v (Prague, 1893)
FS	*Franciscan Studies*
FZ	*Fasciculi Zizaniorum*, ed. W. W. Shirley (*RS*, 1858)
HJ	*Hibbert Journal*
HJB	*Historisches Jahrbuch*
HS	*Hérésies et Sociétés dans l'Europe pré-industrielle, 11ᵉ–18ᵉ Siècles*, ed. J. Le Goff (Paris & La Haye, 1968)
HZ	*Historische Zeitschrift*
IP	*Istoričeski Pregled*
JEH	*Journal of Ecclesiastical History*
JGMO	*Jahrbuch für die Geschichte Mittel—und Ostdeutschlands*
JMRS	*Journal of Medieval and Renaissance Studies*
JTS	*Journal of Theological Studies*
JWCI	*Journal of the Warburg and Courtauld Institutes*
LMA	*Le Moyen Age*
LV	Late version of Wyclif Bible (see p. 243)
MA	*Medium Aevum*
Mansi	J. D. Mansi, *Sacrorum conciliorum nova et amplissima collectio* (Florence & Venice, 1759–98), 31 v.
MBPH	R. I. Moore, *The Birth of Popular Heresy* (London, 1975)
MGH	*Monumenta Germaniae Historica*
MH	*Medievalia et Humanistica*
MOPH	*Monumenta Ordinis Praedicatorum Historica*
MRS	*Medieval and Renaissance Studies*
MS	*Mediaeval Studies*
NMS	*Nottingham Medieval Studies*
NT	New Testament
OT	Old Testament
PBA	*Proceedings of the British Academy*
PL	J. P. Migne, *Patrologia Latina* (Paris, 1844–64)
PP	*Past and Present*
RB	H. Grundmann, *Religiöse Bewegungen*, 2nd edn (Hildesheim, 1961) (1st edn, 1935)
RBPH	*Revue belge de Philologie et d'Histoire*
Relazioni	*Relazioni del X Congresso internazionale di Scienze storiche* (Florence, 1955)
RES	*Revue des Études slaves*
RHE	*Revue d'Histoire ecclésiastique*
RHL	*Revue historique et littéraire du Languedoc*
RHPR	*Revue d'Histoire et de Philosophie religieuse*
RHR	*Revue de l'Histoire des Religions*
RPTK	*Realencyklopädie für protestantische Theologie und Kirche*, 3rd edn (Leipzig, 1908)
RQH	*Revue des Questions historiques*
RR	*Ricerche Religiose*

RS	*Chronicles and Memorials of Great Britain and Ireland during the Middle Ages* (London, 1858–97) (The Rolls Series)
RSCI	*Rivista di storia della chiesa in Italia*
RSI	*Rivista storica italiana*
RSLR	*Rivista di storia e letteratura religiosa*
RSPT	*Revue des Sciences philosophiques et théologiques*
RTAM	*Recherches de Théologie ancienne et médiévale*
SCH	*Studies in Church History*
	I Ed. C. W. Dugmore and C. Duggan (London, 1964)
	II Ed. G. J. Cuming (London, 1965)
	III Ed. G. J. Cuming (Leiden, 1966)
	IV *The Province of York*, ed. G. J. Cuming (Leiden, 1967)
	V Ed. G. J. Cuming (Leiden, 1969)
	VI *The Mission of the Church and the Propagation of the Faith*, ed. G. J. Cuming (Cambridge, 1970)
	VII *Councils and Assemblies*, ed. G. J. Cuming and D. Baker, (Cambridge, 1971)
	VIII *Popular Belief and Practice*, ed. G. J. Cuming and D. Baker, (Cambridge, 1972)
	IX *Schism, Heresy and Religious Protest*, ed. D. Baker, (Cambridge, 1972)
	X *Sanctity and Secularity: the Church and the World*, ed. D. Baker, (Oxford, 1973)
	XI *The Materials, Sources and Methods of Ecclesiastical History*, ed. D. Baker, (Oxford, 1975)
SDAB	*Sitzungsberichte der deutschen Akademie der Wissenschaften zu Berlin*
SHF	*Société de l'Histoire de France*
SHR	*Scottish Historical Review*
SM	*Studi medievali*
SSAWL	*Sitzungsberichte der sächsischen Akademie der Wissenschaften zu Leipzig*
STC	A. W. Pollard and G. R. Redgrave, *A Short-title Catalogue of Books printed in England, Scotland & Ireland, 1475–1640* (London, 1926)
TAPS	*Transactions of the American Philosophical Society*
TDH	*Tractatus de hereticis*, ed. A. Dondaine, in 'La Hiérarchie cathare en Italie', *AFP*, xx (1950), pp. 234–324
TR	*Theologische Rundschau*
TRHS	*Transactions of the Royal Historical Society*
TLZ	*Theologische Literaturzeitung*
UBHJ	*University of Birmingham Historical Journal*
WEH	W. L. Wakefield and A. P. Evans (ed.), *Heresies of the High Middle Ages* (New York & London, 1969)
WS	*Wyclif Society*
ZFB	*Zbornik Filozofskog fakulteta u Beogradu*
ZFK	*Zeitschrift für Kirchengeschichte*
ZFZ	*Zbornik Filozofskog fakulteta u Zagrebu*
ZG	*Zeitschrift für Geschichtswissenschaft*
ZRG	*Zeitschrift für Religions- und Geistesgeschichte*

Reading List

This list is confined to bibliographies and to suggested English literature for introductory reading.

Bibliographies

A. Armand-Hugon and G. Gonnet, *Bibliografia valdese*, in *BSSV*, xcIII (Torre Pellice, 1953).

P. de Berne-Lagarde, *Bibliographie du Catharisme languedocien* (Toulouse, 1957).

H. Grundmann, *Bibliographie zur Ketzergeschichte des Mittelalters*, in *Sussidi eruditi*, xx (Rome, 1967); repr. in *Hérésies et Societés dans l'Europe pré-industrielle, 11ᵉ—18ᵉ siecles*, ed. J. Le Goff (Paris & La Haye, 1968), pp. 411–67.

Id. *Ketzergeschichte des Mittelalters. Die Kirche in ihrer Geschichte: Ein Handbuch*, ed. K. D. Schmidt and E. Wolf, II, G. i (Göttingen, 1963). (Short analysis with extensive bibliography.)

Z. Kulcsár, *Eretnekmozgalmak a XI–XIV században*, Budapest, 1964.

G. Leff, *Heresy in the Later Middle Ages* (Manchester, 1967), II, pp. 741–77.

E. van der Vekené, *Bibliographie der Inquisition: ein Versuch* (Hildesheim, 1963).

WEH, pp. 820–46.

Introductory work in English

Texts in Translation

R. B. Brooke, *The Coming of the Friars* (London, 1975), pp. 140–59 (see also intro., chs 3, 4, 5).

R. I. Moore, *The Birth of Popular Heresy*, London, 1975.

J. B. Russell, *Religious Dissent in the Middle Ages* (New York & London, 1971). (Brief extracts.)

WEH. (The most extensive and varied collection in existence.)

General

A. P. Evans, 'Social Aspects of Medieval Heresy', in *Persecution and Liberty: Essays in Honour of George Lincoln Burr* (New York, 1931), pp. 3–20

R. Knox, *Enthusiasm* (Oxford, 1951). (The medieval section is the weakest of the book but the writing is stimulating and elegant.)

G. Leff, *Heresy in the Later Middle Ages* (Manchester, 1967), I, prologue, pp. 1–47. Supersedes his 'Heresy and the Decline of the Medieval Church', *PP*, xx (1961), pp. 36–51.

R. I. Moore, *The Birth of Popular Heresy* (London, 1976), introduction. (The contemporary analogy between heresy and illness should be noted.)

J. L. Nelson, 'Society, Theodicy and the Origins of Heresy; towards a reassessment of the medieval evidence', *SCH*, IX, pp. 65–77.

J. B. Russell, 'Interpretations of the Origins of Medieval Heresy', *MS*, xxv (1963), pp. 26–53. *Religious Dissent in the Middle Ages* (New York & London, 1971). (Includes material from modern historians.)

WEH, pp. 1–55. (A precise factual account by W. L. Wakefield.)

J. H. Mundy, *Europe in the High Middle Ages 1150–1309* (London, 1973), ch. 14. (Effective and interesting in relating heresy and society.)

Bogomils and Paulicians

N. G. Garsoïan, *The Paulician Heresy* (The Hague and Paris, 1967).

N. G. Garsoïan, 'Byzantine Heresy: a Reinterpretation', *Dumbarton Oaks Papers*, xxv (1971), pp. 101–12. (Not available to me when I wrote on this subject.'

D. Obolensky, *The Bogomils* (Cambridge, 1948).

Eleventh-Century Western Heresy

C. N. L. Brooke, 'Heresy and Religious Sentiment, 1000–1250', *Bulletin of the Institute of Historical Research* xli (1968), 115–31; repr. in his *Medieval Church and Society* (London, 1971), pp. 139–61.

R. I. Moore, 'The Origins of Medieval Heresy', *History*, LV (1970), pp. 21–36.

J. B. Russell, *Dissent and Reform in the Early Middle Ages* (Berkeley & Los Angeles, 1965).

Lesser Heresies of the Twelfth Century

G. W. Greenaway, *Arnold of Brescia* (Cambridge, 1931).

N. Cohn, *The Pursuit of the Millenium* (London, 1957). (A stimulating essay in psychological interpretation of millenial expectations in popular movements from the eleventh century to the sixteenth. Needs to be read with grave caution; best on aberrations on the margin of heresy linked to the crusading movement. See further above, p. 47–8).

J. B. Russell, *Dissent and Reform in the Early Middle Ages* (Berkeley & Los Angeles, 1965).

WEH, pp. 1–55. (Historical sketch by W. L. Wakefield.)

Waldensians

E. Comba, *History of the Waldenses of Italy from their Origin to the Reformation*, trans. T. E. Comba (London, 1889). (Old and romantic, but has some historiographical significance.)

M. Deanesly, *The Lollard Bible* (Cambridge, 1920), chs 1–3. (The Waldensian movement outlined in relation to its use of vernacular Scriptures.)

G. Leff, *Heresy in the Later Middle Ages* (Manchester, 1967), II, pp. 448–71. (Survey introducing little-known foreign literature. The comparison of Waldensians and Cathars (pp. 453–4) does not take adequate account of the varying intensity of persecution mounted against them, and is misleading on the geographical extent of the Cathar movement. It is also doubtful whether organization accounts for Waldensian staying power.)

B. Marthaler, 'Forerunners of the Franciscans: the Waldenses', *Franciscan Studies*, n.s., xviii (1958), 133–42.

WEH, pp. 1–55. (Historical sketch by W. L Wakefield.)

NOTE There is a lack of detailed up-to-date work on the Waldensians in English.

Cathars

B. Hamilton, *The Albigensian Crusade* (London, 1974) (Historical Association pamphlet, G 85).

M. Loos, *Dualist Heresy in the Middle Ages* (Prague, 1974) (Came to hand after this book was written and demands closer analysis than can be given here. Wide-ranging exposition, concerned to stress continuity between eastern dualism and Catharism, valuable for English readers for its knowledge of secondary lit., esp. on Bogomils, Paulicians and the Bosnian Church, and has utility for surveying briefly French and Italian Catharism. Marred in early section by a hypothesis of Marcionite influence on Paulicians (Garsoïan is preferable), by occasional lack of rigour in use of evidence and undue blandness on Cathar internal history. Ch. 19 on Bosnia and the general critique of Borst should be noted.)

S. Runciman, *The Medieval Manichee* (Cambridge, 1947). (Wide survey covering non-Western dualist heresy; marred by hypothesis of descent of Cathars from Mani.)

J. N. Stephens, 'Heresy in Medieval and Renaissance Florence', *PP* liv (1972), pp. 25–60. (Interesting attempt to trace heresy, Cathar and other forms, in one city.)

J. R. Strayer, *The Albigensian Crusades* (New York, 1971). (Lucid on crusade and Languedoc, but should not be used, except as light background, on heresy itself.)

W. L. Wakefield, *Heresy, Crusade and Inquisition in Southern France, 1100–1250* (London, 1974). (Up-to-date, succinct analysis with good bibliography.)

H. J. Warner, *The Albigensian Heresy* (London), I (1922), II (1928). (Seriously outdated, but still has value through its use of original texts.)

WEH is especially strong on Cathar texts (with introductions).

Persecution and the Response of the Church

J. Blötzer, 'Inquisition', in *Catholic Encyclopedia*, VIII (New York, 1910) (Harsh on H. C. Lea, but makes interesting points.)

B. Bolton, 'Tradition and Temerity. Papal Attitudes to Deviants, 1159–1216', *SCH*, IX, pp. 79–91.

A. P. Evans, 'Hunting Subversion in the Middle Ages', *Speculum*, XXXIII (1958), pp. 1–22.

H. C. Lea, *A History of the Inquisition of the Middle Ages* (New York, 1888) 1963 reprint. (This is an old classic, seriously outdated on heresy itself, but yet worth browsing in for many facts and for its account of the machinery of persecution. Protestant bias in Lea's reflections is obvious, but does not necessarily affect factual accuracy.)

E. W. Nelson, 'The Theory of Persecution', *Persecution and Liberty: Essays in Honor of George Lincoln Burr* (New York, 1931), pp. 3–20.

J. B. Pierron, 'Poor Catholics', *Catholic Encyclopedia*, XII (New York, 1911).

A. C. Shannon, *The Popes and Heresy in the Thirteenth Century* (Villanova (Pa.), 1949).

Free Spirit

B. Bolton, 'Mulieres sanctae', *SCH*, x, pp. 77–95. (Background.)

R. E. Lerner, *The Heresy of the Free Spirit in the later Middle Ages* (Berkeley, 1972). (Standard account for northern lands.)

R. W. Southern, *Western Society and the Church in the Middle Ages* (Harmondsworth, 1970), s. 7: Fringe Orders and Anti-orders. (For the background of the beguines.)

Joachim of Fiore and Joachimism

M. E. Reeves, 'The *Liber Figurarum* of Joachim of Fiore', *MRS*, II (1950), pp. 57–81. (Uncommonly illuminating.) Id., *The Influence of Prophecy in the Later Middle Ages: a Study in Joachimism* (Oxford, 1969). (Standard account and major work, best used for reference on Joachim or individual Joachimite episodes.)

R. W. Southern, 'Aspects of the European Tradition of Historical Writing. 3. History as Prophecy', *TRHS*, 5th ser; XXII (1972), pp. 159–80.

Spiritual Franciscans

D. L. Douie, *The Nature and the Effect of the Heresy of the Fraticelli* (Manchester, 1932).

M. D. Lambert, *Franciscan Poverty* (London, 1961).

G. Leff, *Heresy in the Later Middle Ages* (Manchester, 1967), I, pp. 51–255.

D. Knowles, *The Religious Orders in England*, I (Cambridge, 1948), ch. 11. (For a short introduction to Franciscan history.)

Flagellants

R. Kieckhefer, 'Radical Tendencies in the Flagellant Movement of the mid-Fourteenth Century', *JMRS*, IV (1974), pp. 157–76.

G. Leff, *Heresy in the Later Middle Ages*, (Manchester, 1967), II, pp. 485–93.

Wyclif

G. Leff, *Heresy in the Later Middle Ages* (Manchester, 1967), II, ch. 7. (Illuminating survey of the bases of Wyclif's thinking.)

K. B. McFarlane, *John Wycliffe and the Beginnings of English Nonconformity* (London, 1952); re-issued as *The Origins of Religious Dissent in England* (New York, 1966). (The political Wyclif and his opponents.)

B. Smalley, 'The Bible and Eternity: John Wyclif's Dilemma', *JWCI*, xxvii (1964), pp. 73–89. (Explains Wyclif's philosophical position and its emotional significance.)

The English Lollards

M. Aston, 'Lollardy and Sedition, 1381–1431', *PP*, xvii (1960) pp. 1–44.

M. Deanesly, *The Lollard Bible* (Cambridge, 1920). (Remarkably unaffected by its age, and of value for Lollardy and heresy generally.)

A. G. Dickens, 'Heresy and the Origins of English Protestantism', in *Britain and the Netherlands*, ii, ed. J. S. Bromley, E. H. Kossmann (Groningen, 1964), pp. 47–66.

J. Fines, 'Heresy Trials in the Diocese of Coventry and Lichfield, 1511–12', *JEH*, xiv (1963), pp. 160–74.

Hussites

R. R. Betts, *Essays in Czech History* (London, 1969). (Ch. 3, on the philosophical background to Hussitism, should not be read.)

M. Creighton, *A History of the Papacy from the Great Schism to the Sack of Rome*, ii (London, 1899).

E. F. Jacob, 'The Bohemians at the Council of Basel, 1433' in *Prague Essays*, ed. R. W. Seton-Watson, (Oxford, 1948), pp. 81–123.

H. Kaminsky, 'The Prague insurrection of 30 July 1419', *MH*, xvii (1966), pp. 102–26 Id., 'The religion of Hussite Tabor', in *The Czechoslovak Contribution to World Culture*, ed. M. Reichigl (The Hague, 1964), pp. 210–23. Id., *A History of the Hussite Revolution* (Berkeley & Los Angeles, 1967). (This detailed and profound book is far from introductory reading, nor does it cover the history of the whole movement. But see ch. 1 for introduction. It may be consulted throughout with profit).

G. Leff, 'Wyclif and Hus: a Doctrinal Comparison', *BJRL*, l (1968), pp. 387–410.

F. Šmahel, '"Doctor Evangelicus super omnes Evangelistas": Wyclif's Fortune in Hussite Bohemia', *BIHR*, xliii (1970), pp. 16–34.

M. Spinka, *John Hus: a Biography* (Princeton, 1968).

Medieval Heresies and the Reformation

M. E. Aston, 'Lollardy and the Reformation: Survival or Revival', *History* xlix (1964), pp. 149–70.

A. G. Dickens, *Lollards and Protestants in the Diocese of York* (Oxford, 1960).

G. H. Williams, *The Radical Reformation* (London, 1962). (See index for short summaries on late medieval heresy.)

NOTE:

M. J. Wilks, 'Misleading Manuscripts: Wyclif and the non-Wycliffite Bible', *SCH*, xi, pp. 147–61 came to hand when this book was in proof. It should be used for its summary of research on the Wycliffite Bible and the author's hypothesis that Wyclif had no hand in it. He argues for '. . . a takeover of an originally independent English bible project by the Wycliffite movement. . . ' (p. 160). But does he show that the initial impetus to translating Scripture came from any source other than Wyclif? C. Cross, 'Popular Piety and the Records of the unestablished Churches 1460–1660', *SCH*, xi, pp. 269–92 suggests some revision on Lollard beliefs and the class of their adherents in the early sixteenth century (see esp. p. 278).

INDEX

Appendices D and E have not been indexed. Books and articles are listed wherever possible under authors, the page reference indicating the point where full title and date of publication is given.

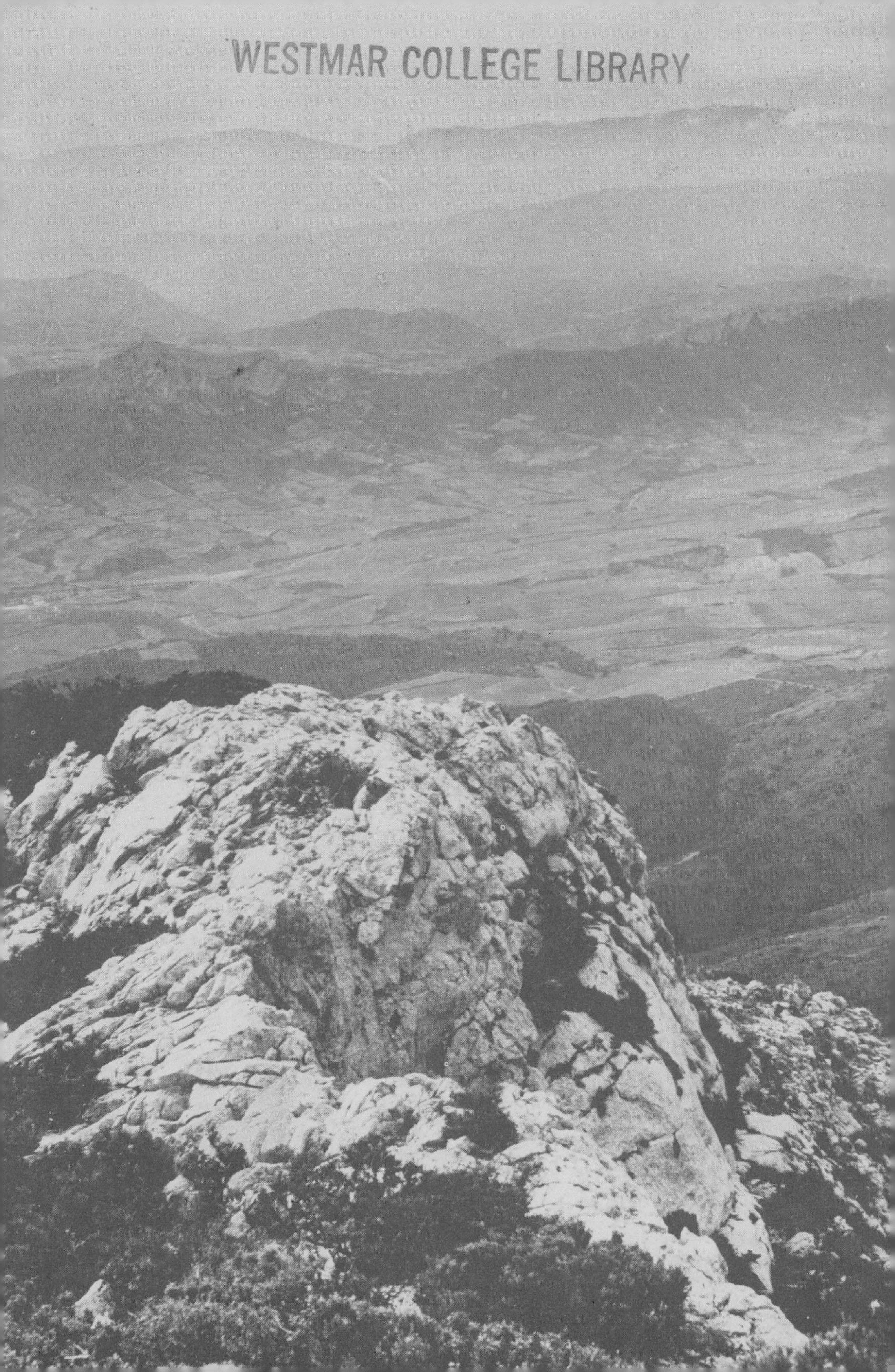